HARRY
OPPENHEIMER

DIAMONDS, GOLD AND DYNASTY

HARRY OPPENHEIMER

DIAMONDS, GOLD AND DYNASTY

Michael Cardo

JONATHAN BALL PUBLISHERS

JOHANNESBURG • CAPE TOWN

Originally published in South Africa in 2023 by
JONATHAN BALL PUBLISHERS
A division of Media24 (Pty) Ltd
PO Box 33977
Jeppestown
2043

Reprinted in 2023

ISBN 978-1-86842-801-4
ISBN (hardback edition) 978-1-77619-296-0
ebook ISBN 978-1-86842-802-1

*Every effort has been made to trace the copyright holders
and to obtain their permission for the use of copyright
material. The publishers apologise for any errors or
omissions and would be grateful to be notified of any
corrections that should be incorporated in future editions of
this book.*

www.jonathanball.co.za
www.twitter.com/JonathanBallPub
www.facebook.com/JonathanBallPublishers

Cover by Sean Robertson
Cover image by Godfrey Argent,
courtesy of the Brenthurst Library
Index by R Sephton
Design and typesetting by Martine Barker
Printed and bound by CTP Printers, Cape Town
Set in Minion Pro

In memory of Jonathan Ball

Surely there is a mine for silver,
and a place for gold that they refine.
Iron is taken out of the earth,
and copper is smelted from the ore ...
But where shall wisdom be found?
And where is the place of understanding?

Job 28: 1, 2, 12

Midas, they say, possessed the art of old;
Of turning whatsoe'er he touch'd to gold;
This modern statesmen can reverse with ease –
Touch *them* with gold, *they'll turn to what you please.*

**John Wilcot,
aka 'Peter Pindar',
satirist and poet, 1738–1819**

Contents

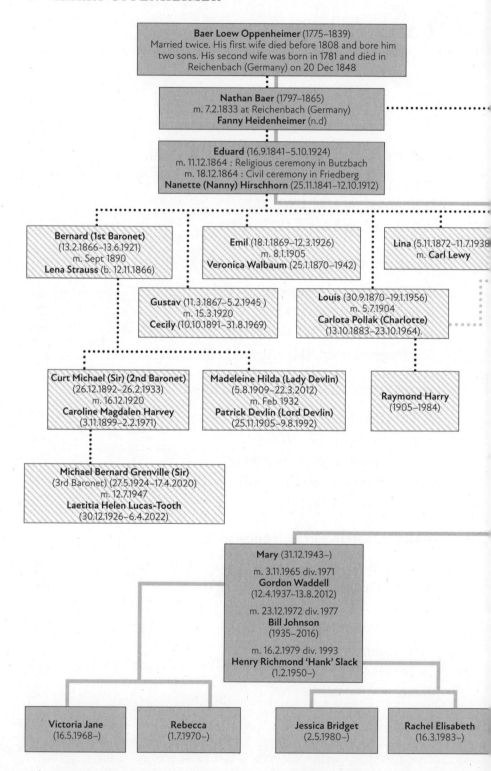

Baer Loew Oppenheimer (1775–1839)
Married twice. His first wife died before 1808 and bore him
two sons. His second wife was born in 1781 and died in
Reichenbach (Germany) on 20 Dec 1848

Nathan Baer (1797–1865)
m. 7.2.1833 at Reichenbach (Germany)
Fanny Heidenheimer (n.d)

Eduard (16.9.1841–5.10.1924)
m. 11.12.1864 : Religious ceremony in Butzbach
m. 18.12.1864 : Civil ceremony in Friedberg
Nanette (Nanny) Hirschhorn (25.11.1841–12.10.1912)

Bernard (1st Baronet)
(13.2.1866–13.6.1921)
m. Sept 1890
Lena Strauss (b. 12.11.1866)

Emil (18.1.1869–12.3.1926)
m. 8.1.1905
Veronica Walbaum (25.1.1870–1942)

Lina (5.11.1872–11.7.1938)
m. Carl Lewy

Gustav (11.3.1867–5.2.1945)
m. 15.3.1920
Cecily (10.10.1891–31.8.1969)

Louis (30.9.1870–19.1.1956)
m. 5.7.1904
Carlota Pollak (Charlotte)
(13.10.1883–23.10.1964).

Curt Michael (Sir) (2nd Baronet)
(26.12.1892–26.2.1933)
m. 16.12.1920
Caroline Magdalen Harvey
(3.11.1899–2.2.1971)

Madeleine Hilda (Lady Devlin)
(5.8.1909–22.3.2012)
m. Feb 1932
Patrick Devlin (Lord Devlin)
(25.11.1905–9.8.1992)

Raymond Harry
(1905–1984)

Michael Bernard Grenville (Sir)
(3rd Baronet) (27.5.1924–17.4.2020)
m. 12.7.1947
Laetitia Helen Lucas-Tooth
(30.12.1926–6.4.2022)

Mary (31.12.1943–)

m. 3.11.1965 div. 1971
Gordon Waddell
(12.4.1937–13.8.2012)

m. 23.12.1972 div. 1977
Bill Johnson
(1935–2016)

m. 16.2.1979 div. 1993
Henry Richmond 'Hank' Slack
(1.2.1950–)

Victoria Jane
(16.5.1968–)

Rebecca
(1.7.1970–)

Jessica Bridget
(2.5.1980–)

Rachel Elisabeth
(16.3.1983–)

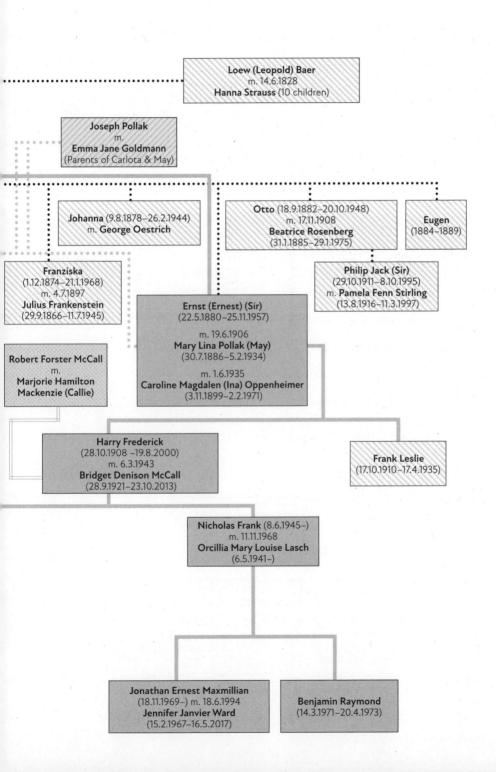

Loew (Leopold) Baer
m. 14.6.1828
Hanna Strauss (10 children)

Joseph Pollak
m.
Emma Jane Goldmann
(Parents of Carlota & May)

Johanna (9.8.1878–26.2.1944)
m. George Oestrich

Otto (18.9.1882–20.10.1948)
m. 17.11.1908
Beatrice Rosenberg
(31.1.1885–29.1.1975)

Eugen
(1884–1889)

Franziska
(1.12.1874–21.1.1968)
m. 4.7.1897
Julius Frankenstein
(29.9.1866–11.7.1945)

Ernst (Ernest) (Sir)
(22.5.1880–25.11.1957)

m. 19.6.1906
Mary Lina Pollak (May)
(30.7.1886–5.2.1934)

m. 1.6.1935
Caroline Magdalen (Ina) Oppenheimer
(3.11.1899–2.2.1971)

Philip Jack (Sir)
(29.10.1911–8.10.1995)
m. Pamela Fenn Stirling
(13.8.1916–11.3.1997)

Robert Forster McCall
m.
Marjorie Hamilton
Mackenzie (Callie)

Harry Frederick
(28.10.1908 –19.8.2000)
m. 6.3.1943
Bridget Denison McCall
(28.9.1921–23.10.2013)

Frank Leslie
(17.10.1910–17.4.1935)

Nicholas Frank (8.6.1945–)
m. 11.11.1968
Orcillia Mary Louise Lasch
(6.5.1941–)

Jonathan Ernest Maxmillian
(18.11.1969–) m. 18.6.1994
Jennifer Janvier Ward
(15.2.1967–16.5.2017)

Benjamin Raymond
(14.3.1971–20.4.1973)

INTRODUCTION

A Reflection on Legacy and Dynasty

When I started my research for this book, Harry Oppenheimer had ebbed from public consciousness. He had been dead 17 years; and in South Africa, a nation often preoccupied with the past, collective memory can fade astonishingly easily. However, the name was shortly to enjoy a revival. In 2017, the London-based public relations firm Bell Pottinger (long since the agency of choice for clients with a chequered past) was exposed as the mastermind behind a campaign designed to stoke racial tensions in the post-apartheid polity. Waged principally through social media, it was constructed around the bogeyman of 'white monopoly capital', a term that conjured up the spectre of South Africa's wealthiest corporate dynasties: the Oppenheimers and the Ruperts. A malevolent monster engorged by centuries of racial capitalism, fuelled by the exploitation of black labour, white monopoly capital had as its archetypes the magnates of a bygone era: Harry Oppenheimer, former crowned head of a gold and diamond empire, and Anton Rupert, founder of the Rembrandt Group. It lived and breathed through their family legacies. Although Johann Rupert (Anton Rupert's heir) stood more directly in the line of fire than Nicky Oppenheimer (Harry Oppenheimer's son), the guns of racial invective were trained on both of them. Bell Pottinger's propaganda offensive served the purposes of its puppet masters: it sought to deflect attention from the project of systematic plunder orchestrated by the African nationalist President, Jacob Zuma, and his associates in business. In due course, their destructive march through the nation's public institutions would be encapsulated in the term 'state capture'. But what struck me forcefully as this sordid saga unfolded was its resonance with the politics of the past, when nationalists of another stripe had focused their ire on the Oppenheimer family.

At the time of Bell Pottinger's unmasking, before its rapid descent into disgrace, I was reading Hansards from the period when Harry Oppenheimer served as the member of Parliament for Kimberley. He represented the United Party (UP). Oppenheimer entered politics in 1948, just as the tide of Afrikaner nationalism swept aside the comparatively inclusive (albeit unassailably white) civic patriotism associated with his boyhood hero, Jan Smuts. Like Smuts, who led the UP, Oppenheimer was imbued with a sense of fealty to the British Commonwealth. However, in the epoch-making election of 1948, Smuts was defeated and the UP was relegated, along with its imperialistic ideals, to the opposition benches in Parliament. That is where Oppenheimer found himself from 1948 to 1957. Under the successive premierships of DF Malan and JG Strijdom (and the doctrinaire Minister of Native Affairs, HF Verwoerd), the National Party proceeded to implement its totalitarian vision of apartheid. The Commonwealth connection was blunted; later it was severed. As the heir to his father Sir Ernest Oppenheimer's corporate kingdom, Harry Oppenheimer may have commanded economic power, but politically he was impotent. Nevertheless, to the National Party he represented an existential threat to Afrikanerdom: he embodied everything its leaders dreaded and detested. Government leaders whipped up fears about the role and reach of influential English-speaking capitalists. To them Oppenheimer personified *die geldmag* (money power), the sinister conglomeration of big capital, which stood to corrupt the *volk* and erode the traditional Afrikaner values of solidarity, piety and integrity.[1] In the heat of political battle, some cabinet ministers threatened to nationalise the Oppenheimers' mines. In the early 1950s, Harry Oppenheimer came to be depicted as 'Hoggenheimer' in the Afrikaner nationalist press, just as his father had been two decades previously.[2] This antisemitic caricature symbolised British–Jewish imperialism and predatory mining finance capital. The Oppenheimers were converts to Anglicanism, but the Jew-baiting reverberated through the House of Assembly. In this moment, the figure of 'Hoggenheimer' – much like the ogre of white monopoly capital – performed a function central to nationalist demonology: it rallied the Afrikaner nation against a common enemy.

I thought of this parallel because it seemed to go to the heart of questions about reputation, legacy and memory, and the historical context in which the lives of public figures are appraised. In producing this biography, I am mindful of two factors that militate against an even-handed hearing for Oppenheimer in the land of his birth. Most importantly, he was a liberal individualist (of a conservative sort, to be sure) in a country where the arc of history bends towards groupthink and nationalism. In South Africa, nationalist myths abound. Among members of the new governing elite, as with their predecessors, there is an impulse to survey the annals of our ancestors and to sanctify or vilify, to celebrate or denigrate. In part, that is just what nationalist rulers do: they enlist mythology and symbolism to present a glorious version of their reconditioned past. Their heroes are deified while ideological adversaries are demonised, and triumphalism replaces the search for truth – fraught as that concept might be – as the purpose of historical endeavour. A man with a complex legacy like Oppenheimer, a liberal in a land dominated by nationalists, is all too unthinkingly reduced to the phantasmagoria of 'Hoggenheimer' and white monopoly capital.

There is another facet to this potentially polarised reception, and that is the growing orthodoxy of 'presentism', the practice whereby historical protagonists are hastily judged on the basis of whether they live up to contemporary mores and values. In some ways, Oppenheimer was a man ahead of his time; in others, he was inescapably a product of his era. He looked upon the 'wind of change' blowing through Africa in the 1960s not as a calamity, but certainly as a phenomenon which might not be unquestionably propitious. Oppenheimer mourned the 'fading' of the Commonwealth, or at least what he perceived to be its original ideals. That was the title of his Smuts Memorial Lecture at the University of Cambridge in 1967.[3] Oppenheimer was no starry-eyed admirer of Cecil John Rhodes, the founder (in 1888) of De Beers Consolidated Mines, but he regarded himself and the Oppenheimer family enterprise – the gold and diamond dynasty – as heirs to the 'Rhodes tradition'. Although Oppenheimer was an articulate opponent of apartheid, and bankrolled the Progressive Party for decades after its formation in 1959 (the 'Progs', a breakaway from the UP, were the liberal opposition to the Nationalist government), he supported a qualified franchise until 1978. In the 1970s and 1980s, he was an evolutionary democrat, a proponent of gradualism and reform; however, his support for non-racial democracy came with all sorts of caveats about black majority rule. And even though Oppenheimer was an enlightened capitalist, certainly by the standards of his peers, on his mines the conditions above and below ground contributed to generations of black hardship. Viewed through this lens, Oppenheimer is hardly likely to pass muster with the 21st-century sloganeers of the decolonisation movement, the statue-topplers, the ideologically pure warriors who want to cleanse the past of ambiguity. Yet his legacy is multifaceted, and he deserves neither obloquy nor hagiography.

Possessed of a refined aesthetic sensibility, Oppenheimer would perhaps have regarded the iconoclasm of today's self-styled social justice campaigners, scouring the past for thoughtcrimes, as brutish. 'When you are brought up in the purple,' he once said to the British writer Anthony Sampson, 'the only thing worth doing is to be some kind of an artist.'[4] With his abiding love of French Impressionist painting and English Romantic poetry, particularly the works of Lord Byron and Percy Bysshe Shelley, there is no doubt that Oppenheimer conceived of his corporate conquests as sublimated artistry. He turned business into an art form, according to Sampson, and 'became an artist in that'. In this world he was known simply by his initials, 'HFO'. A rare example of a scion who inherited both a streak of creative genius and a passion for commerce, HFO vastly expanded the inheritance left to him by his father. The corporate patrimony came in the form of the Anglo American Corporation, founded by Ernest Oppenheimer in 1917, and its sister company, De Beers.

But HFO was much more than an imaginative industrialist whose riches brought him global recognition. He was prominent in public life. Among his many roles, besides serving as a parliamentarian, Oppenheimer was the Chancellor of the University of Cape Town from 1967 to 1996. After the Soweto uprising of 1976, which marked a turning point in South African history, he founded the Urban Foundation with Anton Rupert. A catalyst for the socio-economic upliftment of black township dwellers, the foundation played a critical role in the process of reform. Through the Ernest Oppenheimer Memorial Trust and the Anglo American and De Beers Chairman's Fund, HFO institutionalised a culture of philanthropy. The multiple black beneficiaries of this largesse – across the spectrum of arts and culture, education and training – were able to gain access to opportunities which the apartheid state saw fit to deny them as a matter of course. Nelson Mandela, with whom HFO developed a friendship in the 1990s, lauded the tycoon for his efforts to develop South Africa. Oppenheimer's 'contribution to building a partnership between Big Business and the new democratic government', Mandela panegyrised, could 'never be appreciated too much'.[5] Even so, HFO's legacy remains contested. As the potentate who held sway over

South Africa's largest mining house for a quarter of a century during apartheid, Oppenheimer's name is tarnished by association with those features of the racially oppressive system which left an altogether more corrosive residue. First and foremost among these is the migrant labour system. It rent asunder families and cleaved the social fabric. In that sense, the architect's epitaph that memorialises Sir Christopher Wren at St Paul's Cathedral – 'If you would seek his monument, look around you' – echoes equivocally in the case of this study's subject.

◆

The opportunity to write Oppenheimer's biography, coupled with the benefit of unrestricted access to the family's personal papers, proved an exciting prospect for me. When I first began exploring these holdings at the Brenthurst Library, they were an unmined treasure trove. I felt a bit like one of those diggers who descended on Kimberley in the late 1870s, or perhaps the Witwatersrand a decade later: armed with my metaphorical pick and shovel, I set upon the archive as if it were the site of a diamond rush, a researcher's El Dorado. Oppenheimer's scholarly attractions are clear. His life history is inseparable from the tapestry of South Africa's 20th-century development. The nation's tangled political, economic, social, cultural and commercial strands are all reflected in HFO's personal patchwork of power. Indeed, the origins and growth of Anglo American and De Beers, two of the biggest and most successful businesses in the history of South African capitalism, warrant separate monographs.[6] But that is not my purpose here. Rather, in threading the story of Oppenheimer's long and varied life, I have sought to concentrate on the individual. I have tried to weave the public and the private, the chronological and the thematic; where the canvas of his corporate craftsmanship is concerned, I have approached it (and eyed the developments, the deals and the dynasty) from the perspective of the biographer, not the business historian.

Despite HFO's historical significance, he has not previously been the focus of a comprehensive life history. There is a dual biography of him and his father, *Oppenheimer and Son*, published in 1973.[7] That book unearthed a great deal of useful material, but it is not the product of critical inquiry; nor, by its nature, was it able to do justice to a significant portion of HFO's career. Oppenheimer wrote an outline of his own memoir after he retired in the mid-1980s. He made a stab at several chapters; however, the manuscript was not completed or published. He was 'setting off on a voyage of exploration', HFO proffered in his introduction, and should it turn out that he had pursued a 'circular route', then he hoped to be 'sensible enough' to refrain from publication.[8] The course he charted was more than adequately linear: Oppenheimer had an acute appreciation of time's relentless forward march. Perhaps it was a natural inclination towards self-restraint, the counterpart of a certain courtliness, which dissuaded him from wider dissemination. During his lifetime Oppenheimer politely fobbed off various approaches from would-be biographers. It was only in 2017 that an edited volume, partly fashioned from his speeches and public statements, appeared under the title *A Man of Africa*.[9] Although that compilation focuses exclusively on HFO's political thought – his business and private life fall beyond its scope – the book provides a considered assessment of Oppenheimer's legacy. He was a 'leader who transcended the business world through a quest to understand the public good', the book's editor, Kalim Rajab, concludes, as he lays the groundwork for a rider: 'But in terms of his progressive political-economic thought and action, his legacy is more strained and should not be whitewashed.'[10]

HFO's life shines a sidelight on the history of South Africa's political economy; it bridged not only the rise and fall of apartheid, but the birth – and reincarnation – of the country. Four days after Oppenheimer was born in 1908, a constitutional convention was launched: it culminated in 1910 in the Union of South Africa, which welded the former British colonies and Boer republics into a unified nation-state ruled by the white minority. Segregation, and the exclusion of blacks from citizenship, was its cornerstone. Over eighty years later, another process of constitutional negotiations got under way. It brought together old antagonists, white and black, to midwife what Archbishop Desmond Tutu evocatively christened the 'Rainbow Nation'. The founding democratic election of 1994 and the Constitution ultimately adopted in 1996 were its progeny. In this way, in his old age, Oppenheimer was able to witness the transition from a racial oligarchy to a non-racial democracy.

Oppenheimer played a contentious part in this metamorphosis. To many on the left, who seek to rationalise democracy's disappointing dividends (even its decay), Oppenheimer and Mandela serve as useful scapegoats for the country's current failures. Symbolised by these two figureheads, the white corporate elite and the black political elite, so the argument goes, struck a Faustian bargain in the course of the negotiated settlement. They conspired to retain the economic fundaments of the old order in the new dispensation. As participants in the Brenthurst Group, a forum convened between 1994 and 1996, some among their number met in the seclusion of Oppenheimer's Johannesburg estate. There, Mandela was co-opted: he sold out the revolution, and the mandarins of white monopoly capital bought off their new rulers with promises of riches. Thus was the privilege of the white minority entrenched and the birthright of the black majority cruelly blighted. It is a version of the past incidentally incorporated into African nationalist mythology – or at least the folklore which surrounds the lack of so-called radical economic transformation trumpeted by that slogan's most ardent propagandists. The truth, as the last two chapters of this biography attempt to reveal, is somewhat more slippery.

There was no economic pact. The reasons for the Rainbow Nation's fracturing are much more intricate than the individual legacies of Mandela or Oppenheimer; nor should they be glibly pinned on the fiendish forces of neoliberalism. Besides, if Oppenheimer's record is to be dissected, then a longer lens is needed. Over the *longue durée*, his advocacy against apartheid and his promotion of democracy were indeed characterised by ambivalences. HFO may have been reviled by successive National Party prime ministers, but his corporate empire was engaged in a delicate dance of dependence with the government; after all, it kept the apartheid economy afloat. In Parliament, Oppenheimer was a fierce critic of the National Party. But he tended to couch his arguments against its racial policies in the language of *homo economicus*. The parlance of social justice was not his natural mode of expression; he avoided impugning the Nationalists' morality, and he steered clear of ethical entreaties for them to change their ways. Instead, Oppenheimer insisted that apartheid made no economic sense; it was impracticable. Industrialisation, HFO declared, would lead to modernisation and democracy, and ultimately the barriers that separated blacks from whites would be broken down. This was the germ of the 'Oppenheimer thesis' elaborated by Anglo American's contingent of intellectuals, many of whom were stationed in the Chairman's Fund. They maintained that racial discrimination and free enterprise were irreconcilable: failure to eradicate the one would inevitably result in the elimination of the other. Yet, as Oppenheimer's critics observed, Anglo American prospered well enough off the back of an unholy trinity: the migrant labour system, which provided the mines with a replenishable pool of grossly underpaid, exploited black workers; the pass laws, which regulated the movement of black people to the cities; and the compound system, which corralled black mineworkers into single-sex living quarters where their conditions were often squalid and inhumane. Anglo American profited from this terrible triumvirate, its detractors asserted, and if the company really wanted to smash the institutional apparatus of white supremacy, it could muster the requisite might.

Oppenheimer was alert to insinuations of collaboration or complicity, and the potential they had to taint his legacy. He believed that his businesses flourished in spite of, not because of, apartheid, and that overall they were a force for progress. It could be justly argued that his companies created millions of jobs, built valuable infrastructure, exerted crucial pressure on the National Party to initiate reforms, and provided a platform for economic growth in the democratic era. The party of liberation inherited the most sophisticated economy on the continent, and the Oppenheimer group of companies played a vital part in its development. Nevertheless, there were sins of commission and omission. The hazardous working conditions that gave rise to the spread of silicosis and silico-tuberculosis are a stain on the gold mining industry. It was not a reality that HFO attempted to grasp fully, or that he confronted head-on. He made the odd trip down to the bottom of his deepest gold mines, but he was no more than an accidental tourist. 'It's quite amusing but I wouldn't like to work there,' he once remarked airily to a journalist.[11] Looking back on his life, Oppenheimer readily admitted that his corporations should have done much more, much sooner, to counteract segregation in the workplace. Anglo American should have pushed harder to house a greater fraction of its black mineworkers in accommodation designed for married couples – a concession that Verwoerd as minister of native affairs reluctantly granted – thereby striking a blow against migrant labour. But these were belated admissions, offered with the benefit of hindsight. To many, the regrets rang hollow: they had seen the consequences of Anglo's inaction, quite clearly, long in advance.

◆

What then of the corporate dynasty? If 2017 was notable for Bell Pottinger's deceptions, then it also stood out for another reason: the centenary of the Anglo American Corporation. But by then the mining finance house had turned into a shadow of its former self. On the world stage, it was dwarfed by its major rivals: Glencore, Rio Tinto and BHP. For 'a shattered modern empire to rival Shelley's *Ozymandias*', Rajab lamented, 'one needs look no further than Anglo American'.[12] Tony Bloom, former chairman of the family-founded Premier Group (which Anglo American absorbed into its stable in the 1980s), echoed the sentiment. The credit for 'Anglo's power and prestige belonged to HFO', he ventured, but Oppenheimer's 'monumental commercial legacy' had been 'squandered by his successors'.[13] The family's ties to Anglo American plc, listed on the London Stock Exchange in 1999, had long since frayed. Neither Nicky Oppenheimer nor his son, Jonathan, would ever run or chair the company. Meanwhile, in 2011, Nicky had sold the family's 40 per cent stake in De Beers to Anglo American for $5.1 billion, thus terminating a relationship which had endured for over eighty years. It was, he said at the time, a 'difficult decision', but one that was taken 'in the best interests of the family'.[14] The diamond market had collapsed in the global recession of 2008–9, and although it was well on the way to recovery, it seemed prudent for the family to re-evaluate its investment strategy.

It is interesting if somewhat idle to speculate about what HFO would have made of this trajectory. The 'Oppenheimer dynasty' (not a label, incidentally, which Harry Oppenheimer would have attached to his family, much less employed) has frequently been portrayed as if it resembled royalty in South Africa. Like his father, HFO was consistently referred to in the press as the 'King of Diamonds', the 'King of Gold', or 'the man with the Midas touch'. In his autumn years, he was treated reverentially in Anglo American as a kind of constitutional monarch. Early on in their marriage, Oppenheimer's wife, Bridget, took on a rather regal demeanour. Locally, the family name is equivalent in standing to the Rothschilds (the 'Kings of the Jews') or the Rockefellers (the 'American royal family').[15] It brings to mind the financial and industrial dynasties sustained by the Morgans, the Fords, the Mellons and the Carnegies, the indissoluble stamp of a name associated with a tradition of philanthropy, handed down from generation to generation. However, as has often been observed of well-heeled dynasties, there tends to be a pattern: the first generation makes the money, the second generation spends it, and the third generation throws it all away. In Thomas Mann's chronicle of the rise and fall of a Hanseatic merchant dynasty, *Buddenbrooks*, there is a progressive loss of entrepreneurial vigour and financial aptitude: decadence is detectable in the third generation and threatens to be fatal in the fourth.[16] In Nicky Oppenheimer's case he managed to preserve and monetise the family's wealth thanks to the shrewdly timed (and priced) sale of its interest in De Beers. Through a new global investment company rooted in Africa, Oppenheimer Partners, Jonathan Oppenheimer seeks to build a long-term portfolio of businesses faithful to his great-grandfather's philosophy. This is the idea, as Ernest Oppenheimer liked to say, that the purpose of business is to earn profits, but to earn them in such a way as to make a 'real and permanent contribution to the well-being of the people' and the development of communities.[17]

Dynasties are dynamic. The economic historian David Landes notes in his fascinating study of the world's great family businesses that tales of money, power and kinship inevitably involve 'drama and passion', especially with the passage of generations: 'as wealth grows, so do the opportunities for disagreement'.[18] In 1935 Ernest Oppenheimer founded E Oppenheimer and Son as a holding company for the family's investments. As I conducted my research for this book, the firm was dissolved. In essence, it has bifurcated. Oppenheimer Generations (Opp-Gen) now represents the interests of Nicky and Jonathan Oppenheimer, while Nicky's sister, Mary, and her daughters, Victoria Freudenheim, Rebecca Oppenheimer, Jessica Jell and Rachel Slack, have elected to further their concerns through Mary Oppenheimer and Daughters (MODO). In some ways, this development has freed the women in the family to flex their financial muscles independently: historically, E Oppenheimer and Son, like the greater Anglo American group, was a patriarchal institution. In HFO's working life, the notion that a female Oppenheimer might carve out a career in the family business (or take the lead in making decisions about investments) would have struck him as peculiar, a departure from gender norms. Today, both jointly and independently, Opp-Gen and MODO maintain a commitment to philanthropy. When the Covid-19 pandemic gripped the world in 2020, each side of the family donated R1 billion to privately administered funds to mitigate the socio-economic impacts of the disease on South Africa. The (renamed) Oppenheimer Memorial Trust, currently chaired by Jonathan, with Rebecca serving as a trustee, continues to make significant grants to public benefit organisations and institutions, principally in the education sector. But the nature of the dynasty has palpably changed.

Ernest Oppenheimer was the dynastic founder. As a risk-taking entrepreneur, he was intimately bound up with the economic development of southern Africa. That fact is reflected in the title of Sir Theodore Gregory's weighty biography of the capitalist colossus.[19] Having assumed the chairman's mantle on his father's death in 1957, HFO became the consolidator and the expander. More conservative and cerebral by nature, he nevertheless built on the bequest and added numerous protectorates to the 'Oppenheimer empire'.[20] HFO did this in two ways. From the early 1960s he diversified Anglo American into secondary industry, a process signalled by the formation of the Highveld Steel and Vanadium Corporation. Nationally, Anglo's operations eventually spanned the gamut of manufacturing, construction, property and finance. Prompted in part by the logic of exchange controls, which forced Anglo to reinvest domestically, the corporation morphed into an industrial conglomerate: in time to come, it completely dominated the South African economy. Almost simultaneously, HFO embarked upon a campaign of international expansion. By the time he relinquished the chairmanship of Anglo American at the end of 1982 (and that of De Beers at the end of 1984), the greater group – a Byzantine beast sprouting manifold appendages – had become a multinational mining combine, with interests in a plethora of minerals and metals ranging from gold and diamonds, platinum and uranium, to nickel and oil. The group boasted footholds all over Africa, North America, South America, Europe, Asia and Australasia. It was a $15 billion empire on which the sun never set. Minorco, the group's flagship international investment company (initially domiciled in Bermuda, subsequently in Luxembourg), was the principal shareholder in Phibro-Salomon, a leading American investment bank and commodities trader. In fact, by 1981, Minorco had become the single largest foreign investor in the United States.

HFO saw it as his manifest destiny – indeed, duty – to sustain and strengthen what his father had created. The extraordinarily close relationship between the two of them – they shared something akin to a telepathic connection – is key to understanding HFO's character, outlook and self-image. 'The notion of there being a "generation gap" did not occur to me,' HFO wrote of his father in the outline of his memoir. 'It seemed to me that it was not for me to choose a career but simply to do my duty in the estate to which it had pleased God to call me.'[21] In his various guises as heir, apprentice, magnate, monarch – the quatrain of this book – HFO often appeared to be navigating through life by the North Star of paternal prescripts. However, in stepping out of his father's shadow, he emerged as his own man; the vicissitudes of personal and professional fortune inevitably moulded him. As I write this, Virginia Woolf's dictum rings in my ears: a good biography, she determined, should be the record of the things that change rather than merely of the things that happen. In this book, I have tried to document the transitions as well as the happenings. By the end of Harry Oppenheimer's life, his ideas about destiny and family had shifted. In matters familial, HFO believed in the virtue of tradition. But he came to an important realisation. It is through change, he discovered – rather than conformity or simple continuity – that the art might most reliably outlive the artist.

I
HEIR

1908–1931, and earlier

ONE

Family Roots

(BEFORE 1908)

Blood and Iron, and the Jews of Frankfurt

Outside Eduard Oppenheimer's modestly appointed tobacconist's shop in Friedberg, north of Frankfurt, the tides of nationalist fervour churned. Otto von Bismarck, the volcanic Prussian Minister-President, had resolved to crush his liberal opponents at home and vanquish his European rivals abroad. Bismarck's goal was to forge Germany's disparate states into a unified nation under Prussian hegemony – through blood and iron if need be. The German Reich was wrought with guns and guile. After engineering wars with the three powers that stood in the way of unification – Denmark, Austria and France – and defeating them in turn, Prussia emerged victorious, and its king, Wilhelm I, was proclaimed the new German Emperor at the Palace of Versailles. Bismarck was to be his Chancellor. And so, in 1871, the German Empire was born. The Oppenheimer empire, by contrast – the fabled corporate behemoth of the 20th century, a colossus studded with diamonds and gold – was then but a speck of ash on the map of greater Hesse.

When the Iron Chancellor welded Germany together like some mettlesome metallurgist, the Oppenheimers' fiefdom was confined to a solitary store in Friedberg. They were merchants of cigars, not minerals or metals. Eduard Oppenheimer and his wife, Nanette (or 'Nanny', née Hirschhorn), were married by the rabbi at Butzbach on 11 December 1862. In 1871 they were the parents of four sons: Bernard (b. 1866),

1

Gustav (b. 1867), Emil (b. 1869) and Louis (b. 1870). Ernst, later anglicised to Ernest, arrived ten years later, on 22 May 1880, following a fecund daughterly interlude. His older sisters, Lina, Franziska and Johanna, were all born between 1872 and 1878. Another son, Otto, followed Ernest two years later, while the tenth and last child, Eugen (b. 1884), died early, aged five. Ernest took his place in a family of progressively prospering German-Jewish traders. His father, paternal grandfather and paternal great-grandfather were all property owners born in Reichenbach, where the Oppenheimers had plied their trade since the late 18th century.[1]

Ernest's grandfather Nathan Baer Oppenheimer, a cigar merchant, initiated the move to Frankfurt in the 1850s. He hoped the free imperial city would offer better prospects for his wares. Only six decades earlier, however, Frankfurt had festered with anti-Jewish hostility. The *Judensau* (Jews' sow), an ancient and obscene antisemitic image, occupied an officially sanctioned spot on one of the town's walls. It depicted a group of Jews demeaning themselves with a fierce sow, including a rabbi licking the pig's excrement. In 1795, a traveller to the Jewish quarter, the *Judengasse* (Jews' Lane), remarked that most of Frankfurt's Jews had a 'deathly pale appearance'.[2] For all that it was 'sombre, humid and filthy', Frankfurt's *Judengasse* produced a thriving tribe of teachers, doctors, traders, and financiers like Mayer Amschel Rothschild (b. 1744),[3] who founded the Rothschild banking dynasty.

By the 19th century, Jews oiled the wheels of Germany's financial institutions. They powered its economic development and spearheaded its turn to industry. In fact, as the historian Fritz Stern observed, perhaps never before in Europe had a minority 'risen as fast or gone as far as did German Jews in the nineteenth century'.[4] Within this minority, the Oppenheimer name was associated with money and political influence. Several Oppenheimers became diplomats. Karl (later Sir Charles) Oppenheimer, a Frankfurt native who emigrated to England in 1852 aged 16, started out in the City of London as a general merchant and ended his career as the knighted British consul general in Frankfurt.[5] These Oppenheimers may have occupied loftier and more luxuriant branches of the extended family tree, but Eduard – an unassuming cigar salesman with foresight and aspirations for his large brood of dependants – would harness whatever connections he could for his children's benefit. It seemed increasingly necessary. For although members of the small German-Jewish elite had played a significant role in the creation of the new nation-state – between 1864 and 1871, they effectively underwrote the costs of Germany's wars of unification – the triumphalist pan-German nationalism that sustained it was ethnocentric and exclusionary.

The Oppenheimers' German roots lay deep and spread wide; indeed, the Jewish community of the town Oppenheim, from where the surname springs, was first recorded in the town's tax register in 1241. And yet, after 1870, as an atavistic, chauvinistic sentiment took hold, the very presence of Jews in the German polity came to be resented and scorned. This was a different kind of nationalism from its more liberal predecessor, which had been shaped by the revolutions of 1848. Now, *völkisch* intellectuals cast the Jew as an insidious enfeebler of traditional Germanic values, the 'principal corruptor of the German soul'.[6] Presciently, Eduard Oppenheimer warned his six sons that Germany was no longer 'a country for Jews to live in'.[7] They must get out, as soon as they were reasonably educated, he instructed them, and seek their fortunes far from Friedberg. England appeared to be the safest destination. In contrast to most of Continental Europe, antisemitism failed to gain a sure political foothold in 19th-century Britain.[8] The first to leave Friedberg was Bernard, the eldest son, a youngster of imperious mien. He made his way to London on an exit permit arranged by Charles Oppenheimer. By some quirk of fate, his path was paved by the discovery of diamonds, thousands of miles away on the southern tip of Africa. It was an exploit that would set in motion South Africa's industrial revolution, reshape its political landscape, and radically alter the fortunes of Eduard Oppenheimer's sons.

Discovery of Diamonds in Kimberley

In 1867, a young boy named Erasmus Jacobs, the son of an impecunious Boer farmer, found a diamond on his father's farm near the settlement of Hopetown on the Orange River. Further findings followed.[9] A mad rush for riches ensued. By 1870, there were over ten thousand diggers from all over the globe spread along the banks of the Vaal River, from its confluence with the Orange River to Klipdrift (later, Barkly West) in the north. They engaged in alluvial digging. But an even greater discovery awaited. Unlike in India or Brazil, the diamonds in southern Africa were not confined to riverbeds. It soon became clear that deep below the earth's surface, in hard rock called blue ground, there were diamond deposits of an entirely different order from what any speculator dared dream. From the beginning of the 1870s, pipes of crystallised carbon bearing vast numbers of gemstones were found. In 1871, diggings were established on the farm Vooruitzicht, belonging to Diederik and Johannes de Beer. Two mines formed in swift succession in the area that became known as Kimberley: the Old Rush (later, De Beers) mine and the New Rush (later, Kimberley) mine at Colesberg Kopje, which sat atop an ancient pipe of diamondiferous lava. The small *kopje* (hill) collapsed into Kimberley's 'Big Hole', one of the deepest man-made cavities in the world. By the end of 1871, five mines had been discovered and were being exploited: Bultfontein, Dutoitspan, the De Beers mine, the Kimberley mine, and, one hundred miles away, Jagersfontein.

The problem for the diggers was how to lay their hands on rough diamonds buried deep underground. Sophisticated machinery – physical, administrative and financial – was needed to extract them. In Britain, the mandarins of empire sprang to attention. They proclaimed Griqualand West, which incorporated the diggings at Kimberley, a Crown Colony in 1871 and annexed it to the Cape Colony nine years later. Meanwhile, the foot soldiers of empire scrambled to stake their own claims. The most remarkable among them was the lanky 18-year-old son of an English vicar, a precocious adolescent possessed of vision and determination. He talked garrulously in a piercing falsetto and he scuttled about the diamond fields. His name was Cecil John Rhodes. Rhodes bought a claim to the De Beers mine and proceeded to establish himself as one of the most formidable entrepreneurs in Kimberley, vying for pre-eminence with Barney Barnato, the rough-and-ready son of a London East End Jewish hawker. Rhodes gobbled up the claims of smaller mining operators. He managed to secure funding from the Rothschild banking family. Rhodes was a force of nature, forever metamorphosing. He was a miner-turned-entrepreneur. He was a successful capitalist who transformed himself into an amalgamator. As a member of the Cape Parliament and prime minister of the Cape Colony, Rhodes rose to become a political luminary 'capable of arousing enormous outpourings both of affection and of vituperation'.[10] These are all descriptors that would, in due course, be applied to Ernest Oppenheimer and the dynasty he created. Theirs was to become a dominion of sorts, consciously moulded in the 'Rhodes tradition'. However, Rhodes played no direct role in Ernest Oppenheimer's fortunes. It was Anton Dunkelsbuhler – a relative, through his wife, of Eduard Oppenheimer's sons – who unrolled for the Oppenheimer brothers a jewelled carpet that stretched from Friedberg, via London, to Kimberley and back to England. Dunkelsbuhler's firm became the 'haven and workshop' of Oppenheimers fleeing European antisemitism.[11]

Anton Dunkelsbuhler and the Jewelled Carpet

Anton Dünkelsbühler was born at Fürth in Bavaria on 24 December 1844. He settled in England in July 1866 and became a naturalised British subject at the end of 1871. A man of refined sensibilities, he sought to cast off the shackles of the ghetto and turn himself into an Englishman as fast as he could, not least by dropping the umlauts from his German surname. 'In the privacy of their own homes they may have observed the traditional Jewish customs,' Ernest Oppenheimer's biographer wrote of Dunkelsbuhler, 'but in their everyday commercial life their ambition was to Anglicize themselves and become "Englishmen of Jewish extraction" like the Rothschilds, the Montagus, and the Samuels.'[12] It was an impulse shared by all but one of the Oppenheimer brothers. Long before they were out of their teens, Bernard, Gustav, Louis, Ernest and Otto all fled Friedberg to climb the staircase of financial and social respectability in London. Kimberley was a staging post along the way. Only Ernest would settle permanently in the diamond-mining centre and reinvent himself as a man both of Africa and of the British Empire. Dunkelsbuhler went to Kimberley in 1872 as a diamond buyer and representative for the merchant house Mosenthal and Company. David Harris, Barney Barnato's cousin and a celebrated diamond dealer himself, called Dunkelsbuhler the largest and most generous buyer on the fields. During the four years he spent in Kimberley, Dunkelsbuhler traded more than £1 million on behalf of Mosenthals. He also made sure to accumulate his own stock of stones. Back in London, Dunkelsbuhler set up shop as a diamond dealer at 97 Hatton Garden. He formed a branch in Kimberley, too, from where a resident buyer would send him a regular supply of diamonds.

Bernard was the first Oppenheimer to join the London office of A Dunkelsbuhler and Company. Now approaching middle age and portly with prosperity, the diminutive founder was referred to as 'Old Dunkels' behind his back. After a short apprenticeship shadowing Old Dunkels, Bernard was dispatched to Kimberley at the age of 13.[13] Louis followed in Bernard's footsteps when he turned 16. Two of the brothers' first cousins from Friedberg, Gustav Imroth and Friedrich 'Fritz' Hirschhorn – they went on to senior positions in the diamond brokerages Barnato Brothers and Wernher, Beit and Company respectively – were already ensconced in Kimberley. They provided a ready-made social network for their relatives. Louis arrived in Kimberley just as Rhodes was in the midst of a mighty battle with Barnato to consolidate control of the diamond trade. With the support of Alfred Beit – a shy, unobtrusive, thoroughly anglicised (and converted) German Jew – Rhodes quickly prevailed. In 1888, he concluded a deal with Barnato which led to the creation of De Beers Consolidated Mines Limited. Rhodes soon held sway over more than 95 per cent of the world's diamond production. His next step was to recalibrate the scales of supply and demand so that the market would not be flooded. Rhodes wanted to dominate production and monopolise distribution. In 1890, he formed the Diamond Syndicate, which was effectively a single channel for diamonds entering the market.[14] It comprised ten firms, each of which signed an agreement to purchase a fixed quota of diamonds. At ten per cent, Dunkelsbuhlers had the fourth largest allocation behind Wernher, Beit and Company, Barnato Brothers, and Mosenthals. It was Bernard Oppenheimer who put his signature to the contract on behalf of Dunkelsbuhlers.

The Witwatersrand Gold Rush and the Emergence of the 'Randlords'

Many of the adventurers who grew stupendously rich in Kimberley – anglicised German Jews like Alfred Beit, Anton Dunkelsbuhler and George Albu; Lithuanian Jews like Samuel 'Sammy' Marks; and British Jews like Barnato, Barnato's nephew Solomon 'Solly' Joel, and Lionel Phillips – extended their sphere of operations to the Witwatersrand after the discovery of gold in 1886. They transplanted parts of their physical and financial infrastructure to Johannesburg in order to exploit the auriferous finds. Ownership of individual mines was centralised among a few holding companies. Given the fixed price of gold and the highly speculative nature of mining investment, concentration of ownership meant more efficient use of technical and administrative resources. The result was that wealth and power were channelled into the hands of a small elite, reinforced by a system of interlocking directorships. Some of these gold barons set up residence in the mansions of Parktown on the ridge overlooking Johannesburg. They became 'Randlords', wealthy and cultured creatures of the Anglo-South African establishment.[15] Others looked upon the city of gold just as they had looked upon the city of diamonds. It was a temporary port of call on their voyage of self-enrichment back to the metropole. Returning to England, they proceeded to acquire Park Lane mansions, racehorses and country houses. Dunkelsbuhler was a sojourner on the British Empire's profitable periphery. After the Rand was opened up, he acquired significant gold interests in association with Goerz and

Company (later, the Union Corporation), linked to the Consolidated Mines Selection Company Limited and the Transvaal Coal Trust Company Limited (later, the Rand Selection Corporation Limited). Dunkelsbuhler sent Bernard Oppenheimer to look after his fledgling gold concerns on the Rand. Louis took over from Bernard in the Kimberley office, and he stayed there for several years before going back to London to manage matters at Dunkelsbuhlers' new, grander headquarters on Holborn Circus. Bernard eventually left Dunkelsbuhlers to join forces with Sammy Marks. Ultimately he returned to England, though he remained long enough in Kimberley to serve in the volunteer force of the Kimberley Regiment when the city was besieged during the Anglo-Boer War. So it came to pass that when Ernest undertook his rite of passage from Friedberg to London in 1896, he fell under the wing of Louis rather than Bernard. It was to prove a portentous pairing. Louis was the brother with whom Ernest cultivated his closest relationship and to whom, he would claim in later years, 'he owed everything in his life'.[16]

Ernest Oppenheimer's Apprenticeship

Ernest was squat and powerfully built, with dark, deep-set, lively eyes. Unlike the more effete-looking Louis, young Ernest was a dynamo. He reached London on his 16th birthday and commenced his apprenticeship at Dunkelsbuhlers as the 'office dogsbody', making tea and keeping his superiors stocked with stationery.[17] In time, with another young recruit – a Parisian, Etienne Fallek – Ernest started sorting diamonds. He considered the crystals to be things of beauty. They were the foundation stones of his career. 'When a man really understands something about diamonds,' Ernest would later declare, 'he becomes a diamond merchant, not a valuator.'[18] From the moment he walked through Old Dunkels's door, Ernest Oppenheimer dedicated himself to becoming the world's pre-eminent diamond merchant. His ambition was vaulting. Louis passed on to Ernest all the correspondence from the Dunkelsbuhlers representative in Kimberley, Leon Soutro, which he devoured. Ernest stockpiled every shard of knowledge possible. He compiled all the statistics of mine production, outputs and returns into his own personal register. Although his education had been limited, Ernest was a quick study. His final school report, issued two weeks before his arrival in London, recorded his results in English, French, geography, chemistry and mineralogy as '*gut*' while his performance in algebra and geometry was '*sehr gut*'.[19]

Louis acted as a kind of mentor to Ernest. Although in outlook and demeanour Louis was more passive than his forceful, thickset younger brother, he helped Ernest to navigate the culture and customs of their adopted homeland. He guided Ernest in the process of becoming a naturalised British subject, and Ernest took his oath of allegiance on 25 November 1901.[20] Intellectually agile but emotionally fragile, Louis was a gentle soul; he shared Ernest's innate reserve, but he lacked his brother's resolute temperament. Yet they shared an intimate bond. They took joint lodgings, first in Belsize Park and then in West Hampstead, and they began building up a dense network of social and commercial ties. At the turn of the century, all the brothers bar one, Emil, were clustered around the Square Mile, dealing in diamonds. A photograph of the quintet taken at Anton Dunkelsbuhler's country house in Maidenhead circa 1902 indicates the 'rising opulence of the Oppenheimer tribe'.[21] Bernard fixes his gaze on the photographer with an air of self-satisfaction. He was by then a diamond merchant of some renown and well established. Bernard was also settled in the private sphere: he had married Lena Strauss in 1890 and she bore him a son, Michael, in 1892. In the photograph, Michael focuses sweetly on the camera lens. The moustachioed Gustav appears distracted and slightly out of place. He was not a great success in business: Oppenheimer lore has it that Gustav 'made a failure of everything he touched'.[22] Otto, the youngest, showed promise. He was spirited, even if he lacked Louis's and Ernest's smarts. In the picture, Otto lounges in a deckchair, a look of insouciance upon his face. Louis stares languidly at the lens while Ernest, for all his solidity, looks faintly askance. There is an open book on his lap. Perhaps his reading had been interrupted. At any rate, Ernest seems vaguely ill at ease. It could be he felt the need to prove his mettle in the hurly-burly of the diamond fields. The opportunity was about to arise.

Louis Oppenheimer decided that the time had come to replace Leon Soutro, the self-seeking Frenchman who oversaw Dunkelsbuhlers' Kimberley office with benign neglect. Soutro paid more attention to increasing his own number of shares in De Beers than to Dunkelsbuhlers' affairs. Ernest was to take over from Soutro on a three-year contract at an annual salary of £500, with the promise of a long vacation in England before his contract was renewed. He arrived in Kimberley in November 1902. The 'turbulent city' was gentrifying, but it retained the frenzied atmosphere of old.[23] Rhodes had died eight months previously, on 26 March, before Ernest could meet the man he had heard so much about and come to revere. Yet Rhodes's legacy loomed large. The country, meanwhile, had been totally transformed. The Anglo-Boer War, which erupted in 1899 and pitted Boer against Brit in a bloody contest for mastery over diamonds and gold, had only just come to its bitter end on 31 May 1902 with the signing of the Treaty of Vereeniging. The former Boer republics in the Transvaal and the Orange Free State were no longer under British military administration; they were now colonies of the British Crown with the promise of eventual self-government. Britain guaranteed a sum of £3 million to repay the republics' war debts, part of a policy of post-war reconstruction driven by Lord Milner (the British High Commissioner and Governor of the aforementioned Crown colonies), which placed new financial burdens on the mining industry. Together with his administrative coterie of young male Oxford University graduates (contemptuously dubbed 'Milner's Kindergarten'), Milner proceeded to lay the foundations of the South African state, which was designed to fulfil the demands of British imperialism.[24] It was a state whose development – economically and politically – Ernest Oppenheimer and his descendants were to mould decisively.

Ernest came to Kimberley with £50 in his pocket and installed himself in lodgings at the home of his cousin Fritz Hirschhorn, a gregarious bachelor who had welcomed Bernard and Louis to the mining town years before. It was a grand house called The Grange, built for Rhodes in 1898, and located at 13 Lodge Road. By now, Hirschhorn was the doyen of diamonds in Kimberley. As the representative for Wernher, Beit and Company, he was a key figure in the Diamond Syndicate, and he was an alternate director to Alfred Beit on the board of De Beers. Rhodes had regarded him as an unrivalled authority on the precious stones. Hirschhorn gave Ernest invaluable insights into the diamond trade. He also provided him with an entrée into the upper echelons of Kimberley society and instilled in him an interest in civic affairs. Hirschhorn was a gracious host and bon viveur. At his dinner table, Ernest was exposed to all the leading lights in the firmament of De Beers. David Harris, a director of De Beers and, after Barnato's apparent suicide in 1897, the occupant of Kimberley's seat in the Cape Parliament, was a frequent guest. Solomon 'Solly' Joel, Barnato's combustible and prodigiously occupied nephew – his numerous recreational interests included horse racing, yachting and the Drury Lane Theatre – was another. Joel had inherited his uncle's financial, minerals and property empire and was the largest shareholder in De Beers. Ernest regarded him with awe. Through Hirschhorn, Ernest also met and learnt from De Beers men more closely involved with the company's day-to-day operations, like its consulting engineer, Gardner Williams. However, it was Rhodes's great friend, the impetuous and infamous Leander Starr Jameson (another De Beers director), who made the biggest impression. Jameson was the man whose untamed restlessness – a trait of 'near-pathological proportions' – spurred him to lead the botched raid against Paul Kruger's republican Transvaal government late in 1895.[25] It had contributed to the causes of the Anglo-Boer War. Jameson gave Ernest some useful career advice: 'If you want to be someone in this town, leave the task of sorting diamonds to others.'[26]

Ernest took Jameson's counsel to heart. In the austere De Beers boardroom with its long table and round-backed leather chairs, he sat in on directors' meetings at Hirschhorn's invitation. With Rhodes's portrait watching over him, Ernest helped capture the minutes. He worked voraciously and sought out new opportunities for Dunkelsbuhler. He travelled to Elandsfontein on the Highveld to inspect the Premier mine, where a massive diamond pipe – purportedly six times bigger than anything in Kimberley – had been found by Thomas Cullinan. It was a critical discovery which ultimately unearthed the legendary Cullinan diamond, the largest rough diamond ever found. On the strength of Ernest's instincts, Dunkelsbuhler bought a sizeable stake in the new venture. Others in the Diamond Syndicate underestimated its significance at first. The increasingly complacent directors of De Beers were caught off guard. The Dunkelsbuhler deal sealed Ernest's reputation as an astute speculator. It also crystallised his growing desire to put down roots in southern Africa. The place, it seemed to him, brimmed with possibilities. For one thing, as a company, De Beers had grown sluggish. It was ripe for an overhaul. For another, the goldfields – in which Dunkelsbuhler, through his controlling shares in Consolidated Mines Selection, had a substantial interest – glittered with prospects. But, first, Ernest was due for his long leave. His initial contract had expired. At the end of 1905, he set sail for England. Ernest looked forward to rekindling old friendships and renewing his ties in London. He would go and visit his parents in Friedberg too. At the back of his mind, however, was a gnawing concern. If he were to return to Kimberley, it would be preferable to do so not as a bachelor but as a married man, the originator of his own dynasty.

Portrait of Emma Goldmann, Harry Oppenheimer's maternal grandmother, 1891. *(Courtesy of Nicky Oppenheimer)*

The Beginnings of the Oppenheimer Dynasty

The previous year, Louis Oppenheimer had married Carlota (Charlotte or 'Lottie') Pollak. The Pollaks were a well-to-do, urbane family of anglicised Austro-German Jews. Charlotte's father, Joseph – a shrewd and practical Viennese stockbroker – had at one time served as president of the London Stock Exchange. Her mother, Emma Jane (née Goldmann), despite her Frankfurt heritage, had been born in the Cape Colony. Emma Goldmann's father, Louis, had gone out there in the 1840s to work with the Mosenthal brothers; before the diamond rush, their company traded in wool and ostrich feathers around Graaff-Reinet and Burghersdorp.[27] Emma Pollak's elder sister, Johanna, married Harry Mosenthal, the man who provided Anton Dunkelsbuhler with his launch pad in Kimberley. There were thus several interweaving strands in the web woven by the German-Jewish diaspora. The other Pollak children – Charlotte's siblings, Harry, Mary Lina, Edith, Leslie, Alice, George and Sybil – had all been born in England and were thoroughly English. In time to come, the paterfamilias,

Joseph Pollak, was to provide an important point of contact for Ernest. He opened another avenue into the City of London's trading floor, its banks and finance houses. Of more immediate interest to Ernest, however, was the Pollak sister who had caught his eye at Louis's wedding – Mary Lina, or 'May', as she was known.

During Ernest's spell in the diamond town, he maintained a correspondence with May Pollak. Now, on his leave in England, he saw a great deal of her. May was headstrong and had a razor-sharp mind. Despite being six years younger than Ernest, she was a woman of cultivated tastes and superior education to her suitor. She planned to go up to Girton College, Cambridge. The more time Ernest spent with May, the deeper in love he fell. There was one hitch: he was almost due back in Kimberley. Impulsively, Ernest decided to propose marriage. May accepted, and a wedding was hastily arranged. The ceremony took place according to Jewish rites at the Pollaks' opulent home, originally built for Sir Samuel Morton Peto, at 12a Kensington Gardens on 19 June 1906. The West London Synagogue of British Jews issued a marriage certificate two weeks later.[28]

Almost immediately, the newly-weds had to leave for Kimberley. Once there, they lodged with Fritz Hirschhorn; but this was not a sustainable arrangement, for the couple planned to start a family. Ernest bought a plot of land down the road from Hirschhorn and engaged contractors to build a house. He paid £2000 for it, and when the dwelling was completed he called it Friedberg in homage to his roots. However, in practice, Ernest aspired to a wholly new life, far removed from Germany and his father's tobacco shop. Then a series of calamities struck. In October 1907, a financial crisis exploded in the United States. There was a run on the banks; panic spread, and contagion seeped into the diamond trade. Demand for diamonds dried up overnight. The Diamond Syndicate found itself with £3 million worth of stock in hand and no way to get rid of it. Meanwhile, only a few months earlier, May had suffered a miscarriage. She was devastated. Then, quite unexpectedly, her beloved younger brother George died. May's grandmother Lina Goldmann wrote to her granddaughter in despair: her heart was 'nearly broken' and her eyes were 'blinded with tears'.[29] It was almost too much for the 21-year-old May to bear. Far away from the familiarity of London – in the dry, dusty and inhospitable streets of Kimberley – she found herself marooned, cut off from the emotional support of her parents and siblings. Her recent marriage to Ernest, who had whisked her off to the other side of the

Ernest and May Oppenheimer on their wedding day,
19 June 1906. *(Brenthurst Library)*

globe with the promise of a fresh start, came under severe strain. After
May's miscarriage Lina tried to console her granddaughter. 'Consider
only that your darling husband is with you, and his love will kiss your
tears soon away.'[30] Two weeks later she wrote again. 'Don't fret any more
about your sad loss,' she soothed May; Ernest was a 'good, loving husband',
and May would be able to find happiness in his 'strong, strong love'.[31] The
commiserations were laced with hope. The time might not be far off, Lina
predicted, 'when a sweet darling child may be to you and Ernest the ties
of a new, everlasting love'. Lina Goldmann's words were prophetic. The
following year May fell pregnant. On 28 October 1908, in her new home
at 7 Lodge Road, she gave birth to a baby boy. His parents named him
Harry Friedrich.

TWO

Manifest Destiny

1908–1927

New Beginnings

Harry Oppenheimer's birth in 1908 provided a lifeline to his parents. May was besotted with her new arrival. She rejoiced in his every move and recorded each step for posterity. Harry's introductory appearance on the stoep at 7 Lodge Road took place on 29 October at 7 am. He cut his first tooth on 10 May. He started crawling six days later, and walked unaided on 18 December. His first word, on 14 November, was 'tiger'.[1] The infant was named in accordance with Jewish rites, and underwent his bris at the hands of Rabbi Harris Isaacs of the Griqualand West Jewish Congregation.[2] For all that Louis Oppenheimer was Ernest's closest sibling, one of the other brothers, Gustav, was chosen as Harry's godfather, together with Fritz Hirschhorn. May's younger sister Edith became Harry's godmother. In the first decade of his existence the contours of Harry Oppenheimer's home life were shaped by his parents' Jewish faith and kinship networks. The conversion to Anglicanism would come later. Eventually, the broader political climate – and the cultural environment in which Ernest Oppenheimer's commercial empire evolved – steered the dynast away from the synagogue towards the Anglican Church. The politics of business and the business of politics in southern Africa came to inflect Ernest's adopted Englishness with a faintly gentile sensibility. In Harry's case, as he made his way through Parktown School in Johannesburg, Charterhouse

Harry Oppenheimer, aged six weeks,
and his mother. *(Brenthurst Library)*

in England, and ultimately Christ Church, Oxford, the inflection was to
become emphatic.

Politics moulded the course of Harry Oppenheimer's life from his
very first breath. Four days after Ernest's heir was born, a constitutional
convention was launched to forge the new South African nation in the
aftermath of the Anglo-Boer War. It led to the adoption of the South
Africa Act of 1909, which yoked together the four colonies – the Cape,
Natal, Transvaal and the Orange River Colony – into the Union of
South Africa. Like Bismarck's Germany, the South African nation-state
formed in 1910 was hammered out of blood and metal, although gold
(and diamonds) substituted for iron. Yet the nationalism envisaged by
the convention's key negotiators, Boer generals like Louis Botha and Jan
Smuts, was not of the blood-and-soil variety. Indeed, Smuts, one of the
principal architects of Union, championed the cause of reconciliation

between Boer and Briton within the framework of imperial governance, despite having led republican Boer forces during the war. The Botha–Smuts strand of moderate Anglo-Afrikaner 'South Africanism' was perfectly compatible with the sort of colonial nationalism espoused by Lord Milner and his Kindergarten, which sought to balance local patriotism with wider imperial loyalties. The most remarkable feature of this supposedly inclusive strain of South Africanism was its enduring whiteness.[3] Segregation was the cornerstone of the South African state. The convention's liberal Cape delegates had wanted to extend their colony's non-racial franchise to the rest of the Union. The colour-blind vote dated back to 1853, when the Parliament of the Cape of Good Hope was founded, and it enfranchised all adult males in the colony (with certain qualifications regarding property ownership) irrespective of their race. At the National Convention of 1908–9, the representatives from Natal and the former Boer republics would, however, hear none of it. Smuts suggested a compromise. No Cape voter would be deprived of his vote on the grounds of colour unless a two-thirds majority of both Houses of Parliament, sitting jointly, decided otherwise. In fact, it was clear that Smuts, apart from not wanting to extend the Cape franchise to the other provinces, 'would have liked to abolish it in the Cape itself'.[4] In its own way, the common South African nationhood minted by the Act of Union was just as sectarian as Bismarck's pan-Germanism, for it was predicated on the near exclusion of blacks from the body politic.

Smuts, South Africanism and a larger loyalty to the British Empire (and the British Commonwealth of Nations after it was formed in 1931) were all formative forces in the lives of Ernest Oppenheimer, his son Harry, and the mining companies that fell under their dominion. Those enterprises were to propel South Africa's economic development and fashion its statehood over the course of the 20th century. But in 1908 such concerns seemed somewhat remote. Ernest's interest in politics was parochial, even if it was sparked by an event of global significance. The so-called Panic of 1907, which crashed the New York Stock Exchange and wreaked havoc in the diamond markets, threw Kimberley onto hard times. One of the large mines, Dutoitspan, was temporarily shut, while workers at the other De Beers mines were put on short time. Many jobs were lost; there was misery and poverty. The panic was blamed on several factors: excessive speculation in copper, mining and railroad stocks, as well as President Theodore Roosevelt's attacks on the 'great malefactors of wealth' in the United States.[5] Nevertheless, it was the business oligarchs who saved the day. JP Morgan, New York's wealthiest banker and a financier whose eponymous company would play a decisive role in Ernest Oppenheimer's career, propped up the banks together with a fellow magnate and philanthropist, John D Rockefeller. In Kimberley, Ernest's philanthropy was channelled more modestly. He and May organised relief soup kitchens for the unemployed. The sight of suffering pricked his conscience, and he resolved to play a bigger role in the public square. Early in 1908, before Harry was born, Ernest stood for election to the Kimberley town council. He duly won a seat and served as a councillor over a period of four years, before being elected as the city's mayor in 1912. Oppenheimer's dual role as a businessman and politician – later, with greater wealth and power, this was to merge into a single identity as a sort of business statesman – had commenced.

The Great War and the Flight from Kimberley

In years to come, Ernest Oppenheimer was wont to quip that his involvement in municipal politics started because he had too much time on his hands: the Diamond Syndicate operated like a well-oiled machine, which freed him up for other pursuits. This was a misleading (if self-deprecating) claim, for Oppenheimer's growing interest in politics dovetailed neatly with his commercial concerns. They reinforced one another. The diamond industry in Kimberley required a well-run town, one that functioned to the Syndicate's – and De Beers' – advantage. Ernest also took inspiration from Rhodes, whose pursuit of profit, for better or worse – and in Kimberley, Ernest would certainly have regarded it as for the better – was carried out within a framework of political and social objectives. Besides, Ernest's exposure to local government politics would benefit him personally. It would entail a broadening of experience: an education in public speaking and the management of committees and officials. Such skills were 'not to be learnt in a diamond merchant's office', Ernest's biographer observed.[6] Plainly, Ernest Oppenheimer's ambitions extended beyond running Old Dunkels's office in Kimberley, and he applied himself with ferocious energy to expanding his sphere of influence. Occasionally, throughout his life, there would be a setback to his physical health – or a personal turmoil, like the death of a loved one – that would temporarily immobilise him, and he would repair to Cape Town or London to recuperate. But in the main, Ernest was inexorably industrious. He was an innovator and a pioneer. In fact, there was almost something of the pirate about him: he seemed always to be in the right place, at the right time, ready to swoop and extract a pound of flesh either for Dunkelsbuhlers or himself. In this way, the Oppenheimer empire – the dominion and the dynasty – was born. Ernest was its founder and builder; Harry would be the consolidator.

In the years leading up to the outbreak of the First World War, Ernest Oppenheimer entrenched his reputation as a force to be reckoned with in Kimberley. He submitted two reports to De Beers – one on diamond cutting and the other on the challenges posed by the recent discovery of diamonds in South West Africa – that showed his 'mastery' of the problems facing the industry.[7] In 1911, Anton Dunkelsbuhler died. He left behind a substantial fortune. His son Walter faded from the scene, and Louis Oppenheimer was promoted to managing director of Dunkelsbuhlers. For all intents and purposes the firm became the 'Oppenheimer family concern'.[8] In 1912, Ernest was elevated as an alternate director to (now, Sir) David Harris on the board of Jagersfontein. That same year he accomplished a long-standing goal which brought him much local kudos: the amalgamation of Beaconsfield (the site of the Dutoitspan mine) and Kimberley into a single municipal entity. Oppenheimer was re-elected as Kimberley's mayor in 1913 and again in 1914, just after the Great War erupted. At an appreciative gathering of townsfolk he was presented with a portrait of himself in mayoral robes amid glowing speeches. (In later years, Harry Oppenheimer would describe the painting as 'so appalling' that even his 'deep filial piety' could not 'persuade him to preserve it'.)[9] In between all this, Ernest became a father for the second time: May gave birth to another son, Frank Leslie, on 17 October 1910. Meanwhile, May's younger sister Edith joined the household at 7 Lodge Road for a stint; she was a comely girl preyed upon by the 'gouty old bachelor' Fritz Hirschhorn, who would come courting nightly, 'without notable success'.[10]

After an inauspicious start to married life in Kimberley, Ernest and May now enjoyed a halcyon period of domestic content. To them, 7 Lodge Road was a cosy sanctuary. In his later years, Harry Oppenheimer could recall the house with precision: its entrance hall draped with green curtains; its small library furnished with a red leather sofa and armchairs; and its patch of garden bordered by a white fence and little gate on which the name Friedberg was inscribed in black letters. 'This was, I believe, one of the best houses in Kimberley in those days,' he reminisced.[11] From the earliest time, the boy knew that his father was the mayor, and of this he was 'very proud'.[12] Over the preceding nine years, Ernest and May had put down roots; they were now settled with their own young family, and Ernest was secure in his career. This brought Ernest satisfaction; it vindicated his decision (and his father's advice) to uproot himself from Friedberg. Ernest had come to Kimberley to start afresh; to put a 'deep, unbridgeable gulf between his childhood and boyhood in Germany and his new life, new aims and new ambitions'.[13] In spite of the fact that Ernest spoke English with a German accent throughout his life, he came to think of himself as a British South African. He was grateful and proud of his British nationality, and his loyalty to the British Empire was filtered through the prism of his emerging South Africanness. Kimberley was his home. And so it came as a body blow when, in 1915, Kimberley's mayor, leading diamond buyer and dedicated family man was hounded out of the city on the back of anti-German sentiment. Everything Ernest had worked for seemed to lie shattered; he thought his family and his future were in peril.

The move by South Africa's Prime Minister, Louis Botha, to take the Union into the Great War against Germany in 1914 rallied the English-speaking population, but it estranged many of the Afrikaner nationalists who had joined General JBM Hertzog's breakaway National Party in 1912. Constitutionally the Union was part of the British Empire and, once Britain declared war, Botha had no choice but to follow suit. The Germans had supported the Boers during the Anglo-Boer War, and among some Afrikaners there was a residual sympathy for Kaiser Wilhelm II's nation. A group of Boer generals, led by General Koos de la Rey, opposed Botha's plans to launch an offensive against the German colony of South West Africa. There ensued an unsuccessful Boer 'rebellion'.[14] Ernest Oppenheimer's fealty to the British Empire was, of course, not in doubt. But his opponents on the Kimberley town council exploited his German origins for political gain. A particularly noxious and pompous councillor, Fred Hicks, launched a scurrilous attack and called for Oppenheimer's resignation as mayor. Oppenheimer rode it out. However, the war subjected Kimberley to many privations, and after the diamond mines ceased production for want of trade – throwing thousands into unemployment – the town was a cauldron of discontent. Oppenheimer took his civic duties seriously. He saw off a battalion of the Kimberley Regiment as it departed to join the South West Africa campaign, and he helped form another battalion in its place. He established the Mayor's Relief Fund, which provided employment on public works projects, and he raised money for it from De Beers. In South

West Africa, Botha's forces were driving back the Germans. In the Union, an uneasy peace prevailed. But below the surface anti-German animosity simmered. When an Imperial German Navy submarine torpedoed the RMS *Lusitania* in the Atlantic on 7 May 1915, the resentment burst aflame. Looting and mob violence exploded on the streets of Kimberley. The uncontrolled anger was soon directed at a specific target: the homes of rich diamond merchants with German surnames. The mob threatened to burn down Friedberg at 7 Lodge Road.

Realising that his position was untenable, Ernest Oppenheimer resigned the mayoralty on 12 May 1915. The following night he evacuated May, Harry and Frank from Friedberg and sent them to stay with Irvine Grimmer, the assistant general manager of De Beers. Still, the mob blazed with righteous indignation. A crowd gathered at the offices of the Diamond Syndicate, smashing windows and tearing down the brass plates that bore the names of Hirschhorn and Oppenheimer. Ernest felt dejected and demoralised. He could not sleep; he feared acutely for his family's safety. On 14 May, he put May and the boys on a train to Cape Town. It was a well-timed escape. The next day, Ernest came under personal attack. As he drove from his office on Stockdale Street, rioters accosted him and smashed the windows of his vehicle. Ernest managed narrowly to escape, but blood was pouring from his head. His wounds were caused by shattered glass. In desperation, he scrambled into the nearby Catholic convent on Currey Street. The nuns of the Holy Family tended his injuries – an act of kindness he would never forget – but the trauma was inscribed. There and then, Ernest made up his mind to leave Kimberley for good. He would join May and the children in Cape Town, with a view to seeing out the war in England.

A year before his death, in an interview with Emily Hahn of the *New Yorker*, Ernest Oppenheimer would recall the events of May 1915, with 'just a trace of the old rancour': 'General Botha had already taken South West Africa, and General Smuts was driving the Germans out of East Africa … and then people suddenly remembered that *I* didn't have an English name.'[15] In fact, Botha seized the German territory on 9 July 1915; and Smuts arrived in Nairobi to take command of the German East Africa campaign on 19 February 1916.[16] But even if these developments had occurred sooner, it is unlikely they would have changed the course of Ernest's fortunes. Decades on, Harry Oppenheimer was inclined to believe that the Kimberley riots were only the catalyst and not the basic cause of his father's decision to quit the town. They were the 'emotional spur' to rational 'underlying motives'. 'The fact was that the Kimberley phase of his life was over and he knew that in order to realise his ambitions he needed a new and wider field of action. This he sought in Johannesburg.'[17]

The Formation of the Anglo American Corporation

In Cape Town, holed up like a refugee at a hotel in Sea Point with May and his two young sons, Oppenheimer brooded. For days, according to Emily Hahn, he 'walked the sands or climbed the rocks and sat looking out over the sea as he struggled with his disappointment and resentment.'[18] He plotted his next move. Ernest decided to stay on in South Africa but resolved never to return to Kimberley. 'More and more', Hahn postulated, 'his mind turned to the gold mines in the Rand.'[19] In 1912, Louis Oppenheimer had become a London-based director of Consolidated Mines Selection (CMS) – the international holding company of the Dunkelsbuhler family fortune, which had substantial coal and gold interests. At the same time, the company's consulting engineer, an American called William Lincoln Honnold whom Ernest had met on the Rand, became its managing director in Johannesburg. Another potential path to wealth and power, gilt-edged rather than diamond-studded, seemed to have been paved for Ernest by Old Dunkels. However, whatever ambitions Ernest had to become a Randlord, he placed them on hold: in the latter half of 1915, he regarded England as a safer haven for his family. The Oppenheimers left Cape Town and set sail for London; once there, they took refuge with May's parents, who were now resident at 21 Portman Square, in a beautiful 18th-century house constructed in the Adam style.

It was during his retreat in London, as the First World War raged on the bloody Belgian battlefields, that Ernest Oppenheimer mapped out his future with his brother Louis. All the brothers were reunited once more save for Otto – since 1908, he had been married to Beatrice 'Beattie' Rosenberg – for he was fighting on the Western Front. Bernard was still a leading diamond merchant, but he was devoting more of his time to a munitions factory that he had built in Letchworth. It provided employment for some three thousand Belgian refugees. In 1917, he also established a diamond-cutting and -polishing factory in Brighton for disabled and discharged soldiers.[20] Meanwhile, Ernest renewed his acquaintance with Honnold, who had moved to London in 1915 to become the wartime director of the Commission for Relief in Belgium. The two became firm friends. Honnold regaled Ernest with stories of the Witwatersrand goldfields. He told him about the gold deposits in the Far East Rand basin, which had piqued the interest of the major mining finance houses. Ernest apprised the London directors of CMS. They decided to send him back to South Africa to conduct a fact-finding mission. So, while May, Harry and Frank acclimatised to life in London, Ernest returned to the Union in 1916. In fact, he would sail back and forth between England and South Africa throughout the war, famously (and narrowly) escaping with his life when the ship he was travelling on, the *Galway Castle*, was torpedoed and sunk on 12 September 1918.

From the Far East Rand basin, Oppenheimer advised the CMS directors to take immediate and maximum advantage of the rapidly expanding opportunities for deep-level gold mining. He negotiated with the Union government to lease the deep levels of the Brakpan mine, whose new shaft was financed by CMS and the Rand Selection Corporation. Lease agreements for Springs and Daggafontein followed. However, the majority of CMS board members were elderly, conservative and disinclined to too much adventurism on the Far East Rand. The chairman summed up their rigid attitude: he was 'not prepared to monkey about' with the capital of the company.[21] While maintaining good relations with CMS, the enterprising Oppenheimer resolved to press ahead under his own steam. He would found a new mining house. Ernest approached Honnold, who in turn enlisted the aid of an American associate, Herbert Hoover, a fellow mining engineer (and future President of the United States). Already a man with useful political connections in the Union, Oppenheimer persuaded Henry Hull – the former Minister of Finance in Botha's cabinet – to travel with him to London to meet Hoover. The encounter, which took place at the Savoy Hotel, was a resounding success. Hoover proceeded to intermediate with two American financiers, the Newmont Mining Corporation and its bankers, JP Morgan and Company, and shook them down for money. Ernest had met Jan Smuts during his mayoralty of Kimberley and now he briefed the emerging statesman on his plans. (At the time, Smuts was in London serving on the Imperial War Cabinet led by the British Prime Minister, David Lloyd George.) By Ernest's account, Smuts looked upon the scheme with 'considerable favour', on the understanding that a 'big South African company' would emerge.[22]

This is precisely what Ernest Oppenheimer intended. Most of the major mining finance houses, which straddled both diamonds and gold, were domiciled in London. Consolidated Gold Fields, the company which Rhodes had chaired alongside De Beers, was formed in London in 1887. The so-called Corner House group, a partnership between Julius Wernher, Alfred Beit and Hermann Eckstein, brought Rand Mines Limited under the roof of the London-based Central Mining and Investment Corporation. It bestrode the Witwatersrand like a colossus. The Johannesburg Consolidated Investment Company (JCI), founded by Barney Barnato and controlled by his nephews Solly and Jack Joel, was run out of London. So, too, was the Union Corporation. The chairman of the General Mining and Finance Corporation, Sir George Albu, lived in South Africa; but his mining house lacked a certain vigour. Ernest Oppenheimer wanted to create a South African mining finance dynamo. On 25 September 1917, he launched the Anglo American Corporation of South Africa with initial capital of £1 million, half of which was subscribed through Newmont and JP Morgan in America and the other half through Ernest's friends and associates in England and South Africa. This was a significant capitalisation, and it indicated that Anglo American planned to be a major player. But it was to be more than that. From the start, its founder conceived that Anglo American should stand in the line of succession of Royal Charter companies that had built the British Empire. Rhodes's British South Africa Company, which sought to create a zone of British commercial and political influence from 'Cape to Cairo', was the lodestar. Business and politics would mesh to drive development. Over and above that, Anglo American would be a family concern; it was designed to be the 'Oppenheimer company'.[23] Having been forced into a humiliating retreat from Kimberley, Ernest Oppenheimer now announced himself as a major figure on the Rand and in the political economy of southern Africa. The Oppenheimer empire had taken shape.

Childe Harry's Pilgrimage

With Ernest predominantly in South Africa between 1917 and 1919, May grew restive. Long after her death, the *New Yorker* described her as 'a most unusual woman', with a 'mind like a razor' and a 'singular understanding of the mysteries of finance'.[24] She must have had admirable reserves of patience, too, to endure an absent husband and two young sons making constant demands on her attention. By the middle of 1919, however, after four years in England and with the war against Germany won, May's patience had worn thin. In February she wrote to Ernest and told him

Harry Oppenheimer with his brother, Frank,
and the family dog in Kimberley, c.1914. *(Brenthurst Library)*

that she had been 'bustling around' trying to obtain passports for her and
her maid, so that she could fix up their journey to South Africa. Harry
and Frank, she said, were 'very well & most excited' by the prospect of
returning to the Union.[25] May hoped to sail on the Union-Castle at the
end of the month or in March. 'A week nearer my departure to join you,
but no definite news of a boat!' she complained a fortnight later, adding
with relief that the so-called Spanish Flu – the 1918 influenza pandemic –
had come back 'but so far we have all escaped'.[26] By April, she had become
increasingly annoyed. Returning servicemen and their wives were being
prioritised for passage. May wrote to William Schreiner, South Africa's
High Commissioner in London, and chided him. In view of the work
her husband had done for the Union, she was 'entitled to at least as much
consideration as a soldier's wife' in securing a passage home.[27] Schreiner
sent her a 'very cold reply', she recounted in turn to Ernest.[28] May wrote
to Smuts for good measure too. At the time, he was at the Paris Peace

Conference, negotiating the Treaty of Versailles and giving thought to the League of Nations. May let Smuts know that a 'man's work should count regardless of whether or not he'd donned khaki'.[29] She became overwrought. Her nerves were 'all ajar' and she 'wanted to cry all day', she confided to Ernest.[30] 'I only hope you'll never do anything more for the South African Government,' she reproached him. 'Why should you spend your time & your money when they can't show me even moderate civility?'[31] Eventually, she received a firm undertaking that they would be able to sail by the end of July. May's mind immediately turned to practical matters. She assured Ernest that he need not purchase a house in Johannesburg just yet; that could wait for her return. She reminded him to go and see the headmaster of St John's College in Houghton: she wanted to send the boys there as weekly boarders as soon as they arrived in Johannesburg, as they really did 'need some discipline'.[32]

It is difficult to imagine Harry Oppenheimer as an unruly child. As an adult he had an air of imperturbability; he always took great care to exercise self-restraint. As a boy, he surely could not have put May to the test too much. In any event he was usually in the care of 'Nursie'. Later, when he was a young man, Harry would often observe his mother with cool bemusement. May was certainly a woman conscious of her social standing. In London, during the Great War, she moved in high society. She dined with eminent politicians like the former Prime Minister of New Zealand, Sir Joseph Ward, whom she regarded as 'an awfully common man with waxed ends to his moustache'.[33] When May ordered boots and clothes for Ernest at Stovel & Mason, she found the shop assistants 'too familiar for words'.[34] Even her brother-in-law Louis was not spared her reproving tongue. May had given a wedding present of £50 to a mutual friend, Bertie Ehrmann, and his bride, but she was 'quite ashamed' of Louis's gift – a 'tiny little silver coffee pot & milk jug & sugar basin, *without a tray*'.[35] 'Of course it is decent silver & comes from Tiffany but it looks too mingy for words,' she gossiped to Ernest.[36] May was opinionated. John Tweed, the 'British Rodin', invited her to his studio to see his bust of Smuts and his relief sketches for the proposed South African war memorial. Tweed showed the architect Herbert Baker's designs to May, which she dismissed as an 'abortion' and 'too awful'.[37] May was also importunate; she was not averse to administering a sharp jab of emotional manipulation. In London she grew fond of a young Royal Air Force pilot, and promised him a job in South Africa after the war. In one of several letters on the subject, May pestered Ernest: 'I hope you are not going to let Roland

Norman down … as he is counting absolutely on becoming your Private Secretary & is only waiting to hear from you *when* you need him. He is buying his Mufti … & he can't afford to waste the money.'[38]

Harry was alert to his mother's foibles – she could be pushy and haughty, domineering and peremptory – and when he was in his early twenties, he recorded her personality quirks in his diaries with the ironic detachment of a wryly amused observer. By his maternal grandparents, Harry was regarded with affection for his subtlety and sensitivity. Joseph Pollak was bearded and bristly. One day he showed Harry a 'horrible simian photograph' of himself aged 25. 'What do you think of grandpa as a young man?' he asked, to which the young boy winningly replied, 'I think you look much nicer now.'[39] This quick-witted reply gave Harry a 'lasting reputation for tact'.[40] In London during the war, Harry spent a great deal of time in the company of his mother's sisters. They would escort him on outings to the theatre, art galleries and museums. They would take him shopping for ornamental goods, and to enjoy tea at Selfridges. It was a curiously sophisticated routine for a youngster, and it shaped his future recreational proclivities. Harry was closest to the youngest Pollak sister, Aunt Sybil, who was 11 years his senior. In later years, he would recall her as 'very fat and very stupid', but also full of 'sweetness and kindness and in her way rather pretty'.[41] Presumably this was not a reflection he shared in full with his grandparents at the time, lest he lose his reputation for diplomacy.

Harry sent news of all his materteral adventures in letters to his father. 'Frank had a lovely birthday yesterday,' he wrote in one missive; 'Grandma & all the Aunts came to tea on his birthday & he had a lovely birthday cake with fruit on the top.'[42] Harry went to a fancy-dress party at his aunt Edith's workplace on New Year's Day, where he was much impressed by a conjuror. He and Frank watched *Cinderella* at the Lyceum Theatre, but he was careful not to bore his father with minutiae.[43] In fact, Harry was a discerning theatre-goer. He particularly enjoyed a parody of *The Merchant of Venice* called *The Merchant of Venison*.[44] His Christmas gifts pleased him: toy soldiers, a fruit knife, a writing case and several books. In fact, Harry was a keen reader of fiction, and he relayed plot twists and character descriptions to his father with a careful eye for detail. Bertie Ehrmann gifted him Aesop's fables: 'Some of them I can't think what the morals are,' he confessed, 'especially the fable about the moon and her mother.' 'If you can think of the moral will you tell me in you're [*sic*] next letter?' he asked his father.[45] If the lesson of this lunar tale is that

A bookish boy with an appreciation for beautiful things:
Harry Oppenheimer, aged ten. *(Brenthurst Library)*

shapeshifters go unrewarded – the moon's mother refuses her daughter's request for a new dress because the moon is constantly changing form – Harry did not need to learn it. He knew it intuitively. Some sixty-five years later, looking back on his life, Oppenheimer jotted down a note for his planned memoir: 'The sense that my father had formed a family and that it was my manifest destiny & duty to carry on … what he had created was central to my outlook & subsequent career.'[46] His sense of duty and destiny was fixed from boyhood. (A jaundiced observer might read something equally definitive into the title of two books that Ehrmann's mother gave Harry and Frank as youngsters. Harry received *The Romance of Modern Engineering*, while Frank was presented with *The Romance of Modern Exploitation*.)[47]

The letters that Harry wrote to his father during the First World War suggest a considerate, perceptive, bookish boy. He was solicitous, asking after Ernest's pruritus and expressing concern about Fritz Hirschhorn's gout. But he liked things just so. When May sought passage to the Union,

Harry commented to his father: 'I will be awfully glad to get out there again.'[48] Yet he had definite instructions. 'Do buy a house so that we don't have to live in a hotel long when we come out to you.'[49] A few weeks later came another request. 'Please arrange for us to stay about a week in Cape Town before we go to Johannesburg.'[50] Harry's manner of expression reflected a quality of calmness and composure. He was tremendously self-assured for someone who had yet to reach adolescence; and he showed signs of a refined sensibility. The bedroom ceilings at 21 Portman Square, painted by Angelica Kauffmann, particularly impressed him. After the Guards' triumphal march through London on 22 March 1919, Harry told his father, 'we had a very good tea.'[51] The 'pink satin old English suit' that Frank wore as a page boy to Bertie Ehrmann's wedding appealed to his aesthetic sense.[52] Aunt Sybil took him to a service at St Paul's Cathedral and he was glad to be seated in the 'choice stalls.'[53] The letters provide some insight into not only Harry's developing character, but also the close relationship between father and son, which moulded him profoundly. It was a bond of almost preternatural intensity. Their correspondence would be replicated over two decades later, during the Second World War, when Harry was stationed in the Western Desert; but at that point business and politics figured alongside combat and domesticity as the pair's chief concerns.

Anglicanism and Anglicisation

In the second half of 1919, Ernest, May, Harry and Frank were reunited in South Africa. Mindful of Harry's plea, Ernest purchased a modest house in Jubilee Road on the Parktown ridge. A semblance of normal family life was restored. Ernest would go on long walks with Harry and tell him stories which a good many years later Harry recognised to have been suitably edited extracts from Voltaire's *Zadig* and *Candide*.[54] The boys were enrolled in the nearby private Parktown School, founded by AR Aspinall after the Anglo-Boer War to cater to the sons of Randlords and the affluent professional class. Aspinall had been determined to 'spread among heathen South Africans the best traditions of the English public school', and his prospectus offered to 'prepare the sons of gentlemen' for admission to Eton, Harrow and the like.[55] The school was an outpost of the British Empire; houses were named after British generals or admirals who had fought in the First World War – Kitchener, Haig, Jellicoe and Beatty. Not quite yet 11 years old, Harry had received most of his education up to this point from governesses. But he adapted quickly to the more formal learning environment. Among his contemporaries at the school was William (later Lord) Holford, who went on to become a renowned architect and urban planner in Britain.

Parktown School was non-denominational, but its ethos was Anglican and church services were usually conducted by Anglican clergymen. By this stage it appears that Harry might have been losing touch with his Judaic roots. There is some confusion as to when exactly Ernest Oppenheimer left the Jewish faith and converted to Anglicanism. After May died in 1934, he married Caroline ('Ina') Oppenheimer – the widow of his nephew Michael, Bernard Oppenheimer's son. But Ina was a Catholic, not an Anglican. In 1938, Ernest wrote to the Anglican Bishop of Johannesburg, Geoffrey Clayton, seeking admission to Holy Communion, which Clayton granted.[56] Yet his conversion is likely to have taken place earlier. According to one version, Ernest undertook a 'spiritual pilgrimage' after a series of personal tragedies in the early 1930s; he found solace in the Bible and was 'baptised into the Christian faith' in 1935.[57] Successive generations of Oppenheimers came to believe that Harry Oppenheimer would almost certainly have celebrated his bar mitzvah when he turned 13 in 1921.[58] In later years an apocryphal story circulated to the effect that Ernest and May had erected a plaque in the Kimberley shul at the time of his bar mitzvah, and that in adulthood (having become a Christian) Harry insisted it be taken down. When the congregation refused, he offered to buy the synagogue, gut it and then rebuild it without the plaque. The story was entirely untrue: records show that there was no such plaque.[59] In any event, the Oppenheimers left Kimberley when Harry was six years old and never lived there permanently again. There is no conclusive evidence that a bar mitzvah took place. In fact, it seems improbable. Frank Oppenheimer was baptised in the Anglican parish church of St Jude-on-the-Hill in Hampstead Garden Suburb on 28 July 1919, just before he set sail with his mother and brother for South Africa, and this is recorded in Harry Oppenheimer's papers.[60] Although no equivalent record exists for the elder brother, it seems unlikely that he would not have been baptised around the same time. Some members of the Pollak family converted to Christianity in the second decade of the 20th century: for example, Harry's aunt Edith was baptised in the parish of St Thomas, Portman Square, in 1915. In wartime London, Aunt Sybil took Harry regularly to St Paul's. When he came to write his unpublished memoir, Harry recalled that Sybil's principal interests were 'in the church and in the breeding of Scotch terriers'. He remarked that her 'religious but not her dog-breeding proclivities exercised an influence on me'.[61]

With three years at Parktown School under his belt, Harry's parents thought it sensible to send him to a public school in England. It was, after all, the preparation which Aspinall had intended. By then, Ernest Oppenheimer was not only a prosperous Randlord and venerable member of the South African economic elite, but he was being earmarked by Smuts for a role on the national political stage. Smuts wrote to him in December 1919: 'I am anxious to have you in Parliament as soon as possible as you will be most useful.'[62] In the event, Ernest was only elected to Parliament in 1924, at which point – in the wake of Smuts's brutal suppression of a strike by white miners in 1922, the so-called Rand Revolt – the South African Party started by Botha and Smuts was relegated to the opposition benches. Ernest had also embedded himself as a member of the British establishment with a knighthood. Details of the accolade were announced in the New Year's honours list published on 31 December 1920. His citation read, 'Honorary Secretary to the South African War Memorial Fund. Took a leading part in recruiting of both combatants and labourers for various fronts during the war.'[63] Ernest immediately selected a coat of arms and motto: *Spero optima* (Hope for the best), a subtle reprisal against the town that had driven out his family: Kimberley's motto was *Spero meliora* (Hope for better). Bernard was recognised for his wartime contributions, too, with a baronetcy. A few days later, on 8 January 1921, May and Ernest sailed from Southampton to New York, and spent two months in America. Harry and Frank were left in the care of family friends, Fred Susskind (a Transvaal provincial cricketer) and his wife, Doff. May's diary entry for 4 March reads, 'Inauguration Ceremony of President Harding'.[64] Her husband was now a figure on the world stage.

It was really May, more than Ernest, who was drawn to the idea of an English public school for her son's apprenticeship. 'But for my mother's influence, my father would have sent us to schools in South Africa,' Harry later contemplated.[65] The chosen school was Charterhouse, founded by a wealthy Tudor benefactor in London in 1611, and transplanted to the outskirts of Godalming in the Surrey countryside in 1872. There was a slight South African connection. At the turn of the 20th century, a cloister was added to the school's Gothic buildings in commemoration of Old Carthusians (as former pupils are known) who had served in the Anglo-Boer War. The foundation stone was laid by Robert Baden-Powell, the hero of the Siege of Mafeking and an Old Carthusian. Harry arrived at

Charterhouse in September 1922, in the 'Oration quarter' (or autumn term), and was placed in Daviesites, the house named for its founder, the Reverend Gerald Davies. The November issue of *The Carthusian*, the school magazine, harked back to an earlier editorial and declared with some self-satisfaction: 'Anyone who has visited Old and New Charterhouse must at once be struck by the increasing vigour with which all our pursuits are taken up: our games are more lively and energetic, our love of exercise shows marked increase, and our school work … it is to be hoped is not behindhand or neglected.'[66]

Harry did not take to games with any great enthusiasm. In later years, he readily confessed that he was 'hopeless at sport.'[67] 'Team games I never could endure and find watching them desperately boring.'[68] But he gained enjoyment from his studies. English, French and German were his strongest subjects. He kept his head down: the Oppenheimer name (Frank joined his brother at the school in 1924) does not appear in the sporting columns of *The Carthusian* or those dealing with the plethora of club and society activities. Nevertheless, Harry was a good student, and he often came within the top quintile of his form. At the end of 1924, in a class of 25 boys, he was placed first in German, fifth in French and sixth in English.[69] In the previous mid-quarter, his housemaster, the Reverend Lancelot Allen, deemed him a 'good, thoughtful boy', while his headmaster, Frank Fletcher, pronounced his performance 'very satisfactory.'[70]

Of the new boys in his intake at Daviesites in 1922, Harry appears to have struck up only one life-long friendship – with Bernard Soltau, a boy whose father had died in a polo accident and left the family in straitened circumstances.[71] Soltau went to Charterhouse on a scholarship and, long after taking a degree at Oxford University, became a parish priest. In the manner of English public schools at the time, Charterhouse prized accomplishment in team sports above all else. Although academic competition was encouraged, schoolwork was treated as a bit of an afterthought. This served to sculpt a certain ideal of masculinity and conduced to a culture of machismo. The green fields of Godalming could be a lonely and alienating environment for a boy who preferred books to rackets or rugby balls. Matters were not helped by the fact that Harry and Frank spent their holidays with their elderly grandparents at 21 Portman Square. 'They were extremely kind but this was not a normal or suitable life for a school boy & the effects took some time to get over,' Oppenheimer wrote in the outline of his memoir.[72] Harry might have been happier if he had passed the holidays at White Waltham, the

Maidenhead country home of his uncle Louis and aunt Carlota, where they lived in a manner that seemed to him 'carefree' and 'certainly attractive to young people'.[73] The couple's son, Raymond, was three years older than Harry and became his 'dearest friend'.[74] Harry regarded Aunt Charlotte (as he called her) with affection, but he only started visiting White Waltham once he left Charterhouse. This odd arrangement arose because during Harry's school years the volatile May had become estranged from her sister Carlota. Oppenheimer would later reflect: 'the Pollaks seem to have been a quarrelsome family and my father and uncle Louis, who in such matters were always extremely weak, either could not or did not bother to compose whatever differences there were'.[75] This became a source of life-long regret. Six decades later, Oppenheimer wrote that 'it was quite wrong' for his parents to have sent him and Frank to 21 Portman Square for their holidays; and he considered that 'it might have made a significant difference to my development' if he had gone to White Waltham instead.[76]

The impact on Frank appears to have been less marked, although of course in the absence of his own memoir or written reflections, it is impossible to be sure. But the schoolboy letters that do exist for Frank suggest a personality quite different from his brother's: he was gregarious, and he wore his heart on his sleeve. Frank signed his letters to his parents with declarations of 'my very best love' and a string of kisses.[77] Harry was more guarded about his emotions and less effusive in his correspondence. When he expatiated to his mother on his day-to-day activities, his relish was reserved for the appreciation of finer things. He went into great detail about his clothes. 'I have been buying myself clothes of all kinds & descriptions,' he told May proudly, including a new dress suit: 'The one I've got is very small for me, I think I must have grown, but I'm going to keep the old one & wear [it] when we just have dinner at Portman Square and keep the new one for going out. I'm getting two pairs of shoes; a black pair & a pair of brown brogues & six new shirts (thin ones) and three stiff dress shirts, as sometimes when I want to be very dressy I wear them with a white waistcoat instead of the pleated ones; also six socks & a pair of gloves & three ties which completes the take of my purchases.'[78]

Harry catalogued his visits to the theatre and museums. His grandfather took him and Aunt Sybil to the Tate Gallery after having watched the farce *Tons of Money*. They walked 'round & round for 2½ hours because Grandpa wouldn't miss a single picture, however uninteresting it was'.[79] Towards the end 'Auntie Sybil & I could hardly crawl', Harry admitted, but Joseph Pollak was 'galloping around like a young chamois'. The old man 'wasn't a bit tired'; 'he really is wonderful for his age', Harry mused precociously. The imminent return to school was a 'frightful bore', but his dancing lessons were a source of pleasure. 'I like them awfully', Harry assured his mother.[80] He took tea with his father's sister Lina Lewy in a 'tiny furnished house' in Eaton Terrace, and he joked with May afterwards that Aunt Lina 'would keep on telling us how "*detestful*" the French occupation of the Ruhr was, & of course Auntie Sybil & I nearly died'.[81] It was not all paintings, plays and high tea, however. There were larks, too. Harry indulged in a midnight feast with Aunt Sybil: 'it was great fun' but not, he added drily, 'calculated to help Auntie Sybil in her efforts to get thin'.[82] Sybil was Harry's mainstay, and in later years he acknowledged that without her his 'schooldays would have been very gloomy indeed'. He thought of her nostalgically 'with gratitude and love'.[83]

Any reader of Harry Oppenheimer's boyhood correspondence could be forgiven for concluding that his personality was fully formed by the age of 15. The self-possession, the fastidiousness, the alertness, the dry, ironic humour – all of these were manifest from a very early age. He was a young English gentleman (by now, his second name had been anglicised to 'Frederick'). 'You must write & tell me what tips to give, & also how I can book a table on board ... the *Briton*,' he instructed May before sailing to South Africa for the holidays.[84] (This was the Union-Castle liner that stowed a dairy cow for the convenience of Leander Starr Jameson when he returned to London in 1907.) Even Harry's interests were calcifying in adolescence. He wrote to his father in Parliament: 'remember to send the Hansards when they come out, and whenever you speak please send me all the newspaper cuttings'.[85] On his application form to Christ Church, Oxford, under a section entitled 'To what work in life is he looking forward?' Harry filled in 'Business'.[86]

While Harry was enrolled at Charterhouse, Ernest purchased a house in Parktown, called Marienhof, not far from Jubilee Road.[87] It had been commissioned in 1904 by the directors of Consolidated Gold Fields for their new managing director, Drummond Chaplin. Built by Herbert Baker, the Randlords' architect of choice (and a protégé of Rhodes and Milner), the house combined Cape Dutch and English vernacular conceits. It stood in twenty hectares of park-like grounds. Ernest changed the name to Brenthurst – the same as the house in Jubilee Road – and enthroned himself there. 'I was very interested to get the plan of the house; it really is awfully big & I'm looking forward ever so much to seeing it,' Harry wrote to his mother.[88] The Brenthurst estate was to become a sanctuary for Harry and Frank. Once a year, the brothers would spend the long school vacation in South Africa. This involved nearly three weeks of travelling by sea each way and three weeks at Brenthurst. These holidays, which Harry would spend discussing business and politics with his father while ambling through the estate, were the 'highlights' of his life; they were 'the only part' which 'seemed real and to which I really belonged'. His school career was 'something to be gone through rather than to be lived'. 'Perhaps this was perceptible to the discerning eye since when it became time for me to leave school and I went to say goodbye to the headmaster that very wise old man, Frank Fletcher, he took leave of me with the somewhat equivocal words, "I'm sure you are going to do very well and you will find that you are much better equipped for life than you could ever be for school."'[89]

It was indeed a piece of epigrammatic sagacity. Hugh Trevor-Roper, the distinguished Oxford historian, was five years younger than Harry and, like him, attended Charterhouse (in Daviesites) and proceeded to Christ Church, though they would only just not have coincided. Trevor-Roper's biographer describes Lancelot Allen, the Daviesites housemaster, as a 'nervous, fidgety man'; Trevor-Roper, he writes, regarded Allen as 'the most reactionary man in the school'.[90] Yet Allen was not without discernment. In 1925, he wrote to the Dean of Christ Church, Oxford: 'HF Oppenheimer as far as character & ability goes is all that you could want: he reads a great deal, & is very intelligent & I think may do something big in years to come. His father (Sir Ernest) is a friend of Smuts & in the S African Parliament: a most interesting man. His name & appearance are the only things that could count against him – but he gets on quite well in this House (although he does not shine in games) thanks to his thoughtful unselfish ways. His younger brother also is a very good fellow who I expect looks forward to coming to you in years to come.'[91] Harry's German-Jewish surname (and presumably his Semitic appearance) did not ultimately weigh against him. Allen made him a house monitor in his final year.[92] By the time he left school at the end of the spring term of 1927, the Oppenheimer heir had been sufficiently anglicised and Anglicanised to earn the Charterhouse stamp of approval. In February 1927, *The Carthusian* recorded that he had been awarded the Holford Exhibition to Christ Church to read Modern Languages.[93] The most carefree period of Harry Oppenheimer's life, at the grandest of Oxford's colleges, lay ahead.

THREE

Oxford: The House

1927–1931

Harry Oppenheimer went up to Oxford University in the Michaelmas term of 1927, three weeks short of his 19th birthday. His journey from Kimberley to Oxford had been the converse of Cecil John Rhodes's – a man whose legacy was carved into the university's physical and cultural landscape. After Charterhouse, which at times he found stultifying, the 'freedom of Oxford' had a salutary effect.[1] At first Oppenheimer read for a degree in Modern Languages, with a concentration in French, but after a year he switched to Modern Greats. This was the original name of the Honour School of Philosophy, Politics and Economics (PPE), which had only recently been established at Oxford, but which soon became immensely popular. In 1932, the *Oxford University Handbook* promised prospective PPE students that a combination of the 'intellectual discipline of Philosophy' and a 'training in History and Economics' would prepare them for 'business, the Civil Service, or public life'.[2] It was exactly the preparation that Oppenheimer sought. Yet, in the end, he found PPE more useful as 'a general background for life'; it gave him 'no specific knowledge for business'.[3] Oppenheimer was naturally studious and intellectually inclined. Even so, he looked upon his four years at Oxford as a period to enjoy rather than as an 'opportunity for any serious work'.[4] As a result, he ended up taking a second-class degree – hardly a nugatory achievement, but certainly not the 'first' of which his old Daviesites housemaster, Lancelot Allen, would no doubt have thought him capable. At Oxford, Oppenheimer was regarded as intelligent but idle; the idleness, in his own view, was not fundamental to his nature. Rather, it was the 'effect of special circumstances'; for the first time in his life, Oppenheimer felt ready to breathe.[5] His lot in life was assured – after Oxford he would return to South Africa and join his father in business, and perhaps politics too. Thus freed from the strictures of Charterhouse and 21 Portman Square, Oppenheimer could for once afford to prioritise his senses over his intellect.

Christ Church is one of the largest and most imposing of the Oxford colleges. Its size and its stateliness bring to mind an air of effortless superiority, which is the attitude many of its students contrive to adopt. Founded in 1525 by Cardinal Wolsey, the college was originally known as Cardinal College.[6] It stood on a site occupied by a priory dedicated to the memory of St Frideswide. After Wolsey was stripped of his office and property in 1529, Henry VIII appropriated Cardinal College (along with Hampton Court Palace). In 1546, the King 're-founded' the college: he designated the former priory church as Christ Church Cathedral of the Henrician diocese of Oxford. It was to serve as the chapel of the new college of Christ Church. The cathedral thus forms part of the college, and the Dean of the cathedral serves as the head of the college. For this reason, Christ Church is often called 'the House' in reference to its Latin name, *Aedes Christi*: the House of Christ. The sobriquet is itself revealing. The writer Jan Morris, who went up to Christ Church as an undergraduate in 1949, once irreverently observed: 'the House' suggests that had the Almighty himself been an Oxford man, 'he would surely have studied at Christ Church'.[7]

Christ Church has long been the college of choice for young aristocrats. John Betjeman, who was an undergraduate at Magdalen in the 1920s, recalled that Christ Church men always gave the impression that they were dropping in at Oxford en route to their hereditary seats in the House of Lords. There was an atmosphere of lavishness about the place, best captured by Evelyn Waugh in *Brideshead Revisited*. With good reason, Waugh chose Christ Church in the 1920s as the backdrop for his champagne-quaffing young aristocratic character, Lord Sebastian Flyte. In the early part of the 20th century, the college attracted foreign princes from Siam, Serbia and India; noblemen from Prussia and Russia; and the sons of wealthy businessmen from America, Greece and the British colonies. Christ Church also seemed to be a training ground for future members of Parliament: some 28 Housemen were returned to the British Parliament in the 1923 election, including a future Prime Minister, Anthony Eden.[8] Their politics leant towards Conservative, although after the General Strike of 1926, the University Labour Club regularly hosted a so-called Pink Lunch, and many of those in attendance were Christ Church men like Patrick Gordon Walker (a future secretary of state for Commonwealth relations) and the economist Roy Harrod. Harrod, a close friend (and later biographer) of John Maynard Keynes,[9] became Oppenheimer's economics tutor and exercised a strong influence over his thinking at Oxford.

This, then, was the milieu in which Harry completed the early part of his apprenticeship for a career in public life. He imbibed the culture wholeheartedly. Many years later, it was often said of Harry Oppenheimer that he did not look or act the part of a conventional tycoon. Contemplative of demeanour and slight of build – he was 5 feet 7½ inches – he would become animated when discussing English Romantic poetry or the 18th-century novel. He was more likely to be found reading the poetry of Byron and Shelley than a trade journal or the financial press, and he looked more like an Oxford don with a substantial independent income than the head of a mining house in jagged-edged Johannesburg. At Christ Church, among the manicured quadrangles – in the shadow of Sir Christopher Wren's majestic Tom Tower – Oppenheimer felt at ease. He went up to Oxford on a scholarship, but his father informed the Dean of Christ Church, Henry Julian White, that his 'financial position' precluded him from accepting it.[10] There is no reply on record from White. However, Christ Church's official historian observes that White was 'said to be a snob and excessively deferential to the influential and famous', so it may well be that Ernest Oppenheimer had his way.[11]

By the time Harry arrived in Oxford, Ernest had been a knight bachelor for almost seven years. Oppenheimer *père* was a member of the British establishment and an emergent plutocrat in the tradition of Rhodes: he was head of the 'new' Diamond Syndicate, formed in 1925, which included Anglo American; he controlled the diamond fields in South West Africa; he had become a director of De Beers in July 1926; and he was consolidating his bid for the chairmanship of Rhodes's old diamond company, which succeeded on 20 December 1929. Ernest's ties opened doors for Harry to aristocrats' country houses and to the gentlemen's clubs that lined Pall Mall. By this point, there were Oppenheimer family connections to the English aristocracy too. In 1920, Bernard Oppenheimer's son, Michael, married Caroline Magdalen ('Ina') Harvey, the daughter of Sir Robert Harvey, a saltpetre magnate and landowner in Cornwall and Devon. In years to come, many of the titled English notables who graced Harry Oppenheimer's dinner table at Brenthurst – from the bankers and men of high finance to the Conservative peers and administrators of Britain's dying empire – would be connected, in some way, to Oxford. This is quite apart from the conveyor belt of Oxford graduates whose hop-off point, in echo of Milner's Kindergarten, was the Anglo American chairman's office in Johannesburg. Somehow, Cambridge men tended to fit in less well.

As an imperial hub, Oxford's spokes radiated far and wide. Oxford was, if not quite the fulcrum, then certainly an essential cog in Harry Oppenheimer's subsequent career. The university played an important role in the development of his mind. Oppenheimer became 'addicted' to reading – 'It's like opium, you see,' he would later tell an interviewer.[12] Oxford deepened his love of literature and ideas. He threw himself into the study of philosophy, in which he was tutored by Gilbert Ryle, the critic of Cartesian dualism who went on to coin the phrase 'the ghost in the machine'. Oppenheimer took prodigious notes on Immanuel Kant's *Critique of Pure Reason*, which he kept for posterity.[13] In Roy Harrod's economics tutorials he learnt about money and banking (he already had a pretty solid foundation), international trade, imperfect conditions and the variations of cost, the trade cycle and economic development.[14] He became enamoured of Keynesian economics and 'mad keen on Liberals'.[15] Oppenheimer's politics were to shift rightwards over the years – in British terms, he would come to identify as a Tory – but at Oxford he dabbled in the welfarist 'New Liberalism' that was being reshaped by the likes of Keynes and William Beveridge. His politics tutor was the historian JC Masterman. In later years, Masterman became a celebrated figure after it was revealed that he ran the double-cross system for MI5 during the Second World War. Recruited into the intelligence service by one of his former students at Christ Church, Dick White, Masterman turned German spies into double agents for the British government.[16] In his spare time, the gregarious Masterman wrote murder mystery novels, played hockey and tennis for England, and later toured Canada with the Marylebone Cricket Club (MCC). But he was also a formidably well-connected mover and shaker in the corridors of power. He boasted in his autobiography that 'there must have been few prominent men in Church and State who had not at one time or another been entertained in Christ Church'.[17] Oppenheimer would draw on Masterman's expertise and networks throughout his life.

Outside his tutorials, Oppenheimer joined the Oxford Union, where nascent politicians made their mark. The Union's presidents alternated between Liberals, Tories and Labourites. During Oppenheimer's time at

Shades of *Brideshead Revisited*: Harry Oppenheimer
prepares to go punting on the Isis, late 1920s. *(Brenthurst Library)*

Oxford, Dingle Foot, Quintin Hogg and Michael Stewart all occupied the
top spot, but only Balliol had more Union officials than Christ Church
between 1919 and 1939.[18] For the most part, however, his Oxford years
marked a period of intense (and expensive) sociability for Oppenheimer.
Although he was not exactly short of money, Harry was 'always pumping
Ernest for more'.[19] He enjoyed treating his friends to champagne picnics
in the Cotswolds and frequenting the inns of Oxfordshire. He would
visit his brother, Frank, who went up to Trinity College, Cambridge.
And he would see a great deal of his cousin Raymond Oppenheimer,
who was at Oxford too. At weekends, they would often motor down
to White Waltham together. Raymond was eccentric. Among his many
unconventional enthusiasms was an obsession with prize-winning bull
terriers, of which he became the pre-eminent breeder. Harry delighted in
his company. Raymond had a lean and studious face like his father, Louis,
but, unlike his father's, Raymond's countenance was forever animated;
he and Harry were amused by the same things, and they would laugh

uproariously together. In 1928, Raymond captained the Oxford University golf team. He had been a scratch golfer at Temple Golf Club since the age of 16, and although he sometimes persuaded Harry to join him on the course, it was not an activity at which his cousin excelled. Normally, Harry was ineffably cool-headed, but on the golf course his equanimity would desert him. His mind could not grasp why he was unable to hit the ball 250 yards down the middle of the fairway every time.[20]

At Oxford, Oppenheimer cultivated several close friendships. The most notable of these was with a cheerful but not especially illustrious old Harrovian, Robin Grant Lawson, who went up to the House at the same time as Harry. Grant Lawson was the son of a former Tory MP, Sir John Grant Lawson, 1st Baronet, of Knavesmire Lodge, whose forebears (in the maternal line) had made a fortune in the Lancashire cotton industry. Oppenheimer got him interested in diamonds. In the long summer vacation of 1928, the pair travelled to South Africa, stayed at Brenthurst and visited the offices of the Diamond Syndicate at Kimberley. In this way, Oppenheimer initiated the trend of involving his friends in the family business. His preference, in time to come, would be to surround himself with like-minded associates whose company and contributions he could enjoy both in the boardroom and in the drawing room. After Oppenheimer left Oxford in the Trinity term of 1931, he invited Grant Lawson to South Africa once more, this time to join him in working for Anglo American.

Another firm friend from this time was Hugh 'Hughie' Vivian Smith, a convivial old Etonian whose grandfather Hugh Colin Smith had been the Governor of the Bank of England in the last few years of the 19th century. Hughie's father, Vivian, 1st Baron Bicester, was a director of Morgan, Grenfell & Co., one of Anglo American's bankers. His uncle Lancelot 'Lancie' Smith had joined the recently established stockbroking firm of Rowe & Pitman in 1898 and was largely responsible for Rowe & Pitman's increasing stature over the course of the next quarter of a century.[21] Whatever Oppenheimer may have learnt about monetary policy, central banking and finance in Harrod's tutorials, his knowledge was immeasurably enhanced by personal exposure to the network of financiers, merchant bankers and stock traders all pursuing 'illusions of gold' in the City of London.[22] At Oppenheimer's behest, Hughie Smith would eventually join Anglo American in Johannesburg, where he and his future wife, Lady Helen Dorothy Primrose (daughter of Ernest Oppenheimer's friend Lord Rosebery), were a fixture at Brenthurst.

Herbert Cecil Benyon Berens completes the trio of Oppenheimer's most constant Oxford chums. He was a gifted cricketer (not a passion Oppenheimer shared), and after Oxford he rose through the ranks of merchant banking. Berens ultimately served as a director of Hambros Bank, a role which Ernest, and later Harry, also fulfilled. Grant Lawson, Smith and Berens would have been among the guests for Harry's 21st birthday party, held at the Spread Eagle Inn in the village of Thame outside Oxford and hosted by Ernest and May in October 1929. The innkeeper, John Fothergill, was an epic character. He had studied at the Slade School of Fine Art and the London School of Architecture, and was a beneficiary of the flamboyant American art collector Ned Warren. When Evelyn Waugh presented Fothergill with a copy of his first novel, *Decline and Fall*, he inscribed it: 'John Fothergill, Oxford's only civilising influence'.[23] Among the guests Fothergill welcomed to his inn for Harry's birthday was General Jan Smuts, whom Ernest had asked to propose the toast. The *Oubaas*, as Smuts was known, could not quite fathom why the birthday party was being given in an unprepossessing pub outside Oxford (rather than in Oxford itself, or London). But the waiters asked no such questions. As Fothergill later recalled, Ernest put them in a 'pleasant pother' by tipping them 25 per cent of the bill, which prompted the innkeeper to muse that 'it's good when the princely and the deserving meet'.[24] The crown prince himself received ten thousand shares in the Anglo American Corporation as his birthday gift.

The day after Harry's 21st birthday, Wall Street crashed. The Roaring Twenties – that decade of prosperity and decadence – came to an abrupt halt. On 29 October 1929 – Black Tuesday – investors traded some 16 million shares on the New York Stock Exchange in a single day. The more stocks people sold, the more prices plummeted. Panic selling ensued. Billions of dollars were lost, and thousands of investors were wiped out. Eventually, the stock exchange collapsed to its lowest point in history. Thus began a chain of events that led to the Great Depression, the decade-long economic downturn that affected every industrialised country in the world.

In June 1931, in the midst of this global economic upheaval, Harry Oppenheimer's Oxford idyll drew to a close. Christ Church had offered an Arcadia of sorts – a blissful period of cultural and intellectual refreshment – and Oppenheimer was to retain a lifelong commitment, both sentimental and financial, to his old college. In the 1980s, he would donate £500 000 towards the building of St Aldates Quad across the road from the main college site, next to Christ Church Cathedral, though he declined the Dean's suggestion to have the new quad named after him.[25] Despite his nine years at Charterhouse and Oxford, Oppenheimer 'did not for a moment' think of England as his home; 'whatever I acquired by way of increased knowledge or development of skills or character during those most important years ... were always regarded by me as the basis for a life and career in South Africa.'[26] His real apprenticeship – shadowing his father in business and politics – would take him beyond the Gothic cloisters. Up to the point that Oppenheimer went down from Oxford in 1931, he had led a charmed life. It was not to last. The global upheavals of the 1930s, and a close succession of personal tragedies, were soon to conflagrate.

II
APPRENTICE

1931–1957

FOUR

Diamonds and Flames

1931–1939

The country to which Harry Oppenheimer returned from Oxford as an adult in 1931 was significantly different from the one that he had left as a child in 1922. The dour and taciturn Afrikaner nationalist General JBM Hertzog had come to power in 1924 in an 'unholy alliance' with Colonel Frederic Creswell's English-dominated Labour Party. However, in the 1929 election, Hertzog's National Party was returned with a clear majority and the so-called Pact government fell apart. Smuts and Ernest Oppenheimer were on the opposition benches in Parliament. Anglo-Afrikaner South Africanism of the Botha–Smuts variety was in retreat. The cultural stream of Afrikaner nationalism, propelled by republicanism, was gradually gathering into a torrent. Meanwhile, the Great Depression swept through the Union of South Africa like a wildfire blazing through the prairies. It soon scorched the sinews of the economy. Demand for diamonds dried up, causing an oversupply of stocks. In 1932, with the exception of state diggings, all diamond production in South Africa would cease. Almost simultaneously a drought ravaged the agricultural sector. Over-capitalised farmers defaulted on their interest payments and commercial banks foreclosed. In the countryside, many were plunged into penury; they swelled the ranks of 'poor whites' drifting to the cities. All around there was misery and mayhem.

Gold was in a crisis of sorts, too. Up to this point the 'gold standard' – the monetary system which linked the value of a nation's currency to a fixed price for gold – had underpinned the system of international finance.[1] But in September 1931 speculative attacks on the pound forced Britain to abandon the gold standard. As the world's largest gold producer, South Africa was expected to follow suit. But Prime Minister Hertzog stubbornly refused. The directors of the mining houses were aghast. After an initial period of uncertainty, they realised that a departure from the gold standard (and a concerted international currency devaluation) would actually prolong the lifespan of the low-grade gold mines, bolster their profits and reduce the costs of labour.[2] Hertzog's political opponents sniffed blood, and soon a powerful campaign was launched with the backing of the Transvaal Chamber of Mines, the Chamber's Gold Producers' Committee and the English-language press. They were determined to curb the raging economic fires by going off the gold standard. In Parliament, Ernest Oppenheimer led the charge. This was the sea of flames into which the imperturbable Oxonian Harry Oppenheimer sailed in 1931. But his equanimity would be put to the test, for the 1930s was to be an infernal decade of personal tragedy, too.

The Long Apprenticeship Begins

There had never been any question in Harry's mind about what he would do after Oxford. He took it as given that he would return to South Africa and apprentice himself to his father, in preparation for taking Sir Ernest's place as head of the family one day. And by now the dynastic founder was fast establishing a monopoly – like Rhodes before him – over the diamond industry. In 1919, with the help of Henry Hull and Sir David Graaff (an entrepreneur who had made a fortune in cold storage and served in General Botha's cabinet),[3] Ernest Oppenheimer acquired all of South West Africa's diamond interests for Anglo American. He did this through a new company, the Consolidated Diamond Mines of South West Africa Limited.[4] Ernest's control over the South West African diamond fields was achieved much to the annoyance and envy of his cousin Fritz Hirschhorn; De Beers had ambitions in the former German colony, but Ernest had pipped it to the post. Then in 1922, Anglo American and Barnato Brothers concluded a deal with the Belgian company Forminière for Forminière's diamond production in the Belgian Congo. Anglo subsequently acquired an interest in the Companhia de Diamantes de Angola, once again with Barnato Brothers' backing. Further acquisitions followed in the West African diamond fields. In 1925, with Anglo American having been requested to leave the Diamond Syndicate, Ernest created a new, rival syndicate with the help of Barnato Brothers. Dunkelsbuhlers and the Anglo American Corporation enjoyed a 'joint and several' participation of 45 per cent in the new syndicate.[5]

Like Rhodes, Ernest was intent on unifying all the major diamond producers in southern Africa – by now De Beers, Premier, Jagersfontein and Consolidated Diamond Mines of South West Africa – under his leadership. He built up Anglo's shareholding in De Beers and became a director of the company in 1926. In 1929, with the support of the Rothschilds, he succeeded in his bid for the chairmanship. In 1930, a new organisation, the Diamond Corporation, was formed to set quotas and purchase diamonds from 'outside producers' (that is, producers outside southern Africa). Based in London, it was effectively a subsidiary of De Beers, and Oppenheimer chaired it. The Diamond Corporation cached the large stock of diamonds rendered unsaleable owing to the worldwide economic meltdown. By 1930, then, Ernest Oppenheimer was the King of Diamonds: they were the cornerstone of his expanding realm. In fact, diamonds were Ernest's first love, and they cast a similar spell – at once intellectual and aesthetic – over Harry. Unsurprisingly, therefore, the crown prince started his training for business in his old home town. Harry and Robin Grant Lawson took a house in Egerton Road, Kimberley, not far from where Harry had spent the first seven years of his life. During the day, Harry would sort and value diamonds, just like his father thirty years before. At weekends, he would go riding – he and Grant Lawson were habitués of the Kimberley Club, togged up in their plus-fours – or take the train to Johannesburg to enjoy its metropolitan merriments.

After a few months in Kimberley, Harry moved permanently to Johannesburg and settled at Brenthurst. For the next twenty-five years, he would see his father every day, unless either one of them was travelling. It was the commencement of Harry Oppenheimer's long apprenticeship as magnate-in-waiting. He began work at Anglo American's head office situated in Anmercosa House on Hollard Street under the supervision of his mother's brother Leslie Pollak. From the beginning Ernest had conceived of Anglo American as a family concern, and he brought Pollak out to South Africa after the end of the First World War to join the business. Pollak's first assignment was to negotiate a mining lease from the government for the West Springs gold mine, and he performed the task so effectively that Ernest made him the managing director of Anglo American. Pollak became Ernest's closest collaborator. From 1923, Pollak devoted increasing amounts of time to pursuing new interests for the corporation, in base metals like copper, lead and zinc, and to expanding Anglo's presence in Northern Rhodesia's Copperbelt, where American mining concerns, led by Alfred Chester Beatty, were dominant.

Pollak was an aesthete. In Johannesburg, he stayed in elegantly appointed rooms at the Rand Club and lived a life of bachelorly routine. But most of his time was spent two blocks away, in Anmercosa House. He was in the office before everyone else reported for duty at 7.30 am, and he was the last to leave at night. Pollak knew everyone by name. He hosted dinner parties so that he could get to know each employee individually, and he took a personal interest in the welfare of the staff. Keith Acutt, who joined Anglo American as an enthusiastic 19-year-old in 1928 and rose rapidly through the ranks under Ernest Oppenheimer's wing, recalled Pollak as a fastidious but kindly man. Noticing one day that an employee looked dishevelled in a rather shabby suit, Pollak immediately dispatched the young man to his personal tailor and told him to order two suits for Pollak's own account. In the early days of Harry's career, Pollak exercised a 'considerable influence' on the dynastic apprentice, according to Acutt.[6]

Another new recruit was Harry's cousin Michael, Bernard Oppenheimer's son. A Cambridge-educated barrister, Michael Oppenheimer had stumbled into financial difficulties in England and had been declared bankrupt. On Ernest's suggestion, he relocated to South Africa to get on his feet again.[7] Ernest's nephew was accompanied by his aristocratic wife, Ina, the author of romantic novels and melodramas like *Apple Sauce* (which she wrote under the pseudonym 'Ina Michael'), and their young son, also named Michael.[8] The trio took up residence on the Brenthurst estate in one of the cottages, Little Brenthurst, that Ernest had rebuilt and redecorated to house his library. The young couple quickly became a staple of Johannesburg society. Meanwhile, Harry's brother, Frank, had decided that he would like to stay on in England, and after going down from Cambridge he joined the corporation's London office.

Although Harry spent a great deal of time shadowing Leslie Pollak at Anglo American, Ernest effectively commandeered his son and moved him into the chairman's office. Business was only one aspect of the overall initiation; politics formed an integral and overlapping part in Harry's tapestry of training. He was tasked with devilling: taking notes, drafting minutes and correspondence, and preparing speeches for his father. Harry would accompany Ernest to many of his official engagements. When Parliament was in session – usually in the first six months of the year – Harry would install himself in Cape Town, either at the Mount Nelson hotel or at his parents' beach cottage, Blue Mountains, in Muizenberg. He was often to be found perched in the gallery above the House of Assembly, watching Hertzog and Smuts across the table from each other, in their green leather benches below, slugging out the issues of the day. In Johannesburg, many key political personalities dined at Brenthurst, where Ernest and May hosted dinner parties several times a week. Ernest Oppenheimer was, of course, a member of Parliament for Smuts's South African Party, and he leveraged that position to advance his mining interests. The magnate had a keen nose both for commerce and politics, and when he detected Tielman Roos blowing with the wind, he pounced. Roos, a charming but enigmatic figure, was a wily opportunist. He had been the Transvaal leader of the National Party, an architect of the Pact government, and Minister of Justice in Hertzog's cabinet before the Prime Minister – wishing to free himself of a man he did not entirely trust – elevated him to the Appellate Division of the Supreme Court as a judge. But the calculating Roos was not finished with politics. He kept his oar in, and when the gold standard crisis erupted in 1931, his entrepreneurial instincts came to the fore. Even before Britain left the gold standard, there were rumours of Roos's return to politics. As economic conditions worsened, he sensed Hertzog's vulnerability and eyed the premiership covetously.

Tielman Roos and the Gold Standard Crisis

At the beginning of 1931, Ernest Oppenheimer fired off a series of letters to Roos after meeting with him in person. Would the good judge be amenable to a seat on the board of De Beers at an annual remuneration of £5450? 'Needless to say you can rely on my supporting your candidature as a Director of the above companies [Consolidated Diamond Mines of South West Africa, the Premier Diamond Mining Company, the Jagersfontein mine, and African Explosives and Industries] for the period of eight years mentioned by you.'[9] Roos responded that it would give him 'pleasure' to work with the diamond magnate.[10] Besides, he wished to 'build up a small reserve' for his family, which necessitated strict terms: Roos insisted on annual director's fees of not less than £6000, paid in instalments of £500 per month.[11] Ernest was happy to oblige: he deemed that Roos might be a useful political ally, sweetened into propinquity by the lure of lucre. But in the end Roos got cold feet. He had consulted with a 'leading judicial authority', Roos reported to Ernest, who cautioned him against swapping the bench for the boardroom. His physical condition weighed upon him too: a recurrence of kidney problems forced Roos to decline the directorships, and he ruefully told Ernest that the 'final word' had been spoken by his health, 'which for the second time stands between me & my ambitions'.[12]

Ernest Oppenheimer was regarded by the more revanchist elements of Hertzog's National Party as the sinister apotheosis of predatory international (by which was meant Jewish) mining finance capital. It is instructive that the imperialist, Smuts-supporting Oppenheimer was prepared to co-opt a republican Nationalist, albeit one who wore judicial robes and dispensed justice blindly. And it speaks of Roos's vanity (and patent avarice) that he seemed so eminently persuadable. This constituted a valuable lesson in realpolitik, and it might have been at the back of Harry Oppenheimer's mind when Roos eventually announced his resignation from the bench. On 16 December 1932, the Day of the Vow, Roos grabbed the limelight with a dramatic speech in which he called for the abandonment of the gold standard. (The Day of the Vow was a sacred holiday for Afrikaners, observed to commemorate the vow taken by the Voortrekkers in 1838 as they prepared to fight King Dingane's Zulu warriors at the Battle of Blood River.) A new government of national unity was needed, Roos said, to take South Africa into a post-gold standard era. The inference was clear: cometh the hour, cometh the man. Roos's health had evidently rebounded and he was ready to make his comeback. In fact, he was willing to court both Hertzog's Nationalists and Smuts's South African Party if it meant either one of them would install him as prime minister in the Union Buildings, the seat of the executive in Pretoria. Roos's gambit paid dividends. A speculative flight from the South African pound ensued, and with it came a domestic run on gold. As investors hoarded the precious metal, gold shares on the Johannesburg Stock Exchange went through the roof. Harry and his brother capitalised on the opportunity: 'Frank & I have invested £500 each in gold shares,' he noted in his diary. 'There is no doubt that gold shares must go up. AAC [Anglo American Corporation] has bought largely – £64,000 in last 10 days.'[13] Hertzog's government was forced to act. On 27 December, it suspended the right to convert notes into gold. The link with the gold standard was severed. When Parliament resumed in the new year, it passed the Currency and Exchanges Act, which linked the South African currency to the pound sterling. This paved the way for an influx of capital and a dramatic economic recovery.[14] A new era had begun.

Brenthurst: English Country House on the Highveld

Meanwhile, Harry Oppenheimer eased his way into the New Year by reading Robert Bridges' poetry after a night of festivity at the Johannesburg Country Club: 'It was the usual sort of show with lots of champagne & indiscriminate kissing and I unexpectedly enjoyed myself very much,' he confided in his diary.[15] Over the holidays, Brenthurst fulfilled its function as an English country house on the Highveld. Among the New Year guests staying on the estate were Lady Sylvia Grant Lawson (Robin's mother); Blanche, Lady Lloyd (wife of George Ambrose Lloyd, 1st Lord Lloyd, the former British High Commissioner to Egypt and later head of the British Council); Lady Mildred Fitzgerald (wife of Sir John Fitzgerald, an Irish beverage and hospitality magnate); and Lady Fitzgerald's daughter from her first marriage, Jean Follett.

The tone and tenor of Harry Oppenheimer's diaries from this period bear a residue of Oxford foppishness. It sometimes seems – as he turns the pages of Thackeray's *The History of Henry Esmond* or Milton's *Paradise Lost* ('immeasurably the best stuff that has ever been written'),[16] or orders himself new jodhpurs and poses with the house party for a photograph in *The Star*[17] – that, for Harry, Brenthurst stood in for Brideshead Castle. And, like Lady Marchmain, May Pollak could be an overbearing matriarch. She was volatile and strident. Her elder son took droll delight in observing the idiosyncrasies of 'Mama', as she is captured in his diaries. Sometimes May's husband and sons would try to engineer her (predictable) reactions to various situations. At an aerial show, Harry unsuccessfully attempted to persuade his mother to take to the air with a pilot in a de Havilland Puss Moth. She changed her mind, however, when Ernest told her there was 'nothing to be frightened of'. 'It turned out the greatest success and she is now as pleased as Punch with herself – full of caustic comments about people who are frightened to fly,' Harry recorded.[18] At a dinner with the business mogul Isidore W Schlesinger and his wife, the film actress Mabel May, Mama was 'thunderously noisy but amiable'.[19] (Also in attendance were the Minister of Finance, Nicolaas 'Klasie' Havenga, his wife, Olive, and their 'dull & spotty-faced niece'.) On another occasion Mama was in 'a vile temper'[20] because the De Beers coach was not available to take the family by rail from Cape Town to Johannesburg; on the train she was 'quite insufferable',[21] reaching an intolerable 'crescendo of unpleasantness' at lunch.[22] May's combustibility often took its toll: 'Papa was not feeling well & did not come to the office; this was entirely due to Mama's behaviour'.[23]

Everyday life for Harry was a blend of business, politics and pleasure. He and his father took their titled visitors down one of the shafts at Anglo's new Daggafontein gold mine, where the ladies' interest was 'keen' but 'scarcely intelligent'.[24] Invariably there was a cocktail party or dinner party at Brenthurst. The regular guests included Anthony Comar Wilson (five years older than Harry, he was a promising recruit at Anglo), Fred and Doff Susskind, and various Pilkingtons (George Pilkington was the yachtsman who had brought Ernest Oppenheimer to safety after the torpedoing of the *Galway Castle* in 1918). 'It was a dreadful evening, men in a vast majority, & Papa driven to a state of "messianic" frenzy by the effort of coping with his guests,' was Harry's postprandial pronouncement in his diary.[25] He read prolifically. Along with his Romantic poets, he favoured biography. Duff Cooper's *Talleyrand* was 'really good',[26] while GM Young's *Gibbon* 'did not promise at all well'.[27] There was room for biology (HG Wells's *The Science of Life*) and economics too, although he was convinced that FA Hayek's *Prices and Production* was 'mysterious nonsense'.[28]

Outside work, Harry would play tennis or golf, attend horse-jumping lessons with Madge Handley, or go to the cinema.[29] He socialised with friends like Charles 'Punch' Barlow and his wife, Cynthia. Barlow was another industrialist in the making: his family business, Thomas Barlow & Sons (South Africa), supplied the local market with Caterpillar mining and construction equipment. Harry, his brother, Frank, and cousin Raymond (when the two of them were visiting South Africa) formed a tight-knit social circle along with Grant Lawson. Occasionally there were girls. Jean Follett, Huldah Pine, Violet Martin and Brigid Arkwright all make an appearance in Harry's diary from the time. In Cape Town he would see a great deal of Mittie Mary Starr Bailey, the daughter of the mining magnate Sir Abraham 'Abe' Bailey and his aviator wife, Mary, who had won the Britannia Trophy in 1929 for the longest solo flight over Africa. They would bathe in the sea at Muizenberg, dine at the Queen's, or dance at the Mount Nelson. 'I didn't get to bed till three o' clock,' Harry wrote after a night on the tiles (or the linoleum, he noted, after rain made dancing outside impossible).[30] But he was prone to jealousy; his nose was put out of joint when he saw Mittie Bailey having 'an absurdly early & inexpressibly revolting lunch' with 'a boy called Manfred Czernin' at the

Waldorf.[31] She had not responded to a letter from Harry inviting her to lunch that same day.

As it panned out, Grant Lawson married the Baileys' daughter in 1934, but the marriage did not last: they divorced after only a year. In matters of the flesh, as in matters generally, Harry was sensitive to appearance. 'I bought a skipping rope in a last attempt to acquire a "svelte" figure & skipped furiously in every room before going to bed,' he recorded of his slimming efforts.[32] And he had high aesthetic standards for others. He lunched with his mother at the Benjamins' 'disappointing' house in Cape Town and talked to a girl who was 'quite pretty' but let down by a 'very common voice'.[33] At a picnic he met Susan Hambro (daughter of the British Army officer Sir Percy Hambro, of the Hambro banking dynasty) and found her 'charming'. Cynthia Hankey, by contrast, was 'quite a pretty little thing but very second-rate'.[34] At a dinner party at the Winchester he was pleased to be seated next to Mittie Bailey but was peeved that on his other side – in all her spotty-faced insipidity – was 'Mrs Havenga's deplorable niece'.[35] Meanwhile, Punch Barlow's sister Sally was 'quite pretty' but had a 'frightful voice' and gave the impression of 'not being quite all there'.[36]

Diamond Negotiations in the Great Depression, and Down the Daggafontein Mine

With such exacting requirements of female companionship, it would be a decade before Harry Oppenheimer found love and settled down. He channelled his energies into business and politics in the meantime. At Anmercosa House, Harry drafted all his father's correspondence with the Minister of Mines, APJ Fourie. He served as the liaison with the Diamond Corporation in London. In Kimberley, he assisted with capturing the minutes of De Beers board meetings. The diamond mines were closed, which jeopardised tax revenues, and Ernest Oppenheimer had resolved to reorganise the industry. He was determined to control production and sales through a single channel. To this end, he spearheaded the creation of two new institutions: the Diamond Producers' Association (DPA) and the Diamond Trading Company (DTC). The DPA was representative of all the large South African diamond producers (including the Union government) and the Diamond Corporation. It set industry policy, bought all diamond production, and sold it to the DTC. The DTC, effectively a subsidiary of the Diamond Corporation, would then offer these rough diamonds for sale to dealers at 'sights' several times a year, mainly in London. The umbrella term used to describe the Diamond Corporation, the Diamond Producers' Association and the Diamond Trading Company – and their collective marketing arrangements – was the Central Selling Organisation (CSO). The CSO was in place by 1934, under the effective control of De Beers.

Many of these arrangements required delicate negotiation with the South African government, in which Harry served as an amanuensis to his father. 'They are all the time trying to take away our power & our business from us,' he complained of the government in one diary entry.[37] But Ernest eventually obtained the government's co-operation, and the Diamond Producers' Association set the policy of the diamond trade for decades to come. In later years, Harry would look back on his father's work for the diamond industry during the Great Depression as 'his greatest business achievement' and the success that made possible 'Anglo American's spectacular growth in the years that followed'.[38] There were even flickerings of diamond fire amid the gloom. In January 1934, a 726-carat diamond was found by a digger, Johannes Jacobus Jonker, in the precinct of the Premier mine. It was the fourth-largest uncut gem diamond ever found. In 1935, Harry Winston, the New York diamond dealer, purchased the Jonker diamond for £150 000 and had it cut by Lazare Kaplan.

At the best of times, the diamond industry was fractious. Ernest had made enemies on his way to the top: men like Fritz Hirschhorn, who had once mentored him, now nurtured resentments over the South West African diamond fields, as did another director of De Beers, P Ross Frames. Harry thought Frames was full of 'senile spite' and he told Fourie – under cover of his father's signature – that there would be no peace in the diamond trade in the face of Frames's 'thoroughly unreasonable attitude'.[39] He drew up memoranda in which he fleshed out his father's thoughts. 'At breakfast Papa came out with the bright idea that if the Government wished to keep the SA £ on a parity with Sterling they should make the Union Government loans … transferable at will.'[40] It was a happy marriage of talents, a productive symbiosis. Ernest operated on intuition: he fizzed with new ideas, but it was his more cerebral son who marshalled them into coherent form on paper. As part of his duties, Harry vetted a speech to be delivered by the president of the Transvaal Chamber of Mines, John Martin, on the future of the gold mining industry: 'We made a few alterations that Martin accepted but generally it was quite an unexceptionable document ... somewhat uninspiring & very stilted in style.'[41]

Ernest Oppenheimer believed that a businessman should be an entrepreneur: he thought that the head of a large company like Anglo American should not be a technician but a 'business statesman'.[42] The notion that Anglo's chairman (or even managing director) should be someone who combined the qualities of entrepreneur, technician and administrator was regarded (if contemplated at all) as an improbable conceit. To Ernest's mind, the chairman should devise and decide upon general policy, and then select – and trust – technicians who were capable of carrying it out. With his lack of technical training – the point of his formal education at Charterhouse and Oxford had been to broaden his mind and teach him to think clearly – Harry imbibed this philosophy. He would learn business by doing business. The technical aspects of mining and engineering, Ernest thought, could quite comfortably remain mysteries beyond his ken.

For all that, Harry was keen to get underground. At the Daggafontein mine, the mine manager took him down the Number Two shaft. It was not his natural habitat. On the way back he hit his forehead on a projecting piece of timber; 'it is most difficult to look where one puts one's feet *and* one's head, I always forget one or the other,' he lamented afterwards.[43] After lunch he was taken to the top of the Number One shaft, and then to the on-site hospital and compound for black miners. Up to the age of 23, Harry Oppenheimer had led his whole life insulated from the hardships of black workers. The so-called native problem, as the Union's interrace relations were then framed, lay blurred on the fringe of his political consciousness. If anything, for Oppenheimer 'race' referred to the group identity of white English-speaking South Africans on one side and Afrikaners on the other. His racial attitudes and politics were far from fully formed. He was not immune to the racial prejudices that were ubiquitous among white South Africans at the time and, indeed, among whites around the globe. He encapsulated his thoughts on the visit to Daggafontein in a passage reminiscent of the writings of Mahatma Gandhi, who, during his years in South Africa, had expressed bigoted opinions about black Africans.[44] With a Gandhi-esque flourish, Oppenheimer declared: 'The hospital was extremely well kept & clean but the compound looked just like kennels; as a matter of fact in some ways the natives *are* very like dogs as I am told that their vegetables have to be so mixed with their meat that they cannot be separated, otherwise the natives will always throw the vegetables away

& in consequence get scurvy.'[45] Such crude views were commonplace on the mines, and they served the mine bosses well. Since the beginning of the industrial revolution in Kimberley and on the Rand, the mines had been central to the development of native policy in South Africa. Dependent on cheap, well-policed, black migrant labour from the rural areas, the mines exploited black workers, who were required to carry passes at all times. In return for low wages they were corralled into compounds where the living conditions were dehumanising, their families rent asunder. In this way, the compound system gave birth 'through Caesarean section' to industrial capitalism.[46]

Mining, Migrant Labour and the Segregationist State

Mining magnates required the assistance of the state to create, coerce and control the black labour force, and after the conclusion of the Anglo-Boer War the process of racial subordination and separation gathered pace. The South African Native Affairs Commission, which was appointed by Lord Milner and which sat between 1903 and 1905, provided the Union government with a blueprint for segregation after the nation was forged in 1910.[47] The Mines and Works Act (1911) imposed the colour bar in industry and reserved higher-paid skilled positions for whites. It was followed by the all-important Natives Land Act (1913), which forbade the purchase or lease of land by Africans outside confined areas known as reserves – a mere seven per cent of the Union's overall land area. The Natives Land Act segregated land ownership and effectively proletarianised vast swathes of the African population, to the benefit of white mine owners and farmers – the power-wielding alliance of 'gold and maize'. The Natives (Urban Areas) Act (1923) entrenched residential segregation in towns. The Industrial Conciliation Act (1924) legalised the collective bargaining power of trade unions but explicitly excluded 'native' workers from its provisions.

To some extent, then, the development of segregation – and all the disruption, suffering and indignity it entailed – was a product of the industrial revolution and the labour requirements of mine owners. But its roots stretched back deeper; they were manifold and tangled. Although the basic tenets of segregation were embedded by the administrations of Botha and Smuts, before the 1920s the key planks of segregationist legislation were seldom interpreted as 'integral elements of a united ideological package'.[48] After 1924, when the Pact government assumed power, the Prime Minister, JBM Hertzog, sought to unify the strands of segregationist ideology and codify them into a coherent legislative agenda. The so-called Hertzog bills, which proposed among other things to abolish the Cape African franchise and establish a Natives Representative Council in its place, were introduced in 1926 and eventually piloted through Parliament ten years later. In 1936, Ernest Oppenheimer assured the honorary secretary of the African People's Organisation in Kimberley that he would 'naturally oppose' the disenfranchisement of Cape Africans.[49] But although there was a backlash to Hertzog's bills from liberals like FS Malan and Jan Hendrik Hofmeyr,[50] very few liberals questioned the merits of segregation or the segregationist underpinnings of the South African state. In fact, some liberals actively promoted segregation as a middle road between racial assimilation and repression.[51] To Harry Oppenheimer in the 1930s, segregation was the natural order. The civil order was ineluctably white, and the economic order was premised on the interests of the white ruling class. It would be some time before his liberal conscience was pricked by recrudescent Afrikaner nationalism.

'Hoggenheimer', Coalition and Fusion

The new session of Parliament commenced on 20 January 1933. Ernest, May, Harry and Frank attended in their finery. The men wore their 'wedding garments', Mama was resplendent in 'a flowing magenta cummerbund', but the other guests, Harry noted disapprovingly, came up short. 'Of course anything of this sort in SA suffers from the fact that practically none either of the men or women possesses suitable clothes.'[52] Hertzog's native bills were in abeyance and talk of Tielman Roos's machinations dominated the corridors. Roos's Day of the Vow sally, it was palpable, would reconfigure Union politics. Smuts had deputed Ernest Oppenheimer to intermediate with Roos on behalf of the South African Party.[53] Smuts actively encouraged the idea of coalition government between his own party and those Nationalists whom Roos believed he could induce to disown Hertzog. As the gold standard crisis reached its apogee in the dying days of 1932, Smuts wrote to Ernest and agreed with him that Roos 'should not be turned down, but rather encouraged'.[54]

Early in January, Deneys Reitz – a senior figure in the South African Party (SAP) and author of *Commando*, a book about his experiences fighting in the Anglo-Boer War – went to see Ernest. Harry summarised the meeting in his diary. 'Deneys Reitz came to see Papa & told him confidentially that it had been definitely decided to make Roos an

offer when he is in Pretoria on Tuesday. Roos to defeat Govt. at once &
Coalition Government to be formed 6 SAP 4 Roos – Smuts to be Prime
Minister, Roos Deputy Prime Minister.'[55] In the week after the opening
of Parliament, Harry and Ernest lunched with two South African Party
MPs – Harry Lawrence and Sidney Waterson – and they were, Harry
noted, 'clearly ... in favour of a Coalition even if Roos had to be Prime
Minister.'[56] As the negotiations between the South African Party and
Roos continued, the Afrikaner nationalist press denounced Ernest
Oppenheimer as the Machiavellian mastermind behind the talks. In *Die
Burger*, he was depicted as 'Hoggenheimer': the grotesque antisemitic
caricature popularised by the newspaper's cartoonist, DC Boonzaier.
Harry noted in his diary: '*Die Burger* takes the line that Papa is pressing
for the acceptance of the Roosite proposals in order to benefit the Gold
Mines & published an attack on him & a caricature of Hertzog refusing to
sit in the "Hoggenheimer" Coalition Chair.'[57]

In point of fact, Smuts was not prepared to serve under Roos. '*Slim*'
(meaning 'crafty' in Afrikaans) Jannie, as Smuts was disparagingly called
by his opponents, approached the negotiations with Roos guilefully. He
kept an open channel to Hertzog. 'There can be no doubt that Smuts
has behaved very badly,' Harry reflected when news of Smuts's double-
dealing filtered back to the South African Party caucus.[58] Ernest expressed
his displeasure to the chief whip, Colonel WR Collins, and complained
that he was 'expected to pay the bill ... or start negotiations' but was
'neither consulted nor considered' in the long run, precisely because he
represented the mining industry.[59] He threatened to resign his seat and
intimated that the South African Party might experience future difficulty
'in collecting party funds'.[60] The furore over coalition led to a cooling
of relations between Ernest Oppenheimer and Smuts. Ernest resented
Smuts's silence on *Die Burger*'s 'Hoggenheimer' attack, and clearly Smuts
felt slighted too: when Smuts's wife, Isie, saw Ernest lunching with
another MP, Gideon Brand van Zyl, she pointedly said to Van Zyl: 'You
are a great supporter of my husband but Sir Ernest is a bit of a Roosite.'[61]
In the end, after much backroom manoeuvring, Smuts entered into a
coalition agreement with Hertzog in February 1933. The following year,
the South African Party merged with the Nationalists to form the United
South African National Party (better known as the United Party). Thus
the 'Fusion' government was born, with Hertzog as prime minister and
Smuts as his deputy. It provoked a chauvinistic backlash. The doctrinaire
DF Malan – a former Dutch Reformed Church minister, founding editor

of *Die Burger* and Nationalist cabinet minister under Hertzog – broke away in righteous indignation to form the Gesuiwerde Nasionale Party (Purified National Party). In Natal, English-speaking jingoes viewed Fusion as a threat to the British imperial connection. They took their leave of Smuts and established the Dominion Party led by Colonel Charles Stallard. The political landscape was transformed. But Harry thought that Smuts had 'bungled badly': if he had come to terms with Roos instead of Hertzog, then the South African Party would have had the upper hand; the National Party would have been 'squashed' at the polls; and Smuts would inevitably have become the de facto prime minister in view of Roos's unsteady health.[62]

For all that the focus of Harry's apprenticeship was business – diamonds, gold and copper in order of importance – politics seemed to enthuse him the most. He spent hours drafting his father's parliamentary speeches. At Ernest's side, he lunched and dined with all the political worthies of the day; and he was quick to form judgements about them. When Smuts spoke on financial matters, Harry believed, he 'showed deplorable ignorance'.[63] Patrick Duncan, the South African Party MP for Yeoville and soon to be the coalition government's Minister of Mines, was 'an utter dud'.[64] Hertzog's Nationalist Minister of Mines, APJ Fourie, was so 'flabby' and 'futile' that 'one never knows whether he has agreed [to something] or not'.[65] Charles te Water, South Africa's High Commissioner in London (and delegate to the League of Nations), was 'much stupider' than Harry had supposed: 'very superficial [and] bombastic; he has the gift of talking snappily & slickly but this is all'.[66] The political arena, with its cut and thrust, appealed enormously to Harry: he saw himself as rooted in the Union's polity and, like Rhodes, he conceived of business and politics as intersecting forces on the same spectrum.

Gold on the Far West Rand, and Visit to the Copperbelt

In business, like Rhodes, Harry found diamonds a source of endless fascination. But the Great Depression had cut a swathe through the market for gem diamonds. A confidential market analysis commissioned by De Beers found that from 1930 to 1932 the price of diamonds plummeted by nearly 50 per cent.[67] At the beginning of 1933, Harry noted in his diary: 'Diamond sales were £300 000, mainly Common goods … It is very disappointing and Papa has cabled Louis [Oppenheimer] for details.'[68] Personally, Harry found his uncle Louis 'hopelessly vague & resignedly

Harry Oppenheimer attends a meeting of the De Beers board in 1934, his first as a director of the company. *(Anglo American)*

helpless'.[69] The shortcomings of the London office, from where Otto Oppenheimer cultivated close links with Belgian diamond producers in the Congo, were a frequent source of grumbling between Harry and Ernest. 'Papa and I discussed diamonds … We then groaned together … about the London office who have … sold a 76c [carat] special stone valued at £60 for £32 to a M. Arpels'.[70] It is not clear which Monsieur Arpels Harry was referring to – Julien, who opened the first Van Cleef & Arpels shop on the Place Vendôme in 1906; either of his two brothers; or one of three sons who joined the business in the 1930s. But gossiping and grousing about figures in the diamond world – producers, dealers, buyers, cutters and jewellers – was to become a congenial pastime for the dynast and his heir. Diamonds were a shared love. Harry's greatest aspiration when he joined the business was, like his father before him, to occupy a seat on the board of De Beers. '[EH] Farrer has … definitely suggested to Papa that I should get the vacant seat on the De Beers board,' Harry wrote excitedly in his diary on 22 February 1933.[71] His wish would be fulfilled at the end of the following year.

If, by 1930, Ernest Oppenheimer was the King of Diamonds, then his sights were also set on becoming King Midas and a copper baron, too. During the 1920s, Anglo American had solidified its position on the goldfields of the Far East Rand. After South Africa departed from the gold standard, the gold mining industry experienced a boom, which spurred the country's recovery from the Great Depression and accelerated its economic development. Anglo played a prominent part in the subsequent expansion of the Far East Rand: the corporation developed its interests in Daggafontein and Springs, and commenced crushing at East Daggafontein and South African Lands ('Sallies') in 1934. Several of the mining finance houses now looked to enlarge their sphere of operations. Most notable among them was Consolidated Gold Fields, Rhodes's old company, which had been re-energised by its imaginative Canadian consulting engineer, Guy Carleton Jones. Aided by advanced technical methods of prospecting, Carleton Jones began to open up new mines on the Far West Rand around Klerksdorp. In 1931, news broke that Consolidated Gold Fields had acquired an option on the Western Areas property, and the following year the company began its drilling operations. FA Unger, Anglo American's chief consulting engineer and a perspicacious Hollander, regarded the development as a very attractive 'gamble', and urged Ernest Oppenheimer to get in on the action: 'The possibilities are immense, and if fortune favours the bold, the outlook for the Witwatersrand will undergo a complete change.'[72] Anglo's chairman did not need any persuasion; he was a born risk-taker. In November 1932, on the basis of geological and magnetometric investigations, Consolidated Gold Fields created the West Witwatersrand Area Limited to develop the 'West Wits Line'. The initial working capital involved was £500 000, and Anglo American made a significant contribution. There was a flurry of activity. 'The market is booming wildly,' Harry enthused in his diary; 'AAC ... [has] got options over some farms in the far West Rand, which are apparently even more promising than [the] Gold Fields proposition.'[73] He sold some of the gold shares that he and Frank had recently bought; 'they may go up more but there is never much harm in taking big profits!' he trumpeted.[74] Anglo American's foray into the Far West Rand and its flotation of the Western Reefs mine, which began producing in 1933, were momentous: they were the precursor to prospection in the Orange Free State south of the Vaal River. In time, the Orange Free State goldfields would become the jewel in the crown of Harry's substantial inheritance as chairman of the Anglo American Corporation.

To the north of South Africa – in Northern and Southern Rhodesia – Ernest Oppenheimer took his cue from Rhodes. He expanded his empire there, too. In truth, much of the pioneering work on copper in Northern Rhodesia had been accomplished by Alfred Chester Beatty through his company, Rhodesian Selection Trust, and Sir Edmund Davis, through his Rhodesia Broken Hill Development Company Limited. But Ernest Oppenheimer had collaborated with both Chester Beatty and Davis on purchasing agreements for Angolan and Congolese diamonds, and now he did the same to further his copper interests. By the end of 1925, the Anglo American Corporation had acquired shareholdings in five of the six concession companies. Moreover, the corporation had been appointed as consulting engineers to all of them. In 1926, Anglo American became consulting engineers to the British South Africa ('Chartered') Company. In consequence, Anglo served as consulting engineers for practically the whole of Northern Rhodesia, including the valuable N'Kana concession and N'Changa mine. Ernest became a director of all the concession companies and quickly assembled a formidable team to drive his burgeoning copper interests. It included a distinguished Canadian geologist, Dr JA Bancroft, who surveyed vast swathes of Northern Rhodesia for Anglo American; Carl Davis, Anglo's consulting engineer, who led a specialised technical department located at Broken Hill (later called Kabwe); and Leslie Pollak, who became managing director in South Africa of the newly formed Rhodesian Anglo American Limited (Rhoanglo). Launched with British capital to consolidate Anglo's concerns in Northern Rhodesia, Rhoanglo was incorporated in London on 8 December 1928.[75]

Against this backdrop, Harry accompanied his father on a visit to the Copperbelt in June 1933, followed by a sortie to the Congolese and Angolan diamond fields. It was a difficult time for the copper industry: prices had fallen to an all-time low in 1932, which served to discourage production. Nevertheless a series of mergers had taken place, leading to the formation in 1931 of the Rhokana Corporation with Rio Tinto's Sir Auckland Geddes as its chairman and Ernest Oppenheimer and Edmund Davis as his deputies.[76] Rhokana had put the N'Kana mine into production, and this was the first port of call for Harry and Ernest before they proceeded to the Rhodesian Selection Trust's Roan Antelope mine.

At N'Kana they stayed at the house of HS Munroe, Rhoanglo's American consulting engineer; 'he made a more favourable impression on me than he had done previously though I cannot say that I like him,' Harry remarked in his journal.[77] The N'Kana plant was 'huge & very impressive', Harry observed, but the explanation of its various processes was not 'intelligible to a layman'. Dr Bancroft took them through the thorny challenges of production, and Harry noted them all down in his journal. He remarked on inconsistencies and contradictions in Bancroft's case: 'Surely it is absurd to argue that if & when development is brought up to normal the mine will still not be capable of giving more than 5000–6000 tons per month.'[78] In effect, he thought Bancroft was conspiring to understate N'Kana's potential in order to get another section, Mindola, opened up. Harry took a keen interest in the 'spirit' on the mine, which he felt was cheerless: there was 'no sentiment whatever of loyalty to the Corporation, rather the contrary in fact'. And he ascribed this in part to the Munroes, who had 'absolutely no idea how to manage the social side of a show like N'Kana.'[79] But the mine's doctor and his wife made up for the miserableness: 'She is really very beautiful in the Greta Garbo type [*sic*], well made up & very pleasant to talk to; he is definitely good looking, a rather exotic person, very nice.'[80]

As he toured Northern Rhodesia, the Belgian Congo and Angola, jotting down his impressions along the way, Harry manifested all the traits identifiable from his correspondence as a boy. He was ever on his toes: alert and heedful, always probing below the surface with searching questions and trenchant comments. His eyes roved constantly but quietly, surveying and processing different stimuli. He was sensitive to personality, tone and atmosphere. One particular dinner party with the Governor of Katanga was a trial: the hostess, Madame Deschact, was 'a little crinkled, mud-coloured woman with thick tinted glasses, no conversation whatever, & a habit of bobbing her head in a most disconcerting way as she shakes hands with one.'[81] He was forever remarking on appearance: one of the dinner guests had 'a rather pretty daughter'; the Governor was a 'v. good looking man'; the Bishop, Monsignor Jadot, was 'enchanting … with an immense beard'.[82] And Harry's observations were often tinged with irony: the American mining engineer at the Lubumbashi copper smelter explained everything very slowly and methodically, but 'appeared to be addressing an invisible audience a long way behind us'.[83] There was still something of the Brideshead dandy about him. From his bed at the Hôtel du Globe in Élisabethville he composed a page-long verse. One stanza ran: 'To me, my bathroom seems both dark and small / But to the cockroach 'tis a marble hall / Nor does the stench of faulty drains affright / The winged horrors flapping round the light'.[84] A few days later he spotted a tarantula in his hotel room. He held back a 'piercing scream' so as not to 'disturb the creature's slumber'.[85] In the end he sought help from 'Papa', who with 'almost unbelievable bravery' 'slew the brute with a single blow of a veldschoon'.[86]

A Series of Tragedies

For almost six years in the 1930s, Anglo American received no revenue by dividend from its substantial investments in De Beers and no revenue by dividend for its considerable investments in the copper fields of Northern Rhodesia.[87] But as gold thrived and the depression lifted, the economy rebounded and Anglo American prospered. Anmercosa House was no longer up to the task of accommodating Anglo's growing staff complement, and in 1935 Ernest Oppenheimer decided that it was time for Anglo to build new headquarters from scratch. He purchased a plot of land in an area of Johannesburg – Ferreira's Camp, or Ferreirasdorp – where the first gold claims had been pegged. Consulting architects were brought in from London, overseen by Francis Lorne of Sir John Burnet, Tait & Lorne; and by 1938 the simple but monumental building – faced with Ficksburg freestone, inset with lawns and fountains, and occupying an entire block of the city – was ready to be unveiled. It was called, quite simply, 44 Main Street, the site of its legendary address. But while the recessionary fires had been doused, Ernest Oppenheimer's family life seemed to burst aflame. In the course of two years, the Oppenheimers were ravaged by a series of deaths.

On 26 February 1933, Harry's cousin Michael Oppenheimer was killed in a plane crash as he surveyed the new developments along the West Wits Line. Meanwhile, May Oppenheimer's health was in decline. She had undergone a number of operations over the years for a variety of complaints. It was Michael's widow, Ina, who was constantly by her side. In January 1934, May accompanied Ernest to Cape Town for the opening of Parliament. Instead of Blue Mountains, they stayed at the Mount Nelson, where it would be easier to get hold of a doctor in case of emergency. Ernest needed to return to Johannesburg for business at the end of the first week of the parliamentary session, but May decided to prolong her convalescence for a few days. However, when the time came for her to go to the station to board the afternoon train to Johannesburg on 5 February, she could not be roused. She had suffered a heart attack: not a serious one, the doctors reassured her family, and she would recover with more bed rest. But at 10 o'clock that same night she went into cardiac arrest once more, and this time she did not recover.

Ernest was devastated by his wife's death. For all May's fitful tempestuousness, she had been a steadfast spouse. She had followed her husband's business dealings with intelligent interest and been a lively companion. Now there was a painful void. Ernest wrote to his friend William Honnold in California: 'I feel very tired and weary and am toying with the idea of retiring. I should not like you to think that I am ill, but I find it very difficult after my bereavement to concentrate on work.'[88] He spiralled into sorrow. At Anglo American, more and more responsibility fell to Leslie Pollak, now the corporation's deputy chairman. But one night at a dinner party, Pollak suddenly took ill. By the morning he was dead; unbeknown to anybody, he had been suffering from pneumonia. Ernest was in London when Harry cabled him the news. Leslie Pollak's death deepened Ernest's gloom and left a vacuum at Anglo. The next most senior manager in Johannesburg was Richard Bein ('RB') Hagart. An able albeit somewhat humourless man with conservative instincts, he had joined the company in 1927, aged 33, after a stint in banking. Hagart was out of town at the time of Pollak's death. In his absence, Harry appointed himself and Comar Wilson as joint managers; it was the first major business decision he took without consulting his father. As Keith Acutt later reflected: 'Harry was confident that his father would approve.'[89]

In London, Ernest tried to soothe his sadness. He spent more time with his younger son, Frank. Frank had always been close to Harry but was quite different in temperament and appearance. He was tall, fair and extroverted, and had inherited his father's lack of self-consciousness. Frank spoke what was on his mind and in his heart; he was affectionate and exuded a certain lightsomeness. But if Frank was light of spirit, he was heavy of flesh; and this is what took him and two friends on holiday to Madeira in April 1935. They wanted to lose weight. The trio checked themselves into the storied Reid's hotel, set on cliff tops overlooking the Atlantic Ocean in Funchal. On the evening of 17 April, after dinner, they went dancing with two Blandy girls – from the wine-making family that was considered island royalty. At about 10.30 pm Frank decided he wanted to go bathing – not in the sea, but at a local lido which was closed for the night. The well-connected Blandy girls pulled some strings. The precise sequence of events that ensued is not clear. Subsequent police investigations sought to spare the Blandy girls' blushes, but it seems that after they had all left the pool to get dressed in the changing huts, Frank decided to continue swimming. When the time came to depart, nobody could find him. It was the pool attendant who discovered Frank lying face down in the shallow end of the pool. One of his friends, John Hallett, tried unsuccessfully to revive him.[90] A doctor was summoned and arrived within half an hour, but it was too late. The cause of death was ascribed to vasoconstriction.

Harry received the news while travelling abroad, and he immediately sent a telegram to Brenthurst: 'I wish I could be together I feel dreadfully miserable and alone All love Harry.'[91] Ernest was disconsolate. Smuts wrote twice to him. He expressed his 'grief and horror' at the passing of such 'a bright cheerful promising lad': the loss, he sympathised, 'must be almost more than mortal man can bear.'[92] And a week later Smuts tried to reassure his old friend: 'I know your indomitable energy. You have always risen above the waves that threatened to overwhelm you.'[93] Yet the deaths in close succession of his nephew Michael, wife May, brother-in-law Leslie Pollak and son Frank did indeed threaten to overcome him. Ernest lost all enthusiasm for business and politics. He went once more to London to try to find his moorings. In Johannesburg, Harry shouldered more of the burden at Anglo American. He had been appointed a director of the corporation the previous year, and now – with Hagart, Unger and an Irish lawyer named Ben Friel – he was a vital cog in its executive committee. It was a baptism of fire. As Harry recalled in later years, 'Unger underrated Hagart's capabilities and Hagart distrusted Unger.'[94] It was Friel's job to keep the peace.

Gradually Ernest regained his fortitude. He found solace in the Bible. He also grew closer to Ina, a devout Catholic, who was in the throes of mourning, too. She was still ensconced in Little Brenthurst, and together the pair would take long walks through the estate and the environs of Parktown. They drew comfort from each other and, on a trip to London, Ernest proposed. On 1 June 1935, at an understated ceremony held at Caxton Hall in Westminster, witnessed by Harry, Ernest and Ina were married. Harry looked upon his new stepmother as 'beautiful and talented'; he was grateful that Ina gave his father the 'strength and the will to continue with his work'.[95] Slowly Ernest turned his attention back to his business affairs. He now had a sole heir, and he was determined to secure the Oppenheimer dynasty. On 1 July 1935, the firm E Oppenheimer and Son was formed. It was to be a holding company that protected the family's financial interests. The new enterprise took over Dunkelsbuhlers' guarantees to producers outside the Diamond Corporation (Old Dunkels's firm had been dissolved) and in years to come it would play a significant role in financing Anglo American's various interests.

Sir Ernest and Lady Caroline ('Ina') Oppenheimer
on their wedding day, 1 June 1935. *(Brenthurst Library)*

The Diamond Invention

The effect of all these deaths on Harry in his mid-twenties must have
been profound. They were a refining fire, of sorts, which subjected him
to enormous pressure and stress. But they toughened and strengthened
him, and hardened some of his softer edges. He was forced to mature. As a
result, there was a subtle shift in his demeanour. He had always projected
an air of quiet self-confidence, but now he seemed to exhibit a greater sense
of gravitas, too. He threw himself into his work. Diamonds preoccupied
him. By 1937, the stockpile of diamonds held by De Beers had swelled to
some 40 million carats: even by pre-recession standards, this was nearly
twenty years' supply. But the Great Depression had virtually extinguished
the public's appetite for diamonds. The precious stones seemed to be
going the way of coral and pearls: women's fashion accessories that were

no longer *en vogue*. It was one thing for De Beers to control the world's supply of diamonds, but if there was no demand for them, then prices would collapse and the whole industry would crash. Harry understood this problem perfectly. He realised that there would need to be a 'diamond invention', to manipulate the psyche of the diamond buyer.[96] And so he turned to thinking about how diamonds might be perceived, not merely as precious stones, but as something that exerted a far greater psychological pull. The answer lay in advertising.

In most of Europe, the practice of presenting diamond rings as gifts to celebrate a wedding engagement had never taken hold. In England and France, diamonds were regarded as the preserve of aristocrats, not the general public. However, in America there was a long tradition of men buying diamond rings for their betrothed (though they tended to purchase smaller and poorer-quality diamonds, averaging under $80 apiece). Harry believed that if a new image were to be created for diamonds, then women could be induced to desire more expensive diamond rings and men could be persuaded to buy them. Harry put this hypothesis to his father, who readily concurred. With Ernest's blessing, he sailed to New York in September 1938. There, on the recommendation of De Beers' bankers, JP Morgan, Harry met with Gerold M Lauck, the president of NW Ayer, a leading advertising agency. Harry suggested to Lauck that NW Ayer should prepare a plan for creating a new public perception of diamonds among Americans. If the plan met with Ernest Oppenheimer's approval, he promised, NW Ayer would be appointed as the exclusive agents for the placement of newspaper, magazine and radio advertisements in the United States. Furthermore, De Beers would underwrite the costs of the research needed to develop the campaign. Lauck immediately accepted the offer. This was a significant initiative on Harry's part: few people in South Africa (or London or Antwerp, for that matter) appreciated the importance of marketing and promoting diamonds at the time.[97]

During its investigations, NW Ayer found that over the decade preceding the Great Depression, Americans had begun buying poorer-quality and cheaper diamonds. It was not only economic recession but changes in social attitudes and 'the promotion of competitive luxuries' that had brought about this shift in consumption patterns.[98] The advertising agency recommended a well-orchestrated campaign to transform diamonds from vagaries of fashion to indispensable ingredients of courtship and measures of love. In short, diamonds were to be romanticised. NW Ayer proposed a variety of advertising and public relations techniques. Diamonds should be glamorised by movie idols and worn as symbols of indestructible love. Magazine advertisements for diamond rings should feature reproductions of famous paintings by artists like Picasso, Derain and Dufy, thus conveying the idea that diamonds were unique works of art. And the British royal family might be enlisted to cultivate the romantic allure of diamonds. NW Ayer's memo stated: 'Since Great Britain has such an important interest in the diamond industry, the royal couple could be of tremendous assistance … by wearing diamonds rather than other jewels.'[99] This was to prove an ingenious suggestion. In 1947, the British royals undertook a well-publicised visit to South Africa; part of their itinerary involved a trip to the diamond mines, where the princesses, Elizabeth and Margaret, were gifted diamonds by Ernest Oppenheimer.

The campaign that NW Ayer duly launched was a remarkable success. It reshaped the way diamonds were perceived, and unleashed, in due course, a massive money-spinner for De Beers. Diamonds had passed from the Roaring Twenties to the Dirty Thirties shorn of their lustre. Now, thanks to Harry Oppenheimer, they sparkled and shimmered. The flames that had leapt at the diamond industry during the Great Depression were in the process of being smothered. Another development proved crucial. It was at this time that boart – small, poorly crystallised diamonds used as an abrasive in cutting tools for industry – came to acquire increasing significance. The invention of the diamond grinding wheel – a metal-grinding surface impregnated with crushed diamond powder – facilitated a quantum leap in the mass production of automobiles, aeroplanes and machinery. In fact, the expansion of the market for boart had led to the establishment in London of Boart Products Limited and Boart Products South Africa in 1936.[100] Demand was about to become even greater, for as the decade drew to a close war clouds gathered ominously in Europe. The forces of fascism were on the march. As the German eagle soared, Britain re-armed at a furious rate. War seemed inevitable. The fires that had blazed around Harry Oppenheimer and then smouldered through the decade – the Great Depression and a succession of personal bereavements – were to take a different form and ignite once more, radically altering the life of Ernest's heir and apprentice.

FIVE
Desert Rat
1939–1942

In the eight years since his return from Oxford, Harry Oppenheimer had been immersed in the world of diamonds, gold and politics. The deaths, in close succession, of his mother, May, uncle Leslie Pollak and brother, Frank, had a profound effect on him. In later years, it was said of Harry that, much like a diamond, he had passed through the refining fire of this period 'strong and determined', maybe even to the exclusion of 'some of the softer things in life'.[1] From his point of view, or at least the vantage point he enjoyed while working on his unpublished memoirs in the 1980s, his life up to the age of 30 had been led in 'a particularly sheltered and specialised environment'.[2] His contacts and experiences – educational, social, commercial and even, to an extent, political – had all been with people from a similar class and cultural background to his own. The outbreak of war in 1939 was to change that.

◆

Seven Votes

The Statute of Westminster (1931) and the Status of the Union Act (1934) conferred greater sovereignty on South Africa. When Generals Hertzog and Smuts joined forces to form the Fusion government in 1934, they skirted the issue of the Union's obligations to the Commonwealth in the event of Britain going to war. It might have been a sticking point, easier and more elegant to avoid. Although in 1938 Smuts was prepared to go along with Hertzog's statement in support of neutrality, this was in all likelihood a tactical move. As Oswald Pirow, the mercurial lawyer who for a time was one of Hertzog's most trusted cabinet ministers (and later his biographer), remarked, Smuts accepted the statement 'merely to gain time', since he believed a European war was still 'some distance off'.[3] However, by the first few days of September 1939, the situation had altered irrevocably. Adolf Hitler had invaded Czechoslovakia six months earlier, and on 1 September Nazi troops marched into Poland. Smuts withdrew his backing for neutrality. He was convinced that Hitler posed the gravest threat to peace and freedom across the world. At 9 am on Sunday, 3 September, the British Foreign Secretary, Lord Halifax, issued Britain's final ultimatum to Germany: withdraw from Poland or face war. Alan Paton, the author who was to develop a friendship with Harry Oppenheimer in later years, wrote in his biography of Smuts's right-hand man, Jan Hofmeyr, that English-speaking South Africa waited, 'tense and anxious', for the decision that would take their young men to war. 'No English-speaking South Africans were more tense and anxious than the Jews, whose future on earth depended on the outcome of such a struggle.'[4]

At 11 am, Britain declared war on Germany. The British Prime Minister, Neville Chamberlain, cabled Hertzog and set out the alternatives: 'You can declare war on Germany, you can break off diplomatic relations with her or you can remain neutral. I beg of you not to follow the third course.'[5] Hertzog's cabinet was deeply split over the issue, but in Parliament Hertzog stuck to his guns. Smuts demurred. A lengthy and divisive debate ensued. But by the end of it, Smuts had carried the House by 80 votes to 67. (Ernest Oppenheimer, who had quit politics the previous year to concentrate on his business interests, was no longer in Parliament to cast his vote.) It was a narrow margin: if seven more MPs had sided with Hertzog in favour of neutrality, then South African history might have taken a very different course.[6] Hertzog resigned as prime minister. Smuts formed a new cabinet, and on 6 September he severed relations with Germany. South Africa was at war.

For Harry Oppenheimer, neutrality would have occasioned a 'grave personal conflict of loyalties'. His personal and public sensibilities – his whole outlook, in fact – had long been shaped by an allegiance to Britain, mediated by the broad South Africanism that Botha and Smuts espoused and the obligations to Empire this entailed. De Beers' imperial heritage, his family's eminent position within what he characterised as the 'Rhodes tradition', his education at Charterhouse and Oxford, his commitment to the very idea of the British Commonwealth of Nations: all of this made it so. His German heritage was of very little personal consequence, nor – until later in life – were his family's Jewish origins. As children, Harry and Frank had been taken on only one occasion by Ernest to visit their aunts in Germany. 'This we enjoyed but the contact with our German relatives, charming and kind though they were, somehow meant virtually nothing to us,' Oppenheimer would later recall. 'They seemed to belong to another world outside our experience and interest and this, I believe, was what my father expected, and perhaps wished. My father's eldest sister, Lina Lewy, for whom he had a special affection, once visited us briefly in South Africa but that was all. When we spoke of our German relations, which was rarely, it was always in terms of affection but in my generation they never formed part of our family life. This went so far that the Nazi slaughter of Jews, though it involved a number of my relatives, affected me on humanitarian and political rather than personal grounds. If my father felt differently he never told me so.'[7] Oppenheimer's fealty to the British Commonwealth, his foreboding of Nazi tyranny and, perhaps too, the painful memory of his family's flight from Kimberley in 1915 galvanised him against Hitler. There was another dimension, both personal and political, to Oppenheimer's firm stance against neutrality. He was a Smuts man.

A Smuts Man

Harry Oppenheimer had been brought up to regard General Smuts as a hero. As a boy, he looked on Smuts with something approaching veneration. Ernest Oppenheimer viewed Smuts as a friend. He was devoted to him politically, although, as Harry would later record, his father was not blind to some of the 'flaws and ambiguities in that complicated character'.[8] Smuts had attended and addressed Harry's 21st birthday party at the Spread Eagle Inn in 1929. On his return to South Africa, during Ernest's spell as the MP for Kimberley, Harry had listened with keen interest from the gallery to Smuts's performances in the House, in between drafting his father's own parliamentary speeches. Harry subscribed to the Smutsian politics of holism, with its peculiar conception of South Africa's role and responsibilities in the British Commonwealth.

A few months before the war erupted, Ernest had invited Smuts, along with Smuts's loyal friend Deneys Reitz, to fly to Goma at the northern end of Lake Kivu. Smuts wanted to see the impressive Nyamuragira volcano. Harry joined the party, and this was his first time in Smuts's company for an extended period. On their journey north, the group stayed for a day or two at Zomba State House, in the capital city of what was then Nyasaland. Smuts, as was his wont, was determined to climb the Zomba Plateau. While Reitz and Ernest decided to forgo any such exertions, Harry accompanied the statesman up to the summit. In Harry's view, Smuts was not a great conversationalist, but he could, 'when he was in the mood, be a very good monologist'. And on the mountain at Zomba, Smuts reflected movingly on his wartime experiences in Tanganyika – not of military matters but of the beauty and splendour of East Africa. Oppenheimer would later recall of their encounter: '"I am glad", [Smuts] said, "to see more of Africa while there is time. Evil forces are moving in the world and the Commonwealth will face a great test. I do not think there will be more such holidays as this for many years to come." Then, as we stood on top of the Zomba Mountain, looking out in the approaching dusk over the glorious, tumbled highland scene, Smuts turned to me and said, "Harry, is it not wonderful to be an African?"'[9]

Only a few months later Smuts repudiated neutrality and took the Union into war. It was a decision, Oppenheimer later wrote, for which he felt an enormous 'sense of personal gratitude'. Hertzog regarded Smuts's move as a great blunder and the 'most fatal mistake ever made by a responsible statesman'.[10] He rejoined forces with DF Malan to form the Herenigde Nasionale Party (Reunited National Party). The Union's entry into the Second World War also served to invigorate and toxify the forces of Afrikaner nationalism, which had been an undergoing a strong cultural revival in recent years. Its high point was the centenary celebrations of the Great Trek in 1938. Many right-wing nationalists, some of whom had imbibed National Socialist theory, disavowed party politics altogether and became involved with fascist or pro-Nazi organisations like Oswald Pirow's New Order, Hans van Rensburg's Ossewabrandwag, or the Greyshirts and Brownshirts.[11] Antisemitism was their cornerstone.[12]

For King and Country

As the dominions mobilised, Oppenheimer volunteered for military service on 26 January 1940. Within a few days he was drafted into the Reserve with the rank of temporary second lieutenant. Two weeks later he attended Course 491G for intelligence officers at the South African

Military College in Pretoria.[13] Oppenheimer assumed full-time service on 17 June and was attached to the Intelligence Section at Defence Headquarters before transferring to the 5th South African Armoured Car Company, in the Tank Corps, in December. Another course followed from 18 September to 15 October. Oppenheimer assiduously kept all his timetables, reports and lecture notes, with neat annotations handwritten in pencil. One such lecture was on 'Bush sense'. 'Those born in the bush should have that sense naturally. If not cultivate it – apply the principles you have learned with resolution and common sense,' the official lecture notes commanded. Next to them, Oppenheimer added by hand, 'get confidence ... stand still & make no noise & you will not be seen in the bush'.[14]

Whatever bush skills Oppenheimer acquired at the Military College, and on subsequent training manoeuvres in the veld north of Pretoria, may have been of modest benefit. When the call came to go 'up north' in April the following year, it was to the Western Desert, not the Abyssinian bush, where the Italian forces had already been brought to heel. Oppenheimer passed his courses with ease, qualifying for promotion to the rank of lieutenant. 'Unilingual', his training officer commented on Harry's lack of proficiency in Afrikaans, before adding, somewhat incongruously, 'Some French & German'. Oppenheimer was deemed an 'intelligent young officer who worked hard with good results'. He was a bit green but would 'go far with more experience in regimental work'.[15]

Guy Young, Oppenheimer's friend, wartime comrade and later business colleague, remembered Harry as a 'good soldier' who proved himself 'cool and calm' under 'all sorts of difficult circumstances'. As an intelligence officer he was 'ideal'. Young reminisced: 'It was an awful waste, though, that with his fantastic brain he wasn't put on the general staff. I said to him once that he was wasted in our regiment. "It is exactly where I want to be," he snapped. Harry joined us in 1940, while we were still in the 5th South African Armoured Car Company, on manoeuvres north of Pretoria. He was as generous as always, lending his huge Packard coupé freely to his friends, or taking us off to dinner at Polly's in Pretoria, where he would order a large jar of Russian caviar. Later that year we amalgamated with the 4th Armoured Car Company to become the 4th SA Armoured Car Regiment under Colonel [Dennis] Newton-King, and early in 1941 we moved to Oribi camp at Pietermaritzburg to prepare for embarkation to Egypt. Ernest and Ina came down to Durban to see Harry off. To Ina's dissatisfaction there were thirteen of us at the farewell dinner at the old Marine Hotel.' In fact, Harry confided to Ina at the time, he found life in the 4th SA Armoured Car Regiment 'gloomy' compared to the camaraderie of the 5th Armoured Cars out in the bushveld. Everyone appeared disgruntled to varying degrees. He found the functions of the intelligence officer under the new dispensation somewhat opaque, and he could not make up his mind, he told Ina, whether 'an attitude of petulance & acidity or a Mr Micawberish placidity' would serve him best. No doubt, Harry concluded, it would be Mr Micawber, as the line of least resistance. In any event he had 'long given up the idea that I might do something of any real use'.[16]

Despondency gave way to the anticipation of adventure when Oppenheimer's new regiment set sail for Egypt aboard the *Empress of Australia* at the end of April 1941. Ernest, Ina and her young son, Michael, saw him off at the Durban docks. Oppenheimer, with his instinct for irony, was amused by Michael's parting words: 'Goodbye, I hope you have a very pleasant time.'[17] The *Empress of Australia* had not yet been converted into a troopship. It was a mass of marble and gilt and quite luxurious in an old-fashioned way. According to Guy Young, Oppenheimer appreciated being able to wine and dine in some style for a little while longer, before being exposed to the aggravations of the desert.[18] From his father, Harry hungrily asked for news of the goings-on at Anglo American and De Beers. 'Don't forget to send me a copy of your speech & generally to keep me in touch with real life!' he wrote in his first letter home. 'I shall write as often & fully as I can so that you shall have a full record of this adventure.'[19]

On 6 May, the *Empress of Australia* arrived at Port Tewfik at the southern end of the Suez Canal. Business was still at the forefront of Oppenheimer's mind. On disembarkation, he had hoped to use his first few weeks to think about industrial diamonds and the renewal of the Consolidated African Selection Trust contract. However, his regiment was soon taken by rail to El Amiriya, just outside Alexandria, for training. The journey from the port was 'unspeakable': the train was dirty and overcrowded, and the temperature was the highest recorded in 88 years. Oppenheimer, obsessive about cleanliness, found the camp 'quite odious'. The washing and sanitation arrangements were almost non-existent. The food was inadequate and it was all 'complete piggery', he complained to his father.[20] The only redeeming feature was that he was sharing a 'very good big tent' with a friend, Major Craig Anderson, who was second-in-command to Colonel Newton-King. Yet, outwardly, Oppenheimer maintained an air of equanimity. When regimental relations became strained, he contrived to remain on 'the best of terms with everyone', he informed his father in an early letter home.[21]

Ina had teamed up with Doff Susskind to start the Caledonian Market, a fundraising scheme geared towards purchasing the troops small conveniences and luxuries. On his voyage up north, Oppenheimer sent Ina a complete list of names of the troops in his regiment and the various signals squadrons. He encouraged her to send them parcels under an assumed name, since he did not wish to be connected with the enterprise. Ina maintained a steady supply of delicacies to the troops, including bottles of champagne, packages of biltong, and tins of *foie gras* sourced from Thrupps. She would send off as many as 60 parcels at a time. Ina and Ernest had also decided, for king and country, to turn the main house at Brenthurst into a military hospital. They moved out and decamped to Little Brenthurst. The Johannesburg hospitals were becoming crowded with men invalided from the front; the couple did not need all the space at Brenthurst, and the house would constitute a meaningful contribution to the war effort. The Brenthurst Military Hospital catered principally to burn victims. In some ways, the initiative was redolent of Bernard Oppenheimer's efforts to assist disabled soldiers during the First World War. Harry approved of the idea and told his father that it was good 'to do something personal like that'.[22] To Ina he quipped that he would have to 'get some lingering disease' and 'come and convalesce there myself'.[23]

The Calm before the Storm

After training, the troops in the 4th SA Armoured Cars found that a great deal of time could pass in the desert without much activity. Out on the sand hills, they spent long hours atop their cars scanning the horizon for signs of movement that were slow to come. 'We are … sitting in the desert doing very little except carry on a losing battle against the dust,' Oppenheimer complained to his father.[24] His regiment was organised in four parts: three squadrons spread along the front line observing enemy movements, with regimental headquarters bringing up the rear. The troops would take turns to patrol the front line a few days at a time. The front cars maintained radio contact with a squadron car that tailed them, and the three squadron headquarters kept contact with radio operators at regimental headquarters. Oppenheimer's job, as intelligence officer, was to sift through all the information sent to him, piece together a composite picture, and then consult with Newton-King and Anderson about what should be relayed to divisional headquarters. This was not quite so simple as it sounded, he informed his father: 'It is all speech, radio telephony, and one has to be careful to talk so as to convey clearly what one means to one's own side, without giving anything away to the enemy who of course have sets listening to us all the time.'[25] Oppenheimer would compile a summary of each day's operations, and he kept an archive of intelligence records. Last but not least, 'but infinitely worst', he remarked drily to his father, he acted as a sort of aide-de-camp and 'conversational foil' to the Colonel.

Grey Fletcher, a cheerful sort recruited into E Oppenheimer and Son after the war, was all of 21 when he met Harry for the first time en route to Egypt. The Oppenheimer name did not mean much to him. He just thought Harry 'seemed quite a nice chap'. Fletcher was troop leader of the 'B' squadron, and he quickly gained the impression that 'the intelligence fellow' in the 4th SA Armoured Cars was 'quite a bright boy'. 'He used to send out written reports to keep you informed about developments along the whole front, which affected your flanking troops, your brigade and division, giving you a cohesive picture of what was going on. That was pretty unusual in my experience of "I" officers, and I think it is one of the reasons why that regiment was renowned. Some of the books about the desert war quote [German commander Erwin] Rommel's intelligence people as saying that the 4th Armoured Car Regiment was absolutely frightful because you never got rid of them. They said whenever you looked up, those cars were watching you.'[26]

The wireless work was carried out in Morse cipher, and the wireless operator in Colonel Newton-King's car was Hugh Skelly. He used Oppenheimer's 'dark and expressive eyes' as a barometer of trouble. 'When he sought refuge in the car during a bombing attack his eyes would tell me whether we were going to have merry hell or peaceful coexistence with the enemy,' Skelly would later recall.[27] Among the soldiers, Oppenheimer gained a reputation for acts of understated generosity. He would leave his tin of Balkan Sobranie (a sought-after tobacco) close to Skelly's seat, which was 'his way of saying, "help yourself"', Skelly recollected. Oppenheimer's orders were often phrased as polite requests. 'He was such a gentle person,' Skelly would later reflect: 'I could never understand why, with all that money, he had volunteered for the field of battle when he could so easily have had a safe job in Cairo or at home.'

Before the Germans launched a major offensive in mid-September, Oppenheimer found himself insufficiently occupied. 'I do hope this war doesn't go on for 10 years', he protested to his father in June, before conceding that Hitler's about-turn on his non-aggression pact with Stalin might significantly alter the war's course. 'Actually I don't think the war can last beyond the autumn of 1942 & it might easily be much shorter. But what do you think?' he inquired.[28] Ernest responded that he was convinced 1942 would 'see the end of it'.[29] In July, the 4th SA Armoured Cars moved to a less isolated camp, where Oppenheimer had the opportunity of seeing many of his and his father's friends and associates. They included Comar and Tony Wilson (the brothers who worked for Anglo), Punch Barlow and Sir George Albu, whose father had founded the General Mining and Finance Corporation. The Albus' Randlord mansion, Northwards, was situated very near to Brenthurst.

The relationship between father and son was intimate and intense. Ernest wrote daily, adding news as he went along, before sending off his letters to Harry every Monday. He kept his heir up to date on commercial, political and household affairs, relaying with relish the gossip from Anglo and De Beers meetings, and signing his letters 'Yours most affectionately, Daddie'. The paterfamilias's wartime letters are shot through with warmth and affection, written in the animated, stream-of-consciousness style that reflected his exuberant personality. Occasionally, there is Harry's same weary humour: 'For all that I am always pleased to go to Kimberley', Ernest confessed to his son after a De Beers board meeting, 'I'm particularly pleased to leave again.'[30]

Ernest treated Harry as a confidant and sounding board, an heir not just to the family business but also to the agreements and *faribels* that had moulded their empire. The people in the Barnato group were 'jealous' and 'mischief-making', he warned Harry, referring to an incident long past in which one of the Joels had wronged Frank Oppenheimer. There was no question of working with them, but they were 'always capable of combining with others against us', Ernest cautioned. 'The control of the diamond trade is worth having & we must remain strong', he emphasised.[31] Diamonds were the magnate's preoccupation, but he wrote at length about the copper mines in Northern Rhodesia and the labour problems there. 'I have neglected the gold mines for too long', Ernest revealed to Harry, but he undertook to 'work rather harder so as to play a more active part in Anglo American affairs'.[32]

On all of these matters, Harry wrote long and considered replies. He gave his input on board appointments. He made suggestions for the Diamond Corporation: 'What about forming a syndicate to buy the diamonds in New York?'[33] And he acknowledged that the time had come to separate the industrial section from the rest of the diamond business, though he was nervous about where that might lead.[34] His father listened attentively.

Harry and Ernest exchanged opinions about the pressing political issues of the day. Already there was talk of Northern Rhodesia and Southern Rhodesia amalgamating with Nyasaland under a new dispensation. Lord Harlech, the former British Colonial Secretary who served as high commissioner to South Africa from 1941 to 1944, kept Ernest abreast of developments and Ernest in turn informed Harry. Politics exerted a gravitational pull over business, and the domestic sphere fell flush within their orbit. Ernest was confident that the fusion of the three territories would come about after the war – the Federation of Rhodesia and Nyasaland, or Central African Federation, was eventually established in 1953 – and he advised Harry that this would affect Anglo American's outlook. Before the war Ernest had bought a number of ranches in Southern Rhodesia – including, most importantly, Shangani – and he established the Shangani Corporation Limited in 1937.[35] Shangani was the property to which generations of Oppenheimers would soon regularly repair, and Harry detected a certain serendipity in its acquisition: 'In view of the political developments foreshadowed by Lord Harlech I'm more glad than ever we bought the ranches.'[36] 'What fun we will have there when this wretched war is over,' he enthused, after learning that Ernest had installed a swimming bath at Shangani.[37]

Father and son shared a passion for Africana. Ernest had started collecting material in Kimberley after the Anglo-Boer War, and at Little Brenthurst he was building up a library. He wrote enthusiastically to Harry of his most recent acquisitions: a cheque forged by Princess Radziwill, a letter from David Livingstone to Robert Moffat, and Winston Churchill's manuscript on his capture and escape during the Anglo-Boer War. Ernest maintained a steady supply of novels and biographies to Harry during his time in the desert. He sent him books on Drummond Chaplin, the former administrator of the British South Africa Company in Southern Rhodesia ('so anxious for the approval of others ... rather like an overgrown schoolboy,'[38] Ernest sneered); Lord Halifax; and George VI. Harry asked for the complete works of Shakespeare and Saint Augustine's *Confessions*. His literary judgements were often withering. The life of Drummond Chaplin was a disappointing book, 'or rather what a disappointing life he had'.[39] The style of Lord Lloyd's *Egypt since*

'*Vuil* [dirty] Hendrik': Harry Oppenheimer
in the Western Desert, 1942. *(Brenthurst Library)*

Cromer was 'laborious and in every way suitable for one who so nearly ended his career as President of the Chartered Company'.[40]

Ernest was solicitous of his son's welfare. 'You must not think that I have not thought of you every day,' he assured Harry.[41] Ernest sent him pipes, tobacco, dustproof apparel, wristwatches and all manner of useful appurtenances. And his concern extended to Harry's sanitation. Harry was meticulous in matters of personal hygiene, and he found conditions in the desert an affront to his dignity. 'The lack of washing is frightful. Will I notice when I begin to stink violently – or is it like Halitosis?' he wondered.[42] Nevertheless, Harry developed a technique to get by on a gallon of water a day. With a mug of water he washed his hands, then his feet, and then he rubbed himself all over with a damp sponge sprinkled with eau de cologne (4711 was his preferred brand). Ernest was horrified. He dispatched a consignment of cologne post-haste. 'Dearest Daddie, You could not have thought of anything more useful or which I would like more,' Harry thanked him. 'If it doesn't exactly make one clean it at least gives the illusion of cleanliness!'[43]

By August, Harry was increasingly frustrated with the monotony of his daily routine. He explained to Ernest: 'I sit by my car in the desert, keep the situation map, go out from time to time to see our various patrols, and otherwise read, sleep and eat tinned food. Not a very exhilarating existence.'[44] The only upside was a day trip to the remote Siwa Oasis. There, an oracle had once told Alexander the Great that he was the rightful Pharaoh of Egypt, and that he would conquer the Persian Empire. Oppenheimer was particularly glad to submerge himself in 'Cleopatra's Bath', the antique natural spring. Yet the tedium of life up north was about to change dramatically.

September 1941: A Taste of Action

On Saturday, 13 September, Oppenheimer heard reports of unusual activity on the German side of the Frontier Wire, the fence built by Benito Mussolini's Italian army, which separated the Allied from the Axis forces. During his night patrols he managed to intercept German wireless transmissions. His regiment was forewarned of the attack that was to come. At dawn on Sunday two strong enemy columns came forward extremely fast. The 4th SA Armoured Cars had been ordered to fall back if the enemy attacked. Their role was reconnaissance, and their Marmon-Herrington cars were no match for a panzer division. The chief weight of the advance was to the right of Oppenheimer's regiment, and the enemy moved so fast that by the time Colonel Newton-King had decided on moving the HQ, it proved too late. Oppenheimer recounted the events to his father: 'By the time we got going the enemy must have been almost level with us and they then turned in and were on our flank as we moved back. I heard a tremendous rumbling noise & then saw a mass of tanks come over a rise on our left at about 1500–1000 yards away. They at once started to shell us & we had nothing for it but to run, with the tanks in hot pursuit. I was right in the middle of this & it was tremendously exciting, like going on a super "Giant Racer" at [Kimberley], and though it's not a game I'm specially keen to play again, I must admit I enjoyed myself. Shells were bursting all around my car.'[45] The chase appeared to go on for ages, but actually it lasted less than 15 minutes. At the height of it all, 45 planes flew over. The 4th SA Armoured Cars managed to put distance between themselves and the German tanks; they straightened themselves out and continued their planned withdrawal.

Guy Young later recalled that Colonel Newton-King was sitting on his armoured car, methodically marking the German tanks' positions on his map, as reports came through from the wireless operators in the squadron headquarters. Within a few minutes, only regimental headquarters stood between the 4th SA Armoured Cars and the Germans. Newton-King carried on marking his map until Oppenheimer could take it no more: 'Sir … there's no need to look at the map reference. If you just look up you can see the tanks quite clearly,' he offered gingerly.[46] An almighty dash ensued. Regimental headquarters was shelled and in the melee the Colonel's car broke down. It had to be set on fire and abandoned. Newton-King, Oppenheimer and their driver were fortunate to be picked up by a passing British 25-pounder, for they would almost certainly have been captured otherwise. In fact, their regimental truck was seized with three soldiers and a pile of personnel records on board. From the German propaganda station at Zeesen, the message went out that the men of the 4th SA Armoured Car Regiment had been captured or killed. Oppenheimer's name was mentioned among the casualties. Explosions continued through the night. By the following morning, however, it became clear that the limit of the German advance had been reached. The Germans had moved too fast for their transport columns, and the commander of the panzer division, Johann von Ravenstein, gave the order to turn back. By 5 pm, Oppenheimer's regiment was back in its original position. It had been a tumultuous 36 hours and the 4th SA Armoured Cars' first real taste of warfare. 'We were I think extremely lucky,' Harry reflected to Ernest afterwards.[47]

Siege of Tobruk

Although Tobruk lay well within Axis-controlled Libyan territory, its port had remained occupied by a small contingent of Allied forces when much of the Western Desert Force was sent off to fight in the Greek and Syrian campaigns. The Allied occupation of Tobruk deprived the Axis powers of a supply port closer to the Libyan border than Benghazi, which lay 900 kilometres west of the Egyptian frontier and was within striking distance of RAF bombers. General Rommel was determined to seize the harbour. The Axis siege had begun in April and continued through two unsuccessful relief attempts by the Allies. On the night of 17 November 1941, the land armada of the British Eighth Army rolled through Mussolini's wire fence into Libya. Operation Crusader, which aimed to destroy Rommel's armour, recapture Cyrenaica and relieve Tobruk, had begun.

The armoured car regiments led the advance: the 4th SA Armoured Cars, the 3rd SA Recce Battalion, the 11th Hussars and the King's Dragoons. For two weeks, Oppenheimer was in the heart of the action. His regiment set off at dusk on a pitch-black, moonless night. At first they were hampered by rain, which turned large parts of the desert into a bog, and the cars could not do much more than five miles per hour. They navigated with pocket compasses to find a seven-yard gap in the wire fence. By midnight they were through. The next day the regiment continued its advance, encountering light enemy fire in the morning and heavier shelling in the afternoon. 'All this was pleasantly exciting but not very deadly,' Harry reported to Ernest.[48] Within two days they were over the Sidi Rezegh ridge. After that, the conflict escalated. On 3 December, Oppenheimer wrote an account to his father:

> Today for the first time for over a fortnight we are out of the battle, but I am too tired & busy for a long letter, & this really is just to say that so far I have been lucky & am well & in good form ... The first two days were comparatively peaceful & by that time we had got over the Sidi Rezegh ridge. Then the fun really began & we dodged in & out of tremendous tank battles, giving a running commentary [on] the position by wireless. This was exciting work as the German Artillery was unpleasantly accurate & the art is being near enough a rapidly moving Tank battle to report it properly without getting in front of either side's guns ... We by no means always succeeded in it but our luck so far has been good ... The first really beastly episode was the German attack on the South African 5th Brigade. We saw all this & it was horrible – & considerably different from the news reports. We got out with nothing to spare, but fortunately very few casualties. Since then we have had an unpleasant job of raiding ... behind the enemy lines in order to interfere with his transport & generally cause 'alarm & despondency'.[49]

On the afternoon of 22 November, the 5th South African Infantry Brigade had attempted to capture part of the Sidi Rezegh ridge. The attempt failed and the Allies were forced to retreat when the 21st Panzer attacked from the north and north-west. The following day, 23 November, was *Totensonntag*, the Sunday of the Dead, when the Germans commemorated those who lost their lives during the First World War. Now the 5th South African Brigade came in the cross hairs of the 15th Panzer. A messy fight broke out, and the 21st Panzer moved in as reinforcement. By the end of the day the 5th South African Brigade had almost been annihilated. It lost two-thirds of its men, most of them taken prisoner, and all of its heavy equipment. The 7th Armoured Division took a hammering, too: it was down to only 70 tanks, and appeared in danger of being surrounded by Rommel.

The 4th SA Armoured Cars, meanwhile, had taken prisoners of their own, and Oppenheimer, who spoke some German, was tasked with extracting information. This was to prove useful to the British Eighth Army at large. Oppenheimer's code name among his comrades was 'Oppenschloss'. One of the signals officers in the regiment would later recall that Oppenheimer managed to loosen the tongue of a 'really truculent young Nazi' (who would only respond with '*nicht verstehen*') by threatening to pack him off to the Polish unit of the 2nd Rifle Brigade.[50] On 26 November, the New Zealanders captured Belhamed and Sidi Rezegh, while the Tobruk garrison took El Duda. That night, the two forces met up near El Duda and temporarily lifted the siege of Tobruk. But the battle raged on. Rommel tried to isolate the British divisions from their transport lines. The units of the British Eighth Army were given new orders. The 4th SA Armoured Cars were sent west of Tobruk to try to disrupt Axis communications along the coastal route. But they were spotted by the enemy and one of their squadrons was bombarded by eight Messerschmitt 110s. The South Africans had no anti-aircraft guns. There was no practical way down the escarpment and they could not reach the coastal road. Colonel Newton-King reluctantly withdrew. The regiment pulled back, under sustained fire, and lost three armoured cars in the process. It was a mauling.

In the first week of December, the 4th SA Armoured Cars were sent to the RAF's El Adem repair base so that their vehicles could be overhauled. Operation Crusader wore on, scrappily but favourably for the Allies. On 7 December, Rommel was forced to withdraw his forces to the Gazala position, and on 15 December he ordered a withdrawal to El Agheila. On 16 December, the 2nd South African Division launched an attack on the port of Bardia, garrisoned by thousands of German and Italian troops, and on 2 January 1942 Bardia fell. Sollum fell to the South Africans on 12 January after bitter fighting. On 17 January, Allied forces surrounded the fortified Halfaya Pass position – including the escarpment, the plateau above it, and the surrounding ravines – and cut it off from the sea. Rommel seemed to have been halted.

Harry Oppenheimer in military uniform during
the Second World War. *(Brenthurst Library)*

For all his professed enjoyment of the conflict, Oppenheimer was glad
once it was over. 'I wouldn't have missed *having* been there for anything,
but it was pretty exhausting, & my curiosity as to what a battle is like is
entirely satisfied,' he declared to Ina.[51] To Ernest he wrote, 'It was pretty
frightening but … exciting & I almost enjoyed it, certainly I wouldn't have
missed it for anything.'[52] The 4th Armoured Cars had been brave in battle
and the British 7th Armoured Division valued their contribution. As a
mark of respect, the regiment was awarded a unique honour: the right
to wear the 7th Armoured Division's famous cloth-embroidered 'Desert
Rat' emblem.

Bir Hakeim and Political Reflections

Between 1 and 7 January, Oppenheimer took leave. He went to Alexandria,
where he stayed in the Hotel Metropole, and to Cairo, where he enjoyed a
traditional Arab dinner at the house of Abdul Gomati, a business associate
of Ernest's. But there was not long to rest. Rommel had managed to regroup
his battered forces. On 21 January he launched another offensive. The

German panzers ran rampant once again. The British Eighth Army sent a signal to Colonel Newton-King. The 4th SA Armoured Cars should attach themselves to the 1st Armoured Division on the road to Masus and provide reconnaissance. 'We are once more very much involved in this war!' Harry exclaimed to Ernest. 'Master Rommel seems to have surprised us – quite inexcusable on our part, I think. We came up full of ideas of Tripoli, & found ourselves caught up, entirely without orders, in a distinctly rapid withdrawal!'[53] The weather was vile – icy winds, rain and dust – and in the circumstances Oppenheimer adopted an attitude of 'almost offensive cheerfulness', agreeing with everyone and hoping for the best.[54] The 4th SA Armoured Cars managed to knock out a number of enemy lorries, but 'as a whole', Harry regretted to tell his father, 'the battle doesn't bear comment'. By 5 February, Rommel's unexpected counterattack had forced the British to retreat 350 miles, from the western border of Cyrenaica to the Gazala Line. The Gazala Line was a series of defensive boxes stretching across the desert behind minefields and wire, from Gazala at the coast to the old Ottoman fortress of Bir Hakeim 50 miles south. Each box accommodated a brigade, and there were regular patrols between the boxes. The 4th SA Armoured Cars were to patrol the desert along the southernmost part of the Gazala Line.

During these lengthy and often uneventful patrols, Oppenheimer had time to ruminate on political events back home. 'Seen from here South African politics appear grotesque,' he grumbled to his father after reading that DF Malan had introduced a motion in the House of Assembly to establish a republic. 'I suppose this buffoonery is meant to be serious,' Harry hissed. However, he predicted that once the Allies had won the war, the sort of fascist regimes favoured by some of Malan's supporters would be 'out of fashion'. In the meanwhile, 'a debate like this must make treason appear, if not desirable, at least quite respectable', he mused to Ernest.[55] On the other hand Oppenheimer found the notion of fundamental societal change in a socialist direction 'absurd', unless it was 'another name for complete change in Native policy'. Within the ranks of South Africa's armed forces serving in the Second World War, there was a small but active contingent of soldiers who had formed a voluntary organisation with socialist leanings. It was called the Springbok Legion. The purchase of its socialism was limited, although a number of the Legion's members were information officers in the popular Army Education Services (AES). The AES was headed by Jan Hofmeyr's confidant Leo Marquard, a liberal teacher and writer whose path would cross Oppenheimer's in years to come. Its mission was to school the troops in the liberal-democratic philosophy of citizenship. The scheme played an important role in promoting anti-fascism. Its post-war legacy was felt in various reformist impulses and initiatives in the United Party and, later, when it was formed in 1951, the Torch Commando, which Oppenheimer partly financed.

The broader ideas embodied by the AES were beginning to shape Oppenheimer's political views and, perhaps inchoately, his thoughts about a more public role in civilian life. He explained to his father that during the course of the war he had been 'able for the first time to see & talk to a lot of men of classes whom in the ordinary way I would never get to know'. 'It's the only good thing in this life,' he concluded.[56] Harry thought that most of these men were content with their lot. They were not socialist revolutionaries. On the contrary, they were prepared to take considerable risks in the fight against fascism. 'Can anyone seriously think that when the war ends men want to get back from this to a social revolution?' Harry asked Ernest in disbelief. In his view, the ordinary Allied soldier was fighting not to change the system, 'but to prevent Hitler's changing it'. Of course, many social reforms were desirable, but the best way to get real progress was by tackling one problem after another: 'individual things that are seen to be wrong, & not by vague blathering about new systems of any sort whatsoever'. What Oppenheimer was setting out in this epistolary meditation was a creed of sorts, a gradualist approach to social change that would characterise his politics during the long period of repression and reform that lay ahead for South Africa.

Thoughts of Home

In April, Oppenheimer was due to attend a four-week course at the Middle East Tactical School in Helwan on German army tactics and prisoner interrogation. He was looking forward to it, but there had been a resurgence of activity in the Western Desert, and he did not want to leave his regiment in the lurch. So he consulted General Frank Theron, whose radiographer daughter Jacqueline had been working at the Brenthurst Military Hospital. Theron insisted that Oppenheimer should proceed with the course. Harry discovered that he was now 'very fluent' in German, but, having left the desert for Helwan, he informed his father, he was surprised to experience 'sentimental regrets at leaving the Regt'.[57]

Behind the scenes, Ernest Oppenheimer was manoeuvring to get his son back home. At the beginning of the war Smuts had suggested to Ernest that, having suffered the loss of Frank, he should keep Harry close.[58] Harry was the heir to the throne. It was time for his desert escapades, noble-minded as they were, to come to an end. General IP de Villiers, the commanding officer of the 2nd South African Infantry Division, was about to be transferred back to the Union to head up the Coastal Area Command, headquartered in Cape Town. At the time, there was widespread public fear of a possible Japanese invasion launched from somewhere along South Africa's long coastline, although Harry thought such an attack lay in the realm of fantasy. Still, Cape Town was closer to Brenthurst than the Western Desert, and the idea of having Harry back in the Union appealed to Ernest. Harry had spent a night at the 2nd Division's HQ on his way back from five days' leave in Cairo at the end of March, and General De Villiers had reported back glowingly to Ernest on his son. General De Villiers 'sang your praises and told me that he was taking up a command in the Union and ... he was asking for you to be put on his staff', Ernest wrote to Harry, glossing over who had made contact with whom.[59]

The official request for Harry to join General De Villiers's staff came through in mid-June and Harry wrote eagerly to Ernest that 'the idea of going back to SA & seeing you is so wonderful'. 'I shall feel something of a snake in the grass to leave the Regt; but all being well I shall have had a good view of 3 major Libyan battles to say nothing of our own private little battle last September, so think I can with decency make room for one of the many soldiers in the Union who, so I am told, are thirsting for blood. But can anything so beautiful really happen?'[60] There was only one problem. Harry was in the midst of one of the very battles he had just mentioned: the Battle of Gazala, which lasted from 26 May to 21 June.

Battle of Gazala and the Fall of Tobruk

By the spring of 1942, both the Allied and Axis powers were preparing for another attack. Churchill wanted a British victory over the Germans before the Americans committed a sizeable number of troops to the war. Rommel believed it was necessary to launch a new offensive in Cyrenaica before the Allied forces' advantage in tanks and manpower became too overpowering, and he had made a personal visit to Hitler in March to seek his permission. The go-ahead was granted on 1 May, but only for an attack to break the Gazala Line and capture Tobruk. Rommel's plan was to launch a feint against the main Gazala Line. While that took place, he would lead the Afrika Korps on an outflanking attack passing to the south of Bir Hakeim, where the XX Italian Corps would lead the charge. The Germans, for their part, would swing north and advance behind the British front line towards Acroma, which lay halfway between Tobruk and the main Gazala Line. Rommel hoped to destroy the Allied armour in the tank battle that was likely to ensue and crush the defences of Tobruk before its defenders could prepare for another siege.

Harry wrote to Ernest on 12 June, telling him that he was 'very well & cheerful but very tired'. The battle had been long and exhausting. The 4th SA Armoured Cars had been busy trying to interfere with the enemy's lines of communication. Some of the regiment's supply vehicles were captured and for three days the 4th SA Armoured Cars were very short of water, just enough to drink 'but no washing or shaving at all'. Harry described the action:

> As was to be expected we were attacked all the time from the air, which was exhausting & fraying, but the casualties we had were certainly not great. The night before last Hacheim [Bir Hakeim] was evacuated. The enemy were all around & it was a difficult … business to get out – not a good affair. The French have been magnificent & cost the enemy far more than their losses. The Senegalese gunners thought the original Tank attacks tremendous fun; they … held their fire until the tanks were almost on top of them, & when they got a hit they laughed till they almost burst … Now that Hacheim has gone the Germans have advanced again in force east of our minefields. There must be a big battle soon – probably today. I just do not understand what is going on. I felt quite certain that Rommel was going to be knocked right out; but the fall of Hacheim is a blow. I still think however that the advantage is with us. We know that Rommel had reckoned on being in Egypt by this time & instead of that he is still fighting in the area of our defence line – so clearly matters have not gone as the enemy intended.[61]

After Rommel's destruction of the Bir Hakeim box, he was able to go on the offensive. On 14 June, General Neil Ritchie, commander of the British Eighth Army, ordered the evacuation of the Gazala Line. The fighting moved to Tobruk. On the morning of 20 June, Rommel launched a full-scale assault on the south-eastern side of the Allied defences, and by the afternoon he was in the port. South Africa's Major General HB Klopper, commander of the Commonwealth troops in Tobruk, was forced into a humiliating surrender. The capitulation dealt a devastating blow to South Africa's prestige, and marked a significant reversal for the Allies, both militarily and psychologically. Churchill held Klopper personally responsible: he told President Franklin D Roosevelt that Klopper had 'got cold feet' and 'waved the white flag twenty-four hours after the German attack began'.[62] Smuts despaired, but his Nationalist opponents rejoiced at the prospect of a German victory. 'One can't help being depressed at the news,' Harry lamented to his father. 'So far we have few details, but many of our friends must have been captured & the fall of Tobruk is a bad blow.'[63] In fact, an entire division had been lost, and for many torturous months back home families had no idea whether their fathers, sons or brothers were alive or dead. Harry's own regiment had not been caught up in the action, but he was concerned about the Wilson brothers (both of whom were taken prisoner) and Punch Barlow. And of course he was anxious about his own destiny too. The thought of his impending transfer to the Coastal Area Command made him 'more than ever determined', Harry confided to Ernest, not to be 'put in the bag'.[64]

After the fall of Tobruk, Rommel turned east and crossed over into Egypt, forcing the Allies to abandon the Marsa Matruh position at the end of June. They retreated to El Alamein, where over the coming months the stage would be set for the most decisive battle of them all, the showdown that was to end any Axis hopes of conquering Egypt. By then, Harry would be back in the Union. His last letter home, dated 10 July, was written from the Armoured Fighting Vehicle Wing at Helwan, while he waited for air passage back to South Africa. Reflecting on his time up north from the safety of Helwan, Harry admitted to his father that he felt almost guilty for being there, under orders to return to the Union. It had been an interesting time, but he had had 'enough of the dust' and he was so thrilled at the thought of going home that he felt 'slightly sick' – 'like waiting to catch the "special" on the first day of school holidays'.[65]

Harry's service in the Western Desert marked him profoundly. It changed him in subtle ways. His political views were sharpened by the fight against Nazi tyranny. His thoughts began to turn more seriously to a life in public service back home. Harry had prevailed upon his adjutant, Sabie de Beer, to teach him Afrikaans, and he was 'getting on quite well', he bragged to Ernest, when he asked his father for a supply of Afrikaans novels, an Afrikaans grammar book and an English–Afrikaans dictionary.[66] Ernest took this as a good sign. 'I shall send you the Afrikaans literature tomorrow,' he replied. 'It is useful to know Afrikaans, particularly if you decide to go into politics after the War, which I hope you will.'[67] The war exposed Harry for the first time to a broad cross-section of society, to men of different classes and backgrounds. 'It's the only good thing in this life,' he had written to Ernest. In later years Grey Fletcher would remark: 'I certainly think the experience helped Harry to become more approachable, to mix better, to appreciate the qualities of ordinary people.'[68]

Oppenheimer had pondered Smuts's stirring words at the summit of the Zomba Mountain in 1939 – 'Harry, is it not wonderful to be an African?' – and he knew in his heart that he was a man of Africa. His sense of Africanness was bound up in the familiarity of the Union: the diamond fields of Kimberley, the gold mines of the Witwatersrand, and the nation's parliamentary pulse in Cape Town. At the core of it lay the domesticity of Brenthurst, the centre of all his worlds. While staying at Little Brenthurst, Ina and Ernest had decided to renovate the living quarters for Harry. He was delighted, particularly with Ina's decision to redo the dining room in light teak, and he asked for photos and plans. 'Your description of Little Brenthurst simply thrills me & makes me feel very home-sick,' Harry wrote to Ernest.[69] To Ina he made a more interesting confession: Little Brenthurst was getting to be 'an immense house & I'm afraid I haven't yet found that wife you're providing for so well! However it's obviously quite essential now.'[70] And so, when, with his usual sense of purpose, Harry took up his new posting at Coastal Area Command, matters matrimonial were not far from his mind.

SIX

Gold Strike

1942–1949

Boom Times

Harry Oppenheimer's wartime experiences in the Western Desert were formative. They exposed him to a broader spectrum of men from social and cultural backgrounds different from his own. On a personal level, the war rounded him: it opened his eyes to privation and punctured his reserve. The fight against fascism sensitised Oppenheimer to the dangerous excesses of chauvinistic nationalisms. It fortified his own brand of civic patriotism – Jan Smuts's South Africanism – and sharpened his interest in the Union's political and economic fortunes. Oppenheimer's return to South Africa in July 1942 meant that he did not participate in the two battles that turned the tide of the Allied forces' campaign in North Africa: the first and second battles of El Alamein. The second of these battles, fought between 23 October and 11 November 1942, saw Rommel's men comprehensively routed by Commonwealth forces and the British Eighth Army under General Bernard Montgomery. Tobruk was avenged. The victory was, in Winston Churchill's words, 'not the end', but 'perhaps the end of the beginning' for the Axis powers.[1] For Oppenheimer, deployed in August 1942 to Coastal Area Command in Cape Town, far from the theatre of action, the Second World War was effectively over.

By 1942 South Africa's war economy was bombinating. There was an enormous increase in demand for industrial diamonds, which were needed for military machinery. De Beers supplied President Franklin D

Roosevelt's administration with one million carats, but the Americans wanted more, and their unfulfilled expectations led to the beginning of the diamond monopoly's antitrust difficulties in the United States.[2] In 1945 the US Department of Justice filed an antitrust suit against De Beers and its associates, which subsequently collapsed owing to jurisdictional issues. As industrial diamonds became more sought after, the demand for gemstones multiplied too.[3] Meanwhile, gold production rose to £120 million in 1942: this served to improve the balance of payments, and it allowed the Union government to repatriate £30 million in overseas debt.[4] Gold stood on the precipice of a post-war boom. Immediately prior to the outbreak of hostilities, following the discoveries in the Far West Rand, prospecting had begun in the Orange Free State. After 1945, this was to lead to the development of the Orange Free State goldfields – an epoch-defining event for Anglo American and Harry Oppenheimer, who became an internationally recognised industrialist in its wake.[5] He was preparing to inherit the magnate's mantle. But Oppenheimer was to strike gold in another fashion during the decade, for in 1942 he met his wife-to-be. Now, at last, he could prolong the line of succession in the Oppenheimer dynasty.

Nothing to See and No One to Talk to

By July 1942, Major General George Brink and Major General IP de Villiers had respectively taken charge of the Union's Inland Area Command and its Coastal Area Command. Coastal Command was tasked with defending an area of South Africa's entire coastline approximately one hundred miles wide. This territory was divided into several smaller commands known as 'fortresses'. There were six such fortresses in all, consistent with the Union's ports at Cape Town, Walvis Bay, Outeniqua (Mossel Bay), Port Elizabeth, East London and Durban. Each fortress had a combined operations room, which gathered information based on reports from coastal air patrols, shipping movements, radar plots, troop locations, and the position of patrol vessels.[6] The operations rooms channelled their information to Coastal Area Command, which in turn allocated military forces to the various fortresses.

On Monday, 3 August 1942, Oppenheimer reported for duty as a general staff officer at Coastal Area Command's headquarters. He had flown out of Cairo on 15 July and arrived in Johannesburg three days later, only to be laid low by a bad cold. Janet Ford, the matron at the

Brenthurst Military Hospital, sent him straight to his sickbed. In any event a proper reunion with Ernest and Ina would have to wait: they had set off for Blue Mountains in Muizenberg, in anticipation of spending time with Harry there. When Harry recuperated, he left for Cape Town and took up residence at the Mount Nelson. The Mother City was in the grip of its cool, wet winter and he did not want to have to wake up early to catch the train into town from Muizenberg. Harry found the hotel 'very pleasant and convenient', he told his father, and besides, 'living far out by unmarried members of the staff is apparently not much smiled on'.[7]

Later in life, Oppenheimer would quip that the difference between Johannesburg and Cape Town was quite elementary: in Johannesburg there was nothing to see, and in Cape Town there was no one to talk to.[8] Yet his tour of duty in the legislative capital proved to be intensely sociable. Wartime Cape Town appeared cheerful if a little 'foolish' to Oppenheimer: its denizens gave the impression of being 'far less interested in the war' than the good burghers of Johannesburg.[9] He took full advantage of the city's breeziness. He saw a good deal of friends like Pippa Wilson, Constance and Tommy Charles, Doris and Gerald Wilks, and Nesta and John Cooper – 'in fact, all the usual crowd', he reported to his father; and he spent pleasurable weekends at the Barlows' historic wine estate in Somerset West, Vergelegen, which Punch Barlow had recently purchased from the mining magnate Sir Lionel Phillips. 'It is a beautiful place though I don't really agree with the popular view that Cynth [Punch's wife, Cynthia] has furnished it wonderfully', Harry confided to Ernest.[10]

As to his new position, Harry was nonplussed. His functions as a duty officer involved sleeping in the office, he groused to his father, 'in case anyone rings up to say the Japanese have landed'. 'I'm not, however, going to allow the risks to intimidate me!' he added nonchalantly.[11] At the behest of the German Naval High Command, the Japanese had launched a submarine offensive in the western Indian Ocean, operating between Durban and the northern end of the Mozambique Channel. Between 5 June and 8 July 1942, Japanese submarines sank 21 Allied merchant ships, mostly in the Mozambique Channel.[12] The nearest sinking to the South African coast occurred just south of St Lucia Bay on 6 July. Yet apocryphal stories abounded of Japanese submariners making it ashore. One such tale involved the secret capture of four Japanese men who had supposedly landed in False Bay and made their way to the Hottentots Holland Mountains. From this elevated vantage point, they apparently conspired to take photographs of the De Beers-controlled African

Explosives and Industries factory in Somerset West below.[13] In fact, the threat of a Japanese invasion launched from the South African coastline declined significantly after the American defeat of Japan's naval forces at the Battle of Midway (4–7 June 1942). The danger was more imagined than real, but it lingered in the collective consciousness until the Allied forces began to assert their naval and air supremacy over the Japanese in the Pacific.

It was clear that the real action lay far beyond the Union's maritime borders. Two months after starting at Coastal Area Command, Oppenheimer was promoted to the rank of captain. The work was not arduous and he found Cape Town congenial. Yet part of him hankered after the field of battle. After the second Battle of El Alamein, all of the 1st South African Infantry Division's brigades returned to the Union for re-training and amalgamation with other units to form the core of a new armoured division. This was the 6th Armoured Division, formed on 1 February 1943 under the command of Major General Evered Poole, and Oppenheimer wanted to enlist in it. He wrote personally to Poole, expressing his eagerness to enrol. 'I should say that it is a pretty fair bet that I shall ask for your services,' Poole responded, but for reasons unrecorded Oppenheimer's return to the battlefront was not to be.[14] It was just as well, for he had fallen for a tall, striking young woman working in the cipher department at Coastal Area Command. Her name was Bridget Denison McCall.

Enter Bridget McCall

Bridget McCall was born in Johannesburg on 28 September 1921, the only child of English parents, Robert Forster McCall and Marjorie Hamilton Mackenzie. Robert was a barrister, educated at Oriel College, Oxford, and a member of the Middle Temple. But by the time he married Marjorie at St Jude's Church in South Kensington in 1912, aged 30, McCall's interest in the law was flagging. He was on the lookout for new adventures. The couple decided to emigrate to South Africa. They arrived in 1920 – attracted, according to the chronicler of McCall family history, by the promise of 'cheap labour' and an 'agreeable climate'.[15] The McCalls settled in Johannesburg, not far from Brenthurst, and Robert proceeded to dabble in various business ventures. He was a braggart, regaling anyone who would listen with colourful accounts of his visits to 'Buck Palace'. Sadly, his imagination was larger than his income. McCall also liked to gamble and drink. He racked up numerous debts and drained away Marjorie's inheritance. Eventually Marjorie drew a line in the sand: she refused to bail out her feckless husband any longer. McCall abandoned his wife and young daughter in Johannesburg and scuttled back to England. (On the ship home, he had the good fortune to meet a wealthy divorcee in search of a husband; she enabled him to start a new life in London.) As a result of this desertion, Bridget grew up fatherless. 'My father didn't feature in my life and from about 1927 I never saw him again,' she would later record in an unpublished memoir, noting ruefully that Robert McCall never made any effort to keep in touch.[16] Marjorie (or 'Callie', as she was known) was a woman of tenacity, determined to prevent her slide from the middle class into the ranks of the working poor. An ebullient actress and singer – during the Second World War she ran a cabaret for the troops and appeared on stage – Callie kept the wolf from the door by working as an itinerant secretary. She laboured and scrimped to ensure that her daughter wanted for nothing. As a result, Bridget enjoyed a relatively privileged childhood. She had a spell at the prestigious girls' school, St Anne's, in the Natal Midlands, subsidised by her mother's sister Hilda Reid. But Marjorie's meanderings meant that Bridget's youth was peripatetic: she attended a school in Cannes and later Wadhurst College in England, before qualifying as a shorthand typist in London.

When war clouds started gathering over Europe in 1939, Marjorie sent Bridget to live with Hilda Reid and her husband, John, in Cape Town. As the Union-Castle liner rounded the Bay of Biscay with Bridget on board, Britain declared war on Germany. The Reids were very stiff and strait-laced and, having no children of their own, 'had no idea what the young liked to do', Bridget would later recollect.[17] Any potential suitor had to be thoroughly vetted by John Reid beforehand; if Bridget was taken out of an evening, she had to be home by midnight and her uncle would be waiting at the door upon her return. But Bridget was not a shrinking violet. Her upbringing had made her practical and resourceful: she channelled whatever resentment might have been fostered by an absent, self-regarding father into a mindset and manner both purposeful and forthright. This reflected in her bearing. In Cape Town she found a job as a shorthand typist at Ohlsson's Brewery. She learnt to play bridge. She frequented the dinner dances laid on for serving officers on their way to the battlefields in North Africa, and she garnered a wide circle of friends. Bridget also had a strong civic instinct. In 1941, she joined the Women's Auxiliary Army Services as a clerical worker in the Cape Town

Harry Oppenheimer and Bridget McCall pose for photographers after the announcement of their engagement, January 1943. *(Brenthurst Library)*

Castle. Before long she was made a sergeant and posted to Robben Island to run the island's army office. Here she encountered death at first hand: one day a young serviceman shot himself and Bridget was dispatched to the other side of the island in an ambulance to fetch him. 'I remember so well he was a tall, dark-skinned man with big sad eyes. He looked at me & said "drive carefully Sgt. I am in great pain".'[18]

Bridget McCall was possessed of a certain stoicism – her childhood had seen to that – and she was also prepared to muck in wherever she could. In 1942, she was promoted to second lieutenant and transferred to the headquarters of Coastal Area Command to work as a signaller in the cipher department. Here she met many officers who had returned from the Western Desert. Some of them became lifelong friends: men like Keith Acutt and Albert Robinson, a civic-minded Cambridge law graduate who had joined Anglo American in 1939 before going off to war. However, the most consequential man to catch her eye was Harry Oppenheimer. By this time Oppenheimer had moved out of the Mount Nelson and was sharing a house, Waterhof, with Punch Barlow near the top of Hof Street in the suburb of Gardens. Harry and Bridget started to see a lot of each other. Over the course of a few months they grew closer. Punch and Cynthia Barlow thought they were a good match. So did many of their mutual friends. Harry sensed he might have struck gold. Now in his 35th year and mindful of his prolonged bachelorhood, a few days after Christmas in 1942 he asked Bridget to be his wife. 'Every minute I know more certainly how completely right I am to want to marry you,' he wrote to her on 4 January 1943.[19] But he perceived a slight apprehensiveness on her part: 'Of course you must be quite sure too before you decide; but I am always hoping that that may be soon – perhaps now. You are quite right when you say that we don't really know one another well. But that is a matter of years. It can only be a case of a little knowledge or a lot of faith – which I dare say is another name for love. My love, H.'[20]

Whatever reservations Bridget may have harboured, she quickly overcame them. On 6 January *The Star* announced the couple's engagement. When Bridget took a leap of faith and accepted Harry's proposal, she did so unreservedly. In a sense, she was marrying up: her upbringing and socio-economic standing were reasonably removed from those of her fiancé. Nor, for that matter, did Bridget's larger-than-life mother share Oppenheimer's punctiliousness about proprieties. (On occasion Harry was embarrassed by his future mother-in-law's flamboyance; he was horrified, for example, when Callie took to wearing a mantilla during her not-so-secret affair with the Argentinian Ambassador to South Africa.) Yet, once Bridget McCall resolved to become Mrs Oppenheimer (and she would never quite lose the thrill of being a rich man's wife), she assumed the role, responsibilities and requisite identity with the firmness of purpose that was her hallmark.

Marrying into the Firm

Harry and Bridget were married by Bishop Sidney Lavis at St Saviour's Anglican church in Claremont on 6 March 1943. 'Wedding' is the single-word entry in Harry's diary for the day.[21] The bride was given away by her uncle, John Reid; he and Aunt Hilda hosted the reception afterwards at their home. Harry asked Ina's son, Michael Oppenheimer, to be his best man, though Comar Wilson (indisposed on the battlefield) had been his first choice.[22] Punch and Cynthia Barlow's sons, Thomas and William, served as page boys, and their daughters, Phoebe and Dinah, performed the role of flower girls. Ernest and Ina were in attendance, along with several of their friends. It was a magnificent late Cape summer's day, and the nuptials marked a joyful occasion, even if – as Bridget reminisced in

Harry and Bridget Oppenheimer on their wedding day,
6 March 1943. *(Brenthurst Library)*

her memoirs – the reminders of war were all around, with the officers from Coastal Area Command kitted out in full military uniform.

When Harry asked Bridget for her hand in marriage, he had said, only half-jokingly, that one of them would have to give up a 'promising' army career; 'and since it is always women's careers that are "sacrificed", it will, I suppose, be you.'[23] But Bridget was under no illusion about whom she would be marrying, or what kind of enterprise she would be marrying into. She was hitching herself to 'The Firm', South Africa's most prominent dynasty. Bridget knew the Anglo American Corporation would 'always be first' in her husband's life: 'I accepted this and it worked well.'[24] And so it turned out. She resigned from Coastal Area Command. Although the bride and groom spent the first night of their honeymoon at Blue Mountains, the rest of it unfolded – in Bridget's recollection – in Johannesburg and Kimberley, 'introducing me to people in De Beers

& AAC'[25] In Cape Town the wedded pair moved into Waterhof. Harry bought Bridget her first car – a second-hand Dodge, since new motor vehicles for private use were unavailable during the war – and she settled cheerfully into life as Harry Oppenheimer's consort. One day the newly-wed was shopping in the central business district when suddenly she fainted. Bridget had fallen pregnant.

Back to Business: The Orange Free State Goldfields

There was a hive of activity on the business front. Throughout the war, Ernest Oppenheimer had been involved in negotiations with the government to renew and reshape the agreements that defined the rights of the various members of the Diamond Producers' Association (including the Diamond Corporation). It was complex and arduous work, made more difficult by the frequently intransigent Minister of Mines, Colonel Stallard, who seemed to model himself on Colonel Blimp. 'I had some more letters from Stallard … does he think I am an absolute idiot?' Ernest wrote despairingly to Harry after his discussions with the minister seemed to falter.[26] In the end, Ernest had his way: the agreement concluded in December 1942 prolonged the life of the Diamond Producers' Association until the cessation of wartime hostilities. The demand for diamonds was booming. In 1940, economic planners had advised the United States government that America needed at least 6.5 million carats of industrial diamonds to equip its factories for wartime production. However, De Beers resisted President Roosevelt's entreaties for so many industrial diamonds: the company did not want to transfer a large portion of its stockpile from London to New York. In America the hoard would be beyond De Beers' grasp; and, in the event of an early German surrender, it might possibly not be depleted, thus putting the Americans at a commercial advantage. Ernest agreed to supply the United States with one million carats and to deposit an additional stockpile in Canada (then a British dominion) for the duration of the war. But he held out against the American request to reopen at least one diamond mine. 'We are still arguing about industrial diamonds and the American authorities are still pressing us through the Government to open a mine,' Ernest complained to Harry. 'Stallard agrees that it is just nonsense and that there is no risk of a shortage of industrials.'[27] However, such was the clamour for gemstones by the middle of 1943 that stocks threatened to dry up. As a result, the Dutoitspan mine was put back into operation on 1 September 1943.

The question of whether the trade in industrial diamonds should be separated from the trade in gemstones had long exercised Ernest's mind. Harry had at first been cautious about making any hard-and-fast decisions, but now he thought the subject required resolution. In fact, he realised that the whole diamond trade would need to be reorganised after the war was over and that this would involve considerable exertion. In gold, too, significant developments lay ahead. In 1936, the Anglo American Investment Trust was formed to deal with Anglo American's diamond interests. In 1937, the West Rand Investment Trust was established to hold all of the corporation's gold interests on the Far West Rand. By 1943 it seemed that a similar vehicle might be needed to cater for Anglo American's burgeoning gold interests in the Orange Free State.

Following Anglo's exploration on the Far West Rand and its successful flotation of the Western Reefs mine, the corporation had begun to take an interest in the area immediately south of the Vaal River in the Orange Free State. As early as 1936, Anglo American and the Western Reefs Exploration and Development Company had – together with the Union Corporation, Central Mining, and Consolidated Gold Fields – purchased options over 145 000 hectares of land in the Bothaville area from the geologist and prospector Dr Hans Merensky. The venture became known as the Free State Western Reefs. At about the same time as Anglo American was prospecting its farms south of the Vaal River, Sir Abe Bailey's South African Townships Mining and Finance Corporation was drilling south of Odendaalsrus. The African and European Investment Company, another long-established group predominantly interested in collieries, had taken up options over ground adjoining that of South African Townships, and began drilling there. This unearthed a valuable vein of gold deposits. In the 1940s, Anglo American entered into various agreements with South African Townships and the African and European Investment Company. The result was that the corporation came to control a consolidated area in the Orange Free State on which five separate gold mines were established: St Helena, Welkom, Western Holdings, President Brand and President Steyn.[28] The Welkom mine crushed its first ore in 1951. The rest of Anglo's mines would come on stream during the course of the 1950s. A deal with the Blinkpoort Gold Syndicate gave Anglo American control of the area incorporating the Free State Geduld mine. The Jeanette and Loraine mines were further acquisitions. Ernest Oppenheimer helped devise the corporate structures and secure the funds required to open these new mines as rapidly as possible, but he needed his son's cool, analytical head to help approach the broader business challenges methodically. It was clear that Harry's energies were being wasted at Coastal Area Command. He was needed back at 44 Main Street.

Harry was approved for indefinite release from full-time military service to resume civil duties with effect from 7 September 1943. He had had a respectable war – acknowledged in due course by the award of the 1939–1945 Star, the Africa Star, the War Medal 1939–45, the Africa Service Medal and, of course, his Desert Rat emblem – but it was time to resume his apprenticeship. Harry and Bridget returned to Johannesburg where they rented a house in Jubilee Road belonging to the Hellmann family. (Brenthurst was still in service as a military hospital, and Ernest and Ina were stationed at Little Brenthurst.) During this period, Ernest appointed Harry as managing director of Anglo American. After the war ended in 1945, Harry also took charge of the committee responsible for the development of the Orange Free State goldfields. According to WD 'Bill' Wilson, a Cambridge University law graduate recruited into Anglo in 1946 – he later succeeded Harry as Anglo's managing director – this was the younger Oppenheimer's 'first major command'. Even though Harry was highly thought of for his intellectual abilities by senior people in the group, he was regarded as relatively inexperienced. '[Harry] encountered and weathered cheerfully many frowns, not only from outside the group, but from powerful figures inside it too, such as FA Unger and RB Hagart,' Wilson recalled.[29] But he demonstrated steely resolve, helped of course by the fact that he was the chairman's son.

Harry looked upon the Orange Free State goldfields as the 'great horizon' for Anglo American – an El Dorado that would make Anglo 'the greatest of the South African mining houses'.[30] For Keith Acutt, the most notable feature of Harry's involvement in the Orange Free State developments was his 'determination' that Anglo should establish superior standards of urban planning, architecture, housing, hospitals, and recreational facilities for both black and white workers in the new mining towns created by the corporation. 'He had always felt that … all people … deserved better standards … In that sense he took it for granted – long before it became a public issue – that … blacks too should be beneficiaries of the capitalist system.'[31] Between 1948 and 1955, Anglo American spent £10 million alone on building accommodation in Welkom and Allanridge: 2758 houses, 37 blocks of flats and 5 hostels.[32] Anglo's single biggest innovation, in terms of the black labour force, was to propose building married quarters on the mines. If successfully implemented, this initiative would have begun to dismantle the baleful edifice of migrant labour and the compound system, which corralled black mineworkers into single-sex hostels. The corporation initially aimed at accommodating ten per cent of its black workforce in this way. Smuts gave his in-principle approval. But he was defeated in the 1948 election and his Nationalist successors – in particular the uncompromising Minister of Native Affairs, HF Verwoerd – refused Anglo permission to house more than three per cent of its black mineworkers with their wives. According to Acutt, Harry reacted to Verwoerd's obduracy with 'great disappointment'; had Anglo's proposal been agreed to, 'the migrant labour system in time would simply have fallen away'.[33] The reality, of course, is much less straightforward than Acutt's pat observation suggests. During Ernest Oppenheimer's lifetime, Anglo American never managed to meet even the low three per cent threshold. Looking back on his life, Harry conceded – with notable understatement – that this was a 'missed opportunity … acknowledged, with regret'.[34]

Perpetuating the Dynasty

While the labour pains associated with the development of the Orange Free State goldfields were stirring, Bridget was experiencing a gestation of her own. On 31 December 1943 she gave birth to a daughter. The couple named her Mary, after Harry's mother. Mary's arrival was not permitted to interfere with her father's priorities, however: he attended the Anglo American New Year's party at the Inanda Club, and when someone asked after Bridget, he responded, 'She and Mary are well at home.'[35] Ernest was enraptured with his granddaughter. He placed a 19-carat pink diamond ring on Bridget's finger; she later recalled of Ernest that he was as 'excited with Mary as if she had been his own daughter'.[36] Eighteen months later there was another addition to the family: this time a boy, Nicholas Frank, soon dubbed Nicky, born on 8 June 1945. By then the Italians had long been vanquished by the Allies. Hitler was dead, and Germany had signed a total and unconditional surrender only the month before. The war in Europe was over. The military hospital at Brenthurst had been disestablished (not before an accidental fire gutted a wing); Ernest and Ina were back in the main house; and Harry and Bridget were comfortably established in Little Brenthurst. The children were a source of delight to their grandparents. 'You cannot imagine the pleasure May [*sic*] & Nick give me,' Ernest glowed to Harry. 'We played together after my return from the Free State, & they both tell me that they missed me, & what is more, I am sure they meant it.'[37]

Mary and Nicky may well have seen more of their grandfather than their father in their early years, for Harry was constantly travelling, and not always with his father in tow. Apart from his regular trips to Kimberley to attend meetings of De Beers, and his monthly visits to the Orange Free State goldfields, Harry was forever shuttling to Northern Rhodesia, the Belgian Congo, Angola, England, Continental Europe and the United States. From Élisabethville he wrote despondently to Bridget, after visiting diamond mines in Bakwanga, that the continuous effort of making 'small talk to people you don't know, in French' was 'rather a strain.'[38] A few months later, in October 1944, with the war still smouldering, he was in London on diamond business, and he checked into the Savoy Hotel. The air raid damage was tremendous and Harry described the city to Bridget as 'practically flattened'. 'At present however only just a very few flying bombs are coming over nightly & nobody seems to take any notice of them. I can hear one now,' he wrote, not altogether reassuringly, to his wife eight thousand miles away.[39] The war had claimed the life of a number of Oppenheimer's friends. Among them was Hector Ian Simson, a lieutenant in the 2nd Transvaal Scottish regiment, whom Oppenheimer had befriended in North Africa through Comar and Tony Wilson. Simson was shot by a sniper. 'I can't get over the tragedy of Ian. Apart from his being so specially nice, I always thought he had the greatest promise of doing big things in life,' Harry lamented to Bridget.[40] The most poignant loss was that of his old Oxford chum Robin Grant Lawson. He died in April 1944, only three months after writing to Harry about how 'very honoured' he was to be asked to be Mary's godfather.[41]

London Life

In bomb-ravaged London, Oppenheimer went shopping. 'As a shopping centre London at present doesn't compare with Johannesburg,' he advised Bridget. 'Shops like Asprey have nothing but very nasty second hand things.'[42] But he was determined to find 'something nice' for his wife, and he procured two hats at Molyneux and a set of linen table mats with her initials embroidered on them. For Mary he bought a party dress so that she would be 'much the smartest young woman in Johannesburg'.[43] For himself he purchased a 'lovely little silver cream jug', dating from 1734, 'mostly to go with our coffee pot'.[44] 'I have been most extravagant & immensely enjoyed it,' he beamed to Bridget after snapping up three 'magnificent & very impractical chairs' from Partridge in New Bond Street – an armchair and two Charles IIs in red lacquer of soft salmon pink.[45] Harry was a great collector. The pursuit of beautiful antiques, period furniture and articles of virtu was an essential and pleasurable part of any successful business trip. So, too, were family visits: he stayed for a weekend with Otto Oppenheimer and his wife, Beattie, in Surrey; dined with Gustav Oppenheimer's wife, Cecily; and spent another weekend with his beloved Aunt Sybil at her country cottage in Hadlow – 'in a way attractive but not my cup of tea.'[46] Oppenheimer always found White Waltham, where Louis had moved the diamond office for the duration of the war, a congenial destination. But his enjoyment was tempered by having to try to sort out Louis and Carlota's muddled financial affairs. And although Raymond Oppenheimer was 'extravagantly' amusing, his conversation about championship-winning bull terriers could be pitched at a rather 'high technical level', in his cousin's discreetly disapproving view.[47]

The theatre was an agreeable diversion. Harry went to see *Hamlet* with John Gielgud in the lead role, Leslie Banks as the king, and Peggy Ashcroft as Ophelia: 'It was brilliantly good, except for the staging which I thought was indifferent,' he reported back to Bridget.[48] Edith Coates was impressive in the title role of *Carmen*, though she 'was of enormous size & really frightening ugliness'.[49] Oppenheimer lunched with the Tory MP Harold Balfour (Ina Oppenheimer's former brother-in-law), at the corporation's offices on Holborn Viaduct.[50] He caught up with Cecil Berens and other Oxford friends. Dinner with Roy Harrod was a fixture. He kept Bridget up to speed with his business engagements, including a meeting with the scientist and Zionist leader, Chaim Weizmann (after 1948, the first President of Israel), on the diamond-cutting industry in Palestine. He attended a state dinner for Alfred Chester Beatty, who in turn hosted an 'immense business lunch' for him at Claridge's the following day: 'There were about 40 people, all very grand & intimidating. I had to make a short speech, which I had not expected, so it had to be genuinely impromptu which I hate, but all went off well.'[51]

In London, Oppenheimer rubbed shoulders with the cream of the British commercial and political establishment. He attended 'an astonishing dinner party' for the chairman of Imperial Chemical Industries, Harry McGowan – 'rather fun & very grand, a mass of cabinet ministers' – and gave a 'little speech' that he found 'rather frightening'.[52] In 1947, Ina's son, Michael, wed Laetitia Helen Munro-Lucas-Tooth, the daughter of the Conservative MP Sir Hugh Vere Huntly Duff Munro-Lucas-Tooth, 1st Baronet. The marriage provided Oppenheimer with another extended-family entrée into Torydom. But his affiliations were not entirely tribal. At the end of the decade, during Clement Attlee's premiership, the noted political hostess Lady Crewe (Margaret Primrose, daughter of the 5th Earl of Rosebery) entertained Oppenheimer at a small luncheon party. Other guests included the writer and MP (and Labour convert) Harold Nicolson, and the former Conservative Foreign Secretary and future Prime Minister, Anthony Eden. Oppenheimer found Eden 'very friendly & charming but not at all impressive'.[53]

Oppenheimer's trip to England in 1944 was long and exacting – nearly three months in all – and it entailed diamond-related sallies into war-battered Belgium and Holland. In the Netherlands, Oppenheimer's engagements included champagne with Prince Bernhard, the commander of the Dutch Armed Forces, and a trip to a nightclub with the directors of the Amsterdamsche Bank and their wives: 'easily the ugliest lot of women I have ever seen'.[54] These annual (and later biannual) trips to London were an important part of Oppenheimer's life. Although he consciously thought of himself as a South African – the notion that he was 'a man of Africa' was an important part of his identity[55] – Englishness was deeply woven into his cultural sensibility. His war (and post-war) visits to London groomed him for his later role, following in his father's footsteps, as a business statesman. They embedded him, a man in his thirties, as a member of the politically connected global business elite. In London, Oppenheimer socialised with the scions of dynastic families, many of them leading lights in the firmament of international banking and finance. On his trip in 1945, one of the 'gaieties', he told Bridget, was a dinner with Jocelyn Hambro (appointed to the board of Consolidated Mines Selection the following year), Hambro's wife, Silvia, and her mother, Beatrice Muir.[56] He dined separately with William Astor, the Conservative politician and heir to the family's Cliveden estate. The Rothschilds, too, were a continuous point of contact, especially Victor Rothschild, who had been a direct contemporary of Frank Oppenheimer's at Trinity College, Cambridge. In the Fens, Rothschild was renowned for driving around in his Bugatti and fraternising with the likes of Guy Burgess, Anthony Blunt and Kim Philby – members of the secret Cambridge spy ring. During the war he had been recruited into MI5 – not by Oppenheimer's mentor, JC Masterman, but by the service's head of counter-espionage, Guy Liddell. (Rothschild was responsible, among other things, for ensuring that cigars gifted to Winston Churchill contained no poison.) A brilliant zoologist, accomplished jazz pianist and unrivalled private collector of 18th-century English manuscripts, Rothschild was a polymath and stimulating interlocutor.[57] He and Oppenheimer saw each other regularly and cultivated a life-long friendship.

At the end of his visit to London in 1945, Harry wrote to Bridget: 'Look after yourself, darling, & the babies. How much I wish you were over here.'[58] It was difficult, amid all his multiple business expeditions, for the couple to settle into a routine with their infants for any length of time. Bridget's one salvation was Shangani, the ranch in Southern Rhodesia that Ernest Oppenheimer had purchased in 1937. Harry had started building a house there, but the original architect died during the war and his successor had taken to the bottle. In 1944, Harry and Bridget decided to go and check on the progress of the house, called White Kopjes. Their visits, usually at the beginning of July and sometimes again at the end of August, were soon to become an annual tradition. Shangani was where Bridget would 'cook and make the beds' and enjoy a more relaxed, informal kind of domesticity.[59] It was also a sanctuary for family and friends. Cynthia Barlow wondered how Bridget succeeded in hosting so many guests with good grace: 'I cannot tell you how much I admire the way you manage it all – wonderful food & the greatest comfort & above all such a happy atmosphere all the time ...'[60] Shangani 'gave so many friends pleasure', Bridget would later recall nostalgically: it was the scene of many 'laughs & excitements'.[61]

The American Allure

Once the children were only slightly older, Bridget would leave them at home – cared for by nannies overseen by Ernest and Ina – and join her husband on his international trips. At the end of the decade they spent a month in the United States, where Harry endured a punishing schedule of business meetings, before going on to England. These visits to America would soon constitute a much-anticipated pilgrimage in their own right. They were as enjoyable a fixture in the diary as the London sojourns; and Bridget and Harry eventually took an apartment at the Carlyle in New York. In New York, Oppenheimer went to see De Beers' advertising agency, NW Ayer. He dined with the firm's chief, Gerold M Lauck, and Lauck's wife at the Colony and then proceeded to the Wedgwood Room at the Waldorf Astoria to listen to the jazz pianist Eddy Duchin. 'A noisier

A diamond is forever: tile prepared for De Beers advertising campaign, 1952. *(Brenthurst Library)*

& more loathsome place I have yet to experience,' he complained in his diary afterwards.[62] Under Lauck's direction, NW Ayer's advertising campaign had proved to be an astounding success. The agency reported to De Beers that between 1938 and 1941 the sale of diamonds in America had increased by 55 per cent. After the war, the advertisers stepped up their efforts. They prepared a strategy document for their client which emphasised the need to take a more 'psychological' approach. Diamond rings were to be marketed as a 'psychological necessity' for a demographic of 70 million people aged 15 years and over.[63] The agency boasted to De Beers that it had showcased diamonds worn by 'stars of screen and stage, by wives and daughters of political leaders, by any woman who can make the grocer's wife and the mechanic's sweetheart say "I wish I had what she has"'.[64] But they needed a pithy slogan to encapsulate the romantic and aspirational appeal of diamonds. In 1947, Frances Gerety, a young copywriter at NW Ayer, struck upon a winning formulation. Beneath a photograph of two lovers on honeymoon, she penned the caption 'A diamond is forever'. Within a year it became the iconic slogan of De Beers, as enduring as the very idea of the diamond ring itself.

Harry and Bridget were joined in New York by Harry's cousin Philip (Otto Oppenheimer's son), who was making a name for himself in the London diamond office, and Philip's wife, Pam. Philip was only three years younger than Harry; Pam was five years older than Bridget; and together the four of them got on extremely well. They had a private tour of Harry Winston's flagship jewellery store. A short, indefatigable man, Winston had made a fortune in the diamond business. Born in 1900 in a walk-up tenement apartment in New York, he left school at the age of 14 and joined his father's jewellery business. He bought diamonds from deceased estates and, having re-cut them, re-sold them to chain stores at a profit. By 1940, Winston was America's largest diamond dealer. He had purchased the Jonker diamond in 1935, opened up his own diamond factories in New York, Puerto Rico and Israel, and was now a leading role-player in NW Ayer's advertising campaign. In 1943, he was the first jeweller to loan diamonds to a Hollywood actress for the Academy Awards. Within a few years he would be distributing more than a quarter of all engagement diamonds in the United States. Winston showed the Oppenheimers around his store. Harry Oppenheimer found his namesake to be a 'tiny, dapper little man, very puffed up with himself', but also 'a first class showman' and a 'great asset to the trade'.[65] The South African took an almost rarefied pleasure in inspecting Winston's wares. To see the 'Star of the East' was 'an immense & wonderful privilege'; by contrast, the Hope diamond was 'very ugly' and even the largest, most brilliant cut of the Jonker diamond was 'disappointing' because, although the colour was perfect, the stone lacked brilliance in Oppenheimer's view.[66]

Afterwards the Oppenheimer cousins embarked on a flurry of engagements with diamond cutters, dealers and jewellers. This was an activity that Harry either relished or – when he was dealing with recalcitrant personalities – resented. Salomon van Berg, the president of the Rough Diamond Company and an authority on industrial diamonds, made a 'comparatively favourable impression'. He was 'altogether a better proposition than the Jolis family' (Jac and his son Albert), but like 'all these people', Oppenheimer noted, 'they want watching'.[67] When Oppenheimer made his trip to New York in 1938, Pierre Cartier was in charge of the eponymous Fifth Avenue store. A decade on, his nephew Claude was running the show. Claude Cartier was 'pleasant & efficient', but his jewellery was on the whole 'disappointing; pedestrian in design & comparatively clumsy in workmanship', Oppenheimer felt.[68] The Tsarina of Russia's magnificent emerald necklace, which Cartier had on display, was 'one of the most marvellous pieces of jewellery' Oppenheimer had ever seen, but for the most part Cartier had 'nothing of the fabulous nature' exhibited by Harry Winston.[69]

In between Oppenheimer's various appointments, there was a whirlwind of social activity. He and Bridget dined with American captains of industry. Louis Cates, the chairman of the Phelps Dodge Corporation, laid on a dinner at his River House apartment with a babble of copper barons. Among the guests were James Hobbins and Cornelius Kelley, president and chairman respectively of the Anaconda Copper Mining Company. 'This was indeed discovering America,' Oppenheimer wrote in his diary afterwards; the 'proceedings were of the nature of a tribal rite.'[70] Dinner with Harry Winston and wife, Edna, revealed that Mrs Winston was a 'much better proposition' than Oppenheimer had imagined: 'small, dark, attractive, coarse face with fine eyes; well dressed; jewellery very fine but not excessively so.'[71] Apart from the dinners, there were regular excursions to the Museum of Modern Art, where Oppenheimer took in the Frick collection and saw 'some magnificent Cézannes.'[72] There were frequent outings to the theatre. Harry and Bridget attended the Broadway premier of *Lost in the Stars*, based on Alan Paton's celebrated novel, *Cry, the Beloved Country*. Paton's book had brought South Africa's racial injustices to international attention when it was published in 1948, and Oppenheimer found the stage performance 'wonderful'.[73] Margot Fonteyn was 'magnificent' in the role of Cinderella at the Metropolitan Opera House, while Edith Piaf in song at the Versailles nightclub was 'excellent': she 'almost but not quite made 2½ hours in a very ordinary nightclub worthwhile'.[74]

Oppenheimer flew to Arizona to view the Morenci copper mine. He visited the Norton Company in Worcester, Massachusetts, which had developed a new process for polishing plate glass with diamond wheels. And he met Fred Searls, the president of the Newmont Mining Corporation. Searls urged him to enter negotiations with the US Atomic Energy Commission, either directly or through Newmont, over the sale of uranium to the American market. But the chief reason for Oppenheimer's business trip was to sound out the main finance houses about the possibilities for attracting American investment to South Africa – and the Orange Free State goldfields in particular. At the House of Morgan he lunched with the combative and curmudgeonly chairman, Russell C Leffingwell, a close ally of President Franklin D Roosevelt during the war, and from 1946 the chairman of the Council on Foreign Relations.

Leffingwell was bookish and witty with a mind that was 'promiscuously rich', but he was prone to delivering himself of fiery opinions.[75] For Oppenheimer he produced an impassioned sermon on why there should be no increase in the dollar price of gold. Oppenheimer found Leffingwell's views 'most violent' and 'quite incomprehensible', although personally he could see 'no good reason' for a higher gold price.[76]

By contrast, Harry found TS Lamont admirably restrained. If it were possible to open up a new source of American capital for the development of the goldfields, Oppenheimer suggested, Anglo would be prepared to 'make an initial deal specially attractive'.[77] In reality, JP Morgan was not in a position to assist Anglo American in quite the way Oppenheimer intended. The conversation with Lamont petered out in 'mutual expressions of good will'.[78] But all was not lost. Oppenheimer made two significant connections on this trip. The first of these was with André Meyer from Lazard Frères, to whom Oppenheimer was introduced through representatives of Newmont. In Meyer, Oppenheimer found a kindred spirit. He was a French-born banker who had come to America as a refugee from Nazi-occupied France. In later years, David Rockefeller called him the most creative financial genius in investment banking. An art collector of some renown, he was also known as the banker's Picasso. Oppenheimer immediately took to Meyer. He thought him highly intelligent and a man of 'considerable acuteness'.[79] Partly this was because Meyer had some experience of the South African gold mining industry, and he assessed two of Anglo American's competitors in terms that Oppenheimer found suitably trenchant. The engineer Bob Hersov and stockbroker Simeon 'Slip' Menell had started the smallest of the major mining houses, Anglovaal, in 1933, and Meyer had had dealings with them. He thought Hersov was difficult and 'dangerous' while Menell was 'easily influenced' but at least energetic and ingenious, an opinion Oppenheimer shared.[80] Oppenheimer and Meyer discussed various potential permutations of capitalisation at length, in particular the introduction to the general American public of a share or bond which might offer a good measure of security and at the same time a speculative interest.

The other major American financier with whom Oppenheimer struck up a rapport was C Douglas Dillon at Dillon, Read and Company – a man who impressed him 'extremely favourably in every way'.[81] Douglas Dillon and his father, Clarence (who co-founded the concern), kept a separate office at 40 Wall Street where they conducted their private investment business, and this is where Oppenheimer joined them for lunch after their initial meeting. Dillon *père* believed that an attractive South African gold mining issue would appeal to the American public and potentially open up the market to further issues. There might, he cautioned, be difficulties in obtaining stock exchange quotations in New York, given the bourse's disclosure and transparency requirements. Oppenheimer was torn. He could see merit in pursuing his discussions with both André Meyer and the Dillons but realised that he would have to make a choice. He sensed that, culturally, Lazard Frères would be more flexible and easier for Anglo American to work with. But even though Oppenheimer had found André Meyer very likeable, he took a 'special liking' to the Dillons, particularly the younger one, and this weighed upon his decision-making.[82] This was a thread that ran through his business life: for all that Harry was cerebral, analytical and measured – in contradistinction to his father's more emotional, intuitive and sometimes impulsive approach – the role of affect was often pivotal in his decision-making.

As things turned out, it was the Swiss – not the Americans – who provided the key source of finance for the Orange Free State gold mines. In 1950, the Union Bank of Switzerland floated a £4 million loan to the Anglo American Corporation, thus providing a valuable source of insurance against the investing public's reluctance to stake additional capital on the Orange Free State mines.[83] But the personal networks that Oppenheimer built with financiers on his trip to the United States were to prove profitable and enduring. Men like André Meyer and the Dillons were – or would become – politically influential businessmen who wielded enormous soft power. Meyer became a close confidant of the future American President Lyndon B Johnson and a financial advisor to the Kennedy family. During the First World War, Clarence Dillon had served as the assistant chairman of the War Industries Board. Douglas Dillon was a well-connected Republican – close to John D Rockefeller III – and worked on Thomas E Dewey's 1948 presidential campaign. In 1953, he would be appointed by President Dwight Eisenhower as the United States ambassador to France. Dillon *fils* later found favour among the Democrats: President John F Kennedy appointed him as Secretary of the Treasury in his administration. It was natural that Oppenheimer should seek to take his place among this coterie of international financiers. Apart from their political clout, they were highly erudite, culturally sophisticated and handsomely philanthropic.

There was an aspect of international diplomacy to Oppenheimer's work, too. In 1934, Ernest Oppenheimer had helped to establish the South African Institute of International Affairs (SAIIA), a think tank devoted to international relations and interstate dialogue. On his trip to the United States, Harry engaged in discussions with Whitney Shepardson, an American businessman who headed the Secret Intelligence Branch of the Office of Strategic Services during the Second World War. (It was subsequently incorporated into the Central Intelligence Agency.) Shepardson was also a director of the Carnegie Corporation's British Dominions and Colonies Fund, and he was anxious to find a first-rate researcher who could undertake work on Carnegie's behalf at SAIIA. Oppenheimer took tea with Shepardson at his 'nice shabby house with an Oxford atmosphere', and he reflected in his diary afterwards on one of their conversational digressions.[84] They had discussed the difficulty of attracting capital to undeveloped parts of the British Empire. Oppenheimer wrote contemplatively: 'The trouble really is that the US Govt (& the British Govt) wants to get people to invest money in the wild outposts *without* the inducement of profit. The Belgians got railways built in the Congo by giving mineral concessions to private Cos. as inducement to provide the money for the railways. Without such inducement *private* capital will not be available for roads & railways where the risk is great & the chances of profit very limited.'[85] Oppenheimer's meditation underscored his view, shaped by what he regarded as the 'Rhodes tradition', of the proper role between the state and the private sector in national development (within a broader international framework). For him, the role of the businessman, like that of the politician, was to marry economic development – through private investment and industry – to statehood and nation-building. That was the essence of business statesmanship.

The Last Hurrah: The Royal Tour of 1947

In South Africa's case, its nationhood and economic welfare were tied to the British Commonwealth. This was an idea promoted by Prime Minister Jan Smuts and many South African industrialists, including Ernest Oppenheimer on the benches of Parliament between 1924 and 1938.[86] Harry's conception of the Union stood in stark contrast to the *völkisch* aspirations of DF Malan's Afrikaner nationalists, many of whom were avowed republicans. They sought sovereignty outside British imperial constraints. Nevertheless, the Smutsian ideal received a great boost – and, also, though few knew it at the time, a 'last hurrah' – when the British royal family undertook a tour to South Africa in 1947 at Smuts's invitation.[87] The tour, which unfolded between February and April and included stops in Basutoland, Bechuanaland, Swaziland, Southern Rhodesia and Northern Rhodesia, constituted the high-water mark of the British Empire in Africa. In South Africa, people of all hues and political persuasions turned out in their thousands to cheer and welcome King George VI, Queen Elizabeth, and the princesses, Elizabeth and Margaret. A highlight was the royal family's visit to Kimberley, where Ernest Oppenheimer led them around the De Beers diamond mine. To mark the occasion, Ernest had decided to give both the princesses a glittering blue-white diamond – a 6.5-carat specimen for Elizabeth and a 4.5-carat diamond for Margaret. Watched over by her father, three-year-old Mary Oppenheimer curtsied shyly as she presented the princesses with their gems. The ceremony went off seamlessly until Princess Margaret piped up, 'What about Mummy?' Ernest had to engage in some fancy footwork to adorn the Queen with something suitable.

The royal excursion to De Beers marked a moment in the history of diamonds that not even the copywriters at NW Ayer could have scripted better. It also put the Oppenheimer family on display, revealing the extent of its political influence and its commercial eminence. In later years, journalists would sometimes describe the Oppenheimers, with a hint of 'colonial cringe', as South Africa's unofficial royal family. Here, on the royal tour, was a fledgling dynasty paying homage to one that was centuries old. By the time of the royal visit in 1947, Ernest had been a decade out of Parliament, although he remained a potent ally of Smuts. Smuts wrote to him in 1948: 'We have worked closely together during these testing years … You have always been … a true friend.'[88] Ernest was proud of what Harry had achieved during his business apprenticeship. It was said of the mining magnate that at the Kimberley Club on the eve of a De Beers board meeting, he once asked rhetorically of his friends: 'If you were born with £3,000,000 and a silver spoon in your mouth, would you work as hard as my son Harry does?'[89] And, since 1931, Harry had indeed applied himself with dedication so that he too, one day, might justly inherit the title of King of Diamonds, a magnate with the Midas touch. But there was another component to his training that required some elaboration – politics, or the art of the possible, in Otto von Bismarck's elegant turn of phrase. It was time for Harry Oppenheimer to stand for Parliament.

SEVEN

'Hoggenheimer' Rides Again

1948–1957

The Fagan Report and the 'Old Block's' Entry into Politics

The period following Oppenheimer's discharge from military service had been momentous on both the domestic and business fronts. His marriage to Bridget, the birth of his children, Mary and Nicky, the move back to Little Brenthurst, and his re-immersion into the business – especially his involvement in the development of the Orange Free State goldfields – absorbed Oppenheimer's energies. Yet he had watched his father meld a life in business with public office, and was minded to emulate him. The war crystallised that intent. Besides, there had never been a clear boundary between business and politics in Oppenheimer's mind. To him, like his father, they served the same purpose: to foster the social and economic development of South Africa and, indeed, the wider region. Later in life, when he was ordering his thoughts for his unpublished memoir, Oppenheimer would reflect that he went into politics for the same reason he entered Anglo American. It was part of the 'machine' in which he was caught up from birth – 'willingly, enthusiastically caught up.'[1] There was, of course, a dynastic aspect to it. Ernest Oppenheimer had been the MP for Kimberley between 1924 and 1938, serving alongside General Smuts. It seemed as natural to Harry that he should follow in his father's footsteps to the House of Assembly as he should to 44 Main Street. In 1946, while he was on a trip to London, the younger Oppenheimer was profiled by the *Financial Times*. That august publication referred to him as 'not a chip off the old block', but 'the old block itself'.[2] It was an echo of Edmund Burke's comment on William Pitt the Younger after Pitt's maiden speech in the House of Commons, and it was a canny observation. Harry was assuming Ernest's mantle, and within a decade it would be entirely his own.

Growing up, the younger Oppenheimer had revered Smuts, and the elder statesman encouraged Harry's political ambitions.[3] Like other veterans of the Second World War, Oppenheimer experienced a political awakening up north. The war sharpened his liberal convictions. In the 1940s, and for a long time thereafter, Oppenheimer's liberalism did not extend to affording equal civil rights to blacks, let alone any scheme for multiracial power-sharing. Rather it meant 'mostly treating them humanely'.[4] He believed in political, but not economic, segregation. This was a conservative and paternalistic kind of liberalism, to be sure, and it gained expression in the gradually shifting approach of the United Party (UP) to the so-called native problem during the Second World War. In 1942, Smuts told a meeting of the South African Institute of Race Relations (SAIRR) that segregation had 'fallen on evil days'.[5] The war was causing a rapid expansion of secondary industry. The resultant influx of black workers to industrial centres inevitably led to breaches of the colour bar, especially in manufacturing. Increased black militancy over poor working conditions, coupled with unhappiness over miserable living conditions, created a cauldron of potential conflict.[6]

Faced with this urban tumult, and accompanying demands by African nationalists for full citizenship rights, the UP sought to effect piecemeal, cautiously reformist, changes to its native policy. In 1946, Smuts appointed a commission led by Judge Henry Fagan to investigate possible modifications to segregation. Fagan observed a huge increase in the number of black women going to the cities – by 1947, black women accounted for one-third of the urban black population – and he concluded that black urbanisation was irreversible. Whites and blacks were becoming increasingly economically interdependent. When the Fagan Report was published in February 1948 – three months before the watershed general election – it rejected the idea of total segregation as 'utterly impracticable' and sought to ease influx control measures.[7] Crucially, the report recommended that black workers should be allowed to settle permanently with their families in urban areas. But on the hated pass laws, which required black workers in urban areas to carry permits at all times, it was ambiguous. African nationalists derided the document. The African National Congress president, AB Xuma, described Fagan's recommendations as an attempt to 'palliate the system' within the framework of existing policy.[8] Afrikaner nationalists in the Herenigde Nasionale Party poured scorn on them. They had in any event established their own commission in response to Fagan, headed by the parliamentarian Paul Sauer. It stated unequivocally that blacks in urban areas should be regarded as 'migratory citizens', ineligible for political and social rights equal to those of whites.[9] The Sauer Report, released in March 1948, advocated a territorial separation of the races. Its prescriptions were crystal clear. In effect, they laid the foundations for apartheid.[10]

This was the backdrop against which Harry Oppenheimer stood for Parliament. He believed the most pressing political priority was the 'immediate implementation' of the Fagan Report's recommendations, and he viewed the proper role of the UP as being 'the political expression of the new industrialised South Africa'.[11] Others in Oppenheimer's circle were of like mind. Albert Robinson, who had befriended Harry on the squash courts at the Springs mine club after he joined Anglo American in 1939, successfully fought a by-election at Langlaagte for the UP in 1947. Both he and Oppenheimer hoped that a number of younger people who, like them, had come out of the army would go into Parliament to 'play a part in the post-war reconstruction'.[12] Oppenheimer himself had resolved to stand for Kimberley in 1946 when the incumbent MP, William Humphreys, declared that he would retire at the end of his term. 'I think it is very important that there should be direct representation in Parliament of the gold and diamond mining industries and it is with this end in view that I propose to seek election,' Oppenheimer announced at the time.[13] The 1948 election would eventually deliver 11 ex-servicemen to Parliament as opposition MPs, 5 of whom were newcomers.[14] It was a cohort of novices that included the future United Party leader, Sir De Villiers ('Div') Graaff. 'Look after my boy,' his mother, Lady Eileen Graaff, asked earnestly of Oppenheimer after the two were elected to Parliament.[15] Graaff gained the UP's only new seat, in the Hottentots Holland constituency.

1948 Election

Oppenheimer's decision to contest the Kimberley (City, as opposed to District) seat, even though he had spent most of his time on the Witwatersrand since his return to the Union in 1931, was well calculated. He had been born in Kimberley; his father had served the town

On the hustings. *Above:* Sir Ernest Oppenheimer endorses his son's bid for Parliament at a United Party meeting in Kimberley, 1948. *(Brenthurst Library) Below:* Harry Oppenheimer on the campaign trail, with Bridget at his side. *(Brenthurst Library)*

conscientiously as mayor and MP over a period of many years; and the Oppenheimer name, synonymous with De Beers, lent an added gleam to the city of diamonds. Besides, while the Nationalists were prepared to field candidates in marginal seats on the Rand – and even UP safe seats – they appeared to regard Kimberley as a lost cause. In 1948, there was no challenger from the Nationalists' ranks. Oppenheimer's opponent for the UP nomination was Graham Eden, a crusty character who had been a long-time city councillor, serving as the mayor of Kimberley between 1944 and 1946.[16] Oppenheimer clearly enjoyed Humphreys's support as the retiring member, and the backing of the party machine. In the end, the race was fairly close: Oppenheimer gained 661 votes to Eden's 550, with a 97 per cent turnout of the UP's Kimberley City branch members.[17] Taking the defeat in his stride, Eden went on to serve as Oppenheimer's election agent in the 1948 and 1953 general elections.

Oppenheimer spent the next two months in a flurry of campaigning and canvassing. His adversaries were two independents: William Trehaeven, who had the backing of the Nationalists, and Fred Hicks, who, as a city councillor, had been an implacable and unpleasant foe of Ernest Oppenheimer. It was Hicks who led the charge in questioning Ernest's loyalties to the British Empire during the First World War. It was Hicks who pushed for Ernest's resignation as mayor of Kimberley in 1915. Now, he cast doubt on Harry's commitment to the people of Kimberley. It was a vulnerability. Oppenheimer could hardly be accused of being a carpetbagger, of course; his roots in Kimberley were too deep and strong for that. But Hicks might easily caricature him as an absent political landlord, a sort of distractible dilettante, flitting in and out of Kimberley for meetings at De Beers before returning to his throne in Johannesburg. How could Oppenheimer represent Kimberley if he had no foothold in the community? As a matter of fact, Oppenheimer had taken care to allay such concerns by purchasing Mauritzfontein on the outskirts of the city in 1945. Originally a remount station for British troops during the Anglo-Boer War, Mauritzfontein had been taken over by De Beers and put to use as a stud farm. Harry and Bridget now planned to a build a house and breed racehorses there. Even so, canvassing notes from Oppenheimer's fieldworkers on the campaign suggest a degree of doubtfulness among voters. 'Mr Oppenheimer has too many irons in the fire. He won't have time to worry about the interests of Kimberley,' was a common complaint. Others were more dubious still: 'Mr Oppenheimer has opened up his stud farm, but probably if elected will remove the whole lot to the Transvaal & forget Kimberley.'[18]

These proved to be the concerns of a minority. In any event they were easily dispelled when Oppenheimer took to the dais with quiet, persuasive charm to relay his campaign message. He was a Smuts man. South Africa must stand firm against the rising tide of narrow nationalism and tribal sentiment. Kimberley needed a champion of industry to represent its interests in Parliament. These were the themes that Oppenheimer stressed. On native policy, he was generally more circumspect, but the *Diamond Fields Advertiser* recorded his repudiation of 'the Nationalist policy of apartheid' and his promise to 'further the aspirations of the Coloured population' if he was returned to Parliament.[19] Oppenheimer's sympathies lay broadly with the liberal wing of the UP. Its figurehead was the Deputy Prime Minister, Jan Hofmeyr. Hofmeyr had famously resigned from the cabinet a decade before, during the Fusion government, over General Hertzog's 'native bills', which removed 11 000 African voters from the Cape's common roll and deprived them of the qualified franchise. On the hustings and in their allied press, the Nationalists relentlessly depicted Hofmeyr as a negrophilic bogeyman: the greatest threat to white supremacy and a man who, if he were to succeed Smuts as prime minister one day, would force 'all our daughters ... to marry natives'.[20] Such was the intensity of the attack on Hofmeyr that Harry and Ernest engaged in preliminary negotiations to establish a pro-Hofmeyr press by purchasing the *Sunday Express*, *Saturday Post* and *Natal Witness*. If Hofmeyr had his own press, Harry reasoned at the time, 'he would at least have something to lean on in the event of a clash, say over Native urbanisation'.[21]

Three weeks before election day, Hofmeyr joined Oppenheimer and the Minister of Health, Dr Henry Gluckman, on a platform at the Kimberley City Hall in front of a multiracial audience. The Nationalists were horrified. 'SA ENTERS A NEW EPOCH! MIN. HOFMEYR'S LIBERALISM TRIUMPHS AT UNITED PARTY MEETING! COLOUREDS AND EUROPEANS ON UP PLATFORM,' screamed a pamphlet distributed in the name of the Nationalist candidate for Mayfair.[22] The audience consisted of 'Natives, Coloureds, Malayers, Indians, Chinese, and Europeans', inveighed the outraged leafleteer; and he gasped in horror at the stage decoration – 'banners condemning Nationalism by the Springbok Legion'.

Oppenheimer successfully mobilised war veterans behind his campaign. Foremost among them was the supremely confident, blond, blue-eyed, square-jawed Adolph Gysbert 'Sailor' Malan, former Royal Air

The member for De Beers: Bridget, Harry and Sir Ernest Oppenheimer on election day, 26 May 1948. *(Brenthurst Library)*

Force fighter pilot and hero of the Battle of Britain. On election day, Malan, whose feats of aerial daring had made him a household name, ferried star-struck voters to and from the polls in his sports car. Oppenheimer admired Malan for his enthusiastic and proficient service. For a spell he became Oppenheimer's constituency operative and political secretary. Malan would drive Oppenheimer between speaking engagements while Oppenheimer sat in the back composing his speeches, fitfully looking up to ask, 'Why are we going so slowly?'[23] Sailor's service eventually brought the pilot a 'hefty dividend', according to his biographer: Oppenheimer rewarded him with an enormous pastoral farm in the northern Cape, 'on which sheep supplanted Spitfires as prime living assets'.[24] In the Kimberley City Hall, Ernest took to the podium alongside Hofmeyr and Gluckman to endorse Harry. 'I say to you all: miners, merchants, civil servants, Coloured people', Ernest told the packed hall, 'if you want to make an old man happy, vote for his son.'[25] Bridget also joined Harry in Kimberley. Together with Ernest they criss-crossed the constituency to drum up support and get out the UP vote on 26 May. All their efforts were rewarded when the ballots were counted: Oppenheimer received 5543 votes to Trehaeven's 3277, giving the UP a sizeable majority. Hicks managed to pick up only 101 votes. Harry was going to be the next 'member for De Beers'.

Hofmeyr's support for Oppenheimer had certainly done the United Party no harm in Kimberley. But as the results trickled in from the rest of the country, it soon became clear – even in those urban areas where the UP had traditionally held safe seats – that a slight swing to the Nationalists was under way. In the rural areas – on the platteland – the swing turned into a landslide as the Nationalists drove the UP out from almost every Afrikaner-dominated constituency. The 'crowning disaster', in Alan Paton's words, was when Smuts lost his own seat in Standerton by 224 votes.[26] The unvarnished truth was that the Nationalists' chauvinist appeals to the Afrikaner *volk*, its blood-and-soil patriotism, and its straightforward support for a total separation of the races – the bedrock of apartheid – had resonated with the electorate. Against this powerful, populist offering, the UP's appeals to a hazy white South Africanism and its prevarications on segregation made for weak tea. When Parliament rose in March 1948, the UP had 89 seats. Now, after the election, it was reduced to 65. Together, DF Malan's Nationalists and Nicolaas Havenga's Afrikaner Party had a tally of 79 seats, enough to form a majority government. Harry was to join Parliament on the opposition – not the government – benches, just as his father had done in 1924.

Aftermath

The defeat of Smuts and his United Party government came as a shock to Oppenheimer. Even the Nationalists had believed the UP would be returned with a reduced majority. In retrospect, the UP had been overconfident. Its campaign was lacklustre and feebly organised. According to Smuts's biographer WK Hancock, the UP branches were lethargic; the party had few paid organisers and no youth movement to speak of. It was 'suffering from a hardening of the arteries'.[27] The Nationalists, by contrast, had a substantial force of paid professional organisers, an active youth league, an impassioned sense of self-belief, and a ruthless compulsion to 'conquer and possess' the South African state.[28] It might be said that Smuts, having entered his 80th year, was, like his party, suffering from political sclerosis. In the notes that Oppenheimer compiled for his planned memoir, he recalled that some UP members ascribed the party's defeat to Smuts being 'too old, too vain, too out-of-touch'.[29] In point of fact it was Smuts's deputy, Hofmeyr, who was made the scapegoat by his more conservative colleagues for the UP's humiliation at the polls. Arthur Barlow, the pugnacious blowhard who occupied the Johannesburg–Hospital seat for the UP, claimed the party was 'sick of having to trail Hofmeyr's conscience about'.[30] 'It was a 'Hofmeyr election', Barlow thundered, and it had 'resulted in a debacle for our party'.[31] So long as Hofmeyr was a party leader, the UP would never regain the platteland. This quickly became the conventional wisdom in the UP. Looking back, Oppenheimer remarked that this focus on recovering platteland seats did not 'seem so foolish back then' as the Nationalists had won only a slender majority. Besides, Smuts believed the election result was a 'temporary aberration' that would soon be rectified.[32] This was the thinking and these were the currents in the UP as Oppenheimer prepared to attend his first caucus meeting on 6 July. There were broadly three factions in the caucus. They comprised the Hofmeyr liberals, most prominently Bernard Friedman (MP for Hillbrow); the anti-Hofmeyr group, most notably Barlow; and a large middle section, some of them sympathetic to Hofmeyr, who, in the words of the future UP leader JGN Strauss, regarded 'Hoffie' as 'too heavy to carry and too dangerous to drop'.[33]

Oppenheimer found himself in the middle. He did not have a close personal relationship with Hofmeyr. Nor was he one of those liberals (like the writer-turned-publisher Leo Marquard or the redoubtable 'native representative' Margaret Ballinger) who thought that Hofmeyr should cut the umbilical cord with Smuts and lead his own party. That strand of liberalism would find a home in the Liberal Party, founded five years later. It was temporarily weakened by Hofmeyr's unexpected death in December 1948, which left his supporters in the UP bereft. Of course, once Oppenheimer started asserting himself in Parliament as the party's adroit spokesman on finance, parallels with Hofmeyr were inevitably drawn. 'A young backbencher assumes the mantle of Mr Hofmeyr', was a fairly typical headline in the English-language press during Oppenheimer's early days in Parliament, when he went toe to toe with the Minister of Finance, Havenga.[34] But whatever hopes might have existed in the UP caucus for a liberal successor to Hofmeyr in the immediate wake of his death, they were not pinned on Oppenheimer. And it was only after a new crop of dynamic, younger MPs won their seats on the UP ticket in the 1953 election that these inchoate liberal forces would cohere into something more distinct.

The First Session

The first session of the Tenth Parliament ran from 6 August to 2 October. From the outset, Bridget was determined to be by Harry's side. 'I had decided that I would have as good a staff as possible in JHB & I would travel with Harry & the children would come second,' she wrote matter-of-factly five decades later in her unpublished, handwritten memoirs.[35] She had seen several marriages break up because 'the wife stayed at home & the husband travelled & both were lonely & often found someone else'.[36] She would not let it happen to hers. Nicky Oppenheimer believed that when his mother took her wedding vows, she made a singular 'commitment to be *Mrs* Oppenheimer'. 'She was very clear in what she was doing … she gave up a lot to be the Great Lady.'[37] Bridget's sense of purposefulness seldom brooked opposition. She was not a woman to let obstacles stand in her way. These qualities were to serve Harry well through six decades of marriage. Bridget was a formidable organiser and a punctilious planner. She oversaw the simultaneous running of several (well-staffed) homes with poise. She hosted a dizzying multitude of lunch and dinner guests with ease and enthusiasm, keeping a record – in scores of blue, black and red Smythson notebooks – of every guest, every seating plan, and every menu.[38] Vivacious and sociable, she was in many ways the perfect foil for her quieter, more introverted husband – and she took to the role of parliamentarian's wife with gusto. Bridget fitted in well at Brenthurst. Ernest was close to her. Ina, by contrast, seemed to exude a certain chilliness. 'I wish Bridget & Ina could become friends,' Ernest wrote to Harry in 1948, 'but neither you nor I can solve that problem.'[39]

Harry and Bridget rented a house on Boyes Drive above St James during the first session, and subsequently purchased a small 19th-century cottage from the art dealer André Bothner at 6 Buitencingle (now Buitensingel) Street. It was on the edge of the Malay Quarter, within walking distance of Parliament, and they christened it 'Turkish Delight'. Bridget immediately proceeded to redecorate the house. 'One of the bedrooms has shot silk taffeta curtains with an aurora pink bed … while the curtains in the study are a Burgundy damask with a raised Empire pattern,' the prolific writer Madeleine Masson waxed unctuously in the *Cape Times*, as she sized up the works of Matisse, Derain and Soutine on the walls.[40] The

Oppenheimers' Cape Town residence was to become a centre of bustle for MPs and members of the press gallery while Parliament was in session.

Oppenheimer, meanwhile, threw himself into his portfolio, having taken over from Hofmeyr as the party's most knowledgeable speaker on financial and economic matters. He made his maiden speech on 18 August. It was a wide-ranging discourse on the state of the Union's finances, focusing on the mines. Oppenheimer took aim at the special tax imposed on the diamond mines during the war. It was 'anomalous' and 'inequitable' that this levy should linger on in a budget purporting to mark the end of wartime finance, he protested.[41] The exchange position was hanging like an 'economic cloud over the landscape' with the deficit running at a rate of £80 million annually and the country dependent on continued borrowing from abroad. What the government should be doing to close the deficit, he suggested, was to assist the gold mines in increasing production since gold formed the greater part of the country's exports. That meant making it easier for the mines to get more manpower and essential machinery. But the government should not treat the gold mining industry as an undifferentiated mass, for it comprised many different companies with many kinds of shareholders. The low-grade mines were making negligible profits, and Havenga's tax relief – Oppenheimer called it a 'crumb from the Minister's table' – would be of little benefit to them; they needed measures that would either reduce costs or raise the price of gold. The idea that the profits of high-grade mines should be used to subsidise low-grade mines was most 'inadvisable'. Huge sums of capital were required – the new Orange Free State gold mines alone would need at least £100 million in 'risk capital' – and no one was going to put up that capital if there was any chance of future profits being used to prop up dying mines. Warming to his theme, Oppenheimer sallied: 'The hon Minister of Finance and I have at least one other interest in common besides mining taxation; we are both interested in breeding racehorses. I think he will see that if the prizes of the Turf instead of going to the winner were to be divided among all the runners that would not attract capital into the bloodstock breeding industry. The position is very much the same when it comes to the finance of new mines.'[42] Then, too, the Orange Free State goldfields required skilled immigrant labour, which the government's immigration policy should take into account. Finally, Oppenheimer turned to 'native wage' increases. If increased wages were to be granted to Europeans, 'then at the same time increased wages should be granted to native workers … because it is just, and … because it is expedient'. Better wages meant more labourers on the mines and that meant more gold production.

This was standard Oppenheimer fare. Ernest had said it all before in Parliament (often scripted by Harry), and Harry had conveyed the same message frequently on a variety of public platforms over the preceding decade. As a maiden speech, however, it was an assured performance. Anthony Hocking, Oppenheimer's first biographer, records that he began his speech quietly, 'almost apologetically ... hands behind his back, nervous at first, but gradually gaining in confidence'.[43] The *Sunday Times* political correspondent observed of Oppenheimer a few years later that he 'affects a semi-apologetic manner, which is a product of complete confidence in his views'.[44] The diffidence was not altogether an affectation. Oppenheimer had a natural reserve. But it was certainly cultivated as part of his signature style, a hallmark of the polished urbanity that many of his subordinates in Anglo American would later seek to emulate.

The Forum, a magazine started with Hofmeyr's help in 1938, called his maiden speech 'excellent'.[45] *Die Suiderstem*, a UP mouthpiece, declared Oppenheimer '*Die man van die dag*' (The man of the day). Bridget kept all the press cuttings and letters of congratulation in one of the seventy-odd scrapbooks she maintained throughout her marriage. One of the missives was from Smuts: 'My dear Harry, Just a line to tell you with what deep pleasure I listened to your speech in the Budget debate yesterday. It went right to the real significance of the present situation ... Your constructive suggestions were also very interesting. My hearty congratulations and best wishes for your career in public life'.[46] Margaret Ballinger deemed it an 'excellent' speech: 'very encouraging to us [native representatives]'.[47] Hofmeyr sent Oppenheimer his 'hearty congratulations', too, telling him that Sir Ernest 'would have been very happy'.[48] It was a promising start to Harry's political career.

Enhanced, no doubt, by his wealth and his power, and Bridget's glamour, Harry rapidly became a name to be reckoned with in the UP establishment. He developed a reputation as one of the most promising backbenchers among the new crop. When the House reconvened in the new year, he spoke in the appropriation debate. The *Cape Times* praised him for 'the cogency of his lucid arguments' and confidently predicted that he would soon be established as 'one of the most eminent speakers ... on economic and financial subjects'.[49] The *Cape Argus* declared that Oppenheimer had made 'easily the back-bench speech of this session': 'Mr Oppenheimer wounds with a gentle smile, and his well-modulated voice suggests expert knowledge rather than prejudiced assertion.'[50] Coming from the English-language press, with its historical links to the mining finance houses,[51] such plaudits might be regarded as perfunctory. Smuts, however, was not a man to pay gratuitous compliments, and he commended Oppenheimer for a 'ripping good speech'.[52] Harry Lawrence, another party veteran and Smuts's former Minister of Justice, commented that Parliament had been greatly strengthened by 'new and young members' such as Oppenheimer, De Villiers Graaff, and Marais Steyn (who had beaten the Nationalists' candidate, Hendrik Verwoerd, in Alberton). These three recruits were destined to 'play leading parts' in the affairs of the party, and in helping it to 'regain ground temporarily lost', Lawrence predicted.[53]

The United South Africa Trust Fund

So it came to pass. Oppenheimer took wry pleasure in being described as a brilliant young backbencher when he was, in his own words, 'a successful middle-aged businessman'.[54] Whatever his age, the UP made sure to capitalise on Harry's energy and acumen. There was one immediate priority: to resuscitate the party's moribund organisational machinery. As the UP's top brass surveyed its electoral wreckage, Oppenheimer was swiftly identified as someone with the expertise to rebuild and steady the ship. He understood the policy environment, he knew how to build and consolidate organisations, and he had unparalleled access to a network of potential donors in the business community. Oppenheimer was co-opted onto various committees: the finance committee, which was to replenish party coffers; a so-called action committee, which was to restore party structures; and a national advisory committee, an independent body that included leading businessmen, and that assisted with fundraising, publicity and propaganda. As Oppenheimer's star rose in the UP, the Nationalists identified him as a significant threat. The result was that he assumed Hofmeyr's mantle in another way: Oppenheimer became the focus of Nationalist opprobrium and a target for vilification. The old antisemitic trope of 'Hoggenheimer' was revived.

The UP was in desperate need of money. Towards the end of 1949, on Oppenheimer's suggestion, the United South Africa Trust Fund – a funding vehicle at arm's length from the party – was created with Smuts's blessing. On 27 January 1950, the fund's trustees – a who's who of prominent individuals in commerce, mining and industry – were appointed with

Oppenheimer as chairman and Smuts's loyal aide Henry Cooper as secretary.[55] The objects of the fund, as set out in its constitution, were to assist in the 'building up of a united democratic South African nation' on the basis of the Union's constitution.[56] The fund sought the 'elimination of racialism' and all factors 'tending to the disruption or the abandonment of democratic principles'. It strove for goodwill and co-operation between the races 'under European leadership', on the basis of full equality between English-speakers and Afrikaners. The fund would promote and defend freedom of speech, language, worship and the 'fundamental rights of man' as recognised by the member states of the United Nations. However, it stopped short of endorsing the Universal Declaration of Human Rights (from whose adoption at the United Nations in 1948 South Africa had abstained, along with the Soviet bloc and Saudi Arabia). The fund would also promote the economic development of the Union 'in the best interests of the people of the country'. In short, there was little to distinguish the fund's purposes from those of the UP. Both advocated a broad Anglo-Afrikaner civic patriotism (or South Africanism), rooted in the language of human rights and private enterprise. Both emphasised white leadership and soft-pedalled the issue of human rights for those who were not white. Like Smuts himself – he had shaped the preamble to the United Nations Charter in 1945 with its explicit mention of human rights – the fund (and the UP) embodied a host of contradictions. The trustees stated baldly that the strength of the fund was the strength of the United Party; the fund could do little to achieve its main objects outside political action on the part of the UP; and its principal goal was really to ensure 'that the United Party is returned to power'.[57]

Oppenheimer spent a great deal of his time rattling the tin can for funds. He wrote to all the major mining finance houses, asking for a commitment of £25 000 each over a three- or four-year period. Such was Oppenheimer's success in mobilising the mining houses that by 31 December 1950 the United South Africa Trust Fund had gathered £173 505.15 into its bank account, of which £149 848 was paid over to the United Party Central Fund.[58] The Nationalists soon caught wind. The prospect of a cash-flush opposition, intent on revitalising its organisation, alarmed them. After all, they were still electorally vulnerable. Their victory in 1948 had largely been secured by a system of demarcation that favoured platteland constituencies. This is where they harvested a bumper crop of votes. But the Nationalists' overall majority was relatively tenuous. The UP received over 100 000 more votes than the Malan–Havenga alliance in 1948. Word of the fund soon spread. It brought to the surface all of the Nationalists' old fears and paranoia about *die geldmag*, represented by the sinister figure of 'Hoggenheimer'.

'Hoggenheimer', the bogeyman embodying Jewish mining capital, was a regular feature of Nationalist rhetoric in the first half of the 20th century, but after the 1948 election the phrase had more or less been retired from service. However, when the news broke about the United South Africa Trust Fund, and Oppenheimer's involvement in it, the Nationalists resurrected the libel with relish. On 19 February 1951, the Nationalist MP for Vereeniging, Dr JH Loock – a former UP organiser and noxious turncoat – rose from his bench in the House to speak 'on behalf of the Afrikaner nation'.[59] He branded Oppenheimer 'the real Hoggenheimer' and the 'power behind the throne' in the UP.[60] Claiming that the United South Africa Trust Fund was already £1 million in the black – 'What is £1,000,000 to some of the mining magnates on the other side of the House?' – Loock denounced the fund as an attempt to 'kill the Nationalist Party' and 'subdue the Afrikaner'. Harry Lawrence shot to Oppenheimer's defence, and the Speaker ordered Loock to withdraw his slurs. But the die was cast. 'Hoggenheimer is back,' the *Sunday Times* declared.[61] Further afield, *The Economist* pricked its ears; 'Hoggenheimer rides again,' it announced.[62]

The Nationalist press went into overdrive. It carried frenzied denunciations of Oppenheimer and the fund by members of Malan's cabinet. The Minister of Lands and Irrigation, JG Strijdom, whose sobriquet was 'Lion of the North', claimed that the fund wanted to get rid of the colour bar in industry. He branded it a threat to 'white civilisation' driven by 'big capitalists'.[63] Two other Nationalist MPs, Nico Diederichs and Albertus van Rhyn, warned that if the gold mines contributed money to the fund, then demands for nationalisation of the industry might become 'too strong for the government to resist'.[64] In Durban the Nationalists organised one of their *stryddag* (struggle day) meetings, graced by the doctrinaire and domineering Minister of Native Affairs, HF Verwoerd. A large painting of an octopus, meant to depict the fund, was prominently displayed. Atop the canvas were the words 'Kill the Trust Fund', and it was surrounded by caricatures of Oppenheimer. Attendees were invited to throw objects, three for a shilling, at the target.[65]

Oppenheimer remained unruffled. In Kimberley, he coolly told his constituents that there was nothing secretive or sinister about the fund. But Loock reprised his attack in the House, calling for an investigation into the 'secret large-scale subsidisation' of political parties by 'certain powerful interest groups'.[66] His rambling speech was punctuated with vicious antisemitism, and the *Rand Daily Mail* observed that Oppenheimer 'tidied him up so neatly' afterwards that there was 'very little left' of Loock's arguments.[67] Oppenheimer patiently explained the fund's aims and objects, heckled throughout his speech by the thuggish Nationalist MP for George, PW Botha. The fund donated money to the UP, he said, because it was 'in sympathy with the party's published policy' and because it admired the UP's war record.[68] The fact of the matter, Oppenheimer claimed, was that the 'great majority' of the population depended on the UP for the 'defence of their liberty': the party had to win back power from the Nationalists, who were a 'menace to the country'.

Oppenheimer was firmly in the Nationalists' cross hairs. They regarded him as a Machiavellian power-broker in the UP, its de facto leader, and an existential threat to the Afrikaner *volk*. In the words of the Nationalist MP for Pretoria Central, Dr JG van den Heever, Oppenheimer was the UP's 'master'; the UP was the 'Oppenheimer party' and it advocated the 'liberalistic Oppenheimer doctrine'.[69] Oppenheimer's putative leadership of the UP – the idea that he was the party's puppet master – was underscored by the fact that Smuts's successor lacked a certain heft. Before Smuts fell ill and died in September 1950, he had anointed as his heir the able and articulate lawyer JGN Strauss, the MP for Germiston (District). Strauss was highly intelligent and an excellent debater, but he did not enjoy the universal confidence of his party colleagues. Many of them believed Strauss was too inexperienced, too abrasive and too aloof to lead the caucus.[70] They would have preferred the charming and affable De Villiers Graaff to succeed Smuts. However, Div did not yet feel ready to assume the leadership.[71] To exacerbate matters, even though Strauss was almost 50, he had a callow, youthful appearance. Coupled with his shyness, it created the impression that he was not altogether in charge, and the Nationalists sensed it. Strauss seemed to wither in the shadow of Oppenheimer and Graaff, or '*die ryk jongelinge*' (the rich young men) as they were later dubbed by the Nationalist press.[72] This heightened tensions over leadership in the UP caucus, all of which came to a head after the 1953 election and in the aftermath of the Torch Commando.

The Torch Commando

Section 35 of the Act of Union entrenched the right of Coloured voters in the Cape to a qualified franchise on the common roll. To amend it, a two-thirds majority in a joint sitting of the House of Assembly and the Senate was required. After the 1948 election, the Nationalists had no such majority. But they were determined to abolish the common-roll voting rights of Coloureds whatever obstacles might lie in their path. Together with the passage of cornerstone apartheid legislation – the Group Areas Act and the Population Registration Act were both enacted in 1950 – the removal of Coloured voters from the common roll became an urgent priority for the Nats. In February 1951, they introduced the Separate Representation of Voters Bill. This was to be a matter of great constitutional import.

The threat to the Coloured franchise served as a rallying cause for politically awakened ex-servicemen. In 1949, the left-leaning Springbok Legion had seen the issue coming down the tracks and met with Smuts and Oppenheimer to discuss it. Despite the Legion's reputation for radicalism, Oppenheimer gave the Legionnaires to understand that he would provide assistance to them.[73] After the introduction of the Separate Representation of Voters Bill, matters gathered steam. In April 1951 a variety of ex-servicemen's organisations – including representatives from the United Party – came together to form the War Veterans' Action Committee. On 4 May 1951, a mass meeting was held in Johannesburg with over four thousand veterans and twenty thousand spectators. Contingents of ex-servicemen and women, including a column of Coloured ex-servicemen, carried lit torches in a march-past to protest against the government's plans. Sailor Malan, no longer in Oppenheimer's formal employ, addressed the crowds. 'It is good to see this support in protest against the rape of the Constitution and the attack on our rights and liberties as free men,' he told the serried throng.[74] These were fighting words, and they tapped into a rich vein of discontent among veterans imbued with the spirit of wartime idealism. Soon there were mass gatherings in all the main cities, and plans were made to deliver a petition to the Prime Minister. Ex-servicemen from across the country travelled to Cape Town, transported in jeep convoys that converged on the Grand Parade, where they formed a 'Steel Commando'. Over sixty thousand spectators cheered them on. The Nationalists, fearing military insurrection, placed machine guns on the roof of Parliament. It was a terrific show of force by the war veterans, and it revealed just how insecure the Nationalists were about their hold on power.

The War Veterans' Action Committee and the Steel Commando morphed into the Torch Commando, established on 28 June 1951 with Sailor Malan as its president and Louis Kane-Berman as its chairman. The 'Torch', as it was colloquially known, represented a broad front of extra-parliamentary opposition to the Nationalists. As such, it was the site of all sorts of competing factions and interests.[75] The UP had been involved, behind the scenes, in the lead-up to its creation. Oppenheimer fought shy of direct involvement, but he could see the movement's potential to galvanise anti-Nationalist sentiment and energise support for the UP. He lobbied discreetly for Sailor Malan to play a leading role. The airman's command, Oppenheimer felt, would defuse the more radical impulses of the leftist Legionnaires. Oppenheimer also persuaded Malan to let Marais Steyn have a hand in drafting the Torch's constitution. At times, the UP felt it necessary to try to keep the veterans in check. One of the calls initially made by the War Veterans' Action Committee was that the Nationalist government should resign and seek a fresh mandate. Oppenheimer and De Villiers Graaff were nominated to dissuade the committee from making this demand. The UP was in no state, they pointed out, to contest an early election.

Oppenheimer appeared on platforms around the country with Torch supporters in tow. In Kimberley, he branded DF Malan a 'pocket dictator' and declared the Separate Representation of Voters Act (enacted on 18 June 1951, but nullified by the Appellate Division of the Supreme Court in March 1952) 'not an act of Parliament, but an act of revolution'.[76] It was a violation of the constitution, he charged. In Pretoria, Oppenheimer was heckled at a public meeting by Robey Leibbrandt, the pugilistic pro-Nazi insurrectionist tried for treason during the war. He asked Oppenheimer if Jews were at the root of all the world's troubles.[77] The Nationalists, for their part, drew a straight line between Oppenheimer, Anglo American, the United South Africa Trust Fund and the Torch Commando. In the House, Loock likened Oppenheimer to Rhodes and Sailor Malan to Jameson: they were involved, he insinuated, in an audacious plan to depose the government. JG Strijdom claimed that the Torch had been formed by 'Oppenheimers Ltd.' to bring down the government.[78] DF Malan launched a bitter attack on Oppenheimer, warning his constituents in Citrusdal that the Torch was sailing under false colours. The organisation was in essence a private army established to unseat the government, he fulminated, funded by 'Mr Oppenheimer and the great money powers' who wanted to replace white labour with black labour so that they could make more money.[79] In Porterville, Malan renewed his attack. Oppenheimer and the shadowy forces of 'money power' controlled the United Party and now they were directing the Torch. Oppenheimer, with his millions, had become a 'power in the land'; he wielded a greater influence than 'any man in South Africa' ever had.[80]

Oppenheimer brushed aside the Prime Minister's claims, protesting that Malan was 'off his rocker'. The Torch was largely self-sustaining, he said, adding with customary understatement: 'my own contribution is in keeping with my means, and I am not exactly poor'.[81] In fact, Louis Kane-Berman would later claim that Oppenheimer had promised to finance the Torch, and that he encouraged the organisation not to dissipate its efforts on fundraising at fetes and the like. However, when Torch leaders started expressing views that diverged from those of the UP – the Torch bitterly resented the UP's support of the Nationalists' 'Whipping Bill', introduced in response to the 1952 Defiance Campaign, for example, and staged a national day of protest against the law – Oppenheimer got cold feet. The money dried up.

The Torch continued to muster its huge base of volunteers behind the UP in the run-up to the 1953 election, as part of its support for a broader 'United Front' that included the Labour Party. But there were clearly unstated tensions between Kane-Berman and Oppenheimer. Keith Acutt, who scrambled up the corporate ladder at Anglo American after starting out as an office boy, joined the Torch as an organiser. He kept Oppenheimer apprised of developments on the ground. Kane-Berman came to regard Acutt, not altogether warmly, as the 'eyes and ears of Oppenheimer'.[82] Another Torch activist, Guy Nicholson, a close companion of Acutt's, met Oppenheimer through Sailor Malan and became a lifelong friend. He went on to join Rhoanglo in 1953. After the UP's dismal showing at the polls that year – it managed to lose another seven seats, though Oppenheimer retained his – the Torch imploded. Sailor Malan retreated to his sheep farm and Acutt went to head up the Anglo American office in Salisbury. The end of the Torch Commando heralded, in Kane-Berman's view, the ultimate collapse of the United Party almost twenty-five years later. The Torch's rapid demise signalled a failure not so much of its own leadership as of the UP's. The official opposition failed to harness a powerful resource optimally, and in that Oppenheimer's faltering support played a role.

Leadership Tensions after the 1953 Election

The 1953 election result came as a devastating blow to the United Party. The UP had regarded the Nationalists' victory in 1948 as a short-lived setback. But five years later the ruling party was returned with an increased majority: it now occupied 94 seats to the UP's 57 in the House of Assembly. Inevitably, blame fell on Strauss. The English-language press led the charge – 'Off with his head,'[83] shouted the *Sunday Express* – but there were plenty of detractors in Strauss's own party scheming to get rid of him. In the caucus, deep fissures existed between conservatives and liberals over the UP's position on the Coloured franchise and its approach to some apartheid bills. A further fracturing occurred once several newly elected MPs – among them Helen Suzman, Zach de Beer (Strauss's son-in-law), Ray Swart, Owen Townley Williams, Jan Steytler, Izak Fourie and John Cope – formed a liberal ginger group within the caucus. Strauss attempted to placate both factions but ended up alienating them in equal measure. The strain of holding these irreconcilable forces together began to take its toll. Strauss grew more unapproachable and reclusive: he rejected invitations to address public meetings, and when he did accept them he became racked with anxiety. He appeared lethargic and depressed. 'Strauss came to see me at the office,' Oppenheimer recorded in his diary. 'He was gloomy & showed no sign of new thought.'[84] The quality of Strauss's contributions in the House became uneven. 'I doubt very much whether he [Strauss] will have sufficient courage to be lucid,' Oppenheimer reflected acidly the day before a major debate.[85]

There were intensified mutterings about Strauss's leadership. Colin Steyn, the party's Orange Free State senator, believed Oppenheimer should take the reins. But Oppenheimer dismissed Steyn's approach as 'absurd'.[86] In part, his patience for the drudgery of party duties was diminishing. A contemporary diary entry captures something of Oppenheimer's exasperation: 'Almost the whole day was taken up with a UP Central Executive meeting. The usual demand for an Afrikaans newspaper; the usual complete neglect of financial limitations; the usual refusal to get down to practical work; the usual eagerness to listen … to rubbish provided it comes from the Afrikaans-speaking platteland.'[87] In the August provincial elections, which Strauss sat out owing to severe flu, the Nationalists captured 12 more UP seats, adding to the party's woes. By September, a consensus had developed that Strauss should step down from his position. 'Talked politics with Harry Lawrence &

Sidney Waterson – "Strauss must go" ... Think we are all in agreement,' Oppenheimer noted in his diary.[88] But who should fill the void? Attention started settling on Div.

At Brenthurst, Div dined with Oppenheimer and Harry Lawrence, laying on the charm. 'It was very pleasant & Div made an excellent impression on Harry L. & me. No-one can be perfect but he is very good & of course another class to Strauss.'[89] Meanwhile, the editor of the *Rand Daily Mail*, Paddy Cartwright, reached out to Lawrence on behalf of other editors and prominent businessmen, and asked him to have a word in Strauss's ear about bowing out. This Lawrence did, but Strauss was unmoved. An 'overwhelming' sense of duty compelled Strauss to stay on, he briefed his followers, besides which he suspected that Div might compromise on the Coloured franchise.[90] Lawrence submitted a more formal proposal at a party meeting in November, but Strauss headed this off once more. By January of the following year, Oppenheimer, having conferred with Div, thought the prognosis was grim. The party had 'no confidence' in Strauss, Oppenheimer wrote in his diary, and discontent was 'very strong just below the surface'; Strauss, however, seemed 'cock-a-hoop', believing that he could rely on '*die volk daarbuite*' (the people out there) if not on his colleagues.[91]

Strauss clung on until November 1956. It was a drawn-out, damaging incumbency facilitated in part by Div's lack of focused ambition – for all his stature, Div was lackadaisical and vacillated over his leadership bid – but also by Oppenheimer's reluctance to get his own hands dirty. It was a combination that made for dilatoriness. Unwilling to wear the crown himself, Oppenheimer might at least have wielded the scalpel on Div's behalf. In fairness, Oppenheimer had latent reservations about Div. He thought that some of Div's speeches were 'without form & quite ineffective'. Div would be 'our best leader & yet one can't help [having] certain misgivings,' Oppenheimer confided in his diary.[92] One of these qualms was that Div could be 'wishy-washy',[93] that he exhibited 'endless caution',[94] being especially paranoid not to alienate the party's staunch supporters (the *bloedsappe*) in the platteland. In later years, Oppenheimer would wryly remark, 'I've always thought that Sir De Villiers Graaff should have had the courage of my convictions!'[95]

Jan Morris profiled Oppenheimer for the *Manchester Guardian*, and described him as a 'queer and magnetic figure' who – despite a 'diffident, lopsided appearance' – projected a sense of bigness and significance as he took his seat among 'the mediocrities' in the House of Assembly.[96]

Oppenheimer brought to the Assembly 'a suggestion of power and authority', Morris observed, and he 'leavened its pitifully provincial manners as a Churchill or Bevan gives stature to the House of Commons'. But it remained only a suggestion. It is true that Oppenheimer briefly assumed the chairmanship of the Witwatersrand UP in June 1957, but this was an administrative job. Unlike Churchill or Bevan, Oppenheimer was unwilling to take on the burdens of direct political leadership. He was perfectly happy to act as a patron, or exercise soft power, or engross himself in the responsibilities of a party functionary, but, beyond that, he balked. It was not for want of vigour and drive, intellectual or physical: Oppenheimer was possessed of enormous vitality. But something within held him back.

Helen Suzman, a feisty, razor-tongued new backbencher who went on to enjoy a long and stellar parliamentary career (fortified by Oppenheimer's support and friendship over the course of several decades), sometimes resented his lack of assertiveness in the UP caucus. 'At times when I was engaged in fierce caucus rows, his diffidence upset me ... But Harry was reluctant to throw his weight about; he probably exerted more influence behind the scenes than he did in caucus.'[97] Zach de Beer, an intelligent and self-assured young medical doctor with dark, hooded eyes, was another of the liberal-minded novitiates in caucus. He shared Oppenheimer's ironic humour and intellectual inclinations, and he quickly earned the elder man's trust and affinity. De Beer would later straddle careers in Parliament and Anglo American. In hindsight, De Beer regarded as unfounded the notion that Oppenheimer's excursion into politics was a 'temporary and almost dilettante period'.[98] De Beer recalled a trip in 1955 with Oppenheimer and Sailor Malan to Shangani, where Oppenheimer spoke frankly with the pair after dinner. 'Now I want absolute candour from you two ... Is there really a purpose in my going on in politics?' he asked.[99] This De Beer understood as a sign of Oppenheimer's political ambition: 'Could he really get to the top, he asked, despite the political disadvantages of his name, his wealth, his "Englishness" and so on? Sailor and I both thought he could – he could overcome all that, he had the ability, the personal charm, the stamina. His question really reveals how immensely keen he was. He was saying, "If I give politics the first place in my life, is it going to be worthwhile?"'[100] The anecdote, as relayed by De Beer, is indeed revealing, although perhaps not for the reasons De Beer imagined. It seems probable that Oppenheimer's question was asked more in doubt than in hope. He was shrewd enough to know that what disadvantaged him politically benefited him commercially. Oppenheimer was always more likely, in a country poised politically between rival nationalisms, to garner success as a businessman rather than as prime minister. And his dominion over E Oppenheimer and Son, Anglo American and De Beers was assured.

A Free Soul

Gavin Relly, of a similar age to De Beer, was a thrusting, politically astute 23-year-old when he joined the staff of Anglo American in 1949. He had already done some work for De Villiers Graaff, and it was not long before Oppenheimer put Relly's talents to use as his own political secretary. In later years, Relly reflected nostalgically on this period as a relatively carefree one in Oppenheimer's life. Ernest was in command of the whole group and personally running the diamond business, so it was a fitting time for Harry to be involved in politics. 'Politics enabled him to be a free soul, to do his own thing, and he derived tremendous enjoyment from that,' Relly mused.[101]

The commitments imposed by Harry's later chairmanship of Anglo and De Beers were much fewer in his parliamentary years. He could pursue his pastimes at greater leisure. He invited Joane Pim, Anglo American's landscape architect, to design an indigenous garden at Mauritzfontein; it was a project that delighted him, even if, in its early stages, the garden looked 'like a diamond diggings'.[102] He expanded his collection of French Impressionist paintings. He cultivated his taste for beautiful clocks, cameras and objets d'art. A new model Leica took his fancy: 'Could not resist buying this & selling my existing camera in part exchange,' he jotted in his diary.[103] An advertisement for a rare antique solid silver Georgian snuffbox depicting a scene from Mazeppa caught his eye. 'I shall try to buy [it],' he wrote, and he was inspired to re-read Lord Byron's poem.[104] Oppenheimer read prolifically and was catholic in his tastes. In addition to Shakespeare and the Romantic poets, a small selection of the reading material mentioned in his diaries in the mid-1950s would include Benjamin Constant's *Adolphe*; the poetry of Baudelaire, 'a pleasant change',[105] he suggested, after all the Afrikaans lessons he had been taking with Sarah Goldblatt, CJ Langenhoven's fiery literary executrix; Julian Huxley's *From an Antique Land*; and Orwell's *1984*, which Zach de Beer had sent him.

He devoted more time to his burgeoning interest in horse-breeding and racing. Bridget had never been much captivated by racing, but gradually she became completely 'fascinated'.[106] They took on Tim Furness, a former tobacco farmer from Rhodesia, as their trainer. At Mauritzfontein, Ernest's friend Lord Rosebery, a British Liberal Party politician and horse-breeder of renown, set them up with two foundation mares in foal and a stallion, Hobo. In 1953 Harry and Bridget scored the first major victory in their distinctive black-and-yellow silks in the Cape Metropolitan Handicap at Kenilworth. Prince Bertrand, 'an extremely clever horse' in Bridget's recollection, who Harry always felt 'could read the bookmakers' boards' and didn't try very hard when he was the bookies' favourite, stormed home to win. Ernest had dreamt that Prince Bertrand would triumph, and placed a hefty bet on him at generous odds of 33/1. Harry, never a prodigious punter, backed him at £5 each way. Bridget was far less optimistic about Prince Bertrand's chances. After the horses had paraded, she retired to the car in the picnic area, where she proceeded to remove her shoes and hat and listen to the commentary on the radio. Suddenly the commentator was calling out Prince Bertrand's name. There was a mad scramble as Bridget rushed off towards the winner's enclosure, only to realise on arrival that she was shoeless and hatless. She dashed back to the car to dress properly. But by the time she had composed herself, it was too late to lead Prince Bertrand in. Nevertheless, the spell was cast. From this moment on, Bridget would later recall: 'We were hooked on racing.'[107] Meanwhile, the first thing Oppenheimer did in the office on Monday morning after Prince Bertrand's win was to dictate a letter to Billie Chapple in the Diamond Corporation's London office. He asked Chapple to purchase an initialled leather briefcase for his trainer's son, Tony Furness, because the boy looked on each horse in training as his personal responsibility.[108] This was a thoughtful and delicate touch, which Oppenheimer often gave to his gift-giving.

Oppenheimer took his pleasures where he could but, in truth, he was not a free soul; he still had multiple obligations outside politics. During his time in Parliament, Oppenheimer was forever in action and on the move, attending board meetings, writing and delivering speeches, and closely involving himself in all aspects of the business. He opened gold mines in the Orange Free State. He plotted the development of uranium production. He shuttled to and from the Federation of Rhodesia and Nyasaland. There he conducted discussions on whether a planned hydroelectric power project should be undertaken at Kafue or Kariba. In Northern Rhodesia, he busied himself with copper concerns. In Southern

Rhodesia, he concerned himself with the Wankie Colliery, Rhodesian Alloys and Anglo's chrome interests. He flew several times a year to London, Antwerp and New York on diamond business. He consulted constantly with his father on sundry matters and transactions. And he was continuously thinking about the organisation of Anglo and De Beers: whose skills and which personality would fit best where.

Harry's demeanour – suave and self-effacing – meant that he seldom expressed himself in public with anything other than consummate restraint. Those who annoyed him, or failed to measure up to his standards, were often met with dignified silence or devastating politeness. Michael Phillimore, a family friend whose young son, Roger, was Harry's godson, wanted to know why he was not progressing up the ranks at Anglo. Oppenheimer recorded in his diary: 'Embarrassing interview with Michael Phillimore. He is worried because he does not get on at the office. I had to try to put our reasons for lack of confidence honestly but politely.'[109] This was a comparatively gentle reflection, for Oppenheimer's public courtesy belied a private acerbity. His diaries reveal a propensity to sardonicism. He was not above a sporadic spot of snobbery. At one 'really appalling' dinner party, most of the guests were unknown to him; 'judging purely on appearance I had not missed much,' he observed tartly.[110] His barbs were often aimed at his colleagues, whose perceived demerits Oppenheimer would assess trenchantly. RB Hagart 'was silly & irritating about the Free State mines – criticising from the depths of his ignorance.'[111] Guy Young, one of the wartime comrades Harry brought into the business, talked 'as though he was running the industrial diamond business', but it was 'a great comfort to know he is not'.[112] Sidney Spiro, who married Diney Susskind, the (much younger) daughter of Ernest's great friends Fred and Doff, and whose career in Anglo Ernest launched, was, in Harry's view, in spite of his great fondness for the man, 'tactless, overambitious & [had] too much bounce'.[113]

Oppenheimer could be a perspicacious judge of character and an able talent-spotter, surrounding himself, like Alfred Milner a half-century before, with a kindergarten of bright, young (often Oxford-trained) male acolytes. Derek Henderson, appointed by Oppenheimer as his personal assistant in 1956, went on to become a distinguished academic and ended his career as the vice-chancellor of Rhodes University. Henderson would 'be very good when he gets less shy,' Oppenheimer pronounced after their first meeting.[114] But Oppenheimer's judgements were not always correct or prescient (or, for that matter, eternally damning). In 1954, he lunched for the first time with Charles W Engelhard Jr, the exuberant American heir to a precious metals and chemical empire. Oppenheimer was unimpressed. 'Engelhart [*sic*] makes a poor impression,' he recorded curtly in his diary.[115] Yet Engelhard ('Charlie', as HFO went on to call him) became a great friend and possibly the most consequential business contact Oppenheimer ever made.

Alongside his political commitments, the range of Oppenheimer's commercial involvements was bewildering. As chairman of the committee responsible for the development of the Orange Free State goldfields, he was intimately involved in Anglo American's new El Dorado. Throughout the 1950s, he presided over ceremonial sod-turnings and mine-openings. In 1953, he opened Anglo American's first uranium plant at the Daggafontein mine. In 1954, he brokered a deal between Jack Scott and Sir George Albu that saw the General Mining and Finance Corporation make its landmark acquisition of Scott's Strathmore Consolidated Investments, thus adding the Stilfontein and Buffelsfontein gold mines to General Mining's stable.[116] The transaction ultimately led to Anglo taking effective control of General Mining. In collaboration with his father, he masterminded the creation of the International Diamond Security Organisation – formed to stanch the flow of smuggled diamonds out of Central and West Africa – and brought in the retired head of MI5, Percy Sillitoe, to run it.[117] And he led the formation of a committee to initiate business in minerals 'of which we know little', he wrote in his diary, 'such as lithium, titanium etc.'[118] In 1955, he helped establish Union Acceptances, patterned on Lazard, as South Africa's first merchant bank.[119] In 1956, he worked hard to interest both Rio Tinto and the Newmont Mining Corporation in co-operating with Anglo on a prospecting concession in the Western Rift area of Tanganyika.[120] In 1957, Anglo opened up the world's deepest gold mine in collaboration with Central Mining and Consolidated Gold Fields. This was the Western Deep Levels mine, south of Blyvooruitzicht and West Driefontein on the West Wits Line.

Oppenheimer also concerned himself with more mundane arrangements. The Oxford economist Professor Herbert Frankel had agreed to help Sir Theodore Gregory with his book on Ernest Oppenheimer and the economic development of southern Africa – for a period of three years at the remuneration of £5000. Rather ingeniously, Frankel sought payment in the form of diamonds, to which scheme Harry Oppenheimer gave his blessing.[121] And throughout the decade, Oppenheimer took the lead in negotiating the renewal of diamond contracts in the Belgian Congo and

Tanganyika. The latter brought him into close contact with the volatile Dr John Williamson, owner of the Williamson mine, and his slippery sidekick, Iqbal Chand Chopra, a flamboyant lawyer. The Williamson mine was to play a critical role in Oppenheimer's early chairmanship of De Beers. In all of this, intermittently, Ernest needed management and mollification. Harry discovered that two family trusties, Ted Brown and Pierre Crokaert, had been dealing in diamonds on a large scale for their own account. He was sure that they were not dealing for themselves, but 'on behalf of Papa'. 'I don't like this sort of thing at all,' he complained in his diary. 'I suppose I ought to try to see that everything is put in good order. I have been too much inclined to ignore what I don't like.'[122] Ernest was also somewhat disobliged when he was not appointed to the board of Union Acceptances, and so Harry relinquished his directorship in favour of his father. 'He was delighted & I was glad I had fixed matters this way,' Harry recorded.[123]

Apace with the business commitments was the never-ending succession of social commitments, which Bridget relished more than Harry. 'This week I have had to go to a great many parties, most of which I found very boring,' Harry wrote to Nicky. 'Mummy, of course, enjoyed herself very much but all this put me in a very bad temper.'[124] Even with all his reserves of energy, Oppenheimer found himself stretched, continually having to juggle political and business commitments. He was a dutiful party campaigner. In 1954, he undertook to canvass on behalf of United Party candidates ahead of the provincial elections in Natal. The newly formed Union Federal Party (an outgrowth of the Torch Commando) threatened to win over English-speaking UP voters there by tapping into pro-Commonwealth sentiment and a desire for greater provincial autonomy. Oppenheimer found himself hopping between public meetings in Pietermaritzburg, Impendle ('to find only 3 people'),[125] Bulwer, Glencoe, Babanango, Nqutu ('listened to with apparent satisfaction by 25 of the [party] faithful')[126] and Durban. But it was draining. In Glencoe he 'was tired & bored & made a dull speech'.[127]

All of this took a toll, as Oppenheimer privately conceded: 'Went to Holy Communion at St George's. My life is too rushed nowadays and I have a bad habit of giving only half my attention to what I am doing because I am at the same time thinking of what I am going to do next. I was concerned to find myself [thinking] like this even in Church.'[128] A day later he had 'pretty well decided that I must get out of politics'.[129] Oppenheimer realised that sooner or later the choice between business and politics had to be made; 'the combination just doesn't work – & as things are I don't spend more than 4 months in the year at home,' he reproached himself.[130] And when Oppenheimer *was* travelling, the occasional domestic drama back home might make its way into the newspapers to tantalise a gossip-hungry public. In December 1955, while Oppenheimer was on a trip to the Belgian Congo, burglars broke into Little Brenthurst and made off with most of Bridget's jewellery collection worth £250 000.[131] 'This is most upsetting,' Oppenheimer wrote in his diary. 'I fear there must have been the most undesirable publicity.'[132] For a private man, it rankled.

Jack Higgerty, chief whip of the UP, persuaded Oppenheimer not to resign his seat. Strauss urged Oppenheimer to stay on and told him that if the UP returned to power, he would be 'assured of an important position' in the cabinet.[133] But, as it turned out, Ernest's health was precarious. He suffered several coronary episodes. By the middle of the decade, Harry could not envisage continuing in Parliament beyond the 1958 election. He had his own sporadic health concerns, mostly 'beastly gout', but with Ernest having turned 75, it was clear that Harry's apprenticeship at Anglo was coming to an end.[134] Dominion would soon be his. When Ernest's brother Louis died in January 1956, aged 85, Harry knew it signified 'a great break'.[135] This was not because Louis had played a powerful role in the business, or because he was a forceful character – Harry reflected, 'in a curious way, in spite of his passivity he [Louis] has … been a great influence on all our lives' – but because his death was a portent of generational change.[136]

As regards the third generation, Mary and Nicky, that brought its own parental obligations and anxieties. Every Monday morning, while Parliament was in session, Bridget and Harry would fly to Cape Town, returning to Little Brenthurst on a Friday evening. The flight took about four hours, with stops in Bloemfontein and Beaufort West, and in summer, with electrical storms, it could be pretty harrowing. Sarel Tighy, a scowling but kindly UP MP, would pass Bridget a port or brandy to steady her 'stomach & nerves'.[137] In January, during the school holidays, the children would stay with Ernest and Ina at Blue Mountains in Muizenberg, and when school resumed, Mary and Nicky would be in their grandparents' care on the estate at Brenthurst. 'Of course when they went to school we only saw them at weekends,' Bridget stated frankly in her memoirs.[138] She mothered at a remove. When Nicky had to undergo an emergency appendectomy in 1954, it was Harry who rushed him to the

Mary Oppenheimer and her parents in London in the early 1950s, on their way to a wedding. *(Brenthurst Library)*

Princess Nursing Home and read him stories during his convalescence. More than once, the role of Florence Nightingale seemed to fall to Harry rather than Bridget. 'At 1.30 am I heard Mary running about & found her very miserable with earache. I was up off & on coping with her till 4.30 when she went to sleep,' reads another of Harry's diary entries.[139] In later years, on being reminded of these episodes, Mary Oppenheimer shifted slightly in her chair: 'I wonder where my mother was during all of this,' she pondered.[140]

Oppenheimer was an attentive enough father at weekends, taking Nicky to shoot guinea fowl or watching Mary ride in horse trials, but in time it seemed more practical to send the children to boarding school in England. Mary was enrolled at Heathfield in Ascot, whence she lobbed cheerfully brisk and amusing missives back to Little Brenthurst. 'We are having great fun here, I am not doing a scrap of work but I managed to come top of my form ... Yesterday all the Old Girls came, we had a wonderful time criticising their clothes etc.'[141] Nicky was exiled to Ludgrove in Wokingham at the altogether more tender age of nine – two months shy of his tenth birthday. For a sensitive boy, it was a harsh initiation into pre-adolescence, and the decision to send Nicky overseas (rather than to Michaelhouse in the Natal Midlands, where his name had initially been put down) caused Harry some anguish. 'I only hope we are doing the right thing,' Harry brooded as Nicky left for England with Bridget.[142] The day after Nicky started school, Harry wrote apprehensively: 'Darling Bridget, I am waiting with some anxiety for your phone call to hear how yesterday went off. Going to boarding school for the first time is very hard & certainly poor Nicky was jolly frightened when we went to lunch at Ludgrove before.'[143] In the end, head prevailed over heart. For Nicky was an heir too, and he required a suitable apprenticeship. To Harry's mind, even a good South African education, as he told a sceptical Zach de Beer, was 'not the best preparation for ... the AAC [Anglo American Corporation]'.[144]

The Liberal Wing of the UP and the Coloured Franchise

Back in Parliament, the United Party's liberal wing was growing restive, for the UP's commitment to the Coloured franchise seemed at times to be ambiguous. In September 1953, some of the party's more reactionary MPs rebelled against Strauss and sought to compromise with the Nationalists on the issue. They were eventually expelled from the UP, but the party line remained ambivalent. DF Malan retired from politics in October 1954, having failed in his quest to remove Coloureds from the common roll. (Even in the twilight of his premiership Oppenheimer thought the grim-faced old *dominee* could deliver a speech of 'amazing vigour & malice' for a man of over 80.)[145] His successor as prime minister, JG Strijdom – 'very second-rank'[146] in Oppenheimer's view – was growing frustrated with the ongoing parliamentary struggles and court battles over the Coloured franchise. Having tried and failed to circumvent the Appellate Division of the Supreme Court by passing the High Court of Parliament Bill, the Nationalists now looked to pack the Senate. In 1955, they introduced the Senate Bill in Parliament. It would increase the size of the upper house so that the Senate could be stacked with Nationalists to manufacture a two-thirds majority. This was how the Nationalists planned to amend the Act of Union. Strauss condemned the bill as a monstrosity that would ultimately lead to a one-party state. However, for fear of alienating the conservatives in his own ranks, he refused to be drawn on whether – if the Nationalists succeeded in scuppering the Coloured franchise – the UP would restore it should the party return to power.

Oppenheimer regarded Strauss's response to the bill as 'all right but not inspired'. It was certainly not as bad as the Prime Minister's 'long & very unimpressive piece of "Afrikaner" tub thumping', but nowhere near as good as Margaret Ballinger's speech, which was outstanding, 'even by her high standards'.[147] His own contribution to the debate came at 3.15 am in a marathon, all-night sitting that started on Thursday, 26 May, and carried on to 9 o'clock the following night. He described the Senate Bill as shameful and ludicrous, a profound assault on the constitution and the rule of law. Such sentiments were not harboured solely by the United Party's liberals: 'There are many people who could never be classed as "liberals" who believe that as a matter of principle it would be wrong for South Africa to transfer the Coloured people from the common roll to a separate roll,' Oppenheimer affirmed.[148] Coloured voters should be kept on the common roll and encouraged to identify their political interests with those of whites, he suggested. In a subsequent debate on the Appropriation Bill, Oppenheimer renewed his call. If the government removed Coloureds from the common roll it would be a 'grave injustice', and the UP would be forced to 'put right' what the Nationalists had made wrong when the party regained power.[149]

Oppenheimer had always steadfastly opposed the Separate Representation of Voters Bill, but this was a much more emphatic stance than the one he had taken a year before when, at a public meeting, he suggested that the educational qualifications for the Coloured franchise were too low. His remarks then had elicited Ballinger's disapproval, a public statement from the UP that Oppenheimer was speaking for himself and not the party, and a headline in *The Star* declaring, 'Oppenheimer Coloured vote view startles, interests and dismays'.[150] Once the Senate Bill was on the table, Oppenheimer's message became clear and unmistakeable. He could sense a turning point. And it was to mould his own intellectual preoccupations – his distinctive brand of liberalism – towards a reimagination of the Senate and, indeed, the constitutional order as a whole.

During the debate on the Senate Bill, Strauss issued a press statement on the future restoration of Coloured common-roll voting rights that Oppenheimer found 'foolish & mischievous', since it was calculated to give the impression that the UP was getting ready to sell out.[151] The progressives in the caucus were enraged. Bernard Friedman, Suzman, Fourie, Swart, Townley Williams, Steytler, Cope and Butcher all wanted to circulate a counter-statement dissociating themselves from Strauss's evasions. But Oppenheimer believed this would lead to the disintegration of the UP. For him, party unity was paramount. He calculated that if Strauss could be persuaded to release a second statement clarifying what he had meant, then the liberal wing could be induced to accept it without breaking ranks – all except Friedman, who Oppenheimer considered was 'out for a martyr's crown'.[152] With passions running high, Oppenheimer, Harry Lawrence and Thomas Gray Hughes tried to calm the waters. They met with Friedman, Steytler and Townley Williams, and Oppenheimer put his proposal to them. Friedman wanted an unequivocal reassurance that the UP would restore the Coloured franchise in its current form. The other liberals seemed prepared to let it slide. In the end, Strauss issued a (somewhat mealy-mouthed) clarification that appeared to satisfy all the malcontents save Friedman, whom Oppenheimer found 'utterly intransigent'.[153] Friedman resigned in disgust.

For his part, Oppenheimer deemed Strauss's statement to be a 'triumph for the liberal wing'.[154] The English-language press was unconvinced. In its opinion, only Friedman had held firm. Oppenheimer regarded these as the views of the 'leftist young men' in the press gallery. He remarked disparagingly in his diary: '[They] see themselves cheated of a sensational story & the collapse of the UP (which they would certainly like to see as the prelude to the formation of [a] much stronger professedly liberal/ leftish party) possibly averted. Their influence on our liberal & idealistic, but inexperienced & publicity crazed, back bench is very serious & our troubles are by no means over ... How intolerant & foolish these academic liberals are. Liberalism deserves more sensible champions.'[155] It was a revealing comment. For neither Oppenheimer nor the UP's liberal elder statesman, Harry Lawrence, was an unreserved champion of the party's progressives. Div suspected all along that the liberals were conspiring with the newsmen, drip-feeding them titbits from the caucus, and Oppenheimer was partially sympathetic to his perspective: 'I have much sympathy with Div but am afraid he is getting too conservative & cautious. The foolishness of the liberals naturally makes him worse.'[156] Oppenheimer would often lay on dinner for members of the liberal wing and the press gallery at his home in Buitencingle Street. At a press briefing after one of these occasions – a dinner with Harry Lawrence and John Cope – Lawrence drunkenly harangued the *Sunday Times's* political correspondent, Stanley Uys, accusing him of trying to turn the UP into a liberal party.[157] Oppenheimer was, of course, more polite. Whatever his misgivings, he encouraged the Young Turks privately and defended them publicly. When Suzman came under heavy fire from her divisional committee to resign in solidarity with Friedman, Oppenheimer invited her to dinner: 'I urged her strongly to stand her ground & told her that at all stages in this crisis she had done the right thing.'[158] And he reiterated this judgement at party meetings, telling Bertha Solomon's constituents in Jeppe that Friedman had no right to cast aspersions on the integrity of UP liberals who stayed on in the party.[159] In later years, Suzman would state that Oppenheimer was the main reason why several liberal-minded UP MPs did not resign in solidarity with Friedman.[160] Oppenheimer's loyalty to members of the party's liberal wing – even if he considered some of their actions and statements 'unreasonable & foolish' – was steadfast.[161] He did not wish to be their leader, however. After dinner with Suzman and Cope at the Café Royale (a regular haunt), he recorded in his diary: 'The "liberal wing" is very discontent & talks (not too seriously) about a new party which it is kindly suggested I might lead!'[162] The very notion seemed fanciful to him.

The Liberal Case against Apartheid

In later years Oppenheimer would often quip to foreign correspondents, 'In a South African context I may seem to be liberal, but at heart I'm just an old-fashioned conservative.'[163] Gavin Relly described him as a 'Whig', certainly no 'wide-eyed liberal idealist'.[164] Oppenheimer was a pragmatic liberal, keenly attuned to the dynamics of power and dismissive of what he termed 'idealistic' or 'academic' liberalism. He held Margaret Ballinger in high esteem, but he was not tempted to join the non-racial Liberal Party (LP), founded in 1953, which elected her its president. Peter Brown, a leading LP light in Natal, was married to Punch and Cynthia Barlow's daughter Phoebe. After lunching at the Barlows' farm, Vergelegen, Oppenheimer wrote in his diary with dry amusement: 'apparently Brown is discontent with Mrs Ballinger on grounds [sic] she is too political & not sufficiently idealistic!'[165] And when the LP's national chairman, Oscar Wollheim, came knocking on Oppenheimer's door for a donation, Oppenheimer 'talked politely without committing' himself. Later, he privately acknowledged that 'obviously I cannot help them to fight … the UP'.[166]

In time, the Liberal Party was to stand on a social democratic platform. Its opposition to apartheid was manifested in extra-parliamentary activism, expressed in the language of social justice, and inflected with a moral appeal. Although the LP had a sometimes fraught relationship with the Congress Alliance, its leaders cultivated close contacts with the ANC hierarchy. Chief Albert Luthuli wrote in his autobiography that the LP had been able to speak with a 'far greater moral authority' than other parties with white members because of the quality of the people at its head – people like Paton and Brown.[167] During the Defiance Campaign, according to John Cope, the UP approached Congress leaders to discover what their terms would be for calling off the passive resistance campaign. The ANC's demands of the UP – that it should publicly undertake to halt the tide of apartheid if it came to power – were hardly onerous, but any possible co-operation between the parties was scuppered by conservatives in the ranks of the official opposition. Not long afterwards, Strauss recommitted the UP to a policy of 'white leadership with justice', a nebulous version of racial trusteeship that was difficult to distinguish from the Nationalists' own programme. The tentative UP–ANC discussions came to a halt.[168]

During the 1950s, liberals outside the United Party warmed to the idea of a multiracial national convention to discuss the country's future. After the 1953 election, the South African Institute of Race Relations (SAIRR) undertook preparatory work for such a convention by inviting an equal number of black and white representatives to a private conference at Adams College in Natal. It was chaired by Leo Marquard. The theme was 'how Africans can be more fully associated with the government and development of the country', and the conference was paid for by Harry Oppenheimer.[169] One of the African delegates was ZK Matthews, the distinguished social anthropologist and ANC leader. Soon afterwards he proposed holding a Congress of the People organised by the Congress Alliance itself, freed from the SAIRR's more conservative ideological strictures. The delegates to the SAIRR conference condemned the migrant labour system, but they failed to reach consensus on a number of other critical issues, like the franchise. The ideological gap between white liberals and 'moderate' ANC leaders was revealed in all its starkness. Neither the UP nor the LP supported the historic Congress of the People at Kliptown in June 1955. This was a highly symbolic and significant moment in South African history, during which the ANC adopted the Freedom Charter as its lodestar. The Freedom Charter signalled a notional commitment to non-racialism with its pledge that 'South Africa belongs to all who live in it, black and white'. But this was somewhat undercut by the Congress Alliance's racially compartmentalised organisational structure: there were separate 'congresses' for Africans (the ANC), Indians (the South African Indian Congress), Coloureds (the South African Coloured People's Congress) and whites (the South African Congress of Democrats). Many of the Freedom Charter's promises were programmatic platitudes inspired by revolutionary socialism. In a section that sent a chill down the spine of UP-supporting industrialists, the Charter pledged that the 'mineral wealth beneath the soil, the banks and monopoly industry' would be nationalised and 'transferred to the ownership of the people as a whole'.[170] Although the LP initially intended to co-sponsor the Congress of the People, the party lost its enthusiasm when it became clear that the compilation of the Freedom Charter – meant to be collated from thousands of inputs after exhaustive public engagement – was far from consultative. The Congress of Democrats, essentially a front for the banned and disbanded Communist Party (it revived, underground, as the SACP in 1953), had stitched up the operation, and the document was largely drawn up by the SACP intellectual Lionel 'Rusty' Bernstein and a small band of his fellow travellers.

The Congress Alliance demanded universal suffrage. This was a sticking point for the UP. The Liberal Party, by contrast, despite having initially supported a qualified franchise for blacks, began grappling with the idea of universal suffrage from the late 1950s. In 1960 the LP adopted universal franchise as party policy. This was a position that Oppenheimer found 'unwise' – an 'abrupt cure' that would be 'more disastrous than the disease'.[171] In 1954, Patrick Duncan, the maverick activist who joined the LP in 1955 and left it in 1963 to become the first white member of the Pan Africanist Congress, went to tap Oppenheimer for funds. He wanted to challenge Margaret Ballinger for her native representative's seat on a ticket of universal franchise. Over lunch, Oppenheimer asked Duncan whether the ANC would accept a common-roll franchise with a Standard 6 qualification. If it was offered immediately, Duncan reckoned, the ANC would 'fall over themselves' to grab it and 'Communism & black Nationalism' would be smashed.[172] Oppenheimer's curiosity was piqued. Through Ellen Hellmann, Suzman's constituency chairperson and a veteran of the SAIRR, Oppenheimer reached out to the ANC leadership. He met with Luthuli and politely suggested that the ANC's call for universal suffrage was too extreme. Luthuli protested that his organisation could hardly alter its key demands in order to coddle white sensibilities. Nevertheless, the engagement proved profitable: Oppenheimer discreetly donated £40 000 to the Treason Trial Defence Fund for those members of the Congress Alliance, like Luthuli, Walter Sisulu and Nelson Mandela, who were put on trial for treason in 1956.[173] Mandela, for his part, looked upon Oppenheimer as a class exploiter, and perceived little to distinguish the Liberal Party, when it was founded in 1953, from the left wing of the UP. In *Liberation*, a mouthpiece of the banned Communist Party, Mandela attacked the Liberals' original franchise policy. The Liberals, he charged, were members of a ruling class which 'hates and fears the idea of a revolutionary democracy in South Africa just as much as the Malans and Oppenheimers do'.[174] Mandela served, for a spell, on the Communist Party's central committee; however, in spite of his anti-liberal, anti-capitalist rhetoric, the royal-born Xhosa traditionalist admired Oppenheimer's regal sensibility. He had no qualms about approaching the magnate for money or, indeed, imitating Oppenheimer's fondness for finery. A fashion-conscious freedom fighter – Mandela 'took great trouble with his clothes', according to his biographer Anthony Sampson – he made sure to use the services of Oppenheimer's tailor, Alfred Kahn.[175]

Beyond the ANC, Oppenheimer initiated contact with ANC sympathisers like the Reverend John Collins, a canon of St Paul's Cathedral in London. During the Treason Trial, Collins established what would become the International Defence and Aid Fund, which funded tens of thousands of legal matters, including trials, appeals and stays of execution. Oppenheimer met the cleric in 1954 and found him 'only moderately intelligent'; 'the publicity he has received has gone to his head,' Oppenheimer sneered.[176] In fact, Collins rather alarmed Oppenheimer by suggesting that their views on race relations were 'identical'. This prompted the parliamentarian to comment drily in his diary: 'I hope this is not repeated from the pulpit of St Paul's.'[177] As the Treason Trial unfolded, there were further engagements between Oppenheimer and ANC principals. Oppenheimer dined with ZK Matthews, his son Joe and a few other ANC luminaries. He wrote afterwards to Quintin Whyte of the SAIRR to say that he 'enormously enjoyed' meeting the African leaders. 'If what they say is to be taken at its face value, they are certainly surprisingly moderate and quite plainly they have ability, particularly of course the Matthews father and son.'[178]

In contrast to the Liberal Party – certainly during his tenure as a United Party parliamentarian – Oppenheimer was always careful to frame his objections to apartheid in terms of realpolitik. Apartheid – or 'separate development' as it came to be styled – was unworkable. It made no economic sense. The whole thrust of economic development in South

Africa tended towards racial co-operation and integration, even if – in the UP's view – residential segregation was desirable and the maintenance of white (or European) 'civilisation' must remain cardinal. As Oppenheimer reflected towards the end of his spell in Parliament, the UP's difference of opinion with the Nationalists was 'not that the idea of separate development is immoral, but that it is a policy that cannot be carried out'.[179] The goal, therefore, was to work towards a dispensation – political and constitutional – that could accommodate South Africa's economic realities. That said, Oppenheimer regarded 'pure colour prejudice' – the desire to retain Africans as hewers of wood and drawers of water, and to limit their opportunities for economic advancement on the basis of skin colour – as 'illogical and immoral'.[180]

Apartheid, as adumbrated in the Sauer Report, sought to reinforce the foundations of white domination by curtailing interracial contact, halting the flow of black urbanisation, throttling black competition in the labour market, and doubling down on the industrial colour bar. The reserves, later known as 'homelands' or 'Bantustans', were to become the 'spiritual home' and 'fatherland of the native'.[181] In so far as blacks were needed to work in factories and on mines, their presence in the cities must be regarded as temporary and regulated through a system of migrant labour. However, the problem with the five commissioners who drafted the Sauer Report – four professional politicians and a cleric – was that not one of them appeared to know the first thing about economics. Their recommendations were precise but impractical. This did not deter the Nationalist government, which zealously proceeded to turn almost all of them into legislation.

As far as Oppenheimer could see, black urbanisation was irreversible. As he told the SAIRR in 1950, in a speech entitled 'The future of industry in South Africa', it could not be halted without jeopardising industrial development and destroying economic growth.[182] That did not mean the industrial colour bar was irrational. The colour bar simply reflected the desire of skilled and comparatively well-paid white workers to protect their living standards. They did not want competition from labourers who were willing to work for much lower wages. The problem lay with the *rigidity* of the colour bar, which was 'the chief impediment to our national progress'.[183] Along with a relaxation of the rigid labour regime, the government needed to realise that a settled black presence in urban areas was inevitable since roughly only a third of the black population lived in the reserves. This was critical for racial harmony and for improving industrial relations in a multiracial society, Oppenheimer told the Duke of Edinburgh's Study Conference on Industrial Relations at Oxford University in 1956.[184]

Two months after the Nationalists took power in May 1948, Oppenheimer was arguing that the migrant labour system was economically unsound (although cheap migrant labour had served the mines well enough up to that point). There was a strong case, he contended, especially on the new mines opening in the Orange Free State, for housing to be provided to the wives and children of up to ten per cent of the black labour force. Oppenheimer warned a joint meeting of the Royal African Society and the Royal Commonwealth Society in London in 1950 that the treatment of blacks as though they were 'temporary citizens from another country' – through the prohibition on housing ownership, pass laws and influx control – was creating 'a grave sense of grievance and frustration'.[185] It constituted, on the government's part, an experiment that was 'bound to fail', and South Africa would have to turn to a policy of unity on the basis of 'individual merit' in the place of 'division on a basis of race'.[186]

In the House, Oppenheimer spoke mostly on finance and mining. He emphasised the need for a steady inflow of foreign capital to generate economic development. He underscored the importance of the gold mining industry as a sort of 'great flywheel' in powering the economy.[187] The mines, he said, stabilised the advance of secondary industry, acted as a guarantor of fair prices to farmers, and protected the whole population against the extremes of economic distress. But his core point was always that apartheid threw sand in the engine of economic progress. Such progress depended on (and conduced to) co-operation between whites and blacks. In the long run, therefore, apartheid was doomed. This was to become Oppenheimer's dominant motif, and a central pillar in subsequent liberal thinking about the relationship between capitalism and apartheid. It brought him into heated confrontation with the Minister of Native Affairs, HF Verwoerd, who wanted to confine black labour to the reserves, and of whom Oppenheimer said: 'When you have a man prepared to slow down his nation's economic welfare on account of political theories, you are dealing with an impractical fanatic.'[188]

In 1952, Oppenheimer and Verwoerd came into conflict in Parliament over Anglo American's desire to provide housing for married black mineworkers in mining villages on the Orange Free State goldfields. Verwoerd was 'unequivocally' opposed to the idea.[189] He feared that it would lead to a proliferation of 'black spots', and he arbitrarily imposed a three per cent quota on such accommodation.[190] During a speech in 1955 – described by opposition members as 'the most significant challenge to apartheid yet heard in Parliament' – Oppenheimer accused Verwoerd of deliberately setting out to arrest the expansion of secondary industry on the Witwatersrand in order to move industries to, or near, the reserves.[191] This would turn the Rand into a strip of 'deserted, derelict towns' once the golden age of deep-level mining came to an end.[192] But Verwoerd was willing to court poverty in the future if it meant ideological purity in the present, Oppenheimer claimed. Instead of some 'rigid system' of territorial separation based on 'talk of groups, or races', a coming together of individuals was needed to deal with practical problems in a 'sensible and humane' way'.[193] This was no attack on white supremacy, however. Oppenheimer reassured the House: 'I think all of us in this House will agree that we must maintain the standard of living of the European people, and it certainly would not help the Natives to lower that standard. I think people would also agree that it is very desirable to have residential segregation. I think everyone in this House is agreed that it is most undesirable to put political power into the hands of uncivilised, uneducated people … I think too that in spite of what the hon Minister of Native Affairs says, the whole population of South Africa is agreed that Native labour has got to continue to be available, to the mines, to our industry, on our farms, and in our houses.'[194] Verwoerd unleashed a fusillade of anti-capitalist condemnation in response, speaking with what one reporter called 'white-hot emphasis'.[195] He accused Oppenheimer of only pretending to care about the future of the Witwatersrand. Once the mining houses had extracted every last bit of ore underground, they intended to speculate on industrial land, Verwoerd charged.

In his clashes with Verwoerd, Oppenheimer drew succour from an unlikely source. In 1955, a report commissioned by the Nationalist government into the viability of the reserves – produced under the leadership of Professor FR Tomlinson – was published. Even though the Tomlinson Report backed Verwoerd's policy on developing the reserves (it proposed expenditure of £104 million to that end), Tomlinson's findings cast doubt on the feasibility of territorial separation. On demographic projections, and taking into account the capacity of the reserves, blacks were always going to outnumber whites in the cities, his report said. In Oppenheimer's view, this undermined the very basis of apartheid. The Tomlinson Report had actually 'blown the policy sky-high', Oppenheimer gasped.[196] Privately, Oppenheimer corresponded with Tomlinson and disclosed that even though he disagreed with the commission's first principles, its report was of 'great value', because it provided a 'highly important and imaginative scheme' for the development of the reserves.[197] The real problem, in Oppenheimer's view, was that the commission could not envisage a 'middle path' between apartheid and assimilation. In the House, Oppenheimer elaborated on the middle path, and harked back to the Fagan Report: 'The finding of the Fagan Commission was not only that a middle path was possible, but that nothing but a middle path was possible ... We in the United Party are quite definitely and clearly a middle-of-the-road party and we utterly reject this facile and brittle antithesis between apartheid on the one hand and complete integration leading to assimilation on the other. We believe that these problems in South Africa will only be solved by a process of evolution and mutual adaptation of racial groups living together and working together. When I say living together I do not mean living together in the same street, but living together in what we are pleased to call the European areas of the country, and working together in the same industries. And we believe that a process of mutual adaptation in a unitary South Africa offers the only solution of these problems.'[198]

How would this process of mutual adaptation unfold? How might the middle path be charted through a set of institutional, or constitutional, arrangements? These questions were top of Oppenheimer's mind in the latter half of the 1950s. The Nationalists' relentless assault on the Coloured franchise – they eventually rammed through the Senate Act in 1955 and amended one of the entrenched clauses in the Act of Union – prompted Oppenheimer to spend a considerable amount of time and energy thinking about alternative constitutional models. In this he presaged (indeed, was a significant intellectual forerunner of) a whole cottage industry devoted to constitutional reform and development in subsequent decades. As he prepared his speech for the UP's Transvaal Congress in September 1956, Oppenheimer jotted down a few illuminating handwritten notes: 'Experience points more & more to the conclusion that a multiracial state requires constitutional guarantees of basic rights & liberties & in particular if & when a time should come in any form to grant increased political rights to developed Non-Europeans it would have to be subject to constitutional guarantees of the continued European character of the State.'[199] The question of whether the UP had the appetite to champion such a scheme, a concrete alternative to apartheid, was to play an important role in the evolution of white opposition politics.

Constitutional Proposals

Oppenheimer became seized with the idea of constitutional reform in the mid-1950s. This was spurred by the Nationalists' packing of the Senate, its onslaught on the Coloured franchise, the barrage of government legislation turning South Africa into a police state, and Oppenheimer's desire to flesh out a 'middle path' for South Africa in the light of the Tomlinson Commission's findings. He wanted to forge a constitutional dispensation that could go some (but by no means all the) way to accommodate black demands for political rights, while taking cognisance of economic realities – chiefly, the permanence of black labour in the cities – and securing the interests of industry.

Oppenheimer set down his initial thoughts in a handwritten memo. In effect, he proposed a common-roll qualified franchise for 'non-Europeans' in urban areas and communal representation in a reconstituted multiracial Senate. He hoped this would temper African nationalism and slake the political aspirations of Africans, Coloureds and Indians while ensuring overall white control through what amounted to a white 'veto' in the Senate.[200] But first he wanted the British Commonwealth establishment's approval. He wrote to his old tutor at Oxford, JC Masterman, and asked his advice on whether the scheme might fly.[201] In July 1956, Oppenheimer travelled with Zach de Beer to England where, outside his address to the Duke of Edinburgh conference, he refined his ideas. In Oxford, he consulted the leading expert on constitutional assemblies in former British colonies, Professor Kenneth Wheare, who encouraged him and deemed the scheme 'workable'.[202] In London, Oppenheimer sounded out the editor of The Times, William Haley, who was personally well disposed to the scheme but cautioned him that it would be roundly condemned as a stratagem for white domination by the British press on the left. And in November, Oppenheimer returned to England as a guest of the Conservative Party's Commonwealth Council in the House of Commons. He took the opportunity to seek out Sir Ivor Jennings, the distinguished British lawyer and Master of Trinity Hall, Cambridge, who gave the proposal his legal imprimatur but expressed reservations about communal representation.[203]

Oppenheimer reported back on his activities to Strauss. Strauss, whose days as party leader were numbered, could spot the plan's attractions but thought the UP would never agree to it. 'Perhaps if I were the leader of the Party I should react in the same way,' Oppenheimer subsequently admitted to Zach de Beer, 'but then I am not the leader of the Party & can have the courage of my irresponsibility.'[204] Oppenheimer then turned to Strauss's imminent successor, Sir De Villiers Graaff. Alas, the patrician farmer was unenthusiastic. Div threw cold water on Oppenheimer's optimism, expressing numerous reservations and recording that he was 'unhappy' with the radical recommendations.[205] Undeterred, Oppenheimer responded to Div from the heart of the Diamond District in New York. He told the soon-to-be party leader that he had missed the point of the scheme, and that his own suggestions did not get to the 'heart of the matter'. Oppenheimer chided him: 'I am trying to do two things; on the one hand, I want through a positive veto in the hands of a simple majority of the Europeans to guarantee the fundamental "white Western" character of the state and create the conditions in which we could take the risk of giving common roll voting rights on a reasonable basis to non-Europeans for the House of Assembly; on the other hand, I want to put a measure of real political powers into the hands of non-Europeans *now* so as to make racial legislation which all non-Europeans object to, impossible without a really big majority of the Europeans. Your plan would do neither of these things.'[206]

Oppenheimer pressed on with De Beer's assistance. He got Ellen Hellmann to do further research on possible voter qualifications. He enlisted the support of UP bigwigs like Harry Lawrence and Sidney Waterson. He roped in Philip Brownrigg from Anglo American's London office to draw up pamphlets; and he took the editors of the *Cape Times* and *Cape Argus* into his confidence. In the end, in keeping with his modus operandi as leader, Div deflected Oppenheimer's proposals onto the UP's constitutional review committee. The committee proceeded to dilute and neuter the scheme ahead of its presentation to a special congress of the party in August 1957. In the end, the UP's eventual 'Senate Plan' proved to be 'nothing more than a firm entrenchment of white supremacy'.[207]

Historians of the UP describe the Senate Plan as so complicated that the average voter could barely comprehend it.[208] Colin Eglin, a committed young liberal who had served as De Beer's campaign manager in the 1953 election and who was elected to the Cape Provincial Council in 1954, accurately summed up the response to the so-called GOP, or Graaff–Oppenheimer Plan. Writing to his friend Pieter de Kock, a whip-smart twenty-something lawyer appointed by Oppenheimer as his political secretary in March 1957, Eglin remarked that 'hardly anyone understands the scheme'.[209] The Liberal Party was scornful and saw it as an imitation of *baasskap*; the 'dyed-in-the-wool' UP members were delighted, not because they understood the plan, but because it belonged to the UP; and the progressives within the UP were 'on the whole disappointed'. The LP was indeed derisive. The party's Transvaal chairman, Jack Unterhalter, called it a 'niggardly and tortuous scheme' that would preserve 'white supremacy for all time'.[210] The Nationalists were equally contemptuous. JG Strijdom branded the scheme 'diabolical' and said it would lead to revolution.[211] Eric Louw, the Minister of External Affairs, believed that the plan proved 'Hoggenheimer is on top again'.[212] And the Afrikaner nationalist press hammered Graaff and Oppenheimer as 'two rich young men' who illustrated the 'shattering impact of money power on politics'.[213] Oppenheimer himself was sanguine. He told Philip Brownrigg that although the constitutional proposals did not go nearly as far as he liked, he was 'pretty satisfied' given the fractious nature of the UP.[214]

In fact, Oppenheimer's partial success in persuading the UP to advance constitutional reform convinced him to stay on in Parliament provided he could shift his constituency from Kimberley to the Rand after the 1958 general election. In June 1957, he was elected to chair the executive of the UP's Witwatersrand general council. Buoyed by the UP's municipal election successes on the Rand, Oppenheimer accepted nomination for a safe seat in Johannesburg North. He scheduled a series of meetings in November and December with his prospective constituents. It seemed now as if he were gearing up for what Eglin called 'the politics of the long haul'. And then, very suddenly, his life changed quite dramatically. On the morning of 25 November 1957, as was his custom, Harry looked in on his father at the main house before he left for the office. Ernest seemed, in Harry's own words, 'particularly well ... very cheerful and full of plans'.[215] An hour later, he was dead. As he took his breakfast, watched over by a servant, Ernest suddenly froze. He clutched at his chest and cried out in terrible pain. He was in the throes of another heart attack. A nurse rushed to help him, but there was nothing she could do. This time, it felled him. At the age of 77, the founder of the Oppenheimer dynasty – the man who had created an empire out of the Anglo American Corporation, dominated the world's diamond trade, and conquered the Copperbelt – was no more. It was time for his son's apprenticeship to draw to a close. And so Harry Oppenheimer vacated his seat in Parliament and took up the chairman's seat at 44 Main Street instead.

III
MAGNATE

1957–1989

EIGHT

The Chairman's Mantle

1957–1964

The Inheritance

When the board of the Anglo American Corporation appointed Harry Oppenheimer to the chairman's seat at 44 Main Street on 5 December 1957, the companies his father had created over the preceding four decades now constituted a formidable group. They dominated South African mining, and were significant players on the world stage, too. Harry had been writing Ernest Oppenheimer's chairman's statements for at least a decade before the dynast died. But in the first such communiqué penned under his own name, the new sovereign could boast that Anglo were 'the largest producers of gold in the world', with annual gold profits in excess of £24 million.[1] Anglo's profits from its gold mines in the Orange Free State alone had more than doubled from £7 143 839 in 1955 to £16 749 783 in 1957, providing the corporation with a sturdy cash reserve. Annual profits from uranium amounted to £7 million. Anglo was responsible for 50 per cent of the Union's coal output. De Beers, effectively Anglo's twin, commanded 90 per cent of the thriving global diamond trade. In 1957 sales through the Central Selling Organisation reached a record high of £76 772 112. Consolidated Diamond Mines of South West Africa, established by Ernest Oppenheimer in 1919, was the most important producer of gem diamonds in the world: in 1957 it produced over 900 000 carats valued at £17.5 million. As for copper, the N'Kana and N'Changa mines contributed over half of the Northern

HFO visits the Free State Geduld mine
in the late 1950s. *(Anglo American)*

Rhodesian Copperbelt's yearly output, which in turn accounted for the
world's third-largest copper supply. In 1957 there were approximately
a hundred companies in the Anglo stable. When Harry Oppenheimer
was profiled by *Reader's Digest* in 1964, the journalist claimed that he
had added another 50 companies to the group's tally: Oppenheimer
was a director of roughly 106 of them, and he chaired around 44. 'The
Oppenheimers collect companies the way other people collect stamps,'
was the flip assessment.[2] But theirs was no accidental empire. During
the first third of his incumbency, between 1957 and 1965, Harry
Oppenheimer systematically laid the groundwork for Anglo's expansion
both as a multinational mining house and as a dominant player in South
Africa's secondary industry.

Ernest Oppenheimer's endeavours to restructure and monopolise
the diamond industry in the 1930s, which Harry regarded as his father's
greatest achievement (together with the development of the Orange Free
State goldfields), made possible Anglo American's subsequent spectacular
growth. Harry Oppenheimer was the beneficiary of an enormous bequest,
both personally and in his corporate capacity. He was anxious to continue
honouring Ernest's multiple charitable obligations. There was a veritable
phalanx of relatives and sundry individuals in England and elsewhere
who relied on Ernest's largesse. Harry asked Billie Chapple in the London

office to make 'quite sure that any pensions or allowances or presents which were normally paid by my father are continued'.[3] Ernest had made Harry the sole legatee of his estate and property. Although the figure mentioned in the will was only £3 600 470,[4] most of the actual fortune was channelled into an impenetrable maze of trusts. In the absence of outright control, the Oppenheimer family was able to stamp its seal of authority on Anglo American and De Beers through an intricate web of minority shareholdings, crossholdings and interlocking directorships occupied by loyal liegemen. At the centre lay E Oppenheimer and Son. Harry Oppenheimer would reinforce the family's influence. Forty years later, in 1998, E Oppenheimer and Son enjoyed a 7.2 per cent holding in Anglo American, which in turn held 32.2 per cent of De Beers. At the same time, E Oppenheimer and Son enjoyed a 2.64 per cent holding in De Beers, which held 35.4 per cent of Anglo American.[5] The freshly minted chairman laid claim to a formidable inheritance – not just materially, but in respect of the founder's accomplishments as a business statesman and philanthropist, too. One of the first things Oppenheimer did to signal his commitment to continuing his father's legacy was to establish the Ernest Oppenheimer Memorial Trust (OMT).

With a donation of £1 million from Harry Oppenheimer's private assets, which matched the issued share capital of the Anglo American Corporation when it was founded in 1917, the Ernest Oppenheimer Memorial Trust was created. It sought to benefit any institution geared towards the advancement of science or art, or of an 'educational, charitable or ecclesiastical nature'.[6] Oppenheimer's contribution was the largest single charitable donation in South African history, apart from the bequest that Cecil John Rhodes left to the University of Oxford for the creation of the Rhodes Scholarships.[7] Any individual from South Africa, South West Africa and the Federation of Rhodesia and Nyasaland – 'irrespective of race, colour or creed' – was eligible to apply for funds. Subsequently, beneficiaries came from Botswana, Lesotho and Swaziland, too. As the apartheid juggernaut rolled on, depriving black people of economic, educational and cultural opportunities – exemplified by HF Verwoerd's hotly despised Bantu Education Act of 1953 – the inauguration of the Ernest Oppenheimer Memorial Trust was a pioneering development. Two notable recipients of the trust's munificence in its early years were the Pius XII College (subsequently the National University of Lesotho), where a student bursary scheme was instituted, and the Waterford School in Swaziland. The headmaster of Waterford, Michael Stern, wrote to Oppenheimer in 1964: 'It was you who really got Waterford off the ground ... in 1962. Now comes this magnificent grant to build and equip our Science laboratories – a bigger sum and sooner than we dared hope for.'[8] In 1958, the OMT initiated an enduring funding relationship with the South African Institute of Race Relations (SAIRR), a research and policy organisation which played a key role in opposing apartheid and disseminating liberal ideas. The institute was awarded a major grant for a national conference on Coloured education. Annual grants followed in due course. In 1960, the OMT made a large capital grant and underwrote a loan, to the value of £60 million, to establish a multiracial college of social services in Lusaka. Opened in 1962 as the Oppenheimer College of Social Services, the facility trained generations of social workers in Central Africa. By the time the inaugural graduation ceremony took place in 1964, the Federation of Rhodesia and Nyasaland had broken up. Northern Rhodesia had gained independence from Britain, and the country's new head of state, President Kenneth Kaunda of Zambia, presided as the guest of honour.

In taking on his father's mantle, Harry Oppenheimer – or HFO as he was routinely referred to as chairman – assumed a heavy weight on his shoulders. As the dynastic successor, he was now responsible for consolidating and expanding a mining empire whose interests lay predominantly in diamonds, gold and copper. But in addition to functioning as a producer of minerals and metals, Anglo American was also an investment company. It boasted hundreds of subsidiaries and associates, and carried on a profitable business providing technical and administrative services to a plethora of companies. Most of the group's operating companies were publicly listed and could raise capital on their own account. Anglo's revenue derived from dividends and interest from its investments in these companies, as well as fees for services provided to them. After the Second World War, Ernest Oppenheimer initiated a policy of De Beers taking participations in Anglo American's new projects. When the Diamond Corporation offloaded its stockpile of diamonds accumulated during the Great Depression, De Beers' profits soared. Anglo needed the capital for the development of the Orange Free State goldfields, and De Beers provided a handy source of investment finance. To this end, the De Beers Investment Trust was formed in 1952. The arrangement proved profitable to De Beers, and established the company on a more diversified basis outside the diamond industry. For HFO, diamonds were his preference and preoccupation. He loved their mystique. In a more whimsical vein, Oppenheimer suggested that people purchased diamonds out of vanity and gold out of stupidity (they were too slow-witted to think of a more effective monetary system, he quipped). 'I think vanity is probably a more attractive motive than stupidity,' was a well-worn witticism.[9] Yet under HFO's chairmanship, Anglo's interests would rapidly diversify beyond diamonds and gold.

Young Blood

One of Oppenheimer's immediate priorities was to bring in new blood. The idea was to take a promising university graduate aged roughly 23, train him widely for five years, make him an assistant manager by the time he was 30, and appoint him to a management position by the age of 40. Anglo was ripe for reinvigoration. The corporation's deputy chairman, RB Hagart, was getting on in years. He was stuck in his ways. As far back as 1948, Hagart had begun to try Ernest Oppenheimer's patience. Although 'RB' was one of Ernest's most trusted lieutenants, he was constantly on the warpath, and he gave the team running the Orange Free State goldfields short shrift. Ernest complained bitterly to Harry: 'Hagart undermines our organisation, sees to it that your directive is as far as possible ignored & simply hates all the younger people & wants to destroy their chances of advancement.'[10] Oppenheimer *père* thought Hagart should relinquish some of his responsibilities. Oppenheimer *fils* regarded Hagart as able and lucid, but also rather humourless, unimaginative and inclined to find reasons why things could not be done.[11] Nevertheless, Hagart pressed on for over a decade after Ernest's demise – his own death came in 1969 – and he was held in considerable esteem by his subordinates, if not fear. The running joke among the younger staff was that one entered Hagart's office on all fours.[12] In November 1957, at the time of Ernest Oppenheimer's death, Hagart was recuperating from an operation at a hospital in New York.[13] By the same token, many of the other senior figures in the organisation were products of Ernest Oppenheimer's incumbency. One of them was HFO's close friend Keith Acutt. As Anglo's resident director in the Federation of Rhodesia and Nyasaland, he faithfully projected HFO's personality, style and policy to the north. Nevertheless, Acutt, who had hardly been born with a silver spoon in his mouth, exercised much more of the common touch than Oppenheimer. HFO paired the dutiful Acutt and (periodically) disobliging Hagart as deputy chairmen of the corporation. Bill Wilson formed part of the corporate patrimony, too. He

The Anglo American executive committee, 1964.
From left to right: RB Hagart, W Marshall Clark, T Coulter,
WD Wilson and HFO. *(Anglo American)*

was possessed of humour and humility and a well-stocked mind. Wilson
was Anglo's 'social conscience'.[14] Colleagues quipped that he might just as
well have been a university professor or an Anglican priest. During Ernest
Oppenheimer's reign Wilson had assisted HFO as managing director.
Under HFO's chairmanship he now performed the role in his own right.
William Marshall Clark, general manager of South African Railways
before Ernest Oppenheimer recruited him into Anglo in the early 1950s,
and Tom Coulter, Anglo's veteran coal supremo, joined Hagart, Acutt and
Wilson on the corporation's executive committee.

There were several other prominent personalities in the Anglo
establishment dating from Ernest Oppenheimer's time. One of them
was Doug Beckingham, Frank Oppenheimer's friend, who helped
steer Anglo's diversification into industry.[15] Pierre Crokaert was an old
diamond hand. Ted Brown – 'that remarkable character', as HFO referred
to Brown in the outline of his memoir – had started on the diamond side
of the business in Kimberley and moved to E Oppenheimer and Son in
the mid-1930s.[16] He became increasingly involved in Anglo's industrial,
engineering and construction concerns. Brown fancied himself as HFO's
enforcer, or 'leg-man', taking charge of the 'hard day-to-day nastiness of
business', with which (he believed) he was temperamentally better suited
to deal.[17] Brown considered the working relationship between members of

the chairman's kitchen cabinet and their bosses – both Ernest and Harry – to be unique: 'We weren't members of the family but we were treated almost as if we were.'[18] Like his father, Harry Oppenheimer conceived of Anglo American and De Beers as a family enterprise. But in 1957 his own children were too young to be involved.

HFO had brought some of his comrades into the group after the end of the war. Guy Young was a jovial ex-journalist on *The Star* whom Harry appointed at twice his previous salary. By his own estimation, Young was 'never a great worker or very clever', or destined for the top, but he appreciated the opportunity to work at E Oppenheimer and Son.[19] Young viewed Ernest and Harry as the 'greatest friends': they would talk for hours about business, and at cocktail parties they were a 'minor disaster' because they would venture off into a corner to talk one-on-one. HFO also drafted Grey Fletcher into E Oppenheimer and Son by way of the 4th Armoured Car Regiment. Fletcher was somewhat of a practical joker, but he had a considerable knack for finance and HFO took a shine to him. Oppenheimer's junior by 12 years, Fletcher was probably HFO's earliest youthful recruit. Young and Fletcher were friends of the new chairman; they knew his virtues and foibles and they interacted with him as a peer. Guy Young believed that one attribute HFO did not inherit was 'the consistent charm of his father'. A leading diamond cutter once told Young that 'Sir Ernest can make an office boy feel like a director. Harry can make a director feel like an office boy.'[20] Keith Acutt referred to these episodic lapses in cordiality as Oppenheimer's 'yellow moods'.[21] In the main, Oppenheimer was conscientiously solicitous towards his closest colleagues. Another intimate friend, Comar Wilson, was based in the diamond office in London. He provided the link with Anglo American in Johannesburg, and effectively became the corporation's senior London agent in 1951. HFO rated his abilities highly, and was well disposed towards him – indeed, Oppenheimer had wanted Wilson to be the best man at his wedding in 1943. But in 1957 Wilson was, like Hagart, in delicate health. Wilson worked alongside a trio of HFO loyalists: Philip Brownrigg, Hugh Vivian Smith, and Esmond Baring of the banking family. The latter two were former stockbrokers from Rowe & Pitman. Wilson's death in 1961 robbed the London office of a notable talent. Baring, whose son Oliver was HFO's godson, died in 1963, aged 49. Oppenheimer described him as a 'wonderful friend'.[22]

Oppenheimer's eagerness to cultivate the aptitudes of bright and enthusiastic striplings was soon given institutional form. As an MP he had taken on young men with quicksilver minds, like Gavin Relly and Pieter de Kock, to serve as his political secretary. Relly parlayed this training into a highly successful career at Anglo American. He steered Anglo's interests in Zambia and later North America, before taking the group baton when HFO retired. De Kock served as the chief official in the chairman's office responsible for personnel and administrative matters, until his career was cut short by his tragic drowning in 1967. Although Zach de Beer was never HFO's political secretary, he too leveraged the political connection and pursued a career that straddled Anglo American and Parliament. In 1957, besides his role as a parliamentarian, De Beer was a medical doctor making £700 per annum from a practice whose future, owing to quarrelsome partners, was uncertain.[23] He needed to supplement his annual income by £600, and HFO made good the shortfall.[24] However, De Beer only formally joined Anglo in 1968. He dabbled in public relations and marketing for the industrial division, became a manager, and in 1972 left Johannesburg for Zambia, where he headed Anglo's operations. In the mid-1950s, Robin Rudd, a recent Oxford graduate (and first-class cricketer), acted as a sort of business-cum-political assistant to HFO. His job consisted of dealing with correspondence, predominantly 'begging letters', attending meetings of the Orange Free State goldfields coordinating committee, drafting statements, shepherding callers through to, and sometimes away from, HFO, and 'generally being on tap'.[25] In effect, Rudd was one of HFO's earliest personal assistants on the business front, followed briefly by Derek Henderson, whose real passion lay in academia.

At the end of 1957 the new chairman formalised a system of personal assistants (PAs) at 44 Main Street. These assistants were intelligent, well-educated, male twenty-somethings who exhibited finesse and the promise of management expertise. For a couple of years they would shadow the chairman and be drawn into the belly of the beast, sitting in on important meetings with full sight of the executive committee's papers. If a PA gained the trust and confidence of his boss, and was possessed of demonstrable skill, he would be fast-tracked into the ranks of management. It was a position that demanded impeccable tact, discretion and loyalty, and what Oppenheimer called 'a touch of the monkey' – a personality quirk or idiosyncrasy that set its incumbent apart.[26] Like the league of administrators nurtured by Lord Milner in his 'Kindergarten', HFO's PAs were usually cut from the same cloth: private-school old boys, Oxford University Philosophy, Politics and Economics (PPE) graduates and, appropriately for the self-styled heir to the 'Rhodes tradition', former Rhodes Scholars.

HFO's first PA as chairman, appointed with effect from 1 January 1958, was the 23-year-old Julian Ogilvie Thompson. The son of a judge on the Appellate Division of the Supreme Court, Ogilvie Thompson – or 'JOT', as he became known in the Anglo American fashion – had been educated at Diocesan College ('Bishops') in Cape Town and Oxford University, where he read for the PPE degree on a Rhodes Scholarship. After going down from Oxford, JOT spent six months in Anglo's London office. There he learnt to sort diamonds. 'No one relied on the assortment but I did learn the nomenclature, which became very useful later on,' he recalled over sixty years later.[27] A spell with Anglo's British stockbrokers, Rowe & Pitman, and its merchant bankers, Lazard Brothers, completed his apprenticeship. It did no harm that JOT's young English wife, Tessa, was the daughter of Thomas Henry Brand. Brand was the managing director of Lazard and would soon succeed his father as the 4th Viscount Hampden. When the Brands visited Johannesburg in 1957, while Ernest Oppenheimer was still alive, they were invited to dine at Little Brenthurst. Their daughter and son-in-law joined them. A towering figure both physically, at well over six feet tall, and mentally, with a mind like a steel trap, JOT was quickly identified as a suitable candidate for the role of HFO's PA. At 44 Main Street, Ogilvie Thompson was stationed in the offices of E Oppenheimer and Son, where he assisted Grey Fletcher with winding up Ernest Oppenheimer's estate. He also paid special attention to the holding company's diamond concerns and busied himself with the financial side of Anglo's affairs, often delivering himself of lengthy written commentaries neatly inscribed on the chairman's set of papers.

From 1958 to March 1961, Ogilvie Thompson set the gold standard against which all future PAs would be judged. When HFO was out of the office, JOT would update him with wide-ranging dispatches. These covered everything from Tiger Fish's opening odds in the 1958 Durban July Handicap (the horse went on to become the Oppenheimers' first 'July' winner the following year) to United Party tidings (a 'rallying speech' from Marais Steyn on the north-west Rand after the UP's defeat in the 1958 election) to Anglo's nascent forestry interests.[28] JOT was prodigiously hard-working. He was also inquisitive, and liked to know everything that was going on. Sometimes his curiosity got the better of him. One day Keith Acutt decided to set him up. Acutt peered furtively into JOT's office before striding over to the chairman's suite. As Acutt predicted, Ogilvie Thompson was soon on his trail. Knocking on his boss's door, JOT inquired of HFO: 'Anything you want me to do?' Oppenheimer politely replied 'no, thank you', whereupon Acutt made a show of crunching up a piece of paper and discarding it in the wastepaper basket. He then headed out to lunch with the chairman. Once the coast was clear, JOT proceeded to retrieve the note. On it was scrawled, 'Must talk to Harry about Julian.'[29]

Scientia potestas est, and in spite of (or perhaps because of) Ogilvie Thompson's thirst for knowledge, he enjoyed a meteoric rise into the upper echelons of Anglo American and De Beers. In 1963, Oppenheimer appointed JOT – not yet 30 years old – to various company boards. JOT wrote effusively to the chairman: 'I know I've said this twice but I do want to … thank you for your overwhelming kindness. I really was absolutely bowled over and, in a way, embarrassed at having connived at it.'[30] Adroit PAs and close associates of the chairman had directorships conferred upon them. Some might be selected for Anglo's board or executive committee. The latter body, Anglo's fulcrum and key decision-making forum, met several times a week and operated as a sort of partners' room: although debates were robust, the emphasis was on consensus-seeking, and resolutions were usually reached without having to be voted upon. Relly was appointed as a director of Anglo American in April 1965; Grey Fletcher followed suit in March 1966; and both of them became members of Anglo's executive committee at the beginning of 1967.[31] Ogilvie Thompson joined the board of De Beers in 1966 and of Anglo in 1970. In 1966, all the directors of Anglo American were also nominees of, and shareholders in, E Oppenheimer and Son.[32] The family holding company, converted from a public corporation to a private concern on 1 February 1966, promoted 'a sense of *esprit de corps*' among senior management and personnel.[33] This served a twofold purpose: it discouraged the possibility of an internal coup, and subverted the dangers of disunity within the ranks should there be a hostile takeover bid. In this way, the Oppenheimer family's control of the group was effectively cemented through a kinship network.

The practice whereby favoured courtiers were drawn into the chairman's inner circle was often characterised as nepotism by Anglo's detractors. Anglo's executive directors, it was remarked, were all friends of Harry Oppenheimer. 'That is certainly true and not something for which I would wish to make excuses,' Oppenheimer wrote in his memoir.[34] 'Indeed it may possibly have been a factor in holding together in an agreeable and profitable association people with very different views, talents and temperaments.' What Gavin Relly referred to as the 'band of brothers' idea was close to HFO's (and Ernest Oppenheimer's) heart.[35] Anglo's critics believed patronising elitism and complacent chumminess made the corporation inefficient. HFO's rejoinder was pointed: 'The one thing that is difficult to explain is how, if all this is true, we … managed to be reasonably successful.'[36] Like civil service mandarins, the convivial club of Anglo boys developed into a distinctive breed. Polished and preternaturally self-confident, they mimicked their boss's mannerisms. They projected a studied modesty, talked softly and listened carefully, often with their heads tilted to one side. They rode at the Inanda Club, swam at the Johannesburg Country Club, and flew across Africa in Anglo's private planes. As Anthony Sampson archly observed, 'Developing Africa was rewarding psychologically as well as financially: it was their wives who were often left to try to mitigate the insoluble social problems of black families in the wake of their industrial progress.'[37] In cultivating a cadre of confidants and consiglieres, Harry Oppenheimer commenced his chairmanship as he meant to go on; and this, perhaps, was to be his most significant attainment in a quarter-century as chair. He shored up, and then expanded, Anglo's economic dominion with the support and loyalty of a carefully selected cohort of close colleagues. Oppenheimer enlarged the group in two ways: through a simultaneous process of international diversification and a rapid branching out into different sectors of South African industry.

Foreign Capital

The pursuit of foreign capital forms a distinctive thread in Oppenheimer's chairmanship of Anglo and De Beers. He understood it to be an iron law of South African economic history that, since the discovery of deep-level gold, the country depended on a steady inflow of foreign capital. That is why Oppenheimer devoted a good deal of time abroad to promoting investment in South Africa. A speech to the London Institute of Directors in 1959, entitled 'Is South Africa a good risk?', is a fairly typical example. (The country was a 'risk well worth taking' given the spectacular rise in national income between 1937 and 1957 – from £375 million to £2 billion – and the diversification into manufacturing.)[38] In his second year as chairman, Oppenheimer reported that Anglo had secured a £4 262 000 loan from Deutsche Bank, the first foreign loan by a German institution in nearly forty-five years.[39] Together with a number of the other leading mining finance houses, Anglo formed the American–South African Investment Company contemporaneously, and the new company's shares – primarily in gold mining – were introduced on the New York Stock Exchange.[40] This contributed materially to Anglo's greatly improved liquidity position. Even in the midst of growing political instability, Anglo was able to keep lines of financing open abroad.

The ideological fanatic HF Verwoerd succeeded JG Strijdom as prime minister when the so-called Lion of the North died in 1958. The contours of public debate continued to be shaped by the two rival forces of racial nationalism. The ruling Afrikaner nationalists stared down Albert Luthuli's African National Congress (ANC). Verwoerd consolidated apartheid with a barrage of legislation, while he shifted the emphasis towards separate development and a Bantustan policy that promised eventual independence to the black homelands. Within the ranks of the ANC, however, there was friction. The Freedom Charter's pledge that 'South Africa belongs to all who live in it, black and white' alienated a hard-core fringe of Africanists. Inspired by the incipient process of decolonisation and the formation of independent African states, they began to speak of 'Africa for the Africans'. In 1959, under the leadership of Robert Sobukwe, this faction hived off from the ANC to create a splinter group, the Pan Africanist Congress. Meanwhile, from the beginning of his premiership, Verwoerd had to deal with sporadic but serious disturbances in black areas in different parts of the Union. On 21 March 1960, a large crowd of Africans protesting against the pass laws moved towards the police station at the Sharpeville location outside Vereeniging. The police panicked and opened fire, killing 69 Africans and wounding many more. The Sharpeville massacre had immediate and far-reaching repercussions. The government decreed a three-month State of Emergency. International condemnation ensued. Money poured out of the country. In 1960 there was an outflow of £90 million in (mostly foreign-owned) private capital. The apartheid state came under global financial fire, causing the government to impose stringent exchange controls and restrict the supply of credit. Between April and December 1960, foreign reserves plummeted from £157 million to £85 million. Yet, as South African reserves of gold and foreign exchange took a nosedive and capital bolted from the country, Anglo American – through its affiliate, the Rand Selection Corporation – succeeded in raising a loan of $30 million in the United States.[41] The initiative was taken by Oppenheimer. He sent two of Anglo's best financial brains, Beville Pain and Maurice Rush, to conduct negotiations in New York in May 1961.[42] They managed to place $30 million of Rand Selection debentures with a number of American insurance companies, thus avoiding the need to obtain a listing on the New York Stock Exchange. The loan was guaranteed by Barclays Bank in London following Oppenheimer's personal intervention: he met Barclays' chairman, Anthony William Tuke, the so-called Iron Tuke, and exercised a 'chilly charm' over the helmsman, who doubled the bank's initial offer of security.[43] The entire sum was then brought to South Africa, where it radically bolstered the reserves of foreign exchange. Oppenheimer believed this demonstrated 'the great value' to a relatively small country of 'possessing financial institutions with international connections'.[44] For his detractors, by contrast, it underscored the liminal nature of the mogul's liberal politics. To them, Oppenheimer was propping up the South African state at the moment of its greatest vulnerability.

Ruth First, the South African Communist Party activist banned by the government after the events at Sharpeville, summed up this view: 'A regular critic of apartheid, he [Oppenheimer] has probably done more than anyone else to fuel the economic machine on which the strength of white supremacy depends.'[45] The economy experienced a boom in the period after Sharpeville, thus proving the historian CW de Kiewiet's dictum that South Africa tended to advance through 'political disasters and economic windfalls'. Between 1960 and 1970 the economy grew at an annual average rate of 5.9 per cent, which strengthened the position of the white establishment. Oppenheimer informed his shareholders that Anglo's net profits after tax swelled by 15.7 per cent between 1961 and 1962.[46] By 1964, Anglo's gold mines had improved their output by over one million ounces of gold to the record sum of 10.6 million ounces. This was accompanied by a substantial rise in profits. The South African economy was 'very prosperous', HFO assured his shareholders: indeed, Anglo's final dividend climbed by 20 cents per share to a total of 120 cents per share in 1964.[47] In 1966, under the headline 'The house that Harry builds', the *Financial Mail* catalogued Anglo's decade of exponential growth.[48] The R170 million book value of Anglo's investments at the end of 1965 was greater than their market value in 1955. At the end of 1965 the market value was more than three times higher than at the start of the decade. The overall value of operating companies in the group stood in excess of R1.2 billion. Anglo was not guaranteed to thrive after Ernest Oppenheimer's death, according to the magazine. Ernest's 'special brand of vision, flair and enterprise' was just right for the pioneering times in which he operated; but Harry Oppenheimer's willingness to delegate, his 'more scientific approach' to management, and 'greater knowledge of foreign industrial and non-mining business' made him, 'perhaps, more suited to today's challenges'.[49]

All of this expansion took place against the backdrop of South Africa's increasing international isolation. On 20 January 1960, Verwoerd told Parliament that the time had come to cut the umbilical cord with the British Crown and establish a republic in South Africa. In a national referendum on the matter, 52 per cent of white South Africans voted in favour of a republic. In due course, with growing condemnation of apartheid in the Commonwealth led by Prime Minister Jawaharlal Nehru of India and President Kwame Nkrumah of Ghana, Verwoerd indicated that South Africa would cease to be a member of the Commonwealth after the country became a republic on 31 May 1961. Oppenheimer digested South Africa's departure from the Commonwealth with discomfort. The ensuing loss of political, economic and military ties was, in his view, a 'disaster'.[50] Nevertheless, he affirmed that Anglo's confidence in South Africa was 'unshaken': the corporation was 'determined' to play its full part in the 'economic development of the country'.[51] In Oppenheimer's view, in the long run economic development would liberalise the polity, dissolve apartheid, and resolve the country's racial problems. To his army of critics like Ruth First, Oppenheimer's pronouncements were vapid and hollow. He was merely shoring up the system of racial capitalism and white domination.

Charles W Engelhard Jr and the North American Magnet

Perhaps for symbolic and sentimental reasons, courtesy of William Honnold, Herbert Hoover, and the financiers at Newmont and JP Morgan back in 1917, North America occupied a prominent place in Harry Oppenheimer's international imagination. Gavin Relly thought that North America was like a 'magnet' to Oppenheimer: HFO believed that Anglo should invest in 'this remarkable economic machine'.[52] And from the start of his chairmanship, that is what Oppenheimer set out to do. In 1958, Anglo American acquired a controlling interest in the Central Mining–Rand Mines group (and staved off a takeover bid by Consolidated Gold Fields in the process) with assistance from the ebullient American minerals and metals mogul, Charles W Engelhard Jr (CWE). In due

HFO and Charles W Engelhard Jr at the races,
late 1950s. *(Brenthurst Library)*

course Anglo hived off Rand Mines, with Engelhard in the chair, to the
Rand Selection Corporation. Henceforth, the fortunes of Engelhard
and Oppenheimer became entwined. From the turn of the century,
Engelhard's German-born father, Charles senior, had built up a world-
class, US-based business processing and refining precious metals. It dealt
in silver and gold, boasted special expertise in platinum, and incorporated
the Hanovia Chemical and Manufacturing Company in Newark, New
Jersey. After Charles senior died in 1950, leaving his son an industrial
inheritance worth $20 million, CWE consolidated the family's concerns
into Engelhard Industries. He brought in Gordon Richdale, an English
financier involved in the formation of Harmony Gold Mining, to inject
some managerial rigour. Engelhard had first visited South Africa in the
late 1940s, where he proceeded to make a small fortune by manufacturing
solid gold artefacts and ashtrays for export to the Far East. At their point of
destination, they were melted down into gold bars. In this way Engelhard
circumvented South Africa's bullion regulations and earned himself a

Jane and Charles Engelhard in the library
at Cragwood, 1960s. *(https://allengelhard.com)*

spot in the pantheon of fictional villains. Reputedly, Engelhard was the
inspiration for the character of Auric Goldfinger, James Bond's larger-
than-life adversary in the 1959 novel *Goldfinger*. (Charles Engelhard and
Bond's creator, Ian Fleming, were well acquainted: Engelhard had drawn
on the financial services of Fleming's family firm, Robert Fleming & Co.,
to incorporate one of his own companies.)

Using his chairmanship of Rand Mines as a springboard, Engelhard
branched out into uranium, coal and copper refining. He acquired large
interests in timber and forestry. These were run in due course – along
with his other South African concerns – by the professional forester
David Gevisser.[53] From the environs of his plush Johannesburg residence,
Court House, and a magnificent country home in the Eastern Transvaal,
Mbulwa, perched high above the forestry town of Sabie, the Platinum

King carved out a lucrative business empire in his adopted homeland. In 1961 *Time* magazine acknowledged Engelhard as 'one of the most powerful businessmen in South Africa'.[54] Just over eight years younger than Oppenheimer, Engelhard was loud, garrulous and flamboyant: a stark counterpoint to the South African magnate. He lived on a lavish scale. A man of boundless appetites, the cigar-toting Engelhard ate and drank lustily, gambled heavily, and pursued a passion for fast cars, boats and aeroplanes. He flew all over the world on his company's private aircraft, a BAC One-Eleven dubbed the 'Platinum Plover'.

Engelhard's fast-paced lifestyle would eventually take a toll on his health; but over a period of seventeen-odd years, in spite of their polar opposite personalities, Engelhard and Oppenheimer cultivated a friendship of some consequence. Their evident dissimilarities were a source of mutual curiosity. They respected each other's commercial acumen and powers of negotiation. There was also a shared sense of filial piety. Their fathers had primed them both from a young age to inherit and, perhaps more importantly, to perpetuate a corporate dynasty. Recreationally, the second-generation heirs had in common an

Sir Philip Oppenheimer shared his cousin Harry's enthusiasm for horse racing. He is pictured here with HFO and Elizabeth II, as the Queen prepares to present the De Beers Diamond Trophy after the King George VI and Queen Elizabeth Stakes at Ascot, 1972. *(Getty Images)*

enthusiasm for horse racing. Engelhard assembled a stable of some three hundred racehorses worldwide; he sent his famous stallion, Ribofilio, to stand at Mauritzfontein; and it was Engelhard who offered HFO and Philip Oppenheimer a share in the Nijinsky syndicate after the legendary racehorse retired to stand stud at Claiborne Farm in Kentucky.[55]

On their frequent trips to South Africa, invariably with an entourage of assistants and courtiers in tow, Engelhard and his glamorous socialite wife, Jane, became habitués at Brenthurst. Born in Shanghai and educated in Paris, Jane Engelhard was stylish and sophisticated; after the death of her first husband, a German-Jewish banker and art collector, Fritz Mannheimer, she settled in New York with their young daughter, Annette. David Gevisser, with whom Jane Engelhard subsequently clashed, described her as 'imperious, ruthless and somewhat frightening'.[56] Even Bridget found Jane's cultured worldliness slightly intimidating. In North America the Oppenheimers' hospitality was reciprocated at the Engelhards' various properties: the Georgian Revival-style manor house, Cragwood, in Far Hills, New Jersey; an apartment in the Towers of the Waldorf Astoria in New York; Pamplemousse, a marble-floored seaside retreat in Boca Grande, Florida; and a salmon fishing camp on the Gaspé Peninsula in Quebec. Once, when HFO arrived at the fishing camp early in the morning with a large book under his arm, Jane Engelhard protested that surely he must be too tired from travelling to read. 'What are you reading?' she asked. 'Shakespeare,' came the reply, 'it's the only way to travel.'[57]

As their association deepened, Oppenheimer and Engelhard began to explore the possibility of a joint venture, to which each would contribute assets of equal value. RB Hagart was all for Oppenheimer making a personal investment outside South Africa and getting Engelhard Industries' shares 'on ground floor terms'; but he offered some words of caution to his chairman: 'I like him [Engelhard], as you do, and I have always found him straightforward, a man of his word, easy to talk to & talking sense. He undoubtedly ... has good business ability & acumen. On the other hand he is something of an exhibitionist & in his personal life I believe there have been "hushed up" scandals. He lives at a fast pace and one wonders how long his health will stand it. He has great enthusiasms – goes into things with enormous energy – but drops them equally rapidly when they bore him or he finds things are not working out his way.'[58] It was one thing for Oppenheimer to transact personally with the American tycoon – even if, down the line, that led to a seat for Engelhard on Anglo's board

Bridget Oppenheimer with a tarpon weighing in
at 99 lb, caught at Boca Grande, April 1962. *(Brenthurst Library)*

– but Hagart doubted the wisdom of 'a large public exchange of shares'
between Engelhard Industries and Anglo American or De Beers. Hagart's
reservations notwithstanding, a relationship of mutual trust and affection
evolved between Engelhard and Oppenheimer. In 1960 Engelhard joined
the board of Anglo and he and HFO exchanged shares in their respective
family holding companies, Engelhard Hanovia and E Oppenheimer
and Son. From a tax point of view, it suited Oppenheimer not to receive
substantial dividends from Engelhard Industries.[59] The stock swap
paved the way for a closer convergence of their commercial interests,
and ultimately provided Anglo with an entrée into North America.[60]
In Canada, through Engelhard's intermediation, Anglo and the Rand

Selection Corporation bought an interest in the Hudson Bay Mining and Smelting Company in 1962; this gave them 400 000 shares, equal to 14.5 per cent of the company's capital.[61] The operation was financed through a $15 million loan from First National City Bank in New York negotiated by Maurice Rush.[62] Hudson Bay produced silver, copper, lead and zinc, and had exploration potential in potash. In 1963, Anglo American opened an office in the Bankers Trust Building on Park Avenue in New York: 'in addition to developing new business', Oppenheimer reported, the Anglo American Corporation (North America) would 'play a successful part in encouraging American investment in Southern Africa'.[63] Rush became the inaugural director of Anglo's North American subsidiary.

Harry and Bridget continued their annual trips to New York in the springtime. Occasionally Mary and Nicky would join them, with boundaries firmly set. When Harry Winston offered to treat the adolescent pair to an outing, Oppenheimer demurred. 'The children are still quite small and I have a dislike of pressing them on to other people.'[64] Invariably, the Oppenheimers would holiday with the Engelhards. In 1962, for example, the foursome kicked off their vacation in Boca Grande before travelling to Niagara Falls. From there, they went to Claiborne Farm in Kentucky to inspect the yearlings. Engelhard's wealth and influence made him a force to be reckoned with in the Democratic Party. After his abortive bid for a seat in the New Jersey State Senate in 1955, Engelhard struck up friendships with John F Kennedy and his soon-to-be running mate, Lyndon B Johnson. He was a generous benefactor of Kennedy's 1960 presidential campaign. Engelhard spent a couple of hours at the Kennedy Compound in Hyannis Port after JFK's nomination. He told Oppenheimer that the presidential candidate was 'much more impressive than I expected him to be'.[65] 'Naturally, I will be giving him and the rest of the Democratic ticket considerable support, both financial and otherwise', Engelhard continued; and he wondered whether Anglo American might do the same, should such a donation be possible 'without complications'.[66] Oppenheimer was ambivalent. 'I'm not sure what sort of President he'd make', HFO reputedly told Zach de Beer after meeting Kennedy for the first time, 'but he has a very fine set of teeth.'[67]

During Kennedy's presidency, Engelhard introduced the Oppenheimers to the grandees of the Democratic establishment. The gentlemanly Senate majority leader, Mike Mansfield, became a regular contact of Oppenheimer's and an admired friend. Through Engelhard, Harry and Bridget were invited to dine with President Kennedy and the First Lady,

Jacqueline Kennedy, at the White House on 2 May 1962.[68] Engelhard suggested that Oppenheimer might follow up the invitation with a gift to the first couple: to wit, Samuel Morse's painting of Colonel William Drayton, then valued at $20 000. 'There is no obligation in this regard,' Engelhard assured Oppenheimer, even though Mrs Kennedy had made it pretty clear that she expected Engelhard to stump up for the painting by Edward Troye of General Cocke on a horse, which had been restored and valued at $25 000.[69] Oppenheimer obliged, and the First Lady thanked Harry and Bridget profusely for the 'unbelievable gift'. It was the picture she 'always wanted more than any other', and it looked 'so superb in the Red Room', where it had 'the place of honor facing the fireplace'.[70] Oppenheimer's invitation to the White House underscored the parochialism of South African politics. For all that he had inherited his father's mantle as a business statesman, it was easier for Harry Oppenheimer to walk through the gates of 1600 Pennsylvania Avenue as a dinner guest of the American President than it was for him to set foot in the South African Prime Minister's official residence, Libertas, in Pretoria. In South Africa, Oppenheimer would not be invited to dine with a Prime Minister or President until 1982, when his old parliamentary foe, PW Botha, then dipping his toes in the shallow waters of reform, at last relented. At that stage another American political powerhouse, Henry Kissinger, would play the intercessor's role.

Charles Engelhard was the US administration's official representative at the independence ceremonies of Algeria, Zambia and Gabon. Meanwhile, another Washington insider with impeccable African contacts, the enigmatic diamond merchant and financier Maurice Tempelsman, started to feature prominently in Oppenheimer's life at this time. He too served as an intermediary between Oppenheimer and the White House. Born in Antwerp in 1929, the son of Orthodox Jews, Tempelsman and his parents had fled Nazi-occupied Belgium for the United States in 1940. In New York Tempelsman's father, Leon, built up a thriving diamond brokerage, Leon Tempelsman and Son, which became an authorised bulk purchaser (or 'sightholder') of rough diamonds from De Beers. A decade after Maurice Tempelsman joined the business in 1945, he began to forge links with African leaders, most notably Patrice Lumumba's nemesis, Mobutu Sese Seko. He was assisted by his firm's high-powered lawyer, Adlai Stevenson – a former Governor of Illinois, the Democratic Party's unsuccessful presidential candidate in the elections of 1952 and 1956, and the United States Ambassador to the United Nations in President

Kennedy's administration. From the early 1960s, with the backing of the State Department, Tempelsman became a conduit for Congolese diamonds into the United States. They were bartered for goods like tobacco or metals like uranium to avoid cash payments. Tempelsman performed his task so well that De Beers was soon using him to sell millions of diamonds to the United States government, despite the company's ongoing difficulties with American antitrust authorities.[71] Tempelsman developed into a highly effective middleman and lobbyist for Oppenheimer in diamond-rich but politically volatile parts of the African continent. When Anglo started producing large quantities of uranium, Oppenheimer involved Tempelsman as a seller to the American market. This put Engelhard's nose out of joint: he wanted his fair share, he wrote to Oppenheimer. 'I in no way wish to hurt or cut Tempelsman out of anything that may be his due but it is really a question of my position in Washington on this matter and that it would have been embarrassing for me to play a subsidiary role.'[72] Tempelsman was a canny operator. His political contacts in Washington were formidable, and he had close links to operatives of the Central Intelligence Agency in Africa. Documents in the United States Justice and State Department files suggest that Tempelsman became Oppenheimer's 'unofficial US representative' in the 1950s.[73] On one version it was Tempelsman, not Engelhard, who initially introduced Oppenheimer to John F Kennedy at the Carlyle Hotel.[74] Oppenheimer's own papers reveal that Tempelsman provided him with the names and contact details of State Department officials when Oppenheimer undertook an unofficial visit to Washington in 1965; and Tempelsman appears to have facilitated Oppenheimer's meeting at the White House with Kennedy's successor, President Lyndon B Johnson, at the time.[75]

Corporate Reorganisation

Oppenheimer's sorties into North America in the early 1960s laid the foundations for a concerted campaign of international diversification by Anglo American. There was simply too little scope for growth in mining within South Africa to satisfy Anglo's ambitions; and the newly independent black states to the north were considered politically risky investments. Anglo began to look outside Africa for new opportunities. HFO sought to forge an affiliated organisation, strong enough to stand on its own, through which Anglo could invest around the world.

Above: HFO pours the first bar of gold produced by Anglo American in the Orange Free State. *(Anglo American)*

Below: HFO down the Western Deep Levels mine, 1960s. *(Brenthurst Library)*

The result was Charter Consolidated. In 1965 Anglo merged Central Mining with two other British-based companies, Consolidated Mines Selection and the Chartered (British South Africa) Company, to form Charter Consolidated (known as 'Charter'), domiciled in London.[76] Bill Wilson left Johannesburg to become its managing director. The creation of Charter was the culmination of a process to which Oppenheimer devoted significant resources of time and intellectual energy. At first he had contemplated an amalgamation of parts of Anglo, De Beers and the British South Africa Company. That proposal raised practical difficulties, and the idea developed along a different route, with a merger of assets belonging to the Chartered Company, De Beers Investment Trust and Rand Selection Corporation.[77] In 1960, Oppenheimer announced the reorganisation of Rand Selection Corporation, with assets of £102 million. This included the entire capital of the De Beers Investment Trust (a wholly owned subsidiary of De Beers Consolidated Mines), whose assets had been enlarged by the transfer, in exchange for shares, of assets belonging to various mining houses or their subsidiaries. The Rand Selection Corporation's portfolio included substantial interests in Anglo, De Beers, Central Mining, the Chartered Company, Engelhard Hanovia and the Johannesburg Consolidated Investment Company (JCI). The expansion of Rand Selection Corporation would make it 'the largest investment company in South Africa', forging another link between Anglo American and De Beers and providing 'a safe and solid medium of investment in the economic future of Southern Africa'.[78] The purpose of Charter Consolidated, by contrast, as Oppenheimer reported in his chairman's statement, was to 'invest chiefly outside South Africa'.[79] Charter would participate in international mining ventures as a finance house in its own right, with its own technical staff in London. For a host of political, economic and cultural reasons, it suited Anglo to have a British affiliate through which to channel or attract opportunities globally. For its part the Anglo American Corporation intended to keep the great bulk of its business in South Africa. One of the first countries upon which Charter focused its attention was Australia, where Anglo American opened an office in Melbourne in 1965. From its small North American core, Anglo American's international interests now multiplied in scope and size.[80] Under Harry Oppenheimer's leadership, Anglo became a globally entrenched mining group.

Gold remained the cornerstone of the Anglo American empire. In 1962, Oppenheimer opened the world's deepest gold mine, Anglo's Western Deep Levels near Carletonville, west of Johannesburg. Meanwhile, the huge revenues generated by Anglo's mines on the Orange Free State goldfields enabled the corporation to diversify more widely into industry and finance. Between 1939 and 1955 the value of industrial output in South Africa increased by 690 per cent, from the equivalent of R282 million to R2221 million.[81] The industrial boom generated greater demand for capital. With Britain afflicted by balance of payments constraints, and Anglo cash-flush, it no longer made sense for the corporation to invest its short-term funds exclusively in the London money market. Conditions were ripe for a local iteration. Ernest Oppenheimer had a hand in the establishment of the state-owned National Finance Corporation in 1949, designed to hold and transfer finance earmarked for the gold mines. In 1955 Anglo rallied behind a private undertaking: it formed Union Acceptances, South Africa's first merchant bank and the progenitor of the local money market.[82] Although Ernest Oppenheimer conceived the idea, HFO played an instrumental role in its execution.[83] Supported by Barclays DCO (Dominion, Colonial and Overseas) and modelled on Lazard, Union Acceptances Limited (UAL) became South Africa's largest merchant bank. In 1957 UAL hived off its discount department and spawned the Discount House of South Africa, which was fundamentally a securities trader.[84] Anglo's growing international presence thus coincided with the early phase of its diversification from mining into industry and finance in South Africa.

Thanks to its rocketing gold revenues, Anglo American was able to establish itself not only as a multinational combine, but also as a diversified industrial and financial conglomerate.[85] By the late 1950s, most of the Anglo group's industrial activity was directly related to gold and diamond mining. Together with Imperial Chemical Industries, De Beers owned significant equity in the explosives and chemicals giant, African Explosives & Chemical Industries (AE&CI), thus renamed in 1944. That same year the De Beers Industrial Corporation (Debincor) was formed to hold De Beers' industrial interests. It relieved pressure from the parent company in satisfying the large capital requirements anticipated of the chemical industry after the war.[86] Boart and Hard Metals, which amalgamated the Boart Products Manufacturing Company and Hard Metals Limited, focused on the use of industrial diamonds in mining and other drilling applications, as well as the manufacture of tungsten carbide tools.[87] Meanwhile, Anglo's acquisition of Lewis and Marks in 1945 – occasioned by developments on the Orange Free State goldfields – had brought the Union Steel Corporation and Vereeniging Refractories into its stable. As manufacturing and construction took off, Anglo resolved to invest more widely in iron and steel production.

Iron and Steel

By 1960, South Africa's iron and steel industry was still dominated by the state-owned Iron and Steel Corporation (Iscor), formed in 1928 despite mining industry fears over a potentially overpriced and inferior state product.[88] However, a number of foreign businesses had begun to enter the South African steel and steel products market. One of them was the Minerals Engineering Company of South Africa, an associate of the Rockefeller family's Colorado-based company. Its plant at Witbank produced vanadium pentoxide (used in steel tools) for export to the United States, but it struggled to turn a profit. In 1959 Anglo acquired a two-thirds share in the enterprise, renamed it the Transvaal Vanadium Company, and put it back on its feet. This opened the door for Anglo to enter the vanadium business and, ultimately, the iron and steel industry. The Transvaal Vanadium Company produced vanadium from titaniferous magnetite ore, but discarded the iron content of the ore as waste in the process. Anglo's metallurgists and chemical engineers sought to do two things: pioneer a method of recovering and exploiting the iron content, and discover a more efficient way to extract the vanadium. (The high titanium content of vanadium made it difficult to smelt the ore using a traditional blast furnace.) In pursuit of these dual objectives, Anglo American established the Highveld Development Company in 1960. Anglo then decided to risk its own capital on building a vanadium-based integrated iron and steel production facility near Witbank, which became known as the Highveld Steel and Vanadium Corporation.

The decision to establish the plant at an initial capital cost of R70 million, by far the largest venture outside mining that Anglo had ever undertaken, was made in 1964.[89] The project was high-risk and investment-intensive. Oppenheimer described it as 'a major single act of faith by private enterprise in the future of South Africa'.[90] The Highveld Steel and Vanadium Corporation, referred to as Highveld Steel or simply Highveld, became the largest vanadium producer in the world. At the outset, according to Francis Howard, HFO's PA at the time, no one could 'make the figures look good'; 'but there was absolutely no doubt in Harry's mind that it was the right thing to do and it ... proved an enormous success'.[91] By the time the plant was completed in 1968, R127 million had been spent on the project. Just over one-third was financed through long- and medium-term loans from various European banks, and 45 per cent through equity capital.[92] Graham Boustred, the managing director (and later chairman) of Highveld Steel, recalled the 'financial agony' of Highveld's start-up years; he regarded HFO's confidence in the project as critical to its ultimate success.[93]

Boustred, who combined technical expertise with a flair for entrepreneurship and the instincts of a born trader, would develop into a formidable industrialist. He first came to Anglo's notice as the hard-nosed managing director of Scaw Metals, a reputable family-run business which produced steel parts and grinding balls for the mining industry. In 1964, as Anglo grappled with Highveld Steel's start-up problems, it acquired Scaw Metals. Scaw had begun to manufacture cast-steel bogies for the railways, and was becoming a major consumer of the kinds of specialised steel which Highveld intended to produce. Besides, Boustred knew his way around the steel business, and Oppenheimer reckoned he would be a valuable asset in his own right. It seemed logical to bring Scaw into Anglo's fold. HFO was a great admirer of Boustred's abilities. A product of private schools, St John's College and St Andrew's College, with a chemistry degree from Oxford, for all his polished credentials Boustred was no Oppenheimer clone. He lacked a certain politesse, the hallmark of Anglo's silken senior managers. Boustred was anything but bureaucratic boilerplate. He could be cantankerous and belligerent. An impatient man not unduly concerned to flatter other people's egos or soothe their sensitivities, he was often hectoring in manner. Boustred acquired a reputation for uncompromising effectiveness. 'He is so difficult that if he were not the best industrialist in South Africa we could not possibly put up with him,' Oppenheimer jested in his memoir.[94] Without Boustred, HFO claimed, Anglo would not have had the confidence to enter so deeply into industry.

◆

The Politics of Business

Although it was clear to Oppenheimer that his chairmanship of Anglo American and De Beers would make it impossible for him to stand for re-election in the 1958 election, his intention was not to quit Parliament immediately. Colin Eglin thought it would be asking too much of

Oppenheimer to continue playing 'his vital role in the [United] Party'.[95] For several days after Ernest Oppenheimer died, the press speculated whether Harry would resign his seat in Parliament. Journalists pondered the possible ramifications of HFO trying to combine his responsibilities as a parliamentarian with his stewardship of Anglo and De Beers. Unsurprisingly, the Afrikaner nationalist press led the pack, with dire prognostications of what might happen if the embodiment of *die geldmag* lingered around the House of Assembly. The most comprehensive – and interesting – treatment of the theme was delivered by *Die Burger's* columnist 'Dawie' in a piece headlined 'Kleinbaas word grootbaas' (Little boss becomes big boss).[96] At the time, 'Dawie' was *Die Burger's* editor, Piet Cillié. Cillié claimed to like Harry Oppenheimer; it was hard not to, he said, since Oppenheimer was companionable, thoughtful and sensitive. But he was not cut out for the ruthlessness of politics, and he should never have attempted to keep one foot in Parliament while maintaining the other in business. Whatever political statements Oppenheimer made were undermined, not enhanced, by his role as a business leader. It would be quite wrong, 'Dawie' charged, for Oppenheimer to continue in Parliament. He was the heir to a £267 million empire, and he should concentrate his energies on commerce. Even so, Harry lacked Ernest's 'elemental personality' – the aesthetic, idealistic streak was more pronounced in the son – and 'Dawie' could not imagine the new chairman as a daring entrepreneur creating and sustaining enterprises. As a piece of analysis, the column was both insightful and inaccurate. Whether it had any bearing on Oppenheimer's decision to abandon his political career was a question mulled over by *Die Burger's* journalists for years to come.

The announcement came on the afternoon of 2 December 1957. 'My father's death has brought me heavy business responsibilities which cannot be discharged properly if I remain actively engaged in political controversy,' Oppenheimer explained.[97] HFO hoped to make a farewell speech in Parliament, but almost immediately he was deluged with troubles on the Copperbelt where the price of copper was dwindling. This was a matter of pressing importance to Anglo American – 'perhaps the most important question with which we have to deal at the present time', he told the manager of Anglo's Bancroft mine, and it became Oppenheimer's immediate priority.[98] He asked the United Party chief whip, Jack Higgerty, for leave for the rest of the parliamentary session provided that 'it does not harm the Party'.[99] Oppenheimer pledged his loyalty to De Villiers Graaff and his ongoing support for the UP. He kept his oar in as a party fundraiser, hitting up Sam Cohen, co-founder of the retailer OK Bazaars, for a contribution to the UP's electoral coffers. He told Cohen it was 'strange' not to be directly involved in the election after having given so much time to politics in the preceding ten years. 'In some ways it is a great relief, but in others I miss the excitement.'[100] The English-language press expressed its profound regret at his parliamentary exit. 'Probably not since Cecil Rhodes used to attend the old Cape House has a businessman commanded more respect in Parliament than the man who today inherits the diamond empire Rhodes founded,' declared the *Natal Mercury*.[101] Yet there could be no greater contrast, it continued, than that between the 'burly Empire-builder with the squeaky voice' and the 'small, sleek, diffident debater' who 'punctured Nationalist dreams with polished wit and a shy smile'.

Harry Oppenheimer's departure from Parliament did nothing to dim his self-image as a business statesman in the mould of Rhodes. Once, when Ernest Oppenheimer and his son were walking through the Company Gardens in Cape Town, they stopped alongside the statue of Rhodes pointing northward with its inscription 'Your hinterland is there'. At the time Ernest remarked that there should be a similar statue on the Zambezi, with Rhodes pointing towards the south. Continuing in his father's vein, Harry regarded himself as a man of Africa, with all that it implied for the economic development of the region south of the Zambezi. In the mid-1950s, under Ernest Oppenheimer, Anglo formed a new finance house, the Anglo American Rhodesian Development Corporation, to promote development in the Rhodesian territories. It made a loan of £1 million to help Rhodesia Railways build new lines and provided another £5 million for the purchase of rolling stock. With Anglo then under fire from Prime Minister Strijdom for sending capital out of South Africa, Harry Oppenheimer could confidently retort that in the preceding decade Anglo had invested £5.6 million in the Rhodesias but received £10.7 million in return. He was minded to cultivate the mutually beneficial relationship.

At the time of these developments, the forces of African nationalism were chafing against British colonial power. There was a rising clamour for decolonisation and the formation of independent black states. In 1957, Ghana gained its independence. On 3 February 1960, the British Conservative Prime Minister, Harold Macmillan, warned members of the South African Parliament that the 'wind of change' was blowing through Africa; the growth of African 'national consciousness', he informed his stunned audience, was a political fact, like it or not.[102] His speech provoked a frisson of horror among Britons at home (and British settlers in Africa) and emboldened Verwoerd politically ahead of the republican referendum. Against this backdrop, the future of the Federation of Rhodesia and Nyasaland, which Anglo American had promoted and funded, hung in the balance. The African nationalist movement in Nyasaland, led by Hastings Banda's Nyasaland African Congress – precursor to the Malawi Congress Party – bitterly opposed the Federation. In Northern Rhodesia, the leader of the United National Independence Party, Kenneth Kaunda, felt the same way. Oppenheimer regarded the Federation as an exciting – perhaps even imitable – experiment in multiracialism, and he wanted it to succeed. 'Harry saw in the Federation a glimmer of hope for a more progressive attitude in southern Africa generally,' Anglo's man on the spot, Keith Acutt, revealed in later years.[103] His reports as Anglo chairman invariably devoted several column inches to developments in the polity. The Federation was not 'going to work … unless African opinion and aspirations in each of the federated territories are fairly represented in the central government,' Oppenheimer told his shareholders.[104] Behind the scenes, Anglo engaged in high-level efforts to shape the course of events, particularly with regard to the Monckton Commission's constitutional and legislative proposals.[105] So did the other main mining house, Rhodesian Selection Trust (RST), through its chairman, Sir Ronald Prain.[106] Anglo was slower than RST to digest the implications of the 'wind of change' speech, and its response to political developments was comparatively 'cautious and conservative'.[107] Oppenheimer remained close to Albert Robinson – the former United Party MP who became the Federation's high commissioner to Britain in 1961 – and Robinson was one of his multiple channels of influence.[108] However, the Tory government's appetite for the Federation was waning. In 1959, Lord Devlin, the British judge who was married to Sir Bernard Oppenheimer's daughter Madeleine, chaired a commission of inquiry into widespread disturbances in Nyasaland. Devlin found that the colonial government had effectively turned the territory into a police state by detaining thousands of activists from Banda's party without trial during a state of emergency. Initially, attempts were made to discredit the Devlin Report, but ultimately it helped persuade the British government that the Federation was not acceptable to the African majority.

Meanwhile, Oppenheimer engaged in a lengthy correspondence with his ally Sir Roy Welensky, the Federation's Prime Minister, who found himself increasingly at odds with Macmillan's administration. Welensky's 'constant friendship' meant a great deal to Oppenheimer; in fact, Welensky proposed to recommend Oppenheimer for a knighthood, but the magnate felt unable to accept his offer.[109] In Northern Rhodesia, Oppenheimer met with Kaunda for the first time in December 1962, almost three years after Prain had made contact, and not until after the outcome of elections which ensured an African-led coalition government in the country. This suggests that Anglo may have been hedging its bets politically, biding its time before committing itself to any particular nationalist grouping.[110] Oppenheimer intimated to Kaunda that Anglo would increase its investments in Northern Rhodesia, provided the company could be assured of political stability. Kaunda 'makes, on the surface anyway, a good impression', Oppenheimer wrote to Welensky.[111] Welensky agreed. As to the future of the Federation, Welensky confessed to having 'no crystal ball'. But he was convinced that Banda, Kaunda and the British First Secretary of State with responsibility for the newly created Central Africa Department, RA 'Rab' Butler, were in for 'a rude shock' when they got down to examining the 'practical problems' of unscrambling the federated egg. Welensky ended on a note of gratitude: 'Come what may I shall always remember the backing you've given me in these very difficult years.'[112] As the Federation was unravelling in 1963, Oppenheimer met Rab Butler to voice his concerns. He followed this up with a long letter to Butler, in which he underscored the need for 'co-ordinated and efficient plans and administration' for the defence and financial stewardship of Northern Rhodesia and Southern Rhodesia: 'We are confident of our ability to adapt ourselves to changing political conditions, and we hope not only to maintain our present interests, but to take a significant part in the further economic development of the Rhodesias ... As I see the overall position, the three essentials are, firstly, joint control at the centre over defence and finance, secondly, to prevent Northern Rhodesia developing into a one-party state, and thirdly, to give the present Southern Rhodesian constitution time to prove itself and provide ... a rapidly increasing share for Africans in government. Subject to these conditions it seems to me just possible, and I hope this is not just wishful thinking, that we may one day see the two countries come together on their own initiative to form some new Federation or Association.'[113] Yet in spite of his best attempts at business statesmanship, Oppenheimer could prevent neither the Federation from breaking up into its constituent parts, nor the Unilateral Declaration of Independence by the Prime Minister of Southern Rhodesia, Ian Smith, in 1965 – a development which Oppenheimer regarded as reckless and foolish.

◆

The Williamson Diamond Mine

Two career-defining moments in Oppenheimer's chairmanship occurred between 1957 and 1964. Both held a special significance for him. The first took place in 1958 when he flew to Tanganyika with the aim of purchasing the Williamson diamond mine at Mwadui. In later years Oppenheimer would look upon this particular transaction as the first big deal he landed independently. Although it was not the most important one of his career, it was certainly 'the most unusual and romantic'.[114] The Mwadui kimberlite pipe had been discovered by an eccentric Canadian geologist, Dr John Williamson, in 1940. From the outset De Beers attempted to buy the Williamson mine, which by 1949 had an output of 195 000 carats, but the reclusive Williamson rebuffed the mining company's overtures.[115] In any event, relations between Williamson and the diamond cartel – represented by the Diamond Corporation – were strained. There were protracted disputes over sales prices and contracts. In 1952, on the initiative of the Colonial Office and the Governor of Tanganyika, HFO went to Mwadui to negotiate directly with Williamson. Bill Wilson, who accompanied him, recalled it as 'an extraordinary visit', punctuated by Williamson's frequent disappearances into the bush, prolific consumption of Chateau d'Yquem, and disconcerting distractibility during meetings.[116] Williamson's long silences would be followed by erratic exclamations and peals of joyous laughter. Nevertheless, the negotiations bore fruit, and the agreement concluded with Williamson was renewed four years later. Anglo American provided technical assistance and advice to the management of the Williamson mine.

Williamson was a curious character. He turned Mwadui into a private city-state, with its own school, police station, shops, recreational facilities, airstrip, and a reservoir for his yacht. Highly intelligent and unpredictable (he carried a pair of scissors in his pocket to snip off visitors' ties should the urge possess him), Williamson was also an avid collector of mongrels and a two-time winner of the Aylesbury Women's Institute Silver Distaff Award for Needlework. In negotiations he would usually be flanked by his legal henchman, IC Chopra, a chameleon who put both Ernest's and Harry's patience to the test. After HFO received the news in 1956 that some 65 000 carats of Williamson diamonds had been delivered to the Diamond Development Company for sorting, he wrote to Billie Chapple with a sense of relief: 'The additional news that Chopra is, in future, to have nothing to do with the deliveries of diamonds is even more satisfactory and both my father and I were delighted to hear it.'[117]

Quite by coincidence Harry Oppenheimer was staying with the Governor of Tanganyika, Sir Edward Twining, at his official residence in Lushoto when John Williamson died on the morning of 8 January 1958. At Mwadui there was great concern: would Williamson's brother, Percy – heir to the largest number of shares in Williamson Diamonds ahead of his two sisters and Chopra – run the mine himself? He was equally as volatile as his fraternal sibling, and just as much of a dipsomaniac. But whereas John Williamson had 'charm', in HFO's view, Percy Williamson was a man of 'no obvious talents or charm', and quite 'out of his depth' in Central Africa.[118] Oppenheimer hastened to send his condolences to Chopra, and conveyed the hope that De Beers might continue to enjoy 'friendly relations' with Mwadui.[119] After reading a news report that De Beers' rival, Selection Trust, had been in touch with the management of Williamson mine to discuss the mine's future, Oppenheimer fired off a missive to Alfred Chester Beatty. 'All this is very vague, but I thought I should write to you ... because I am most anxious that we should co-operate very closely in anything affecting the diamond business.'[120] HFO was concerned that whatever became of the Williamson mine, central marketing arrangements in the trade should be maintained – a desideratum that he impressed upon Governor Twining. In truth, Oppenheimer was determined to acquire control of the Williamson mine. As the months dragged on with confusing reports emerging from Mwadui, HFO felt it was time to pay his respects to the new owners. In June, accompanied by Tony Wilson and Ogilvie Thompson, Oppenheimer took the company Heron from Johannesburg to Mwadui. On arrival they were greeted by the acting mine manager, Gay du Toit, and Chopra, but Percy Williamson was unavailable: the day before, he had managed to get spectacularly inebriated at the mine club and now he was nursing a hangover.

Once the crapulent Williamson had recovered, it became clear he had no appetite for Mwadui. As soon as he met Oppenheimer and Wilson, Williamson launched into a tirade: 'I hate this place, I hate Tanganyika and everyone here; to get clear of them I'll give away my shares!'[121] But his outburst was for show; he was as mercurial as his brother. In reality, Williamson wanted a worthwhile offer. Oppenheimer returned to South Africa and instructed GHR Edmunds – auditor of De Beers and chairman of the South African board of Standard Bank – to go and conduct an evaluation. On 4 July, the De Beers negotiating team made its opening bid: £4 million. Chopra seemed tempted, but Williamson was affronted: he walked out of the meeting. A little while later he returned. If the offer was free of death duties – increasing the purchase price to just over £5.6 million – he would consider it. Representatives from De Beers consulted with senior members of the Tanganyika government; it had been decided to bring in the government as a 50 per cent shareholder with funds loaned by De Beers. As matters gathered steam, Oppenheimer swooped in to close the deal. On Sunday, 6 July, he returned to Mwadui. His window of opportunity was narrow. Percy Williamson had resolved to go back to Canada come hell or high water on the Tuesday. After dinner with the irascible Williamson and a still-scheming Chopra on the Sunday night, Oppenheimer got down to the laborious business of drafting their terms of agreement. (In later years, he claimed to have written the contract on loo paper.) Tony Wilson was at his side, but there were no lawyers to assist them. Oppenheimer worked until 1 am. Eventually he produced something he regarded as satisfactory. De Beers would purchase the whole of the equity – 1200 shares – for £5 645 451 and transfer 320 shares to the government of Tanganyika in lieu of the local duty payable by John Williamson's estate. Williamson and Chopra consented. De Beers' lawyers, Webber Wentzel, pronounced the contract watertight; there was no need for any alterations. The following month, an agreement was struck between De Beers and the Tanganyika government for the latter to acquire a further 280 shares at a cost of £1 317 212, thus making it an equal owner of the Williamson mine. This 50-50 ownership arrangement set a precedent that was to become important in the future. It enabled De Beers to manage and control production from the Williamson mine, and to ensure that its output would be sold through the Central Selling Organisation. All told, it was Oppenheimer's first triumph. As Ogilvie Thompson, his PA at the time, subsequently reflected: the acquisition gave HFO 'understandable pleasure' and 'confirmed to the outside world … that De Beers had a worthy successor to Sir Ernest in the chair'.[122]

The General Mining–Federale Mynbou Deal

Oppenheimer's other masterstroke during this period was to engineer the deal that gave an Afrikaner mining concern, Federale Mynbou, the controlling share in Sir George Albu's General Mining and Finance Corporation. This provided Afrikaners with a significant stake in the gold mining industry for the first time – in return for De Beers' continued dominion over diamonds. The background to the General Mining–Federale Mynbou transaction is complex. After Anglo American brokered negotiations between Jack Scott and George Albu in 1954, Anglo proceeded to acquire a 22 per cent shareholding in General Mining. This was enough to give the corporation a controlling interest. However, by the time Albu died in February 1963, General Mining was in a sclerotic state, blighted by static profits and hamstrung by an elderly, conservative board and management. Albu's death afforded Anglo the opportunity to restructure and re-energise General Mining. Federale Mynbou happened to be waiting in the wings. In fact, its managing director, Tom Muller, recalled in later years that the initiative to collaborate with Anglo 'really came from our side during the time Sir Ernest was still alive'.[123]

In the mid-1950s, Federale Mynbou was a fledgling mining house. It had been formed in 1953 under the umbrella of Federale Volksbeleggings, whose goal was to support Afrikaner entrepreneurs and mobilise Afrikaner capital and savings, thereby strengthening Afrikaner economic nationalism.[124] In 1955 Sanlam, the Cape-based Afrikaner insurance company, became a shareholder in Federale Mynbou. Soon after its formation Federale Mynbou's chairman, William Bedford Coetzer, went to see Ernest Oppenheimer, accompanied by Muller. At that stage their enterprise was increasingly active in coal mining, and they sought Anglo's co-operation in making strategic acquisitions. A degree of collaboration ensued. In 1957, Federale Mynbou won the Electricity Supply Commission's tender for the supply of coal to the newly commissioned Komati power station in Middelburg. Anglo American owned coal-bearing ground in the middle of Federale Mynbou's two tracts of land next to the site of the development. In exchange for Anglo's property, Federale Mynbou gave the corporation roughly a 40 per cent share in the Blinkpan colliery – created to exploit the coal deposits – and a seat on the board of Blinkpan for Gavin Relly.[125] By 1962, Federale Mynbou's coal interests were rapidly expanding. The company gained a controlling concern in Trans-Natal Coal Limited, a significant industry player and rival to Anglo. Federale Mynbou then turned its attention to asbestos and acquired key holdings. Diamonds were next in its line of sight; and that is what caused Harry Oppenheimer to renew Anglo's acquaintance with Tom Muller. In 1963, Federale Mynbou took a 17.5 per cent interest in the Terra Marina Diamond Corporation, whose other major Afrikaner shareholders, notably Sanlam, held 70 per cent.[126] Terra Marina sought diamond concessions in Namaqualand and off the West Coast at sea. Muller tried to persuade Sam Collins, proprietor of the Marine Diamond Corporation which mined diamonds off the West Coast, to join Terra Marina. Concerned about the potential threat to its monopoly, after tough negotiations De Beers reached a separate agreement with Collins. For Oppenheimer the warning lights were flashing. A few years earlier Afrikaner financial interests had sought to gain control of JCI, which would have given them a foothold in diamond mining (35 per cent of JCI's interests were tied up in the diamond industry).[127] Anglo blocked the move and acquired a 50 per cent stake in JCI through the Rand Selection Corporation. Like his father, HFO had life-long experience of shutting out competitors from the diamond industry, or absorbing them into the Central Selling Organisation. That is precisely what he set out to achieve when he invited Tom Muller and his wife to a banquet in the Diamond Pavilion at the Rand Easter Show. There, in his most charming and persuasive manner, Oppenheimer suggested to Muller: 'You said you were interested in making an acquisition. I think perhaps we might have a discussion about that.'[128]

The nub of the subsequent discussions was this: in exchange for Federale Mynbou essentially abandoning its diamond ambitions – and provided that Terra Marina marketed its diamonds through the Central Selling Organisation – Federale Mynbou would acquire a significant stake in General Mining. Lured by the promise of gold, Muller and Coetzer turned their back on diamonds. In August 1963, Anglo American and Federale Mynbou formed a joint venture, Main Street Investments, in which each of them acquired a 50 per cent interest. Anglo American placed its 22 per cent shareholding in General Mining into the new vehicle, which increased its holdings in General Mining to 40 per cent via the market. Federale Mynbou exchanged a substantial basket of Trans-Natal Coal shares, and some other bits and bobs, for a 50 per cent shareholding in Main Street Investments.[129] Muller was appointed as managing director of General Mining, and Coetzer joined the board. Albert Robinson, who had recently returned to South Africa with a knighthood, was made deputy chairman of General Mining. Together, they worked to relieve the managerial rheumatism that had taken hold under the chairmanship of Calvin Stowe McLean.

The formation of Main Street Investments provoked a backlash in sections of the Afrikaner nationalist press in the north of the country – most notably, *Die Vaderland*, and organs effectively controlled by Dagbreek Press – which were sympathetic to Hendrik Verwoerd. The Prime Minister launched a scathing attack on Anglo American, and described the group as more dangerous than the Sons of England Patriotic and Benevolent Society.[130] His tirade was an indirect assault, according to the *Sunday Times*, on Coetzer and Muller and their southern backers at Sanlam, who were seen to be working too closely with the 'liberal enemy'.[131] To Verwoerd and a zealous coterie in his cabinet, Harry Oppenheimer was the personification of 'Hoggenheimer' and the Anglo American Corporation was the imperialist enemy of Afrikanerdom. Oppenheimer's nationalist denigrators were able to tap into a (shrinking) well of anti-capitalist sentiment which had coexisted, counterintuitively, with the rise of the Afrikaner economic movement and *volkskapitalisme* in the 1930s and 1940s. Oppenheimer had made concerted efforts to learn Afrikaans during the war and in Parliament, and he kept a close eye on the Afrikaans press. He could see that the brouhaha was unsettling Muller – a prominent member of the Afrikaner establishment – and so he approached the new managing director of General Mining with an idea. 'Look, I can see that this is very embarrassing for you people. I will sell Federale [Mynbou] one per cent of my fifty per cent in Mainstraat [Main Street Investments], so you will have fifty-one per cent and can say you now control the majority of votes in General Mining.'[132] Muller regarded this as a 'very great gesture'. He went to see Verwoerd and explained the proposal in confidence. 'He didn't comment very much but he was very friendly and certainly didn't have any criticism … I think Dr Verwoerd appreciated what a big thing it was for Afrikaans business.'[133]

In August 1964, Oppenheimer, Muller and Robinson announced that Federale Mynbou would acquire the controlling interest in General Mining through Main Street Investments, with effect from the beginning of 1965. Federale Mynbou proceeded to take ownership of General Mining's assets valued at between R200 million and R250 million.[134] This was a significant step for a company formed only 11 years previously with capital of R120 000. The English-language press fell over itself to lavish praise. *Sunday Times* reported the deal as a 'personal triumph' for

Oppenheimer, 'an important step forward in his proposals for closer business co-operation across the South African language barrier'.[135] Without 'Mr Oppenheimer's act of guidance', the *Rand Daily Mail* contended, the deal would never have been brokered.[136] Afrikaans newspapers in the Naspers group, historically aligned to Sanlam and the National Party in the Cape, were equally well disposed. In Bloemfontein, *Die Volksblad* billed the deal as another economic 'breakthrough'; the days when Afrikaners had to be 'satisfied with just the crumbs of the country's riches' were gone for good.[137] Even the Minister of Economic Affairs, Nico Diederichs, conferred his imprimatur. Far from being swallowed up by Anglo American, Federale Mynbou had captured an 'important share of a world hitherto beyond its grasp'.[138] However, in a long editorial, AM van Schoor of *Die Vaderland* struck a cautionary note. The transaction was not a major victory for Afrikaner interests. In fact, it dealt a death blow to an ideal which had started with the Afrikaner economic empowerment organisation, the Reddingsdaadbond, in 1939: namely, the independent acquisition by Afrikaners of their own place and share in the mining industry. Federale Mynbou was now only a name. Its Afrikaner character would disappear, submerged into the greater whole of General Mining. Ratcheting up the rhetoric, Van Schoor continued: 'There will certainly be greater opportunities for money-making ... But the original idea is dead, buried in Hollard Street, in a 24-carat-gold coffin.'[139] For Oppenheimer, by contrast, the tie-up was a 'breakthrough': he had successfully co-opted the competition.

The transaction sparked renewed controversy. Hard-line Afrikaner nationalists believed their ethnic confrères in business had been duped and assimilated into a subservient relationship with English capital by Anglo's smooth-tongued 'Hoggenheimer'. There were some English-speaking South Africans who thought, with more than a touch of jingoist self-satisfaction, that Oppenheimer had cut Federale Mynbou a discount deal in an act of statesmanlike generosity. The notion that Anglo American 'gave' General Mining to Federale Mynbou 'at a fraction of its value' still persists among scholars of South African economic history.[140] Yet the shares in General Mining were not passed on to Federale Mynbou by way of charity. Federale Mynbou acquired Anglo American's stake in General Mining at market prices.[141] Then, too, decades after the transaction was concluded, commentators would look upon it as a precursor to the post-apartheid government's black economic empowerment policy. Yet the analogy is misleading. The deal was not actively encouraged by

Verwoerd's government nor was the equity in General Mining handed over to Afrikaner businessmen like a free lunch in a gold-ribboned box. Albert Robinson, Oppenheimer's devoted friend, regarded the tie-up as 'the most important act of financial statesmanship' by the magnate during his chairmanship of Anglo.[142] The claim is overstated. The deal enabled Anglo to procure better management for General Mining and protect De Beers' diamond monopoly. It was thus a shrewd commercial gambit propelled by enlightened self-interest.

The General Mining–Federale Mynbou deal certainly illustrates Oppenheimer's political foresight. He sought, with some measure of long-term success, to buttress the moderating tendency within Afrikaner nationalism. In this way he helped tilt the balance of forces in favour of what subsequently became known as the *verligte* (or enlightened) as opposed to the *verkrampte* (or reactionary) camp in the Afrikaner ruling class. Seen from this point of view, Oppenheimer's actions were politically strategic. Some analysts believe they ultimately served to legitimate and facilitate the negotiated settlement in the 1990s.[143] Indeed, from the mid-1960s, sections of the Afrikaans press wrote sympathetically about Oppenheimer's wealth and commercial prowess. This might be attributed to the assiduousness of Anglo's public relations machine in the run-up to the announcement of the deal. The popular magazine *Die Huisgenoot* carried a series of admiring articles with titles like 'The power of De Beers',[144] 'Anglo American Corporation: The colossus of our business world',[145] and 'Our country's richest man'.[146] The Oppenheimer family was depicted as a paragon of glamour. *Die Brandwag* pronounced Mary Oppenheimer the 'Pearl of Parktown'.[147] By holding out the hand of co-operation to Afrikaner business interests – and by exposing Federale Mynbou first-hand to the challenges of the gold mining industry – Oppenheimer reckoned that he would gain a more sympathetic ear from the government both for Anglo American and for the English-dominated Chamber of Mines. The entry of Afrikaners into the Chamber of Mines, which represented the collective interests of mine employers and managed all wage negotiations and collective bargaining, defused the National Party's residual antipathy to the mining industry. Muller's election to the presidency of the Chamber in 1968 was a symbolic breakthrough in this regard. In short, Oppenheimer's championship of the General Mining–Federale Mynbou deal was driven principally by pragmatic – rather than by idealistic – considerations. A similar motive force propelled his progressive politics in the 1960s and 1970s.

NINE

Progressive

1959–1973

'If I could have been in the government, I think I would have been very inclined to stay in politics and try to make other arrangements about business.'[1] That is how, later in life, Harry Oppenheimer reflected on his succession to the chairmanship of Anglo American and De Beers. Shorn of his parliamentary platform, Oppenheimer nevertheless remained a prominent figure in the polemical arena. He instinctively grasped the calculus of power. Business, as an agent of economic development, might conceivably drive the process of social change, but the power-brokers in cabinet could smooth or stall its course. Throughout the 1960s and beyond, Oppenheimer harnessed his international prestige and global networks to shift the tide of domestic politics. He came to be recognised as the most important 'non-cabinet member of the cabinet'.[2] In his chairman's statements for the Anglo American Corporation, HFO frequently analysed the country's political economy in greater detail than he reported on commercial developments and company profits. They constituted an alternative state of the nation address. As South Africa's pre-eminent capitalist, Oppenheimer's words carried weight with Western heads of state. He wielded enormous soft power. Over the *longue durée*, Oppenheimer engaged in a kind of corporate shuttle diplomacy to bring about reform, weaving his way from Washington to Whitehall. In 1962 he dined with President John F Kennedy at the White House. Two years after Kennedy's assassination, he was received with remarkable informality in the same venue by JFK's successor, the burly, bear-like President Lyndon B

Johnson. LBJ, Oppenheimer observed (somewhat appalled), held court in the presidential bathroom, 'dressed in pyjamas in the process of having his hair cut', before continuing the discussion from his bed.[3] The architect of the Great Society condemned apartheid in a tone the businessman found 'harsh'. HFO replied that South Africa needed to find a pragmatic way of dismantling racial discrimination without incurring the risk of black-on-white retaliation or destroying the parliamentary system. But he cautioned that undue foreign interference – or outright censure of the Nationalist government – would hinder, not help, the cause. President Johnson was a champion of racial equality at home, but his views on South Africa's cauldron of injustice were tempered by Oppenheimer and their great mutual friend, Charles Engelhard.

The British Prime Minister Harold Macmillan consulted Oppenheimer on the eve of his famous 'Wind of Change' speech.[4] Harold Wilson, Macmillan's Labourite successor (after the brief interposition of Sir Alec Douglas-Home), sought Oppenheimer's counsel on Rhodesian affairs in the wake of Ian Smith's Unilateral Declaration of Independence in 1965.[5] The magnate enjoyed a closer ideological rapport with Wilson's Tory rival, Edward Heath, elected to the premiership in 1970. Oppenheimer stressed to Heath that politicians in South Africa would have 'the utmost difficulty' in taking any positive steps towards progressive change.[6] The solution, he averred, lay in the business community paying higher wages to upskilled black labourers: their promotion into the ranks of management would ultimately break down racial barriers. Oppenheimer was granted a private audience with the world leader he most revered, President Charles de Gaulle, at the Élysée Palace, before de Gaulle's resignation in 1969. The imposing French statesman sat at his desk and opened the conversation brusquely. 'Que voulez-vous de moi?' he demanded of Oppenheimer. Caught slightly off guard, HFO responded diffidently that de Gaulle was a 'very great man'. He wanted to know if de Gaulle's experiences in managing the Algerian conflict held any lessons for South Africa. (At the back of Oppenheimer's mind, he drily conceded, was the thought 'You're a public monument and I've come to see you as I might come to see the Eiffel Tower'.)[7] President Johnson had argued forcefully that South Africa's racial policies were 'an affront to the civilised world'.[8] By contrast, de Gaulle took the line that white South Africans were tasked with '*une oeuvre civilisatrice*'. But it would be a civilising mission only in so far as people of other races could share in it to the full extent of their ability and willingness. Oppenheimer deemed de Gaulle's approach to be 'absolutely splendid'.[9]

Oppenheimer continued to expound the same anti-apartheid views that had threaded his speeches in the House of Assembly, eschewing moralism for the measured arguments of *homo economicus*. On international platforms – if he were addressing the Royal Institute of International Affairs at Chatham House in London, for example – he might tailor his pronouncements in order to pre-empt a rebuke from the South African government. In consequence of this ambidextrous strategy, a waggish columnist at *Africa South* – the left-leaning anti-apartheid magazine founded by Ronald Segal in 1956 – attached the adjective 'multi-facial' to Oppenheimer's politics, a riff on his professed support for multiracialism.[10] As the 'wind of change' blew through the rest of Africa, there were continuities and ruptures in the polity at home. Like the African National Congress (ANC), from which the Pan Africanist Congress (PAC) had splintered, the white parliamentary opposition was vulnerable to scission. De Villiers Graaff failed to arrest the United Party's ongoing ossification. He offered a pale imitation of the ruling party's platform of white supremacy. After the 1958 election, the United Party mustered only 53 seats in Parliament to the National Party's 103. Meanwhile, members of the UP's liberal wing could no longer bear their party's prevarications on 'native policy', and in 1959 they broke away to form the Progressive Party under the leadership of Jan Steytler. It was a classically liberal party, upholding free enterprise, civil rights and the rule of law. During the 1960s, the Progressives advocated a colour-blind (or non-racial) qualified franchise, opposed the Bantustan policy, and rooted their resistance to apartheid in the principle of 'merit, not race'. They also proposed various constitutional safeguards for minority groups, a hedged sort of liberalism which placed the 'Progs' increasingly at odds with the more radical Liberal Party. The Liberals switched their support to universal suffrage in 1960.

Against this backdrop, Oppenheimer relinquished his membership of the UP, threw in his lot with the Progs, and bankrolled the fledgling party. He remained the most influential figure, outside Parliament, in opposition politics. Oppenheimer presented the public face of liberal capitalism, with its unshakeable conviction that racial discrimination and free enterprise were incompatible. The so-called Oppenheimer thesis held that 'failure to eradicate the one' would 'ultimately result in the destruction of the other'.[11] Industrialisation would gradually

Knocking out apartheid's industrial policy: HFO gives
Prime Minister BJ Vorster a glass jaw in this Bob Connolly
cartoon from the late 1960s. *(Brenthurst Library)*

but ineluctably lead to modernisation, the emergence of an urbanised
black middle class, democracy and racial equality. In a seminal essay
published in 1966, several core tenets of the liberal creed were explicated
by Michael O' Dowd, *primus inter pares* among a slew of socially engaged
and sometimes eccentric intellectuals employed by Anglo American
primarily to think.[12] They also fostered a culture of corporate citizenship.
To Anglo's attackers, the Oppenheimer thesis played an obstructive role
in 'dividing and confusing' the critics of foreign investment in apartheid
South Africa.[13]

The 1960s were the apogee of grand apartheid. The seismic upheaval
unleashed by the Sharpeville massacre subsided into a period of
impregnable authority for the National Party – backed by its erosion of
civil liberties – and unprecedented economic prosperity for the white
minority. The ANC and PAC were banned in 1960, and Oliver Tambo
proceeded to establish the ANC in exile. A police raid on Lilliesleaf farm
in Rivonia in 1963 led to the arrest, trial and imprisonment of almost all
the underground leaders of the ANC and the Communist Party (SACP),
several of whom were sentenced to life imprisonment alongside Nelson
Mandela on Robben Island. Although the ANC turned to armed resistance

in 1961 with the formation of a military wing, Umkhonto we Sizwe (a move echoed by the PAC with Poqo), within a year after the Rivonia Trial ended in 1964 the liberation movements in South Africa were 'smashed and eviscerated'.[14] The UP and the Progs both suffered debilitating electoral setbacks in October 1961 and again in March 1966, as the National Party reached out to English-speakers fearful of the *swart gevaar* (black peril) and neutralised white opposition to apartheid. The Liberal Party – an electoral minnow – disbanded in 1968 in the wake of the Prohibition of Political Interference Act, which forbade blacks and whites to belong to the same political organisation. By the end of the decade whites, who accounted for less than one-fifth of the total population, boasted nearly three-quarters of national income. And yet, in spite of the seemingly invincible nature of the apartheid regime, by the late 1960s tiny cracks were forming below the surface. On 6 September 1966, Prime Minister HF Verwoerd was stabbed to death by a parliamentary messenger, Dimitri Tsafendas. His successor, the former Minister of Justice, BJ Vorster, was a hard-boiled securocrat; but he wanted to make the outside world less antagonistic towards South Africa. Vorster therefore pursued a policy of détente with other African states and made minor concessions in respect of 'petty' apartheid. He desegregated some public amenities and allowed multiracial international sports teams to tour the country. Vorster's apparent moderation alarmed the right-wing Verwoerdian nationalists in the ruling party. It set the stage for a showdown between what the Potchefstroom academic WA de Klerk identified in 1967 as the Nationalists' *verligte* and *verkrampte* factions. As fissures appeared in the edifice of Afrikanerdom, in the early 1970s the economy began to falter owing to structural vulnerabilities and global pressures. Industrial strife, coupled with the rise of the Black Consciousness Movement, paved the way for a cycle of repression and reform and a major turning point in South African history. In the background, Oppenheimer positioned himself – and his corporate empire – as pragmatic mediators in the momentous events that were to follow.

◆

The Private Sphere

As Harry Oppenheimer became a ubiquitous presence in civic life, the Brenthurst estate developed into both his private haven and an extension of his public sphere. For several years after Ernest Oppenheimer's death, Harry and Bridget remained in Little Brenthurst while his stepmother, Ina, occupied Brenthurst proper. In due course, a new residence, Blue Skies, was built for Ernest's widow on another section of the grounds. Ina and Bridget's relationship was punctuated by protracted periods of frostiness. There were squabbles over dogs. Bridget once blotted her copybook by gifting Ina with a tome whose foreword the dowager had written. Bridget had failed to look inside. Putting some distance between their abodes was mutually desirable. Joane Pim, designer of the gardens at Mauritzfontein, was commissioned to revivify the Brenthurst estate before Harry and Bridget moved into the main house. On Christmas Eve 1962 the last step to the terrace of Brenthurst was put in place – leading out onto 'gentle slopes and patches of brilliant colour', *The Star* recorded – and over a weekend in January the re-landscaped gardens were opened to the public to help raise funds for the African Children's Feeding Scheme.[15] Ina remained actively engaged in her pursuits – writing, flower arranging and photography – until injuries sustained in a motor car accident took her life in 1971. Bridget's mother, Marjorie McCall, died in 1967.

Harry continually added to his father's archive of Africana. He was forever purchasing books, maps and manuscripts; and he started building up an impressive array of Lord Byron's works – including some of the poet's letters and first editions – from Bernard Quaritch and Chas J Sawyer, among other antiquarian booksellers. Oppenheimer acquired a number of French Impressionist paintings to add to Ernest's old masters. He augmented his collection of silverware and chinaware. He furnished Brenthurst with several Louis XV chairs, chests and console tables; and he commissioned the twenty-something South African sculptor Louis le Sueur to create a large bronze sculpture for the gardens (plumping for the youngster over the more established Henry Moore and Marino Marini).[16] Several times a week Harry and Bridget hosted a black-tie dinner for a carefully curated selection of friends, colleagues, opposition politicians, assorted worthies, and whichever celebrated author, artist, academic or aristocrat happened to be passing through Johannesburg. Bridget kept a detailed record of her dinner guests, the number of times in any given year that they graced the dinner table, and the victuals and vintage wines she served. Once a year there was a grand ball. The lady of the manor busied herself with charity work and keeping her various major-domos in check. She excelled in the role of grande dame. In testimony to her grandeur, Bridget sat for a painting by Queen Elizabeth's portraitist Pietro Annigoni

Bridget Oppenheimer and HFO lead in Hengist, winner of the
Johannesburg Summer Handicap (Grade 1) in 1959; Tiger Fish was
the Oppenheimers' first Durban July Handicap winner that same year.
(Brenthurst Library)

in 1966. Horse racing grew into a shared passion. Harry and Bridget made
regular trips to Mauritzfontein, where a veterinary surgeon, Tremayne
Thoms, was installed as the stud manager. Mauritzfontein produced a
number of Grade 1 winners for the couple in the 1960s, including King
Willow. He notched up the Oppenheimers' second Durban July Handicap
victory in 1965.

Harry and Bridget travelled overseas often, venturing from Anchorage
to the Amazon, from Melbourne to Honolulu, and to wherever Anglo's
expanding empire established its latest outpost. There were jaunts to
Shangani every August with the children and the children's friends. In so
far as HFO took an annual holiday, this was it. In 1968, he added another
property to the family's portfolio: Milkwood, a sprawling, terracotta
mansion set in three hectares of verdant, subtropical grounds manicured
by the doyen of Durban City Parks, Cedric van Ryneveld. It opened onto
the Indian Ocean at La Lucia, north of Durban. Bridget's idea was to use
Milkwood as a base during the Natal winter racing season. The house was
constructed on a strip of land purchased from one of Anglo's property
investment companies. 'I must admit to having been a bit taken aback

by its size,' Harry wrote to his daughter as the dwelling took shape.[17] It comprised ten luxurious bedrooms with en-suite facilities, a huge swimming pool, and every amenity imaginable. The house was going to cost 'a very great deal of money', Harry calculated, but the outlay would be worthwhile. 'I believe we're all of us going to get an immense amount of pleasure out of it,' he enthused to Mary. By the time construction was finished, Milkwood was South Africa's most expensive seaside villa, chalking up a sum of R500 000. This prompted the *Sunday Express* to rhapsodise about an oceanside retreat on 'so superb a scale' that it would have 'stunned even the late Cecil B de Mille'.[18]

The children came of age. Mary completed her schooling at Heathfield, and Nicky proceeded from Ludgrove to Harrow. His name had been down for Eton since he was only a year old, but HFO's contemporary at Oxford Alan Barber, the principal of Ludgrove, thought Harrow a better bet.[19] In England, Raymond Oppenheimer made White Waltham a more congenial environment for Nicky's half-term exeats than 21 Portman Square had been for Harry's. Raymond became, in Bridget Oppenheimer's view, a 'surrogate father' to Mary and Nicky.[20] A great deal of the siblings' immediate family life was sacrificed on the altar of Anglo American and De Beers, with all the time-consuming rituals and sacraments which the House of Oppenheimer imposed upon their parents. Mary joined the other debutantes at the Queen Charlotte's Ball in 1961, accompanied by her godfather, Keith Acutt. Afterwards she was treated to a lavish coming-out party at Hugh and Helen Vivian Smith's property, the Durdans, near Epsom. Following a brief stint in Paris, Mary returned to Johannesburg and took her first job as a trainee in the accounts department at Anglo American. Another position at the Ernest Oppenheimer Memorial Trust was more to her liking. The 'diamond girl', 'diamond heiress' or 'diamond princess', as Mary was regularly referred to in complimentary press profiles of the time, was clever and captivatingly coy. She did not want for potential suitors – many of them sportsmen – including her horse-riding instructor, Bill Johnson. But the man who won her over was a rugby player, a powerfully built fly-half, and a famous one at that. Gordon Waddell, third son of a Glaswegian stockbroker, was the shrewd and driven product of Fettes College and Cambridge University, where he read for a law degree. Between 1957 and 1962 Waddell earned 18 caps for Scotland, toured twice with the British Lions and played for the Barbarians a dozen times. In 1962 he travelled to South Africa with the Lions and met Mary at a party. Romance blossomed and a courtship across the continents ensued. Waddell was introduced to Harry and Bridget. In 1963 he met up with them and Mary on a trip to the United States, where he was pursuing an MBA at Stanford University. After he graduated the following year, Waddell spent five weeks with the family at Shangani. Contemporary photos of the square-jawed Waddell on the Rhodesian ranch show him looking remarkably at ease, in a kilt, staring confidently at the camera. On a visit to London, Mary accepted his marriage proposal. But the engagement was kept under wraps for a few weeks: on the day of the Durban July Handicap in 1965, Mary announced the news to her parents. 'We certainly had a memorable weekend with King Willow and Mary's engagement all on the same day,' Oppenheimer wrote to Colin Eglin.[21] The plutocrat rewarded his future son-in-law with a golden-bronze Maserati sports coupé.

Mary and Gordon's nuptials on 3 November 1965 were hailed as Johannesburg society's wedding of the century. As soon as their engagement was announced Bridget was bombarded with letters from admirers hoping to feast their eyes on the proceedings. 'Of course, Mary is regarded as the uncrowned Princess of the Republic of South Africa, and I am sure that on the day of her wedding she will be as regal and lovely as a Queen,' one Mrs R Chaitowitz penned breathlessly, adding that she had an 'obsession' to see Mary in her 'shining hour of glory'.[22] The wedding itself was a high-priced piece of pageantry in downtown Johannesburg's Anglican cathedral, presided over by a procession of vergers, robed priests and the Bishop of Johannesburg garbed in gold and scarlet. As an ever-swelling crowd thronged the streets amidst intermittent rain showers, the city became gridlocked. Some women tried to reach out and touch Mary's bridal gown, with its twenty-foot train, for luck. The police struggled to enforce crowd control, and as the melee grew, several spectators were hurt in the scrummage to see the couple pass. By the end of the day, abandoned hats, handbags and shoes lay strewn near the cathedral grounds. Happily, the reception at Brenthurst afterwards – attended by nearly a thousand guests – proved to be a more governable affair.

On the Waddells' return from their honeymoon in Beirut, Gordon slotted comfortably into the Oppenheimer dynasty. 'He's much more of an Oppenheimer than I'll ever be,' Mary was reputed to have said. Waddell was given a position in Anglo's finance division, where he rapidly inserted himself in the corridors of power. It helped that he was the boss's son-in-law, but he was also able and, according to some of his nonplussed colleagues, relentlessly self-assertive, if not arrogant. As one

Above: Curious onlookers try to catch a glimpse of Mary Oppenheimer before her wedding to Gordon Waddell, 3 November 1965. *(Brenthurst Library) Below:* Mary Waddell and her mother, Bridget, at the wedding reception afterwards. *(Brenthurst Library)*

observer noted, employees who expected Waddell to serve as a kind of prince consort, 'taking up a corner office between lunch engagements and golf dates', were in for a rude surprise.[23] He was blunt and ambitious. Supervisors handed him various opportunities to fail, but he made a success of them all. Within two years of his marriage to Mary, Gordon was ready to undertake an overseas 'tour of duty' in Anglo's New York office.[24] Waddell's rise in Anglo was lightning-fast. In 1969 he joined the board; two years later he was made an executive director. Meanwhile, he and Mary started their own family. A daughter, Victoria Jane, was born in 1968, followed by another, Rebecca, in 1970.

Harry and Bridget's first grandson, Jonathan Ernest Maxmillian Oppenheimer, arrived in 1969. He was Nicky's heir. From Harrow, Nicky had proceeded to Christ Church, Oxford, where, like his father, he read for the PPE. Unlike his progenitor, Nicky's 21st birthday party was held at White Waltham rather than the Spread Eagle Inn. If Jan Smuts was no longer around to lend a sense of gravitas to the occasion, then this was more than compensated for by the presence of a bevy of nubile noblewomen, including Lady Caroline Percy (a member of the Prince of Wales's set) and another of Prince Charles's subsequent girlfriends, Lucia Santa Cruz (the beautiful and brainy daughter of the Chilean Ambassador to the Court of St James). 'South Africa's most eligible bachelor' was how the recently launched *Scope* magazine tagged Nicky in an interview.[25] He had returned to South Africa for military service in Kimberley. Yet Nicky's heart was already set on Orcillia 'Strilli' Lasch, the free-spirited daughter of a wealthy Johannesburg businessman and internationally competitive glider pilot, Helmut 'Helli' Lasch. He had first met her on the golf course at the Johannesburg Country Club when he was 13 and she was 17, but now – in their twenties – the age gap did not seem so formidable (though Harry and Bridget were less convinced of the fact). The wedding ceremony, on 11 November 1968, was altogether more low-key than Mary and Gordon's: Nicky and Strilli exchanged vows at the small St George's Anglican church in Parktown, where the Lasch family and the Oppenheimers had both been parishioners for some time. There was no frenzied press pack trying to uncover their honeymoon destination – Australia – and on their return to Johannesburg Nicky settled unassumingly back into work at 44 Main Street, to which he had reported earlier in the year as his father's 'bag carrier'.[26]

In spite of his interests being more sporting than cerebral – principally, cricket, golf and helicoptering – in some ways Nicky took after his

Nicky and Strilli Oppenheimer on their wedding day,
11 November 1968. *(Brenthurst Library)*

father. He shared Harry's self-effacing manner, and there was a quality
of diffidence about him. (In HFO's case this modesty perhaps ran only
skin-deep: it belied vigorous views on people, business and politics, as
well as a latent streak of intellectual vanity.) However, Nicky's tutelage at
Anglo differed from his father's thirty-five years before. The corporation
was now a diversified conglomerate. Its complexity was much more
challenging to master. The nature of Nicky's relationship with his father
was also different. Bridget regarded Harry's bond with Ernest – the way
in which they exchanged ideas and intuited each other's thoughts – as
'one of the most remarkable I have ever seen'. 'Certainly Harry & Nicky
did not have this wonderful rapport,' she added.[27]

Meanwhile, Strilli acclimatised to life as an Oppenheimer at less
than Gordon's full throttle. Relations between Strilli and the regimental
Bridget were sometimes strained, as they were between Bridget and Ina.

Strilli disliked playing the hostess at business dinners – 'Entertaining to us is a pleasure, not a duty,' she told the features writer Chloe Rolfes early on in her marriage – and she readily admitted to being a less-than-efficient lady of the house.[28] In her scrapbook Bridget underlined in red ink that part of the profile which stated: 'Perhaps her [Strilli's] standard of comparison is her mother-in-law … of whom it has been said, more than once, she could organise an army.' Strilli had an idiosyncratic approach to gardening and decorating – two cornerstones of Brenthurst domesticity – and her tastes and inclinations did not always accord with those of her in-laws. When she and Nicky took occupation of Little Brenthurst after Mary and Gordon moved to a house in the suburb of Morningside, Harry commented that Strilli was 'mad about the library'. But he felt that, 'left to themselves', Nicky and Strilli 'would certainly have produced something in the "stinkwood *kis* and *rusbank*" [traditional chest and settee] style'.[29] Strilli gave birth to a second son, Benjamin Raymond, in 1971, and he and Jonathan were proudly unveiled to the press. 'Meet Ben and Jake: Oppenheimer grandsons,' the *Sunday Express* announced.[30] The joyousness was painfully short-lived. Two years later Benjamin died, a victim of the rare Tay-Sachs disease. His traumatic passing cast a pall over Little Brenthurst. Harry and Bridget were abroad at the time and did not hasten home for Benjamin's funeral. Their remoteness further complicated the family dynamic.

The Public Square: Progressive Party

Opposition politics had their own complicated dynamics. Oppenheimer's departure from Parliament in 1957 was a blow to the liberal ginger group in the United Party. When JGN Strauss was forced out as UP leader in November 1956, the move was actively championed by conservative MPs like the party's supremo in Natal, Douglas Mitchell, but it carried the caucus's broader support. Nevertheless, the liberals were ambivalent about Strauss's successor, De Villiers Graaff. Although Div was elected unanimously and enjoyed the two Harrys' (Oppenheimer and Lawrence) imprimatur, progressive MPs like Helen Suzman regarded him as lazy and indecisive. He owed his hidebound backers like Mitchell a political debt, and he was unlikely to stick his neck out for the liberals. Even so, the UP's progressive wing looked to Oppenheimer as a moderating influence on Graaff. The heir to the Anglo American throne was considered an indispensable ally in reforming the UP from within.[31] In the first 18 months of Oppenheimer's chairmanship of Anglo and De Beers, his priorities understandably lay beyond the mind-numbing minutiae of factional party battles. Pieter de Kock kept him abreast of developments, and corridor gossip, regardless. 'The news you send about the state of affairs in the United Party is depressing though not I am afraid surprising,' Oppenheimer wrote to De Kock in May 1958.[32] The feud between the UP's two wings was growing increasingly bitter. The party's drubbing at the polls in the 1958 election did not lead to any serious introspection. Instead it emboldened the reactionaries. They sought to out-Nat the Nats, which put paid to any hopes of internal reform. Mitchell and other prominent right-wing MPs resolved to drive the liberals out, or at least provoke a purge of the party's most pervicacious progressives, by engineering a feud over policy.[33] The restoration of the common-roll franchise for Coloured voters, and the whole question of whether African representation in Parliament should be catered for via a common or separate electoral roll, continued to be divisive issues in the UP.

Contestation over policy came to a head at the UP's national congress in Bloemfontein in August 1959. Together with Zach de Beer, Colin Eglin (who had been elected to the House of Assembly in 1958) apprised Oppenheimer of Mitchell's machinations in the run-up to the conference. In fact, Oppenheimer travelled to Cape Town to raise his concerns with Graaff. He told Div that should the party renege on its commitments regarding common-roll representation, he would be forced to 'stand outside' the UP.[34] Oppenheimer had little confidence that Div would hold the line. After his discussion with the UP leader, Oppenheimer informed Harry Lawrence of their 'pretty frank' talk: he doubted whether Div could be kept on the 'side of the angels'. 'I am not optimistic – he seems convinced that the only thing is to accept, or appear to accept, the Nat view on race relations.'[35] At the congress, the faction-fighting intensified while Graaff stared on like a passive bystander. Steytler, the party's Cape leader, and Helen Suzman were subjected to barracking when they conveyed their views. Delegates voted in favour of parliamentary representation for Africans (by whites) on a separate roll, an apparent reversal of the party position – though it was more often honoured in the breach – adopted in 1954. On the final day of proceedings, Mitchell moved that the UP should oppose the 'acquisition and alienation' of more land for the government's avowed purpose of giving it to 'Bantu tribes'.[36] His resolution received overwhelming support. Despite Mitchell's caveats, the progressives interpreted this as a repudiation of General Hertzog's promise back in

1936 that Africans would be compensated for the curtailment of their franchise rights with an extra six million hectares of land. It was the straw that broke the camel's back. A significant number of liberal UP MPs resolved to quit the party. Licking their wounds, Steytler, Suzman, Eglin, De Beer, Sidney Waterson, Owen Townley Williams, Ray Swart and Clive van Ryneveld repaired to room 309 of the Maitland Hotel. The self-styled 'progressive group' released a press statement that rejected Mitchell's resolution and threw down the gauntlet to Graaff by threatening a split. It was the precursor to their resignation from the UP – save for Waterson, whom Graaff persuaded to stay – and they were subsequently joined by fellow MPs Ronald Butcher, John Cope and Boris Wilson. However, they retained their seats in Parliament.

Oppenheimer had been kept in the picture throughout. Pieter de Kock briefed him on the progressive group's organisational evolution and teething problems. Meanwhile, Eglin and De Beer had made Brenthurst their first port of call after the UP's Bloemfontein congress, in pursuit of the baronial benediction. Oppenheimer assured them of his backing. On 2 September 1959 he matched word with deed and issued a statement widely covered in the press: 'After careful consideration of the issues involved, and of the statements issued by Sir De Villiers Graaff and Dr J Steytler, I find myself in general sympathy with the progressive group. In the circumstances, I think it would be improper for me to remain a member of the United Party and I have accordingly tendered my resignation.'[37] The UP warhorse, Harry Lawrence, who was holidaying in Italy, telephoned Oppenheimer at Brenthurst while Eglin and De Beer happened to be lunching there. He was urged to join the progressive insurgency. Oppenheimer later cabled Lawrence in Rapallo, told him that the idea was to launch a new party in November, and encouraged him to issue a public statement in reinforcement of the dissidents.[38] On his return to the Union, Lawrence resigned from the UP and bestowed his considerable political heft on the progressive group. In London, *The Times* applauded Oppenheimer's resignation from the UP as a 'courageous action' from a man who had 'long and consistently' supported the view that industrial integration was an undeniable fact.[39] An editorial in the *Cape Times* predicted that with Oppenheimer's 'background support' and Lawrence's endorsement, the progressives would make a 'formidable parliamentary group' regardless of whether they had a 'substantial following in the constituencies'.[40]

This was a naive prognostication. Even if they kept their seats for the remainder of the term, which all 11 of the defectors did, the progressives would need to coax their constituents into returning them at the next election. With Oppenheimer's arm's length involvement, the splinter group metamorphosed into the Progressive Party, launched at the Cranbrook Hotel in Johannesburg on 13 and 14 November 1959. However, the party managed to hold on to only one seat in the 1961 election. Although Helen Suzman's victory in the Houghton constituency was momentous, the Progs' overall losses constituted a severe blow. Only two years after its formation, the Progressive Party was all but extinguished at the polls, and for the next 13 years the outspoken and courageous Suzman would be its lone parliamentary representative – a 'bright star in a dark chamber' shining a light on the injustices of apartheid.[41] Almost single-handedly, Oppenheimer kept the Progs financially afloat in the 1960s. In 1966, the party's annual revenue into its central coffers was R68 000, R50 000 of which was doled out by Oppenheimer in monthly instalments of R4000.[42]

For more than a decade after its inception, the Progressive Party limped along from election to election, hamstrung – Eglin confided to Oppenheimer – by inefficient organisation and a lack of 'clearly defined objectives'.[43] By the mid-1960s, there were leadership difficulties, too. Ray Swart warned Oppenheimer that Steytler was trying to shepherd the scattered flock of independent-minded Progressives from the remote sanctuary of his farm in Queenstown, without notable success. Despite these shortcomings, Steytler, an old hand with deeply held liberal convictions, led the party through three successive electoral blowouts before voluntarily bowing out at the national congress in 1971. The candidates best placed to succeed him were Oppenheimer's two closest confidants in politics, De Beer and Eglin. From the mid-1950s, they had been firm friends involved, to varying degrees, in one another's domestic triumphs and tribulations. In the study at Brenthurst 13 years later, a frank assessment was made of the contenders' respective merits. The upshot, Eglin wrote in his memoirs, was that he would make himself available as leader, while De Beer assisted him on the managerial side of the party.[44] Oppenheimer undertook to smooth over arrangements with Eglin's employers, the firm of quantity surveyors Bernard James and Partners. Eglin was a man of rock-solid dependability, a tireless slogger committed to the long obedience. But his leadership was not without its flaws. He was a dull orator, gruff, and often irascible to friend and foe alike.[45] Eglin had the 'bedside manner of an angry crocodile', according to the Progressive Party campaign manager, Peter Soal.[46] Yet he injected

Shining a light in dark times: cartoonist Bob Connolly illustrates
HFO's support for the Progressive Party, 1970s. *(Brenthurst Library)*

energy and confidence (and new sources of funding) into the party and
steered it to an electoral breakthrough in 1974, when the Progs bagged
six additional seats in former UP-held constituencies – including one for
Gordon Waddell in Johannesburg North. Eglin and Swart approached
Oppenheimer to stand as the Progressive Party candidate in Parktown,
a call enthusiastically echoed by the *Rand Daily Mail*. But HFO's hands
were tied on the business front, and he dismissed the suggestion out of
hand.[47]

From 1959 to 1974, and through the Progressive Party's successive
reincarnations (the Progs absorbed UP defector Harry Schwarz's Reform
Party in 1975 to form the Progressive Reform Party, and merged with
another UP breakaway to create the Progressive Federal Party in 1977),
Oppenheimer was the party's chief financial backer, sounding board and
arbiter. In short, he was its rock. Oppenheimer endorsed Progressive
candidates on the hustings, most regularly Helen Suzman in Houghton.
He rallied the troops with motivational speeches at party congresses. He
was continually roped into hosting fundraising dinners at Brenthurst, or
asked to drum up money in the business community. This did not always
have the intended consequence: many potential Prog patrons clung on

to their cheque books, assuming that 'Harry O' would bail out the party come what may. When he was appealing to donors, Oppenheimer's 'short & brilliant' talks stood in contrast to Steytler's 'honest albeit not very intelligent speeches', Suzman observed tartly to her elder daughter, Frances.[48] Oppenheimer was a sympathetic friend to Suzman. Although she was possessed of a hardened carapace and a waspish tongue, Suzman's solitary battle against the brutish Nats in Parliament took its toll. Many of her former colleagues on the United Party benches were indolent and ineffectual. 'Had dinner at Harry O's & got a lot off my chest,' Suzman confided to Frances, 'He's still very Prog & has finally shed his lingering admiration for that slob De Villiers [Graaff].'[49] Oppenheimer's words of solace and acts of generosity were legion. When Harry Lawrence lost his seat in 1961, Oppenheimer proposed that he should join the boards of various Anglo American companies so that he could afford to continue his involvement in politics.[50] After Lawrence's death in 1973, Oppenheimer arranged for De Beers to pay his widow, Jean, a monthly allowance.[51] And over the years several other party leaders, among them Steytler and Frederik van Zyl Slabbert, would benefit from HFO's loans and largesse.[52]

Molteno Commission and the Qualified Franchise

The Liberal Party historian (and former party activist) Randolph Vigne wrote of the Progressives that, having gained the 'inestimable advantage of financial support' from Oppenheimer, they launched their new party on almost identical policy grounds to those of the Liberals six and a half years earlier.[53] In addition to providing funds, Oppenheimer helped shape the Progressive Party's core principles and policies, a continuation of his intellectual labour in the UP. When the Progressives were drafting basic statements on social and economic policy ahead of their inaugural congress in November 1959, Oppenheimer was consulted, and alterations were made to accommodate his advice on a 'proper standard' for extending rights to African trade unions.[54] Oppenheimer informed Harry Lawrence that he was in favour of abolishing pass laws and influx control, but suggested the Progs should make it clear in their labour policy that the migrant labour system, 'especially in regard to the mining industry', could not be abolished immediately.[55] In 1960, the Progressive Party established a commission under the chairmanship of the distinguished lawyer and former 'native representative' in Parliament, Donald Molteno, to make recommendations on its constitutional and franchise policy. Molteno had joined the Liberal Party soon after its inception in 1953 and become its national vice-chairman, but his disquiet with the Liberals' extra-parliamentary activism (and their move towards endorsing universal suffrage) led him to resign his membership in 1957.[56] He found a more congenial home among the incrementalist Progs.

Oppenheimer was invited to serve on the Molteno Commission alongside various historians, economists and luminaries of constitutional law. There was a sprinkling of 'non-white' commissioners: an African academic, Selby Ngcobo; the Coloured principal of a teacher training college, Richard van der Ross; and an Indian economics lecturer, Dr S Cooppan. The terms of reference for the commission – which sat between 1960 and 1962 – stipulated that it should aim to enable the people of South Africa to 'live as one nation in accordance with the values and concepts of Western Civilisation'.[57] Its constitutional proposals were to include an entrenched Bill of Rights that would guarantee funda-mental human rights and individual liberties, and a framework for an independent judiciary operating under the rule of law. Legislative and executive powers and functions were to be decentralised and devolved to the provinces, laying the groundwork for the Progs' commitment to federalism. Through a reform of the Senate, the commission was mandated to devise constitutional checks and balances and prevent domination by one racial group over another, 'white or non-white'. Meanwhile, the parameters of the franchise were straitened. Only suitably 'qualified' citizens of a 'defined degree of civilisation', regardless of race, should be eligible to vote on a common roll and hold office in Parliament.[58] It was the commission's duty to determine the appropriate qualifications. This then was the earliest systematic attempt by a political organisation to devise a constitutional model for a democratic South Africa, one which could be refined through negotiation at a national convention. In his foreword to the first volume of the Molteno Report, Steytler claimed it was the 'first real plan to equate our political system' with the 'long-established and highly successful economic multi-racial character of our land'.[59] In fact, the ANC, founded in 1912, had a much longer history of constitutionalism.[60] Its 'African Claims' document, produced in 1943, provided a framework for constitutional government and included a Bill of Rights. Throughout its existence the Congress Alliance – like the Liberal Party, for that matter – advocated a Bill of Rights and championed a national convention to hammer out a non-racial constitutional dispensation. However, the latter idea only really took shape at the All-In

African Conference in Pietermaritzburg in March 1961, where Nelson Mandela issued a clarion call in his keynote address. Despite the fact that the Freedom Charter was animated by a constitutionalist intent, this vade mecum of the liberation movement did not attach much constitutional flesh to its long, bony list of demands.

ZK Matthews and AB Xuma both declined Molteno's invitation to serve on the commission since the ANC was committed to universal franchise, and the commission's terms of reference ruled that out. The majority of commissioners proposed a graduated, non-racial common-roll franchise for all South Africans over the age of 21 conditional upon educational, income-related or property qualifications. Cooppan and Van der Ross believed the suggested options were too limiting and submitted separate, dissentient minority reports. Oppenheimer and Zach de Beer, on the other hand, did not think some of the formulations offered a sufficient guarantee of a 'fair degree of civilisation'.[61] In their own joint minority report, they proposed higher minimum educational and economic qualifications for the common roll. In recognition that their proposals were unlikely to enfranchise more than 'a small percentage of non-European voters in present circumstances', the duo provided for additional representation to the House of Assembly on a special voters' roll. This would be contingent on a literacy test and earnings of £15 per month continuously for two years. The latter – but not the former – proposed amendment was endorsed by the Progressive Party at its national congress in 1960.

In echo of Oppenheimer's ill-fated Senate Plan, which foreshadowed aspects of the Molteno Commission, Molteno elaborated a scheme to reform the composition and function of the Senate. The goal was to safeguard against racial domination, particularly the 'oppression of racial minorities'.[62] Although they welcomed the system of checks and balances introduced by Molteno's multiracial Senate, Oppenheimer and De Beer disagreed on its proposed composition. They insisted on areas of auxiliary legislative competence – regarding education, employment, housing and public amenities – that might be subject to a racial veto. For instance, they argued, a measure prohibiting the provision of separate institutional facilities, even on an equal basis, or one having the effect of reducing skilled wage rates, might be strongly objected to by whites. In the end, official Prog policy closely mirrored the commission's majority recommendations on the qualified franchise, Bill of Rights, and constitutional safeguards for racial groups. Since the party strove to achieve basic educational standards for all, universal suffrage – it was implied – would ultimately, at some far-off point, prevail.

To the Liberal Party's chairman, Peter Brown, the Progressives' gradualist platform reeked of racial paternalism. It proved they remained a 'White party with White views, convinced that a White-orientated policy holds the answer'.[63] Brown's Liberal colleague Patrick Duncan was scathing. He described the Molteno Report as a 'pretentious and ambiguous document' that 'proved … the slogan "merit, not colour", was a lie'.[64] In terms that would be used more or less verbatim over four decades later – after South Africa had adopted a non-racial, democratic constitution in 1996 – Duncan savaged the Molteno plan as 'another of these tortuous devices for maintaining, behind a democratic-looking mask, the substance of White privilege, White wealth and White power'. Indeed there was a world of difference in style and content between the liberalism of the Liberal Party and the liberalism of the Progressive Party in the 1960s. With such a shallow pool of potential voters – whites were, on the whole, politically, socially and racially conservative – the Liberals were less bothered than the Progs with becoming a going electoral concern. They sought to build a non-racial organisation and focused on increasing their black membership. The majority of delegates at the Liberal Party's national congress in 1961 were black. The Liberal Party engaged in extra-parliamentary activism such as boycotts, sit-ins, and campaigns against black-spot removals in Natal and sham 'self-rule' in the Transkei. The party was concerned with broader issues of social justice, and its policy documents grappled with issues like land redistribution and other measures of state intervention to deracialise the economy.

The Progressives, by contrast, believed that Parliament offered the real route to reform. It was the legitimate vehicle to jettison apartheid. They focused on increasing their parliamentary representation, and this involved the drudgery of carving off slivers of support from the coalface of the conservative white electorate. The Progs therefore wore their liberalism lightly. The Progressive Party conceptualised a civil order in which blacks could participate to the extent that white fears about black domination – and potential threats to the minority's economic interests – were assuaged through constitutional safeguards. The vast majority of whites looked upon the notion of universal suffrage with horror. It was not a vote-winner. In this context, the qualified franchise was a pragmatic policy choice. *Die Transvaler*, voice of the National Party, regarded Molteno's recommendations as 'so revolutionary that one wonders how the Progressive Party can hope to get popular support from the whites in South Africa'.[65] Albert Luthuli, at the other end of the political spectrum, responded to the Molteno Report by dismissing the qualified franchise as a tool to 'perpetuate group privilege at the expense of the African people'.[66] For Oppenheimer, like Eglin, the graduated franchise was an educational regulator, and it offered a sensible middle path between apartheid and black majority rule. Oppenheimer did not deny that universal suffrage was 'an end to be worked for', as he told his audience when he delivered the University of Cape Town's TB Davie Memorial Lecture in 1962.[67] But it could not be adopted without incurring 'unacceptable risks' until the standard of education and living in general was far higher.[68] The Progressives eventually abandoned the qualified franchise in 1978 when another constitutional commission – headed by a charismatic rising star in the caucus, Van Zyl Slabbert – recommended universal suffrage and full citizenship rights regardless of race.[69]

From Oppenheimer's perspective in the 1960s, multiracial polities should stick as firmly as possible to the principle of 'individual merit' and accept, as the *Financial Times* captured his sentiments, that this meant a 'white political majority now' and a 'black political majority in the future'.[70] He considered the Monckton Commission's proposals for equal parliamentary representation of blacks and whites in the Federation of Rhodesia and Nyasaland to be harmful and impracticable.[71] What was required was an 'immediate substantial share' for Africans in the Federal Parliament and a 'progressive approach' to the non-racial common-roll franchise.[72] The deliberations of both the Monckton Commission and the Molteno Commission unfolded as the Belgian Congo attained its independence. The so-called Congo crisis, triggered by the mutiny of the army in 1960, and which unravelled into a constitutional impasse, led to the flight of thousands of whites. Many of them sought refuge in South Africa. For Oppenheimer the events in the Congo illustrated that 'primitive, uncivilised people cannot be trusted with the running of a modern state'.[73] Only those who had a 'reasonable standard of education and civilisation' were equal to the task.[74]

Relations with Afrikanerdom

As soon as Oppenheimer's support for the Progressive Party and involvement in the Molteno Commission became public knowledge, the Afrikaner nationalist press reprised the chorus of an old tune.

Oppenheimer would dictate Prog policy on behalf of the Anglo American Corporation. The Progs were serving the interests of monopoly capital. Oppenheimer's new political home was an instrument of *die geldmag* and an enemy of Afrikanerdom.[75] 'Hoggenheimer' rode again.

As this response revealed, Oppenheimer's economic empire existed in 'awkward tandem' (to use Anthony Sampson's perceptive phrase) with the Afrikaner political monopoly.[76] The awkwardness could be traced back to the brouhaha over the United South Africa Trust Fund in 1951. The episode marked an acrimonious start to a complicated relationship between Oppenheimer and the Nationalist government, which would undergo many vicissitudes over forty-odd years. Frequently antagonistic, predominantly ambivalent, the affiliation was to prove inextricable. Politically prepotent Afrikaners were separated from economically ascendant English-speakers by ethnicity, language, cultural customs, religion, socialisation through school, university and work, and often even residential suburbs. 'Social distance, arrogance and condescension on the part of the English, suspicion and paranoia on the part of the Afrikaners': that is how the scholar Heribert Adam characterised a relationship based on 'mutual disdain, sometimes mutual contempt'.[77] However, in Oppenheimer's case, he made a partial attempt to bridge the divide. While in Parliament, he learnt Afrikaans and attempted to speak it on public platforms. In the early 1960s, he brought talented Afrikaners like Wim de Villiers into the inner sanctum of 44 Main Street to advise him on mine productivity and wages paid to black workers. De Villiers, a straight-talking engineer with a PhD, had managed Anglo's Rhokana copper mine in the 1950s. He was an avowed National Party supporter, but he believed big business should stay out of politics. De Villiers was appalled by the pittance Anglo American paid its black workforce. He was also critical of the culture at Anglo. 'I felt the emphasis on Oxford graduates was wrong,' De Villiers declared; the system of personal assistants encouraged upstarts to 'play politics' and prevented them from 'getting to grips with problems on the shop floor'.[78]

In 1964, Oppenheimer asked a former Governor of the Reserve Bank, Michiel de Kock, to join the board of Anglo American. Oppenheimer cultivated Afrikaner journalists like Stanley Uys and Otto Krause, both of whom, admittedly, wrote for English publications – the former as a political correspondent for the *Sunday Times* and the latter as editor, from 1962, of *News/Check*. Oppenheimer's attitude towards Afrikaners was hardly contemptuous. He regarded the doyens of Afrikaner big business

HFO with Anton Rupert (far right) at a game reserve in
Swaziland, 1970s. *(Brenthurst Library)*

as indispensable partners in the process of political reform. Most notably,
he enjoyed a long and productive philanthropic association with the
Afrikaner tobacco and luxury goods titan, Anton Rupert, founder of
the Rembrandt Group.[79] Rupert and Oppenheimer 'did many things
together', the Afrikaner philanthropist would later recall, a note of
empathy in his voice: 'If he needed my help, he would ask for it. I did the
same.'[80] Oppenheimer grasped the long-term political benefit of bringing
Afrikaners into the gold mining industry through the General Mining–
Federale Mynbou deal. By the early 1970s there was a discernible shift
in attitude towards Oppenheimer in sections of the Afrikaans press. The
prolific journalist Kas van den Bergh even suggested that Oppenheimer
might serve in the cabinet as minister of mining, while Anton Rupert took
on the economic affairs portfolio and Punch Barlow handled finance.[81]

Although Oppenheimer was often vilified by National Party cabinet
ministers and members of Parliament between 1948 and 1957, in the
outline of his memoir he referred to – and then crossed out – 'Prime
Minister's & some others' NP [National Party] kindness' in the chapter that
was to deal with his parliamentary career.[82] Whether he was referring to
DF Malan or JG Strijdom is not clear. In the erased section Oppenheimer
listed Klasie Havenga, BJ 'Ben' Schoeman (Strijdom's Minister of

Transport), and TE 'Eben' Dönges (Strijdom's Minister of the Interior). The suave, softly spoken Dönges had paid handsome tribute to Ernest Oppenheimer on the occasion of the tycoon's 70th birthday in 1950. Dönges praised the dynast for his unswerving loyalty to the nation and his contribution in attracting overseas capital for economic development. Not all of Dönges's cabinet colleagues took such a rosy view of English-speaking entrepreneurs. It was one of those curious contradictions that marked the uneasy relationship between Afrikaner nationalists in political power and their ideological opponents who wielded economic power. The Nationalist government might engage in sabre-rattling about *die geldmag*, but they were partners in a dance of dependence with corporate empires like Oppenheimer's which kept the apartheid economy afloat. In the course of his chairmanship of Anglo and De Beers, Oppenheimer would regularly consult successive ministers of finance and mines, as well as governors of the Reserve Bank. Hilgard Muller, the former ambassador to London whom Verwoerd appointed minister of foreign affairs, was a frequent contact. Oppenheimer might not have enjoyed private audiences with Verwoerd, and their political exchanges might have been rancorous, but on shared public platforms they were able to bury the hatchet – even if only for appearances. Two months before Verwoerd was assassinated, Oppenheimer attended a banquet at the Johannesburg Stock Exchange in Verwoerd's honour. A photograph of the two, chatting amiably, appeared in the *Sunday Express* captioned 'Premier and millionaire'.[83] During the 1960s, the baleful spectre of 'Hoggenheimer' would be invoked from time to time – with decreasing regularity – to score political points, but the Afrikaner architects of apartheid and the English-speaking captains of industry coexisted peaceably enough, with intermittent acts or expressions of kindness.

The political attacks on Oppenheimer were prompted both by his Progressive ties and by commercial considerations. The General Mining–Federale Mynbou deal raised fears about Anglo's attempts to co-opt Afrikaners. In 1963, Anglo proposed a joint investment with Iscor in what would become Highveld Steel, but the state steel producer rejected the offer for a combination of technical, economic and political reasons.[84] The rejection was unwise, for the venture would have given Iscor dominion over the local steel industry. By the 1960s, the Iscor board was dominated by members of the Afrikaner Broederbond – the secret society whose number included cabinet ministers, civil servants, clergymen, wealthy businessmen, farmers and trade unionists, and which provided

The Premier and the millionaire: HFO with Prime Minister
HF Verwoerd (far left) at a Johannesburg Stock Exchange banquet,
June 1966. *(Brenthurst Library)*

a fulcrum for the apartheid state.[85] Iscor's Broeders contemplated Anglo
with suspicion: they believed the company's overtures were a gambit to
dilute Afrikaner control of the iron and steel sector. Iscor's board and
management did not wish to reach out and grasp Anglo's velvet-gloved
hand lest they be crushed by its iron grip. When the Highveld Steel plant
was officially opened in 1969, Iscor's chairman, Hendrik van Eck, graced
the occasion with his presence but, unusually, not a single cabinet minister
attended. The *Financial Mail* remarked that both Oppenheimer's and
Graham Boustred's speeches were 'cautious' and directed at 'assuaging
the politicians'.[86]

Critically, Anglo's original proposal to Iscor triggered an investigation
into the power and reach of the Oppenheimer empire by Iscor's
commercial manager and Broederbond member, Professor PW Hoek.
In 1964, a delegation from the Broederbond urged Verwoerd to launch
an official probe into Anglo's outsize holdings and role in the economy.
However, according to Hennie Serfontein in his early exposé of the
secret organisation, Verwoerd did not think such an inquiry was in the

republic's best interests, and he rejected the idea.[87] With the backing of the right-wing cabinet minister Albert Hertzog and other senior Broeders, including the Broederbond's chairman and director general of the South African Broadcasting Corporation, Dr Piet Meyer, Hoek pressed ahead anyway. He used Iscor's resources to conduct an illicit investigation into the Anglo American Corporation.

The Hoek Report claimed to offer a comprehensive indictment of the Oppenheimer empire, and attempted to unpack Anglo's economic stranglehold. The spectre of 'Hoggenheimer' loomed over the document. Hoek painted a dire portrait of the 'British-Jewish capitalists ... controlling our economy'.[88] Anglo was large enough to thwart apartheid policies, Hoek warned. As a critical supplier of key minerals to the defence industry, the group should be brought under stricter government control. Anglo's operational boundaries in South Africa should be limited, and restrictions placed on foreign associates like Charter Consolidated. In short, the Hoek Report called for state action to clip Anglo's wings. But apart from Hoek's assertion that Anglo paid a disproportionately low level of tax, there was nothing particularly noteworthy (or revelatory) about his findings. The report was completed after Verwoerd's death and handed over to the Prime Minister's successor, BJ Vorster. Unmoved by its recommendations, Vorster kept the Hoek Report under wraps. In fact, Vorster favoured a more conciliatory approach to Anglo American. Partly this stemmed from the realisation that if the state were to persecute Anglo, it would hamper Vorster's halting efforts to improve South Africa's standing abroad. Moreover, in the late 1960s, South Africa had begun to create a local armaments industry, and Vorster needed Anglo's co-operation in the steel and engineering sectors in order for it to take off.

In any event, by this stage the battle lines between the *verkramptes* and *verligtes* had been drawn. Vorster's noises about improving foreign relations and strengthening ties with black states, and his moves to allow racially integrated international sports teams to play in South Africa, marked him out as a *verligte*. In May 1968 a group of *verkramptes* disseminated two anonymous smear letters in Pretoria, damning Vorster's policies as 'liberalistic'. Hertzog was becoming an increasingly divisive figure on the reactionary fringe of the National Party, and in August Vorster felt confident enough to drop him from his cabinet. That same month Vorster was the guest of honour at a Chamber of Mines banquet where Oppenheimer proposed a toast and thanked the premier for 'promoting South African unity'.[89] Albert Hertzog and two of his fellow travellers, Jaap Marais and Louis Stofberg, were expelled from the National Party in 1969. It was left to the marginal and ultra-conservative Herstigte Nasionale Party (HNP), formed as a splinter group by Hertzog, to try to flog the Hoek Report ahead of the 1970 election. There were leaks to the press. Hoek denied his authorship; he even took out an injunction to stop the dissemination of the report. The HNP's mouthpiece, *Die Afrikaner*, accused Vorster of 'protecting' Oppenheimer.[90] The National Party, in its view, had sold out to the hated 'Hoggenheimer'. However, for all the heated rhetoric, neither the HNP nor the Hoek Report managed to gain much traction.

The South Africa Foundation

The apartheid government had plenty of leverage over Anglo American, through state contracts and corporate taxes. Like the emperor of Fiat in Italy, Gianni Agnelli, Oppenheimer mitigated his risk. He financed a range of political (and quasi-political) groups and protagonists in the 1960s, some of which – most notably the South Africa Foundation (SAF) – were not exactly at loggerheads with the state. Others were. During the 1960 State of Emergency, Oppenheimer ensured that anti-apartheid campaigners detained without trial would remain on Anglo's payroll, and privately assisted ANC activists via ad hoc payments. Oppenheimer wrote a cheque for £200 to Frieda Bokwe, ZK Matthews's wife, and suggested that Zach de Beer be approached to take up Matthews's cause in Parliament.[91] Nelson Mandela was less successful in his bid for funds. He asked Oppenheimer for money so that he could arrange transport to the All-In African Conference in 1961. HFO was one of the few white businessmen to meet Mandela before the firebrand was jailed. He received Mandela with great politeness in the Anglo chairman's office, and he was impressed by Mandela's sense of power. But Oppenheimer turned down the request. 'How do I know', he asked Mandela, 'that after giving you assistance you will not be eliminated by the PAC?'[92]

It would be ungenerous to infer that the corporate titan only backed sure-fire political winners; his dedication to the Progs gives the lie to that. (Although, to be sure, in later years, as South Africa's first post-apartheid president, Mandela could rely on Anglo American to entertain his fundraising pitches far more sympathetically.) Nevertheless, Oppenheimer spread his bets. After the formation of the Progressive Party, he helped to establish and sponsor the far-from-progressive South Africa

Foundation. This was a controversial public relations outfit launched in December 1959. It took shape months after the emergence of the boycott lobby in Britain, which subsequently morphed into the pro-sanctions Anti-Apartheid Movement (AAM). Although it functioned like a semi-quango, the South Africa Foundation was set up as an apolitical, private-sector agency directed towards keeping the country's international lines of communication open. Financed by large corporations, it brought together English-speaking and Afrikaner businessmen and harnessed their networks overseas. The foundation's founding objectives were to promote 'international understanding of the South African way of life', champion 'Western European' civilisation, and engage in 'positive campaigns' that targeted 'opportunities for investment'.[93] Although the SAF did not ostensibly defend or promote apartheid, it co-operated with South African government officials and staff at foreign embassies to counter the AAM's narrative. The foundation opposed the call for boycotts, sanctions and disinvestment.[94] In a booklet castigating the South Africa Foundation's backers for being 'collaborators' with the apartheid regime, the Anti-Apartheid Movement branded the SAF an 'astonishing alliance of Nationalist and Opposition, State and private capital'.[95] The AAM claimed that Oppenheimer was 'running munitions factories' for the apartheid government out of African Explosives & Chemical Industries, and lamented that whatever power mining finance capital had to oppose the government it was 'totally unwilling to use'.[96]

The South Africa Foundation published and distributed publicity material, lobbied the press, and organised and funded trips to South Africa for foreign correspondents and opinion-formers. Ultimately, the SAF served to launder the country's reputation abroad. At first it was led by Sir Francis 'Freddie' de Guingand, Field Marshal Bernard Montgomery's chief of staff during the Second World War, a director of scores of companies including Rothmans, and an old business associate of Oppenheimer's. De Guingand had been a regular at the Little Brenthurst dinner table in the 1950s. His second-in-command was a pillar of the Afrikaner establishment: the chairman of the Industrial Development Corporation (before Iscor), Hendrik van Eck. At the inaugural meeting Oppenheimer was provisionally elected as a trustee, along with Anton Rupert, Punch Barlow, Michiel de Kock, AL Geyer (a director of Nasionale Pers), and sundry other prominent industrialists, bankers, former diplomats, and movers and shakers in state-owned enterprises. Charles Engelhard chaired the foundation's American committee while the British shipping tycoon and major Tory donor, Sir Nicholas Cayzer, presided over its London counterpart. Several major British and American companies, including General Motors, Chrysler, Union Carbide and Caterpillar, subscribed to the foundation. Soon there were SAF representatives in Paris and Bonn, too.

Over the course of the 1960s the SAF arranged for grandees like Field Marshal Montgomery to visit and applaud white South Africa. By its tenth anniversary, the foundation claimed to have helped 'stem the tide of ignorance, criticism and misrepresentation against the Republic'.[97] By this stage Oppenheimer does not appear to have been terribly active in the foundation, and as time wore on he pulled back. He was 'positively not' involved in the SAF, according to Julian Ogilvie Thompson: 'He thought the South Africa Foundation was an apologist for the government, and he played no part in it at all, [though] I suppose we paid our dues as a group.'[98] Under the presidency of Jan Marais from 1974 to 1977, the SAF became more closely allied in outlook and purpose with the Department of Information – the apartheid government's 'dirty tricks' bureau overseen by the oleaginous Eschel Rhoodie, later embroiled in the infamous 'Information scandal'.[99] Nevertheless, in the mid-1970s Oppenheimer remained a paid-up member of the foundation.[100] 'There was a time when I seriously considered resigning,' HFO told an interviewer many years later, 'but I thought it would do no good by making a song and dance, and I never took any part in it.'[101]

To his left-liberal critics Oppenheimer's involvement in the SAF, active or not, exposed the Janus-faced character of his politics. Apartheid was 'ugly enough', according to the editorialist at *Africa South*. But with SAF's 'foundation cream' covering her pimples and a 'gold cigarette-holder and tastefully-mounted diamonds to finish her off' – a somewhat heavy-handed reference to Oppenheimer's mining interests – apartheid appeared like a 'worn-out whore decked by the House of Dior'.[102] Oppenheimer's sponsorship of the foundation, the writer claimed, was incompatible with his backing of the Progressive Party. Zach de Beer was more cautious: he welcomed the establishment of the SAF provided it did not 'try to whitewash government policies' and confined itself to informing overseas investors of the 'innate soundness' of the South African economy.[103] On other occasions, the SAF attracted 'considerable venom' from Progressive Party politicians.[104] Oppenheimer's concurrent contributions to the South Africa Foundation and the Progs were not, as far as he was concerned, contradictory. They were part of a broad front of initiatives to secure the country's long-term stability. Besides, his deep pockets contained several discrete compartments. Months after the Progressive Party and the South Africa Foundation were founded, Oppenheimer donated the significant sum of £20 000 towards the United Party's referendum campaign against the establishment of a republic.[105]

Press Baron and Philanthropist: Building an Alternative Nation

Outside Oppenheimer's support for the Progressive Party and his pervasive presence on the public square, he confronted the apartheid hegemon in more oblique ways. Under his chairmanship, the Anglo American Corporation acquired shareholdings in the two South African media houses that dominated the English-language press. The liberal English newspapers sought to tell the truth about apartheid. They were a persistent thorn in the side of the Nationalist government. The regime was discomforted by journalistic truth-telling, much as it was embarrassed by Suzman's questions in Parliament. ('It is not my questions that are embarrassing; it is your answers,' Suzman countered memorably.) Oppenheimer often quoted the influential American journalist Walter Lippmann to the effect that there could be no freedom for a community which 'lacked the information by which to detect lies'. It was a line he used during his lecture on 'the press and society' at the University of Cape Town (UCT) Summer School in 1973.[106] Indeed, Oppenheimer regarded press freedom as a prerequisite for an open society, and he resisted Nationalist attempts to infiltrate and subjugate this liberal bastion of opposition to apartheid.

From an early stage the Fourth Estate had been inextricably tied up with mining interests. Rhodes was one of the key subscribers of the Argus Printing and Publishing Company; and Corner House (forerunner of the Central Mining–Rand Mines stable) controlled the Argus Group. In 1958, Anglo's takeover of Central Mining gave it a significant stake in the Argus Group, whose newspapers included the *Cape Argus*, *The Star* in Johannesburg, the *Daily News* and *Sunday Tribune* in Natal, the *Diamond Fields Advertiser* in Kimberley, the *Pretoria News*, and *The Friend* in Bloemfontein. Through Argus, Anglo American also enjoyed an interest in Bantu Press, with its thriving string of black newspapers like *The World*. Oppenheimer was not entirely detached from decisions affecting his press holdings: he told Jim Bailey, Sir Abe's son, the proprietor of *Drum* magazine and the *Golden City Post* (both of which targeted black readers), that 'having consulted with the other shareholders in Bantu Press', Anglo had decided against Bailey's suggested merger with *Drum*.[107]

In 1960, Anglo acquired control of the Johannesburg Consolidated Investment Company (JCI), which took its shareholding in the Argus Group to around 40 per cent. In 1971, Argus obtained a controlling interest in the other main English-language newspaper group – South African Associated Newspapers, or SAAN – home to the *Rand Daily Mail* and *Sunday Times*, among other broadsheets. Two years later, the formerly independent *Cape Times* and *Natal Mercury* entered SAAN's fold. By 1973, then, Oppenheimer had joined the ranks of industrialists-cum-press barons, with a monopoly over the English-language press. When Oppenheimer delivered his lecture on press freedom at UCT, the editor of East London's *Daily Dispatch*, Donald Woods, suggested that HFO and Punch Barlow had the Argus Group in their pockets. Unfortunately that was not true, Oppenheimer smoothly replied; if it was, he would make sure the Argus titles were more like the *Daily Dispatch*, a newspaper he professed to admire.[108] Oppenheimer insisted that Anglo American did not set out to control the press; and, in the main, Anglo was a disinterested shareholder.[109] The corporation balked at interfering in the commercial and editorial independence of the newspapers under its sway, although its action – or inaction – over the closure of the *Rand Daily Mail* in 1985 later brought Anglo much criticism. Oppenheimer tended to keep his own business dealings with the Fourth Estate at a remove, apart from warding off (through the good offices of Max Borkum and Gordon Waddell) a hostile takeover bid for SAAN in 1975. On that occasion he joined a group of businessmen in setting up the Advowson Trust. The trust financed a 20 per cent stake in SAAN to complement the Argus Group's holdings, thus guaranteeing a majority share in Anglo's favour. This served to thwart the ambitions of the Afrikaner entrepreneur Louis Luyt, a bulldozer of a man who had made his money out of fertiliser and beer. Luyt was a staunch supporter of the National Party. It later emerged that he was put up as a useful idiot by the Minister of Information, Connie Mulder, and head of the Bureau for State Security, General Hendrik van den Bergh, to wrest control of SAAN. Had Luyt succeeded, SAAN's organs would have turned into the 'unquestioning catspaws' of the Nationalist government, in the words of the *Rand Daily Mail*'s editor Raymond Louw.[110]

Oppenheimer manifested his particular brand of liberalism in an array of philanthropic endeavours whose beneficiaries were multiracial.

In this way he contributed to building an alternative nation to that envisaged by the apartheid government, one in which race was not an obstacle to opportunity. Sometimes these initiatives were funded from Oppenheimer's own war chest, or the coffers at E Oppenheimer and Son, or the Ernest Oppenheimer Memorial Trust (OMT). Often they were sponsored by funds established in terms of Anglo American's burgeoning, benevolent bureaucracy. In its profit-making pursuits Anglo was almost like a state within a state, with its own diplomatic envoys, intelligence operatives and mine police. 'More like a government than a company,' was the verdict passed by the British magazine *Investors Chronicle*.[111] Similarly, the sheer scale of the corporation's non-profit-making activities – the scope and reach of its philanthropic networks and the social capital they created and disbursed – fashioned Anglo into a parallel state, a provider or underwriter of social services and cultural and educational opportunities. In the 1960s and 1970s, Oppenheimer helped lay the foundations of a vibrant multiracial civic order – even though, unlike some of his more far-sighted white contemporaries, his civic ethic stopped short of full citizenship rights for blacks.

In the field of corporate citizenship, Oppenheimer made a significant contribution to public life. The Chairman's Fund at Anglo American pioneered modern corporate social investment in South Africa. By the time Oppenheimer assumed the chairmanship, Anglo had a long-established tradition of giving to charitable causes and making funds available for social upliftment. Its support, beginning in 1930, of the Johannesburg Child Welfare Society, and the African Children's Feeding Scheme, founded by Father Trevor Huddleston in 1945, are two examples. The impetus behind these initiatives was best captured by Ernest Oppenheimer in his chairman's statement of 1954: Anglo's purpose, he wrote, was to generate profits for its shareholders, but to do so in a way that made a real and lasting contribution to the welfare of communities in which the company operated. In the mid-1950s, Ernest Oppenheimer raised £3 million from the major mining groups to build 15 000 houses for the inhabitants of Pimville and Moroka rendered homeless by Verwoerd's policies. Most of these philanthropic endeavours were coordinated informally through the chairman's office, but by the early 1970s Anglo American and De Beers had formally combined their social investment funds into a single vehicle administered by a committee of senior executives from both companies.[112] De Beers explained that this concentration of funds would enable the group to make substantial grants for capital development projects in education and social services, while continuing to support the many annual appeals from national and local charity and welfare organisations.[113] In 1971, the budget of the Chairman's Fund was R1.4 million, two-thirds of which came from Anglo American. In 1973, the fund's budget was increased by 60 per cent and its work was assigned to a full-time social development team headed by a company executive. Michael O'Dowd became the chairman of the Anglo American and De Beers Chairman's Fund. In a section devoted to 'social responsibility' in his chairman's statement for 1974, Oppenheimer stressed that the time was 'ripe' for the group to do more 'in view of the social changes' taking place in South Africa.[114] The plan was to initiate special projects in 'education, technical training and the socio-economic progress of rural areas'.

As early as the 1960s the Chairman's Fund spent between 50 and 70 per cent of its budget on education and at least half of the expenditure was earmarked for black learners deliberately underfunded by the Department of Bantu Education.[115] The Chairman's Fund became South Africa's biggest corporate social investor, and the largest private-sector contributor to schooling – spanning early childhood education, school reconstructions and teacher training – for disadvantaged South Africans. Elite private institutions were not neglected. In 1955, Oppenheimer personally benefacted £6300 for the construction of a new sixth-form block at Michaelhouse.[116] (Bill Wilson, a Michaelhouse old boy and at the time Oppenheimer's assistant managing director, joined the Michaelhouse board of governors almost simultaneously.) Highbury, a long-established preparatory school in Natal, received R15 000 from the Chairman's Fund in 1969.[117] Oppenheimer chaired the Industrial Fund – the brainchild of Bill Wilson, which sought to improve scientific facilities at private schools – and Michaelhouse and Kearsney College respectively commissioned and opened new science laboratories under its aegis in the early 1960s.

Meanwhile, the Ernest Oppenheimer Memorial Trust funded theatre and the visual arts as a driver of social transformation. By the mid-1960s, black writers who had reinvigorated the iconic *Drum* magazine – the likes of Nat Nakasa, Can Themba and Lewis Nkosi – were subjected to censorship, banning or exile. So too were black artists. As the government strangled domestic expressions of black cultural and political life, the OMT sponsored the 'Art of the Nation' exhibition in 1963. (Later this was known as 'Art South Africa Today', a biennale of contemporary South

African art.) The exhibition showcased paintings and sculpture by artists of all races, and celebrated a 'common culture' deemed 'typically South African'.[118] In 1976 the Market Theatre, a non-racial playhouse known as the 'Theatre of the Struggle' for its anti-apartheid ethos, opened its doors in downtown Johannesburg, thanks in part to funding from the OMT and the Chairman's Fund. While the Chairman's Fund tended to focus on bricks-and-mortar work, the OMT invested in individuals. In the early 1970s, Richard Rive, the Coloured novelist who wrote about the Sharpeville massacre in *Emergency*, pursued a DPhil at the University of Oxford with the OMT's material support. A fellow writer, Sipho Sepamla, was another beneficiary. The OMT paid for him to attend drama school in the United Kingdom. Oppenheimer provided private patronage to a gamut of black creative artists. He championed the work of photojournalist Peter Magubane, the talented documenter of the Sharpeville massacre and the Rivonia Trial, whom Oppenheimer met in the 1960s and endorsed in testimonials.[119]

The OMT funded the Bureau of Literacy and Literature, founded by the South African Institute of Race Relations (SAIRR) as part of its adult education programme. The bureau launched as an independent voluntary organisation in 1964.[120] It ran literacy classes on the mines, conducted teacher training, helped African writers with publication, and offered African language courses for whites with primers produced in the vernacular, as well as in English and Afrikaans. An OMT grant, channelled through the SAIRR, enabled the republication of *The African Who's Who* by the former ANC secretary general TD Mweli Skota.[121] In 1964 the OMT brought out the distinguished educationalist (and former headmaster of Charterhouse and Eton) Robert Birley, to conduct research and teach at Orlando High School in the black township of the same name. Birley stayed on until 1967 as a visiting professor of education at the University of the Witwatersrand. The OMT-sponsored bursary programme, whose early recipients included future politicians and journalists like Lionel Mtshali and Aggrey Klaaste, put hundreds of South Africans through university. By 1969 it had sustained 169 undergraduates ranging from librarians to doctors, of whom 102 were black.[122] Through the OMT, Oppenheimer became the largest and most enduring non-state funder of education in South Africa, a legacy kept alive by his children and grandchildren.[123]

The Open Universities and the Chancellorship of UCT

Oppenheimer's role in higher education extended beyond providing scholarships, making endowments and subsidising research. He was a frequent guest on South Africa's liberal, English-medium university campuses – Cape Town, Natal, Rhodes and the Witwatersrand – which were at the forefront of opposing apartheid, particularly over issues of university autonomy. From the late 1950s onwards the so-called open universities, thus named because they admitted black students, were targeted by the Nationalist government. The Extension of University Education Act (1959) barred African, Coloured and Indian students from registering at any open university without ministerial permission. As the Nationalists tried to enforce segregation at the open universities and bring them under their thumb, Oppenheimer became a torch-bearer for academic freedom and a sought-after speaker at graduation ceremonies. He regarded the English-speaking campuses as 'the few points of real liberty' left in South Africa, and for that reason dismissed the academic boycott as 'damn silly'.[124] A succession of honorary doctorates was bestowed on Oppenheimer in the 1960s, starting with the University of Natal (1960), followed by the University of the Witwatersrand (1963), Rhodes University (1965) and, abroad, the University of Leeds (1965). The Leeds award, which came in the wake of a £250 000 donation from Oppenheimer to establish a research institute in African geology, proved controversial. The student union's left-wing committee members decided to boycott the degree ceremony. Its vice-president lambasted Oppenheimer for sponsoring the South Africa Foundation and making 'tacit statements' against racial discrimination while implementing apartheid laws in his factories and mines.[125] The stayaway flopped. Over two hundred students gathered outside the graduation venue with banners stating 'Congratulations Mr Oppenheimer – we are not the reds, we are the majority'.[126] In a move that typified Oppenheimer's fleet-footed brand of diplomacy, he subsequently hosted five Leeds students on an all-expenses-paid trip to South Africa to see the country for themselves. They met with politicians and journalists, including Helen Suzman and the editor of *Die Burger*, Piet Cillié. 'It is all more complicated than we imagined,' one of the visitors confessed in a manner that would have made the South Africa Foundation proud.[127]

The titular head of the University of Cape Town, Albert van der Sandt Centlivres – an old-fashioned Cape liberal with a deep commitment to academic freedom – died in September 1966, and the chancellorship fell vacant. The political atmosphere was so charged, according to UCT's official historian, that the race to replace Centlivres took on a partisan complexion: all three contenders for the position drew their core support along party political lines.[128] Judge Marius Diemont (United Party), Leo Marquard (Liberal Party) and Oppenheimer (Progressive Party) accepted nomination. In October, the head of the UCT Department of Economics, Professor HM Robertson, urged Oppenheimer to put his name forward and 'help us keep our liberal tradition'.[129] Later that month, Clive Corder, the chairman of the UCT Council, approached Oppenheimer on behalf of the Convocation – the body of staff and graduates that would elect Centlivres's successor – to make himself available for the position. Corder mentioned in passing that De Villiers Graaff had been touted as a potential candidate too. As was his wont, Div dithered. He failed to make his intentions clear, and muttered vaguely to Corder about finding a compromise candidate instead. Corder wrote in exasperation to Oppenheimer about the United Party leader's 'procrastination & deviousness'.[130] Oppenheimer was unwilling to enter into a contest with Div for the chancellorship, so he sought clarity from his old friend and attempted to defuse the 'somewhat awkward situation [that] seems to be arising'.[131] Graaff gave his former benchmate the run-around for a little while longer – Oppenheimer told Zach de Beer that Div's aim was not to secure the position for himself, 'but to prevent my taking it' – before bowing out of contention.[132]

Although Diemont ran as someone divorced from party politics, De Beer jibed that he was a 'time-server' who wanted to be 'Chief Justice under the Nats'.[133] Diemont had Graaff's backing, and a United Party councillor, Brian Bamford, organised an extensive letter-writing campaign in support of his candidature. Diemont appealed to a bloc of conservative voters who might have regarded Oppenheimer as the lesser of two evils in a straightforward contest with Marquard.[134] De Beer served as Oppenheimer's election agent, lobbied furiously on his behalf, and harvested a slew of prominent endorsements in the press. It was a hotly contested campaign that provided many wondrous examples, in the words of the *Rand Daily Mail*'s Laurence Gandar, of 'political gut-fighting', all the more deadly for being conducted in 'coldly courteous academic language'.[135] Oppenheimer's positioning as the candidate of the centre – less inclined than Diemont or Marquard to be drawn into taking public stands on controversial issues but nevertheless mindful of the university's character and determined to preserve it – worked in his

HFO is installed as the Chancellor of the University of Cape Town,
30 May 1967. Behind him, from left to right, are UCT's Deputy Principal,
Professor DP Inskip; Principal and Vice-Chancellor, Dr JP Duminy; and
chair of the Council, Mr CS Corder. *(Anglo American)*

favour. Having defeated his competitors, Oppenheimer was inaugurated
as the chancellor of UCT on 30 May 1967. It was a function he fulfilled
diligently over a period of 29 years, into the post-1994 democratic
dispensation. Oppenheimer capped thousands of graduates, provided
steady support to successive Vice-Chancellors – JP Duminy, Sir Richard
Luyt and Stuart Saunders – and imbued the university's official stance on
academic freedom and institutional autonomy with his personal gravitas.

Shortly after Oppenheimer's installation, the government imposed
banning orders on Bill Hoffenberg, a popular medical scientist at Groote
Schuur Hospital and UCT. In part, this was a calculated attempt to sever
Hoffenberg's ties to student leaders in the National Union of South African
Students (Nusas). The ban provoked a huge public outcry, with poster
demonstrations, protest meetings and petitions from university staff

and students. Oppenheimer led an official UCT deputation, comprising Duminy, Corder and the head of the medical school, Professor JF Brock, to lobby the Minister of Justice, Peet Pelser, for a rescission of Hoffenberg's banning orders. Their plea fell on deaf ears. Nevertheless, this high-profile advocacy of Hoffenberg's cause was a conspicuous display of solidarity in opposition to the Nats. By contrast, Oppenheimer was largely absent during the infamous 'Mafeje Affair' of 1968. This episode was prompted by the government's refusal to allow UCT's appointment of a black social anthropologist, Archie Mafeje, as a senior lecturer. In protest, students staged a sit-in at the university's administrative hub, the Bremner Building, over several days. UCT's Senate refused their request for a 24-hour shutdown of the campus and the occupation was eventually abandoned. Meanwhile, UCT's Council capitulated to the government's demands and withdrew Mafeje's appointment. It was an overhasty surrender, which sullied the institution's liberal reputation in some quarters and haunted UCT for years to come. (Several decades later, in an attempt to make amends, a plaque was erected on the steps leading to the Chancellor Oppenheimer Library in remembrance of the Mafeje Affair.)

As a neo-Marxist orthodoxy began to permeate the open universities in the 1970s, unsettling traditional liberal pieties about the incompatibility of capitalism and apartheid, a section of UCT students questioned the progressive patina of Oppenheimer's politics. In 1973, in the wake of the Schlebusch Commission of Inquiry, the government served banning orders on several Nusas leaders. Oppenheimer accused the government of abusing its powers, trampling civil rights underfoot and bringing South Africa closer to a police state. BJ Vorster upbraided Oppenheimer for his remarks and even De Villiers Graaff saw fit to censure him. However, for a group of radical left-wing students on campus, Oppenheimer was trading in platitudes. They accused him of assuming a 'progressive façade'; in reality he was the epitome of 'racist capitalism' who underpaid his black workers and treated them like chattel.[136] Oppenheimer's reliance on the iniquitous migrant labour system, the barrack-like compounds on his mines, the strict reinforcement of tribalism, and the destruction of family life to which these practices gave rise – all of this, in the students' view, opened a yawning chasm between their Chancellor's words and deeds. Righteous anger flowed from the campus onto the streets of Cape Town, where students carried an effigy of Oppenheimer with placards excoriating him as an arch-exploiter. 'Hunger breeds hatred, Give rights and money, Don't give to charity – pay a decent wage,' they chanted.

Oppenheimer brushed off their reprovals. 'I don't resent criticism, it keeps you up to scratch', was his nonchalant response.[137] Notwithstanding the occasional student opprobrium, Oppenheimer and UCT enjoyed a mutually beneficial relationship. It brought significant material benefits to the university, including the establishment of the Centre for African Studies with a R2 million grant from Anglo and De Beers. The African Studies Library and (much later) the Chancellor Oppenheimer Library followed. Oppenheimer's chancellorship conferred on him a degree of 'academic lustre', according to UCT's official historian.[138]

Decolonisation and the Conditions for Progress in Africa

Oppenheimer had always conceived of himself as a man of Africa, the heir to Rhodes, an apostle of the British imperial and Commonwealth connection. He thus watched with apprehension as the wave of African independence and decolonisation movements swept through the continent in the 1960s. It was a topic to which he returned repeatedly in his university addresses. In 1961 Oppenheimer advised graduands at the University of Natal that there was no magic charm to transform 'primitive tribesmen' into 'freedom-loving democrats'.[139] In the absence of an 'educated and sophisticated' electorate, the principle of one man, one vote was likely to demolish freedom, democracy and civilisation in the settler colonies. Oppenheimer believed that colonialism had produced significant benefits for Africa in terms of governance, economic development and infrastructure, and education and health care. He insisted that the 'white tribes of Africa' were Africans and not Europeans, and he deplored those 'modern liberals' who seemed 'to suffer from a sense of guilt over the colonial past' and who thought 'in a doctrinal way' that to expiate their guilt 'they must support everything black – including the black dictatorships'.[140] In 1962, in the course of a wide-ranging discourse delivered during UCT's TB Davie Memorial Lecture, Oppenheimer expounded on these themes under the rubric of 'the conditions for progress in Africa'.[141] The critical question, he concluded, was whether African nationalists would 'prove capable of completing the work of the Colonialists'. 'In these new African countries are individual men and women to become increasingly free to realise their potentialities? Or is Africa, like Europe when the Roman colonial system collapsed, to sink back into the tyranny and chaos from which the Europeans rescued it?'[142]

As the first South African to deliver the Smuts Memorial Lecture at the University of Cambridge in November 1967, Oppenheimer mourned the 'fading' of the Commonwealth.[143] The Commonwealth was an idea, he reflected wistfully, that until recently had been central to his political thinking and planning as an industrialist. South Africa's departure from the Commonwealth was a matter of profound regret for Oppenheimer. However, as the sun set on the British Empire, and Britain pivoted to 'pursuing the shadow' of a larger, more inclusive Commonwealth, he felt the substance of the old British Commonwealth had been abandoned. The Commonwealth was no longer an organisation based on political, military and economic unity. It lacked any 'emotional content'. Indeed, it was difficult to generate a sense of pride or loyalty in an international association whose reason for existing rested on the 'somewhat uninspiring objective of avoiding discrimination between its members'. The Commonwealth's material decline might be regarded as a measure of its 'moral greatness', Oppenheimer consoled his audience. Personally he drew cold comfort from that notion, but then he was a 'rather old-fashioned person', he confessed. Certainly he would have appeared as such to the small band of placard-waving students who protested against his arrival.

Oppenheimer's musings on colonialism and the evanescence of the Commonwealth might appear antiquated over a half-century later. Yet they were not, as he freely conceded, particularly progressive in their time. Even so, Oppenheimer was no unreconstructed imperialist jingo. In 1970 he offered a reasonably balanced appraisal, given contemporary mores, of Cecil John Rhodes's legacy, in the first Rhodes Commemoration Lecture held at Rhodes University. Oppenheimer suggested that in founding Rhodesia, Rhodes was inspired by a 'great vision', but he acknowledged that Rhodes's methods involved 'harshness' and 'trickery' and a ruthless destruction of Matabele power.[144] Rhodes might have been susceptible to 'crude imperialist conspiracy', as evidenced by his first will, but the idea that he devoted his life to the pursuit of an illusion by 'morally reprehensible means' was a 'gross distortion of the truth'. Rhodes used profits from diamonds to build railways, to kickstart gold mining on the Witwatersrand, to establish South Africa's fruit farming industry, to pioneer the manufacture of explosives and fertilisers, and to contribute to the 'cost of colonising Rhodesia'. 'I am glad to think that long after Rhodes' death', Oppenheimer reflected in an allusion to his own dynasty at De Beers, 'his policy of using diamond profits for the general development of the South African economy has been revived to the considerable benefit both of shareholders and the country.' In Oppenheimer's view, Rhodes was a man of apparent contradictions. Nevertheless, there was a logical and consistent pattern of thought to Rhodes's statements and actions. He subordinated everything to one great idea: the development of a 'great modern industrialised state' in South Africa, anchored in the British Empire. Rhodes's vision of an industrialised society in which all civilised men could enjoy equal rights remained valid. In the long run, according to Oppenheimer, it was the only way the nation could prosper.

In his lifetime Oppenheimer, like Rhodes, became the object of anti-imperialist ire. The Ghanaian publication *Voice of Africa*, which enjoyed President Kwame Nkrumah's patronage, denounced Oppenheimer as the continent's 'richest settler' and 'worst exploiter of the African masses': that particular edition was so widely circulated in South Africa that the police's notorious Special Branch sought to track down its distributors.[145] Unlike Rhodes, Oppenheimer had to accommodate himself to Africa's post-independence black heads of state for his commercial empire to flourish. He quickly struck up a good rapport with the President of Zambia, Kenneth Kaunda. 'I like him very much. He's a very attractive person,' Oppenheimer told an interviewer three years after Kaunda came to power.[146] Kaunda admired Oppenheimer for his intellectual ability, and neatly summed up their friendship: 'He's a capitalist, I'm a socialist, but I like to look at a man's own character and it is that which attracts me to him.'[147] On his visit to Washington DC in 1965, Oppenheimer outwardly agreed with a senior official from the US State Department on the need to strengthen Kaunda's hand. The idea was to help Kaunda forge closer political and economic ties with President Julius Nyerere of Tanzania, by road or rail links among other things. 'I said we were deeply interested in the maintenance of stable conditions in Zambia and Tanzania and preventing communist infiltration, and would certainly co-operate within our means in any scheme envisaging these aims,' Oppenheimer recorded after the meeting.[148] Yet privately he thought the mandarin's views were 'entirely unrealistic'. The real interest of the Western powers, to Oppenheimer's mind, was not to encourage closer relations between Zambia and Tanzania, but to induce Kaunda to live in harmony with Rhodesia, 'whether he likes Ian Smith's Government or not'. Oppenheimer believed the State Department and the Central Intelligence Agency harboured 'comfortable illusions' about Tanzania. 'In fact, the influence of Chinese communists in Tanzania is great and

HFO and Sir Seretse Khama (third from right)
at a meeting in Gaborone, 1968. *(Anglo American)*

growing and I should say that the worse the connections are between
Tanzania and Zambia, the better.'

Whatever his reservations about the Tanzanian polity, Oppenheimer
cultivated Nyerere, whose integrity he lauded. He also courted President
Seretse Khama of Botswana. After the discovery of diamonds in 1967, with
the Orapa and Letlhakane pipes, the economy of Botswana practically
became an Anglo fiefdom. Oppenheimer led the negotiations with Khama,
and when De Beers opened the Orapa diamond mine in 1971, HFO had
the entire Botswanan cabinet flown in for the ceremony. Debswana, the
mining company established by De Beers in 1969, was still 50 per cent
owned by the government of Botswana half a century later. It has served
the landlocked nation well, contributing massively to Botswana's gross
domestic product, foreign exchange earnings and employment numbers
(apart from all the schools, hospitals and community facilities built on
its dime).

Unsurprisingly, Kaunda, Nyerere and Khama all eagerly hosted
Oppenheimer in their State Houses on his business trips. Nyerere and
Oppenheimer would spend the evening discussing their shared love
of Shakespeare. They dined together with the newly installed British

HFO and President Kenneth Kaunda,
late 1970s. *(Anglo American)*

Prime Minister, Edward Heath, at Chequers in 1970, an event recorded
by *The Guardian* under the headline 'Sanction soup'. With more than
a hint of a sneer, the left-wing publication identified Oppenheimer as
a 'well-known arms manufacturer and critic of apartheid'.[149] If Kaunda
and Nyerere harboured any such misgivings about Oppenheimer's
politics, they kept it to themselves. Zambia led Africa's campaign against
the apartheid state, and Tanzania provided the ANC in exile with its
African headquarters; yet the two Presidents treated the arch-capitalist
Oppenheimer as an esteemed dignitary in their countries. Both leaders
concocted an ersatz philosophy of African socialism, with economically
ruinous consequences. Initially Kaunda promised that Zambia's copper
mines would remain in the hands of private enterprise. He soon wavered.
Kaunda accused the mining companies of distributing 80 per cent of their

profits each year in dividends. Oppenheimer put the Zambian President to rights. Of Anglo's gross mining profits in Zambia since independence, between 1964 and 1967, 64.8 per cent had been paid to the Zambian government by way of royalties and taxation.[150] In 1969 Kaunda signalled his intention to nationalise the copper mines. HFO immediately jumped on the company Gulfstream to Lusaka. Anglo laid on a banquet for the mining minister, hoping to persuade him against nationalisation. Alas, despite having accepted the invitation, the minister was a no-show. The next day Oppenheimer happened to bump into him in the street; the political worthy was full of good cheer, and he greeted HFO with a broad smile and a warm handshake. 'I'm terribly sorry we missed you at dinner last night,' Oppenheimer probed gently. 'Ah, yes,' came the minister's deadpan reply, 'I wasn't feeling hungry.' A few days later the Zambian government acquired a 51 per cent stake in the Zambian Anglo American Corporation's mines. Zamanglo was compensated for the loss and initially retained the management contracts for its mines, but full-scale nationalisation followed in 1974. It turned out to be a catastrophe. The move coincided with a crash in the copper price. Nationalisation sapped the mines' profitability and dragged the country from copper-bottomed prosperity into worst-case penury. 'I would not be human,' Oppenheimer wrote to Kaunda, 'if I did not regret the loosening of the direct ties between our group and Zambia which is the inevitable consequence of these developments.'[151] Nevertheless, HFO retained a fond regard for Kaunda, and he expressed the hope that Anglo might still make a contribution to the country's development and welfare. Kaunda, the sentimental socialist, found Oppenheimer's message 'most touching', but kept to his destructive course all the same.[152]

Black Wages and Industrial Relations

Until the 1970s the six finance houses that dominated South Africa's gold mining industry paid no significant increases to their African mineworkers, the majority of whom were migrant labourers from Malawi and Mozambique. These mineworkers formed the backbone of the sector. They risked their lives underground in scorching confines, yet earned starvation wages. In fact, between 1889 and 1970, the real wages of black mineworkers fell while those of white mineworkers improved by around two-thirds.[153] African wages on the gold mines were effectively higher in 1915 than in 1970.[154] In 1970, white mineworkers earned on average twenty times more than their black counterparts. When Wim de Villiers relocated from the Copperbelt to Johannesburg, he was shocked to find that black mineworkers were pocketing the equivalent of £6 per month in 1961; in 1896, black wages on the mines averaged £3 16s.[155] As the largest and wealthiest mining house, Anglo American lobbied the Chamber of Mines, with varying degrees of determination, to raise black wages. However, Anglo only broke ranks with the Chamber on this score for the first time in 1985, by which point African workers had been granted collective bargaining rights.[156] From the early 1960s Oppenheimer identified South Africa's 'greatest need' as 'more pay for natives', a point he drove home at the Rand Easter Show in 1963.[157] In Parliament the Minister of Bantu Administration, MDC de Wet Nel, responded somewhat pointedly: 'The Oppenheimers ... should not only talk about higher wages but should pay their workers more.'[158] Oppenheimer countered that the basic earnings of black mineworkers employed in Anglo's Free State and Western Transvaal gold mines had increased by between 15 and 20 per cent from 1961 to 1963. However, it was only in 1972 that Anglo started to address systematically the slow-burning question of low wages for the 165 000 black workers employed on its gold and coal mines.

In March of that year Bill Wilson was appointed to chair an employment practices committee, consisting of the heads of Anglo's operating divisions. The committee's mandate, HFO reported, was to formulate and implement a strategy for improving the working conditions of the 'Black employees of the Group'.[159] The committee would also consider the social ills produced by the migrant labour system and Anglo's severely regimented mine compounds. Alex Boraine, a Methodist minister with progressive sensibilities – the Progs had approached him to stand as their candidate in Durban's Berea constituency in 1970 – was brought on board as a full-time consultant to assist with the work. Boraine was a vocal critic of black mine labourers' working and living conditions. As president of the Methodist Church from 1970 to 1972, he regularly visited mine compounds: the cleric took fire at mine management, and his reproving views were often quoted in the press. It was Oppenheimer who took notice of Boraine. HFO sounded him out over dinner at Milkwood, facilitated his consultancy at Anglo, and accommodated the clergyman, his wife and their four young children at Blue Skies on the Brenthurst estate, while Boraine found his feet at 44 Main Street.[160]

These developments were spurred by economic tremors, which

Oppenheimer feared might produce an earthquake. There was a major slump in the share market in 1969. Anglo's investments, taking quoted shares at market value, fell by 14.5 per cent.[161] 'Harry O' had lost around R250 000 a day over the preceding twelve months, the *Sunday Times* rumoured, reducing his personal fortune in Anglo American and Charter Consolidated from R166 million to R84 million.[162] More significantly, between 1970 and 1972, after five decades of steady progression, real gross domestic product per head in South Africa rose by only 0.9 per cent; and the rate of growth of national income showed signs of impending contraction.[163] The country was reaching the end of an era in which a high growth rate could be achieved by sucking more and more African peasants into the industrial system to do unskilled work for low wages. As South Africa entered a new decade, there was an acute skills shortage alongside rising black unemployment. Meanwhile, long-term demographic projections suggested that the white population would shrink relative to the black population, thus exacerbating the skills crisis. In London, Oppenheimer told the South Africa Club in April 1972 that this marked a fundamental 'turning point' in the South African economy.[164] The oil crisis of 1973, triggered by the embargo which Arab nations imposed on countries that supported Israel during the Yom Kippur War, caused the price of oil to surge. Inflation rocketed. Increased economic volatility coupled with slower growth and skills shortages pressed home the need, Oppenheimer told an audience at Chatham House, to upskill black workers, increase black wages, and provide black South Africans with access to previously denied opportunities.[165] 'Everyone, without regard to race or colour, should receive the same pay for the same work,' Oppenheimer announced to the Trade Union Council of South Africa in 1971.[166] Counterintuitively, the period of economic stagnation in the early 1970s coincided with a mini-boom in mineral resources. Oppenheimer counselled his shareholders that higher export prices for gold and diamonds obliged the mining industry to make 'better use of the black labour force': it would be prudent, he signalled, to pay black workers 'commensurately higher wages'.[167] In 1974, Oppenheimer accurately predicted that the demand for skilled black labour would unleash 'a major economic revolution', which would transform South African society and 'powerfully alter the way of thinking in all political parties'.[168] Indeed, from the late 1960s, Oppenheimer had emphasised that South Africa would not be able to realise its economic potential so long as the productivity and wages of black labourers were held back by an outmoded system of industrial relations. This included legal prohibitions on the use of labour, and a deficient system of education and technical training. The 'refusal to train and use African ... labour fully and effectively lies at the root of our economic problems', Oppenheimer claimed.[169]

The work of the employment practices committee bore fruit. In 1973, Anglo raised the wages of black mineworkers by 60 per cent on average, while De Beers raised them by 70 per cent.[170] Black workers were invited to join Anglo's pension scheme on the same terms as white workers. Oppenheimer announced a substantial expansion in Anglo's training facilities and an allocation of R60 million by the gold division to introduce 'higher standards of accommodation' for black workers.[171] He made no pretence of liking the migrant labour system with its 'serious social and economic disadvantages', Oppenheimer professed, but given the scale and complexity of the practice there was 'no realistic prospect' of phasing it out on the gold mines for the foreseeable future. (In Kimberley, the De Beers mine now drew its black labour force from the municipal township.) To the *Rand Daily Mail*, Anglo's new tack reflected a mixture of 'progressive idealism' and 'practical business sense'.[172] The *Financial Times* declared Oppenheimer's line on African workers to be 'cool' and 'constructive'.[173]

In contrast, industrial relations on the mines were decidedly hot. Flowing from the re-evaluation of its employment practices, Anglo introduced a new system of job grading and restructured its pay scales. In one infamous instance this had fatal consequences. On 4 September 1973, some 200 black machine operators – men who drilled the holes for explosives – downed tools at Western Deep Levels' Number 2 shaft. Their pay had been hiked by 46 per cent, but they were upset that the earnings of mineworkers on a lower pay grade – underground locomotive and winch drivers – had shot up by 60 per cent. They wanted a wider wage differential. Violent rioting broke out, mine management called in the police, and before peace was restored 12 black miners had died: 11 were shot by the police and one was hacked by fellow workers. There was an immediate fallout. Gold shares tumbled. Anglo and the head of its gold division, John Shilling, came under fierce attack. (Shilling later recalled that Oppenheimer was a 'sheet anchor' during the episode, 'always understanding and ready with advice'.)[174] In London the anti-apartheid campaigner Peter Hain led a large demonstration outside South Africa House. Over a hundred Wits students invaded 44 Main Street in protest, while their peers at UCT convened a mass meeting and demanded that Oppenheimer resign his chancellorship. Oppenheimer responded to the president of the UCT Students' Representative Council, Laurine Platzky, with a detailed account, written in his own hand, of exactly what had happened at Western Deep Levels and why. He also invited Platzky and another student leader, Nigel Willis, to lunch at Brenthurst where he listened attentively to their concerns. The correspondence was reproduced in *Bolt*, a quirky literary magazine which sported a cover illustration of HFO as Count Dracula. (Anglo promptly cancelled its subs.) For Eddie Webster, a sociologist at the University of Natal deeply involved in labour issues, Oppenheimer's missive was full of 'half-truths and omissions'. For too long, Webster charged, liberal critics such as Oppenheimer had hidden behind the rhetoric of anti-apartheid criticism, thus obscuring the 'very real collaboration' between the mine owners and the 'basic institutions of labour repression in South Africa'.[175]

Anglo supported a judicial commission of inquiry into the killings at Western Deep Levels. The company initiated its own investigation and undertook to improve communication between mine managers and workers over its new employment policies. One of the problems, Oppenheimer acknowledged in his letter to Platzky, was the absence of an 'adequate workers' organisation' – that is, black trade union – through which to channel communications.[176] The violence at Western Deep Levels was the harbinger of more brutal conflict involving black mineworkers, often with complex and multifaceted causes, which bedevilled the mining industry in the 1970s and 1980s. A contemporaneous study found that from the eruption at Western Deep Levels to the end of June 1976, there were 192 deaths from mine violence and 1278 injuries.[177] However, the discontent on the mines was not fomented in a vacuum. In January, 2000 black workers went on strike at a brick factory in Durban. The strikes soon spread to East London and Johannesburg. By the end of 1973, as many as 100 000 workers had participated in a rolling wave of industrial action. It was the biggest and most protracted manifestation of worker militancy since the 1946 African mineworkers' strike, and it sowed the seeds of the black trade union movement, which was to become a critical player on South Africa's political stage. (Although the formation of trade unions by black workers was not illegal, until 1979 they could not be formally registered; as such, black unions did not enjoy the legal right to strike.) Alongside this tumult, the Black Consciousness Movement (BCM), associated with Steve Biko and the South African Students'

The cousins: Jonathan Oppenheimer and Victoria Waddell with their mothers, Strilli Oppenheimer (far right) and Mary Waddell (second from right), c.1971. *(Brenthurst Library)*

Organisation, began to flex its muscles. It raised the political temperature. In 1972 more than 1400 delegates attended the inaugural conference of the Black People's Convention in Pietermaritzburg. With the political mercury rising, the economy stagnating and black labour convulsing, South Africa was a time bomb waiting to explode. The detonation came on 16 June 1976. Large-scale riots broke out in the black township of Soweto, and pandemonium ensued. It was clear to Oppenheimer that urgent reforms were needed. This was to become the key theme in the next phase of HFO's public life, as he took on the role of reformer and nudged the government to make an accommodation with the 'economic revolution'. South Africa's 'silent revolution', as one contemporary analyst termed it, would ultimately herald political change.[178]

TEN

Inside the Anglo Powerhouse

The Four Columns

'I chose my father with discretion,' Harry Oppenheimer once explained to an interviewer from the South African Broadcasting Corporation. 'And … like the prayer book says, I have sought to do my duty in the station in which it pleases the Lord to call me.'[1] Propelled by a conscious sense of manifest destiny, Oppenheimer provided a fillip to the gold and diamond dynasty. His ambitions proved to be more imperial than Sir Ernest's. By the time HFO vacated the chairman's seat at Anglo American at the end of 1982, he had fashioned the so-called greater group into a massive multinational conglomerate with assets worth an estimated $15 billion.[2] Anglo was the capitalist world's largest producer of gold, platinum and vanadium. Its manifold interests were sprawled across the globe, part of a corporate empire spanning North America, South America, Europe, Asia, Africa and Australasia. In South Africa, owing to a battery of moves into manufacturing, construction, property and finance during the 1960s and 1970s, Anglo straddled the economy. Beyond diamonds and gold, and platinum and uranium, Anglo boasted vast holdings in a range of base metals. Its diversified portfolio included coal, iron and steel, chemicals and explosives, pulp and paper, beer and bricks, banks and insurance houses, hotels and commercial offices, motor car manufacturers and distributors, and all manner of large retailers. Even before Anglo American started gobbling up the assets of foreign firms that disinvested from the country in the late 1980s, companies in the Anglo stable controlled over 50 per cent of the listings on the Johannesburg Stock Exchange.

In southern Africa, during the period of HFO's chairmanship from 1957 to 1982, the Anglo American group produced after-tax profits of R13 300 million, paid dividends to its shareholders amounting to R7 100 million, and contributed over R5 400 million to the fiscus in taxes.[3] Critics looked upon this embarrassment of riches with cynicism and rancour: they believed that three key institutions of apartheid – migrant labour, pass laws and the compound system – kept Anglo's argosy afloat. These were the mechanisms through which, it was argued, the group controlled and exploited cheap black labour as a major source of its profit. Oppenheimer, the enlightened liberal capitalist, was wont to reply that Anglo American (and South Africa) would have been much more prosperous in the absence of these regressive and restrictive policies. Why, then, did Anglo not use its awesome financial and economic might to strike at the foundations of the racial order? In reality, although big business was by no means devoid of leverage, or incapable of exercising moral suasion, it lacked the political power required to bring down the whole edifice of racial oppression. At most it could chip away at the bedrock. Even so, Oppenheimer was the first to admit that the companies under his control 'didn't do as much as we should have done'.[4] His guarded admission somewhat soft-pedalled the ambiguous nature of Anglo's legacy. Yet any reckoning of the group's societal ledger must take into account the fact that, at the same time that Anglo was playing a cardinal role in South Africa's industrialisation, it was leading the pack in trying to ameliorate industrial relations, uplift communities of different races, and pioneer new forms of corporate citizenship. In this way Anglo contributed significantly to building the most urbanised, industrialised and developed country on the continent of Africa – a formidable endowment for the first democratic, post-apartheid government.

When HFO retired from the chairmanship of De Beers Consolidated Mines at the end of 1984 – he stayed on to lead De Beers through a global recession – Cecil John Rhodes's old company still effectively ruled the world of diamonds. From 1957 to 1983 production from the group's diamond mines expanded almost sevenfold to 21.4 million carats. Sales of diamonds through the Central Selling Organisation soared tenfold to R1 771 million, though in 1978 (before the market downturn) they reached a record high of R2 219 million.[5] De Beers' after-tax profits surged six times higher to R530 million; and the value of its investments multiplied no less than thirty times to R3 278 million.[6] These were remarkable accomplishments by any measure of comparison. As a dynast of the second generation, Harry Oppenheimer not only maintained the family's fortune, he grew it exponentially. *Fortune* magazine credited HFO with being one of the world's ten wealthiest men in 1968, a claim repeated in the local press under simpering headlines such as 'Oppenheimer's R344-million smile'.[7] More than two decades later, *Fortune* began to include the Oppenheimer family on its list of dollar billionaires; in 1990, with estimated riches of $1.3 billion, the dynasty ranked above the Benettons of Italy.[8] Like the Cadburys and Rowntrees in Britain, and the Fords, Mellons and Carnegies in America, the Oppenheimers constituted a powerful industrial and philanthropic dynasty in South Africa.

In 1965 the group was buttressed by four columns: the Anglo American Corporation, De Beers Consolidated Mines, the Rand Selection Corporation, and Charter Consolidated. HFO had played a critical role in the conceptualisation and design of the latter two entities: they drove Anglo's investments inside and outside South Africa, respectively. By the mid-1970s, the Mineral and Resources Corporation (Minorco) formed another pillar, and occupied an expanding corner of the Anglo realm. Born out of Zambian Anglo American (Zamanglo), and transferred to Bermuda in 1970 after the nationalisation of the Zambian copper mines, Minorco came to displace Charter as the principal vehicle for Anglo's strategic investments abroad. Although the group's internal control structure was highly decentralised, a lattice of pyramided holding companies, interlocking shareholdings and cross-directorships rendered the Oppenheimer empire if not impregnable, then certainly well garrisoned by loyalists. Anglo, De Beers, Charter and Minorco (Rand Selection was ultimately absorbed into Anglo) were bound together by crossholdings. Taken together, the various minority holdings added up to a substantial majority share in each company. As a result, one financial weekly observed, any international corporate giant attempting a takeover of Anglo on a stock-swap basis was bound to end up in 'the awkward position of having Oppenheimer' as its single biggest shareholder.[9] The Anglo trademark evoked the Oppenheimer name. Yet by the time HFO stood down, the diversification and reorganisation of the group into numerous, fairly autonomous operating divisions – coupled with its sheer size and complexity – meant that Anglo's continued status as the 'Oppenheimer company' was far from certain. Nicky Oppenheimer was waiting patiently in the wings; but when his father departed from the throne, the heir apparent was still of an age that the financial press could plausibly dub him 'Not-yet Nicky'.[10] As HFO prepared to relinquish the chairmanship, questions of succession greatly exercised his mind.

Banker to the Gold Mining Industry, and the Post-Sharpeville Industrial Boom

After HFO's first decade in the hot seat, the *Financial Mail* conducted a survey on the 'Anglo power house'. It found that between 1958 and 1968 the market value of the Anglo American Corporation's investments had risen by a staggering 619 per cent, to £478 million.[11] Anglo dwarfed its rivals. At the beginning of 1961, the market capitalisation of the corporation's issued ordinary shares amounted to two-thirds of the market capitalisation of the rest of the mining finance houses combined. Thanks to Anglo's profitable new mines in the Orange Free State, the corporation completely dominated South Africa's gold mining industry. Oppenheimer had centralised power by bringing the Central Mining–Rand Mines group into Anglo's stable, and he followed suit with the Johannesburg Consolidated Investment Company (JCI). By the end of the 1960s Anglo had minority shareholdings in three of the four other main mining groups – Gold Fields, General Mining and Union Corporation – and enjoyed representation on their boards. Only family-owned Anglovaal remained free of Oppenheimer's grasp, a fact keenly appreciated by its founders, Bob Hersov and Slip Menell. They planned to hand over the family silver (or gold) to two of their own sons, Basil Hersov and Clive Menell, undiluted by Anglo's acquisitiveness.

As early as 1961, Slip Menell's urbane heir, Clive, an enlightened latter-day Randlord in the Oppenheimer mould, conceded that Anglo was the 'undisputed leader' of the industry and its foremost financier.[12] If Clive Menell and various other English-speaking titans of industry looked to the patrician Oppenheimer as a sort of political and cultural exemplar, a pillar of the anglophone establishment, then they must surely have felt a pang of envy over the Anglo powerhouse's reach. In the 1960s Anglo produced 40 per cent of South Africa's gold and about a third of its uranium. Anglo held lucrative diamond interests through De Beers. JCI controlled the world's largest platinum mine at Rustenburg. Perhaps most significantly of all, as Clive Menell acknowledged, by the 1960s Anglo had emerged as one of the great financial institutions of its time, a banker to the gold mining industry. Over the remaining course of HFO's

Banker to the gold mining industry: HFO poses in front
of a mining headgear, 1964. *(Anglo American)*

chairmanship, Anglo would extend its sphere of influence beyond mining
into industry and finance. The process was lubricated by a large cash flow
from the Orange Free State goldfields and the prosperity afforded by
Anglo's investments in diamonds and copper. A dizzying diversification
drive lay ahead.

Once the dust had settled from Sharpeville, the economy took
off. Investors piled into South Africa from the United States, Britain
and Western Europe, often bearing new technology. Multinational
corporations like Chrysler, Ford, General Motors, Hoechst and Siemens
established local operations. Growth rebounded, albeit contrary to
conventional wisdom, to rates less eye-watering than before, and not quite
so exceptional by global standards.[13] (The really dramatic phase of South
Africa's economic upswing occurred between 1945 and 1964, when GDP
growth averaged 8.3 per cent a year.) By the mid-1960s, the share of GDP
accounted for by industry, including manufacturing and construction,
had long surpassed the combined share of agriculture and mining. It now
topped 30 per cent.[14] While some mining houses, notably Anglovaal, had

diversified into industry from the start, divarication occurred chiefly in the 1960s and 1970s. Anglo rode the wave.[15] Between 1960 and 1968, the value of Anglo's industrial interests in South Africa rose by approximately 470 per cent, from R50 million to R285 million.[16] According to Duncan Innes, the Marxist mapper of Anglo's monopoly, Anglo American created new monopolies in various branches of manufacturing and construction, and thus extended its influence not just economically, but also 'politically and ideologically'.[17]

Leftists of a more polemical bent tended to converge with purveyors of the 'Hoggenheimer' motif in their portrayal of Anglo. The Oppenheimer group, they insinuated, was a predatory, hydra-headed, hyper-capitalist monster, and it exercised undue political influence. Granted, Anglo came to permeate the economy, which positioned it as a powerful political broker in the era of reform. Whether it gained any great ideological purchase over racial nationalists of different stripes – herd thinkers who exalted the executive power of the central state and mistrusted market forces – is a thornier proposition. Nevertheless, Anglo's economic supremacy was not attained entirely by design. Protected domestic markets and restrictions on investment abroad meant the group had little option but to diversify beyond mining and reinvest its profits at home. Rigid exchange controls encouraged the concentration of ownership. As international pressure to end apartheid intensified in the second half of the 1980s, disinvestment by blue-chip American and European firms reinforced the trend. Anglo snapped up Ford's business and most of Barclays'. In 1987, four conglomerates – including Anglo American and Anton Rupert's Rembrandt – controlled 83 per cent of all companies listed on the Johannesburg Stock Exchange (JSE).[18] Anglo alone was responsible for 60 per cent of the JSE's total market capitalisation.[19] In the outline of his memoir, HFO claimed that Anglo's turn to manufacturing did not, at first, appeal to him 'temperamentally'.[20] A conservative at heart, he doubted whether a mining house – especially a gold mining house – was equipped for the task. Nevertheless, as Anglo gained confidence outside its mining comfort zone, and as investment opportunities snowballed, the group expanded insatiably. Anglo's engorgement would have ramifications for its overall coherence, organisational structure and sustainability as a family concern. Meanwhile, by the end of the 1980s, the *New York Times* deemed that 'Oppenheimer's collection of multinationals' outnumbered those of Nissan and Siemens.[21]

Anglo's Industrial Empire

The spadework for Anglo's escalating expansion into industry was undertaken during the first seven years of HFO's chairmanship. In 1964, in a section of his annual statement headed 'Outside traditional fields', Oppenheimer announced the completion of a low-carbon ferrochrome plant in partnership with the Swedish steel titan, Avesta Jernverks Aktieborg.[22] The work was undertaken by an Anglo subsidiary, Transalloys Limited. This was one of several collaborations with foreign companies which gave Anglo access to advanced technology. In fact, Anglo was spreading so 'rapidly in the field of secondary industry', Oppenheimer proclaimed, that the corporation had formed a new finance and investment company, the Anglo American Industrial Corporation (Amic).[23] Amic's role would be to consolidate Anglo's industrial holdings. Almost simultaneously, through Boart and Hard Metals, Anglo established a new construction company, Amalgamated Construction and Contracting. The corporation's entry into the commercial property sector – 'on a large scale', Oppenheimer advised – would be showcased by a mammoth project: the development, in tandem with South African Breweries, of four blocks in the Johannesburg central business district into one integrated building.[24] This was to become the Carlton Centre.

Soon after its formation Amic made a successful bid for Scaw Metals, which became a wholly owned subsidiary. Under Anglo's wing Scaw's business mushroomed. In 1966 Anglo financed the construction of a R10 million steel rolling mill. Scaw was soon manufacturing over ten per cent of the world's supply of grinding balls. With Anglo's resources behind it and Graham Boustred's continued stewardship, Scaw's total assets ballooned to R40 million by 1969; a decade later, the company was valued at about R90 million.[25] Scaw became one of the country's leading profit-earners and an exporter of international renown. It supplied over twenty nations with rolled steel and foundry products, and furnished the American market with undercarriages for railway freight cars. Anglo's acquisition of Scaw had been prompted in part by its plans for the Highveld Steel and Vanadium Corporation: it needed Scaw's management expertise in the steel business. After some serious teething problems, Highveld Steel blasted off. It garnered R50 million from exports between 1969 and 1971, and ramped up Anglo's group profits.[26] By 1970 Highveld was the fourth-largest industrial concern in South Africa, with assets valued at R138.4 million.[27] That same year, Leslie Boyd, a Scottish-born metallurgical engineer with an earthy sense of humour and wide experience of managing steel plants in Australia, Holland and India, moved to Witbank. He became, in turn, Highveld's general manager and managing director. Under Boyd's watch, the corporation went from strength to strength.

Anglo had partnered with Davy United in Britain to develop Highveld's Witbank plant. The overall production process marked an innovation in steel-making: it combined and adapted existing foreign technologies.[28] Even before the steel works were up and running, Highveld secured contracts with American and European manufacturers of ferro-vanadium. All of its planned vanadium production was committed until the end of 1971.[29] Iscor watched in trepidation. In 1966 the state-owned steel producer estimated that approximately 30 per cent of its orders were placed by companies within Anglo's orbit; it stood to reason that these contracts would be redirected to Highveld.[30] HFO's assessment of the situation, as relayed to Gordon Waddell, was that Iscor officials were so accustomed to their monopoly that they had become 'emotionally excited by our competition'.[31] Yet Highveld was a prominent public company, and it would be 'quite impossible politically', Oppenheimer professed, for the government to be seen trying to spoil its chances.[32] Even so, he was anxious not to burn his bridges.

HFO was troubled by the cabinet's conspicuous snub of Highveld's opening in April 1969 – not a single minister turned up at the unveiling of the Witbank plant – and he resolved to proceed with caution. In July he lunched with the general manager of Iscor, Hans Coetzee. The day after their meeting he followed up with a conciliatory letter. 'I am convinced that in the national interest, as well as for normal business reasons,' he wrote, 'Highveld should be ready to reach a friendly understanding with Iscor covering the whole field of their mutual interests, and I would certainly do anything I could to bring this about.'[33] Coetzee was non-committal. In fact, Iscor's management had chosen to meet Highveld's challenge head-on. None other than Professor PW Hoek, author of the shelved Hoek Report, had designed a commercial strategy to protect Iscor's market, maintain the sphere of Afrikaner influence, and frustrate Anglo's ambitions.[34] This led to the creation of an investment company, Metkor, controlled by Iscor, in 1969. Metkor established holdings in various engineering concerns that were significant consumers of steel, such as Wispeco, African Gate, and Tube & Pipe Industries. Since Metkor was managed and directed by representatives from Iscor, they channelled business Iscor's way. If Iscor would not join its enemies, and could not beat them, then it would mimic them instead. HFO was famed for his maxim 'By control I don't mean 51 per cent of the shares'; by accumulating minority stakes in downstream companies, and stacking their boards with friendly directors, Metkor was simply putting his proverb into practice. Iscor was playing Oppenheimer at his own game. During his meeting with HFO, Coetzee indicated that Iscor, through Metkor, might now wish to acquire a stake in Highveld, despite having rebuffed Anglo's overtures a few years previously. Oppenheimer played his cards close to his chest. There would be 'considerable difficulties' in carrying through such a transaction in the current circumstances, he suggested, but 'careful and sympathetic consideration' would be given to any future proposal.[35]

For all his willingness to reach an accord with Iscor, Oppenheimer balked at the prospect of the Afrikaner political monopoly transmogrifying into an economic monopoly. It offended his capitalist sensibilities. Already the state had moved into coal, oil and gas through Sasol. Another parastatal, Foskor, produced phosphates for the agricultural sector. The Industrial Development Corporation drew the government into a wide range of manufacturing activities but tended – in the words of Sanlam's chairman, Andries Wassenaar – to enter into direct competition with the private sector 'instead of assisting it'.[36] Increasingly, the 'commanding heights' of the economy, apart from mining, seemed to be under the state's thumb.[37] HFO aired his misgivings in the AAC chairman's statement of 1969: 'Recently the state-controlled sector of the economy has been growing fast, and directly and indirectly has been moving into areas which used to be reserved for private enterprise. In South Africa it has never been the practice to nationalise privately owned industries, but the agencies of the state are now increasingly stepping in to acquire control of private business by the means of market operations … In these circumstances I believe that Highveld's entry into the basic steel industry will serve a useful subsidiary purpose in preserving South Africa's reputation at home and abroad as a country in which private enterprise is still welcomed and encouraged.'[38] However, while Oppenheimer might have been sincere in championing private enterprise and decrying state encroachment into the economy, he was also a well-practised pragmatist. Before long, Highveld and Iscor reached an accommodation. The catalyst, curiously, was the UK Labour government's decision to nationalise the British steel industry.

The newly formed British Steel Corporation agreed to cede its inherited South African assets but decided to retain a shareholding. All the while, the arms embargo against the apartheid government – initiated by Harold Wilson's administration under United Nations pressure – remained in force. (HFO was openly critical of Britain's refusal to sell arms to South Africa: at an Institute of Bankers dinner, he launched a 'scathing' attack on the Labour government, and correctly predicted – two years in advance – a 'change of wind' rather than a 'wind of change' after the Tories won the next election.)[39] As state spending soared on munitions and police machinery, the local steel and engineering industries assumed a greater measure of strategic importance to the pariah nation's fast-growing arms industry. The Nationalists were determined not to let them slip from their control, especially after the establishment of the Armaments Development and Production Corporation (Armscor) in 1968. A complex series of transactions and mergers involving British Steel ensued, which united Iscor and Anglo American at the negotiating table. The upshot, in 1970, was the creation of International Pipe and Steel Investments South Africa (Ipsa), in which Metkor held a 50 per cent share, British Steel owned 35 per cent, and Anglo claimed 15 per cent.[40] Ipsa soaked up control of South Africa's biggest structural engineering company, Dorman Long. It acquired Stewarts and Lloyds, the largest local manufacturer of tubes and pipes. The formation of Ipsa ensured that South Africa's strategic steel and engineering industries would not fall prey to a foreign government. Tellingly, it also signalled an 'effective truce' between Iscor and Anglo, which prevailed over the steel industry for a decade or more.[41] Oppenheimer described the partnership, with customary delicacy, as 'an interesting example of co-operation between private enterprise and the agencies of the state'.[42]

The dark satanic mills proliferated. In 1972 the Mondi mill in Merebank, Durban, became fully operational. It was opened by the Deputy Prime Minister, BJ Schoeman.[43] Anglo had leant on its equity partner – the British paper giant, Bowater – for technical assistance. The Mondi Paper Company began producing paper to the value of R25 million per year, and most of the company's production replaced imports.[44] When Anglo established Mondi in 1967, the South African paper industry was monopolised by one player, South African Pulp and Paper Industries (Sappi), owned by Union Corporation. Now there was competition. However, since Anglo controlled the Argus Group, Mondi had a captive market for its newsprint. The company produced for export, too, and quickly penetrated markets in South America and the Far East. Mondi acquired a subsidiary, South African Board Mills, which manufactured

HFO and Gordon Waddell (second from left) on a site visit
to Mondi, early 1970s. *(Anglo American)*

paper board for the packaging, printing and stationery industries. This
was a field in which Anglo, through its holding in the Central News
Agency, enjoyed several diverse interests.

Mondi, like several other notable Anglo subsidiaries – Scaw Metals,
Highveld Steel, Boart and Hard Metals, Transalloys, and Forest Industries
and Veneers – was among the group's most important industrial ventures.
The Merebank mill involved a large initial outlay of capital, at R50 million.
In addition to the subsidiaries, a raft of associated companies – effectively
under Anglo's scaffold – engaged in all manner of manufacturing.
Debincor's AE&CI was the sole supplier of a wide range of chemicals
and explosives, and a leading producer of fertilisers, plastics, textiles
and ferro-silicon (an alloy used by Highveld in the production of steel).
In 1966 AE&CI commissioned a large petrochemical plant. This was
followed by a new R77 million ammonia plant and ancillary plant for
the manufacture of nitric acid, ammonium nitrate and urea, targeted for
completion in 1974.[45] AE&CI was an employer of note and the country's
largest industrial concern, with total assets of R204 million in 1969.[46] By

1978 its market capitalisation was almost R500 million, well ahead of its industrial rivals.[47] South Africa's dependence on AE&CI was immense. As the *Financial Mail* noted in 1969, if AE&CI shut down tomorrow, the repercussions to South Africa would be far more serious than those of the recent coal miners' strike to Britain. 'All mining and much of industry would come to a standstill; agricultural output would dwindle miserably. If the shutdown continued for long, we'd be in danger of starvation.'[48]

AE&CI was an industrial behemoth in its own right. But in the 1970s a spate of mergers involving Anglo American, both within manufacturing and between manufacturing and mining, vastly expanded Anglo's industrial kingdom. The most momentous of these was the amalgamation in 1971 of Rand Mines and Thomas Barlow & Sons, the business which Oppenheimer's wartime housemate, Punch Barlow, had inherited from his father. As far back as 1960, Punch had proposed to HFO that Barlows should take ownership of Rand Mines and manage Central Mining. Oppenheimer confided to Charles Engelhard that he found the idea 'startling' and not particularly attractive; however, if Barlows could bring new industrial business to Central Mining, then that aspect of the proposal 'might be very acceptable', he conceded.[49] A decade on, Barlows was the third-biggest industrial concern in South Africa. Its tentacles were attached to heavy earth-moving equipment, steel, timber, building supplies, motor vehicles, electrical appliances and electronic equipment. A tie-up with Rand Mines now seemed rather appealing. Barlows proceeded to acquire Rand Mines for R40 million, at the time the largest such transaction in South African history. The new company, Barlow Rand Limited, was a leviathan, and Anglo, together with its subsidiaries, controlled nearly 25 per cent of Barlow Rand's shares. It proved to be a fruitful deal for Anglo. Between 1972 and 1974 Barlow Rand more than doubled its net profits to R53.9 million, becoming the country's highest industrial profit-earner and second-largest industrial concern, with assets valued at R564 million.[50]

While Barlow Rand raked in the profits, gold enjoyed a revival. Since 1934 the price of gold had been fixed at $35 per fine ounce, and it suited the United States to keep it that way. President Charles de Gaulle, in Oppenheimer's opinion the quintessential Western statesman, took a different view: he believed the gold price was artificially constrained by the hegemony of the dollar. Even after de Gaulle left office, France sought to contrive a large-scale devaluation of the dollar against gold. To achieve this it bought more and more bullion. The US government held the line, but in 1971 President Richard Nixon, faced with persistent deficits in the balance of payments, was compelled to close the gold window. He formally unpegged the US dollar from gold. Foreign governments were no longer able to convert their dollars into gold at the official price. The dollar was devalued by increasing the gold price to $38 an ounce. This was the first step towards jettisoning the Bretton Woods system of fixed exchange rates and abolishing the fixed gold price. The result was a bonanza both for the apartheid regime and for South African mining houses: countries scrambled for gold reserves, the market price ceased to be fixed, and Pretoria quietly restricted gold production to increase its pound of flesh. The gold price soared, and the oil crisis of 1973 pushed it up even further. By the time HFO delivered his chairman's statement in 1974, the price had doubled to $170 an ounce. This was 'an event of utmost significance', Oppenheimer gleefully reported.[51] The value of South Africa's gold output leapt from R1 161 million in 1972 to R2 560 million in 1974, and Anglo's mines alone were responsible for 40 per cent of production. Although the economic boom would peter out after 1974, and GDP per capita would start to decline as Oppenheimer predicted – indeed, growth averaged 3 per cent a year in the 1970s and just 1.5 per cent a year in the 1980s – gold's resurgence strengthened Anglo. It facilitated further mergers and acquisitions involving the corporation's weaker industrial rivals.

In 1973 Oppenheimer reported major investments, through Amic, in iron, steel and alloys, chemicals and explosives, construction, drilling tools, timber, paper and board, and motor vehicles.[52] Moreover, Anglo claimed substantial minority shareholdings in a variety of large, diversified industrial concerns. In 1962, Anglo bought its first shares in the Tongaat Hulett group; the country's largest producer of sugar cane, Tongaat Hulett's other interests included aluminium, building materials, consumer foods, edible oils and agri-processing. By way of a 32 per cent stake in South African Breweries (SAB), Anglo secured a foothold in the food and beverages market. In the early 1970s, SAB embarked on its own diversification drive. In 1974 the largest retail transaction in South African history saw the brewer acquire OK Bazaars, the chain of mass-market stores started by Sam Cohen and Michael Miller in 1927. Forays into fashion followed: SAB acquired Scotts Stores in 1981 and the Edgars chain in 1982. Hotels were another concern. The Southern Sun group, which operated several hotels in South Africa, was formed by the merger in 1969 of existing SAB hotel interests with those of the colourful, headline-hogging hotelier Sol Kerzner. An industrial company of sizeable proportions, SAB thus offered Anglo a smorgasbord of goods beyond barley and hops. Concurrently, the McCarthy Group, in which Amic built up its holdings to 23.3 per cent by 1982, developed into South Africa's premier retail motor organisation. It held the sole franchise for the distribution of Mercedes-Benz, BMW, Citroën, Mazda, Peugeot and Toyota, among others. In 1976 Anglo formed the Sigma Motor Corporation in partnership with Chrysler South Africa. It was able to draw on the 'expertise and model ranges' of leading producers in North and South America, Europe, Australia and Japan, Oppenheimer recorded.[53] After Sigma acquired Pacsa, the company which manufactured Peugeot and Citroën vehicles in South Africa, it became one of the country's biggest motor manufacturers, with assets well in excess of R100 million.

Steeped in mining, Oppenheimer's preference was for Anglo or its subsidiaries to initiate physical business – greenfield or brownfield projects – rather than buy its way into industrial peers. That is why he found the Highveld Steel project such a source of fascination. Graham Boustred had shown his mettle with Scaw and Highveld. His success thrust him to prominence. Boustred became a director of Anglo in 1972; and in 1974 he was made chairman of both Highveld Steel and Vereeniging Refractories. He joined Anglo's executive committee at the same time. Meanwhile, because of the rapidly increasing requirements of the Electricity Supply Commission (Escom) and its growing opportunities in export markets, Oppenheimer forecast that Anglo's coal-related capital expenditure would balloon from R47 million in 1975 to R169 million in 1979.[54] At the end of 1975 AAC's coal interests were amalgamated into the Anglo American Coal Corporation (Amcoal), a globally dominant coal producer. Boustred became the new company's chairman. In this capacity he drove the creation of the Richards Bay Coal Terminal, one of the world's prime coal export terminals. It opened in 1976 with an initial capacity of 12 million tons per annum, rising to 20 million tons in 1979. This made coal an important source of foreign exchange. HFO described the opening as a 'milestone in the history' of South African industry.[55]

On the construction front, Anglo merged four large civil engineering firms in 1965 to form a holding company and group subsidiary, LTA, with assets exceeding R13 million.[56] Between them, LTA and Murray & Roberts carved up the local construction industry. LTA built roads, railways, bridges, tunnels and power stations for the state, and hotels and office blocks for the private sector. It led the consortia that completed the Orange–Fish River Tunnel and the massive Cahora Bassa Dam. Envisaged as the largest hydroelectric scheme in southern Africa, the Cahora Bassa project appealed to HFO's sense of scale. 'It's important to get this development going, not only for Mozambique but for our own country,' HFO told Wim de Villiers, LTA's inaugural chairman.[57] As Mozambique was a Portuguese territory (until 1975), Oppenheimer met with the Portuguese Prime Minister, Marcello Caetano. He offered Caetano's government an initial $10 million loan on favourable terms to help finance its involvement (the credit was not drawn), and clinched the bid in LTA's favour over the American competition.[58] While in Lisbon, Oppenheimer paid a visit to the hospital where the recently displaced premier, António de Oliveira Salazar – incapacitated by a stroke – was receiving medical attention. This diplomatic gesture, captured by press photographers, gained Oppenheimer the goodwill of Caetano's government. It was a typically deft touch.

After construction, Cahora Bassa would supply Mozambique with low-cost power and channel an export surplus to South Africa equal to 10 per cent of the Electricity Supply Commission's contemporary requirements. Although that obviated the need for Escom to build another coal-fired power station, the state-owned entity was not wildly keen on the scheme. Escom executives regarded the importation of energy across national boundaries – especially from a Portuguese outpost riven for several years by guerrilla warfare – as an outlandish notion. It was HF Verwoerd who railroaded cabinet into giving the go-ahead: he was enticed by strategic, rather than economic, considerations.[59] Despite the wider significance of Cahora Bassa, Oppenheimer generally preferred LTA to concentrate on bread-and-butter projects. He complained to Ted Brown that LTA's chairman, Henry Olivier, was too focused on 'great international schemes' and insufficiently seized with the 'less spectacular' building and construction projects out of which LTA made its recurring profits.[60] In fact, HFO proposed to Brown that he should resign his chairmanship of Zamco, the international consortium in charge of the Cahora Bassa development, in favour of Olivier. Brown could then take over the reins at LTA. This was the sort of exercise in corporate musical chairs to which Oppenheimer's tactful disposition inclined him. Instead of getting rid of the balsa wood, he often opted to move around the furniture. 'It seems to me that in this way it might be possible to deal with a very awkward situation in an elegant way without scandal or unduly hurt feelings,' Oppenheimer assured Brown.[61] Where tricky decisions regarding senior deployments were concerned, HFO shied away from conflict. He preferred the sideways manoeuvre to the frontal assault.

Property and Finance

At the same time that Anglo was spinning profits from manufacturing and construction, the corporation broadened its property and financial interests. Anglo had long owned large areas of farming land, acquired – for the most part – in connection with its mining activities. In 1969 the company consolidated its farming interests into Soetvelde Farms. Two subsidiaries, Dawn Orchards and Debshan Ranches, were involved in extensive vegetable and ranching operations. Viniculture was another concern. In the late 1960s, the Anglo powerhouse purchased and restored Boschendal – formerly Rhodes Fruit Farms, or 'Cecil's farm', as Bridget Oppenheimer preferred to call it – and emerged, in time, as a successful producer of wines. In 1987 the restyled Anglo American Farms added the Barlows' estate, Vergelegen, to its portfolio, and Vergelegen's vintages became, like Boschendal (and Boschendal's Le Pavillon) wines, well-established, high-profile brands.

A variety of property schemes took shape. In partnership with Creative Homes of Cape Town, Anglo developed South Africa's first residential marina at Muizenberg. On launching, the estimated capital cost of the Marina Da Gama project was R15 million.[62] Meanwhile, work on the Carlton Centre forged ahead, with input from American architects and structural engineers. However, the much-maligned Anglo octopus failed to wrap its tentacles around the construction site: LTA lost the tender bid to its chief rival, Murray & Roberts. Although HFO was not involved in the executive management of the project, he chaired the Carlton Centre for a period of ten years, initially with South African Breweries' managing director, Ted Sceales, as his deputy. The massive R88 million office, shopping, hotel and exhibition complex drew in SAB and Anglo as equal partners with equity of 45 per cent apiece. Barclays DCO stumped up the other 10 per cent after HFO persuaded the bank's chairman, Arthur Aiken, to come on board. Over time, the Carlton Centre put Anglo's relations with SAB to the test. There were endless obstacles raised by town-planning by-laws, objections from neighbouring property owners, construction complications and project overruns. All of this created tension. In 1969 SAB acquired a 38 per cent stake in Retco Limited, South Africa's largest property development company; and Dick Goss, Sceales's successor, suggested to HFO that Retco should take over SAB's shareholding in the Carlton Centre. This proposal caused Oppenheimer to express 'some reservations' – he wanted SAB as a backstop should Retco struggle with cash reserves – but the transaction went ahead regardless.[63] SAB eventually (and expensively) sold out to Anglo in 1971, deterred by spiralling costs and peeved that its own hotel operator would not be entrusted with managing the Carlton Hotel.

The Carlton Centre was, Oppenheimer proudly stated, the 'largest city development scheme' ever undertaken in South Africa.[64] It transformed the urban landscape of downtown Johannesburg. Doug Hoffe, Anglo's property guru and point man on the project, believed that the Carlton Centre appealed to the 'innermost values of the Oppenheimer business philosophy': it was visionary, it set new standards, and it opened up fresh challenges in construction and property management.[65] The office block was a reinforced concrete skyscraper which towered well over 200 metres above street level and broke several records. Occupation of the building, with Barclays as a prime tenant, commenced in 1971, and the Carlton Hotel was officially opened in 1972. As the Carlton Centre took shape, Anglo's property portfolio burgeoned to such an extent that the group created a new commercial property company, Anglo American Properties Limited (Amaprop). Amaprop brought under one roof South African Townships; Rand Mines Properties, the third-largest township developer in the country; Anmercosa Land and Estates, which owned several Anglo-occupied office blocks; and a host of smaller concerns. It became South Africa's second-largest property company, with net assets valued at R52 million.[66]

Anglo's partnership with Barclays in the Carlton Centre project was just one aspect of the group's multifaceted banking relationships. From the corporation's earliest days it had transacted with the two imperial banks, Barclays and Standard. Representatives from Anglo sat on their boards, and Anglo held a stake in each of them. Indeed, HFO was a long-serving director of Barclays International; a 'shrewd and sensitive' financier, he wielded a powerful influence on the bank's approach to South Africa.[67] After the death of the Iron Tuke, Anthony William Tuke, his son Anthony Favill Tuke perpetuated the line of the Quaker banking dynasty: he chaired Barclays in Britain from 1973 to 1981. On matters pertaining to South African politics and Barclays' local considerations, Tuke took his cue from HFO – a confrère in the global financial patriciate. They interacted closely at a time when Barclays was under fierce attack from anti-apartheid campaigners lobbying for disinvestment. Oppenheimer encouraged him to stay the course. In 1986, after both Oppenheimer and Tuke had formally retired, Barclays decided to pull out of South Africa. Together Anglo and De Beers snapped up 30 per cent of Barclays' local offering while their insurance partner, the Southern Life Association, took 25 per cent. Although this led to a closer identification of Anglo and Barclays in the public imagination, the association had much deeper roots. In the 1970s, under HFO's command, Anglo cultivated multiple banking connections in parallel. Its financial networks began to multiply. In fact, the group came to play an outsize role in the financial services sector.

In 1973 and 1974 Anglo was enmeshed in a series of transactions involving, firstly, the Dutch-owned Nedbank group and, secondly, Barclays, whose South African operations were restructured and spun off as Barclays National Bank. Through this process Anglo yielded up Union Acceptances Limited but gained a stake in the Nedbank group. In 1974 Anglo's plain-Jane stepsister, the Rand Selection Corporation, tied the knot with the Schlesinger Organisation. Built up by the diminutive insurance and entertainment tycoon, IW Schlesinger, one of South Africa's most remarkable industrialists, the organisation was overseen after IW's death in a somewhat desultory fashion by his heir, John. In practice, John Schlesinger gave free rein to his right-hand man and chief executive, the masterly but mercurial Mandy Moross. Moross focused on Schlesinger's property and financial side. When the Schlesinger Organisation wedded Anglo, its substantial dowry included cash-rich insurance businesses under the umbrella of the African Eagle Life Assurance Society, as well as the country's fastest growing hire-purchase bank, Wesbank.[68] The marriage did not prosper. Punctuated by spats, it faltered after only two years, derailed by mismatched expectations. Nevertheless, the union gave Anglo an opportunity to exchange Wesbank for a sizeable stake in Barclays National Bank. This made Anglo the largest local shareholder in Barclays' South African offshoot. By the end of HFO's reign, then, Anglo had carved for itself a position of 'considerable influence' in South African finance.[69]

Anglo's entry into commercial banking had its origins in Union Acceptances Limited (UAL). The affable and avuncular Sidney Spiro, a long-standing Oppenheimer loyalist and Anglo executive committee member since 1963, managed Anglo's merchant bank at its inception;

latterly he chaired it. UAL flourished under Spiro's wing. His business and social talents equipped him well for the role, while the tightening of exchange controls, which locked capital inside the country, was good for business. UAL soon forged a reservoir of talent, and was able to compete on an equal footing with established peers in London. The bank diversified into mutual funds, management consultancy and real estate development. It attracted local competition. By 1961 there were four domestic merchant banks; in spite of that, seven years later Union Acceptances was still the largest of them, with total assets of R142 million.[70] When Spiro left UAL in 1969 to succeed Bill Wilson at Charter Consolidated, the lender's fortunes took a turn for the worse. It was plagued by management difficulties. In some measure these problems were kindled by HFO. He brought in Strilli Oppenheimer's uncle Roger Berry from Twentieth Century Fox's film business, to serve as managing director. Berry had no previous banking experience and was not up to the task.[71] His team of general managers grew restless and resentful. Oppenheimer failed to quell the uprising. Any precipitate action, he explained to Spiro, would be 'quite wrong' from a public relations point of view, and also 'not fair to Roger'.[72] Oppenheimer came under fire. The managing director of Lazard, Mark Norman, pushed and prodded from London. He had little confidence in Berry's ability to establish his authority as an 'accepted leader' among the general managers; and he suggested that Berry be sidelined in favour of someone who would manage the business 'professionally, skilfully and vigorously'.[73]

HFO temporised, an instinctual impulse when tough choices had to be made involving senior managers. He assured Norman that Berry would be able to continue for a few months, 'without anything going drastically wrong'.[74] As it turned out, Berry resigned after less than a year in the role; and his successor, another Oppenheimer appointee, did not last much longer. By the early 1970s Union Acceptances was beset by intractable management challenges. That is probably what encouraged HFO to extricate Anglo from front-line merchant banking.[75] In 1973 UAL merged with Syfrets Trust (effectively controlled by the insurance company Old Mutual, with a 23 per cent shareholding) to form Syfrual. Syfrual merged in turn with the Nedbank group, proprietor of South Africa's fourth-largest commercial bank.[76] The product, Nedsual, was a vast financial conglomerate with R1600 million in assets, which made it the third-largest financial institution in the country, behind Barclays National Bank (R1830 million) and Standard Bank (R1630 million).

Although Anglo's holdings in Nedsual were diluted to 8 per cent, which HFO regarded as a 'pure investment' rather than a 'strategic holding', Anglo gained a seat on Nedbank's board.[77] The merger beefed up Anglo's authority in the banking and financial sector.

From the 1960s, the *toenadering* (rapprochement) between the Oppenheimer empire and the Afrikaner financial establishment (principally Sanlam, through the General Mining–Federale Mynbou deal) helped to defuse ethnic antagonisms in business. Progressively, it took the sting out of the attacks against Oppenheimer in the Afrikaner nationalist press, and it recalibrated white politics. Yet even in the mid-1970s Oppenheimer was dubious about just how far the Anglo-Afrikaner accord should go, or what it might reasonably achieve. HFO's correspondence with Anthony Favill Tuke reflected his misgivings. 'All of us here like the idea of our having an interest in your South African bank,' HFO informed Tuke in 1974, after Barclays had spun off its local operations.[78] But he doubted the wisdom of acquiring such an interest in partnership with Sanlam, as Tuke had suggested. Oppenheimer elaborated: 'We've tried hard (& still do) to work closely with the Afrikaans interests in the mining field but frankly this "partnership" (about which *they* did a great deal of talk when it first began) hasn't worked out in practice. The basic reason is that the Sanlam group in all its ramifications is not only concerned with business in the normal sense, but with capturing a greater proportion of the South African economy for Afrikaans interests politically well-disposed to the Government. Whereas we, if we bought shares in your South African bank, would want for sound business reasons, as well as for historical & sentimental reasons, to emphasise the advantages of its membership of your international group'.[79] In the wake of the state-appointed Franzen Commission, domestic banks were under pressure to reduce the holdings of their foreign owners and become more perceptibly South African. Oppenheimer maintained that Sanlam would interpret this injunction narrowly. Sanlam would seek to 'Afrikanerise' Barclays National Bank and ally it with Volkskas, another central player in the Afrikaner nationalist establishment.[80] In turn, this was likely to produce friction between Anglo and Sanlam, which Oppenheimer was eager to avoid. Whereas, should Anglo acquire a minority holding *without* Sanlam, it would be regarded as 'a natural extension of a long-standing association with no implication of a basic change of control'.[81]

Oppenheimer's mistrust of Sanlam would be magnified in the coming years. It was fuelled by the insurer's rumbling ambitions in the mining sector, which the General Mining–Federale Mynbou deal had failed to quench. In this regard, one of the most dramatic, drawn-out, intricate and impassioned takeover battles in the history of South African mining unfolded between 1974 and 1976: an overcrowded contest for control of the British-owned Union Corporation. At various stages, Barlow Rand, Gold Fields, General Mining and Anglo American were all in the fray. By the end of it Sanlam had vanquished all-comers. General Mining, then very much a strategic concern of Sanlam's via Federale Mynbou, acquired a 51 per cent share in Union Corporation after furious lobbying by Sanlam's Andries Wassenaar. He secured additional financial backing from the Afrikaner powerhouses Volkskas and Rembrandt.[82] The General Mining–Union Corporation tie-up paved the way for the creation of a mining mammoth, Gencor, in 1980. At one stage Anglo American gave its support to General Mining's bid, on condition that Anglo would be compensated with Union Corporation's platinum and paper businesses, Impala and Sappi, respectively. However, that was not a concession General Mining was willing to make, and its managing director, Wim de Villiers, pressed ahead sans Anglo. Oppenheimer believed that in taking over Union Corporation without Anglo, General Mining had broken the letter and spirit of the agreement he brokered with Federale Mynbou in 1964. At the time, it was accepted that should either Anglo or Federale Mynbou ever be faced with the prospect of acquiring a dominant position in any of the other mining groups operating in South Africa, then 'we should discuss the matter with the view to that business being undertaken jointly'.[83] After taking legal advice, Oppenheimer let the matter go.[84] Be that as it may, in June 1974, when HFO was corresponding with Barclays' chairman, Anglo's grievance with Sanlam over Union Corporation had not yet been triggered. In any event, Anglo would obtain a respectable slice of Barclays National Bank unencumbered by the Afrikaner insurance group. But the route to Anglo's shareholding in Barclays traversed a notable detour involving the Schlesinger Organisation.

In March 1974 Anglo American announced a R160 million bid for Schlesinger Insurance and Institutional Holdings, conducted though the medium of the Rand Selection Corporation. Since HFO had come to regard Rand Selection as a 'pale imitation' of Anglo – its role was really to raise funds for group projects without diluting AAC's own equity – he hoped the deal would give Anglo's affiliate a rather 'special and different character'.[85] The financial press was all atwitter. The merger would boost Anglo's assets by R800 million to well over R5000 million, with 'mind-boggling ramifications' in terms of 'sheer economic power', crowed one journalist.[86] Schlesinger's gross assets in Britain, the *Financial Times* noted, were worth R200 million.[87] The transaction was mutually beneficial; for some time John Schlesinger had been looking to reduce his holdings in the family business, and in fact Mandy Moross approached Anglo first.[88] While retaining managerial autonomy, the Schlesinger Organisation stood to benefit from Anglo's prestige and networks in Europe. Anglo would gain a strategic position in life assurance, a portfolio largely outside its ken. Apart from offering a 75 per cent stake in African Eagle Life (whose subsidiaries included two other insurers, Guarantee Life and South African Eagle), Schlesingers came to the banquet table laden with several sumptuous dishes. Anglo sank its teeth into a 69 per cent holding in Wesbank; a 47 per cent interest in Sorec Ltd, the second-largest property company in South Africa; and a 55 per cent holding in Schlesinger European Investments. The merger rallied leftist critics of Oppenheimer's politics. Peter Randall, a parliamentary candidate for the Committee of Social Democrats in the 1974 election, used it as a hook for his campaign. He condemned the coupling as a vivid illustration of 'monopoly capitalism', which gave the lie to the 'Progressive Party myth of equality of opportunity under a capitalist system'.[89] Randall's tiny band of campaigners tried to festoon Anglo's headquarters with protest pamphlets but were stopped by security guards.[90] HFO, who would continue to be demonised as the archetype of 'white monopoly capital' long after his death, was unmoved. 'I think that if we're going to have companies in South Africa which can compete around the world,' he countered, 'we've got to have big concentrations.'[91]

The more rousing remonstration came not from without but from within. John Schlesinger soon expressed his dismay to HFO over Anglo's apparent unwillingness to participate 'in any meaningful way' in Schlesingers' British businesses.[92] He thought Mandy Moross was being mistreated by Anglo's top brass, particularly Gavin Relly. 'Mandy is without doubt the most highly motivated man that I have ever encountered but with that comes a considerable sensitivity and a need to be allowed to get on with the job,' Schlesinger complained.[93] For all his business finesse, Moross had a reputation for truculence. Donald Gordon, the larger-than-life founder of insurance heavyweight Liberty Life, had done a deal with John Schlesinger in the 1960s; as the junior partner in the relationship, he found Moross arrogant and condescending.[94] Oppenheimer readily conceded 'Mandy's ability and determination', but he thought IW's son was labouring under a misapprehension. Going into the merger, Anglo had seen its role as passive shareholders and 'sleeping partners', yet the corporation was being called upon to make substantial sums of money available and to accept large and undefined risks.[95] All the Schlesinger companies were facing difficulties, Oppenheimer observed. Wesbank had to provide for bad debts on 'a quite abnormal scale', and African Eagle was over-committed in property development.[96] The relationship deteriorated. Moross tendered his resignation from the board of Rand Selection Insurance Holdings after bad-mouthing by Anglo executives got back to him.[97] Oppenheimer declined to accept it but struggled to mask his irritation: 'It would be idle to pretend that our ... deal has turned out entirely as we all hoped it would, and some sense of disappointment on everyone's part is natural and unavoidable.'[98] The key thing was to 'work together' and put the Schlesinger Organisation on a sound footing. However, the differences between the two organisations proved irreconcilable. Dissatisfaction gave way to disrelish, and in February 1976, under the headline 'Why Mandy is morose,' *The Economist* declared that Anglo's 'pending divorce' from the Schlesinger Organisation left 'an awful lot of mess to tidy up'.[99] In South Africa, the Schlesinger *res publica* disintegrated. Moross left to form AIM Management Group, which became one of the largest players in the United States mutual fund industry. Sorec Ltd was incorporated into Amaprop. The insurance companies were absorbed into Anglo American Life, which later merged into Southern Life. The most critical development was Anglo's decision to exchange Wesbank for 15 per cent of the issued share capital of Barclays National Bank.[100] By acquiring this stake, Anglo helped Barclays counter the criticism of exclusive foreign ownership. Anglo also set the stage for its later buyout of Barclays. Meanwhile, the group's strong ties to Standard Bank and Nedsual laid the basis for a powerful alliance and served to erect a financial wall seemingly 'impregnable to attack by Afrikaner financial interests'.[101]

◆

Structure, Culture and Succession

By 1976, companies from the Anglo group dominated every sector of the South African economy save for agriculture. The top five mining houses were all Anglo investment companies. In manufacturing Anglo either controlled or had a significant minority share in five of the top ten industrial performers. The group owned two of the top ten property companies. In construction, Anglo's creation, LTA, stood toe to toe with Murray & Roberts for market share. In finance, Anglo had strengthened its ties with Barclays National Bank, Standard Bank and Nedsual; the group had also managed to bring one of the country's top three life assurers, African Eagle, under its wing.[102]

The bewildering speed of Anglo's growth – linked to its diversification into every nook and cranny of the economy – meant the group grew 'like Topsy', in Gavin Relly's words.[103] In so far as Oppenheimer thought too much administration inflated costs and detracted from the spirit of entrepreneurialism, he was not a 'management man'. But by the 1970s he realised that many of Anglo's corporate arrangements had become redundant or outdated. The corporate and financial structure of the group needed to be made fit for purpose. Its approach to human resource management and administration had to be professionalised. Accordingly, as Oppenheimer expanded the Anglo American empire, he presided over a parallel process of corporate consolidation and reorganisation. This was largely actioned by Gavin Relly after his return to Johannesburg from Canada. Anglo's gold, coal and corporate services divisions were restructured in the mid-1970s. In 1977 Anglo merged with the Rand Selection Corporation in a transaction underwritten by De Beers. The contractual participations which Rand Selection enjoyed in new business undertaken by Anglo had turned out to be something of a liability, for Anglo's alter ego lacked the resources to follow through. Although the investments of Anglo and Rand Selection were much the same – and therefore their dividend flow pro rata was similar – Rand Selection did not have Anglo's lucrative management business to generate an income stream. Besides, after the disintegration of its marriage to the Schlesinger Organisation, Rand Selection was left without any special *raison d'être*. The amalgamation of Anglo and Rand Selection nevertheless occasioned a major change in the structure of the group: De Beers became by far the largest shareholder in Anglo.

The other side of the organisational coin was the 'decentralisation of 44 Main Street'.[104] Long-range planning, as far as it occurred, had traditionally been the preserve of Ernest Oppenheimer and his son. It was usually conducted in the sanctuary of Brenthurst, where the tranquillity of the gardens lent themselves to contemplation. Only in the latter years of HFO's chairmanship did senior Anglo executives begin to meet annually at Mbulwa, Charles Engelhard's old property, to consider more formally divisional plans that might have long-term implications for the group's coherence. As chairmen, both Ernest and Harry were intimately involved in the day-to-day process of decision-making for the entire group. However, as Anglo expanded, it became impossible to take every decision at the centre. Consequently, a greater degree of responsibility was devolved to the heads of the operating divisions. They were given the latitude to generate new business, while HFO retained ultimate control of group strategy, investments and policy-making in his person, a role shared and supported by the members of Anglo's executive committee. In 1974 an operating committee (Opco) was appointed with Relly in the chair, flanked by Julian Ogilvie Thompson and Gordon Waddell. It took responsibility for the daily running of the organisation vis-à-vis personnel development, finance, and the management of the operating divisions' (and group companies') performance against their budgets.[105] Opco formulated methods of greater decentralisation of authority to the operating divisions, and worked towards a better integration of their technical and administrative functions.

If Anglo's organisation and group structure underwent something of a revolution during HFO's tenure, then its institutional culture appeared to be fixed in aspic. When the merger with the Schlesinger Organisation occurred in 1974, the *Financial Mail* wondered how Mandy Moross's team of individualistic, young and flexible financiers with their 'go-go image' would adapt to Anglo's 'staid' and 'conventional' style: 'Will oil and water mix in this case?' the magazine asked dubiously.[106] The answer, delivered two years later, was a resounding no, although that had just as much to do with commercial as cultural considerations. Anglo's tone and tenor, as perceived by newcomers and strangers to 44 Main Street, radiated from the chairman's office. Loyalty, tradition and discretion were at the heart of Anglo's executive culture. It was not HFO's practice to have wide and intimate contacts in the organisation; partly because of his instinctive reserve, he preferred to mix among a small band of brothers. Outside Anglo, HFO had long been a member of the Freemasons, the world's oldest fraternal organisation, whose codes and rituals seemed shrouded in secrecy to outsiders. He was initiated into the Richard Giddy Lodge in Kimberley in 1943, and by 1958 had 'advanced to the second and third degrees'.[107] From time to time the coterie of liegemen who enjoyed Oppenheimer's patronage would be invited to take lunch in his elegantly muralled private dining room. Here, at the black-lacquered table, white-gloved stewards would serve ambrosia, the food of the Anglo gods, washed down with a choice of sumptuous wines. It was an experience, some wistful Anglo executives still recall, worthy of any Michelin-star restaurant.

At Brenthurst, black-tie dinners every other night provided Anglo's social fulcrum. These occasions were the corporate glue that bonded Anglo's upper echelons. Bridget Oppenheimer was responsible for putting them together, and she ensured their seamless execution. Many of the corporate wives, especially the younger ones, felt intimidated by the chairman. They had a particular dread of being seated next to him at dinner. Small talk was not HFO's strong suit; he became bored very easily. He would begin fiddling with his cufflinks – a tell-tale sign of his waning interest in the conversation – and then a glazed look would descend over his usually alert brown eyes. Coupled with a rictus grin, this cast of glassiness betrayed his utter boredom. Bridget, for all her grandeur, could be a warm and engaging hostess. She put her visitors at ease and made an art of hospitality. However, the one shortcoming that 'BDO' could not abide was a disregard for punctuality. Guests who failed to arrive at the appointed hour could expect a chilly reception and a blistering aside in one of her personal notebooks. Brenthurst dinners followed a particular rhythm. Visitors would move from the drawing room to the dining room once their champagne glasses had been deplenished. At 8.30 pm sharp the first course was served. The Brenthurst estate boasted a phenomenal wine cellar, curated from terroirs everywhere on earth. After the De Beers director (and HFO's friend) Baron Edmond de Rothschild purchased Château Clarke in 1973, Rothschild's Bordeaux wines featured regularly on Bridget's menus. Château Haut-Brion was another favourite. Dinner having drawn to a close, the women would make an exit, leaving the men to smoke cigars and hash out the issues of the day over a balloon of cognac.

Anglo's tribal customs might have seemed stuffy or antediluvian, even by the standards of the day, but it would be unfair to portray the organisation as sclerotic. Acuity and youthfulness were still highly prized commodities, nowhere more so than in the chairman's office. In January 1970, Adrian Doull, a thoughtful 25-year-old with some experience in Anglo's group financial planning department, was driving with his wife and four-month-old baby from Durban to Cape Town, due to start an MBA, when Gordon Waddell tracked him down at his hotel in Port Elizabeth. Waddell offered him the job as HFO's personal assistant, and Doull quickly abandoned his plans for further study in preference for the position. Oppenheimer took Doull into his confidence 'to a remarkable extent'.[108] PAs were implicitly trusted to preserve the chairman's 'privacy and confidences'. Moreover, HFO solicited his personal assistants' views and ideas, and listened to them attentively. Doull's successor, Nick Diemont (son of HFO's rival for the UCT chancellorship, Judge Marius Diemont), had been at Anglo for roughly six months when he asked Doull if he could hitch a ride with the UCT Chancellor on the Anglo jet: Diemont needed to attend his own LLB graduation ceremony in Cape Town, where Oppenheimer was due to cap him. The chairman happily obliged. Sometime later, Zach de Beer approached Diemont to be HFO's PA. Diemont regarded Oppenheimer's interest in young people partly as a function of his 'almost boyish enthusiasm for new ideas'.[109] Like other PAs, Diemont was given an insight into his principal's more private side. On a trip to England, where they stayed with Raymond Oppenheimer at White Waltham, HFO took Diemont on a tour of Oxford. He showed Diemont around his old rooms at Christ Church, and recalled his student days with fondness and nostalgia.

Oppenheimer's encouragement of young people within Anglo extended beyond his inner circle of PAs. Tony Trahar, an industrious, Wits-educated chartered accountant, joined the financial planning department as a management trainee in 1974, aged 25. His university studies had been sponsored by Anglo, and Sidney Spiro was a family friend. About a year after he first attended a Brenthurst dinner, Trahar decided to reciprocate the invitation. At the time a bachelor living with his widowed mother, he took a slug of his salary and bought two bottles of French champagne and a prime cut of beef.[110] On an icy Johannesburg winter evening, the Oppenheimers arrived on the dot of 8 pm, accompanied by Otto Krause, Patsy Curlewis (one of the few people in the Oppenheimers' circle of intimates whose friendship was uncoloured by deference), and Robin Crawford (a De Beers man) and his wife, Jenny. Unfortunately, Trahar neglected to tell the cook when to put the beef in the oven, and by 8.30 pm Bridget was glancing unnervingly at her watch. A partially cooked piece of beef eventually emerged at 9 pm, by which time the dinner-goers were pretty well oiled. The evening concluded with HFO and a bibulous Patsy Curlewis standing around the fire singing German drinking songs.

Trahar was one of a number of Young Turks, all born in the 1940s or early 1950s, who had the ear of the chairman, and who were drawn into the family's social orbit. They would go on to occupy very senior positions in Anglo. As chief executive and then chairman of Mondi in the 1990s,

Trahar grew the Anglo subsidiary into one of Europe's most successful pulp, paper and packaging groups. In 2000, he succeeded Ogilvie Thompson as the chief executive officer of Anglo American plc, the product of a merger between the Anglo American Corporation and Minorco. When Trahar led the merged entity in London – Anglo moved its primary listing to the British capital in 1999 – his counterpart as managing director of De Beers was Gary Ralfe, a tall, spruce Cambridge graduate whose university studies had likewise been paid for by Anglo. The corporation sent him to the Fens on a scholarship; and although he was not obliged to return the payment in kind, on his homecoming in 1966 Ralfe launched into a career at 44 Main Street. After a stint in Anglo's gold division, where he teamed up with the 'new boy', Nicky Oppenheimer, Ralfe devoted himself from 1974 to the diamond business.[111] The partnership with Nicky continued, and his proximity to the family grew closer. Ralfe's political affiliations were an added distinction: a Progressive Party enthusiast and fluent French-speaker, he had accompanied Helen Suzman and Colin Eglin on a trip to Senegal in 1972 and served as their interpreter.

By far the most politically attuned of the Young Turks was Bobby Godsell, a subtle thinker with strong liberal convictions and a concern for corporate citizenship. He went to Anglo armed with a degree in sociology from the University of Natal and a record of involvement in Durban's Young Progressives. Godsell joined the corporation in 1974 as one of two assistants to Alex Boraine, tasked with advising Anglo's employment practices committee on improving the lot of black workers. Initially he was embarrassed about his association with a 'big capitalist organisation' fabled for its complicity in migrant labour. 'I used to tell people that I worked for Boraine, not Anglo', Godsell grinned many years later.[112] Boraine's other adjutant was the British-born Clem Sunter. A former Wykehamist and Oxford PPE graduate, Sunter had already enjoyed a brief innings at Charter Consolidated as a management trainee, which he followed up with a spell in Lusaka working for Anglo. Unlike Sunter, Godsell was hardly sprung from the Anglo mould; the son of an artisan father and bookkeeper mother, he received his schooling at Grosvenor Boys' High in Durban, a government school in the tough working-class, harbour-side suburb of the Bluff. But he quicky gained HFO's confidence as someone with keen political insights. Godsell had his finger on the pulse of South Africa's tumultuous industrial relations. Sunter, for his part, became well known in the 1980s for the 'high road' and 'low road' scenarios he developed, the two alternative futures of interracial negotiation or confrontation that lay open to South Africa. Oppenheimer tended to look upon these exercises in scenario planning with wry bemusement. After one of Sunter's presentations, HFO turned to him with a quizzical expression on his face – his head tilted to one side – and gently probed, 'All very interesting, but should it be done in office hours?'[113] Godsell became chief executive of Anglo's gold and uranium division in the 1990s, and continued at the helm of its spun-off successor, AngloGold (later AngloGold Ashanti), into the new century. Sunter chaired the same division, and ended his career at Anglo as head of the Chairman's Fund.

Of all the twenty- and thirty-somethings who entered Anglo's portals between 1966 and 1974, a slightly built, quiet, gentle American, Henry 'Hank' Slack, would be drawn nearest to the family. A former history student at Princeton University (he had tutored two of Charles and Jane Engelhard's daughters in the course of a university vacation), Slack first met HFO in 1969, at the Engelhards' home Cragwood. He was all of 19 years old at the time. Spurred by his own interest in South Africa and jollied along by the Engelhard connection, Slack wrote directly to HFO just prior to graduating and asked him for an internship. In 1972 he joined Anglo's investment research department; what started as a short-term placement morphed into a career, and four years later Slack landed the position as HFO's PA. This was a role he performed until his principal's retirement. 'Harry Oppenheimer would encourage young people to encourage other young people,' Slack recalled of this period under HFO's tutelage.[114] Slack, Trahar, Ralfe, Godsell, Sunter and a few other contemporaries – most notably Tony Lea, a financial boffin, and Roger Phillimore, one among HFO's plethora of godsons – together constituted an informal caucus. Keith Acutt jokingly dubbed them 'Revco', the committee of revolutionaries. If they took an idea or scheme to HFO, he would give it careful consideration. The chairman exercised power like a benevolent monarch – his approach was deliberative and consensus-seeking – and the rebels enjoyed access to his court. Phillimore, silver-tongued and amusingly sharp-witted, had been given a leg-up by his godfather. HFO set him up in England after his university studies in South Africa, and arranged a berth for him at Charter Consolidated. 'I started on 1 November 1972 at the princely sum of £90 a month, my first exercise in exploitation,' was his later breezy recollection.[115] Phillimore eventually moved back to Johannesburg via the Luxembourg office of E Oppenheimer and Son, and performed several key roles at

Anglo – including a stretch as secretary to the executive committee. His crowning glory in the group was as Minorco's joint managing director with Tony Lea (during which period Slack chaired Minorco's three-man operating committee), until various corporate ructions led to Phillimore's departure in 1992.

The Young Turks would only assume high-ranking leadership positions in the late 1980s and 1990s, after HFO's retirement. Nevertheless, at 44 Main Street there was a slow but perceptible changing of the guard. Ted Brown and Doug Beckingham retired from the Anglo board in 1974. John Shilling, who took over the coal division from Tom Coulter in 1963 and ran it until 1969, resigned from the board in 1975. After RB Hagart's death, Bill Wilson had been appointed deputy chairman alongside Keith Acutt in 1970; but at the end of 1975, with his autumn years approaching, he relinquished the role, though he retained his directorship. Zach de Beer, Guy Nicholson and Peter Gush, Anglo's thirty-something finance director, all joined the board in 1974, at the same time as Nicky Oppenheimer. Nicky was not yet 30 years of age, and even though the expectation was that he would follow in his father's footsteps as chairman one day, thus guaranteeing the family's continuity, that eventuality seemed far off. In the interim HFO was starting to feel his age. The first time he perceived the onset of senectitude was on a late summer day in March 1977. Sitting on his terrace at Mauritzfontein, then aged 68, Oppenheimer surveyed with pleasure the oasis of green which he and Joane Pim had sculpted out of the dusty Kimberley wilderness. 'I realised that I could never again in my lifetime build such a garden.'[116] In the wake of this melancholy but not altogether disagreeable reflection, HFO began to envision and plan for his retirement. Gavin Relly joined Acutt as Anglo's deputy chairman on 26 May 1977, and he replaced HFO as chair of the executive committee on 2 November 1978.

Relly was in many ways Oppenheimer's anointed successor. He was the right age and projected the requisite gravitas. An eloquent, widely liked, straight-shooting veteran of the organisation, he had served in various locales – including Zambia, which was a good testing ground of character, in HFO's view. Relly had an excellent grasp of the greater group, and although he could not match the broad sweep of Oppenheimer's intellectual curiosity, he was erudite and had a keen appreciation of South Africa's peculiar political dynamics. A gregarious man, Relly related well to people and was remarkably comfortable in his own skin. He was a natural leader and a trusted confidant, valued by his mentor for his qualities of integrity and loyalty. That is not to say Oppenheimer was oblivious to the chinks in Relly's armour. Charles Engelhard had once likened Relly's boardroom negotiation tactics to those of a fisherman trying to catch a fish by beating it repeatedly on the head with a fly, and HFO had chuckled mirthfully at the comparison. Perhaps the more intriguing question was who would ultimately step into Relly's shoes. The obvious candidates, as matters stood in 1978, were Waddell and Ogilvie Thompson. Despite his surname, Nicky was still an unknown quantity. He was self-contained and self-effacing, kindly and decent; but in an environment of cut-throat competition, which rumbled beneath several polished layers of clubbable collegiality, some of Nicky's co-workers muttered that his activities remained a mystery. With all the corporate intrigue at 44 Main Street, Anglo sometimes resembled a Florentine palace during the rule of the Medicis; the *principe ereditario* was always susceptible to attack. In fact, Nicky was quietly mastering the diamond business and grappling with the intricacies of E Oppenheimer and Son.

In Waddell's case, any claims to the throne that he might have staked by virtue of his marriage to Mary should, in theory, have been upended by the couple's acrimonious divorce in 1971. Mary had liberated herself from the gilded cage of Brenthurst by wedding Waddell at the age of 21, but her marriage to someone who (for all his charisma) turned out to be temperamentally incompatible imposed confines of its own. Talk of their separation trickled into newsprint in March 1971, and soon there was a torrent of reportage. As Mary and Gordon grew estranged, Mary spent increasing amounts of time with her riding instructor. 'Will Mary marry Bill Johnson?' the *Sunday Express* speculated in gossipy fashion, as Johnson's wife unburdened herself to the press over her own imminent divorce.[117] Johnson denied the rumours cavalierly: 'I'm paid to ride Oppenheimer horses, that's all I do.'[118] Bridget regarded Bill Johnson as an upstart and a calculating paramour; she was furious that her daughter's dirty linen was being aired in public. Sharply critical of her offspring at the best of times, Bridget made her displeasure abundantly clear to Mary. HFO's disapproval was communicated in a more restrained fashion. He instructed Doull to write to Johnson: 'Mr Oppenheimer would not think it right, in present circumstances, that a horse registered in his name should be entered or ridden by you in shows.'[119]

After a brief reconciliation in Rome in May, the marriage broke down irretrievably. In August, photos appeared in the press of Mary leaving the marital home with some of her belongings, as she decamped, sans daughters, to stay with her friends Robin and Liz Wilson. Gordon filed for divorce on the grounds of desertion, and Mary subsequently sought refuge from the media storm in London. Both the rupture itself – the shattering of a public facade – and the intrusive interest of the press pack weighed heavily on the family. HFO and Bridget put pressure on Mary not to oppose the matter in court, in order to avoid further bad press. Even so, the court proceedings proved discomforting. The judge awarded Gordon sole custody of Victoria and Rebecca, a most unusual and unexpected order. It was a huge blow to Mary, and profoundly unsettling for the girls.

At the time, Mary's parents blamed her for the collapse of the marriage. In their view, it was a violation of public presentability, a source not only of sorrow but shame. Effectively, they sided with Gordon. When Mary and Nicky were growing up, HFO had not always been the most attentive father: he was often absent, and with hindsight he felt a measure of contrition about his paternal shortcomings. However, his and Bridget's failure to support Mary in the divorce from Gordon was to become HFO's greatest regret. Meanwhile, long after the dissolution of her daughter's marriage, Bridget's regard for Waddell ('Waddsy', as she affectionately called her former son-in-law) remained pointedly undimmed.

Mary's relationship with Johnson did not carry her parents' blessing. Bridget thought that Johnson would never fit in with the family, and she seldom missed an opportunity to intimate as much. When the lovers tied the knot in a low-key ceremony performed by the district commissioner of Manzini in Swaziland on 23 December 1972, not a single member of the Oppenheimer family attended. Mary Johnson settled into her new, more carefree existence – snippets of which featured in a regular column she penned for the *Rand Daily Mail* between 1973 and 1976 – but for all his bluff charm Johnson had his limitations, and the couple split up in 1977. Another divorce unfolded in the unforgiving public glare.

Eventually, Mary's fortunes changed. By the end of the decade she had settled down with a partner deemed altogether more suitable by her parents, one who (like Waddell before him) had earned their affections. On 16 February 1979, the Episcopalian Bishop of New Jersey, Mellick Belshaw (Hank Slack's cousin), presided over Mary's wedding to Slack at a small chapel in Bernardsville, NJ, in a ceremony attended by HFO, Bridget and Nicky. The reception afterwards was held at Cragwood, Jane Engelhard's residence. In 1980 Mary gave birth to a third daughter, Jessica Bridget; Jessica's sister, Rachel Elisabeth, followed three years later. Soon after they were married, Hank and Mary successfully sought joint custody

Hank Slack and Mary at Cragwood on their wedding day, with
Bridget Oppenheimer and HFO, 16 February 1979. *(Brenthurst Library)*

of Victoria and Rebecca (in the face of initial pushback from Gordon),
and the two eldest girls gradually began to spend more time under their
mother's roof than their father's.

When the union with Gordon unravelled, unnamed newspaper
sources sympathetic to Mary pinned the break-up on Waddell's 'dedication to his work at Anglo'.[120] Some of his colleagues might have hoped
that Waddell's career prospects would be diminished by the divorce, but
those aspirations evaporated quickly. Waddell held on to his ambitions
for upward advancement, and HFO held on to his fondness for his former
son-in-law. He was, after all, the custodian of Oppenheimer's two eldest
granddaughters. Waddell entrenched himself in the Anglo establishment.
He joined the Progressive Party in 1971 after taking out South African
citizenship, and he won the Johannesburg North seat for the party in
the 1974 election. Waddell successfully combined a political calling with
his executive responsibilities at Anglo and JCI. In 1979 Relly wrote to
Oppenheimer that it was 'probably time that Gordon was seen as the
heir apparent' at JCI; two years later Waddell succeeded Albert Robinson
as chairman of the mining house.[121] Such a prestigious position was a
perfect stepping stone, many thought, to the highest office at Anglo.

By the end of the 1970s, Zach de Beer was another prominent figure stalking Anglo's corridors. After a spell as HFO's viceroy in Zambia, he returned to head office as the chief of manpower resources. But HFO believed the former parliamentarian could make his most valuable contribution in politics rather than in business. As it happened De Beer was returned to Parliament by the Progs in 1977, as the MP for Parktown, while he was still in Anglo's employ. Relly deprecated this 'half-in-half-out' arrangement as 'not particularly satisfactory for any of us'. He felt De Beer should stick to politics, at least until the 'convulsions' in the National Party had played themselves out.[122] In the event, De Beer resigned his seat in 1980 to devote himself to Anglo. He took up the chairmanship of Anglo American Life. Yet Oppenheimer never regarded De Beer, who was capable but languorous, as a serious contender for the top job at 44 Main Street. A much likelier prospect was Ogilvie Thompson, who served on the operating committee, and whose estimable intellect and flair for finance HFO held in high regard. 'I think perhaps the cleverest executive we have ever had in the group,' Oppenheimer observed of JOT in his memoir.[123] Ogilvie Thompson's strength lay in his absolute mastery of the group's affairs, his icy decision-making abilities, and his prodigious work ethic. He did not quite possess Relly's rounded political outlook: indeed, JOT had a reputation for expressing mildly reactionary views around the boardroom table on occasion, partly for his own entertainment. Nor was he famed for his genial people skills. Slow-wittedness irked him, and he was a master of the put-down. 'The scourge of secretaries who dare to show up in pantsuits' was how one financial publication characterised JOT, a stickler for propriety.[124] But nobody questioned Ogilvie Thompson's brilliance or his dedication to the group. On one occasion many years later, Oppenheimer was spending part of his summer holiday at his private game farm, Ntoma, in the Eastern Transvaal, when his PA at the time, Clifford Elphick, sensing his boss's growing boredom, suggested they go and visit JOT on his nearby farm in the Klaserie Reserve. There, in the scorching midday heat, they found Ogilvie Thompson seated at a steel table in a reservoir, knee-deep in the water. He was sporting a pith helmet with a solar panel attached to it. This ingenious contraption powered a fan which blew a breeze onto JOT's forehead, cooling him as he worked furiously through multiple piles of Anglo and De Beers papers.

E Oppenheimer and Son held shares in various diamond trading companies and played a connective role in the selling side of the diamond business. This is where Ogilvie Thompson learnt his métier and mastered the group's corporate and financial structures. Twenty years on, his salary

Tony Trahar and Anthony Oppenheimer. *(Brenthurst Library)*

was still being paid by the family firm. It was an association which stood him in good stead. When HFO was beginning to contemplate retirement, he wrote confidentially to Philip Oppenheimer, then president of the Central Selling Organisation, and elaborated on JOT's virtues. Of the senior men in Anglo and De Beers who had become shareholders in E Oppenheimer and Son, HFO told his cousin, 'it is only Julian who has the temperament, intelligence & imagination to be, or look on himself, as our partner in the full sense'.[125] Relly was 'a first rate man'; but even though he was 'pleased & grateful' to be a partner in the family concern, no matter how many shares he held in E Oppenheimer and Son, he would never be able 'to feel "in his bones" what a private firm like ours is really about'. Relly would 'never be an entrepreneur', in Oppenheimer's judgement.

The reason for HFO's lengthy exposition was that he had been brooding over the future of both Nicky and Philip's son, Anthony, in the group. The two scions differed from their fathers in certain respects, in leadership style and aptitudes. Their immersion in the business had taken place in a very different context from HFO's apprenticeship to Ernest or Philip's initiation by his father, Otto. At the time, Anthony Oppenheimer was making his way up the ladder in the diamond industry; like Nicky, he was surrounded by company officials who appraised him, not as a dynastic successor with divine rights of kingship, but merely as a colleague with whom they competed for promotion. Increasingly, as powers of decision-making came to be dispersed to professional managers in Anglo's operating divisions, HFO worried about the family's ability to keep a meaningful measure of control over the greater group. It was only through a 'properly organised family firm' that they could hope to succeed, he emphasised to Philip. At the height of the gold frenzy in 1980, when the price of gold surged to a record $850 an ounce, E Oppenheimer and Son had attained a market value in the region of $450 million. That was certainly not without its effect, HFO noted, but by itself it was not enough to bulletproof the family's interests in the group. He explained further:

> You & I still have great prestige handed down from our fathers; but this dates from earlier times when the Group was smaller & simpler and it was possible to be well informed about all its ramifications and when necessary to exercise a decisive influence on all issues of real importance. The situation into which Anthony & Nicky are entering is very different, much larger and very much more complicated. This size and complication, together with the business fashion of the present time, has resulted in ever tightening control by professional managers – with virtually no financial interest in the business – and this makes it more & more difficult for those managers who are supposed to be responsible for central group policy to exercise an effective measure of control over the managers who bear direct responsibility for the major divisions on the periphery. Indeed we have reached a point where you in London & I in South Africa, together with Julian in the next generation, are just about all that stands in the way of this process being completed, with all its risks not only to the position of our family firm but to the coherence of the Group as such. Anglo American has no 'outside' directors (unless you, I and Nicky should be classed as 'outside' directors, since it is only the three of us who are not, directly or indirectly, employees of the company) and while in De Beers there are outside directors (Edmond & Evelyn [de Rothschild]) … they can hardly be said to be very effective.

HFO believed that if the family was to maintain a degree of significant control, then it had to draw a clear distinction between the functions of family members, together with trusted associates (like JOT) who qualified as partners in E Oppenheimer and Son, and those 'of employees of Anglo/De Beers/the CSO'. 'We must not think that this cannot be achieved unless Anthony & Nicky are leading officials as well as key directors in the major companies of the group.' It would be possible for the family to keep effective control over major policy decisions (and the choice of senior administrators), HFO reasoned, so long as it did not try to control day-to-day administration.

In short, Oppenheimer was convinced that for Anthony, just as for Nicky, the right thing was to withdraw from line management and exercise his influence as a director of various group companies instead. 'I do not think that when we go, either Anthony or Nicky should necessarily aim at becoming Chief Executive in their respective fields. They could however, *if we take the necessary steps* ... be in a position ... to exercise, as directors of the major companies of the Group, an important influence when it comes to policy decisions.' Philip might counter, HFO foresaw, that this would leave Anthony with too little work and too much time on his hands. But that was not necessarily a bad thing. It was important to have time to think; and as HFO looked back on his own life, he believed that 'had I reserved more time for my books, my pictures, my horses and my family, I would have enjoyed myself more & have no less money'. What motivated him was being in the rare if not unique position of being able to control the policy of a group of the size and diversity of Anglo and De Beers through a private family firm, with all that it implied for his sphere of influence beyond business in the 'usual, narrow interpretation of the word'. The 'necessary steps' to which HFO referred included expanding the size of Anglo's board and finding 'suitable men' as 'outside directors': allies who would reinforce the family's influence and help resist the centrifugal forces that were becoming powerful within the group. 'This is urgent and we cannot afford to wait for existing directors to die off in order to make room for new appointments,' HFO told Philip. 'After all in the normal course of nature we are likely to be among the first to die off!'

Once his pen had gleaned his teeming brain, HFO proceeded purposefully. He wrote to Anthony and tactfully suggested that his nephew should give up his line-management responsibilities.[126] Having arranged that, Oppenheimer approached his old liegeman, Pierre Crokaert, to resign his seat on the De Beers board. Crokaert's exit would make way for Anthony, and HFO knew that he could rely on Crokaert's lifelong friendship for 'an understanding reaction to this difficult request'.[127] Oppenheimer then proposed to increase Anglo's board to a maximum of thirty directors, of whom at least five would be 'outside

HFO bids farewell to the staff at 44 Main Street on his retirement as
chairman of Anglo American, 1982. *(Anglo American)*

directors', 'men or women of wisdom and ability' with expertise outside
mining, he announced in his annual chairman's statement.[128] In 1981
Rupert Hambro joined the board; an executive director of Anglo's long-
time British banking associates, Hambros Bank, Jocelyn Hambro's son
was a dependable Oppenheimer ally. The appropriate arrangements were
made to take care of the partners at E Oppenheimer and Son. Nicky
would continue to be a presence at 44 Main Street, where his managerial
responsibilities remained suitably amorphous. By June 1982, HFO felt
confident that he had put in place the necessary measures to facilitate his
retirement. On 1 June he announced his decision to step down from both
the chairmanship and the board of the Anglo American Corporation,
effective from 31 December. After 48 years as a director and 25 years as
chairman, it was a 'matter of sadness … not, however, a matter of regret',
he said in a statement widely carried in the international press.[129] On the
steps outside 44 Main Street, HFO delivered his farewell address in front
of over three thousand staff members, from high-flying executives to
lowly messengers. The government even gave Anglo a dispensation from
the Riotous Assemblies Act for the sovereign's last hurrah.

Hank Slack occupied the board seat left vacant by HFO. Gavin
Relly assumed the chairmanship on 1 January 1983. He was 'a man of

Nicky Oppenheimer, Sir Albert ('Robbie') Robinson, and Evelyn de Rothschild. (*Brenthurst Library*)

exceptional ability, experience and understanding, and a very old friend', Oppenheimer assured the shareholders.[130] Keith Acutt bowed out of the deputy chairmanship (though not the board) simultaneously. Ogilvie Thompson and Nicky Oppenheimer filled the vacuum as joint deputy chairmen. In this way, the path was cleared for the Oppenheimers' continued dominance of Anglo American. Not that Nicky took the line of succession at Anglo for granted: 'These days it's not enough to have the Oppenheimer name,' he volunteered in a rare interview. 'If you can't run with the ball, you're going to be dropped from the team.'[131] But by a curious twist of fate – in fact, he had rather insisted on it – Nicky, not Anthony, ended up succeeding Philip Oppenheimer as chairman of the CSO in 1985. He was appointed deputy chairman of De Beers at the same time.

HFO remained a venerable presence in the background. Right to the end of his life, the *éminence grise* would spend the better part of the day in the office. A consummate wielder of soft power, HFO exerted his authority like a constitutional monarch. When the maverick journalist Denis Beckett first met Oppenheimer towards the end of his chairmanship of Anglo, that was the term bandied about. Beckett was invited to dinner at Otto Krause's flat with Harry and Bridget and another newsman, Ton

Vosloo, editor of the Afrikaans daily *Beeld*. After the Oppenheimers had left, Vosloo joked, 'Now that the constitutional monarch has gone we can take off our jackets.'[132] It was a fitting descriptor. At Anglo, even if he was no longer running the show, HFO's successors would take no decision of consequence without consulting him first. Just as Harry Oppenheimer had inherited the deeds to a formidable corporate edifice, he in turn bequeathed a house of many mansions. He built on to the Anglo powerhouse several flourishing chambers, covering the gamut of economic activity. But that was only one aspect of the group's frontage; for during HFO's tenure, Anglo American vastly expanded its sphere of operations to become a multinational combine, a major investor in mining, energy and commodities companies around the world. This was part of a long-term strategy of internationalisation developed for both economic and political reasons. By 1982, Anglo's empire extended to all four corners of the earth.

ELEVEN

Corners of the Realm: De Beers, Charter and Minorco

Anglo's Overseas Territories

During Ernest Oppenheimer's chairmanship, the greater group's interests outside South Africa were concentrated in Southern Rhodesia, among the diamond fields of South West Africa and Angola, and along the Central African Copperbelt between Northern Rhodesia and the Congo. De Beers monopolised the global diamond trade through the Central Selling Organisation (CSO), and for that reason the name 'Oppenheimer' – like the diamond empire with which it was synonymous – had an international footprint. However, in spite of the Anglo American Corporation's appellation and original financial backing, Anglo was essentially a sub-Saharan enterprise, styled in the tradition of Cecil John Rhodes's British South Africa Company, and anchored in the vision and values of the British Commonwealth. HFO dismissed as 'quite wrong' the notion that his father was an international mining financier: 'There was nothing international in his thought or outlook, and he saw his financial success as a by-product of his part in building up South Africa ... [as] a member of the Commonwealth.'[1] HFO shared his father's philosophical and sentimental attachment to the Commonwealth, and he conceived of the corporation's broader developmental mission in the same way. But his commercial perspective and individual sensibility were far more cosmopolitan than those of Anglo's founder. South Africa's withdrawal from the Commonwealth, coupled with the risk profile of Africa's newly independent states, changed the nature of the beast. Anglo's conception of itself and its backyard were altered. The 'wind of change', the corporation understood, meant that it would have to cast its investment net more widely. While Harry Oppenheimer regarded himself as a man of Africa, he was a creature of the metropolitan Anglosphere too. To begin with, he intended to establish a commercial empire with bridgeheads in London, New York, Toronto and Melbourne.

The Square Mile was one of HFO's natural habitats, as it had been for his diamond-dealing forebears. Even before Oppenheimer assumed the chairmanship of Anglo in 1957, he had chosen for his London residence a flat in stately Belgravia, not far from where the former British Prime Ministers Stanley Baldwin and Neville Chamberlain once lived. No. 80 Eaton Square, a Grade II-listed building in an area noted for its classical Georgian architecture, was situated on a prime stretch of real estate overlooking a rectangular expanse of colourful, tree-lined gardens. Today, the blue plaque attached to one of its exterior stucco walls reveals that George Peabody, international financier and philanthropist, died there. Furnished by Lenygon & Morant under Bridget Oppenheimer's supervision, the apartment radiated grandeur. It was where HFO entertained heads of state, among them Britain's Prime Minister in the 1980s, Margaret Thatcher. The flat also provided a domestic refuge and soothing sense of routine: every day, as he was chauffeured into work, HFO would try to complete *The Times* crossword before he reached the office. Ever since Oppenheimer started sorting diamonds in 1931, London had been a vital hub of his commercial universe. After his collaboration with Charles Engelhard on the Central Mining–Rand Mines takeover in 1958, North America began to exercise a comparable gravitational pull. New York was the dazzling drawcard in that particular galaxy, despite the fact that Hudson Bay – Anglo's earliest transatlantic concern – was located in Canada. That is what prompted Anglo to open an office in Manhattan in 1963. Oppenheimer would often use the Engelhards' apartment in the Waldorf Towers as a base, until HFO purchased his own apartment in the Carlyle Hotel, a bastion of Upper East Side sophistication. It had been dubbed the 'New York White House' during President John F Kennedy's administration. 'The apt [apartment] is *very* nice & exactly what we want,' Bridget Oppenheimer wrote after spending her first night there.[2]

The opportunities afforded by Australia's many different ores, gems and minerals were equally enticing to HFO. After Anglo opened an office in Melbourne in 1965, Charter Consolidated spearheaded the group's worldwide investments in mining, from Malaysia through Mauritania to Mexico. The tightening of exchange controls in South Africa made an affiliate organisation, based in London, a more viable all-terrain vehicle than the Anglo American Corporation. By the mid-1970s, the group had gained a foothold in South America. At that point, the Mineral and Resources Corporation (Minorco) was earmarked for a higher-profile placement on Anglo's international rostrum. In 1976 Anglo American was involved in over 250 companies with mining concerns in 22 different countries: its portfolio ranged across 48 gold mines (some of which produced uranium), 31 prospecting companies, 29 diamond companies, 28 coal mines, 22 copper and nickel mines, 10 oil ventures, 7 platinum mines, 5 tin mines, 5 iron mines, 2 chrome mines, 2 lead mines, 2 vanadium mines, and one mine each in asbestos, potash, soda, lime, tungsten, manganese and silver.[3] The group's interests were dotted around the length and breadth of the globe, in pockets and on plains where English was not the lingua franca. Anglo American, it might be justifiably said, had become an empire on which the sun never set.

Oppenheimer's range and reach were extraordinary. In 1976 he met with the Shah of Iran, Mohammad Reza Pahlavi, and the Iranian Prime Minister, Amir-Abbas Hoveyda. According to a confidential memorandum penned by Oppenheimer, they discussed potential joint prospecting operations and the possible development, by Anglo, of a copper mine on behalf of the Iranian government.[4] The Iranian Revolution put an end to that. Although the South African government gave its blessing to the meeting – indeed, Charles 'Pop' Fraser, South Africa's Consul General in Teheran, facilitated it, and the two nations enjoyed close trading ties – it was really the parochial shackles of apartheid South Africa that opened up HFO's international vista. As South Africa's horizons shrank, Anglo American's purview broadened. This enabled the company to play a commanding role on the world stage. At times Anglo appeared to be a state actor in its own right. The group's international ambitions were spurred (and partly financed) by the huge revenues generated by the Orange Free State goldfields, the Zambian Copperbelt and De Beers' diamond empire. By the end of Harry Oppenheimer's reign, Anglo had emerged as the world's pre-eminent mining group. It became, through Minorco, the single largest foreign investor in the United States. These were feats scarcely imaginable in Ernest Oppenheimer's day.

The Diamond Empire

The diamond trade had always been the most internationally oriented aspect of the group's business, and the most familiar and fascinating facet for Oppenheimer personally. It was the most profitable part too. In 1969, ahead of the introduction of the freely floating gold price, De Beers' net consolidated profit came in at R112.3 million, three times higher than that of the Anglo American Corporation, at R36.5 million.[5] Even after the gold price was unfixed, diamonds led the pack in terms of profits. The structure of the gold industry prior to the so-called Nixon shock of 1971 meant that gold was produced for sale to the South African Reserve Bank at a fixed price. Coal was sold through the various coal owners' associations or directly to Escom. Anglo had no need to trade in these two commodities. The diamond business, in contrast, revolved around purchasing, selling and marketing in a diversity of locales, and all the personal relationships – with producers, dealers, cutters, polishers, jewellers and advertisers – that went along with it. The precious stones took Oppenheimer regularly to diamondiferous districts all over Africa, and to sorting or cutting centres in London, New York, Amsterdam and Antwerp. In 1968 he visited Tel Aviv, an important cutting and polishing hub, for the first time. The promotional campaign around diamonds, kickstarted by HFO and NW Ayer in 1938, required that Oppenheimer should have at least a passing acquaintance with what was happening at the retail end of the trade, and with consumer preferences and design trends internationally. As De Beers' advertisers targeted new markets in the 1960s, Japan became the second-largest consumer of diamond engagement rings after the United States. HFO undertook his first trip to the country in 1968, accompanied by Albert Robinson. (Bridget insisted that they all wear kimonos on their first night, to HFO's embarrassment and everyone's amusement.) At that point only five per cent of betrothed Japanese women received a diamond engagement ring. By 1981, after an intensive advertising campaign by the J Walter Thompson agency, some sixty per cent of Japanese brides wore diamonds.

Scientific research was another frontier of knowledge. In the early 1950s De Beers enjoyed a worldwide monopoly over natural diamonds, both gemstones and industrials. It controlled every known pipe mine in the world – all located in southern and Central Africa – and had put in place arrangements, either directly or indirectly, with the governments of Angola, the Congo, Sierra Leone and Tanganyika to purchase rough diamonds found by independent diggers and fortune hunters. The Central Selling Organisation, De Beers' London-based affiliate, restricted the supply of uncut diamonds through a single channel of distribution and mopped up the surplus into a stockpile. This astounding degree of market (and price) control conferred upon De Beers the status of a cartel; the shorthand for its extensive sphere of operations and many incarnations was the 'diamond empire'. But in December 1954, the American conglomerate General Electric threw a spanner in the works. In a cloak-and-dagger operation, it devised a process for synthesising diamonds in a laboratory. This imperilled De Beers' market dominance. Although the artificial diamonds were expensive to manufacture, and initially only really amounted to a form of abrasive grit, they were still suitable for industrial purposes like grinding and shaping tools. Outwardly De Beers executives responded calmly, but inwardly they wondered fretfully whether the market might soon be flooded with man-made, industrial-grade diamonds. And what if, one day, synthetic gemstones could be mass-produced? The diamond cartel would fracture and shatter. Even HFO struggled to retain his air of imperturbability. He gave the order for scientists at De Beers' diamond research laboratory to crack the code and replicate the GE process post-haste.

In 1958 a team of De Beers scientists succeeded in their task. Oppenheimer was delighted. Henry Dyer, who headed the so-called Adamant research group, and his squad of fitters, turners, lab assistants and technologists were invited to Brenthurst to celebrate their eureka moment at a cocktail party. It was 'an unprecedented and terrifying experience', Dyer recollected, but the team's wives were happy: they were presented with diamond brooches.[6] After this success, a protracted dispute with General Electric ensued over patents. De Beers eventually agreed to pay $8 million plus royalties for the right to manufacture diamonds under the process invented by General Electric. De Beers also entered into a series of cross-licensing agreements with the American behemoth, which made it difficult for other companies to compete in the production of synthetic diamonds. De Beers was now in a position to face down prospective challengers. HFO authorised the establishment of a synthetic diamond plant at Springs. He bought a factory from the Swedish electrical company ASEA replete with patents, technology, and a hydraulic press capable of synthesising diamonds. And in 1963 De Beers took advantage of favourable terms offered by the Irish government to open a factory in the town of Shannon. It had the capacity to produce

HFO inspects synthetic grit at the opening of the diamond factory
in Shannon, 1963. *(Brenthurst Library)*

750 000 carats of synthetic diamonds annually worth around £750 000,
and HFO attended its unveiling.[7]

By 1970, more than half the diamonds produced worldwide were
synthetic. However, unlike prices for gem diamonds, which rose
consistently until 1980, the cost of industrial diamonds fell sharply. In
May 1970 General Electric announced that it had managed to synthesise
gem-grade diamonds weighing over one carat. Once again, Oppenheimer
took a sharp breath. But the opportunity cost of production was too high,
and General Electric realised that even if more cost-effective methods
were found, the market for diamonds might collapse. After all, the appeal
of gem diamonds (and the profits that flowed from their sale) depended
on the contrived rarity and romanticism of the stones. The more gem
diamonds there were in circulation, the cheaper they would become.
Mass production in a factory might rob them of their carefully cultivated
allure, and the diamond illusion would be smashed. Rather than risk being
'destroyed by the success of our own invention', as one General Electric
executive encapsulated matters, the corporation promptly abandoned
its plans to invest hundreds of millions of dollars in hydraulic presses to
synthesise gem diamonds.[8]

In so far as De Beers' vice-like grip on the diamond industry was monopolistic, HFO regarded it as a monopoly of public benefit. Price fluctuations, which were normal in the case of other raw materials, would be 'destructive of public confidence' in the case of pure luxury items like gem diamonds.[9] Well-heeled customers expected their diamond jewellery to retain its value. The monopoly, Oppenheimer claimed, was also beneficial to producers, a line echoed by liberal economists. They argued that the Central Selling Organisation's practice of selling uncut diamonds in parcels at sights – the parcels consisted of a number of stones of different types and values from various producers – served to smooth the price of individual diamonds and, therefore, the income streams of different producers.[10] The benefits of price smoothing were passed on to diamond producers: losses incurred by the undervaluation of individual stones were invariably offset by the overvaluation of others. In the long run, the price of diamonds could not be kept artificially high through restrictions on production. Supply was the critical lever. As far as the stockpile was concerned, Oppenheimer believed the CSO simply ran a buffer pool; he doubted whether this was an 'immoral device' or even really monopolistic.[11] If super-profits of an unreasonable nature arose, he maintained that the government could always tax them; but it would not be justified, in HFO's view, for the state to force through lower prices by diktat.

By the time Ernest Oppenheimer died, he had managed to funnel almost all the world's rough diamonds through a carefully engineered system: he had turned the 'diamond invention' into a powerful instrument for preserving the price of diamonds.[12] HFO was concerned to keep it that way, in homage to his father's legacy. Of course, the system was not infallible. Smugglers and illicit buyers could evade it. That is why Ernest recruited the former chief of MI5, Percy Sillitoe (possibly via HFO's old Oxford tutor John Masterman), to set up the International Diamond Security Organisation in 1954. In due course, Sillitoe's account of IDSO would furnish the framework for Ian Fleming's only work of non-fiction, *The Diamond Smugglers*.[13] On De Beers' dime, Sillitoe spent six weeks investigating all the major diamond producers in West Africa, Tanganyika, the Congo, Angola, South West Africa and South Africa. He looked for gaps in security on the mines, and proposed various measures from the installation of closed-circuit television at the Williamson mine to the ubiquitous use of X-ray machines – to plug potential leaks. The greatest challenge was posed by illegal diggers in Sierra Leone, where diamonds were abundant. Smugglers fenced the goods to unlicensed buyers across the border in Liberia, and government officials steered them on to the market in Antwerp, where they were easily laundered. From there they found their way into the jewellery stores of London, Paris and New York. Sillitoe proceeded to hire half a dozen intelligence officers from the British secret service. They employed a variety of aggressive methods, including bloody ambushes by subcontracted mercenaries, to snare their prey. Undercover diamond buyers were stationed in Monrovia, Brazzaville and Burundi to curb the exodus of despoiled gems. However, only two years later, IDSO was disbanded. The cartel set up its own corporate security system, and Sillitoe returned to his sweet shop in Eastbourne whence he had been exfiltrated from retirement. Whether his mission had been accomplished or his services had become an embarrassment and Oppenheimer terminated them – reports of sanguinary campaigns in Sierra Leone, marked by machine-gun fire and flares, seeped back to Johannesburg – is a moot point. Sillitoe's cameo is interesting for two reasons. One is that, through the old spymaster, a madcap mercenary, Fouad ('Flash Fred') Kamil, thrust his way into Oppenheimer's life; the other is that, after Sillitoe's departure from the scene (although not because of it), the potential threats to De Beers' diamond monopoly multiplied.

Kamil was a resourceful young Lebanese trader operating in Sierra Leone, where Sillitoe enlisted him into IDSO. For years Kamil, a venal though charming sociopath, had extorted money from merchants and travellers along the 'Strangers' Trail', the route through the swamps of Sierra Leone to Liberia. Sillitoe offered him an attractive deal: in return for ambushing diamond smugglers and handing over the contraband to a tributary of De Beers, Kamil and his collaborators would receive one-third of the diamonds' value in cash. Even after Sillitoe's exit, Kamil remained on the diamond empire's radar. In 1965, De Beers allegedly flew Kamil to Johannesburg. At 44 Main Street, on Kamil's version of events, he was contracted to establish and operate a clandestine network of investigators and informers. Their role would be to recover stolen diamonds and stem illicit diamond buying.[14] This he reportedly did for a period of three years until he was summarily dismissed. Aggrieved and embittered, Kamil took refuge in Beirut and plotted his revenge. He fired off a series of letters to De Beers demanding compensation, and threatened to blow up the group's headquarters if his ultimatums were not met. As his missives went unanswered, Kamil became increasingly unhinged. In 1972, he concocted a deranged scheme to extort money from De Beers: he would hijack a South African airliner with a member of the Oppenheimer family on board, take him or her hostage, and then insist on meeting HFO personally to negotiate the ransom.

Posing as a photographer, Kamil journeyed to South Africa with a Lebanese policeman, Abou Yaghi. There they refined their dastardly plan. The pair learnt that Gordon Waddell was scheduled to fly back to Johannesburg from London, via Salisbury, one coming Wednesday. He became their chosen victim. On 24 May 1972, Kamil and Yaghi boarded a South African Airways aircraft in the Rhodesian capital, armed with sticks of dynamite. On the descent, they showed their hand and demanded that the pilot re-route to Khartoum. But there was insufficient fuel to fly that far. Besides, it soon became clear, once the stewards had sifted through all the passengers' passports, that Waddell was not on board. In fact, he had caught an earlier flight home. Kamil's plans began to unravel in tandem with his mental state. After briefly returning to Salisbury, the hijackers ordered the captain, Blake Flemington, to head for Malawi. From there Kamil intended to fire a fusillade of threats: if Oppenheimer did not make his way to Blantyre to resolve the situation, De Beers' offices would be blown sky-high, and HFO's daughter, Mary, would be kidnapped. But the Malawian President, Hastings Banda, was on the verge of departing for a holiday in London, and he refused to brook any such impertinences. Once the skyjacked jet was safely on the tarmac, he gave the command for its wheels to be flattened, and for sharpshooters to surround it. Kamil and Yaghi were cornered. After a dramatic 24-hour siege – during which Flemington and the hostages managed to escape – the hijackers gave themselves up. They were sent to prison. In Malawi, Kamil served only a few months of his 11-year sentence before being pardoned, but it was long enough for his resentment to fester. Kamil began to think of Harry Oppenheimer, a man the mercenary had never met, as the architect of his incarceration and ignominy. The magnate, he decided, must be brought to book.

For years after his release from prison Kamil waged a bitter vendetta against De Beers, Anglo and the Oppenheimers. He tried to blackmail company directors. Every so often he would make death threats, or have funeral wreaths delivered to the homes of Oppenheimer family members. Based on his espionage contacts, Kamil was drawn into a convoluted plot to discredit the British Liberal Party leader, Jeremy Thorpe, and the London-based anti-apartheid campaigner Peter Hain.[15] This turned out to be a covert operation masterminded by the Bureau for State Security (BOSS), the South African state intelligence agency. In a bizarre twist, the head of BOSS, Hendrik van den Bergh, tried to pin responsibility for the black op on Oppenheimer himself, according to one of his agents, Gordon Winter.[16] A rumour began doing the rounds that Anglo American was financing a smear campaign against Thorpe: at the time, the British press reported on claims by Norman Stone, a former stable hand and model, that Thorpe had been his emotionally abusive lover. No less a personage than Harold Wilson repeated the insinuations against Anglo in the House of Commons, only a week before he unexpectedly announced his resignation as prime minister. Oppenheimer dismissed Wilson's allegations as the 'wildest fantasy', and speculated on Kamil's connivance.[17] Three years later, in 1979, Kamil exorcised multiple other demons in a rambling autobiography.[18] He insisted that, after his release from prison, De Beers paid him over £50 000 in compensation for his services. Yet the cartel continued to disclaim him. In 1994 a controversial documentary, 'The Diamond Empire', was aired by the American public service broadcaster, PBS. Billed sensationally as a chronicle of 'how one family, the Oppenheimers of South Africa', had gained control of the 'supply, marketing, and pricing of the world's diamonds', it rehashed several of Kamil's averments.[19] Of his activities on behalf of De Beers in Sierra Leone, Kamil alleged that he had kidnapped, interrogated, beaten and starved diamond smugglers: 'We did everything we could to extort the information from them ... So to put it bluntly, we were a terrorist group.'[20] De Beers' department of corporate communications swiftly rubbished the assertions. But to ensure that everyone was on the same page, the director of the unit, WJ Lear, shared a memorandum with HFO's PA, Clifford Elphick: 'For the record, Kamil was not employed in any capacity, whether as a security official, detective or otherwise, by either De Beers or Anglo American.'[21] Kamil lived out his days in Brazil, occasionally lobbing long-distance grenades at De Beers, and making sporadic – though not especially consequential – attempts to intrude on Oppenheimer's life.

The demise of IDSO by 1957 coincided with the rise of several other hazards to the diamond empire aside from smugglers and bandits. It became progressively harder for De Beers to act as the industry's international policeman. Decolonisation and the advent of African independence meant that the Central Selling Organisation could no longer rely on tractable colonial governments to preserve elaborately tailored contractual agreements. Various post-colonial African leaders condemned apartheid and preached socialism while they plundered their countries and amassed large personal fortunes. In the interests of propriety and ideological integrity, they preferred to deal with the diamond cartel indirectly. Agreements between the African liberators and the CSO were concluded via innocuously named subsidiary companies like the Diamond Development Corporation, and Mining and Technical Services Limited, which were registered in places as far afield as Switzerland, Luxembourg, Liechtenstein and the Bahamas.[22] It was left predominantly to Philip Oppenheimer in London to navigate this complex political terrain, supported by two old Africa hands in the Diamond Trading Company, Monty Charles and Teddie Dawe. They handled negotiations with the Marxist government in Angola after the Portuguese revolution and the nationalisation of Diamang, the company formed in 1917 to exploit Angola's diamond mines. Elsewhere on the African continent, HFO played a more hands-on role. He came up with the idea for a Government Diamond Office (GDO) in Sierra Leone. Established in 1959 as a public–private partnership with the Diamond Corporation, the GDO continued to exercise sole responsibility for the export and marketing of Sierra Leone's diamonds long after the country gained its independence from Britain in 1961. Effectively, this meant that De Beers was able to buy up the production of its rival, Sierra Leone Selection Trust. As such it was a masterstroke on Oppenheimer's part, and he took great pride in the achievement. In South Africa's diamond-rich neighbours, Botswana and Lesotho, HFO conducted the initial talks with President Seretse Khama and Prime Minister Joseph Leabua Jonathan, respectively. After the discovery of the Orapa pipe in Botswana, Lesotho struck pay dirt with the Letšeng la Terai mine high up in the Maluti Mountains. It was developed by De Beers at a cost of $45 million, the company's biggest investment in a mine outside South Africa. Oppenheimer found the idea of a highlands diamond haul 'especially romantic'.[23] De Beers opened the Letšeng mine in 1977, but closed it five years later with less than 20 per cent of the open-pit mineable ore having been treated – a premature move since the mine turned out to be profitable under new operators in the 1990s.

Not every head of state was as amenable to Harry Oppenheimer's overtures as President Seretse Khama (and Khama's deputy and successor, Quett Masire) or President Nyerere in Tanzania. In the former Belgian Congo, the world's largest producer of industrial diamonds, the powers that be required some mollification. An accommodation was reached with Mobutu Sese Seko, President of the Democratic Republic of Congo (subsequently Zaire) from 1965, smoothed by Maurice Tempelsman, Oppenheimer's friend and Mobutu's ardent backer. When Mobutu nationalised the diamond mines in 1973, HFO flew into Kinshasa to meet the President with Pierre Crokaert, who had been intimately involved in safeguarding De Beers' Congolese interests since Ernest Oppenheimer's day. HFO and Crokaert wanted to ensure that production from the Société Minière de Bakwanga, the state-owned diamond company that succeeded Forminière, would continue to be channelled through the Central Selling Organisation. After complex negotiations, Mobutu found common cause with the duo. The CSO would enjoy sole purchasing rights over Zaire's diamond output through a company called Britmond, the British Zaire Diamond Distributors Limited. Crokaert recalled that HFO was 'quite impressed by Mobutu'. 'He didn't know anything about the diamond business of course, but he seemed a determined and authoritative man, and he certainly was the undisputed leader of the country.'[24] This was a staggeringly euphemistic characterisation of the Zairean President – a brutal and rapacious autocrat who ransacked his nation – but in the course of commerce such niceties were immaterial. The diamond empire was in need of reinforcement.

Zaire's *entente cordiale* with De Beers endured for many years, to each partner's mutual benefit. However, some of Mobutu's cabinet ministers began whispering in his ear that the nation might secure a higher price for its diamonds if the middlemen were eliminated. In 1981 Mobutu withdrew Zaire from its agreement with the CSO, only the second African nation to cut itself loose after Ghana two decades previously. He issued a decree which gave the state mineral marketing agency, Sozacom, the exclusive right to market Zaire's substantial diamond production. De Beers fought back. The cartel saturated the market with industrials, thereby dramatically reducing the gains from Zaire's diamond exports, and it stationed several dealers across the border in Brazzaville, where they soaked up Zaire's smuggled small gem production at inflated prices. Gradually, it dawned on Mobutu's ministers and the chief of Sozacom that they were receiving far less for Zaire's diamonds than they had been getting from the CSO. They took the initiative to reopen negotiations, and in February 1983, with Tempelsman's assistance, a new contract was signed. Mobutu submitted his country unto De Beers' protective embrace once more. For Oppenheimer, the whole episode had been an opportunity *pour encourager les autres*. To the *Financial Times*, he commented pointedly: 'the Zaire experiment should be looked upon as a warning rather than an example'.[25]

By far the most menacing development in the history of the diamond empire was the discovery of a trove of diamonds in Siberia in the late 1950s. According to legend, a Russian geologist stumbled upon a Soviet kimberlite pipe for the first time by tracking a fox with a blue-stained belly to its lair. By 1959, 120 pipes had been discovered. Even though the Siberian stones were extremely small in size, they were of a high quality, and they accounted for 20 per cent of the world's gem-grade diamonds. In time, Soviet production would make up nearly a third of global output. Once the world learnt of the Siberian explorations, De Beers' shares plummeted from 114s 6d to 82s. HFO feared that the Soviet Union might flood the market with stones and bring the whole industry crashing down. Philip Oppenheimer immediately set off to conduct negotiations. The Western capitalists and the Kremlin's communist czars forged an ungodly covenant in secret. The Soviets agreed to sell all of their rough diamonds to the syndicate at prices higher than the market rate – the initial contract was reputedly worth $25 million – provided the route from mine to sight was heavily disguised. Several layers of holding companies and conduits – a set of corporate matryoshka dolls – distanced Moscow from De Beers. As observed by Stefan Kanfer, the diamond empire's chronicler, this smokescreen allayed the Soviets' disquiet, since they had only recently severed official diplomatic, trade and economic ties with South Africa. 'This arrangement would give the Soviet delegate license to pound his fist on the tables of the United Nations, denouncing monopoly, condemning the racist capitalists of South Africa, and urging a boycott of the country's exports – even as his country was wholesaling its stones to the enemy'.[26] The CSO's guaranteed revenues were far too good to spurn.

For all their posturing, the Soviets were easily absorbed into the diamond cartel. In fact, they were eager to do business with Oppenheimer. In 1965, plans were drawn up for HFO to visit Moscow, a few months after he met President Lyndon Johnson at the White House. In this instance the intermediary volunteering his services was a French businessman, François Saar-Demichel. Ten years previously he had won a lucrative contract to import Soviet wood pulp for French paper manufacture. A generous donor to President Charles de Gaulle, habitué of the Élysée Palace, and influential foreign policy advisor on East–West relations, Saar-Demichel had been recruited as a KGB agent in the early 1960s. He was regarded by the high-ups in the Lubyanka Building as the 'most successful French recruitment in Moscow'.[27] Anglo's representative in Paris, Serge Combard, liaised with Saar-Demichel and subsequently informed Oppenheimer that the chairman of Gosbank (the state bank of the USSR), Alexei Poskonov, looked forward to hosting the South African. 'He confirms that your visit would be unofficial inasmuch as they would not send you a direct invitation. However from your arrival in Moscow until your departure you would be the guest of the Soviet government.'[28] The Soviets had established a synthetic diamond factory in Kiev, and they were anxious to discuss the possibility of a marketing agreement on industrial diamonds, as well as the potential for technical co-operation. Gold was on the agenda too. According to a confidential memorandum prepared for Oppenheimer, the Soviet monetary authorities wanted to solicit HFO's views on 'possible common action in the direction of a price increase'.[29] Here, the interests of Gaullist France, the USSR and South Africa intersected. And there were hopes that the interlocutors might see eye to eye on a 'common price' for platinum, in the vicinity of $125 per troy ounce, the Soviets suggested.

In spite of the fact that the USSR condemned South Africa's racial policies, the compiler of the memo noted that there were sufficient common interests in the economic field, particularly in mining, to warrant confidential agreements. The Kremlin, the self-styled champion of black African nationalism, was only too delighted to collaborate with the apartheid nation's most famous white capitalist and his business empire. In this way, the Soviet approach was not unlike that of African socialists like President Kaunda in Zambia or President Nyerere in Tanzania. As long as the price was right, even the most ideologically unbending overlords were prepared to disregard their own rhetoric. The key thing in the USSR was to keep up the appearance, at all times, of 'the private character' of HFO's visit.[30] To this end, it would be prudent for Oppenheimer not to be accompanied by any technicians from Anglo American or De Beers. If HFO provided particulars of his passport and three photos, he was assured, the Soviet Embassy in Paris would grant him a tourist visa. Conscious that he could hardly slip behind the Iron Curtain without potentially causing diplomatic difficulties, or at least raising eyebrows in Pretoria, Oppenheimer thought it wise to inform the South African government of his plans. From the Union Buildings came an equivocal response. 'They are not prepared to say yes or no,' HFO's PA, Francis Howard, informed his boss: should the visit take place, the Nationalists wished to react as they saw fit 'on the consequences to be borne'.[31] As if he had stepped unshod upon the Siberian tundra, Oppenheimer instantly got cold feet. He called off the expedition. It was only in 1993 that HFO travelled to (post-Soviet) Russia for the first time. However, Muscovite theatregoers were convinced that they had caught a glimpse of Harry Oppenheimer at the Bolshoi Theatre on at least one occasion. Gordon Waddell was indisputably there in November 1980. The BBC's Moscow correspondent, John Osman, was surprised to see Oppenheimer's former son-in-law at a performance of the opera *Boris Godunov*. 'Just passing through,' a sheepish Waddell muttered to Osman during the intermission.[32] It was an unlikely story. 'You don't just pass through Moscow and get good seats at the Bolshoi ballet by accident,' commented William Gutteridge, a contemporary expert on Soviet–South African relations.[33] The next day there was no trace of Waddell, and the Soviet authorities denied any knowledge of his visit.

From time to time the Russians bristled at the cartel's apparent autarky, and they indulged in acts of insubordination. In 1984 large quantities of cheaply priced Soviet gems were dumped onto the Antwerp cutting market. De Beers reminded the Russians where their bread was buttered. By the end of the year, HFO could assure the *Wall Street Journal* of a return to normalcy: 'The Russians are acting responsibly. They do not want to disrupt the market.'[34] Wherever its empire extended, De Beers seemed to be able to crack the whip with unerring effectiveness. Israel was a case in point. Harry and Bridget visited the Holy Land for the first time in 1968, accompanied by Edmond de Rothschild, one of Israel's most generous benefactors, and Rothschild's wife, Nadine. Although the visit was low-key – the only public reception was a cocktail party arranged jointly by the Israel Diamond Exchange and the Israel Diamond Manufacturers Association – the diamond-cutting industry attached great significance to the trip.[35] Oppenheimer met Israel's founder and first Prime Minister, David Ben-Gurion – a statesman he ranked alongside de Gaulle – and he subsequently became a steadfast friend to the Israeli nation. In 1986, HFO opened a facility established by the Israel Diamond Institute and named in his honour, the Harry Oppenheimer Diamond Museum in Ramat Gan.

During the diamond boom of the late 1970s, however, the Israelis were proving to be recalcitrant. Israeli buyers moved into Africa and began buying directly from smugglers. The Intercontinental Hotel in Liberia was turned into an extension of the Israeli bourse. Simultaneously, De Beers discovered that some of its American and Belgian clients had been reselling their parcels on to cutters in Tel Aviv at a markup of 100 per cent. Israeli banks were underwriting the diamond purchases with loans at interest rates far below inflation, and the country was starting to amass a stockpile which rivalled the CSO's. On De Beers' reckoning, the Israeli store of diamonds stood at six million carats in 1977 and was growing at the rate of half a million carats a month. The Israeli stockpile needed to be liquidated if De Beers was to maintain its ascendancy. One of the institutions that were financing the diamond purchases was Barclays Discount, a local subsidiary of Barclays Bank. HFO used his directorship of Barclays International to communicate his displeasure. De Beers opted for a more retaliatory response. The cartel levied a temporary surcharge of 40 per cent on all diamond buyers. Overnight, uncut gemstones became prohibitively expensive to buy and difficult to sell. Israeli banks had extended more than $850 million in credit – roughly one-third of Israel's foreign exchange – and now they were compelled to charge higher interest rates and demand additional collateral. De Beers proceeded to blacklist 40 of its clients who had been selling their consignments to the Israelis. Squeezed by rampant interest rates and hampered by the surcharge, Israel's major dealers were forced to eat into their stockpile to repay their loans. Smaller dealers went bankrupt. By 1980 the blitzkrieg was over; it was known by Israeli diamond dealers as the *bren* (burn). One ruined dealer complained: 'When the *bren* happened people said, "Who does Oppenheimer think he is, God?" Today they know.'[36]

De Beers' net attributable profit soared to R856 million in 1980.[37] To many diamantaires it seemed as if the diamond empire would rule until the Second Coming. But not even De Beers, or the Oppenheimer dynasty, could exercise the divine right of kings in perpetuity. In the 1980s and 1990s, the emergence of major Australian and Canadian diamond mines, overseen by independent-minded owners, subjected the monopoly's supply-controlled approach to enormous heat and pressure. In the new millennium, under Nicky Oppenheimer's chairmanship, De Beers would have to revise its operational model and abandon the cartel. In the last few years of his father's imperium, the diamond empire's problems were already mounting. The discovery of massive deposits of diamonds in the Argyle region of Western Australia narrowly preceded the worst downturn in the history of the industry since the Great Depression. In 1981 sales of diamonds by the CSO fell by 46 per cent to $1472 million.[38] De Beers' profits took an equivalent nosedive. As the company ran low on cash reserves, it had to borrow large sums of money at stratospheric interest rates to finance its stockpile. For the first time in 38 years, De Beers was forced to cut its dividend from 50 cents to 25 cents a share. Meanwhile, test drillings indicated that the Argyle pipes would be able to produce up to 50 million carats of diamonds a year, more than De Beers' entire annual production. The CSO desperately needed the Australian contract. In fact, the situation was so precarious that the emperor himself, not a mere emissary, was required to bring the Antipodeans to heel. HFO led the negotiations with CRA Limited, the major shareholder in the Argyle mine, and built up good relations with CRA's deputy chairman, Rus Madigan. There was a great public furore. The opposition Labour Party claimed that the cartel was trying to cheat Australia out of the true value of the Argyle diamonds. Prime Minister Malcolm Fraser threatened to put the kibosh on any deal. But in December 1982, after frantic lobbying, the transaction went through: the Argyle Diamond Mine, the world's largest diamond mine, would channel almost all of its gem-quality stones, and three-quarters of its other qualities, through the Central Selling Organisation. Coming in the middle of the recession, and amidst Zaire's defection from the CSO, it was a coup for De Beers. As one newspaper remarked, the decision added Australia to the long list of diamond-producing countries that opposed South Africa for its racial policies but found commercial links 'irresistible'.[39] The successful conclusion of the contract was Oppenheimer's swansong as chairman of De Beers. Julian Ogilvie Thompson, the man destined to take over the position when HFO retired from it at the end of 1984, regarded the deal as a 'considerable achievement, particularly for Harry'.[40] There was an element of symmetry to the affair, for when Charter Consolidated pioneered Anglo's programme of international diversification in the mid-1960s, Australia was its first port of call.

Charter Consolidated and the Shift to Minorco

When Oppenheimer formed Charter Consolidated in 1965, he envisaged it as Anglo's foreign mining arm. Anglo would provide technical advice and consulting services to Charter, as it did to De Beers. In London, Anglo, De Beers and Charter all shared premises on Charterhouse Street, the narrow thoroughfare discreetly tucked away from the babel of activity on High Holborn and Farringdon Road. When Minorco later joined them, the four pillars of the Oppenheimer empire were situated like the 'corners of a cloister': De Beers and Minorco occupied one side of the city block, Anglo and Charter commanded the other.[41] Every working day, scores of employees, suspended almost ten metres above ground level in a glass-encased, split-level skywalk, would shuttle between the two office complexes like an army of ants.

Bill Wilson put Charter on its feet between 1965 and 1969 before returning to Johannesburg, where he became Anglo's joint deputy chairman after RB Hagart's death. The two corporations, Anglo and Charter, worked hand in glove. Charter's primary focus was on mineral exploration, initially in Australia and then in Malaysia. HFO was enthused by Charter's early prospects: between April and May 1966, he visited these outposts of Anglo's empire to appraise his buds and shoots. Charter subsequently opened up a copper mine at Akjoujt in Mauritania. For this purpose Charter claimed a 75 per cent stake in Somima, the Société Minière de Mauritanie. There followed a gargantuan collaboration with Imperial Chemical Industries (ICI): Charter helped ICI set up a large-scale potash mine in North Yorkshire. The estimated capital cost of Cleveland Potash, Oppenheimer announced, would be £25 million.[42] The mine came into production in October 1973.[43]

By 1968, HFO could report on prospecting by the greater group and its associates in several African countries, the United Kingdom, Canada, the United States, Mexico, Australia and Malaysia.[44] Charter started prospecting for silver and copper in Chile and Peru, which marked the group's arrival in South America.[45] In Brazil, exploration for diamonds by De Beers and gold by Anglo through local companies led the group to open an office in Rio de Janeiro in 1973. HFO, Bridget, Julian Ogilvie Thompson and his wife, Tessa, visited Belém, São Paulo and Rio in November 1972. The sojourn confirmed Oppenheimer's belief that Brazil had 'considerable potential', and that it made sense for the group to invest a small proportion of its assets there.[46] In 1975 Anglo American do Brasil (Ambras) acquired a 49 per cent interest in Mineração Morro Velho, the oldest gold-mining company in Brazil. Accompanied by Maurice Tempelsman, Oppenheimer met with President Ernesto Geisel prior to the transaction.[47] In the context of Brazil's authoritarian military state, their meeting spelt 'automatic official acceptance' of the deal.[48] The Morro Velho complex of mines at Nova Lima became Anglo's anchor project in the country.[49]

In all of Anglo's and Charter's combined endeavours, Anglo provided technical assistance to Charter through a wholly owned London-based subsidiary, Anglo American International (UK). On occasion Anglo

HFO discusses the operations at Morro Velho. With him are
Dr PJ Pienaar (right), Julian Ogilvie Thompson and
(standing) JR Rossouw, 1974. *(Anglo American)*

and Charter would split their equity participations equally, as they did
in the case of the Société Minière de Tenke Fungurume (SMTF). This
was an international consortium stitched together in 1970 to exploit
copper and cobalt deposits in Tenke Fungurume, in the Shaba (formerly
Katanga) region of the Democratic Republic of Congo (renamed Zaire
the following year). In 1971 HFO reported that Charter was continuing
to make 'satisfactory progress', posting net profits of £12 998 000 for the
year ended 31 March 1970.[50] Yet below the surface there were problems.
One of the greater group's weaknesses was its persistent lack of success in
independent exploration. Anglo, Charter and Zambian Anglo American
(Zamanglo) came together as shareholders of the newly created Australian
Anglo American in August 1971, even though, after six years down
under, HFO had to admit Anglo had not yet been successful in turning
up a mineral deposit that could be worked at a profit.[51] In November,
under the headline 'More like a government than a company', the British
financial magazine *Investors Chronicle* noted that Anglo had not made a

major mineral discovery in years.[52] The exception was the Orapa diamond mine in Botswana, unearthed by a team of geologists from De Beers in 1967. Often Anglo would buy its way into other mining houses' ventures. Indeed, in the early 1970s Anglo's interests in mining finance houses like JCI, the Rio Tinto-Zinc Corporation (RTZ) and Union Corporation meant the group benefited from new discoveries even when it did not participate in their development. Charter, too, got into the habit of riding on other corporations' coat-tails, not least of all Anglo's.

On Charterhouse Street there were differences of opinion between the administrative division of Charter (mostly remnants of Central Mining and the British South Africa Company) and the AAC-dominated technical department over who ultimately ran the show. Did the buck stop with Anglo American in Johannesburg or Charter Consolidated in London? Should Charter develop along the traditional Anglo path, or confine itself to managing a portfolio of investments – a sort of resuscitated Central Mining? In the absence of a distinctive corporate identity, compounded by the hazy delineation of roles and responsibilities, these were contentious questions for Charter's top executives. Sidney Spiro took over the reins from Bill Wilson in 1969, but he did little to dispel the confusion; it soon became apparent that his skills were better suited to merchant banking. After Spiro was elevated to the chairmanship of Charter in 1971, Murray Hofmeyr became managing director. Born in 1925, the product of Pretoria Boys' High, Hofmeyr had read for the PPE at Oxford University on a Rhodes Scholarship (obtaining a double blue for cricket and rugby in the process), but his path to 44 Main Street was circuitous. He started his career as a schoolteacher, worked for a spell at an investment firm, and joined Anglo in 1962, well into his thirties. But within three years Hofmeyr was a manager in the Lusaka office; he subsequently took over from Gavin Relly as the resident satrap when Relly left Zambia for North America. In 1970 Hofmeyr was appointed to the Anglo board. HFO had high hopes for his superintendency of Charter. One of Oppenheimer's bugbears was that Charter initiated almost no business on its own. Cleveland Potash arose from De Beers' relationship with ICI. The Tenke Fungurume project stemmed from Maurice Tempelsman's contacts at the Diamond Office, the beating heart of Belgium's diamond trade. 'I only wish Charter *would* initiate some business & now with you it will,' Oppenheimer wrote pointedly to Hofmeyr.[53] HFO was happy for Charter to flex its entrepreneurial muscles independently of Anglo, provided the company's overriding loyalty and locus remained within the greater group. But he felt Charter's executives were insufficiently enterprising.

Murray Hofmeyr faced numerous hurdles. Charter was committed to two major ventures in politically perilous environments – Somima in Mauritania and Tenke Fungurume in Zaire – where, against its better judgement, the greater group had taken on too many risks. 'We blunted our reputation with those projects, as well as losing a great deal of money,' Gavin Relly would later lament.[54] For many years the technical stumbling blocks at Charter's third big endeavour, Cleveland Potash, seemed insurmountable. In each instance Charter had taken a participation out of proportion to its resources.[55] But in 1973 HFO was already beginning to look beyond Charter as the principal lever in Anglo's international apparatus. His attention turned to Zamanglo.

After the nationalisation of the Zambian copper mines, the Zambian government compensated Zamanglo's shareholders for their loss to the tune of £73 million (with a further £22 million in 1974, when Anglo's management contracts were terminated).[56] The payout, at market value, was made in American dollars, without any restrictions on repatriation. Zamanglo quickly re-registered in Bermuda, the British colonial tax haven in the Caribbean. Its new location and engorged coffers meant that Zamanglo was well placed and partially resourced to fulfil Anglo's international aspirations. It was a 'convenient instrument', HFO told a sceptical Hofmeyr, through which the group could channel its combined resources towards major international projects that required 'very large sums of money'.[57] Naturally, Charter's new bailiff saw the shift to Zamanglo as a threat to his bailiwick, entailing a diminution of Charter's role. But HFO countered that it was unreasonable for Charter to claim an 'absolute right' to take the lead in any new business initiated by the group internationally. 'In practice the probability is that Charter will play a disproportionately large role in running any Zamanglo business, but naturally not an exclusive role.'[58]

In fact, Charter's star was on the wane. Over the next six years HFO would revise his ideas about the company's form and function. This process culminated in the adoption of the so-called SVA (Sponsor/Vendor/Acquirer) scheme in 1979, which transferred various strategic group investments from Charter to Minorco. Henceforth, Minorco replaced Charter as the group's flagship investment company internationally. In 1975 Oppenheimer announced the expansion of Zamanglo into the field of natural resources; accordingly, its name was changed to the Mineral and Resources Corporation. Minorco would become an 'international mining concern' and assume a greater role in new business undertaken by Anglo and Charter.[59] After the disasters in Mauritania and Zaire, Charter gradually lost credibility as a mining company. Hofmeyr relieved Spiro of the chairmanship in 1976; in the run-up to Spiro's departure, HFO gave considered thought to a well-remunerated sinecure for the former merchant banker.

When Hofmeyr's turn came to stand down – he returned to 44 Main Street in 1979 – Oppenheimer battled to find takers for the Charter chairmanship, a role he had once personally fulfilled. The man who ultimately navigated Charter through uncharted waters in the 1980s as its chief executive was Neil Clarke. Dispatched to London from Anglo's finance office in Johannesburg, the reserved and carefully spoken Clarke later rose to prominence as chair of the British Coal Corporation. 'The growing realisation in Charter that Neil is going to be the boss is accompanied by universal dismay,' Relly wrote resignedly to HFO in July 1979; he asked, in passing, whether Oppenheimer had considered reclaiming the chairmanship himself.[60] Three months later, after a protracted process much mistrusted by Charter's executives, the SVA was signed and sealed. It had involved complicated technical work around the valuation of assets, exchange control and taxation in multiple jurisdictions, as well as organisational restructuring – much of it coordinated by one of the Young Turks, Tony Lea. Clarke had never witnessed HFO 'so closely involved in something before'.[61] He was impressed by Oppenheimer's determination to get the scheme approved, and his willingness to adapt it to 'meet all sorts of parochial interests', provided the greater group's overarching purpose would be fulfilled. Not all of Clarke's minions shared this rosy view: many felt that HFO had simply transferred his allegiance from Charter to Minorco. When the SVA was launched in London, Oppenheimer presented it to three different groupings on the same day: the Charter staff, the press, and an assembly of investment analysts. In essence, the scheme had four core components. Charter would sell the greater part of its investments in Africa, Australia, Brazil and Canada to Anglo, Minorco and De Beers, and receive £29 million in cash. Anglo and Charter would buy out ICI's 50 per cent share of Cleveland Potash, but Anglo alone would assume all further liabilities for the money pit on the North York moors. Charter would become a more narrowly focused British industrial concern, with a 28 per cent holding in the chemicals giant Johnson Matthey, and some medium-sized mining projects in

Europe. And Minorco would take over Charter's role on the international stage. Hovering in the background, an important catalyst to Minorco's restructuring, were Anglo's North American concerns.

North America: The Engelhard Connection

HFO regarded North America as a prize corner of the Anglo realm. It was not possible to run an international business empire, he believed, without a major stake in the United States. The US made good business sense: unlike South Africa, it was politically and economically stable. Rich in mineral and energy resources, it offered opportunities for high returns on investment. And in the event that the ship sank in South Africa, it would be sensible for Anglo to have a decent fleet of business interests (and safe harbour) in the Western Hemisphere. Following Anglo's arrival in New York, the group established a separate arm in Canada – the Anglo American Corporation of Canada (Amcan) – which in 1966 opened an office in Toronto.[62] Amcan's major interest was Hudson Bay Mining and Smelting. By the end of the decade, Anglo enjoyed a 28 per cent shareholding in the company. But the jewel in Anglo's North American crown derived from Oppenheimer's association with Charles Engelhard. The irrepressible tycoon cemented his friendship with HFO during the 1960s: indeed, he came to play a central part in Anglo's fortunes north-west of the Atlantic. After the initial exchange of shares in their private holding companies, Engelhard Hanovia and E Oppenheimer and Son, Engelhard and HFO drew their corporate empires into closer synergy. Anglo American began to build up a shareholding in Engelhard Hanovia, the controlling force behind Engelhard Industries. In turn, Engelhard Hanovia acquired minority shareholdings in various companies affiliated to Anglo American. In December 1966 Engelhard joined Anglo's executive committee. The following year Anglo increased its stake in Engelhard Hanovia to approximately 50 per cent. The negotiations were led by HFO and Engelhard, each with his own individual style and approach: Oppenheimer was logical and methodical, Engelhard was more inclined to the sweeping gesture and intuitive leap. Yet such was the level of trust and understanding between the two men, Engelhard's lawyer, Ed Beimfohr, later recollected, that they felt it unnecessary to record every detail in writing.[63] André Meyer, the financier from Lazard Frères who had made an impression upon Oppenheimer on their first encounter in 1949, was a key figure in the proceedings; and through this set of negotiations HFO met Meyer's colleague and mentee, Felix Rohatyn. A refugee from Nazi-occupied France like Meyer, 'Felix the Fixer', as Rohatyn became known – not least for his role, during the mid-1970s, in preventing the bankruptcy of New York City – combined sober rectitude with tremendous flair. A renowned art collector with heavyweight political connections, Rohatyn would become one of Oppenheimer's best-liked American acquaintances.

Among Engelhard Hanovia's attractions was Engelhard's tie-up with the world's largest trader of commodities, Philipp Brothers, a firm which specialised in buying and selling minerals, metals and ores on the international market. Back in 1960 Oppenheimer had written to Engelhard that 'some sort of link' between Engelhard Industries and Philipp Brothers might possibly lead to 'useful co-operation between Philipps and Anglo American one day'.[64] And so it came to pass. André Meyer brokered a merger between Philipp Brothers and the Minerals and Chemicals Corporation. It provided the latter with access to Philipp Brothers' immense cash flow for development projects, and the former with a listing on the New York Stock Exchange. In 1963 Engelhard acquired roughly 20 per cent of the common stock of the newly formed company, Minerals and Chemicals Philipp (MCP).[65] In September 1967, the joint venture was taken a step further: MCP joined forces with Engelhard Industries to create the Engelhard Minerals and Chemicals (EMC) Corporation. EMC boasted a vast and diversified business, covering precious metals in many applications, the mining and beneficiation of non-metallic minerals, and the marketing of basic ores, minerals and metals. It became a money-spinner of note, with after-tax profits of over $28 million by the end of its first year of existence.[66]

Through Engelhard Hanovia's 44 per cent holding in the publicly listed EMC, Anglo saw that it could acquire a major position in Philipp Brothers; and this, undoubtedly, lay behind Anglo's decision to raise its stake in Engelhard Hanovia to 70 per cent in December 1969. As a prelude to the deal, HFO assured Engelhard that Engelhard Hanovia would become the principal vehicle through which Anglo conducted business in the United States. It was an adaptation to their existing arrangements which Engelhard found 'extremely attractive'.[67] By this stage the American mogul's health was failing. He was grossly overweight. An arthritic hip caused him chronic pain and made walking difficult, even with the support of his trademark ebony cane; and apart from all his other compulsions and dependencies, like drinking endless bottles of Coca-Cola, Engelhard relied heavily on painkillers to make it through the day. He knew that time was not on his side. Anglo's buyout, most of it conducted in hard cash, provided Engelhard with a windfall. Over the years his extravagant tastes had contrived to burn a hole in his pocket the size of a small platinum mine. With the money from Anglo, Engelhard was able to put his estate in order and provide for his family in the event of his death. Besides, with no male heir of his own – Engelhard had five daughters – he was anxious that his business empire should be conserved by a trusted dynasty. So long as he was alive Engelhard would continue to run the show in association with EMC's often overshadowed, frequently embattled president, Milton Rosenthal, and in consultation with HFO's executives.

The transaction pulled 'Harry's men' closer into Engelhard's orbit. Gavin Relly, who went to head up Anglo's Canadian operations in 1970, occupied a seat on the EMC board. HFO told Engelhard tactfully that contact between Anglo and the Engelhard empire could no longer be limited to personal consultation between the two of them on 'matters of broad policy'.[68] There needed to be thorough contact at all levels with respect to business dealings. To Basil Hone, an Anglo man in New York with one foot in Engelhard Hanovia, Oppenheimer spelt out matters clearly: if 'Charlie' was under the impression that communication between Anglo and EMC should take the form of 'woolly personal letters exchanged between him and me', then he needed to be disabused of the notion immediately.[69] But HFO was unwilling to set matters straight personally, at least not directly; his respect and affection for Engelhard precluded any clumsy conversations. Similarly, Oppenheimer demurred from addressing his friend head-on about the myriad personal extravagances and chaotic corporate structure of EMC, where Engelhard, as chief executive, rode roughshod over Rosenthal. 'Naturally it would be very much better and more pleasant if these matters could be tackled without any intervention from me,' HFO suggested to Relly.[70]

To add to the chaos, the Philipp Brothers' executives started stewing with resentment. As the world turned to spot traders to move scarce natural resources around the globe quickly and efficiently, EMC's sales soared, spurred on by the oil crisis. Between 1972 and 1974, EMC's consolidated net earnings leapt from $36.6 million to $110.2 million.[71] The problem, if it could be called that, was that 80 per cent of EMC's revenue was being generated by Philipp Brothers single-handedly. They were bringing home the bacon. Increasingly, the people from Philipp Brothers looked upon their counterparts at Engelhard Industries as profligate and parasitic.

There was a clash of cultures and personalities. In some measure it was HFO's personal relationship with the head of Philipp Brothers, Ludwig Jesselson, that helped smooth the waters. 'Harry, in his wisdom, showed his hand behind the scenes,' Jesselson remarked.[72] Jesselson, a noteworthy Jewish philanthropist who had escaped Nazi Germany in 1934, developed a friendship with Oppenheimer. On one of HFO's visits to Israel, Jesselson served as his guide to the country. In 1982 they travelled together to Lake Tiberius, toured Jerusalem with the mayor, Teddy Kollek, visited the Holocaust memorial at Yad Vashem, and enjoyed an hour-long audience with the Prime Minister, Menachem Begin.

Charles Engelhard died on 2 March 1971, aged only 54. He and Jane had hosted President Lyndon Johnson and his wife, Lady Bird, at Pamplemousse in Boca Grande the week before his death; the strain of entertaining, coupled with insomnia, took a heavy toll on the ailing plutocrat. Bridget and Harry departed at once from Brenthurst to attend the funeral in New Jersey. At St Mary's Abbey in Morristown, HFO was ushered to the front of the church as an honorary pallbearer. Bridget slotted into a pew behind President Johnson. 'A sad end, but it was planned suicide on his part,' she observed on notepaper from the Carlyle afterwards.[73] Engelhard's demise was a turning point of sorts for Anglo in America. It more or less coincided with the US Department of Justice's renewed attack on the group for alleged antitrust activities. For HFO, Engelhard's death was a source of sorrow: he had lost the only real business partner, outside the greater group, he had ever had, as well as one of his most treasured friends.

At first, doing business in North America proved culturally and commercially challenging for Anglo. The environment was intensely competitive; and, unlike in South Africa, Anglo was a bit player. The corporation's asset base was small: there were no Orange Free State goldfields, Kimberley diamond fields or Zambian Copperbelt churning out a huge cash flow from a broad base. This meant that Anglo struggled to establish unique operating enterprises. Moreover, ever since the adoption of the Sherman Antitrust Act in 1890, the 'Magna Carta of free enterprise', the US government had harboured a deep suspicion of the power of large corporations.[74] Anglo's whole corporate structure was anathema to Uncle Sam. Antitrust legislation was a niggly thorn in Anglo's side. De Beers, of course, steered clear of the United States: it conducted sales to American sightholders outside the country. While the US Justice Department had been forced to abandon the antitrust case which it lodged against De Beers in 1945, the government kept both the diamond cartel and Anglo in its sights. Before Engelhard's death, the department started asking questions about HFO's relationship with him. But despite its best investigative efforts, the Justice Department found that when Engelhard had interests in the diamond business, Oppenheimer owned no part of them; and when Anglo bought control of Engelhard Hanovia, the Platinum King's holding company was no longer involved in the diamond industry.

The Justice Department tried another tack. A grand jury was sworn in to probe claims that De Beers was trying to gain monopoly control of the US market for diamond drilling stones – industrial diamonds used in tools that drill for oil and other minerals. A single American company, Christensen Diamond Products, supplied the US with most of its diamonds for petroleum drill bits; and, through a tangled web of go-betweens, De Beers' Luxembourg-based subsidiary, Boart International, appeared to be in cahoots with Christensen. In 1971, Bob Clare, senior partner at the law firm Shearman & Sterling, had sniffed the way the wind was blowing. He advised Anglo to close its office in New York and transfer its operations to Toronto. HFO took the decision to shut the office forthwith – 'an example of Harry's great realism', according to Ronnie Fraser, Anglo's chief liaison with Philipp Brothers – and at the beginning of 1972 Anglo decamped to Canada.[75] For a period of almost four years, Anglo executives gave the United States a wide berth; they dared not set foot on US soil. A watch began at the airports for directors of both Anglo and De Beers: on arrival, they would be taken into custody and subpoenaed to make depositions to the grand jury. On one occasion, the Immigration Department, acting on a tip-off, forced down a Hudson Bay aeroplane en route from Toronto to Mexico. Officers went through the aircraft looking for Anglo American directors, but came up short. EMC board meetings were moved to London or Toronto. For Harry and Bridget, whose springtime trips to New York were a highlight of their social calendar, this effective embargo was a nuisance. One of the Rothschilds on the De Beers board was so put out by the virtual ban – he liked shopping on Fifth Avenue – that he relinquished his directorship.

The antitrust suit was hampered by jurisdictional wrangles and some fleet-footed manoeuvring on the part of De Beers. Boart International sold back to Christensen Diamond Products all the stock that it owned in the company, and De Beers managed to clean up its US links. The Justice Department's case was fatally undercut. The matter was eventually settled in 1976, and the Justice Department had to make do with a token victory. An Irish subsidiary of De Beers and two American distributors of diamond abrasives entered into a consent judgment. It prevented them from fixing the price of diamond grit or entering into collusive bids. In total, they paid a trifling $50 000 fine. The verdict was meaningless: by that stage, most diamond grit was produced synthetically, and De Beers could not hope to monopolise the supply. For HFO, the resolution of the case felt like a new beginning. A weight was lifted from his shoulders, and he could get back to expanding his American empire.

Minorco: A Major International Mining Finance Group

As Charter's standing in the greater group diminished, Minorco's position strengthened. When Zamanglo assumed its new name and expanded role in 1974, the rebranded entity retained its Zambian copper interests through a 49 per cent holding in Zambia Copper Investments. But Minorco's horizons shifted beyond Africa to the Americas, along with its Zambian start-up capital conveniently deposited in Bermuda. Ultimately, the company re-domiciled in Luxembourg. Minorco acquired Anglo's 29 per cent interest in the Engelhard Minerals and Chemicals Corporation. All the while, thanks in large part to Philipp Brothers, EMC continued to flourish: in 1978 the company recorded earnings of $142.2 million.[76] In Canada, the reorganisation of the group's international interests gave Minorco 50 per cent (and, later, the entirety) of Amcan, which in turn held 45 per cent of Hudson Bay. HFO toured the Great White North with Amcan's chief (and concurrently Hudbay's president), Peter Gush. They surveyed lead and zinc prospects in the Yukon, as well as the remote Stikine copper deposit in British Columbia. In the Yukon, the geologist's camp consisted of little more than a wooden shack, which looked pitifully small against the mountain beyond. But the cook was enormous, and he had spent the previous two weeks preparing food worthy of his distinguished visitor. Loath to give offence, HFO manfully attacked the huge steaks on his plate until he could cope no longer.[77]

By 1980 Minorco could boast a 234 per cent increase in its net earnings, to $114.8 million, and a 64 per cent rise in its operating profit, to $24.7 million.[78] In partnership with Hudson Bay, Minorco launched a successful bid for complete control of Inspiration Copper in Arizona. In HFO's view, this step signalled a 'fuller realisation' of Minorco's role as an international resources company.[79] Another joint venture between

Minorco and Hudson Bay resulted in their 50-50 ownership of Terra Chemicals, a fertiliser and agricultural chemicals business based in Iowa. There were oil and gas companies, too, like Trend International, a Denver-based outfit with interests in America and Indonesia. Meanwhile, Inspiration Coal, another Minorco investment, snapped up coal properties in Kentucky. Over the years, Hudson Bay swung its investments almost entirely away from Canada to the United States. The only concerns really run from Toronto were Hudbay's Manitoba mining operations. As a result, it made sense to settle on the US as an operational base. At HFO's prompting, this led to the reconcentration in America of Minorco's joint interests with Hudson Bay under the name of Inspiration Resources. Hudbay's Canadian operations became a division of the US parent.

By 1981, Minorco's assets were spread over a wide range of mining, energy and commodities companies. Their combined value was $2 billion. Philipp Brothers, with profits of $467 million off revenues of $23 billion (mainly from oil trades), was the biggest prize of all. It accounted for almost 90 per cent of EMC's total revenues. But in May 1981, after years of mutual ill feeling, EMC's constituent parts split in two: Engelhard Industries and the Minerals and Chemicals division were spun off as the Engelhard Corporation, and Philipp Brothers went its own way as the Phibro Corporation. Minorco retained a 27 per cent interest in each of them. Shortly after the separation Phibro pulled off a dazzling feat. For a mere $483 million it secured 100 per cent of Salomon Brothers, America's largest private investment bank and the world's leading bond-trading firm, dubbed the 'King of Wall Street'.[80] The average partner at Salomon, whose money had been legally frozen in the firm's capital fund until that point, scooped up about $7.8 million. How an American concern could fold so smoothly into the Oppenheimer empire was a question many asked. 'Rhodes had shown the way: every man has his price,' came the answer.[81] Salomon Brothers' business went from strength to strength just as the global economy turned and metal trading fell out of bed. As financial markets hummed during Ronald Reagan's presidency, at least until the crash of 1987, Phibro-Salomon became a cash cow for Minorco. In August 1981, *Fortune* reported that Minorco was the single largest foreign investor in the United States.[82] The claim was backed up by research from a US-based non-governmental organisation, the Africa Fund; and Thomas Lippman, the *Washington Post* correspondent, repeated it in an article entitled 'A South African empire reaches to US'.[83]

Given that ultimate authority for Minorco lay at the doorstep of 44 Main Street, Johannesburg, a nondescript mining outpost thousands of kilometres away, this was an astonishing conquest. It was a neat inversion of the age-old order: the periphery had colonised the metropole.

In his Anglo chairman's statement for 1981, HFO extolled Minorco's virtues: it now had a large asset base, little debt and much-improved cash flow. These were factors which significantly enhanced its position as a 'major international mining finance group'.[84] With 35.8 per cent of Charter in its portfolio and a cornucopia of strategic investments like Phibro-Salomon, Minorco had developed into an aggressively expansionist corner of the Anglo American realm. Through the SVA, Charter had been reduced to a mere dependency – a sort of disempowered protectorate. And although Anglo's grip on Minorco was beyond doubt – Ronnie Fraser was its president, HFO its chair, and Anglo's shareholding stood at 42.8 per cent in 1981, with De Beers accounting for another chunk – the company had a transatlantic flavour. At HFO's suggestion, the majority of Minorco's directors were prominent North American businessmen. This gave the company an independent identity. Minorco's initial outside directors brought heft: Citicorp chairman Walter Wriston; Bob Clare; Felix Rohatyn; and Cedric Ritchie, chairman of the Bank of Nova Scotia. HFO cultivated personal relationships with each of them. He had a knack for making admirers of his associates. Just as he had endeared himself to Ludwig Jesselson, Oppenheimer charmed Phibro-Salomon's joint chief executive, John Gutfreund, a gruff, aggressive, profit-hungry trader. Gutfreund took no prisoners. He eventually squeezed out his Phibro counterpart, David Tendler, and his brazen financial exploits were immortalised in the book *Liar's Poker*.[85] No matter how much they might differ in disposition from the cerebral King of Diamonds, chairmen of Fortune 500 companies, state governors, US senators, local politicians and even workers on the shop floor all seemed curiously susceptible to HFO's other-worldly brand of mannerly, self-assured reserve.

Striking Back against the Empire: Minorco and Consolidated Gold Fields

Yet it would be foolish to mistake Oppenheimer's reserve for meekness. He was a hard-headed businessman, with a highly developed sense of *amour propre* and a keen fascination with power and prestige. HFO was an empire-builder – he consciously saw himself in the tradition of Rhodes –

and empires, whether territorial or commercial, are seldom built without a measure of subjugation. When Lippman wrote his story, he acknowledged that Oppenheimer had a long-standing reputation as a liberal, 'at least in the South African context', and that he had used his personal wealth and power to oppose apartheid and improve black living conditions. But Lippman included a dissenting quote: Oppenheimer was perceived in some quarters as a 'profiteer', whose fortune had been accumulated on the 'backs of low-paid black miners'.[86] Such criticisms would gather steam as pressure mounted to sever US–South African business ties in apartheid's dying decade. In America they dovetailed with latent misgivings about Anglo as a mammoth monopoly, by virtue of its affiliation with De Beers. One of the multinational companies that drove this narrative against Anglo, entirely for self-serving reasons, was London-listed Consolidated Gold Fields (Consgold), Anglo's nearest rival and the world's second-largest gold producer. Consgold's imputations were somewhat hypocritical, given that its South African interest – Gold Fields South Africa (GFSA) – had a reputation for being the country's most hidebound mining house, accustomed to responding with brutal force to strikes by black mineworkers. In 1989 Consgold's chairman, Rudolph Agnew, a former cavalry officer with a languid air, dispensed with his customary urbanity and denounced Anglo American in witheringly scornful terms. Anglo was 'manipulative and a self-professed believer in cartels', he charged.[87] The group's companies were run by a small number of executives to satisfy the ravening financial ambitions of the Oppenheimer family. 'They are not driven by creativity or the desire to uncover new resources,' Agnew fulminated. 'It is a management style that, in mining circles, is known as "the dead hand of Anglo American".' Oppenheimer, Agnew averred, was an industrialist in the mould of Citizen Kane, who lorded over the Anglo American empire from his Xanadu at Brenthurst. In contrast, Agnew depicted himself as a modest company man. 'As much as any laborer in the mines, I am simply a paid hand,' he guilefully protested.

Agnew's remarkable gush of vitriol had long been bubbling. It was unleashed by a hostile takeover bid which Minorco instigated against Consgold on the morning of 21 September 1988. At the time this was the largest such attempt in British corporate history, with an opening offer of £2.9 billion, and it spurred a tenacious fightback by Agnew. In fact, Agnew's rage had been simmering at a low intensity for some time before it reached boiling point, ever since Minorco's putsch was presaged eight years earlier. In 1980, at the same time that cash-rich

Minorco was embarking on a binge of acquisitions, Anglo and De Beers surreptitiously launched a 'dawn raid' against Consgold and gobbled up just over 29 per cent of its shares. The shareholding was later transferred to Minorco. The dawn raid left Consgold with a predator in its pantry: among the British company's other assets, it enjoyed a sizeable stake in the Newmont Mining Corporation, Anglo's original American backer. But it also exposed the mining house to Anglo's predations on South African soil, since Consgold owned 49 per cent of Gold Fields South Africa, and Anglo already had an 11 per cent stake in GFSA. Even though HFO felt the basic structure of the mining industry in South Africa in the late 1970s was sound and should not be disturbed, the earlier discussions between GFSA and Union Corporation, before the General Mining–Union Corporation tie-up, had run up a flag. They showed that a change in GFSA's ownership was possible. In August 1979 Oliver Baring, HFO's godson and a partner at Anglo's stockbrokers, Rowe & Pitman, tipped off his godfather that Consgold's shares were being steadily bought up in London.[88] Anglo decided to follow suit. According to Julian Ogilvie Thompson, it all started in a rather desultory way, with a view, at worst, to making a profit should a takeover bid be launched and, at best, to warding off such a bid, whether from another South African group or, as was improbably rumoured, from oil-rich Americans or Arabs. In fact, Anglo's actions seem to have been quite calculated: if Consgold was acquired by a rival South African mining house, then Anglo's predominance in gold production would be threatened. Thus, it was the 'internal politics' of the South African gold mining industry that came to spark one of 'the most far reaching and bitter corporate battles' ever.[89]

Between November 1979 and February 1980, in an operation spearheaded by Ogilvie Thompson and authorised by HFO, Anglo and De Beers quietly channelled R60 million to six affiliated companies, and instructed them to buy Consgold shares on command. This coordinated strategy was used to circumvent Britain's Companies Act, which required any purchase of more than 5 per cent in a company to be publicly declared. By 8 February, the greater group's collective interest in Consgold stood at just under 15 per cent.[90] At 8.30 am on Tuesday, 12 February, Rowe & Pitman gave the signal: it was time to begin the buying blitz. As 30 of the firm's stockbrokers dialled their telephones in unison, the Anglo consortium grabbed 16.5 million Consgold shares, close to an additional 15 per cent of the company, in less than half an hour. Consgold was blindsided. When the operation had been completed, HFO telephoned

David Lloyd-Jacob, Consgold's managing director of finance, to break the news. 'I'm terribly sorry we had to act so confidentially,' he intoned benignly. Consgold was to rest assured that Anglo had full confidence in the management of the company; there would be no fundamental changes to its overall control. Publicly, Lloyd-Jacob responded in a most sporting fashion. He brushed the whole thing off as a non-event. 'I have absolute confidence in Mr Oppenheimer. He is one of the most charming and delightful people I know.' There was, of course, an ironic tinge to these comments: 'I did not ask [Mr Oppenheimer] why he had bought the shares,' Lloyd-Jacob continued. 'He seemed to be in rather a hurry.'[91]

With a little over 29 per cent of Consgold bagged, HFO delighted in the outcome. He was tickled by the boldness of the subterfuge. When Oliver Baring asked him, 'Wouldn't your father have been pleased?' HFO jokingly responded, 'No, he would have been furious – he would have expected us to buy the lot.'[92] Standing between the Oppenheimer empire and total control of Consgold were British takeover regulations: they required anyone who had acquired a shareholding of 30 per cent or more to make a formal tender offer to the other shareholders. Such a move would have been costly and attracted undesirable attention. Eight years later, circumstances were different. Minorco had cash in hand. The corporation had already reduced its shareholding in Phibro-Salomon by half, the result of a strategic decision to focus on minerals and natural resources. Then, in September 1987, Salomon Inc. agreed to buy out 12 per cent of Minorco's remaining stake in the firm. (Gutfreund had dropped Phibro from the establishment's name and purged all public memory of the commodities trader after Tendler's departure, 'executing the inhabitants and then razing the town', as *New York Magazine* evocatively described his actions.)[93] Uber-investor Warren Buffett simultaneously purchased a 12 per cent stake in Salomon, and Minorco walked away with $809 million.[94] Oppenheimer had approached Felix Rohatyn to sell Minorco's block of shares back in April, and Gutfreund had dragged his feet. When the transaction was finally announced on 28 September, at $38 a share (a $6 premium over Salomon's stock price at the time), Oppenheimer's timing proved to be inspired. Three weeks later the stock market crashed unexpectedly. On 19 October 1987, 'Black Monday', the Dow Jones Industrial Average fell by 508 points, the largest one-day percentage drop in its history. There was carnage on the floor of the New York Stock Exchange. The value of Salomon's shares plummeted. But by then Minorco's money was in the bank.

Cash-flush Minorco now set its sights on Consgold. A merger between the two companies would establish the largest and most powerful mining house in the world. In 1988, the Oppenheimer empire encompassed 600 corporations, assets of more than \$20 billion, and 800 000 employees. Minorco was its international centrepiece. Nor were Minorco's marriage prospects entirely unpropitious. Since the dawn raid, Anglo had managed to establish reasonably amicable relations with Consgold in London. The two mining houses coexisted harmoniously enough, although in Johannesburg, under GFSA's conservative principal (and sometime president of the Chamber of Mines), Robin Plumbridge, there was a lingering suspicion of Anglo. Agnew, as Consgold's chief executive, had agreed to what he later derisively termed 'the corporate equivalent of an exchange of prisoners': he joined Anglo's board, while Ogilvie Thompson and Neil Clarke were appointed directors of Consgold.[95] In South Africa Gold Fields found itself partly fused to Anglo's familial corporate structure. The partners muddled along. But when Minorco launched its all-out bid for Consgold in September 1988, with financing from the Bank of Nova Scotia, Geneva's Swiss Bank Corporation, New York City's Chemical Bank and West Germany's Dresdner Bank, the atmosphere eventually turned mephitic.

'After protracted talks, we came very close to a friendly transaction. Only much later did the bid turn hostile. At that point, this thing fell on one issue,' Hank Slack subsequently regretted of the failed merger.[96] By then, he, Roger Phillimore and Tony Lea were all directors of Minorco. They were willing to serve under Agnew but, Slack later acknowledged, 'in our stupidity, we were not prepared to make Rudolph Agnew the chief executive officer of the new entity'. The deal foundered on a title. Consgold thought Minorco's negotiators were acting in bad faith, that they had no intention of sharing management responsibility. Agnew envisaged his unsaddling by Oppenheimer's mounted troops. In consequence, Consgold's board rejected the proposal. When Minorco's bid turned unfriendly, Consgold matched the hostility in spades. 'All hell broke loose,' in Phillimore's recollection. 'We ended up with a scrappy, demeaning, anti-South African, anti-Oppenheimer, scorched earth response. It was absolutely bloody horrible.'[97] Minorco was mercilessly attacked for its South African connections. Anglo, De Beers and Minorco were cast as conjoined triplets, spawn of the Great Satan: the outcast apartheid state, whose very lifeblood was *their* variety of racial capitalism. In response, Minorco feebly tried to downplay its South African links.

It did so, oddly, by wheeling into service a plucky and purposeful South African-born Briton, Sir Michael Edwardes. Edwardes had joined Minorco's board in 1984 and now he emerged as its frontman. With Edwardes front and centre, the mining house acquired a 'tweed suit' and an 'English accent'.[98] As the chairman of British Leyland, Britain's largest car manufacturer, from 1977 to 1982, Edwardes had taken on the trade unions and become a key player in the Thatcherite revolution. He was a high-profile businessman and a pillar of the British establishment. His cachet and credentials, so the thinking went, would make him the acceptable face of Minorco's bid for Consgold. Personally, Oppenheimer could not comprehend why Edwardes had been roped in to take the lead. But he kept his own counsel. Although HFO was extensively consulted on the takeover – and actively supported it – by this stage he was retired and mellowed, and he tended to defer to his successors. He was disinclined to make any interventions that might be deemed obtrusive.

As Consgold fought back against Minorco's unwelcome overtures, it marshalled an army of attorneys, investment analysts and corporate detectives on both sides of the Atlantic to build a wide-ranging legal case. A no-holds-barred crusade to sway the court of public opinion unfolded concomitantly. Lobbyists and spin doctors were rallied to the cause. There were fierce attack ads and relentless whispering campaigns. In London the Anti-Apartheid Movement (AAM) added its voice to the chorus of naysayers. Anglo's wealth had been built on the exploitation of cheap black labour and a Machiavellian manipulation of monopolies, the organisation charged. 'A takeover of Consolidated Gold Fields by Minorco would represent a Trojan horse for South Africa situated at the very heart of Britain's financial and industrial establishment,' the AAM warned darkly.[99] Fearmongering about the apartheid regime's intentions abroad might justifiably provoke a wave of moral panic; in case that failed to produce the desired effect, the Third Reich could be invoked by way of caution. De Beers, it was alleged, had sold industrial diamonds to Nazi Germany. A shabby and fallacious hearsay circulated by the rumour mill, this marked a low point of the saga. Day in and day out, the *Financial Times* and other newspapers carried front-page stories about Anglo's quest to conquer an ancient rival. The Oppenheimer empire was subjected to an unprecedented level of scrutiny. Amid the slurry of accusations, Britain's Office of Fair Trading began a preliminary investigation into De Beers' diamond monopoly, the first of its kind by any European authority. The assault was all too undignified for Ogilvie Thompson. He angrily denounced the 'worldwide orchestrated programme of vilification and abuse against Minorco, Anglo American, De Beers, [and] Harry Oppenheimer'.[100]

On 2 February 1989, after a gruelling winter siege, Minorco finally broke through: on that day the British Monopolies and Mergers Commission ruled the Consgold deal could go ahead. A major roadblock was cleared. Regulatory approvals in other jurisdictions followed. Minorco sweetened its offer to £3.2 billion (up from $4.9 billion to $5.65 billion, in dollar terms). Once again, Consgold repudiated it. In any event, there was still an American hurdle to overcome: Newmont, Consgold's largest shareholder, had filed an antitrust suit against Minorco in a US district court, and a preliminary injunction blocked Minorco's path. Meanwhile, the whiff of apartheid hovered over Minorco. Three years previously, the US Congress had enacted the Comprehensive Anti-Apartheid Act, which imposed a raft of sanctions on South Africa. Although President Reagan vetoed it, the House and Senate overrode him. The legislation did not prevent Minorco from doing business in the United States, but that meant little to American workers, who would have been hard pressed to identify Johannesburg on a map: they were told a takeover would jeopardise their jobs. Consgold's attorneys approached the matter from yet another angle. They directed a 26-page letter to President Reagan, laying out their case. The buyout, they argued, would hand South Africa the lion's share of global gold production, and of titanium and zirconium too – strategic minerals essential to the American defence and space industries. If Minorco managed to get its claws into Consgold, that might open the door to price-fixing and restrictions on production. US national security interests would be threatened.

On 16 May 1989 Judge Michael Mukasey of the New York District Court in Lower Manhattan delivered his verdict. He ruled that the injunction, which effectively barred Minorco from taking over Consgold, had to remain in place. Through Mukasey's ruling – 'Judge Mucousy', JOT sneered in private – the US had struck back against the Oppenheimer empire. Minorco's plans were pulverised. 'What we have proved in New York', Agnew crowed in response, is that 'South African control is just not acceptable in large areas of the world.'[101] His triumphalism would be short-lived. Only three months later Consgold was sold to Britain's biggest conglomerate, the renowned corporate raider and asset stripper Hanson plc. It fetched a much lower price than Minorco's offer. For Oppenheimer the botched bid was a personal blow. A few months after announcing his retirement in 1982, he had told a group of senior Anglo staff that it was in Minorco's and Consgold's interests to work together closely.[102] He regarded a tie-up as mutually desirable. Looking back on his career in later years, with the benefit of hindsight and a touch of revisionism, Oppenheimer recast the failure as the group's 'luckiest' escape: 'I'm very sorry for the loss of prestige ... but it would never have worked. I don't think we could have got on with the people involved. We would have had continual miseries, and I think it's much better as we are.'[103] By then, he could afford to be sanguine. But, at the time, HFO experienced the whole affair as an unseemly humiliation. He thought Minorco's leadership had bungled the deal, and the unrelenting negative publicity rankled him. His empire had been sullied. He found it 'insufferable' to be attacked on the grounds of South African connections, HFO told the *Financial Times*, 'particularly by a group which has been very active in South Africa and which has certainly not been in the forefront of opposition to the apartheid policy'.[104] He could barely conceal his disdain. But the hint of bitterness was understandable, for, unlike GFSA, Oppenheimer and his South African business empire had spent the previous fifteen years pursuing a reformist agenda. Apartheid was in terminal decline and, together with his corporations, HFO helped accelerate its death.

TWELVE

Reformer

1974–1989

Questioned by an interviewer from *Forbes* magazine in December 1972 on the 'danger of a black uprising', Oppenheimer brushed the notion aside: 'Oh no. Americans shouldn't worry about that. None of these things is in the time scale that you ought to think about when you invest.'[1] Less than four years later, young black protesters in Soweto exploded in anger. The Soweto uprising was the biggest and most significant rebellion against apartheid since Sharpeville 16 years earlier. It shook the foundations of the racial order. Although Prime Minister BJ Vorster's government moved quickly to reassert control, the aftershocks reverberated widely. For Oppenheimer, the insurrection was a watershed, and it heralded a change in his approach to public life. If South Africa was to be spared the kind of bloody revolution which had installed Marxist governments in Angola and Mozambique, he reasoned, then it must embark on a programme of socio-economic reform – a precursor to peaceful political change. That conviction led Oppenheimer to establish the Urban Foundation (UF) with Anton Rupert in 1976. Backed by the corporate sector's money and skills, the UF sought to improve the living conditions of township dwellers and to anchor a stable, propertied black middle class in the cities. This, HFO hoped, would give black people a stake in the economy, lay the groundwork for an orderly political transition, and foil violent regime change. In 1979 Vorster's successor, PW Botha, initiated a series of socio-economic reforms which fired Oppenheimer's optimism. Away from the public glare he reached out to the Afrikaner leader and offered him support. Yet, amid intense domestic and international pressure to end apartheid (marked by the escalation of black resistance at home and a vigorous sanctions and disinvestment campaign abroad), politically Botha barely budged. In spite of a floundering economy and major political upheavals, he remained intransigent to the bitter end. 'If the ship sinks, which I don't think it will, I will go down with it,' Oppenheimer told *The Economist* in 1982, a line he repeated on more than one occasion during that turbulent decade.[2] He exercised all the soft power at his disposal to help steady the ship and chart a course towards democracy. He did this both institutionally – in Anglo American and the UF – and, during and after his retirement, through his personal contacts with the former US Secretary of State Henry Kissinger, the British Prime Minister Margaret Thatcher, and PW Botha himself, as well as a variety of influential friends in industry and politics. But when the lineaments of change did eventually take shape on the horizon, on 2 February 1990, it was a moment that took even HFO by surprise.

Before the Storm: Black Consciousness, White Fears, and the Frontline States

The economic downturn of the early 1970s, widespread industrial action following the Durban strikes, and black discontent over low wages and racialised labour market inequalities all created a pressure-cooker environment in the second half of BJ Vorster's prime ministership. The rise of the Black Consciousness Movement (BCM) was another acute stress. Between 1975 and 1976, several leaders of the South African Students' Organisation (SASO) and the Black People's Convention (BPC) were put on trial for breaches of the Terrorism Act. They used the opportunity to expound the core tenets of the BCM. By then, Steve Biko, the movement's leader, had developed a sophisticated critique of white liberals, which he articulated in various essays, most notably 'Black souls in white skins?' and 'White racism and black consciousness'. In Biko's view, liberal incrementalism, coupled with suffocating paternalism, blunted black consciousness and stunted revolutionary change. Liberals' rigid insistence on colour-blind non-racialism was a mask for the perpetuation of white privilege. It erected a barrier to black liberation. Biko censured white liberals for verbalising the complaints of blacks 'beautifully', all the while skilfully extracting what suited them from 'the exclusive pool of white privileges'.[3] As the ideology of Black Consciousness evolved, its focus broadened to the impact of capitalism and imperialism on the socio-economic conditions of black people.[4] Intellectually, Oppenheimer could appreciate the trenchancy of Biko's analysis. But emotionally he intuited a deep-seated anxiety among white South Africans, particularly white liberals. They feared that the summary abandonment of white minority rule would 'not only involve the giving up of a privileged position' (which sooner or later, Oppenheimer conceded, 'has to be given up'), but the destruction of free enterprise and the parliamentary system, too.[5]

As the SASO–BPC trial unfolded, Vorster's faltering attempts at détente with neighbouring African states heightened the tension and called into question the life expectancy of white rule. Oppenheimer applauded the Prime Minister's 'courageous efforts' to improve South Africa's relations with her neighbours.[6] The need for détente, he maintained, was made more urgent by developments in Mozambique and Angola. Nor could it be divorced from the government's domestic policy of consulting with black homeland leaders. 'Indeed,' Oppenheimer told Anglo's share-holders, 'the establishment and development of dialogue between the races in South Africa is essential to the success of the détente policy externally.'[7] The difficulty was that the geopolitics of southern Africa were shifting unpredictably. In 1974 the Caetano government in Portugal was toppled in the Carnation Revolution, a military coup orchestrated by left-leaning officers in the Armed Forces Movement. This paved the way for pro-Marxist black nationalists to seize power in the former Portuguese colonies. Almost overnight, the *cordon sanitaire* that had long given white South Africans psychological comfort was erased. In Mozambique, Frelimo's victory and Samora Machel's installation as president rallied the liberation movement's comrades in the ANC. After Frelimo's success, SASO and the BPC staged a celebratory rally in Durban, replete with publicity flyers which revelled in the defeat of settler colonialism next door and invoked the prospect of revolutionary violence on home soil. In Angola, Vorster became embroiled in a covert and costly invasion as he tried, unsuccessfully, to prevent the Cuban-backed People's Movement for the Liberation of Angola (MPLA) from gaining the upper hand over its anti-communist rival, the National Union for the Total Independence of Angola (Unita). In South West Africa, a territory under South African control, the South African Defence Force engaged in low-intensity combat with the South West Africa People's Organisation (Swapo), which fought for Namibian independence. In Rhodesia, the long-term prospects for white supremacy were dimmed by full-scale guerrilla warfare between Ian Smith's defence forces and black nationalists supported by Frelimo.

HFO was a bit player in some of the unfolding action. In Zaire he held long, meandering meetings with President Mobutu Sese Seko and Mobutu's ally Holden Roberto, president of the National Liberation Front of Angola (FNLA). Though its leadership was largely in exile, FNLA, like Unita, received financial aid from the American government to oppose the MPLA. The encounters proved inconclusive, but Oppenheimer thought both Mobutu and Roberto were receptive to Vorster's policy of détente, and he offered to brief the Minister of Foreign Affairs, Hilgard Muller, on their talks.[8] In South West Africa, owing to De Beers' extensive diamond interests, HFO kept his finger on the pulse of political developments. From 1975 to 1977, under the chairmanship of the former National Party MP Dirk Mudge, the Turnhalle Conference broached the subject of South West Africa's constitutional future. Oppenheimer had his oar in. He went on to support Mudge's Democratic Turnhalle Alliance (DTA), Swapo's main opposition. Edmond de Rothschild asked HFO to meet Kuaima Riruako, the Herero chief who joined the DTA. In addition to the French and the Israelis, Rothschild informed Oppenheimer, 'it looks as if some conservative African governments and also the Saudis prefer this Association to ... SWAPO'.[9] HFO duly met with Riruako, who wanted party funding, but he opted to channel his support through Mudge instead. 'Whether or not the DTA could win an election in Namibia is a matter about which it is most difficult to judge,' Oppenheimer replied to Rothschild, 'though I would certainly think that in the interests of the country as well as in our [De Beers'] particular interests it would be very desirable that they should.'[10] Clearly, the Anglo empire's strategic interests were not always in conflict with those of the South African government, and in the Union Buildings Hilgard Muller was one of HFO's most sympathetic contacts, usually willing to lend his ear.[11]

As Oppenheimer surveyed regional developments with mounting unease, he came to the obvious conclusion. 'We simply cannot afford to go on like this,' he warned a symposium of the United States–South Africa Leader Exchange Program (US-SALEP) in March 1976.[12] Oppenheimer realised that South Africa could not remain immune from the break-up of colonial empires and the formation of independent black states. At the same time, the only certain outcome of South Africa's defeat in Angola, he asserted, would be 'the extension of the African power vacuum' into the richest and strategically most important country on the continent. The South African government needed to couple the backyard diplomacy of détente (and presumably support for the adversaries of Frelimo and the MPLA) with a clean-up of its own doorstep. The apparatus of racial discrimination had to be dismantled. Apartheid had to go. Yet it was impossible, Oppenheimer continued, for 'even the most ardent liberal' to imagine that the immediate alternative to white rule in South Africa was a 'true democracy' in which racial differences meant nothing. A middle path between apartheid and assimilation, an old expression of his from the 1950s, must be found. A multiparty system, underpinned by the non-racial qualified franchise, was the way forward. As Oppenheimer argued in the Chairman's Lecture at the London Stock Exchange in May 1976: 'To my mind, the maintenance of parliamentary government, with opposition parties freely expressing their views, is more important for the defence of individual freedom than is the attainment of full democracy on a one-man, one-vote basis.'[13] In the long run, it would be essential to devise effective guarantees for a multiparty system as a precondition of change. In the interim, as a show of good faith and in the interests of interracial unity, Oppenheimer suggested to the US-SALEP conference, the Nationalists should commit themselves to a programme for ending racial discrimination. In a quid pro quo, opponents of separate development might be persuaded to suspend their criticism of the government, pending concrete action.

Oppenheimer's ruminations were given pride of place on the opinion pages of the *New York Times*.[14] But in South Africa, his 'plan for unity', as it was labelled by the press, was flayed across the political spectrum, by friend and foe alike.[15] De Villiers Graaff, determinedly leading the United Party into oblivion, saw it as an attack on white hegemony. He was reportedly 'incensed' by the proposal.[16] So too was Andries Treurnicht, the *verkrampte* National Party parliamentarian whom Vorster had recently appointed as deputy minister of Bantu education. Mangosuthu Buthelezi, Chief Minister of the KwaZulu homeland, founder of the Inkatha cultural movement, and a gradualist drawn increasingly closer to HFO, registered his objections. On the left, Mohammed Timol, an activist whose brother Ahmed had infamously perished in suspicious circumstances while in police detention six years earlier, panned the suggestion. The mere elimination of racial discrimination, Timol accurately foresaw, would be insufficient. Africans, Indians and Coloureds demanded 'a complete transformation' of the 'political, social and economic order'.[17]

Oppenheimer gave voice to his ideas on the eve of the Soweto uprising, just as the Cold War generated hot flashpoints among some of the so-called Frontline States bordering, or near to, South Africa. This loose coalition of countries, incorporating Angola, Botswana, Lesotho, Mozambique, Tanzania and Zambia, was committed to ending apartheid and white minority rule in Rhodesia. It was also rife with infiltration by foreign powers pursuing vested interests. In Zambia and Tanzania, where President Kenneth Kaunda and President Julius Nyerere comingled crippling socialist policies with misty-eyed Pan-Africanism, the Soviet Union and China vied for influence. 'KK' also built bridges with the US. In Mozambique and Angola the red peril loomed large. Both Moscow and Beijing supplied arms to Frelimo and the MPLA, and Cuba reinforced the MPLA with thousands of combat troops. Oppenheimer decried the tightening grip of Marxist movements on the newly independent black states and on African thought in the white-controlled South. They had become 'a real impediment', he emphasised at the London Stock Exchange, to the peaceful solution of South Africa's problems.[18] It was one thing for Britain to have a democratic socialist government in the context of a multiparty system – as it then did, under Jim Callaghan's premiership – but the left-wing hold over southern Africa was 'quite another' matter. Oppenheimer bemoaned the purchase of left-wing ideas in Africa, gained not by winning intellectual assent to socialist doctrine, but by conflating leftist ideology with African grievances and aspirations. He used a stock exchange analogy for his audience's benefit: the expansion of left-wing influence in Africa had not been organic, he declared; instead it had come about by way of 'a number of takeover bids'. The churches, too, had been complicit: they had largely been 'taken over' by ideologues, and had redirected their energies from 'saving souls' to supporting a 'particular concept of social justice'.

Although Oppenheimer did not name the culpable clerics, in South Africa this might have been a reference to the Christian Institute (CI), an ecumenical organisation led by the Afrikaner cleric Beyers Naudé. Naudé struck up a relationship with Biko and reached out to Black Consciousness groupings. With the support of the South African Council of Churches, the CI had convened the Study Project on Christianity in Apartheid Society (Spro-cas) between 1969 and 1974. Directed by Peter Randall, Oppenheimer's social-democratic detractor during the 1974 election, Spro-cas was a think tank geared to envisioning alternatives to apartheid. It was liberal in character, but its ecumenism was coloured by radical notions of social justice. Randall's strand of Christian faith – and his sceptical attitude towards 'white' monopoly capital – was not in tune with Oppenheimer's conventional Anglicanism, which tended to treat Western civilisation, industrialisation and economic growth as formative components of the just social order. Oppenheimer's religious beliefs suffused his politics in a much subtler way. Desmond Tutu, the politically rumbustious Anglican Dean of St Mary's Cathedral in Johannesburg (and later Archbishop of Cape Town), worked closely with Naudé and participated in the Spro-cas commissions. He had approached Oppenheimer back in 1956 to subsidise his theological studies. At the time, Oppenheimer sent Tutu a cheque for £200 and wished him well in helping to build 'a spirit of greater tolerance and understanding' in South Africa.[19] The magnate and the mendicant continued to enjoy occasional contacts in the dark days of apartheid. Tutu was one of four black leaders who kept Oppenheimer in touch with 'black opinion' during the 1970s and 1980s. The others were Chief Buthelezi; Lucas Mangope, the leader of the Bophuthatswana homeland; and Nthato Motlana, the Mandelas' family doctor and a businessman whose Black Community Programmes in Soweto, particularly the health centres, were partly financed either directly by HFO or by the Anglo American and De Beers Chairman's Fund. Despite their mutual goodwill, there would be significant political differences between Oppenheimer and Tutu in the 1980s, especially regarding economic sanctions and disinvestment.[20]

As the churches lent their moral support to black liberation movements and embraced Marxist-Leninist dogma in the name of social justice – much like the Catholic advocates of liberation theology in Latin America – Oppenheimer vocalised white South Africans' deepest fears. They were afraid of a one-party state controlled by an authoritarian, black, communist government. In order to assuage white anxieties, Oppenheimer believed that South Africa should frame its dilemma not simply in terms of a gradual and peaceful transition to black majority rule. 'We are faced with the very much more difficult question', Oppenheimer concluded at the London Stock Exchange, 'of how to do justice – politically, socially and economically – to all races without destroying the great achievements of the long period of exclusive white rule.'[21] That necessitated the maintenance of free enterprise and private property as the bedrock of society: they secured the conditions for economic prosperity, which went hand in hand with 'racial peace'. For Oppenheimer, what had to be avoided at all costs was a destructive race war, a nihilistic Marxist revolution, and a single-party system under black majority rule without checks and balances. In order to obviate that disaster, the Nationalists needed to bring the 'melancholy catalogue of injustice' – the pass laws, the migrant labour system, and racially discriminatory legislation – to an end, sooner rather than later. They also needed to find a better accommodation with moderate black leaders.

The American Connection

In the United States, Oppenheimer's message resonated with establishment Republicans. President Richard Nixon's administration, under the lead of his omnipresent National Security Advisor and Secretary of State, Henry Kissinger, pursued a policy of détente vis-à-vis the Soviet Union. But it also attempted to counter the fungal spread of communism globally. This entailed a pivot towards southern Africa and a measure of sympathy for the continent's white tribe. In Rhodesia, with Vorster's backing, Kissinger encouraged Ian Smith to let some steam out of the pot. He pressured Smith into hastening the country's peaceful transition to black majority rule. After Nixon's ignominious resignation in 1974, Kissinger was retained by President Gerald Ford. He stayed on as secretary of state until Jimmy Carter, a Democrat, took over the presidential reins in 1977.[22] For most of Kissinger's incumbency as secretary of state, De Beers' difficulties with the American antitrust authorities precluded face-to-face encounters with Oppenheimer in Washington. Nevertheless, outside politics, the two had mutual friends – most notably, Charles and Jane Engelhard's daughter Annette. Once Oppenheimer was able to travel freely to the US, he and Kissinger met in person and began to see each other frequently. In calibrating the application of realpolitik to South Africa, Kissinger would come to draw heavily on Oppenheimer for information and advice.[23]

In April 1976 Kissinger toured southern Africa. In Lusaka, he delivered one of the most significant speeches in the history of US foreign relations. His plea for 'a peaceful end to institutionalised inequality' in South Africa, and his words of praise for Kaunda, brought the lachrymose Zambian leader to tears.[24] American policy towards South Africa, Kissinger promised, would be based upon the premise that 'within a reasonable time' there would be 'a clear evolution toward equality of opportunity' and 'basic human rights for all South Africans'.[25] Behind the scenes, Oppenheimer facilitated at least one episode in the sequence of Kissinger's African shuttle diplomacy. Through the offices of Anglo American, he arranged for Joshua Nkomo, the leader of the Zimbabwe African People's Union (Zapu), to meet the US Secretary of State in Lusaka. More so than Robert Mugabe, the bookish but bloodthirsty guerrilla leader who later prised control of the Zimbabwe African National Union (Zanu), Nkomo adopted a conciliatory pose. He appeared to be an evolutionary moderate, prepared to bring an end to the bloodshed of the Bush War by negotiating a settlement with Smith's regime; and he attracted support and funding from corporate sources, including the 'unpleasant and unacceptable face of capitalism', 'Tiny' Rowland's Lonrho.[26]

Nkomo was Kaunda's friend and ally. After consulting HFO, Zach de Beer gave the go-ahead for Nkomo to be ferried from Salisbury to Lusaka on Anglo's jet. 'It should be noted that Anglo has previously used its executive jet to bring ANC leaders out of Rhodesia into Zambia for discussions with Pres Kaunda,' the US Embassy in Lusaka confusingly suggested, possibly in reference to Bishop Muzorewa's African National Council.[27] State House in Zambia had also previously used Anglo as a communications link for messages to ANC leaders, according to the embassy. Naturally, the matter had to be handled discreetly. Anglo was 'very sensitive' about any potential disclosure of its role in the arrangement, the American officials cautioned. They understood that Anglo was 'deeply involved with Nkomo in financial support', the details of which were 'carefully shielded'. The immediate significance of Nkomo's meeting with Kissinger is hazy. But in September, the US Secretary of State returned to southern Africa, and this time he proceeded purposefully to Pretoria. Backed by Vorster, whose patience with Smith was wearing thin, Kissinger cornered the Rhodesian into accepting black majority rule within stipulated time frames. That set the stage for the Geneva Conference and the Lancaster House negotiations. Although it had been his own diplomacy which closed off all of Smith's escape routes, Kissinger subsequently reflected, he did not relish having to tell his interlocutors that 'their way of life was coming to an end'.[28] A few months after Kissinger's intervention, Zapu and Zanu established a joint platform known as the Patriotic Front. Meanwhile, Oppenheimer kept an anxious eye on Anglo's commercial interests in Rhodesia (and on Nkomo). He met Kaunda in March 1977, and told him in no uncertain terms that Nkomo had damaged his reputation and popularity by allying himself with Mugabe.[29] The message was relayed to the Zapu leader and back-channelled to the US Embassy.

Oppenheimer's insights on the politics of the region were equally valued by the civil rights leader Andrew Young, whom President Carter appointed as the first black US ambassador to the United Nations in 1977. Oppenheimer was struck by Young's simple message – that if businessmen knew segregation was bad for business, then they should use their power to root it out of the workplace – and he invited Young to address the South African Chamber of Commerce on the theme.[30] Young was eager for Carter to meet HFO. He told Carter's National Security Advisor, Zbigniew Brzeziński, that Oppenheimer and Anglo American were 'the closest thing to a true opposition in South Africa'.[31] 'I see him as a friend, a committed humanist, and a powerful ally in our efforts to promote nonviolent change in South Africa,' Young motivated his submission. It does not appear that the meeting went ahead. Ideologically, Oppenheimer was much more in sympathy with Carter's successor, President Ronald Reagan – one of a troika of like-minded world leaders elected contemporaneously, together with Thatcher in Britain and Helmut Kohl in West Germany. Reagan's monetarist assault on Keynesian orthodoxy in the 1980s chimed with Oppenheimer's own economic philosophy.

Between March and April 1976, Milton Friedman, winner of the Nobel Prize in Economics that year, and later an advisor to the Reagan administration, visited South Africa. He dined at Brenthurst during his stay and picked the industrialist's brains. 'This is wealth and affluence with a capital W and a capital A,' Friedman rhapsodised afterwards, 'a magnificent estate landscaped to the tee, Japanese gardens, rose gardens, swimming pools, tennis courts, you name it, and a house which is itself an art museum filled with priceless original paintings by all of the great artists of the world.'[32] The eminent economist found HFO 'extremely interesting' and 'highly knowledgeable' about global finance. Bridget was 'a rather large robust woman', he observed, with a 'great interest in horses and horse racing'. On his return home, Friedman mulled over his visit for *Newsweek*. The free marketeer expressed abhorrence for apartheid but he submitted two caveats: first, 'how complex the actual situation is', and, second, how vital it was for America's national interests 'not to be absorbed into the Soviet camp'.[33] By comparison with the Soviet Union and many post-independence black governments, Friedman opined, South Africa was a 'model' of freedom and enlightenment. He thought that Kissinger, 'a great man who has no talent for economics',[34] was rushing Rhodesia into black majority rule. Apart from the swipe at Kissinger, it is hard not to detect a vestigial trace of Oppenheimer's thinking in Friedman's meditations. However, what neither the monetary theorist nor the mining magnate adequately grasped was the raw fury kindled by festering black resentment. That would soon be unmistakeable.

The Soweto Riots and the Birth of the Urban Foundation

Three weeks after Friedman penned his piece, South Africa reached a fiery crossroads. The dramatic events of 16 June 1976 signalled a turning point in the country's history. They were a seminal moment in the decline of apartheid. On that day, some fifteen to twenty thousand black schoolchildren took to the streets of Soweto in protest against an incendiary instruction that Afrikaans be enforced as the medium of instruction in half of all subjects not taught in the vernacular. In fact, the townships were a tinderbox waiting to be ignited. There was already a widespread feeling of frustration among urban blacks about their state of political powerlessness, economic impoverishment and social distress. On 16 June, black students gathered en masse with placards bearing slogans such as 'Down with Afrikaans', 'Viva Azania', and 'If we must do Afrikaans, Vorster must do Zulu'. The rallying cries of the Black Consciousness Movement punctuated the air. When the police tried to disperse the crowd with tear gas, the schoolchildren retaliated by throwing stones. Overwhelmed and undertrained, the officers opened fire using live rounds. Zolile Hector Pieterson, a schoolboy not yet in his teens, was the first child to be killed. After that, chaos erupted. Within a week, at least 176 people lay dead and over 1100 were injured. Over the next few months, violent rioting broke out in black settlements across the country, from Pretoria to Port Elizabeth to Cape Town. A seemingly endless cycle of repression and rebellion ensued. Workers engaged in large-scale stayaways. In September, over half a million black workers withheld their labour on the Witwatersrand alone. It was only towards the end of the following year that the nationwide unrest died down. By that point more than 600 people had lost their lives, many of them gunned down by police.

Journalist Sam Nzima's photograph of Pieterson's lifeless body being carried by a friend while Pieterson's dazed sister runs desperately alongside them was published in newspapers around the world. It made a martyr of the boy, and brought the horrors of apartheid to international attention in a striking way. For Oppenheimer, the Soweto uprising marked a profound shift in his thinking. He re-evaluated his approach to South Africa's racial quandary and his interaction with the Nationalist government. Oppenheimer sensed that black urban dwellers, ground down by decades of racial oppression and socio-economic deprivation, were ripe for revolution. If the government could not (or would not) defuse the situation by initiating a programme of upliftment and reform, then the private sector would have to take the lead, and nudge the state along. In reality, like a back-seat driver, business steered the apartheid regime into the era of reform, while reassuring South Africa's political masters that it was their own hands on the steering wheel. Oppenheimer's new slant provided the impetus for the 'businessmen's conference on the quality of life in urban communities', convened at the Carlton Hotel on 29 and 30 November 1976. Ultimately, it led to the establishment of the Urban Foundation – a crucial vehicle for social change and political reform in South Africa.

The Urban Foundation's parentage was mixed, but Oppenheimer was certainly the driving force behind its conception. Clive Menell and his wife, Irene, Oppenheimer's progressive Parktown neighbours, were also involved; they were inspired by an act of business statesmanship abroad. After the 1967 Detroit Riot, which pitted poverty-stricken black protesters against police, Henry Ford II bankrolled the formation of the 'New Detroit' committee with an initial $2 million grant from the Ford Foundation. The committee was set up by members of the American corporate elite to coordinate urban renewal projects in the wake of the insurrection, and to take the sting out of radical Black Power activism. Anglo drew similar inspiration overseas. The corporation sent a delegation from its industrial relations team, led by Chris du Toit, to attend the United Nations Conference on Human Settlements in Vancouver between 31 May and 11 June 1976. Galvanised by the proceedings, Anglo planned its own conference on sustainable urban housing for November. The Menells learnt about it from Freddie van Wyk, the director of the South African Institute of Race Relations, and George Palmer, editor of the *Financial Mail*. They persuaded Nick Diemont to expand the scope of the symposium. Diemont then sold the idea on to Zach de Beer and eventually Oppenheimer himself. In this way, the Menells managed to 'hijack' Anglo's conference.[35]

With an eye on political strategy, Oppenheimer decided to cast the net wider. He enlisted the support of Afrikaner big business. On his way back from the United States, where Kissinger had stressed to him how disturbed the American government was by the Soweto riots, HFO stopped off in London. There he called on Anton Rupert at Rupert's Grosvenor House suite, and coaxed the Afrikaner tycoon on board. 'I don't think it took him too long to convince me – we were *ad idem* from the start', Rupert later recalled.[36] Next Oppenheimer turned his attention to Wim de Villiers, then running the General Mining–Union Corporation, and talked him into participating. 'Lang Dawid' de Villiers, managing director of Nasionale Pers, agreed to act as a liaison with Pretoria, but it soon became evident that the Minister of Bantu Administration, MC Botha, was unwilling for government officials to get involved. Manie Mulder, head of the West Rand Administration Board, and other civil servants were instructed not to attend. Such was the lingering lack of trust between the public and private sectors. BJ Vorster chided 'Lang Dawid' for doing Oppenheimer's bidding: 'I don't trust him. Everything he stands for is inimical to what I stand for,' the Prime Minister thundered about HFO.[37] But in spite of his objections, Vorster did not attempt to scupper the conference, and in November 1976 more than two hundred prominent business people descended on the Carlton Hotel. They included Oppenheimer, Rupert, and a welter of miners, bankers and retailers, like the supermarket supremo Raymond Ackerman. Several black invitees, many of whom had made a name for themselves in civic life, were in attendance. Among them were Franklin Sonn, a Coloured high school principal and later rector of Cape Town's Peninsula Technikon. Ellen Kuzwayo, the women's rights activist who served on the Soweto Committee of Ten (precursor to the Soweto Civic Association), and whose research on black women and community development Oppenheimer sponsored out of his own pocket in the 1980s, was another.[38]

Rupert cut to the heart of the matter in his closing address: 'We cannot survive unless we have a free market economy, a stable black middle class with the necessary security of tenure, personal security and a feeling of hope for betterment in the heart of all of our peoples.'[39] What this meant in practice for black urban dwellers was more jobs, better training, a living wage, greater commercial opportunities, improved housing prospects and expanded home ownership, and the provision of decent recreational facilities. An urban development foundation, Rupert concluded, was required to coordinate the private sector's endeavours, and to act as a catalyst in transforming black township communities into 'stable, essentially middle-class societies subscribing to the values of … free enterprise'.[40] Thus was the Urban Foundation born, ushered into life by two titans of the business world, with Oppenheimer as chairman and Rupert as vice-chair. One was the embodiment of the English *geldmag*, the other was the face of Afrikaner capital. It was a pairing that would have been inconceivable fifteen years earlier, and certainly not when Rembrandt listed on the Johannesburg Stock Exchange in 1956. At that time, Oppenheimer still bore the brunt of 'Hoggenheimer' taunts outside

Parliament. But by 1976 the sands had shifted appreciably. In the corporate sphere, the Anglo-Boer War had been consigned to the past, and the armistice had led to a *toenadering* (rapprochement). The realigned forces now constituted a significant bloc, one that could gently exert pressure on the National Party to reform. It was time, the government would soon learn, to adapt or die.

Great care was taken to strike the right political balance at the conference – to ensure, in Diemont's words, that it was not seen as 'a left-wing plot to discredit the government'.[41] Even so, the occasion generated tensions. Richard van der Ross, rector of the University of the Western Cape, proposed that the assembled employers should commit to doing away with the colour bar in industry. After intensive discussion, mediated by Oppenheimer, it was agreed that Van der Ross's proposal would be accommodated in the UF's re-drafted credo. Accordingly, the *Rand Daily Mail* framed the conference proceedings under the headline 'Businessmen reject job reservation', which prompted Wim de Villiers to rattle off a litany of complaints. He grumbled to Oppenheimer: 'The only gain has been to placate those who did not fully appreciate the fact that inclusion of a political objective would emasculate the Foundation before it got off the ground.'[42] The government now regarded the UF as a political pressure group, De Villiers protested, and this made him 'extremely pessimistic about the viability of our venture'. Oppenheimer thought De Villiers was over-reacting. 'What is important', he replied, 'is that the whole of the press, other than the *Rand Daily Mail*, and particularly the press which supports the Government, saw in the conference an effort to work with the Government and not against it.'[43] By and large, the Fourth Estate was on the UF's side. The press's overall assessment was best summed up by the editor of the *Sunday Times*, Tertius Myburgh, a Dutch Reformed Church elder with close government contacts. 'If the Urban Foundation can harness the efforts of Blacks, the resources of big business, and the co-operation of the authorities,' he enthused, 'it could mean a major step towards dignity and peace in South Africa.'[44] The key thing, Oppenheimer underscored to De Villiers, was to get on with the business of establishing the foundation. They needed to find a suitable executive director, and let the UF show through its actions that it had no party political aims – that it was simply trying to do its best to improve conditions for black people in the urban areas.

On 14 December 1976, the Urban Foundation was formally registered as a non-profit organisation. Among its 25 directors were Clive Menell,

Zach de Beer, Dr FJC Cronjé (chairman of Nedbank), the black business leader Sam Motsuenyane (president of the National African Federated Chamber of Commerce), and Vuka Tshabalala (the first black advocate to practise in Natal).[45] The UF thus represented a broad multiracial coalition of interests. Symbolically, Oppenheimer and Rupert's partnership at the top united the English and Afrikaner business communities. The foundation's ability to exert political influence was strengthened by the individual membership of high-profile Afrikaner businessmen like Sanlam's Andries Wassenaar and Fred du Plessis, as well as the corporate membership of the Afrikaanse Handelsinstituut, the largest Afrikaner business organisation. Oppenheimer and Rupert felt that it was critical for the Urban Foundation to be run by someone of ability and standing, who would be politically acceptable to the government. They chose Jan Steyn, an impeccably credentialled Afrikaner judge, to serve as the foundation's inaugural chief executive. Steyn had a strong commitment to social justice, demonstrated by his work for Nicro, a non-profit organisation with a long history of promoting human rights and penal reform. He took a leave of absence from the bench. 'After having been cushioned for the previous thirteen years in the seat of judicial office, I suddenly found myself facing the prospect of being tossed into the turbulent waters of race relations and conflicts with authority,' Steyn later mused.[46] Under Steyn's stewardship, the UF notched up several successes. Apart from its function as a conduit for the funding of housing, education and other community services like the electrification of schools, the foundation produced high-quality research on urbanisation. It coupled long-term development with short-term amelioration. The UF promoted the idea of 99-year leaseholds for blacks living and working in the townships, which effectively allowed them to buy and sell property and bequeath it at will. Pressure by the foundation eventually led to the introduction of full freehold rights for blacks. This signalled a reversal of the government's long-held belief that Africans were temporary sojourners in white cities, and the foundation could largely claim the credit for it.

Anglo and De Beers were the Urban Foundation's biggest donors, initially accounting for a third of its income. Even though the foundation represented a broad constituency, many saw it as yet another appendage of the Anglo octopus. In truth, Anglo's reach, wide as it was, could only penetrate so far and with so much effect. Oppenheimer had realised this from the start. A body that could tap into a network only partially within Anglo's orbit would be able to attract more numerous sources of funding and harness multiple spheres of influence. Steyn proved to be a formidable fundraiser. Within five years the foundation was receiving funds from more than 150 businesses. Rembrandt was a mainstay, but Gencor, Barlow Rand, the banks, and retailers like Pick n Pay and Woolworths all contributed handsomely over the long run. Foreign companies with South African operations came to the party: Ford gave R1 million over four years, and British Petroleum and Shell donated almost as much. By 1985 the UF had raised R227 million in donor funding.[47] The foundation's international exposure led to offices being opened in London and New York. These turned out to be not so much satellites seeking further sponsorship, but primarily lobbying instruments. Like the South Africa Foundation, the UF's foreign arms tended to campaign hard against economic sanctions and disinvestment.[48]

To be sure, despite the Urban Foundation's institutional independence and diverse membership, there was a close convergence between its aims and outlook and Oppenheimer's own reform agenda. His intention for the UF, like the Free Market Foundation, also established in 1976, was that it would 'spread the message of free enterprise to young blacks'.[49] Blacks were to be persuaded of the tangible benefits of capitalist-led development. In HFO's view, the growth of a stable black middle class would be the best bulwark against revolution, the inevitable consequences of which (to wit, Angola and Mozambique) were too ghastly to contemplate. Besides, the Oppenheimer thesis had long held that racial discrimination and free enterprise were essentially incompatible. Given the composition of the UF, he felt, perhaps it would have more success in driving that message home to the government. The foundation embodied Oppenheimer's ethos, and it was plugged into the broader Anglo bureaucracy. HFO was a hands-on chairman. In 1979 Steyn contemplated resigning from the bench to devote himself full-time to the UF, a move encouraged by Oppenheimer. He promised to match Steyn's judicial remuneration and benefits. HFO got Anglo to underwrite guarantees that, once Steyn eventually left the foundation itself, he would 'be offered business positions which would carry the necessary annual income'.[50] When Steyn decided to take the plunge and peel off his judicial robes, Oppenheimer suggested a seat for him on the board of Anglo.[51] Mike Rosholt, the chairman of Barlow Rand (and, after HFO, of the Urban Foundation too), was an industrialist who saw himself very much in the Oppenheimer mould. Rosholt told HFO that he was glad about Steyn's decision to quit the bench, as 'he [Steyn] would have been virtually impossible to replace' at the foundation.[52] The

Barlows boss volunteered a number of suggestions for other boards Steyn might join – Barclays Bank was one – so that the former judge could become 'even better known', and 'better understand the workings of the private sector'.

Oppenheimer took a keen interest in the administration of the UF, in its budget allocations and policy direction. He agreed with Robin Lee, a director of the foundation, that the staff complement should be increased and that a proper executive committee should be established, since the interest of some board members had begun to wane.[53] One of those with a dwindling attention span was Rupert himself. He had redirected his zeal towards the Small Business Development Corporation, a non-profit lender established in 1981 to support small and medium enterprises. Confidentially, Steyn informed Oppenheimer that Rembrandt's founder had become 'somewhat remote' from the UF's activities, owing to his 'very rare attendance at meetings' and the 'abdication of his functions' to his alternate, Tienie Oosthuizen.[54] Rupert was less than enthusiastic about Steyn's plans to take on board directorships, especially the one at Barclays. 'You will forgive me if I speculate that the identity of the bank concerned may have played a significant role in this respect,' Steyn commented drily to HFO. 'Afrikaner nationalism still rears its ugly head from time to time,' he added disapprovingly.[55]

In fact, one of the UF's great accomplishments was its success in undermining Afrikaner nationalist ideology – as expressed in legislation – by producing pragmatic, evidence-based, strategic research to prod government policy in a reformist direction. Steyn regarded the foundation's efforts to lobby Piet Koornhof (the Minster of Co-operation and Development derisively known as 'Piet Promises') on the so-called Koornhof bills as a case in point.[56] This legislative package aimed at granting more local government power to urban blacks while tightening the laws on influx control. The UF forced what Joseph Lelyveld, the *New York Times* correspondent and keen Oppenheimer observer, called a 'tactical retreat'. The pullback came, Lelyveld wrote, after Koornhof received a 'painstaking analysis' of the proposals from 'a team of legal experts brought together by the Urban Foundation'.[57] As apartheid came up against economic reality in the 1980s, its ideological moorings began to slip. Nationalist officials and politicians no longer had a lodestar to guide their every decision. 'In this context of uncertainty', the UF's policy director, Ann Bernstein, noted, the government was likely to be influenced by policy recommendations which offered it 'a way out of its many impasses'. This was far more effective, she continued, than 'generalised calls for change'.[58] By avoiding open confrontation, the Urban Foundation managed to chip away at the foundations of apartheid. Apart from securing property rights for urban blacks, the UF prompted the abolition of influx control in 1986. Oppenheimer won grudging respect from erstwhile adversaries. When Koornhof was given his new ministerial appointment in 1978, he thanked Oppenheimer for the magnate's good wishes and ended his note somewhat beseechingly: 'I rely on your co-operation and prayers'.[59] The Deputy Minister of Foreign Affairs, DJ Louis Nel, wrote to congratulate HFO after reading the foundation's annual report.[60] Nel expressed sincere appreciation for the UF's work.

The Urban Foundation's gradualist approach was scorned by the left and the BCM, which saw it as a form of Vichy-like collaboration with the system of oppression. In September 1977 Biko was arrested and brutally interrogated. Biko's death, which resulted from injuries inflicted by the police, turned him into a martyr of the struggle and emboldened his followers. Alive to the potential blowback, in October the government banned, among other anti-apartheid organisations, SASO, the BPC and the CI, and two leading black newspapers, *The World* and the *Weekend World*. But a few months before its proscription, SASO had made its attitude to the UF clear. At a joint conference with the BPC, SASO passed a resolution which condemned the activities of the Urban Foundation. It accused the UF of sabotaging black interests by 'creating a black middle class'.[61] Notwithstanding such radical remonstrances, there is reason to believe that the UF's developmental initiatives built bridges between pragmatic whites and moderate blacks. They were now 'tramping around some of the same intellectual and practical spaces', according to Cyril Ramaphosa's biographer.[62] (Ramaphosa, the unionist who would go on to play a critical role in post-apartheid politics, not least of all as one of the ANC's key constitutional negotiators, and later as South Africa's president, served for a spell on the UF's Transvaal regional board, at the instigation of his friends Clive and Irene Menell.) In sum, the UF created a united multiracial front in business. It helped to improve the quality of life of urban blacks. Above all, the foundation served to bridge the gulf between the government and the private sector. It turned the tide of mistrust and contributed to the sea change which prefigured apartheid's fall. The foundation played a 'crucial' role in the process of political reform.[63]

*Co-operation or Confrontation? Women for Peace
and Opposition Politics*

The Soweto riots had a galvanising effect on Bridget as well as Harry. In September, Bridget approached Cecile Cilliers, an Afrikaans-speaking journalist, to launch a multiracial, apolitical organisation named Women for Peace (WFP).[64] Inspired by the Ulster Women's Peace Movement, it was aimed at promoting dialogue and using 'the power of women ... to explore all avenues in seeking peaceful change'.[65] Although it started life modestly in the drawing room at Brenthurst, by November WFP had attracted over a thousand women from all racial groups to its inaugural conference. They shared the pain and fears which had been stirred up by the Soweto uprising. The new movement received the blessing of Deborah Mabiletsa, the president of the Black Women's Federation, an organisation opposed to racial discrimination. In a country where black women and white women were largely strangers to one another outside the constraints of the servant–master relationship between maids in domestic service and their 'madams' in white households, WFP opened new avenues of communication and helped break down racial barriers. By the end of its first year, the organisation had attracted more than three thousand members, white and black, all working on small-scale, local projects to promote interracial harmony and equality of opportunity. WFP established numerous branches and concentrated its work on 'Centres of Concern' – community meeting places like church halls – where women could gather and learn practical skills such as literacy, sewing, typing or cooking.[66] In the Indian 'group area' of Lenasia, the Centre of Concern focused on feeding and caring for pensioners. Other centres in black townships set up libraries and stocked them with books. WFP lobbied large retailers to open discount stores near the townships; since township dwellers tended to spend disproportionately more of their income on basic foodstuffs for want of easy access to supermarkets, this initiative targeted a reduction in the cost of living. The organisation's most celebrated and enduring project (and Bridget's hobby horse) was its nationwide advocacy and distribution of the 'Wonderbox', a low-energy insulation cooker which worked on the haybox principle pioneered by women during the First World War. Over a period of several years, Bridget, her wing woman, Dailinah Khoza, and their team of volunteers traversed many of the region's most inhospitable rural areas in a Toyota HiAce van. They dished out Wonderboxes and gave practical cooking demonstrations using nutritious foods. These excursions, which often involved sleeping in bunk beds or similarly rustic accommodation, brought Bridget's no-nonsense demeanour to the fore. In Brits, the Wonderbox missionaries were received by townswomen dressed in their Sunday best. They were puzzled to find Bridget sporting an apron and walking shoes. 'But we expected a young, thin woman called Mrs Oppenheimer,' they quibbled. 'Bad luck,' Bridget snapped back, 'you have a tall, grey-haired, fat lady for Mrs Oppenheimer instead!'

It would be facile to dismiss WFP's welfarism as the work of do-gooders tinkering on the margins, well-meaning liberals inspired by the Victorian idea of social upliftment through self-help who merely reinforced the racial order. Certainly, that is what some of their contemporary critics thought. Even the Black Sash, the liberal women's campaign group which became radicalised in the 1980s, scoffed at Women for Peace. Soon after the formation of WFP, the Black Sash president, Sheena Duncan, accused the body of having 'no fire' in its belly; she characterised it as a 'harmless little organisation going nowhere fast.'[67] True to form, Bridget was pithily unapologetic. She would not allow 'militants' to use WFP as a 'political battlefront'. 'Our policy is … one of representation not confrontation … [and] we will not be dictated to by the Black Sash or any other group represented in the organisation.'[68] Despite her recently raised awareness of apartheid's cruelties, Bridget believed that WFP had to treat the Nationalist government not as an enemy to be overthrown, but one whose intransigence might be overcome if the organisation remained non-aligned and non-antagonistic. One of WFP's first actions had been to send a delegation to the hard-hearted Minister of Justice, Jimmy Kruger (who infamously said of Biko's death that it left him cold), to voice its concerns about the government's handling of the conflagration in Soweto. He received them cordially. Bridget's initial approach to Cilliers had been calculated – she wanted buy-in from the Afrikaner community – in the same way that HFO reached out strategically to Anton Rupert before launching the Urban Foundation. WFP mirrored the UF's modus operandi. The National Party's policies might 'lie in ruins', but the ruling party still had the support of the vast majority of Afrikaners; they were a 'tough, obstinate and courageous people', HFO informed his audience at a meeting of the Foreign Policy Association in New York in October 1977.[69] Peaceful change would never come about so long as Afrikaners believed their identity would be threatened if they ceased to hold on to political power. Oppenheimer tailored his approach to the Nationalists accordingly. Bridget echoed Harry's views on a non-conflictual path to change. But she was much less politically minded than he was: it is probably more accurate to describe Bridget's attitude to 'race relations' as conventionally colonial rather than progressive or liberal. Nevertheless, WFP did expand her racial horizons and sensitise her to racial injustice in ways that were personally unprecedented.

The care that HFO took not to upset the government over the UF should not be interpreted as co-option on his part, or a desire to appease the Nationalists. On the contrary, he remained implacably antagonistic to their political philosophy. Oppenheimer's support for the Progressives and their adversarial, Westminster-style of opposition politics was absolute. He was heartened by the party's quantum leap in 1974. After the general election of that year, Helen Suzman was joined by five Progressive benchmates after 13 lonely years in Parliament: Colin Eglin; René de Villiers, the former editor of *The Star*; Rupert Lorimer, who bagged the Orange Grove constituency; Frederik van Zyl Slabbert, the Afrikaner 'golden boy', who took Rondebosch by 1568 votes; and HFO's former son-in-law, Gordon Waddell. 'I am immensely delighted at these wonderful results,' HFO telexed Suzman; of course, they were 'based on your long years of courage [and] hard work', he applauded her.[70] Six weeks later, another Anglo man, Alex Boraine, won a by-election for the Progs in Pinelands, despite HFO having warned him: 'You haven't a hope of winning this seat.'[71] Six Progressives became seven in the House of Assembly. A fundamental realignment of the opposition caused the Progs to grow even bigger. Harry Schwarz, expelled from the United Party (UP) for bucking the party line, swelled the ranks of the Progs in 1975 with his band of Reform Party apostates. Two years later, the merged Progressive Reform Party (PRP) underwent another name change. In June 1977 the UP finally disbanded. It had been marooned in the political wilderness by a directionless captain in De Villiers Graaff, a defective strategic compass, and a bevy of defectors who preferred to throw themselves overboard rather than be shipwrecked. In fact, many of them jumped ship to the PRP. They responded to Eglin's appeal for *verligte* opponents of the Nats to join in a unified opposition. The upshot was the formation of the Progressive Federal Party (PFP) in September 1977. It cannibalised the remnants of the UP and returned to Parliament, after the election in November, as the official opposition with 17 MPs to the National Party's 134.

No stranger to mergers and acquisitions in corporate life, Oppenheimer viewed the Progressives' strategy of growth by absorption in a positive light. Politics, he saw, were now reshaping into a clearer (albeit lopsided) contest between two opposing visions: the dead end of apartheid and the salvation of liberal democracy. HFO remained a party man. He continued to make what Eglin called 'tremendously generous' contributions to the PFP's coffers;[72] and he subsidised the appointment of individual staffers like Nic Olivier, the party's national director of research.[73] Oppenheimer had long been accused by the Nationalists of having captured Prog policy, but in at least one important respect he toed the party line. Right up until 1978 HFO justified his support for the qualified franchise on the basis that it was a regulatory mechanism which sought to facilitate the gradualness of change over time. The timespan would end at that indeterminate point when every adult, black and white, had satisfied the educational requirements for full citizenship. Oppenheimer reiterated his stance at the Foreign Policy Association in 1977. It was one thing for foreign powers to press for an end to racial discrimination in South Africa, he submitted, but quite another for them to seek to impose a 'simplistic system based on majority rule and one-man-one-vote as the only reasonable solution'.[74] In May 1978, Oppenheimer addressed the International Monetary Conference in Mexico City, delivering a speech entitled 'Why the world should continue to invest in South Africa', where he reprised this theme. He insisted that nothing could be more 'absurd' than to expect foreign investor confidence would surge in the event of 'a rapid change-over to majority rule based on one man – one vote'.[75]

Only six months later Oppenheimer fell in line with the PFP's new constitutional policy. Formulated under Slabbert's direction, it represented a bold departure from the past. A committee chaired by Slabbert proposed a process of constitutional negotiations, underpinned by several core principles: universal franchise, federal government, a Bill of Rights, the sharing of executive power between majority and minority parties, a minority veto, and a constitutional court as the final arbiter of disputes.[76] On the question of the vote, the Progs were heavily swayed by input from Nthato Motlana. But there was also a broader realisation, sharpened by the Soweto uprising, that whatever the merits of the qualified franchise might have been in the past, 'political attitudes and constitutional realities', in Eglin's words, had changed the game in favour of universal suffrage.[77] Oppenheimer became a wary convert. He threw his weight behind Slabbert, too, when Eglin stood back for the younger, more dashing, more relatable Afrikaner as party leader in 1979, the outcome of a palace coup partly orchestrated by Waddell. Oppenheimer's relationship with Slabbert was by no means as warm and intimate as his friendships with De Beer, Eglin and Suzman. For his part, Slabbert felt Anglo American could have stumped up more money for the party.[78] But HFO saw in Slabbert a politician with crossover appeal, and he supported his leadership with optimism.

PW Botha and the Promise of Reform

The shifts in opposition politics were matched by ructions within the ruling party. They opened a window of opportunity for Oppenheimer and the private sector to lobby for reform. In September 1978 BJ Vorster resigned the premiership, ostensibly for health reasons, but in actuality because he had sanctioned (and lied about) government expenditure on secret propaganda projects abroad – the so-called Information Scandal – to buy political influence overseas. However, the pressure piled on Vorster for a host of different reasons: the bitter battles between *verligtes* and *verkramptes* in his party, the ongoing debacle in Angola, his cabinet's mishandling of the Soweto uprising, and an embarrassing exposé of the inner workings of the Broederbond, authored by two political journalists, Ivor Wilkins and Hans Strydom.[79] Into the breach stepped the hawkish Minister of Defence, PW Botha, a charmless, surly, belligerent bully. He succeeded Vorster as prime minister. A quarter of a century before, Oppenheimer had jousted with Botha in the House of Assembly – they were both elected to Parliament in 1948 – and he regarded him, according to Patrick Esnouf, HFO's personal assistant in the mid-1980s, as a 'brute'.[80] But Botha had one redeeming virtue: he was a pragmatist, attuned to the demands of the Cape's more enlightened Nationalists – the Afrikaner corporate elite – and he was unshakeably uninterested in the arcane, often acrimonious ideological debates about the essence of apartheid which tended to divide their counterparts to the north. To HFO's pleasant surprise, Botha turned out to be someone with whom – to borrow Thatcher's aphoristic appraisal of President Mikhail Gorbachev – he could do business.

Ever since Oppenheimer diagnosed the 'fundamental turning point' in the South African economy in 1972, Anglo American had focused its developmental initiatives on three broad fronts. Firstly, it espoused corporate social responsibility. Through the Chairman's Fund, the group poured money into 'special projects' for black beneficiaries, spanning education, technical training and rural development. For example, it sponsored the first black technical training college at Umlazi, a township south-west of Durban.[81] Mangosuthu Buthelezi had approached

HFO and Chief Mangosuthu Buthelezi at the official opening of the
Mangosuthu Technikon, 1982. *(Anglo American)*

Oppenheimer personally about the Umlazi facility, and in 1979 – at a
cost of over R5 million, the largest such project yet undertaken by the
Chairman's Fund – the Mangosuthu Technikon partially opened its doors
for teaching, though the construction work was incomplete.[82] Soon after
the events of June 1976, the Fund started building a teachers' training
college in Soweto. At the University of Cape Town, the Chairman's Fund
subsidised research on urban low-cost housing, with a view to lobbying
local authorities. In this way its work dovetailed with that of the Urban
Foundation.

Secondly, the corporation sought to train and upskill its own black
workers, hike their wages, and improve their conditions of employment.
That is what Bill Wilson's employment practices committee set out to do
in 1973. It led to the implementation of a uniform system of job evaluation
and the development of new pay structures in all of Anglo's mines. In
1975 the real earnings of black miners rose, overall, by 44 per cent.[83]
Higher wages meant that workers opted for shorter stints on the mines.
To Oppenheimer's mind this represented a 'significant amelioration of
the hardships of the migrant system'.[84] Anglo commissioned T Dunbar

Moodie, a sociologist at Wits, to document the living conditions of workers above ground, in the mine hostels, kitchens and beer halls. Moodie's inventory of woes – described by *The Times* in London as 'a chronicle of degradation, humiliation and near-institutionalised homosexuality' – jolted Anglo into action.[85] In 1977 Oppenheimer reported on improved conditions on the mines, 'particularly in the design of housing [and] the provision of further accommodation for senior black personnel and their families'.[86] Of course, it would be a mistake to take Anglo at its word. The pernicious effects of the migrant labour system were certainly not effaced during HFO's chairmanship. When it came to mine amenities, local mine managers – concerned with getting gold out of the ground and little else – frequently had different ideas from those of the pointy-shoed humanitarians at head office; and they could hamstring or hamper reform. For the most part Anglo did outshine its peers; but to many critics the group demonstrated a deficit of 'commitment and imagination' in addressing the plight of workers.[87] In 1976, Anglo would have had to spend R130 million – a few months' profit – for it to house ten per cent of its migrant labour force. But that never came to pass. In matters of health and safety, Anglo often fell feebly short. It failed to implement adequate measures to minimise the loss of life underground, or to stem the spread of lung diseases like silicosis and silico-tuberculosis. One of Suzman's constituents, KM Samela, wrote to her emotively: 'In 1963, that multi-millionaire of world fame, Harry Oppenheimer, ruined my life with TB in his gold mines.' 'Surely,' he reproached her, 'you people have left a hopeless impression on me.'[88] To such *cris de coeur* the white liberal establishment could find no satisfactory response. Anglo made greater strides on other fronts. In 1978 a working party of black employees and management representatives investigated complaints of racially discriminatory employment practices in the group. This led to the introduction of a range of programmes for black employees identified for job advancement. One of them was Anglo's long-running cadet scheme, which recruited, trained and developed high-performing black matriculants to form a pool of potential managers in the fields of finance and engineering.[89]

Thirdly, in the wake of the 1973 strikes, heightened black militancy on the mines, and the disaster at Western Deep Levels, Anglo adopted a forward-looking industrial relations policy, championed by Oppenheimer and crafted primarily by Alex Boraine and Bobby Godsell. This resulted in the creation, early in 1975, of a 'manpower resources division', which absorbed the greater part of the personnel division, the Employment

Practices Office, and the industrial relations function as a whole.[90] Outside 44 Main Street, Anglo made the case for industrial relations reform among its competitor companies in the Chamber of Mines and in discussions with the government. Anglo appealed for the recognition of black trade unions and the removal of the colour bar in industry (referred to as 'job reservation' for whites), which drove up the price of skilled labour. Such changes, Anglo proffered, would curb wildcat strikes, improve workforce productivity, and immunise the mines from labour unrest. In contrast to Anglo, several of the other mining houses, notably Gold Fields and (after 1980) Gencor, were reactionary and repressive in their approach.[91] They resisted Anglo's tack. Oppenheimer was the first South African industrialist to legitimise the fledgling black union movement. In a keynote address to the Institute of Personnel Management in 1974, he affirmed that black workers should enjoy the same trade union rights as white workers.[92] He called for a wide-ranging review of labour laws by a multiracial commission consisting jointly of the public and private sectors. And he maintained that no statute prevented employers from recognising and negotiating with black unions. Over the next decade, Anglo came to play a decisive role in the unionisation of the mining industry. As an employer of note – by the mid-1980s, Anglo employed more than a quarter of a million people on its gold mines, 25 000 in its diamond mines, and 100 000 more in platinum and coal – the group's actions reverberated widely.

In 1976 Oppenheimer joined the board of the newly established Institute for Industrial Relations, the first mainstream institution to appoint black unionists as trustees. His imprimatur conferred prestige. More importantly, Oppenheimer's dual emphasis on modernising the country's obsolete machinery of labour relations and championing the free enterprise system (despite Anglo's status as a monopoly) made a much greater impression on PW Botha than on any of the Prime Minister's predecessors. Traditionally, the Nationalists had been obsessed with capturing the commanding heights of the economy through parastatals like Iscor, and with pursuing a policy of *dirigisme*. Botha broke the mould. Convinced that South Africa faced a 'total onslaught' by communist agitators, the *Groot Krokodil* (big crocodile), as Botha was nicknamed for his fierceness, was highly receptive to the lexicon and leadership of free enterprise. He was much taken with the contemporary tract penned by Sanlam's Andries Wassenaar, *Assault on Private Enterprise: The Freeway to Communism*.[93] By the time Botha visited Soweto in 1979 – the first

Prime Minister to do so – he had slowly started coming round to the view that political stability and economic prosperity (fostered by a free-market economy, not state-led development) required a stable, black middle class. On this he and Oppenheimer were in accord. But whereas Botha assumed black embourgeoisement would placate the ungovernable urban underclass, forestall revolution and entrench white domination, Oppenheimer maintained it would expedite the regime's demise.

At the start of his premiership, Botha embarked on a series of reforms which seemed to vindicate Anglo's endeavours. They gave Oppenheimer hope. In 1979 Piet Riekert's Manpower Commission, appointed by the government, accepted that black urbanisation was irreversible, thirty years after the Fagan Commission had reached the same conclusion. Although it remained straitjacketed by the shibboleth of influx control, the Riekert Commission recommended that blacks permanently resident in urban areas – termed 'insiders' as opposed to homeland 'outsiders' – should be afforded additional workplace rights and limited representation in local government. This signalled an advance. Botha's administration eventually conceded that there were more disadvantages than benefits to influx control. Spurred on by the Urban Foundation, among others, it gave the green light to the Abolition of Influx Control Act in 1986.

Within the Institute for Industrial Relations, Oppenheimer argued for a commission of inquiry into labour laws. In 1977 Vorster's government appointed a commission on labour legislation headed by Professor Nic Wiehahn, into which Chris du Toit funnelled Anglo's inputs. Two years later the Wiehahn Commission released its report. It was to revolutionise industrial relations in South Africa. One of Wiehahn's central recommendations was the abolition of statutory job reservation. The commission advocated the principle of equal pay for equal work. It endorsed the official recognition of black trade unions and supported the legalisation of collective bargaining. Parliament went a long way towards enacting the commission's proposals in the Industrial Conciliation Amendment Act of 1979. At one point it seemed as if Botha's cabinet might waver on equal trade union rights by insisting that only 'permanent urban black South Africans' should qualify.[94] That would have excluded three-quarters of the labour force. HFO led a deputation of objectors, including Godsell and Graham Boustred, to meet the Minister of Labour, Fanie Botha. 'Fanie received us alone, and what amazed me was the reverence with which he greeted and interacted with HFO,' Godsell reflected.[95] When the Labour Relations Amendment

Act was passed in 1981, it deleted all references to race and enabled the registration of trade unions for white and black workers alike, with no limitations. To Oppenheimer, the reforms advocated by the Riekert and Wiehahn commissions signalled that a process of change had begun, 'from which there can be no going back', he assured his audience at the 50th anniversary conference of the South African Institute of Race Relations (SAIRR).[96] The apartheid glacier was breaking up. Liberal institutions like the SAIRR, HFO advised, would have to reassess their role: they must become 'more directly and positively engaged' in promoting the process of reform. These utterances reflected a shift in Oppenheimer's approach to the battle of ideas: outright opposition to the government was giving way to constructive encouragement. However, over the coming years, PW Botha's many deviations from the reformist path would put HFO's faith to the test.

It is a moot point whether Oppenheimer's intervention with the Minister of Labour tipped the scales, but the enactment of Wiehahn's reforms contributed significantly to the rapid proliferation of black trade unions in the 1980s. They became a political force to be reckoned with. For Anglo this proved to be a double-edged sword. HFO suspected that if Anglo's mines were in the vanguard of unionisation, their pro-union advocacy might come back to bite the group. In the absence of representative democracy, he predicted, black trade unions would become surrogate political parties. That could make for hostile workplace showdowns between management and mineworkers, rather than the peaceful resolution of labour disputes. So it came to pass. The unions became an instrument in the struggle against apartheid, as a battering ram in the ANC's campaign to make South Africa ungovernable. For Anglo, this phenomenon manifested itself most dramatically during the 1987 mineworkers' strike, a major confrontation between the black National Union of Mineworkers (NUM), led by the union's general secretary, Cyril Ramaphosa, and mine management over the NUM's demand for a 30–55 per cent wage increase. Ramaphosa grievously miscalculated: he assumed the strike would be quickly won, but by the third week over 50 000 workers had been dismissed. At the height of national political unrest, Anglo's mass dismissal of striking black mineworkers (a decision it later partially reversed) dented the corporation's image and almost destroyed the union.[97]

Total Strategy, Total Onslaught

Botha's receptiveness to the doyens of capital was crowned by his hosting of the Carlton Conference in November 1979. It brought together cabinet ministers, senior civil servants and English-speaking business leaders to discuss the creation of 'reciprocal channels' between government and business.[98] The Prime Minister outlined a 'total strategy' to meet the 'total onslaught', one which drew on the capabilities of the state and the whole of society to ensure white survival. The strategy melded defence with development, and envisaged swingeing steps to strengthen state security while promoting private-sector-led economic growth and limited racial reforms. These reforms would include an end to some of apartheid's pettier restrictions. New economic opportunities would be created by enabling corporations to employ blacks in hitherto restricted jobs. To an assembly of businessmen weaned on free-market orthodoxy, it all sounded perfectly reasonable. In the *Daily Telegraph*'s somewhat fusty framing: 'It was Mr Oppenheimer who connected, before most of his English-speaking fellow tycoons in South Africa, the emancipation of the black man with the good offices of capitalism.' Now 'enlightened Afrikaners' were catching up. The consequent demand for skilled and semi-skilled black labour, and the attendant financial rewards, were bound to bring about 'an almost irresistible social revolution'.[99] Casting his eye over the audience, the correspondent for *Time* magazine mused that 'Botha seemed to have won them over'. Oppenheimer, the convocation's kingpin, conveyed a sense of optimism and cheer: 'I've got more hope for the future of South Africa than I've had for many, many years,' he declared.[100]

The 'total strategy' had its limits. Botha's sweeping review of 'petty apartheid', which eventually culminated in the repeal of laws prohibiting interracial sex and interracial marriage, failed to mollify the opponents of separate development. They rightly viewed the changes as cosmetic, half-hearted attempts to apply an inhuman system more humanely while keeping the structures of racial oppression intact. Be that as it may, Botha's tentative reforms sent a shiver down the spine of hardliners in his cabinet, who regarded them as evidence of treason. The battles intensified between the *verkramptes*, clustered around the party's Transvaal leader, Andries Treurnicht, and the reform-minded *verligtes*. As Botha tried to calm stormy waters by browbeating his opponents into submission, his reform agenda stalled. According to the *Financial Mail*, the mouthpiece of the English-speaking commercial class, the public and private sectors' so-called Carlton Contract appeared to lie 'shredded'.[101] A follow-up meeting to the Carlton Conference was scheduled for November 1981, and Zach de Beer told HFO that 'some pre-planning and lobbying' was essential to get the government back on course.[102] At the gathering, in front of Botha, Oppenheimer laid his cards on the table. 'We must frankly admit', he intoned, 'that the high hopes of two years ago have been followed by a general sense of disillusion.' It was only in the field of industrial relations that 'solid progress' had been made. Urgent reforms were needed, Oppenheimer exhorted, to make the labour market more flexible, black technical education more accessible, and housing opportunities more plentiful. Unless the government was able to devise acceptable political arrangements for urban blacks, he concluded, it was virtually certain that their growing industrial power would be used for political purposes, with 'gravely disruptive effects on the whole economy'.[103]

Botha listened impassively. In all Oppenheimer's time as sovereign ruler of the country's most powerful business empire, he had never been asked to break bread with a sitting Prime Minister. Once, after Oppenheimer had lunched at Nasionale Pers as the guest of 'Lang Dawid' de Villiers, Botha had flown into a rage: he threatened to boycott the media house's dining facilities. Yet on 6 September 1982, HFO and Bridget were invited to Botha's state residence, Libertas, for dinner with the premier and his wife, Elize. The change of heart had been in the offing since the first Carlton Conference, but it was ultimately Henry Kissinger who persuaded Botha to extend the olive branch. Kissinger and Oppenheimer had corresponded with increasing regularity over the preceding five years. In 1978 Oppenheimer approached Kissinger for assistance with an idea that had been pitched to him by two members of 'Revco', Bobby Godsell and Hank Slack: an American-led investigation into constitutional alternatives for South Africa. What the Young Turks had in mind, Oppenheimer explained, adding his own gloss, was a study to determine whether constitutional changes could be devised that might 'reconcile the claims of justice with the facts of practical politics'.[104] Several follow-up meetings ensued. Notes from one of these encounters, jotted down by Julian Ogilvie Thompson, are instructive. 'Kissinger sees the real problem in Southern Africa as how to avoid a war ... not least because pictures on television of blacks and whites killing each other would have a terrible effect on American society', JOT recorded.[105]

Although these exploratory talks yielded few tangible outcomes, Kissinger and Oppenheimer kept in contact. In December 1981 Kissinger wrote to Oppenheimer that the South African Ambassador to the US, Donald Sole, had suggested he visit the republic in September of the following year. 'The trip would not make nearly as much sense if you were not available for much of the time,' the former Secretary of State advised.[106] He was anxious to meet people from various walks of life and to learn about the nation's dynamics. Would Oppenheimer help to facilitate the process? Kissinger inquired. HFO went one step further. In his capacity as chairman of the South African Institute of International Affairs (SAIIA), he arranged for Kissinger to address a SAIIA conference on the subject of 'American global concerns and Africa'.[107] Harry and Bridget played host to Henry and his wife, Nancy, on the Brenthurst estate. 'Before I knew it', Kissinger recalled, 'he had organised my whole itinerary ... in the most selfless fashion imaginable ... and [made] his house available for meetings ... Our two families became very close during that visit.'[108] Bill Paley, the media tycoon who built the Columbia Broadcasting System (CBS), and Annette Reed, Charles Engelhard's daughter, joined the party. Meanwhile, Kissinger's growing closeness to Oppenheimer was complemented by a thawing of relations between the King of Diamonds and the *Groot Krokodil*.

Oppenheimer left no written record of his impressions of that night at Libertas. But the proceedings must have been relatively congenial – HFO would have been at pains not to beard the lion in his den – for they opened up a channel of written communication which foreshadowed further meetings. One of the sticking points at the time was the issue of political rights for 'non-whites' in a new constitutional dispensation. The matter came to a head in the whites-only referendum of 1983. Long before then, it cleaved the National Party caucus and provided the catalyst for Treurnicht's breakaway. The President's Council – a multiracial body comprising whites, Indians and Coloureds, which replaced the Senate in 1981 – suggested that there should be an appropriate division of power between the three racial groups (that is, excluding Africans) as long as whites retained overall control. This was to take the form of a tricameral parliament, in which each of the three groups had its own chamber with power over its 'own affairs'. To the troublemaking Treurnicht, an obdurate ideologist, the whole notion of power-sharing was a red rag. He thought Botha was leading his cabinet like a Prog. Treurnicht proceeded to launch a clumsy attack on the *hoofleier* (supreme leader). The *broedertwis* (fraternal feud) proved irreconcilable. Botha saw it as an opportunity to rid himself of the defiant dogmatist. He issued an ultimatum. The upshot, on 20 March 1982, was that Treurnicht and 18 other Nationalist MPs hived off to form the Conservative Party.

In many ways, the schism within Afrikanerdom should have strengthened Botha's hand; instead, over the remainder of his imperial presidency (the Prime Minister's functions were subsumed into the position of State President in 1983) Botha's 'total strategy' unravelled. To some extent it was unstitched by his own leadership shortcomings: an erratic authoritarian suffering from a persecution complex, Botha cycled between repression and reform. But his constitutional proposals also aggravated the crisis of state legitimacy. Outside the confines of the legislature, on the civic square, they galvanised opponents of apartheid to intensify their struggle. The *Rand Daily Mail* remarked that 'Phoenix-like, anti-apartheid black organisations are rising up again'.[109] On 29 August 1983 the most impactful among them, the United Democratic Front (UDF), was born. While Botha's ham-fisted attempts at constitutional reform were met with scorn by most blacks, they polarised the PFP and the white business community. Slabbert saw through the reformist veneer – the government was 'selling the sizzle and not the steak', he maintained – and he led his party's opposition to the scheme.[110] The plebiscite was framed narrowly to white voters: 'Are you in favour of the implementation of the Republic of South Africa Constitution Act as approved by Parliament?' Harry Schwarz believed a 'no' vote in the referendum of 2 November 1983 would make the Progs appear reactionary and confuse the voters. He was one of several party bigwigs who found the arguments in favour of a 'yes' vote to be seductive if not necessarily persuasive.

A phalanx of the English-language press concurred. According to Michael Spicer, Gavin Relly's right-hand man in public affairs (and later chairman of Anglo American South Africa's board), Relly welcomed the tricameral parliament as 'a way station' that would make further political change 'inevitable'.[111] At a meeting hosted by Oppenheimer and addressed by Slabbert during the referendum campaign, among the businessmen present there was little enthusiasm for Slabbert's arguments. Chris Saunders, the chairman of Tongaat Hulett, rallied behind the 'yes' vote and gave it a very public thumbs-up.[112] Some anglophone thought leaders and a handful of Anglo's own panjandrums were inclined to spoil their ballots. Ten days before the referendum, GR 'Bozz' Bozzoli (the former Vice-Chancellor of Wits), Peter Gush (then head of Anglo's gold division), Jan Steyn and Denis Beckett (editor of *Frontline* magazine, which HFO

Portrait of a dynasty: HFO poses in front of Sir Ernest Oppenheimer's portrait on the occasion of Anglo American's 50th anniversary, 1967.
(Anglo American)

A major act of faith: HFO visits the plant at Highveld Steel during the company's difficult start-up phase. With him are Ted Brown (far left), Graham Boustred (third from left), and Doug Beckingham (third from right), mid-1960s. *(Anglo American)*

A meeting of the Anglo American executive committee, 1977. Anti-clockwise from HFO (far right) are Gavin Relly, Julian Ogilvie Thompson, Peter Gush, Chris Griffith, Graham Boustred, Gordon Waddell, Guy Nicholson, Zach de Beer, Dennis Etheredge and Robin Crawford. *(Anglo American)*

The magnate and his heir: HFO and Nicky Oppenheimer in Anglo American's executive committee room, 1981. *(Anglo American)*

End of the reign: Accompanied by Bridget and his granddaughter Victoria, HFO bids farewell to Anglo American staff on the steps of 44 Main Street, in 1982. He is flanked by Gavin Relly, and in the frame are Sir Philip Oppenheimer (far right) and Sir Keith Acutt (far left). *(Anglo American)*

Nelson Mandela
and HFO at a
function to mark
HFO's retirement
from the De Beers
board, 1994.
(Anglo American)

The chairmen:
Julian Ogilvie
Thompson (seated),
Gavin Relly (left),
HFO (right), 1990.
(Anglo American)

HFO and Alan Paton at the opening of the Brenthurst Library, 1984. *(Brenthurst Library)*

A panoply of Progs, 1998. From left to right: Tony Leon, Colin Eglin, Helen Suzman, Frederik van Zyl Slabbert, HFO, Zach de Beer and Harry Schwarz. *(Brenthurst Library)*

HFO and Bridget pose for a photographer in the Blue Room at
Brenthurst, 1965. The smaller of the drawing rooms, it is
where HFO kept all his best art. *(Getty Images)*

On the grounds of Xanadu: HFO and Bridget in front of the
main house at Brenthurst, 1965. *(Getty Images)*

HFO, Mary Slack
and Bridget
Oppenheimer
on the day of
Mary's wedding
to Hank Slack,
16 February 1979.
(Brenthurst Library)

HFO and Bridget on Bridget's 60th birthday, 1981. Hank and Mary Slack
hosted a ball to mark the occasion. Peter Duchin was flown out to provide
the musical entertainment. *(Brenthurst Library)*

The gold and diamond dynasty, 1997. From left to right: Jessica, Rebecca, Rachel, Mary, Strilli, Jennifer, Victoria, Bridget, Nicky, HFO and Jonathan (in front, kneeling) with Jessica's dog, Oscar. *(Brenthurst Library)*

Not one to bounce the bairns upon the knee: 'Grandpa' with Victoria and Jonathan, c.1980. *(Brenthurst Library)*

Three generations of Oppenheimer men: Jonathan, HFO and Nicky admire gold bullion from the Isabella gold mine in Zimbabwe, 1990s. *(Anglo American)*

had twice bailed out of financial difficulty) dined at Brenthurst. Beckett pushed for the spoilt vote, and by the end Gush and Steyn were leaning heavily on his side. 'We watched Harry come within an inch, and then close the subject on the fact that he could not now turn his back on the Progs ... Some you win and some you lose,' Beckett later shrugged.[113]

Botha's constitutional reforms were patently a stratagem to entrench white control. Steeped in the tradition of divide and rule, the tricameral parliament was an exercise in co-optive domination. Invited for a second time to address the Foreign Policy Association in 1984, Oppenheimer explained the rationale behind his 'no' vote to a US audience: 'My reasons were, firstly, that I feared it might prove unworkable, and secondly ... I thought that the introduction of a measure of power-sharing with the Coloureds and Indians without ... the blacks was bound to increase interracial bitterness and tension.'[114] As popular resistance to apartheid intensified, HFO's prognostications proved well founded. Violence flared throughout the decade; an urban revolt between 1984 and 1986 caused Botha to impose a partial State of Emergency in 1985, and he renewed it nationally the following year. Botha was riding a tiger, and he evidently had no idea how to dismount it. But at least now a line of communication had been opened; Oppenheimer would try to coax the combative curmudgeon into climbing down.

HFO in Retirement: The Public and the Private Spheres

In retirement, away from frontline politics, Oppenheimer kept up his varied involvements in public life. As chancellor of the University of Cape Town (UCT), he continued to cap graduates every year; and in the tumultuous 1980s – when the liberal campuses were a hotbed of anti-apartheid activism – HFO served the university diligently as a sensible and sober figurehead. In 1979 UCT reached its 150th birthday. Oppenheimer made a personal donation of R150 000, which went towards an academic support programme geared to black students. In the years that followed, he matched financial aid with moral succour to UCT's 'Vice-Chancellor on a tightrope', Stuart Saunders.[115] Together they opposed the Universities Amendment Bill. Introduced in 1983, the law replaced the permit system for black students with a regime of ministerially determined quotas. Oppenheimer also assisted Saunders in securing additional student accommodation. A generous donation from HFO enabled the university to establish a new, non-racial hall of residence, the Woolsack.

Dr Stuart Saunders caps HFO with an honorary degree (Doctor of Literature) at the University of Cape Town, 1985. *(Brenthurst Library)*

Oppenheimer heeded the liberal call to action on several fronts – in his support for the Progs, the 'open' universities, and wider philanthropic causes – but as a press baron, with the power to keep the flame of liberalism alive in print, he exercised an abundance of caution. HFO always maintained that he did not interfere in the management and editorial decisions that affected his newspapers. Not every journalist was convinced. Once, at a meeting of the Young Progressives in the early 1980s, Oppenheimer had raised his hand in support of a resolution calling on the government to free political prisoners. A journalist in the audience, John Matisonn from the *Sunday Times*, knew immediately that he had stumbled upon a newsworthy nugget. But his editor, Tertius Myburgh, spiked the story. 'My understanding, and [the news editor Steve] Mulholland's,' Matisson wrote, 'was that Myburgh had effectively called to offer Oppenheimer a veto.'[116] There is no way to corroborate such a claim, but if Oppenheimer was guilty of interposing himself, then many of Matisonn's colleagues would have hoped for an equally interventionist approach where the future of the *Rand Daily Mail* was concerned.

By 1984 the *Rand Daily Mail*, the most outspoken of the anti-apartheid,

English-language newspapers, was losing money hand over fist: its projected loss for 1985 stood at almost R20 million.[117] Relly and Waddell (then chairman of JCI, SAAN's major shareholder) were of a mind to close the newspaper, along with the equally ailing *Sunday Express*.[118] SAAN's chairman, Ian Macpherson, and managing director, Clive Kinsley, did not need much persuasion. They disliked the *Rand Daily Mail*'s pugnacious politics. On 15 March, the newspaper's beleaguered editor, Rex Gibson, announced to his staff that the *Rand Daily Mail* would cease publication on 30 April. The closure might have made commercial sense, but politically it was short-sighted. It dented Anglo's reputation. The *Sunday Express* had broken the Information Scandal story wide open. The *Rand Daily Mail*, among its many exposés, had revealed the brutal circumstances of Steve Biko's death in detention. Their coverage was internationally lauded. Foreign correspondents looked to the *Rand Daily Mail* as a reliable source for their reports. Its disappearance, many felt, would silence a voice of liberal stature and knock down an interracial bridge-builder. The director of the International Press Institute, Peter Galliner, pleaded with Oppenheimer to save the publication. HFO agreed that the newspaper's demise was 'a great misfortune'. But it was not correct, he submitted, that either he personally or Anglo's executives collectively had played 'any part in the difficult decision' by SAAN's board to shutter it. He would be 'very pleased indeed' were it possible for the *Rand Daily Mail* to be saved, but the decision to close it was 'forced on the company' on account of the newspaper's continuing, unsustainable financial losses.[119]

Oppenheimer's protestations of powerlessness failed to convince the organ's flag-bearers. After all, as Raymond Louw, a former editor the *Rand Daily Mail*, pointed out, ten years previously HFO had played a role in preventing the newspaper from falling into Louis Luyt's wily clutches. 'A small flame of anger, even contempt, burned inside me,' Allister Sparks, another former editor, confessed. 'Here was this man with the power to save our great newspaper … yet he didn't want to get involved by exercising that power.'[120] To be sure, the death of the *Rand Daily Mail* could not have occurred at a worse time. Not only did its passing make the middle ground more difficult to occupy, but it conduced to a loss of morale in the midst of battle, as *The Star*'s former editor Harvey Tyson lamented.[121] PW Botha revelled in the closure. In later years Oppenheimer reportedly expressed regret over the newspaper's fall.[122] However, in an interview published in 1993, he shed a rather different perspective on his thinking. While he felt a 'close sympathy' for the views articulated by the *Rand Daily Mail*, HFO suggested that by addressing itself to 'too distant a goal' and by attacking apartheid 'almost exclusively on moral grounds', while not placing enough emphasis on 'the damaging effects of apartheid on the economy', the newspaper had offended conservative whites and opened a chasm between black opinion-formers and white businessmen.[123] Perhaps the publication's lukewarm reception of the Urban Foundation back in 1976 had rankled Oppenheimer after all.

Away from the noisy marketplace of ideas, HFO retreated into a brown study, surrounded by the works of Byron and Shelley and an extensive collection of Africana. It included the original manuscript of Alan Paton's *Cry, the Beloved Country*; letters from David Livingstone (and one from Leo Tolstoy to Mahatma Gandhi on the nature of passive resistance); Thomas Baines's notebooks; and a manuscript by Winston Churchill on the Anglo-Boer War. By the time of Oppenheimer's retirement the accumulation of maps, books, pamphlets and manuscripts had grown so large that it was no longer feasible to store them all at Little Brenthurst. Coupled with an increasing volume of requests from researchers to access the holdings, this prompted the decision to build a separate library on the estate, one with appropriate climate-controlled facilities. The building was also intended to house the offices of the Brenthurst Press. Established in 1974 to publish fine, limited-edition books based on the collection of manuscripts and artworks, within its first decade the press had produced illustrated volumes on, inter alia, Baines's sketches, 19th-century Cape watercolours, the invasion of Zululand, the War of the Axe, and the defence of Ladysmith and Mafeking.

Designed by the architect Hans Hallen, the Brenthurst Library was officially opened by Alan Paton on 23 February 1984. The library conveyed, like its originator, a sense of age and authority. It contrived to blend classical touches with African materials, making extensive use of red and black Transvaal granite. Set into the domed roof are four large circular windows filled with translucent marble, their sills lined with gold leaf. The reception area is cross-vaulted like a Romanesque crypt; its cast-aluminium sculptured door is redolent of the entrance to an Italian baptistery. Among the many priceless artworks, a huge and darkly powerful mural, 'The Bridge', created by the Australian artist Leonard French, provides a focal point. It depicts the division between black and white South Africans which, at the time of the mural's installation, still had to be overcome. Today, a bronze bust of HFO by Rhona Stern (a gift

Raymond Oppenheimer with his beloved bull terriers.
(*https://culturabullterrier.com*)

from Anglo American upon his retirement) stands on a travertine plinth in the library gardens. However, a plaque might just as suitably echo Christopher Wren's epitaph, for the Brenthurst Library is an impeccable testament to Oppenheimer's personality and principles. In his lifetime it provided HFO with hours of joy in quiet contemplation, as the library's former director Marcelle Graham fondly recalled. A discreetly located private study still houses his first editions. Every day HFO would walk down from the main house – usually followed by one of his whippets – to spend a morning or afternoon out of Bridget's sight, enraptured in reading.

HFO had a palpable sense that he was in the autumn of his life. In 1984 his beloved cousin Raymond Oppenheimer died. He had been one of HFO's few intimate friends, bound not solely by family ties but, from Oxford days, by a shared appreciation of the whimsical and the waggish. Oppenheimer started writing his memoirs. Although he produced a comprehensive outline, the manuscript remained incomplete and unpublished at the time of his death. Its biblical title was 'Help thou mine unbelief: Some recollections and reflections', a meditation on faith and doubt as he looked back on his life and career, his successes

HFO, seemingly shrunken, celebrates his
80th birthday, 1988. *(Anglo American)*

and his failures. But it was also an allusion to HFO's Christian beliefs, the Anglicanism that had shaped his personal ethic and public outlook since the conversion from Judaism many years before. In the chapter that was to be devoted to 'recreation', Oppenheimer acknowledged that he was 'indeed lucky to be able to live in a degree of privacy', in beautiful surroundings, with a wife 'much younger than myself' who 'puts up with my shortcomings & eccentricities' and 'has an exaggerated idea of my virtues & beliefs, such as they are'.[124] Bridget had been such an integral part of his corporate life, hosting innumerable dinners and accompanying him across goldfields and diamond mines – and indeed continents – to meet captains of industry, statesmen, kings, queens and commoners. Some of it had involved social drudgery. She had often taken on the heavy lifting of making small talk and the responsibility of shielding her husband from dullards and bores. Now the couple settled into a less frenetic social routine. They still travelled prodigiously. Twice a year they would go to London and New York. In London HFO pursued his recreational interests; he spent hours poring over the catalogues from Sotheby's and Christie's, and he liked lunching with the chairman of Christie's, Charles Allsopp. Mary and Hank took over some of the obligations of entertaining, and the dynamic between Harry and Bridget began to shift imperceptibly. As he grew older, HFO seemed to shrink. His visage became more elfin. Of course, Bridget had always been much taller than he, with a commanding demeanour to boot, but, as HFO mellowed with age, he could appear to observers to be under the whip – tilting his head to one side and deferring to 'Bwidgie', as he called her, the effect of a slight rhotacism.

Although HFO was affable, even avuncular at times, he was not the kind of grandparent to bounce the bairns upon his knee. He often struck his grandchildren as someone remote and inscrutable, and he preferred to express his love through gifts. Once, when a teenage Victoria was seated next to him at dinner, HFO smiled benignly at her and proceeded to turn down the volume on his hearing aid. To a child, Bridget could appear ineffably intimidating. A boisterous young Jonathan Oppenheimer, tearing around the estate at Brenthurst on his motorcycle, was more likely than not to take off in the other direction when he saw his grandmother approaching. 'I was a hooligan in the garden!' he later reminisced.[125] At St George's, the Parktown church where both Harry and Bridget and Strilli Oppenheimer's family had long been parishioners, Jonathan and his parents sat separately from his grandparents: there was hardly any interaction between them. HFO and Bridget were of the view that children should be little seen and seldom heard; and if they did speak, in the company of adults, it should be to impart something amusing or interesting. Effervescent Rebecca, who bore an uncanny resemblance to her grandmother, reliably produced the goods: the ten-year-old was 'the life & soul of the party', Bridget proudly recorded after a combined function for Mary's birthday and New Year's Eve festivities.[126] Victoria, then on the cusp of her teens, was poised and solicitous. She watched her grandfather giving his farewell speech on the steps of 44 Main Street, and she took a keen interest in the family history. Jessica, though still small, seemed to have inherited the matrilineal fascination with all things equestrian. She and her younger sister, Rachel, lived with Mary and Hank in Fourways, just outside Johannesburg, on a farm called White Hills. It stabled about fifty horses. Sometimes the extended family would holiday under one roof at Milkwood; and Milkwood is where Harry and Bridget began to spend longer stretches during the Natal winter racing season. This was a dry decade as far as the Durban July Handicap was concerned: after Principal Boy won the race in 1975, the couple had to wait another 17 years for their fourth 'July' winner, Spanish Galliard, trained by Dennis Drier. By way of consolation, another of their star performers, Bodrum, notched up several Grade 1 victories in the early 1980s.

Over Christmas, Harry and Bridget would return to Milkwood, where a party of British house guests – in flight from the northern hemisphere winter – typically joined them in the New Year. HFO's old friend Julian Amery – a Tory MP, long-time member of the Conservative Monday Club, and chairman of Le Cercle, the secretive, right-wing, foreign policy forum – was a fixture. He and Oppenheimer had corresponded on Commonwealth affairs going back to the 1950s, and Amery and his wife, Catherine (Harold Macmillan's daughter), dined frequently with Harry and Bridget in London. An enthusiastic drinker and diehard imperialist – his maxim was 'between the revolution and the firing squad, there is always time for a bottle of champagne' – Amery kept Oppenheimer up to date on the machinations in Thatcher's cabinet.[127] Amery was one of several linkmen connecting Oppenheimer and the Iron Lady. Oppenheimer's opinion 'weighs more with me than any other South African', Amery wrote to his political principal; he enclosed correspondence from HFO which warned against the negative impact of sanctions and alluded to a potential meeting between Thatcher and PW Botha.[128] In South Africa Oppenheimer helped facilitate contacts for Amery. Slabbert was a fellow guest at Milkwood in January 1986, and after the holiday had ended, Oppenheimer took Amery to Johannesburg to dine with Fritz Leutwiler, the former president of the Swiss National Bank, who was – in his own right – Thatcher's 'main contact' with PW Botha.[129] Also present were the 'top hamper' of Anglo executives – Amery's description to Thatcher – as well as Gerhard de Kock, the Governor of the Reserve Bank, Anton Rupert and Fred du Plessis.[130] Several of Thatcher's and Oppenheimer's mutual friends made their way to Milkwood. Victor and Teresa 'Tess' Rothschild made repeated trips, though they took the unusual precaution of travelling to South Africa under assumed names. Gordon Richardson, the former Governor of the Bank of England, was another; on learning that Richardson was off to Milkwood, Geoffrey Howe, Thatcher's Foreign Secretary, suggested that the Prime Minister write to Botha recommending Richardson as someone who 'had your confidence' as a potential intermediary.[131] A prominent Tory donor, Sir 'Chips' Keswick, chairman of Hambros Bank, and his wife, Lady Sarah – keen racehorse owners like the Oppenheimers – were also regular returnees to Oppenheimer's seaside villa.

Crossing the Rubicon, and American Pressure to Reform

Oppenheimer had no intention of settling down to life as a well-heeled pensioner, detached from current affairs. In any event his opinions on the South African imbroglio were highly sought after, and he made frequent appearances on international television networks – among them the BBC and ABC's *Nightline* programme hosted by Ted Koppel – as well as on radio.[132] After Botha's speech at the opening of Parliament in 1985, in which he promised to grant freehold rights to blacks and reconsider the system of influx control, Oppenheimer wrote diffidently to the State President. 'Together with the great majority of South Africans I was immensely impressed by your speech,' HFO complimented him.[133] The blandishments were calculated. Overseas, the sanctions and disinvestment campaign was gaining momentum, and Oppenheimer warned Botha that only one set of measures would subdue it. The government must inaugurate a process of multiracial negotiations. Unless Botha's administration made progress towards a constitutional dispensation that included Africans outside the homelands, then his social and economic reforms would fall flat. Cataclysmic violence would probably be inevitable. Ideally, HFO suggested, the negotiations should include both Mandela and Buthelezi, whose private correspondence with Botha the Zulu chief had shared with Oppenheimer. (In one of these missives, dated November 1984, Buthelezi assured the State President that he had 'ventured forth from hard-line Black political thinking', and now publicly told his people that they would 'have to think about abandoning their one-man-one-vote ideal ... and seek political solutions through the politics of compromise and negotiation'. Buthelezi appealed to Botha for the state to strengthen his hand by releasing Mandela as he waged 'the real Black political struggle', between Inkatha and 'the ANC's Mission in Exile'.)[134] It had taken HFO 'courage' to impart his thoughts – 'perhaps you may rather call it impertinence', he flattered Botha – and, amid humble assurances of goodwill, Oppenheimer offered his unreserved assistance. 'It seems to me just possible that some

HFO receives his Decoration for Meritorious Service
from President PW Botha at Tuynhuys, 1985.
(Brenthurst Library)

of the connections I have … might in certain circumstances be used to
advantage in an entirely unofficial and confidential way.'

The correspondence appeared to soften Botha's attitude to
Oppenheimer. In March, a week after the announcement of the *Rand
Daily Mail's* impending closure, Botha awarded HFO an honour, the
Decoration for Meritorious Service, for his 'outstanding contribution
to South Africa's industrial and economic progress' and 'the welfare of
its people'.[135] The citation drew attention to HFO's role in setting up the
Urban Foundation. Harry and Bridget made a point of attending the
ceremony at Tuynhuys. Nevertheless, in spite of the positive signals,
Oppenheimer would learn to lower his expectations of the *Groot
Krokodil*, especially after the events of 15 August 1985. On that date
Botha managed to shoot himself in the foot with a bazooka. Overnight,
he hardened international sentiment against South Africa. The reason

for this turn of events was Botha's infamous 'Rubicon' speech. Billed as a 'manifesto for a new South Africa' – a crossing of the Rubicon – the address was more truculent tirade than portentous peroration. Instead of announcing far-reaching reforms, Botha strayed from his prepared text and castigated his critics. He rejected unambiguously the principle of one man, one vote in a unitary system: it would lead whites down the road to abdication and suicide, he admonished his audience. Botha scotched any hopes of Mandela's release from prison. Wagging his index finger in a trademark gesture of irascibility, Botha snarled at the millions of people watching him live on television not to 'push us too far'. It was, in Oppenheimer's own words to Roger Smith, president of the automotive giant General Motors, a 'disastrous' performance and a public relations catastrophe.[136] Immediately after the speech Chase Manhattan Bank – chaired, until four years previously, by Oppenheimer's friend David Rockefeller – announced that it would stop rolling over South Africa's debts. The country was now deemed to pose an unacceptable investment risk. No new loans would be made and all outstanding loans and deposits would have to be repaid as they fell due. Several other banks in the United States and Europe followed suit. The result of Botha's ruinous Rubicon speech was a liquidity crisis, a tanking rand, an immediate exodus of capital, and runaway inflation: indeed, the abrupt withdrawal of Western economic support dealt Pretoria a crucial blow.

Like Leutwiler, who helped mitigate the fallout with the backing of German and Swiss banks, Oppenheimer regarded Chase Manhattan's actions as overhasty. He conveyed his sentiments to Rockefeller. Their political views were not always in harmony: a few years beforehand, the American dynast had claimed that African socialism posed no threat to Western business interests, and HFO had scoffed at that assertion as 'obvious nonsense'.[137] Rockefeller and his daughter Peggy Dulany usually stayed at Brenthurst on their sojourns in Johannesburg. Oppenheimer found Rockefeller Republicanism perhaps a little too leftist for his tastes; certainly he felt that way about Dulany's more radical brand of liberalism. Yet Botha had managed to alienate both progressive East Coast Republicans *and* conservative US congressmen and business interests. Historically opposed to economic sanctions, they were forced to re-evaluate their stance. Oppenheimer had always held, with some justification, that trade and financial sanctions could only work by destroying the economy. In his view, they were bound to jeopardise ordinary people's livelihoods. Sanctions would worsen unemployment and poverty – for blacks in particular – thus fuelling further violence. But in an atmosphere charged with moral outrage, where corporates felt compelled to signal their repugnance of apartheid, it became harder to listen to Oppenheimer's logic dispassionately. The call for sanctions intensified. Pressure mounted on blue-chip foreign companies to pull out of South Africa and dispose of their local assets.

Nevertheless, Oppenheimer believed Botha might still correct his course if the luminaries of American industry sugar-coated their demands. He held intensive discussions with Roger Smith and Michael Blumenthal (Carter's former Treasury secretary, and chairman of the Burroughs Corporation) to plot the way forward. Smith and Blumenthal chaired the US Corporate Council on South Africa. This group was formed towards the end of 1985 by the heads of ten of the biggest American companies operating in South Africa to resist the disinvestment drive. It included IBM, Johnson & Johnson, Mobil, Citibank and Caltex. As signatories of the Sullivan Principles, the voluntary code which rejected racial discrimination in the workplace and promoted racial equality, these corporations used their joint might to lobby for reform. The US Corporate Council sought Oppenheimer's advice on how to deal with Botha: on what to say and how to say it.[138] The most pressing need, Oppenheimer and Smith agreed, was a move by Botha to abolish the pass laws and the Group Areas Act. In April 1986, Oppenheimer accompanied Smith to meet Botha at Tuynhuys, the State President's offices in Parliament. The meeting was not a great success. Smith sensed that a 'siege mentality' had settled in; the government, he reflected, was not 'doing what I hoped they would'.[139]

These encounters with Botha agitated HFO; it was the one time, those who knew him well could see, that he appeared slightly out of kilter. Botha often seemed to smoulder with resentment, and he made it clear that he felt hard done by. The State President found it difficult to rise above self-pity, and Oppenheimer's diplomatic interventions had only a limited impact. Botha did institute further reforms between 1986 and 1989: he desegregated amenities, did away with influx control, and restored South African citizenship to a number of black people resident in the homelands. But he made no serious attempt to kickstart a process of political change. In October 1986 Smith announced that General Motors, the largest American company doing business in South Africa, would sell its local operations. A cold numbers man, with a large black workforce back in Michigan and the Reverend Leon Sullivan (drafter of the Sullivan

Principles) an inexorable presence on his board, Smith had come to the conclusion that the game was not worth the candle. General Motors had been losing money in South Africa for years. Too little progress, Smith declared publicly, had been made in ending apartheid.[140] The US Congress had overturned Reagan's veto of the Comprehensive Anti-Apartheid Act earlier in the month, inflicting a body blow to Pretoria, and now the trickle of companies disinvesting turned into a flood. The day after Smith's announcement, the chairman of IBM, John Akers, followed suit. By the middle of 1987 over 120 corporations had disinvested from South Africa. In April 1989 Mobil, the biggest remaining American operator, announced that it would sell its assets to Gencor.[141]

Throughout this period, key figures in Anglo's intelligentsia engaged with American opinion-formers in an attempt to move the needle on South Africa. In 1985, with Oppenheimer's backing and involvement, Bobby Godsell approached Peter Berger, a renowned sociologist at Boston University, to lead a study on post-apartheid possibilities. Over the course of the following two years, a team of 20 South African and American scholars collaborated on a project named South Africa Beyond Apartheid (SABA). The inquiry sought not to be prescriptive: it aimed to produce an accurate account of how South Africa's competing political actors conceived of their social reality and envisaged change, rather than a comprehensive set of recommendations. Nevertheless, the researchers shared four key convictions. Apartheid was morally reprehensible and should be abolished. South Africa's white racial oligarchy must be succeeded by democracy, not another form of tyranny. In the transitional process it would be crucial to preserve the productive capacity of the economy. Finally, the costs of the transition, 'especially in human terms', should be kept to a minimum.[142] From the South African side, the researchers represented a broad cross-section of middle-ground thinking. Many of them would rise to prominence in public life after the fall of apartheid, including Jakes Gerwel (Nelson Mandela's director general in the Presidency), Reuel Khoza (chairman of Eskom in the late 1990s and of various corporate boards), Helen Zille (journalist-turned-politician who led the Democratic Alliance, successor to the PFP, from 2007 to 2015, and governed Cape Town and the Western Cape, respectively, as mayor and premier) and Paulus Zulu (a distinguished social scientist). The report on SABA's survey was presented to the South African government, the Broederbond and the US Assistant Secretary of State for African Affairs, Chester Crocker; the ensuing book, entitled *A Future South Africa:*

Visions, Strategies, and Realities, was widely read after its publication in 1988.[143] It was a useful mapping exercise – an example of the kind of intellectual labour, enriched by international networks, with which few of Anglo's corporate peers in South Africa concerned themselves at the time.

Meeting the ANC

In adopting certain political positions or in speaking out on contentious issues publicly, Oppenheimer refrained from talking on behalf of Anglo. Harry O and the Anglo powerhouse might be one and the same in the public imagination, but it was important, HFO realised, to give Relly the necessary breathing space to make his own decisions and to articulate his views independently. He had no intention of 'blowing down the necks of those who come after me', HFO assured senior Anglo staffers on the eve of his retirement. However, after 51 years in the business, he would not be able to relax his 'devotion to the group'. To lose touch with all his old friends and colleagues, he confided, would seem to him 'a sort of death'.[144]

When he stepped down at Anglo, Oppenheimer was a man approaching the age of 75. Although his continued influence was indisputable, there were others at 44 Main Street who played an equally active role externally in trying to shift the political tides. During HFO's chairmanship, he had occasionally participated in informal discussions about a new constitutional framework for South Africa. He began acquainting himself with theories of consociationalism, a form of democratic power-sharing between groups divided by race, ethnicity, language or religion. At one stage he believed consociational models offered 'us our best, if not our only, chance'.[145] In 1981 he met Lucas Mangope at the Bantustan leader's residence, accompanied by Judge Victor Hiemstra, the Chief Justice of Bophuthatswana; Professor Marinus Wiechers, a constitutional law expert; Albert Robinson and Hank Slack. They engaged in open-ended talks on the subject. And the following year, at Brenthurst, in the same vein, he brought together an eclectic mix of businessmen (Gavin Relly, Graham Boustred, Mike Rosholt and Dick Goss), politicians (Slabbert), academics (Lawrence Schlemmer, the Natal University sociologist who directed Buthelezi's think tank, the Inkatha Institute) and journalists (Harald Pakendorf).

Bobby Godsell and Hank Slack were usually present on these occasions, and often they served as HFO's political emissaries. Oppenheimer was a member of the Buthelezi Commission, a multiracial body established by Chief Mangosuthu Buthelezi and assisted by two foreign academics, Heribert Adam and Arend Lijphart, which explored possible options for the political, economic and administrative future of KwaZulu and Natal. However, Godsell was really HFO's point person there: he attended all the sessions and took detailed notes. The Buthelezi Commission released a comprehensive report in 1982. It essentially argued for consociational democracy and a form of inter-regional federalism.[146] The federal proposals were expanded upon at the KwaZulu/Natal Indaba of 1986, which enjoyed significant buy-in from the PFP and much of the white business community. Oppenheimer embraced the recommendations of the Buthelezi Commission wholeheartedly.[147] He had a high regard for Buthelezi, whose opposition to sanctions and views on democracy and free enterprise broadly echoed his own. The Chief Minister was a regular visitor to Milkwood. HFO funded the Inkatha Institute at its inception and contributed intermittently to the parent body. Buthelezi thanked him for a R50 000 donation in 1985; the funds, he said, were 'a magnificent gesture of goodwill' and 'a personal vote of confidence'.[148] As ever, Oppenheimer's munificence was not entirely one-sided; more or less simultaneously, he gifted Nelson Mandela's firebrand wife, Winnie, R15 000 for the clinic she had founded in Brandfort, the small Free State town to which she was banished in 1977.[149]

At Anglo, several executives stepped into the political space opened up by HFO's departure. Although he was no longer in Parliament, Zach de Beer stayed close to Eglin and the Progs. Godsell was a ubiquitous mover and shaker in Anglo's ever-expanding apparatus of public affairs. He cultivated links with up-and-coming black unionists like Cyril Ramaphosa. In 1986 a group of progressive executives drawn overwhelmingly from Anglo's board established contact with the UDF. They formed the kernel of the Consultative Business Movement (CBM), set up in August 1988 to facilitate dialogue with a wide spectrum of political movements and civil society organisations. Neither Oppenheimer nor Relly participated in the CBM, which mainstream business tended to regard as subversively leftist, but Relly encouraged Anglo directors like Murray Hofmeyr to take on leading roles. Spicer eventually became its deputy chairman. Between 1989 and 1990, the CBM convened a national consultative process involving business people and members of both the UDF and the trade union federation Cosatu (the Congress of South African Trade Unions). It broke down barriers between industrialists and anti-apartheid activists.

HFO and Gavin Relly at the old Western Deep Levels
No. 1 shaft, 1986. *(Anglo American)*

Behind the radical, socialist rhetoric of the so-called Mass Democratic Movement there was a 'good deal of pragmatism' and preparedness to listen to the concerns of business.[150]

Relly did occasionally feel suffocated by the spectre of Oppenheimer looming over his shoulder. HFO's successor once bristled at a reporter's line of questioning: 'I don't intend to have to fill his boots. I intend to fill my own.'[151] Yet Oppenheimer was the cobbler who had fashioned the corporate leather, and he could not but watch Relly's footsteps closely. Politically, Relly beat his own path, both on Botha's constitutional reforms and in his approach to the ANC. Before the imposition of the State of Emergency, there had been tentative efforts by several businessmen to make contact with the ANC in exile. In 1985 Anglo's chairman undertook to lead a delegation of corporate leaders and opinion-formers to meet the ANC in Zambia. The encounter would be unprecedented; at a time when the apartheid state and ANC operatives in South Africa were fighting a war marked by escalating violence, it also seemed momentous. When news of the impending trip leaked out, PW Botha blew his cool. He talked menacingly of treason. Some of those who had initially agreed to join the expedition – Anton Rupert, Fred du Plessis, Mike Rosholt, and Chris Ball of Barclays – dropped out for one or other reason. Oppenheimer was given pause for thought; Botha's reaction made him twitchy. HFO worried about Anglo antagonising the State President. He also had misgivings about Relly meeting members of an organisation whose leader, Oliver Tambo, had issued a seditious New Year message, 'Render South Africa ungovernable'. Besides, the ANC was avowedly committed to armed struggle. Oppenheimer made it known that he considered the trip unwise. However, he did not force the issue, nor did he insist that Relly abort the mission. That was not his style. As a result, on the morning of 13 September 1985, Relly and his envoys descended from the Anglo Gulfstream at Kenneth Kaunda's presidential game lodge, Mfuwe. The businessmen in Relly's group had been whittled down to De Beer and Tony Bloom, the debonair, Harvard-trained lawyer who chaired the Premier Group. He was also an eloquent Prog activist and close friend of Waddell's. Hugh Murray, the entrepreneurial editor and publisher of *Leadership*, a corporate magazine, and Peter Sorour, director general of the South Africa Foundation, were lobbyists. Like Oppenheimer, they vocally assailed the campaign for sanctions and disinvestment. Two Afrikaner journalists, Tertius Myburgh and *Die Vaderland*'s Harald Pakendorf, rounded off the pack. Watched over benignly by Kaunda, whom Relly had got to know well during his Zambian stint for Anglo, the group met their opposite numbers from the ANC: Tambo, Thabo Mbeki, Chris Hani, Pallo Jordan, Mac Maharaj and James Stuart.

By all accounts the atmosphere at the meeting was remarkably cordial. Relly recalled it as 'one of the nicest days' he had ever spent, a 'picnic among South Africans talking about their future together'.[152] In such relaxed environs, with Kaunda serving them mid-morning tea and scones, it was easy for the two sets of interlocutors to dispel their mutual misconceptions. They might have differed on core economic issues like nationalisation and some of the Freedom Charter's more vaguely worded exhortations, but there were sufficient reassurances to make the businessmen feel buoyed. 'Nobody is going to start nationalizing swimming pools,' the *Washington Post* quoted Mbeki afterwards.[153] For Africa's sun-struck white tribe, reared to regard private property as sacrosanct, the symbolism was comforting. For his part, Mbeki left with high hopes from the exchange. But there was precious little follow-up from the other side – Relly got cold feet as the ANC's 'People's War' ratcheted up – and it left Mbeki bitterly disappointed. Nevertheless, as Mbeki's biographer reflected, the encounter established a dialogue between South Africa's 'industrialists and its future rulers' about the shape of things to come. By the time the ANC assumed power in 1994, after the fall of the Berlin Wall and the collapse of communism, the Zambian rendezvous had facilitated an 'unexpected consensus'.[154] The old white corporate elite and the new black political elite concurred on the inevitability of liberal-democratic governance.

Should Oppenheimer have seized the initiative and joined Relly's deputation? It certainly would have sent a potent message to Botha. In later years HFO conceded that 'probably I was wrong not to be more enthusiastic about it'.[155] However, at the time he regarded the trip as a press stunt. HFO preferred to exercise power in a more understated fashion. He eschewed the grand gesture and never forcefully imposed his will. This could be a shortcoming. In later years Bloom wondered what would have happened if, for example, Oppenheimer had 'taken the gloves off' at the two Carlton Conference meetings and, 'in front of the whole business establishment, torn into PW Botha and the cabinet, calling them out in graphic terms'.[156] It would have made a major impact both domestically and abroad. Yet Oppenheimer was not without courage. When, two weeks after the Zambian trip, Bloom placed a full-page advertisement in the Sunday newspapers calling for an end to apartheid, the start of negotiations, and 'full South African citizenship [for] all our peoples', Oppenheimer did not hesitate to endorse it.[157] The appeal was reproduced in several of the world's leading newspapers. Of the ninety-odd South African businessmen who signed it, few would have been bold enough to add their signatures had HFO not led the way. Many of Oppenheimer's contemporaries refused to lend their support; yet, 'with no sense of irony', Bloom sniggered, they scrambled to cosy up to the ANC as soon as it won power.[158]

For all his initial apprehension, Oppenheimer told Thatcher at a private meeting on 24 September (initiated by Victor Rothschild) that Relly's foray had done no harm, and perhaps even some good. But on the 'central issues' – in all likelihood, the structure of the post-apartheid economy – HFO believed the ANC had shown itself to be 'entirely unrealistic'.[159] Besides, he observed, black support for the ANC was much exaggerated. Buthelezi was the dominant black political personality in South Africa, and his importance should not be underestimated. Oppenheimer confirmed Thatcher's instincts; in any event, she regarded the ANC as a bunch of communist terrorists. Anyone who thought the organisation could ever form a government – she would handbag those who disagreed with her – was 'living in cloud cuckoo land'.[160] Oppenheimer's understanding of the ANC, like Thatcher's, had been shaped at second hand. His contacts across the African continent and discussions with senior black leaders like Buthelezi, Motlana and Tutu meant he had some idea about the culture and creed of the movement, of both its exiles and 'inziles'. But it was well over twenty years since he had met Luthuli and Mandela. For the most part the banned ANC, the ANC that had taken up violent struggle through Umkhonto we Sizwe, represented unexplored and dangerous territory to him. *Hic sunt dracones*. Although unfamiliarity and risk were hardly qualities that deterred Oppenheimer in commercial life, his conservative political instincts held him back from reaching out to the liberation movement's leaders. Although he might not have realised just how ideologically in hock the ANC was to the South African Communist Party's primitive brand of Stalinism, HFO fully absorbed the ANC's ambivalence towards private enterprise. He was shrewd enough to take the measure of the organisation. Oppenheimer knew the ANC's Zambian charm offensive masked a deep-seated aversion to the idea of economic freedom as he understood it. The ANC, he suspected, was no different from any other African liberation movement that spurned free enterprise as a form of 'neo-colonialism' and advocated, instead, some malignant mutation of socialism with a superficial 'African' twist. As he told the American Chamber of Commerce, the ANC sought to impose an economic system that would 'destroy everything that we in this room stand for'. He duly counselled business to offer the ANC neither 'moral' nor 'material support'.[161]

In the post-Rubicon crucible HFO did meet a black trade unionist who would go on to play a prominent leadership role in the unbanned ANC. In June 1986, Anton Harber, the editor of the *Weekly Mail* – an anti-apartheid newspaper started as an 'alternative' to the mainstream press after the closure of the *Rand Daily Mail* – wanted to do something out of the ordinary to celebrate his publication's one-year anniversary. So he decided to invite two very different men, 'in the middle of the toughest political battles of the time', to share a stage in appreciation of the media's role in society.[162] One was Oppenheimer, the elderly epitome of English

The unionist and the industrialist: Cyril Ramaphosa and HFO
at the Market Theatre, 1986. *(Africa Media Online)*

mining capital and an early promoter of black trade union rights (he had, incidentally, made a modest contribution of R5000 to the *Weekly Mail*'s start-up costs); the other was Cyril Ramaphosa, a young, fiery, rabble-rousing revolutionary riding to prominence in the NUM.

The meeting would be fraught with significance. It took some time for Godsell and Esnouf to convince HFO (against his better judgement) that he should appear on a joint platform with a unionist he had never met. Eventually, they won Oppenheimer over. On a brisk winter's evening, Oppenheimer and Ramaphosa made their way to the Market Theatre. Oppenheimer had expected a genteel audience. There would probably be a fair turnout of bohemian, corduroy-jacketed UDF types, he envisaged, but the mining town's grey-haired *bien pensants* – the chattering classes – could be relied upon to fill the theatre's seats. What confronted HFO on arrival was a raucous crowd of black mineworkers and union officials cheering on their leader. They danced and ululated and sang anti-capitalist anthems. After the introductions, Ramaphosa was the first to speak. He had little to say about the media and went straight on the attack. The mining industry, he goaded his followers, provided 'the furnace in which race discrimination was baked'. 'Today it relies absolutely on the exploitative migrant labour system and on police oppression to operate.'[163] Oppenheimer, ever so slightly discombobulated, managed to project an air of imperturbable good cheer. Taking to the stage, a sparkle in his eye, he responded with barbed grace: 'The fact that Mr Cyril Ramaphosa is here to talk as he did talk tonight – a most touching and moving speech, made all the more touching by the neglect of the facts – the fact that we were both here to talk together is something which gives me very great pleasure.'[164] Afterwards, Esnouf imagined his job was on the line. 'It was a total ambush ... I felt that I ought to resign,' he reflected over thirty years later.[165] But Oppenheimer assuaged his underling's unease. He was quite used to a spot of bother, HFO assured his PA; after all, he had spent ten years in Parliament being heckled by the Nats.

Four Steps to Democracy

Oppenheimer's meeting with Ramaphosa displayed a capacity for shrewd pragmatism on both their parts. In a small but symbolically powerful way, it demonstrated that discordant voices could be heard without a collapse into chaos or violence. For a racially divided society, that was surely going to be the operative principle of democracy once apartheid had been dismantled. Ongoing political violence drove home the urgency of a negotiated transition but reduced the likelihood of one. The problem was that PW Botha stubbornly refused to accept the logical conclusion of his reforms. He moved no closer towards negotiating the shift to a new democratic order. It did not take a Gramscian scholar to observe that the old was dying, the new could not be born, and in the interregnum a variety of morbid symptoms plagued South Africa. Many lost faith in Parliament's prospective role as midwife. On 7 February 1986, during the no-confidence debate, Slabbert abruptly announced his resignation from Parliament. He had met Mbeki and other high-ranking ANC officials in Lusaka shortly after Relly opened the floodgates, and had been 'charmed out of his pants'.[166] One of the effects of this meeting was that it crystallised Slabbert's pessimism with the tricameral parliament: real change, he began to think – the eventual abolition of apartheid – would only come through a process of negotiation instigated and brokered outside the halls of Parliament. Parliament itself had become, in his memorable phrase, a 'grotesque ritual of irrelevance'.

Slabbert had apprised Eglin of his intentions shortly before the sitting, but the news hit their colleagues like a bombshell. At Milkwood, a month before, Slabbert had mentioned nothing of his plans to Oppenheimer, although Boraine later claimed that Slabbert 'did try to raise the matter' with HFO at some point.[167] The move stunned grassroots Prog activists and shattered party morale. A week later Boraine followed suit, compounding the blow, though he had been urged to seek the party leadership in place of Slabbert, and he briefly toyed with the idea, testing his support. Slabbert's desertion of the battlefield infuriated many, not least of all Helen Suzman. For many years afterwards she refused to speak to him. He was, as the *Sunday Times* described him, the captain who had helicoptered off the ship at the height of the storm, 'leaving officers and crew in the lurch'.[168] Eglin tried to weather the squall manfully; his colleagues elected him unanimously to reclaim the helm. Surveying the scene of disaster, Oppenheimer expressed his distress. He lamented the fact that Slabbert's departure had harmed the PFP and subjected it to a 'severe and undeserved ordeal'.[169] However, HFO assured the doubters, Eglin would steady the vessel. He pledged his support to the old political warhorse and lauded him as a 'good soldier', 'a man of courage whose reliability and loyalty to [the] party have been tried in the fire'.[170] These were fine-sounding words, but whether they could rally the party faithful was another matter. Many party members perceived Eglin as an 'abrasive party retread', ill-equipped to fill the gap left by the more charismatic Slabbert.[171] On the eve of the municipal election, some of the PFP's traditional voters asked, not unreasonably, why they should support a party which had failed to inspire the confidence of its own leader.[172] In due course, there was a heavy price to pay at the polls. In the 1987 general election the PFP haemorrhaged seven seats; worst of all, it lost the status of official opposition to Treurnicht's insurgent Conservative Party. The election result signalled, as *Time* aptly termed it, a 'lurch to the right'.[173]

Within the ranks of the Progs there was bitter disillusionment. Eglin, bruised and battered, the object of much backbiting, was unsure whether to make himself available for re-election as party leader. Oppenheimer wanted to do right by his ally, and so when Eglin broached the subject of his resignation with Godsell, HFO wrote to him at once. He wanted to 'make quite sure' that there was 'no misunderstanding on this issue between such old friends as we are'.[174] 'I have always, from the beginning, given my support to the Party and the various leaders it has chosen,' HFO continued; and he was not about to abandon that policy now. Oppenheimer admired Eglin's 'dignity, devotion and courage', and the Progs' line during the election campaign, he reassured him, had enjoyed HFO's 'enthusiastic support'. 'If therefore you are prepared to carry on as leader and feel you can hold the Party together you will, for what it may be worth, continue to have my full support.' Oppenheimer's personal backing was obviously worth quite a lot. The obstacle, of course, was that after the Progs' electoral disaster Eglin doubted his ability to carry the party along with him; he had expressed his reservations to senior colleagues, and Oppenheimer had caught wind of them. Zach de Beer was on standby, just as he had been when Eglin succeeded Jan Steytler in 1971. In the event that Eglin stood down, Oppenheimer informed him, De Beer would be a worthy successor: 'He is an old and dear friend ... and I have great admiration for him. If he were chosen and ... willing ... I should certainly give him any support in my power.' But so long as the Progs remained an 'effective' party, Oppenheimer concluded, he would carry on supporting them no matter their choice of leader.

The letter was vintage HFO. For all the carefully couched caveats designed to soothe Eglin's ego, the subtext was unmistakeable: his time was up. In June 1988, with talk that another general election might be held the following year, Eglin announced that he would stand down from the leadership. De Beer succeeded him, and Eglin became party chairman. Further changes were afoot. By 1988 Helen Suzman had been in Parliament for 35 consecutive years. At a dinner held to honour her in March, HFO praised Suzman's 'fine brain', 'high courage' and 'hatred of all cruelty and injustice'; she was, he said, living proof that the struggle for a just society in South Africa was 'not a lost cause'.[175] In fact, at the age of 71, Suzman felt she was in the twilight of her parliamentary career. The impression was strengthened in April 1989 when the PFP merged with two small opposition groupings: the Independent Party, founded by the former National Party MP and Ambassador to the United Kingdom, Denis Worrall, and the National Democratic Movement, started by another Nationalist defector, Wynand Malan. Suzman was unenthusiastic. She did not see why De Beer should have to share the leadership with Worrall and Malan, or why the Progs' identity must be submerged into a renamed outfit, the Democratic Party. It would be an unwieldy troika, she predicted. Besides, in terms of voters and financial resources, the PFP brought the most valuable dowry to the marriage. Suzman described the union mordantly as 'the biggest hijack since Entebbe', with no 'Jews around to rescue it'.[176] At the end of the parliamentary session in 1989, Suzman made it known that she would not contest the general election in September. It was the end of an epic innings. Suzman had become 'a world figure', HFO told her preferred successor in the Houghton constituency, Irene Menell, and without her Parliament would be a 'different and poorer place'.[177] He reiterated the message in a handsome festschrift for Suzman entitled *Values Alive*.[178] The Ernest Oppenheimer Memorial Trust and the Chairman's Fund together paid homage to the liberal doyenne by endowing the Helen Suzman Chair of Political Economy at Wits University. Given that Suzman had spent eight years teaching economic history at Wits before launching her political career, it was an appropriate way in which to memorialise her legacy.

If Suzman's exit from Parliament felt like the end of an era, that is because it was – in ways that neither she nor her fellow Progs, let alone the Nationalists or Conservatives, could yet fully comprehend. By the end of the decade, after an extended period of economic decline and political turmoil, there was a broad view among the well-informed that apartheid was in its final throes. But no one could quite predict the denouement or foretell what would follow. Behind the scenes, beyond the parliamentary precinct, there were talks about talks about talks taking place simultaneously on multiple fronts. Every vaguely reform-minded Tom, Dick and Harry – white politicians, businessmen, academics and journalists, both English and Afrikaner – was hastening to Lusaka (or Dakar) or London for exploratory discussions with ANC grandees. The heaviest-hitting Harry kept his distance. But he recognised that the ANC was 'an extremely important organisation', and he hoped that it would renounce violence so that the government could 'find a means of negotiating' with it.[179]

In 1988 the ANC published its 'Constitutional Guidelines', and followed them up with the Harare Declaration one year later, which made encouraging noises about constitutionalism and human rights. Meanwhile, business engaged in various forms of lobbying. In London, shortly before its battle royal with Minorco, Anglo's great rival, Consolidated Gold Fields, initiated secret talks between members of the Afrikaner intelligentsia and high-ranking ANC officials, most notably Mbeki. These discussions, conducted at Consgold's secluded countryside manor house, Mells Park, were fed back to the head of the South African National Intelligence Service, Niël Barnard. They played a pivotal part in the transition.[180] In Cape Town Barnard and the Justice Minister, Kobie Coetsee, beat a path to Mandela's prison cell – with PW Botha's consent – to sound out the grey eminence and lay down conditions for negotiation. Still, the path ahead remained shrouded. Economic sanctions were biting, but despite four years of unprecedented internal and international pressure, there was no serious indication of the National Party preparing to relinquish power, nor of the ANC being poised to wrest it militarily.

In 1989 the fog of confusion lifted; it would turn out to be the most fateful year in the history of South African politics. On 18 January PW Botha suffered a serious stroke, though its seriousness – and the political repercussions thereof – would only become clearer later. On 31 January Oppenheimer addressed the World Economic Forum in Davos. He chose, for the title of his speech, 'Four steps to democracy'.[181] Having asked the question on everyone's lips – 'how … are we to move forward?' – HFO offered a four-pronged prescription. Firstly, the government should repeal the Group Areas Act, the Population Registration Act, and other racially discriminatory legislation. Secondly, it would have to prioritise equal educational opportunities for all. Thirdly, there had to be a more equitable spread of private property – of home ownership in the first instance, 'but of the ownership of shares in public companies also'.[182] Fourthly, it was necessary to remove all the hurdles that hindered the development of black-owned small businesses; finance had to be made more readily available to expand the informal sector. Even for a 'Davos man' *avant la lettre*, the recipe seemed to lean heavily on the ingredients of capital. But in giving primacy to economic considerations, Oppenheimer was making a critical point: whites would only mobilise behind political change if – on top of guaranteed civil rights – they could be assured of economic security. He put it plainly to his audience: the ruling white minority would never accept peaceful change unless they were convinced that the post-apartheid state would be one in which 'minority as well as majority rights are assured', with 'a free and dynamic economy based on the system of private enterprise'.[183] In short, whites would not accept the exchange of one tyranny for another. 'Group rights must be guaranteed,' Oppenheimer cautioned, but then group membership must be determined by 'free individual choice' and not 'the accidents of race and colour'.

In August 1989 Botha's steadily declining health led to his resignation and replacement as state president by an unlikely reformer, FW de Klerk. A blue-blooded Nationalist and ideological conservative educated at the Afrikaner citadel of Christian National Higher Education, Potchefstroom University, De Klerk surprised both his own cabinet and the parliamentary opposition with his openness to the concept of a negotiated transition. De Klerk began to claw back power from the securocrats who had surrounded Botha. The determining event in De Klerk's unfolding glasnost and perestroika, however, was the fall of the Berlin Wall on 9 November 1989. It gave him the impetus to act. With the break-up of the Soviet Union and the collapse of the communist bloc in Eastern Europe, the ANC lost its major sponsor. Umkhonto we Sizwe was deprived of military aid. The red peril was neutered, the prospect of 'total onslaught' was obliterated, and the National Party – it seemed – would be able to negotiate from a position of relative strength. President Gorbachev's bold political positioning served as an exemplar; it encouraged De Klerk to seize the initiative. Even so, when De Klerk took to the parliamentary podium on 2 February 1990 and announced a series of sweeping changes, his speech astonished the nation. It was a *pronunciamento* packed with thermonuclear intensity. Everything Oppenheimer and the Progressives had been arguing for looked like it might come to pass. Indeed, the political space which they occupied was colonised: as two rival groups of nationalists limbered up to talk to each other, it appeared the liberals might be squeezed off stage. In fact, De Klerk's speech heralded the 'ironic victory' of liberalism, for liberal ideas furnished the building blocks of the new democratic order.[184] In his later years, Oppenheimer liked to repeat a self-deprecating conceit: his career had been a commercial success and a political failure. Now, in the last decade of his life, there was a chance that truism might be turned on its head.

IV

MONARCH

1990–2000

THIRTEEN

Negotiating the Rainbow Nation

1990–1996

President FW de Klerk's speech at the opening of Parliament on 2 February 1990 struck the world like a thunderbolt. In a matter of minutes he ripped up nearly all of his predecessors' policies. De Klerk announced the unbanning of the ANC, SACP and PAC. He promised the unconditional release of Nelson Mandela and other political prisoners, and he signalled his government's intention to negotiate a new constitutional dispensation. The address was designed to catch the ANC and the Mass Democratic Movement off guard, and in some measure it succeeded. In Stockholm the ANC president, Oliver Tambo, readily conceded that De Klerk's peroration had gone a long way towards creating a climate conducive to negotiations. 'South Africa suddenly became a new country,' Mandela's biographer Anthony Sampson enthused. 'The underground came overground, banned people proclaimed themselves, the ANC ... flags waved, and the papers published photographs of Mandela.'[1] Oppenheimer too was caught up in the euphoria: at the age of 81, ten years Mandela's senior, he had not thought he would live to see the change. In the last decade of his life, thirty years after their initial encounter, Oppenheimer developed a friendship of sorts with Mandela, or 'Madiba', as the world came to embrace him, after his Xhosa clan name. HFO was far from impervious to 'Madiba magic', the goodwill which Mandela radiated and engendered, a spell cast by his personal magnetism. It served as a kind of mesmeric anaesthesia, dulling the racial trauma of the past and blunting the new nation's birth pangs.

Whereas Oppenheimer had been struck by Mandela's air of power in 1961, now he was taken with his 'very great charm'.[2]

Was Oppenheimer hoping, on the eve of Uhuru, to insure his economic empire against political retribution? Did he actively court and co-opt Mandela, a presidential probable, in order to preserve the fundaments of the old racial order in the non-racial democracy to come? Sections of the ANC thought so: in later years the party's unreconstructed racial nationalists – and even some members of its 'Tripartite Alliance' partner organisations, Cosatu and the SACP – talked of a new bogeyman, 'white monopoly capital'. It was personified by anglophone Randlords like Oppenheimer, Afrikaner industrialists like Anton Rupert, and their respective corporate dynasties. Just as menacing as 'Hoggenheimer' of yore, this fiendish entity was designed to thwart 'radical economic transformation'. White monopoly capital, so it was claimed, upheld the power structures that privileged whites and oppressed blacks; it perfused the social order with its avarice. In reality, the claims about white monopoly capital were stoked by conspiracy-mongers with a partisan agenda and bore all the hallmarks of historical revisionism, notably a tendency to distort the facts. Oppenheimer did not play any role of consequence in Mandela's long (and winding) walk from the left of the economic spectrum towards the pragmatic centre, signposted by his rejection of nationalisation in February 1992. Nor did Oppenheimer steer the ANC's macroeconomic policy shifts after the liberation movement came to power in 1994. HFO's most noteworthy soft-power intervention, initiated immediately before the ANC's accession to the Union Buildings, was the establishment of the Brenthurst Group. This forum brought together senior white businessmen, Mandela and other ANC leaders on sporadic occasions from 1994 to 1996 to discuss economic issues, and it fed into a broader stream of dialogue between the government and big business. However, its impact has been vastly exaggerated by left-leaning economists.

Just prior to the advent of democracy Oppenheimer warned that it was 'extremely dangerous' to be 'ruled by people who have no material stake in the country'.[3] That sentiment led him to champion an incipient form of black economic empowerment (BEE) in 1996, through Anglo's unbundling and sale of JCI to two separate consortia of black investors, one of which was led by Cyril Ramaphosa. (Ramaphosa served as the ANC's secretary general from 1991 to 1996, before he resigned the position to enter business.) BEE became one of the ANC's flagship policies, though it quickly degenerated into a patronage scheme – a system of elite enrichment for the politically well-connected, and a vehicle for state capture. HFO failed to foresee the predatory practices to which BEE gave rise. He would have been aghast at the turn of events. For not only did BEE achieve little for the immiserated black majority – in the long run, it deterred fixed investment, put a ceiling on growth, and amplified inequalities – but it also corrupted governance, thus undermining South Africa's viability as a going democratic concern.

Oppenheimer was born on the eve of the National Convention, which foreshadowed the creation of the Union in 1910. This constitutional forum fashioned the South African state and propagated the idea of shared white South Africanism – based on conciliation between Boer and Brit – as the axis of nationhood. Now, over eighty years later, the nation was to be reconceived, midwifed not by segregation and white domination, but by racial reconciliation and the certainty of a common South African citizenship. These precepts were to be coupled constitutionally with the values of human dignity, non-racialism and the rule of law. The polity would witness the birth of the 'Rainbow Nation', to use Desmond Tutu's vivid metaphor. Yet even as the constitutional settlement gestated, from the launch of the Convention for a Democratic South Africa (Codesa) in 1991, through the Interim Constitution of 1993, to the adoption of the final Constitution in 1996, the feel-good notion of 'rainbowism' had its doubters: they believed the unfolding process would culminate in an interracial 'elite pact'. The argument gained traction in the wake of Mandela's death in 2013, as the country began, under his ANC successors, to go to rack and ruin. Neo-patrimonialist nationalists and disaffected leftists were *ad idem*: the democratic transition of 1994 and the constitutional settlement, they contended, might have transformed the country's politics, but nothing had been done to shake the foundations of white economic power. Not only was the bedrock intact; it had been fortified to boot. *Die geldmag* had transmogrified, and now it feasted like a parasite on the economically disempowered black masses. Mandela was a 'sell-out', rang the refrain in certain quarters. He had made too many compromises with the forces of 'neoliberalism'. Madiba had abandoned the Freedom Charter and surrendered to big capital, entrenching white privilege and black poverty into the bargain.

There was even a tacit implication that Oppenheimer figured as a kind of constitutional monarch in the transfer of power – not in the jocular way that Ton Vosloo had intended in the 1980s, but in the sense of an omnipotent sovereign whose fingerprints tainted the negotiated settlement – the inverse of the Midas touch. At one level this tendentious reading of history is superficially plausible. Mandela did cosy up to rich liberal mining financiers like Oppenheimer (and, more so, Clive Menell, at whose secluded Cape mansion, Glendirk, Mandela spent his first Christmas as president in 1994). Mindful of the need to attract foreign investment into a shattered economy, he reached out to them in a way that would have been inconceivable to Afrikaner nationalist heads of state, from DF Malan to FW de Klerk. Yet the negotiated settlement that emerged in South Africa was far from the sort of political compact that Oppenheimer would have deemed desirable, or even likely, when De Klerk turned the tide of history in 1990. For starters, it sealed in a winner-takes-all form of democracy with watered-down provisions for federalism. What HFO had long envisaged was a version of consociational democracy, some model of power-sharing which guaranteed minority rights and factored in the regional realities of South Africa's multiracial, multi-ethnic state. Certainly, that was the golden thread of his thinking in the 1980s, from the Buthelezi Commission through the KwaZulu/Natal Indaba to his speech in Davos in 1989.

If Oppenheimer was the hidden hand negotiating the Rainbow Nation – a process in which liberal politicians like Colin Eglin and Zach de Beer performed a hands-on, albeit circumscribed role – then he would probably have been disappointed with his handiwork. For the settlement was politically flawed: it led quickly to the development of a dominant-party system and an environment in which corruption flourished, law and order crumbled, and service delivery stalled. 'I don't think this government so far has shown enormous ability at national administration,' HFO volunteered, with characteristic understatement, in 1997.[4] Economically, the settlement was neither fish nor fowl. The Constitution enshrined property rights, with a provision for expropriation subject to compensation, but the inclusion of a host of second-generation rights gave the state ample scope for *dirigisme*. As such, the document could scarcely be termed neoliberal. Despite Mandela's turn away from nationalisation, the settlement was silent on privatisation: in retrospect this was a failing, for profligate state-owned enterprises came to blight the post-apartheid economy. In the last years of his life, despite his reservations about the ANC, Oppenheimer praised Mandela and professed to be 'immensely pleased at what has taken place'.[5] Indeed, the real rot only started to manifest itself after the turn of the century, and Oppenheimer was to be spared the shattering of the Rainbow Nation myth.

De Klerk's Damascene Moment and the End of White Minority Rule

Oppenheimer told Patti Waldmeir, the *Financial Times* correspondent who chronicled South Africa's democratic transition and later analysed it in her book *Anatomy of a Miracle*, that he was 'amazed' and 'thrilled' by De Klerk's seminal address.[6] He harboured a 'starry-eyed' notion, HFO commented exuberantly, that De Klerk must have undergone a Damascene conversion before delivering it. How else might one explain this volte-face by a 'genuine conservative'? In Oppenheimer's view, De Klerk could have battened down the hatches, cracked down on the resistance movements, and mounted a military defence of apartheid for years to come; instead, he did a 'spectacular thing' and abandoned what for him had been mother's milk. De Klerk's change of heart, HFO surmised, was due to the President's realisation that apartheid had become patently unworkable. Its injustices were incontrovertible. Steeped in the Gereformeerde Kerk (Reformed Church), or 'Dopper', theological tradition, which developed a moral justification for apartheid, De Klerk tied the morality of separate development to its viability. 'Of course a thing like that, if it doesn't work, *becomes* immoral,' especially to its ethical champions, Oppenheimer reflected.

In some ways this was an *ex post facto* rationalisation of Oppenheimer's own style of opposition politics – his approach of 'putting moral arguments in economic terms', as he described it to Waldmeir – though it could equally be said that the so-called Oppenheimer thesis had been vindicated by the march of history. Since his days as a member of Parliament, Oppenheimer had argued that apartheid would prove economically unsustainable, and that capitalist development would unstitch the feudal racial order. He was correct. Apartheid might have dovetailed with economic growth and white prosperity in the 1950s and 1960s, but its inefficiencies and contradictions – the fact that it held back black skilled labour and strangled productivity – could no longer be managed or contained from the mid-1970s. The 'economic revolution' which Oppenheimer foresaw in 1974 dissolved racial hierarchies and cleared the path for political change.

In order to grow, South Africa's industrial economy depended on technical progress, better human capital, and advances in productivity

– not the exploitation of cheap, unskilled black labour. HFO knew it, and he tried to steer Anglo American accordingly, in spite of the prescripts of the political ruling class. By 1986 many of the major economic institutions and policies underpinning apartheid had been dismantled, paving the way for the transition to black rule. According to the foremost economic historian of South Africa, Charles Feinstein, by then the retreat from 'the economic dogmas of previous decades' was 'largely complete'.[7] There had also been a significant relaxation of social apartheid. PW Botha could take credit for a good deal of this. 'He did things of the very greatest importance,' HFO conceded to Waldmeir; however, Botha's 'unattractive' personality tended to militate against such kudos being given. In the long run, as Oppenheimer had predicted, capitalism made a mockery of apartheid. Yet Botha's socio-economic reforms could not prevent stagnation, or balance-of-payments constraints, or disinvestment. Those particular crises required political solutions. In 1989 foreign pressures were mounting; the economic crisis was becoming acute; and South Africa was teetering, De Klerk told his brother, Wimpie, 'on the edge of the abyss'.[8] That is what galvanised Botha's successor into action once the window of opportunity blew open, courtesy of communism's collapse. Regionally, the withdrawal of Cuban troops from Angola and the successful conclusion of negotiations for Namibia's independence helped tip the scales. Margaret Thatcher, through Robin Renwick, her subtle and skilful ambassador to South Africa, assured De Klerk that if he gave Mandela his freedom, then Britain would lift sanctions and the ban on new investment that she had reluctantly imposed. The promise provided a fillip to South Africa's last apartheid President.

In the dying days of her premiership Thatcher continued to seek Oppenheimer's advice on South African matters. However, on one visit to the country she had to make do with lunch in HFO's private dining room at 44 Main Street rather than dinner at Brenthurst. HFO rang up Bridget from the office to synchronise their diaries. 'Bwidgie, Mrs Thatcher is coming to South Africa in two weeks' time, and Robin Renwick has asked us to have her to dinner. Can we make it the Wednesday night?' he asked her, almost apologetically.[9] 'No, we're busy,' came the curt reply, followed by the click of the receiver. He tried again. 'Bwidgie, why can't we host Mrs Thatcher on Wednesday night?' The answer was that Bridget had organised a farewell dinner for one of the retiring gardeners who worked on the Brenthurst estate; the invitations had gone out, and not even the arrival of the Iron Lady could make Bridget bend her iron will.

Nevertheless, Harry and Bridget rolled out the red carpet for Thatcher when she travelled to South Africa to receive a national honour, the Order of Good Hope, from De Klerk in 1991, a few months after her forced departure from 10 Downing Street. On that occasion the dinner invitees reflected something of the nascent Rainbow Nation's colourful kaleidoscope: alongside the familiar names on Bridget's guest list – Helen Suzman, Gavin and Jane Relly, Julian and Tessa Ogilvie Thompson, Albert and Madeleine Robinson, Frederik and Jane van Zyl Slabbert – appeared members of the black elite. One of them was Aggrey Klaaste, editor of the *Sowetan* newspaper. Another was Richard Maponya with his wife, Marina, a cousin of Mandela's. A multi-millionaire who had built up a retail empire in spite of apartheid prohibitions, Maponya was the first black racehorse owner to be granted colours. Oppenheimer had proposed him to a hesitant Jockey Club in the early 1980s, and Maponya's runners eventually took to the track in a distinctive set of black, green and gold silks – a nod to the ANC's own insignia. Fresh crayfish were on the menu for Thatcher. 'Very good dinner & greatly enjoyed,' Bridget recorded afterwards.[10]

Ten months after Thatcher's visit (and three months after the first plenary session of Codesa) De Klerk sought affirmation from the white electorate to continue the process of negotiations. The referendum, held on 17 March 1992, was designed to hobble the backlash from Andries Treurnicht's Conservative Party (CP), which had been stoked by the party's victories in recent by-elections. Anglo American and other big corporates campaigned vigorously in favour of a 'yes' vote. Under the auspices of the Private Sector Referendum Fund they sponsored a series of full-page advertisements warning against the dire international repercussions of a 'no' vote. At the same time, Oppenheimer and Relly issued hard-hitting statements in support of ongoing negotiations, as did Zach de Beer on behalf of the Democratic Party (DP).[11] De Klerk's gamble paid off handsomely: 69 per cent of white voters gave him a mandate to proceed. 'Today we have closed the books on apartheid,' the President announced victoriously.[12] While that was indisputably true, De Klerk had assured the white electorate of future power-sharing arrangements alongside a justiciable constitution. Many voters gave him the go-ahead on the strength of that undertaking.

However, in the Multi-Party Negotiating Process (MPNP) that followed Codesa, De Klerk's middlemen failed to embed power-sharing or minority rights in the Interim Constitution, never mind, as had once been floated, a minority veto. Before De Klerk and Mandela signed the Record of Understanding on 26 September 1992, an agreement was reached to establish a Government of National Unity (GNU) for a period of five years after the first democratic election. That is as far as power-sharing went. Confronted by the 'fierce urgency of now', the National Party (NP) rushed to strike a settlement. A massacre of ANC supporters at Boipatong in June 1992, and another at Bisho in September, fuelled political unrest, jeopardised negotiations, and piled pressure on the government. In April 1993 the assassination of Chris Hani, the SACP's popular general secretary, by Janusz Waluś, a white, right-wing Polish extremist with links to the CP, led South Africa to the edge of the abyss. The effect, far from stalling negotiations as the white revanchists had hoped, was to speed up the process. Mandela calmed the angry masses in a televised address, thereby averting a potential racial conflagration. Meanwhile, with Anglo's backing, Bobby Godsell quietly persuaded the Chamber of Mines to donate a substantial sum towards the costs of Hani's funeral, which James Motlatsi (Godsell's close contact and then president of the National Union of Mineworkers) had been tasked with organising.[13] In some ways the ANC's bargaining power was enhanced in the aftermath of Hani's assassination. The NP found itself cornered into making more and more concessions. Outwitted and outmanoeuvred by their counterparts in the ANC, the NP's negotiators soon acquiesced in simple majority rule. They lacked the fire in the belly needed to secure constitutional guarantees on power-sharing; at the same time, the 'strong currents in the river' favoured the ANC, and they swept away all obstacles with ease.[14]

Meanwhile, the liberal flirtation with consociationalism petered out. At Codesa, Colin Eglin had presented the DP's policy on 'the meaningful participation of political minorities', which the party understood as the product of citizens associating voluntarily to express their individual rights collectively, rather than as racial groups. He proposed a number of constitutional mechanisms to give political minorities access to power, 'a form of power-sharing by rotation'.[15] These included special voting majorities that would give minorities a say on matters to do with language, religion and culture. However, the DP did not press the issue, and most of the party's proposals on political minorities were consigned to the ash heap of history. Nevertheless, the incorporation of core liberal-democratic principles into the Interim Constitution signalled, in some measure, an ironic victory for South Africa's political minnows, wedged as they were between the Scylla and Charybdis of rival racial nationalisms.

For decades the DP's predecessor parties had been making the case for a comprehensive Bill of Rights that protected individual freedoms. Ever since the Molteno Commission they had advocated curbs on legislative and executive power. They had proposed constitutional checks and balances to counter majoritarianism, put forward measures to strengthen judicial independence (including a move away from the executive appointment of judges), and championed the devolution of authority to regional governments. The ANC, a party wedded to the Marxist-Leninist dogma of the 'National Democratic Revolution', and steeped in the practice of democratic centralism, did not look upon many of these proposals with unbridled enthusiasm. Several other parties in the MPNP cleaved, like the ANC, to the notion of a unitary state. They refrained from referring to 'federalism', the so-called f-word.[16] However, the ANC's concession on the creation of three spheres of government, and the dispersal of powers to provinces, opened the door to a weak version of the system. South Africa would not be *remotely* a federation', as Joe Slovo, the ANC's most consequential negotiator (and the SACP's master tactician), crowed; what the ANC had yielded to was 'devolution, without losing control'.[17] Although the ANC achieved substantially what it wanted from the Interim Constitution – a path to hegemonic power – it was the MPNP's liberal actors who provided many of the conceptual tools that enabled the ANC and the NP to find common ground. They helped limit the scope for majoritarian abuse. This was an achievement made more impressive by the fact that the negotiations operated on the basis of 'sufficient consensus', a bromide interpreted bluntly by the ANC's chief negotiator, Ramaphosa: 'It means that, if we and the National Party agree, everyone else can get stuffed.'[18]

In contemplating the transition as it unfolded, Oppenheimer held firm to the staples that had long animated his involvement in politics. For him the key determinants to democratic success, whatever shape the Interim Constitution might take, provided the political direction of travel was tolerable, were the maintenance of free enterprise and private property. 'The fact is that in the majority of new African states', HFO had emphasised at the World Economic Forum in 1989, 'a new tyranny has limited individual freedom, wrecked the economy ... and produced a state of endemic violence and sometimes starvation.'[19] The sort of economic thinking that led to such destruction, HFO reasoned, needed to be countered. Very few people in developed countries looked to nationalisation of industry or central planning to raise social and economic standards, he contended; but this fact had gone 'largely unnoticed or ignored' in the 'Third World countries of Africa'. Oppenheimer scorned the notion that by following Kwame Nkrumah's injunction 'Give me first the political kingdom', African nationalists would be able to conjure up a land of milk and honey. 'Nothing could be further from the truth,' HFO insisted to the delegates at Davos. He believed that unless the ANC dispensed with the Freedom Charter's ideological obsolescences – nationalisation, first and foremost – majority rule in South Africa would probably spell the same kind of oppressive governance that it did in other parts of the continent. Therefore, big business should make a concerted effort, Oppenheimer and Anglo's top brass agreed, to help remove the scales from the ANC's eyes. In Mandela they found someone who, if not entirely clear-eyed on the economy, was at least prepared to look in their direction. As a free man, he stressed the need for consultation with the jittery business community. Two weeks after his release from prison Mandela summoned Gavin Relly to the residence he shared with Winnie in Soweto. It was an amiable and symbolically important meeting, though the commanding heights of the economy were not discussed.

Befriending Mandela

As it happened, neither Anglo nor Oppenheimer induced Mandela to turn his back on nationalisation, which he famously did in February 1992, in the rarefied atmosphere of Davos, spurred on by the socialist leaders of China and Vietnam. 'They changed my views altogether ... I came home to say: "We either keep nationalisation and get no investment, or we modify our own attitude and get investment."'[20] Over the preceding two years Mandela had been wined and dined, indeed lionised, by the world's leading bankers and industrialists, none of whom had any truck with nationalisation. Nevertheless, it was the sympathetic delegates from the left who turned him at Davos. The initial auguries were mixed. In November 1989 Mandela had been visited in prison by Richard Maponya. After their meeting Maponya told reporters that Mandela was concerned about South Africa's sluggish growth rate. The struggle icon, Maponya added, 'did not believe in nationalisation'.[21] The comment rattled some of Mandela's comrades: they saw the Freedom Charter being betrayed.[22]

However, two months later, Mandela reaffirmed the ANC's commitment to nationalising mines, banks and monopoly industries.

On 11 February 1990, the day he walked out of the gates of Victor Verster Prison, Mandela delivered a wooden speech on the Grand Parade in Cape Town. It was full of platitudes, and he called for the intensification of the struggle and the 'fundamental restructuring of our political and economic systems'.[23] Oppenheimer regarded it as 'abominable', 'so absolutely a speech without vision'.[24] The sentiment was shared by De Klerk and Thatcher: the British Prime Minister was dismayed by the 'old ritual phrases', and she scotched a planned statement.[25] However, the following day, at his first press conference, hosted in the gardens of Archbishop Tutu's official residence in Bishopscourt, Mandela revealed a less dogmatic, more conciliatory and charismatic aspect to his personality. It was this side of Mandela that HFO warmed to: there was a mutual respect and admiration between these two men of gravitas, and it evolved into close fellow feeling, even genuine warmth. They met at a lunch hosted by Helen Suzman, with several other tycoons in attendance; she had visited Mandela on Robben Island, cultivated a rapport with both him and Winnie over many years, and championed his release. Mandela 'charmed the bloody lot of them', Suzman later recalled.[26] The impression was confirmed by Oppenheimer: 'He has charming manners and a nice presence … you simply felt that you were meeting a very agreeable, sensible person.'[27] Shortly after capping Mandela with an honorary Doctor of Laws at UCT, Oppenheimer invited him to dine at Brenthurst, and soon the ANC president (Mandela was elected to the position in 1991) became a regular dinner guest.

These affairs tended to be intimate. After Mandela's separation from Winnie in 1992, Bridget made a point of inviting Madiba to dinner regularly. He appeared lonely and in need of solace, and Bridget was solicitous about his welfare. It was only on larger, more formal occasions, legend had it, that her invitations were accompanied by a caveat: 'Oh, and Nelson, wear a tie, please, not one of your silly shirts.' Clifford Elphick was present on almost all of these occasions. A sporty, affable go-getter who had started out as a management trainee in Anglo's finance division, he was seconded as HFO's private assistant in 1988. Elphick rapidly became the magnate's blue-eyed boy: in the 1990s he doubled up as the managing director of E Oppenheimer and Son, having learnt the ropes from Grey Fletcher. He helped build up the firm's private equity interests outside South Africa. Elphick's recollection of these early encounters was

Flanked by Dr Stuart Saunders and HFO, Nelson Mandela beams
after receiving his honorary degree (Doctor of Laws) from the
University of Cape Town, 1990. *(Anglo American)*

that Mandela 'seemed to think South Africa was a rich country'; however,
'quite quickly, the reality of a bankrupt nation emerged ... He realised
that this thing wasn't going to work without capital investment.'[28] When
Mandela and Oppenheimer met, nationalisation was never on the agenda.

At first, Mandela's economic pronouncements could be ambiguous
and even vacuous. 'When you talked about the future of the country,
particularly on the economic side,' Oppenheimer reflected, 'he said a great
many things that seemed to me very silly ...'[29] HFO offered his views,
nudged and cajoled but never hectored, and subtly underscored the point
that in office the ANC's political philosophy would be constrained, like
the Nats before them, by what was economically practical. The party
might campaign in the poetry of struggle, but it would have to govern
in the prose of realpolitik. Even before Mandela's light-bulb moment
at Davos, a variety of structured engagements between the ANC and
the private sector prompted a shift in the organisation's economic
thinking, away from the model of growth through redistribution towards
reforms premised on attracting fixed investment. The presentation and
dissemination of the Mont Fleur scenarios, the product of a think tank
hatched in the Western Cape winelands, as well as Nedcor–Old Mutual's
South Africa: Prospects for a Successful Transition – both of which drew

Jonathan Oppenheimer and Clifford Elphick at Bridget and HFO's anniversary dinner, March 1993. *(Brenthurst Library)*

inspiration from Clem Sunter's earlier 'high road, low road' scenario-planning exercise – fed into this process.[30]

By the time Mandela ascended to the country's presidency, HFO had come to think that there was no 'difference ... in principle' between the two of them on broad economic issues: 'I believe in private enterprise, but I've never been the sort of person that believes that any regulation ... comes from the devil.'[31] Oppenheimer began to get a good sense of Mandela. A few months before the Interim Constitution was finalised in November 1993, shortly after the date was set for South Africa's first democratic election, Oppenheimer confidently told an interviewer from the *Financial Times*: 'I don't think there's any risk of a government dominated by the ANC nationalising the mines or Anglo American.'[32] Certainly, Anglo 'shouldn't expect gratitude' from the ANC for its role in criticising the old regime, Oppenheimer conceded, but he doubted that 'white' business would be singled out for punishment. 'I think this will be a government with which business people can work comfortably. You know, we've had a great deal of experience working with very, very difficult governments in Africa – a great deal more difficult than this one is likely to be.' Not even talk of antitrust policies, or the break-up of monopolies and unbundling of conglomerates, fazed him. Anglo's rival Gencor had recently announced a wholesale restructuring, widely seen as the first step in the transformation of corporate South Africa. But HFO waved it aside. 'I think it's absurd to say that a holding company just in principle should only invest in one industry ... personally, I wouldn't dream of accepting a policy of unbundling.' These were to prove thorny issues once the ANC introduced stringent competition legislation in 1998, and they were navigated by Julian Ogilvie Thompson. Having fended off the challenge from Gordon Waddell, who left South Africa for England in 1987, ostensibly for political reasons – 'he said he didn't want anything more to do with any of us', JOT later recounted – Ogilvie Thompson took over the reins at Anglo when Relly retired from the chairmanship in 1990.[33] At the same time, JOT remained in the saddle at De Beers.

Although Mandela and Oppenheimer discussed economics, they dwelt more on politics and history. Madiba asked HFO about his days in Parliament and why Smuts had deferred dealing with the 'native question'. He displayed an impressive knowledge of Suzman's lone battles in the House of Assembly and of the Progressive Party's metamorphosis. Mandela was well informed; he asked probing questions. Oppenheimer found him companionable. Yet HFO was not one of those businessmen who lavished patronage upon Mandela, like the brash, self-made insurance tycoon, Douw Steyn, or the casino capitalist, Sol Kerzner, who had made a killing out of the Bantustans with his gaudy hotel resorts-cum-gambling-dens, catering to white pleasure-seekers. Steyn put Mandela up in his flashy mansion after his split from Winnie, and Kerzner partly financed the honeymoon of Madiba's daughter Zindzi, in addition to making 'other strategic donations' to the ANC elite.[34]

Mandela tended to regard successful white businessmen as fellow chiefs: he once surprised a group of Johannesburg's corporate overlords by referring to them as the 'traditional tribal leaders in this area'.[35] Some of them, in turn, established a patron–client relationship with the ANC. They sponsored the return of ANC exiles to South Africa and helped set them up financially, a phenomenon which spawned a sense of entitlement among the prodigal sons and daughters of the revolution: it encouraged the notion that they could acquire money without earning or declaring (or, in public life, accounting for) it. Many businesses poured money into causes favoured by the ANC. Donald Gordon's Liberty Life Foundation channelled a good deal of funds to such ends. The Anglo American and De Beers Chairman's Fund could also be relied upon to offer a sympathetic ear and an open cheque book. Madiba magic exerted a remarkable magnetism in matters monetary. 'Your father was a man who in his quiet and unassuming manner almost castigated me', Mandela told Nicky Oppenheimer in 2003 (when De Beers donated the historic Rhodes Building in Cape Town to the Mandela Rhodes Foundation), 'for ever doubting that he would respond generously to calls for support of worthy causes.'[36] Nevertheless, some of this munificence masked the beginnings of capital (and personal) flight by white titans of commerce after the ANC took power. 'Gordon, like Kerzner, had taken one look at the ANC and decided to emigrate', wrote RW Johnson, the Durban-schooled political scientist who had returned to South Africa after a long career at Oxford University.[37] He recorded South Africa's democratic transition and Mandela's presidency for various British newspapers, a task performed with a more jaundiced eye than many of his star-struck colleagues on *The Guardian* or *Observer*. Since it took time for would-be émigrés to 'rearrange their affairs' and establish a new base in another country, many of them 'threw money at the ANC', Johnson jibed, while they quietly went about selling their businesses and moving money abroad.

In spite of onerous exchange controls Oppenheimer had externalised much of his private wealth by the 1970s, thanks to the creative financial brains at E Oppenheimer and Son. It was a course of action initiated during the early years of BJ Vorster's premiership, when Anglo was in the government's cross hairs and the status of the Hoek Report remained in the balance. Gordon Waddell almost put the kibosh on the plan, reputedly, when he announced these developments to the Governor of the Reserve Bank in an official letter. E Oppenheimer and Son essentially became an administrative company, handling the family's day-to-day affairs and expenses, with lawyers, bookkeepers and drivers on its payroll. The Oppenheimers' business interests, in contrast, were managed by a holding company, the Luxembourg-based Central Holdings Limited, registered in 1968. Central Holdings owned E Oppenheimer and Son. Dresdner Bank, the German banking corporation which assisted South Africa with international gold trades and provided credit to the country in the 1970s,[38] was brought in as a ten per cent shareholder of Central Holdings to discourage possible retaliatory action by the Nationalists. Nevertheless, even if his financial holdings had largely been offshored, HFO retained a significant number of physical assets in South Africa. He remained heavily invested in the country's success. Oppenheimer kept a South African passport only, and he did not entertain emigration lightly. 'If a great many obstacles were put in the way of our having a successful and expanding business here ... there would be pressure to do it elsewhere,' he acknowledged in 1993. Even so, he was 'absolutely tied' to South Africa and believed in 'sticking to your roots'.[39] Having looked into his crystal ball, Oppenheimer fell back on an old line: 'If the ship sinks, I shall drown, but I'm not going to jump overboard'.[40]

The 1994 Election: ANC Hegemony and the DP's 'Dreadful' Defeat

Mandela was a consummate and unabashed fundraiser for the ANC and other causes close to his heart: he thought nothing of picking up the telephone and leaning on white industrialists to empty their wallets. On the eve of the first democratic election, set for 27 April 1994, Mandela approached twenty top businessman for R1 million each, and all but one of them complied. Mandela knew that Oppenheimer's loyalty to the DP, the party of Eglin and De Beer, was unshakeable; he stopped short of requesting wire transfers from Brenthurst to Shell House, the ANC's headquarters in downtown Johannesburg. Others were less inhibited. Before the election the PAC's secretary general, Benny Alexander (later known as Khoisan X), arrived with an entourage at 44 Main Street and put up a 'spirited and lively' case to HFO as to why he should donate funds to the party.[41] Alexander appealed to the former parliamentarian's democratic sensibilities, though he readily admitted that, in power, the PAC would confiscate Oppenheimer's properties and nationalise Anglo's mines. HFO greatly enjoyed the meeting, but Alexander walked away without a pledge.

Throughout this period Oppenheimer remained in regular contact with Chief Mangosuthu Buthelezi. They saw each other often at Milkwood. Buthelezi's KwaZulu-Natal-based cultural movement contested the founding election as the Inkatha Freedom Party (IFP), but right up until the eleventh hour its participation was far from guaranteed. A proud man of royal birth with considerable *amour propre*, Buthelezi had had his nose put out of joint early on in the transition. When Inkatha was formed in 1975, the ANC had hoped it would serve as a sort of Trojan horse for the banned organisation inside South Africa. But the Zulu chief was his own man: during apartheid he had adopted contrarian views on sanctions and the armed struggle, and now he fought for a post-apartheid settlement that embraced an extreme form of federalism – one that would give KwaZulu virtual autonomy and secure his regional power-base. The ANC regarded Buthelezi as intransigent, at best, and a homeland stooge, at worst. Rumours soon spread that a sinister 'third force' of state security operatives was aiding and abetting the IFP to foment violence against ANC supporters. The conflict that raged between Inkatha and the ANC turned the rolling green hills of KwaZulu-Natal (and the Transvaal's migrant hostels) into bloody killing fields. Despite Buthelezi's early overtures, it was not until almost a year after Mandela's release that he and Madiba met.

Buthelezi felt snubbed and humiliated. He became alienated from the negotiating process. In fact, Buthelezi believed he was being deliberately marginalised, that the multiparty negotiations were a facade for bilateral talks between De Klerk and Mandela, and that the Zulu kingdom was being disrespected by the so-called Xhosa Nostra. His resentment grew. Egged on by hard-line white advisors, Buthelezi resorted to acts of brinkmanship. He quit the MPNP, threatened civil war if an unpalatable constitution was foisted on KwaZulu, and joined forces with a motley crew of ultra-right-wing groupings that included the separatist umbrella organisation, the Afrikaner Volksfront, led by General Constand Viljoen. Oppenheimer believed that Buthelezi had been badly treated during the transition, though he conceded to an interviewer that the IFP leader was a 'prickly fellow'.[42] He was mindful of Buthelezi's ability to upset the apple cart, a fact brought home to observers when the IFP marched goadingly on Shell House – replete with traditional weapons – on 28 March 1994, an episode which led to bloodshed and left 53 demonstrators dead. Before the slaughter, HFO had relayed his concerns about Buthelezi's burgeoning bellicosity to Mandela. When two international mediators – Lord Carrington, the former British Foreign Secretary, and Henry Kissinger – flew to South Africa in mid-April in an attempt to resolve the political deadlock and broker the IFP's electoral participation, Oppenheimer quietly lent them his support. But their efforts were a failure. Buthelezi wanted the election delayed – an impossible demand since the date was set in stone – and after a few days of frantic but fruitless manoeuvring, Kissinger returned home dejected by the miscarriage of his 'catastrophic mission'.[43]

The shuttle diplomacy continued, courtesy of Anglo's fleet of unmarked private planes. 'Enter a small, shy, hard-of-hearing 86-year-old retiree recovering from pneumonia, who prefers to spend his day betting on the horses, playing with his whippets and surrounding himself with 19th-century antiques', the American newspaper *USA Today* declared effusively, under a hyperbolic headline: 'South Africa's secret freedom fighter'.[44] 'Hours later Mandela and Buthelezi are smiling, hugging, and proclaiming the beginning of the new South Africa. Details of the deal remain unclear … but the crisis was ended.' HFO, the publication postulated, had saved the day. For good measure, it quoted one Joseph Hlongwane, a community leader from the township of Crossroads in Cape Town. Hlongwane lauded Oppenheimer: 'He's God's gift to the black man … His skin may be white but he's one of us.' UCT political scientist Professor David Welsh acknowledged HFO's clout: 'When Harry Oppenheimer speaks, the entire country listens.' Oppenheimer had indeed played a part behind the scenes, but the decisive intervention, Welsh subsequently explained, was made by a portly Kenyan theologian, Buthelezi's long-time friend Washington Okumu. He had arrived with the Kissinger–Carrington team but had not departed with them. Okumu was the *deus ex machina* who persuaded Buthelezi to contest the election, six days before the ballot, by playing on his vanity and his more pragmatic instincts.[45] The IFP leader would not want to end up on the historical scrapheap, Okumu tactfully suggested, nor be remembered as an embittered spoiler.

The run-up to the April election passed in a haze of drama, dread and delirium. Political violence continued unabated: in March, as the campaign was in full swing, an average of 17 people lost their lives per day. Meanwhile, bomb explosions, orchestrated by the neo-fascist Afrikaner Weerstandsbeweging (Afrikaner Resistance Movement), rocked several towns. They failed to deter millions of voters from heading to the polls. On voting day, South Africans of every hue – rich and poor, black and white – snaked their way around open fields and roads in interminable queues, waiting patiently to exercise their rights as equal citizens. The atmosphere was jubilant.

Squeezed between the ANC and the NP, the DP understood that its best hopes lay in the Western Cape, which is where the party's energies and comparatively meagre resources were channelled. The DP tried to chart a centrist course, exemplified by an advertisement which positioned the party logo in the middle of the page, with text on the left warning, 'If the left get in, there'll be nothing right', and text on the right cautioning, 'If the right get in, there'll be nothing left.'[46] But the fact of the matter was that during the transition the NP's magpie nationalists had stolen many of the liberals' best ideas. They had swooped down upon the DP's carefully cultivated middle ground and nested there. Thousands of white voters who had supported the Progs in the 1987 election – voters who might reasonably be expected to endorse the DP – now made their mark for the NP. By doing this, they believed they could maximise opposition to the ANC's prospective hegemony. Some of the DP's left-wing voters plumped for the party on the provincial ballot but gave their national vote 'to Mandela' for sentimental reasons.[47] To Oppenheimer, voting for the NP, the party which had devised apartheid (and weaponised the 'Hoggenheimer' slur against him), was unthinkable. Like Zach de Beer, he never quite shook off his aversion to the Nats. Nor did Mandela's liberally sprinkled magic dust blind Oppenheimer to the ANC's soft underbelly. HFO proudly announced that he had cast his ballot for the DP. As he explained to one reporter, historically the ANC had gone in for 'a great deal of violence', which was repellent to him, and besides, he 'didn't take to' the ANC's 'alliance with the Communist Party'.[48]

The 1994 election amounted to little more than an ethnic census. Voting took place broadly along racial lines. The great majority of Africans backed their liberators, the party of Uhuru, and gave the ANC an overwhelming mandate nationally of 62.7 per cent. The NP had confidently predicted that it would bag over one-third of all the votes cast, but in the end it had to settle for a dispiriting 20.8 per cent. Nevertheless, more than 60 per cent of Coloured and Indian voters lined up behind the NP, which (in the case of the Coloured electorate) enabled it to claim the consolation prize of power in the Western Cape. In the main, whites turned to De Klerk's party as a safe haven in the storm of non-racial democracy, thus ensuring the runner-up berth for the NP nationally. But white votes were distributed among several minority parties: the DP, CP and Vryheidsfront (Freedom Front), founded by Constand Viljoen just two months before the election. With less than a week to campaign, the IFP managed to win power in the reconfigured province of KwaZulu-Natal, and it gained over ten per cent of the vote nationally. This was a creditable performance, though the IFP's over-reliance on Zulu traditionalist support concentrated in one province represented something of a personal blow to Buthelezi. As one of the country's most recognisable black leaders, he had banked on having broader appeal. However, by far the most bitter disappointment was felt by the DP, which netted a paltry 1.73 per cent of the national vote, yielding only seven seats in Parliament. This was scant reward, the party faithful brooded, for thirty-five years of dogged opposition to apartheid and a history of trying to attenuate racial polarisation. De Beer, elected sole leader of the DP after the troika leadership disintegrated, had gone into the campaign communicating an ambivalent message about his long-term availability for the position. Debilitated by strong medication for cardiovascular disease, he appeared to lack energy and enthusiasm; the fires which had once burned so brightly within him, reckoned Tony Leon, his spirited successor, had been 'all but extinguished'.[49] Even so, the electoral outcome fell far short of De Beer's personal expectations. It posed a devastating setback to the DP.

Afterwards, De Beer wrote an anguished and self-abasing apology to the party's financial linchpin. It was, he confessed to HFO, the most difficult letter he had yet had to write in their forty-odd years of friendship. 'We are appalled by the dreadful result we achieved,' De Beer submitted sheepishly, and he proceeded in the same penitent vein. He felt 'distinctly ashamed' of himself and 'desperately guilty' towards Oppenheimer (and other donors) for having 'misled' them 'so grossly'. 'It is one thing to be a little over-optimistic; but this simply bears no relation to anything we discussed. The nearest I can come to an explanation is that, where our traditional supporters are concerned, they fell for the line that the Nats could offer a more effective opposition to the ANC than we could, and they found it easy to accept this because the Nats had in effect adopted our policy. As far as the "new" voters are concerned, we made no dent on the blacks, and the Coloureds [and] Indians are even more scared of the ANC than the whites are, and voted accordingly. It is hard to hold one's head up, but I must try. There is still a small nucleus, and it has to be kept alive, at least until some new strategy can develop.'[50] In truth, it was not only a new strategy that the DP required to turn its fortunes around. It also needed an injection of new blood at the top if it was to reclaim and reinvigorate liberalism. After the party leader's customary consultation with HFO, De Beer came away thinking, like Eglin had six years previously, that it was best to fall on his sword. Two days after penning his *mea culpa* to Oppenheimer, De Beer announced his immediate resignation as party leader.

Tony Leon was poised to fill the void. The son of Ramon Leon, a former judge on the Natal bench (Leon senior and his second wife, Jacqueline, were social acquaintances of Harry and Bridget in Durban), Leon Jr had, by his early thirties, made a rapid ascent up the greasy pole of politics, thanks to a combination of acumen, ardour and ambition. Much to Suzman's surprise and irritation, Leon trounced her chosen successor, Irene Menell, in the Prog nomination contest for Houghton in 1989. He went on to fill Suzman's vacancy in Parliament. De Beer had accompanied Leon to Brenthurst shortly after Leon was elected to lead the Progs' Johannesburg city caucus in 1988, and for the Young Turk it was the beginning of a 'significant and enduring relationship' with the Oppenheimers.[51] At a party fundraiser after the Progs' 1987 electoral eclipse by the CP, HFO had rallied the troops with a quote from Churchill's ringing dictum 'In defeat, defiance; in victory, magnanimity', and Leon had been struck by it.[52] Faced with a battle for the DP's survival, defiance (and a combative commitment to championing 'muscular liberalism') is what the pugnacious Leon offered when he assumed the leadership from De Beer in 1994. Oppenheimer affirmed and supported Leon in the role, relishing the political anecdotes and titbits which the newly minted leader passed his way. 'Tell me, Tony, how much money would help you achieve your political objectives?' the diminutive elder statesman asked of Leon as he set out to rebuild the party.[53] Leon plucked a figure from thin air, and asked for R600 000. But the request was acceded to so graciously and effortlessly that Leon wondered what would have happened had he asked for ten times more.

The Brenthurst Group: The ANC and Big Business

While the DP had been all but wiped out at the polls (and written off by the press in a series of bleak epitaphs), the ANC emerged from the election with almost unquestioned political and moral authority: a liberation dividend reinforced by Mandela's aura of saintliness. The ANC completely dominated the GNU. De Klerk occupied one of two deputy president positions – Thabo Mbeki filled the other post, purposefully – and initially the cabinet included members of the NP and IFP. However, the ANC effectively ruled as if the other parties were not there. That is what led De Klerk to quit the multiparty government after only two years. Few in civil society were perturbed by the ANC's majoritarian instincts, or its evident habituation to a one-party-dominant state. Fewer, still, appreciated the vital importance of political opposition. What was desperately needed for democracy to take root, a prerequisite either gainsaid or ignored, was countervailing forces to ANC hegemony – the ruling party's pursuit of control, not only over the organs of state, but over social and cultural institutions, like the press and universities, too.

During the ANC's salad days, big business enjoyed a complex and contradictory relationship with the government. On the one hand it helped to offset the party's calcified credo of socialist economics, thus bolstering the Rainbow Nation's democratic prospects. But in another sense the accommodation that big business found with the government (and, through it, with organised labour), in statutory bodies like the National Economic Development and Labour Council (Nedlac), served to sanction ANC hegemony. Corporatist institutions such as these drowned out the voices of small business and the unemployed, and set the country up for problems down the line. Unlike Nedlac, the Brenthurst Group, convened in the studious seclusion of Oppenheimer's Brenthurst Library, was an informal initiative which brought together senior representatives from big business with ANC movers and shakers under Mandela's leadership. The aim was to foster dialogue, establish trust, and build consensus on South Africa's economic future. The engagements were benignly overseen by the plutocrat and the President, rather than actively propelled by them. Nevertheless, here was the moment, its leftist detractors charged, when a coterie of powerful white capitalists and emergent black rulers, embodied by Oppenheimer and Mandela, struck a Faustian bargain. In secret, they hammered out a pact, the effect of which was to leave the structures of economic power largely undisturbed. The Brenthurst Group brought Mandela to heel, so the left's conventional wisdom went. White business captured the ANC's economic policy-making process; it emasculated the Macro-Economic Research Group (the SACP- and Cosatu-friendly outfit which advised the ANC), and caused the party of liberation to stray from a 'broadly social-democratic' trajectory onto a 'conservative, neoliberal' path.[54] The truth was more prosaic than such conspiracy theories permit. The ANC's major economic shifts were occasioned, in essence, by the collapse of communism and the force of global pressures, among them the fiscal and monetary prescriptions of the World Bank and the International Monetary Fund. The party's economic repositioning predated the formation of the Brenthurst Group in 1994. In point of fact, the intermittent conclaves in the Brenthurst Library made a marginal, but not material, impact on ANC thinking. It is worth noting that neither Oppenheimer nor Mandela had much to say during the meetings.

The impetus for the Brenthurst Group came from the ANC. It was Alec Erwin, the former trade unionist soon to become Mandela's deputy minister of finance, who contacted Bobby Godsell at the end of January 1994, at Mandela's behest, and got the ball rolling on the get-togethers. Mandela was keen for the ANC's economics brains trust to meet with 'a group of leading businessmen', Ogilvie Thompson wrote confidentially to Donald Gordon, 'to lay the foundation for a constructive pattern of relationships' with the business community after the election.[55] The first meeting was hastily arranged, and took place on 22 February. Alongside Mandela and Thabo Mbeki, the ANC fielded its key economic planners – Erwin, Trevor Manuel, Tito Mboweni – together with Franklin Sonn and a national executive committee member, Cheryl Carolus; they were flanked by a mini-federation of trade unionists, Mbhazima 'Sam' Shilowa, John Gomomo and Jay Naidoo.[56] The business attendees constituted the crème de la crème of white corporate power: HFO, Clive Menell, Warren Clewlow (Barlow Rand), Marinus Dalling (Sanlam), Mike Levett (Old Mutual), John Maree (Nedcor), Conrad Strauss (Standard Bank), and a slew of executives from the Anglo American stable: Ogilvie Thompson, Nicky Oppenheimer, Michael Spicer, Donald Ncube (business's sole black representative), Godsell, and Anglo's in-house economist, CJ Buys. 'Their collective industrial power represents virtually the entire formal economy of South Africa,' gasped one journalist, two years later, after the existence of the secret synod became known. 'And their collective reticence,' she added, 'has all the singularity of a Carmelite monastery.'[57]

Mandela kicked off the discussion by stressing that the ANC had an 'open mind' on the Reconstruction and Development Programme (RDP), the party's socio-economic policy framework drafted by Naidoo.[58] The RDP set ambitious targets for land redistribution, housing, and the provision of basic services, but it was essentially an election manifesto rather than a systematic plan. The economic section was 'riddled with ambiguities': it promised massive state spending while pledging to avoid undue inflation and balance of payments difficulties.[59] The RDP was widely disseminated and endlessly consulted upon by the Tripartite Alliance partners; international financial institutions scrutinised the document, and it was submitted for approval to the governments of Britain, America, France, Germany and Japan. By the time the RDP White Paper was gazetted in November 1994 – Naidoo became the minister responsible for its implementation – it had undergone multiple revisions. The draft before the businessmen assembled in the Brenthurst Library, Mandela reassured them, was not a statist blueprint; the idea was to 'empower civil society' to play an active role in delivery, and the ANC had consciously sought to avoid stressing development at the expense of growth. '*There was a guarantee of no radical policies that could damage our economy*,' Spicer underlined optimistically in his notes on Mandela's opening remarks.[60]

Oppenheimer spoke next. He paid personal tribute to Mandela, and affirmed that a 'close understanding' between business and the ANC alliance was desirable. There was an 'urgent need to tackle poverty', HFO concurred, but he cautioned that poverty should not be addressed in such a way as to discourage growth. Manuel then expanded on the RDP's salient features. HFO's approach in the inaugural meeting of what was to be the genesis of the Brenthurst Group, and in the dozen or so encounters that took place over the following two years, was decidedly hands-off. He sat back, performed a sort of ceremonial role, contributed infrequently and gnomically, and gave Strauss free rein to chair the gatherings on business's behalf. The two sides traded courteously in generalities. It was left to JOT to underscore that reconstruction and development hinged on economic growth; he suggested that the word 'growth' be inserted into the title of the RDP. He also raised specific concerns about the policy's costing, cross-subsidisation proposals, and 'excessive element of state planning' – a charge vigorously but diplomatically denied by Erwin and Mboweni.

'It was an almost wholly useless exercise', Godsell later recalled of the Brenthurst colloquies, 'because on both sides people were excessively polite.'[61] A week after the election, he penned a confidential note to the business delegation; it now included a number of ranking magnificoes unable to attend the first meeting, notably Anton Rupert, Donald Gordon, Meyer Kahn (South African Breweries) and Dave Brink (Murray & Roberts). Godsell called on them to think in terms of a 'bold gesture', perhaps an offer to fund and implement selected development programmes.[62] 'We need ... to establish ourselves as effective partners in helping the new government discharge its development commitments,' he counselled. 'Only then will we be able to help shape economic policy.' Whether that kind of close and creative collaboration materialised is open to debate. At the outset, Anglo had no inside track on Mandela's cabinet appointments: Mandela sounded out Oppenheimer on the finance spot, but Spicer received his information about likely cabinet ministers second-hand from Peter Sullivan, editor of *The Star*, and passed it on to JOT.[63] Once the new government was installed, the Anglo American and De Beers Chairman's Fund, like other corporate social investment vehicles, paid its dues by financing housing and infrastructure projects and community development initiatives. A year into Mandela's presidency, Ogilvie Thompson announced that Anglo would spend R20 billion on its export-focused build programme, a welcome boost to the country's foreign exchange reserves. During Mandela's tenure Anglo paid R6.6 billion in corporate taxes, and its contribution did not go unheeded:

the Minister of Minerals and Energy, Penuell Maduna, opened the Harry Oppenheimer Diamond Trading School, for example, and there were several other ribbon-cutting affirmations by the Union Buildings' new occupants.[64] Yet it would be straining credibility to say that big business was the puppeteer pulling the strings of national economic policy. It is true that the Brenthurst businessmen proposed several amendments to the RDP to make it more investor-friendly – including a firmer commitment to fiscal discipline, deficit reduction and trade liberalisation – but those suggestions were hardly original or unique, nor did they make the critical difference. 'ANC policy evolved in a convoluted way', Spicer recollected, 'and we often struggled to understand where it was headed.'[65]

The Brenthurst Group engaged in wide-ranging discussions. Mandela called a meeting to discuss the 'excess number of civil servants', many of whom, JOT recounted the President bemoaning, 'simply "play cards"'.[66] Yet the first occasion on which business requested a meeting, Strauss observed at the time, was as late as July 1995, to register its concerns over the Labour Relations Bill.[67] Up till then, the ANC had made all the running. Godsell's minutes and Spicer's notes provide no evidence that big business extracted significant concessions from the ANC at meetings of the Brenthurst Group. Oppenheimer, like the other businessmen present, would have hoped for a fully liberalised economy relieved from the burden of exchange controls. That was never on the table. The labour regime which emerged out of the cabinet-approved Labour Relations Act (and later the Employment Equity Act, a reinscribed form of job reservation) was rigid: it protected and benefited workers, not their employers (or, for that matter, the unemployed).

In 1996, the government more or less abandoned the RDP in favour of a macroeconomic strategy more closely aligned to the 'Washington Consensus'. Initiated by Erwin and championed by Manuel, it was named GEAR (Growth, Employment and Redistribution). GEAR was the outcome, in one academic's overwrought view, of 'an intense ideological "onslaught"' and 'religious crusade' by 'powerful right-wing pressure groups', who emerged as ideological conquerors in June 1996.[68] Quite possibly the ANC's retreat from the RDP was accelerated by the Brenthurst Group's corporate conquistadors. Roughly nine months before GEAR's release, some of them revived the dormant South Africa Foundation – unlike the Brenthurst Group, the SAF was an entity which had never concealed itself from public view – and in March they presented an SAF document, 'Growth for All', to Mandela. It made the case for a flexible, two-tier labour market system, privatisation of state assets, and export-driven growth. The ANC responded with horror. Mboweni led the attack, particularly on the SAF's call for labour market deregulation, and he slammed the proposals as 'dangerous'.[69] Mbeki, who ran the engine room of government while Mandela bestrode the decks as honorary captain, was publicly silent but privately infuriated. He found the 'Growth for All' document high-handed, prescriptive and pre-emptive. He stewed over the timing of its release. GEAR, Mbeki anticipated, would be seen as a defensive response to 'Growth for All', and thus raise the hackles of the labour movement and the left. Ironically, at the same time that the government's switch from the RDP to GEAR drove a wedge between Mbeki, Cosatu and the SACP, Mbeki fell out with the SAF and 'the Anglo crowd'.[70] He felt alienated by their conduct and bristled at what he perceived to be racial slights. (Strauss, frustrated by his failure to nail down a slot in Mbeki's diary, had famously vented to Mbeki's PA: 'If he cannot manage his diary, how can he manage the country?')[71] At that point, Mbeki effectively shut the door on any kind of special partnership with big business.

The Elite Pact

GEAR and the SAF's 'Growth for All' document shared clear ideological resonances.[72] Be that as it may, the ANC's change of macroeconomic gear had long been in the offing, the product both of pragmatism and of pressures that emanated from outside the business community. In any event, it was Mandela (or, more accurately, Mbeki) in the driving seat. They navigated the government's policy direction – not Oppenheimer, or any of the other business barons belonging to the Brenthurst Group. The notion that Mandela and Oppenheimer covertly brokered an economic pact is a fantasy, a self-serving fiction invented by the left to explain why the Rainbow Nation's glory faded, and why 'the revolution' was derailed. The only accord reached between South Africa's black and white elites was the Constitution; there was no comparable economic covenant, and nothing that the Brenthurst Group lobbied for (or the SAF, or any other business grouping, formal or informal) bound future ANC governments. Much of the ANC's later policy orientation – from its ambivalence on property rights to its stance on mineral rights to its interventionist Mining Charter – betrayed a profound hostility to the private sector. It showed complete ignorance of, or indifference to, the factors conducive to investment. However, what can be said with some degree of confidence is that several members of the black elite rushed headlong into the arms of white businessmen in anticipation of enrichment. Many of them looked upon the Oppenheimers and the Menells in their vast suburban mansions, surrounded by all the accoutrements of affluence, and decided that they too wanted to be captains of industry. Yet this desire to emulate successful white capitalists was seldom accompanied by any evident inclination towards industriousness or willingness to acquire skills through the necessary apprenticeship. The white business establishment, like its totemic leader, Oppenheimer, believed that to be governed by a class of economically disempowered people was potentially perilous. At the same time, white-led corporations felt an understandable compulsion to demonstrate their progressive bona fides to the new government. But the solution which the mining and finance houses like Anglo and Sanlam seized upon, a model later legally codified by the ruling party as BEE, only accentuated the economic inequalities it purported to redress.

In the early days of democracy a clique of ANC worthies gravitated to Brenthurst. Mandela, of course, regularly visited Oppenheimer's Xanadu for dinner, and as president he reciprocated the hospitality at his official residence in Pretoria, Mahlamba Ndlopfu (formerly Libertas), where Harry and Bridget dined alone with him. After one such occasion, arranged because Mandela wanted to ask HFO's advice on who the next Governor of the Reserve Bank should be, Bridget reported back on the presidential patter to her old friend Albert Robinson, whose acquaintance she had first made at her mother's flat in Cape Town in 1942. (Oppenheimer undertook to brood on Mandela's request, but the President subsequently disregarded his input when he appointed Mboweni to the governorship.) In later years Robinson and Bridget kept up a daily correspondence by fax. Like HFO, Bridget enjoyed gossip and had strong opinions, though, in sharp contrast to him, she was colourfully outspoken and not especially discreet. The Oppenheimers' London flat in Belgravia was a mandatory port of call for the ANC's post-apartheid exiles: Mendi Msimang, South Africa's High Commissioner to the UK, once got so inebriated at 80 Eaton Square that HFO's faithful manservant, Antonio Peres, practically had to scrape him off the floor before depositing him into a taxi. 'A good man who had had bad problems with drink but he has been cured,' Mandela told Bridget, an assessment which she relayed to Robinson.[73] Mandela told HFO that Msimang, like all 'the good people' in the ANC, intended to go into business; 'they all want to make money', the President

The new Governor of the Reserve Bank, Tito Mboweni, meets HFO
on the verandah at Brenthurst, 1999. *(Anglo American)*

lamented. 'Take Cyril [Ramaphosa], Tokyo [Sexwale], [Nthato] Motlana.
He [Motlana] is my doctor – I have known him for many, many years but
if I have a medical problem I have to ring the Stock Exchange to talk to
him!!!'[74]

Motlana was an old associate of HFO's and one of BEE's pioneering
beneficiaries. Sexwale was likewise an early BEE aspirant. An erstwhile
political prisoner on Robben Island, he became a major player in ANC
regional politics after his release; later, Sexwale's moving tribute to Chris
Hani (a close friend) thrust him into national prominence after the SACP
leader's death. In 1994 Sexwale was elected as the first premier of Gauteng.
However, following clashes with Mbeki, he resigned his premiership
less than four years in; he abandoned politics and proceeded to take
advantage of empowerment opportunities instead. Sexwale had, in any
event, been a director of Thebe Investments, the empowerment vehicle
set up in 1992 by the ANC's head of finance, Vusi Khanyile. Mvelaphanda
Holdings, the company created by Sexwale upon his retreat from politics,
focused initially on diamonds and platinum, reputedly on HFO's advice.
Anglo American sold off assets to give Mvelaphanda a leg-up, and in
2000 Sexwale's organisation acquired a 22.5 per cent stake in Northam
Platinum from Anglo and Anton Rupert's Remgro.

By the mid-1990s, Sexwale and his wife, Judy, were the darlings of Johannesburg's old mining liberals. They graced the dining rooms of many a Parktown mansion. The dashing, forty-something Premier, who moonlighted as a talk show host on the popular AM station Radio 702, was an avid caller at Brenthurst. He made himself at home there. After a small dinner party hosted for Henry Kissinger, attended by the Sexwales, Bridget vented her spleen to Robinson: 'Tokyo ... said, "Take away [the] asparagus, I need meat!"'[75] She added disapprovingly in her guest book: 'Tokyo demanded meat! Then [he] left to do a programme on [Radio] 702 & interviewed Henry after the women left, on the phone!!"'[76] The behaviour of the new black elite frequently left the queen consort reeling in bewilderment: there were minor breaches of etiquette that offended her sense of decorum, any number of imposed desiderata, and – most frustrating of all – last-minute no-shows which threw out her carefully crafted seating plans. Ramaphosa's wife, Dr Tshepo Motsepe, was 'too tired to come!!'[77] Bridget huffed after a dinner in honour of Chryss Goulandris and her husband, Tony O'Reilly, the Irish press baron. Two years earlier, in 1994, O'Reilly's publishing company, Independent Newspapers, had purchased control of Argus Newspapers from JCI and Anglo for R125 million.

Anglo's unbundling of JCI acted as a stimulus to the profusion of BEE transactions involving the ANC's very own entrepreneurs. Sanlam had set the ball rolling on BEE in 1993 when it sold off ten per cent of Momentum Life to a consortium led by Motlana. A year later, Anglo followed suit when it sold 51 per cent of Southern Life's shareholding in African Life to Real Africa Investments, an empowerment vehicle driven by Don Ncube. Anglo then split JCI into three companies and put up for sale a 35 per cent stake in two of them – JCI and Johnnic – to different consortia of black investors. JCI remained a mining company, denuded of its platinum and diamond assets, and refocused instead on gold, ferrochrome and base metals. It was purchased for R2.9 billion by the African Mining Group (AMG), a consortium stitched together by another former inmate of Robben Island, Mzi Khumalo. AMG narrowly trumped a bid by New Africa Investments Limited (Nail), a company chaired by Motlana with Ramaphosa as his deputy. The sale of JCI and Johnnic made Oppenheimer a courted figure. Both Khumalo and Ramaphosa made sure to attend the dinner for Kissinger while their rival bids for JCI were under way; and when Mbeki dropped in at Brenthurst to meet Kissinger a few days later, Bridget had her hands full trying to ensure that Mbeki's and Motlana's paths did not cross. Motlana had turned up unexpectedly, supposedly to see Peggy Dulany, another of the Oppenheimer house guests. All of a sudden Brenthurst felt like Piccadilly Circus, a thoroughfare besieged by ANC politicos. HFO sought refuge from the bustle in his study. 'Harry & I had lunch lurking in the dining room at the end of the big table – not on the verandah in case we were seen,' Bridget gabbed to Robinson.[78] She retreated to her room 'in case of further invasions'.

Although Nail lost out to Khumalo's consortium on the purchase of JCI, by only 50 cents per share, Ramaphosa had already had his cake and eaten it when Anglo sold its stake in Johnnic. Johnnic was an investment holding company: it consolidated JCI's publishing and media interests alongside the non-mining, industrial concerns such as SAB and the Premier Group. Nail muscled its way into the National Empowerment Consortium (NEC), which spearheaded a successful R2.6 billion bid for the company. In a move that raised eyebrows, the NEC received a seven per cent discount on the market value of Johnnic's share price. But even though Anglo had parted ways with JCI and Johnnic, it kept the crown jewels for itself: JCI's diamond assets went to De Beers, and the platinum interests were earmarked for Anglo American Platinum (Amplats), the separately listed amalgamation of the corporation's platinum concerns. Khumalo's course with JCI soon proved to be troubled – he got into bed with Brett Kebble, a venal corporate raider who outmanoeuvred him and effectively looted JCI for personal gain – but Ramaphosa, despite his own rocky road with Johnnic, parlayed the deal into a profitable business career. Oppenheimer admired Ramaphosa's ingenuity and intellect. HFO thought the one-time trade unionist had outplayed the Nats during the negotiations, and he believed those qualities might serve Ramaphosa well in business. Ramaphosa embarked on the Johnnic transaction with no money of his own and proceeded to become, like many politically savvy BEE beneficiaries with affluent white backers, an immensely wealthy man.

Oppenheimer had spotted the opportunities presented by unbundling at an early stage. In 1993, when he expressed misgivings about the ANC's injunction to unbundle, HFO hastened to add a rider: 'Just as I thought it was extremely wise to facilitate the growth of Afrikaans economic power, I also think it is going to be highly desirable … to facilitate the growth of black economic power. And if I saw an opportunity for that and it involved [the] unbundling of something, I would look at it very seriously. But … this doesn't mean the people at Anglo think like this; they may not at all because I've been retired for a good many years.'[79] Not unexpectedly, the people at Anglo thought exactly along the same lines. 'I tried to do for the blacks what Harry did for the Afrikaners,' Ogilvie Thompson reflected on the JCI and Johnnic deals long after his retirement.[80] Yet the parallels are far from perfect. From the mid-1960s, the General Mining–Federale Mynbou tie-up facilitated an Anglo-Afrikaner accord in the corporate sphere – an elite pact of sorts – which, over time, became a vehicle to drive reform. Those party to it sought to develop a black middle class. Through the Urban Foundation, for example, proponents of the Boer-and-Brit *entente cordiale* lobbied for broader economic inclusion, which helped to break the political logjam. But the BEE transactions pioneered by white corporations in the 1990s had the opposite effect. Transferring ownership of lucrative shares to ANC-allied beneficiaries entrenched patronage networks in the state and reinforced the ruling party's hegemony. It served less to expand the black middle class than to foster a form of black crony capitalism, a rigged game of favoured insiders and ill-starred outsiders. Through BEE, a small black elite became exceedingly rich without the quid pro quo of starting new enterprises, adding value to the economy or creating jobs – all of which did little to mitigate the marginalisation of the poor, unemployed black masses.

Few, if any, of the moguls that emerged from the laboratory of BEE in the 1990s were genuinely entrepreneurial. The most successful turned out to be Patrice Motsepe, founder of African Rainbow Minerals. Motsepe's path to mega-riches was paved in 1997 by his purchase, from Anglo, of several older, loss-making shafts at the Freegold mine in Welkom and at Vaal Reefs near Orkney. In the absence of a bank willing to finance the deal (to the tune of $8.2 million), Anglo went on risk for payment, based on a future return of profits, and provided Motsepe with management resources and toll treatment agreements. 'He was very polite,' Motsepe later recalled of HFO, 'but he said to me, "What makes you think you are going to make money where Anglo has not?"'[81] Motsepe's self-belief would ultimately be vindicated. Supported by a seasoned mine manager, André Wilkens (courtesy of Anglo), he made the mines profitable, paid Anglo back within three years, and proceeded to build on his success. In due course, the BEE billionaire would channel a portion of his growing wealth to philanthropic causes.

For many other practitioners of BEE, however, charity began at home and stayed there. Curiously, the spirit of *ubuntu* – the African philosophy which ties together ideas of humanity and community – seldom translated into institutionalised philanthropy where BEE was concerned. Instead, the empowerment policy gave rise to a form of comprador capitalism. It led to a glut of undesirable socio-economic consequences. For that, whatever its good intentions in seeking to build the Rainbow Nation, Anglo must bear some sliver of responsibility. The group was, perhaps, too eager to earn the new government's approval; too anxious to prove its progressive credentials to the ANC. What of Oppenheimer's motives? At this stage of his life, HFO confessed, he only wished to be remembered as being 'reasonably kind and, if it isn't too grand a word, wise'.[82] 'Everybody wants to be loved,' he continued, offering a rare glimpse of public vulnerability. On a charitable interpretation, perhaps that impulse, coloured by enlightened self-interest, is what underpinned HFO's efforts to provide South Africa's new political rulers with a material stake in the economy. Would these actions serve to safeguard his legacy? The final reckoning lay ahead.

FOURTEEN

The Final Reckoning

1996–2000

As Harry Oppenheimer approached the last years of his life, his thoughts naturally turned to matters of legacy. Anglo American had long occupied an ambiguous position in the public imagination in so far as its 'struggle credentials' were concerned. During the dark decades of apartheid Anglo had been the most politically progressive of the mining houses. HFO was a consistent critic of the Nationalist government and its policies. However, his companies had managed to thrive under white minority rule; and, more to the point, Anglo's detractors declared, the corporation had served to buttress the edifice of racial oppression. Neither Anglo nor the wider business establishment, they insisted, no matter what the 'Oppenheimer thesis' might hold, had ever posed a serious threat to the maintenance of white supremacy. When, in 1994, Oppenheimer relinquished his directorship of De Beers, Nelson Mandela paid tribute to him at a farewell dinner. Yet, the President saw fit to qualify his praise: 'The dazzling achievements of the mining industry and of your great corporations', he said, turning his steely gaze on Oppenheimer, were 'bound up with a profoundly unjust labour system.' 'The problems it has bequeathed us are deeply rooted and will require commitment and dedication to eradicate.'[1] Early on in the transition, HFO expressed the view that, in retrospect, Anglo should have done more to stand up to the old regime and improve the welfare of its black workers. As he told a team of interviewers from the *Financial Times* (the exchange appeared under the headline 'Old man and the sea change'), 'Whenever you look back and say did we do everything that should have been done, you never have ...'[2] Anglo's moral balance sheet (and the whole issue of business's complicity in apartheid) would be pored over by the Truth and Reconciliation Commission (TRC) in 1997, when it probed the extent to which white corporations benefited from the system and pondered whether they had done enough to oppose it.

Destiny and dynasty were the major themes of Oppenheimer's life. Ever since he was a boy, HFO had been seized with the notion that his father had founded a family business. It was his manifest destiny and duty, HFO believed, to continue it. But could the dynasty survive his death? Would De Beers, the diamond empire built by the Oppenheimers upon foundations laid by Rhodes, still glister in the approaching epoch, like the externally flawless Millennium Star, the most beautiful diamond (HFO said) that he had ever seen? Did Anglo American, the corporate behemoth breathed into life by Ernest Oppenheimer, stand poised to expand and prosper? And would the companies remain under the family's effective control? These were the questions that filtered through Oppenheimer's mind as he put his affairs in order and prepared, in Shelley's words, for death to set 'his mark and seal / On all we are and all we feel / On all we know and all we fear'. As the poet poignantly penned:

> First our pleasures die – and then
> Our hopes, and then our fears – and when
> These are dead, the debt is due,
> Dust claims dust – and we die too.
>
> All things that we love and cherish,
> Like ourselves must fade and perish;
> Such is our rude mortal lot –
> Love itself would, did they not.[3]

HFO enjoyed his pleasures to the end, though episodes of ill health, beginning with a serious throat infection early in 1997, caused him intermittent discomfort and distress. He read, he attended meetings of the Roxburghe Club in London – the oldest society of bibliophiles in the world, whose small, invitation-only membership was restricted to readers with distinguished library collections – and he pottered about 44 Main Street, where he was treated with a combination of reverence and affection.

HFO continued to travel around the globe, but he spent more time with friends and family in his various homes, a kindly if retiring host exhibiting flashes of warmth and wit. And, of course, with Bridget by his side, he pursued his love of horses. The couple bought a stallion, Fort Wood, who sired a champion named Horse Chestnut. Horse Chestnut was conditioned into a majestic galloping machine by an up-and-coming trainer new to the Oppenheimer stable, Mike de Kock. The only horse in the history of South African racing to win the J&B Met and Triple Crown in the same season, Horse Chestnut swept all before him, and he went on to compete internationally. 'The best [thing] that's ever happened to Harry and I,' an emotional Bridget remarked on receiving one of Horse Chestnut's many awards. 'Here we are, in our old age, enjoying every moment.'[4] The enjoyment was palpable. Nicky Oppenheimer reflected: 'I am not sure what gave my father most pleasure – breeding a champion or observing, benignly, the pleasure it gave my mother.' He suspected that if anyone had asked his father what provided him with the greatest 'buzz' in the 1990s, HFO would have answered, 'democracy in South Africa and a champion racehorse.'[5]

So much for his pleasures. What of HFO's hopes and fears? He was a man of Africa, rooted in its southernmost nation-state, with a monarch's desire to protect his corporate kingdom – a regent who, though no longer on the throne, exercised indirect rule from Brenthurst. In the late 1980s, Oppenheimer had wondered whether change was coming too late to his home country. In the outline of his memoir, he dwelt on the dangers of democracy deferred: should it arrive brutally and belatedly, HFO predicted, 'all my father & I worked for will be swallowed up in disaster and my family will have [to] build an entirely new way of life with different aspirations – a different lifestyle – & different risks.'[6] But now that the political transition had taken place – peacefully, in the main – and the Rainbow Nation had spluttered into life, there were indications that the infant did not enjoy rude health. Crime soared, high levels of unemployment persisted, and HFO worried about the possible drift to one-party rule.[7]

Meanwhile, Anglo was undergoing a rebirth of its own. While the ANC was still equivocating on nationalisation, Anglo had moved to protect some of its assets by transferring them into the control of subsidiaries and affiliated companies located outside South Africa, principally Minorco. In 1993, by means of a $1.4 billion asset swap, Minorco took over the South American, European and Australian operations of both Anglo American and De Beers.[8] In exchange, Minorco gave Anglo all of its African assets. This meant that ownership of Anglo's holdings outside Africa now resided with Minorco: they were placed slightly beyond the ANC's unpredictable grasp. Back home, JCI was unbundled, the platinum interests were spun out into Amplats, and in June 1998 Anglo consolidated all of its gold mining concerns in South Africa into the separately listed AngloGold. The empire was being broken up, and soon South Africa would no longer be the centre of the imperium. In 1999, following on from a $10 billion merger with Minorco, Anglo moved its primary listing to London, where the cost of borrowing was lower and the pool of available capital was larger. Less trumpeted as a justification, but tacitly acknowledged among Anglo's executive apparatchiks, was the fact that the London listing provided Anglo American plc (as the merged entity was called) with additional political insurance against the ANC. As Anglo's move heralded a new dawn, another light shimmered in the gloaming.

Only days before HFO's death, Nicky presented to his father an audacious plan to privatise De Beers. He proposed that the family should radically increase its shareholding in the diamond empire, financed by a reduction of its stake in Anglo. The deal would unwind a complicated web of crossholdings, which other investors blamed for the lacklustre performance of their shares. But it would also mark the beginning of the family's retreat from Anglo. Just before Oppenheimer died, it appeared as if the family's dynastic hold on Anglo might begin to fade and perish. However, HFO did not live long enough to witness the denouement.

The Truth and Reconciliation Commission and Anglo's Apartheid Ledger

The architects of the negotiated settlement realised that if South Africans were going to come to terms with their dark past – if the Rainbow Nation's fledgling democracy was to stand a chance – then there would need to be some kind of cathartic ritual of disclosure and propitiation. The upshot was the establishment of the Truth and Reconciliation Commission (TRC) in 1995. The TRC's mandate was to investigate the causes, nature and extent of the political killings and human rights abuses – the abductions, atrocities and acts of torture – which took place from March 1960 to May 1994. The commission was given the power to grant amnesty to perpetrators of gross human rights violations who made a clean breast of their crimes and sought absolution. The whole exercise, like similar initiatives undertaken in Latin America and various other conflict-ridden societies transitioning to democracy from authoritarian rule, worked on the assumption that truth-telling would lead to healing. Confession, forgiveness and symbolic acts of restitution (rather than retributive justice) would set the nation free. They would inaugurate a more just future.

Chaired by Archbishop Desmond Tutu, with Alex Boraine (a former Methodist cleric and Anglo employee) as his understudy, the TRC was suffused with the spirit of religiosity. It combined the sanctity of the church and the authority of the courthouse with the emotional intensity of the ancient Roman Colosseum. In written statements and at public hearings, thousands of apartheid's victims recounted deeply moving stories of death and dehumanisation. The world wept with them as they relived their pain. It was a heart-rending spectacle expertly choreographed by Tutu – a cleansing ceremony designed to exorcise South Africa's demons, a necessary prophylaxis against collective amnesia. Although its task was vast (and time frames tight), the commission's terms of reference were relatively restricted: it had to focus on politically motivated murders and gross human rights violations committed over a 34-year period, and its findings were to be made in accordance with established legal principles. Yet, even before the TRC began its work, powerful voices within the ANC tried to impose their partisan assumptions and demands upon the body. The campaign was not without effect. Many of the TRC's commissioners and researchers were fellow travellers of the disbanded UDF – Tutu had been the organisation's patron – and they demonstrated a degree of bias towards the ANC.[9] Mangosuthu Buthelezi and members of the IFP were given short shrift by the commission; and when FW de Klerk delivered his testimony, he was treated with such contempt that Tutu and Boraine later apologised publicly.

In the midst of the TRC hearings, Kader Asmal, regarded by the ANC as one of its intellectual heavyweights, published a tendentious tract entitled *Reconciliation through Truth: A Reckoning of Apartheid's Criminal Governance*.[10] Having spent most of his adult life exiled in Ireland, where he taught law at Trinity College Dublin and chaired the Anti-Apartheid Movement, Asmal returned to South Africa in 1990 and became a professor of human rights law at the University of the Western Cape. In 1994 Mandela appointed him to his cabinet as minister of water affairs and forestry. Disputatious and domineering, Asmal had little trouble in ensuring that his book received extensive coverage in the press. He and his co-authors pressed a narrowly ideological point of view, and they made a great show of their solidarity with the ruling party's aims and outlook. Controversially, Asmal drew parallels between apartheid and the Holocaust. He bemoaned the fact that the concept of 'the corporate war criminal' remained 'under-explored in South Africa'.[11] And he rammed the point home with an unsubstantiated claim that, in the 1980s, Anglo's directors had privately fretted that their company would be remembered as the IG Farben of apartheid. This was a reference to the German company which formed the industrial backbone of the Third Reich, using slave labour from the concentration camps. For good measure Asmal singled out Oppenheimer for alleged thoughtcrimes: he quoted from Anthony Hocking's biography of HFO, to the effect that the magnate had 'never subscribed to the view that apartheid was morally wrong'.[12]

Albert Robinson wrote indignantly to Bridget. 'To say – in Asmal's book – that Harry never said that apartheid was morally wrong is a pernicious libel and a lie.'[13] She was understandably protective of her husband's reputation. 'You are quite right about Asmal,' Bridget fired back. 'I find it appalling but Harry seems relaxed & says they don't know that you could be anti-apartheid & not pro-ANC.'[14] Oppenheimer's unruffled response touched upon a core truth: Asmal's invective, much like the TRC's modus operandi, was thoroughly rooted in the ANC's Manichaean world view. The ANC had been on the right side of history (the less said about its uncritical support for Soviet communism the better), and this conviction – this moral certitude – often manifested itself in an overweening sense of self-righteousness. It was as if the ANC had enjoyed a monopoly on the struggle against apartheid – the party readily airbrushed the PAC and the liberals out of its triumphalist version of history – and often ANC adherents spoke and conducted themselves as if they possessed a monopoly on virtue too. When apostles of the ANC recounted the parable of the businessman and apartheid, they would inevitably reveal, just like those revisionist historians and neo-Marxist scholars from two decades before, that South Africa's white corporate class had been supping with the devil all along. It was always a matter of *collective* responsibility.

And yet when it came to Oppenheimer, Asmal had simply repeated a contentious conclusion drawn by the mining mogul's biographer. In spite of the preening professor's polemics, his comment about HFO was neither libellous nor especially mendacious. Perhaps that is why Oppenheimer remained unfazed. In the 1950s, as a United Party MP, he had indeed stressed that the *idea* of separate development was impractical rather than intrinsically immoral. In part, this was a rhetorical device. As the

UP's spokesman on finance and economic affairs, Oppenheimer tended to marshal his arguments against apartheid by using the nomenclature of an economist. He believed this was likely to make more of an impression on the opposite side of the House than if he were to shower the Nats with moral entreaties or berate them for their presumed depravity. HFO was putting an essentially moral case, or so he justified it to himself, in economic terms: whites and blacks were economically interdependent – the national egg could not be unscrambled – and everybody, regardless of skin colour, should be afforded the wherewithal to develop their skills and capabilities. It was a liberal, if not moral, imperative. To be sure, this approach was shot through with contradictions, not least of all the liberals' (specifically the Progressives') long-time insistence on the qualified right to vote. But Oppenheimer believed economic development was bound to break down the barriers that separated South Africa's different race groups: the National Party, he contended, was deluded in thinking that it could bend the arc of history away from justice. Eventually reason would prevail.

A journalist once asked Oppenheimer if he felt uncomfortable about 'a sense of complicity with apartheid', to which he replied: 'No, I don't think I did feel that – perhaps because I haven't got so much sensitivity as I ought to have had, but also because if you were really going to take that line you would have had to leave South Africa. And that was something I never contemplated … But I can't pretend that I sat there feeling in an agony of moral despair … that's just because perhaps my personality wasn't like that. On the other hand, I don't think we'd have done as well by the economy if I had felt like that all the time.'[15] This was Oppenheimer talking as a hard-nosed businessman. Even though he had challenged the apartheid government by expressing his oppositional views publicly, Anglo's ex-chairman maintained that the group's ability to influence the state was limited. It was all well and good to say that Anglo should have refused to pay its corporate taxes, he noted, but that was 'easier said than done'. 'The government has the power.' Besides, at the height of apartheid, far from Anglo having had a 'direct line' to the Union Buildings, anything it said was 'assumed to be wrong and dangerous to Afrikaners', HFO continued. 'So we … didn't have an easy way of influencing things by talking to the government.'

Asmal's broadsides might well have prompted the TRC to put business under the moral microscope.[16] The commission conducted a series of 'institutional hearings' to explore broader issues of societal responsibility stemming from white minority rule. Representatives from business were summoned to account for their sector's past behaviour, and the process was replicated (with varying degrees of hostility and assumed culpability) in hearings involving faith-based organisations, the legal community, the health sector and the media. The TRC's point of departure, captured in its final report, was that apartheid could only have become entrenched if large numbers of 'enfranchised, relatively privileged' South Africans (to wit, whites) either 'condoned or simply allowed it to continue'.[17] It seemed to be an eminently reasonable contention.

Naturally, given its historical size and sway, Anglo was firmly in the TRC's firing line. Bobby Godsell oversaw the compilation of a 19-page written submission in mitigation of expected sentence: it was part apologia, part *mea culpa*.[18] The document underscored Anglo's contribution to the economy. Over a period of eighty years, the corporation's gold producers alone had provided '7 million employee/years of employment', paid R98 billion in tax, and earned South Africa R557 billion in foreign exchange. Anglo had aspired to be a good corporate citizen through the disbursements of the Chairman's Fund and the actions of the Urban Foundation, providing multiracial opportunities for education, training and development. From the 1970s, the group had increased black wages and pioneered the recognition of black trade unions. Compared with the other mining finance houses, Anglo had, as HFO once described it, been 'reasonably in the forefront of ethics'.[19] Indeed, Anglo's top brass had consistently opposed apartheid in their public statements, which had led to the company being scorned and sometimes stonewalled by the government. Even so, the authors of the submission conceded, there were 'missed opportunities' and a gap between 'word and deed'. Anglo had failed to 'fully exploit' the three per cent housing allocation for black migrant labourers and their families on its gold mines; it could have done more to tackle the 'social prejudices' that hampered the recruitment and promotion of black and female candidates into 'important surface occupations'; and it should have desegregated the workplace much earlier than the mid-1970s.

Anglo's alternating line of defence and concession was repeated at the business inquisition, where Nicky Oppenheimer, Julian Ogilvie Thompson and Godsell entered the lion's den on the corporation's behalf. Under HFO's leadership, they asserted, Anglo had opposed apartheid on the grounds that it was 'both morally wrong and economically disastrous'.[20] Nicky proceeded to issue an apology. 'With hindsight it's quite clear that we at Anglo did not do everything we could have or should have ... for that we must express our apologies and our remorse.'[21] But expressions of corporate contrition did not cut the mustard. Russell Ally, an economic historian and member of the TRC's human rights violations committee, led the charge against Anglo. He recycled many of Cosatu's and the broader left's talking points. Ally insinuated that Anglo had propped up the apartheid government financially in the aftermath of Sharpeville. The corporation 'practically gave away' General Mining to Federale Mynbou, he suggested, to cement the links between English and Afrikaner capital, thus strengthening the forces of Afrikaner nationalism; and it had created the Urban Foundation in order to co-opt a budding black bourgeoisie and 'prevent fundamental change'.[22] All of it was decidedly slanted and in some instances plain wrong. The TRC was looking for villains, and Anglo matched the identikit. Even Boraine, Godsell's old boss at Anglo, stuck the knife in when Godsell gave testimony on the Chamber of Mines' behalf. (Godsell was the Chamber's then president.) Apart from profiting from a terrible troika – migrant labour, pass laws and the compound system – the mining industry, Boraine noted, had racked up a deplorable health and safety record. In addition to thousands of cases of tuberculosis and silicosis, it bore responsibility for the death of 69 000 miners in accidents between 1900 and 1993.[23]

The truth of the matter was that the mining industry – exemplified by Anglo American, for all that the corporation had, in terms of ethics, outshone its peers – did have a case to answer. For the better part of a century, it had paid deplorably low wages to black workers and subjected them to abysmal working and living conditions. However, the TRC more or less used the institutional hearings to issue a blanket condemnation of the entire business sector. Unlike the perpetrators of gross human rights violations who were granted amnesty in their individual capacity, the TRC recommended that businesses should be held collectively liable for punitive taxation, no matter the nature of their past transgressions. Its reasoning was fundamentally flawed. The commission equated any profitable activity under apartheid with business having benefited from 'the system', the monstrous hybrid of racial capitalism, and this in turn the TRC conflated with the private sector's moral culpability. The only way in which any business could have avoided censure by the TRC was to have disinvested entirely from the South African economy.[24] There was no acknowledgement, as Ann Bernstein (formerly of the Urban Foundation, now at the Centre for Development and Enterprise) reasoned in her submission, of the fact that business had provided jobs for millions of people, created infrastructure, 'unleashed democratising pressures', and sustained a base of activity for post-apartheid economic growth.[25] Many business representatives, eager to ingratiate themselves with the new government, bowed and scraped, mouthed a few apologetic platitudes, and sought to move on quickly. It was left to Johann Rupert, heir to his father Anton's Rembrandt empire, to ask a pointed question. 'Would you have preferred Ernest Oppenheimer to have settled in Australia rather than in South Africa?' he asked of the commission in an exasperated tone.[26]

The Season of Farewells

HFO had retired as chairman of De Beers in 1984, but he held on to his directorship for another decade, until 27 December 1994 – exactly 60 years after his original appointment. His devotion to diamonds meant that the formal separation from De Beers was always going to be the hardest parting and the longest farewell. In the Kimberley Mine Museum, Oppenheimer took his leave of Rhodes's old company. 'How wonderful De Beers is!' HFO proclaimed to the gathering of friends and colleagues, as he reminisced about his personal history with the diamond cartel.[27] 'I would certainly not have become a director at the age of twenty-six without a big element of nepotism,' he confessed. But he had heard it said that 'enlightened nepotism' was one of 'the quickest ways to efficiency'. It was both a warm-hearted meander down memory lane and a commanding performance, at once poignant and rousing. 'Grown men were in tears,' Gary Ralfe later recalled.[28] 'Even the King of Diamonds is not forever,' one journalist quipped, under the headline 'The going of Harry O'.[29]

Sir Philip Oppenheimer died in 1995. He had started working for De Beers in the early 1930s, not long after HFO commenced his own career, and he had played an instrumental role in building up the Central Selling Organisation/Diamond Trading Company. At Philip's memorial service in St George's, Hanover Square, HFO praised him for his kindness, courage and, above all, loyalty. Philip's greatest business achievements, his cousin suggested, were his success in convincing the Soviets to let De Beers market their diamonds, and the way in which he had dealt with unregulated production in Sierra Leone.[30] It was the end of a long and productive relationship. Other long-standing friends, like Patsy Curlewis, grew old and met their maker. Gavin Relly died unexpectedly in January 1999: unbeknown to him, he was riddled with

Patsy Curlewis strikes a dramatic pose alongside
Rebecca Oppenheimer, 1993. *(Brenthurst Library)*

cancer. A few months later, Zach de Beer followed him to the grave.
Through all this, Harry and Bridget kept up their closest friendships, and
they took care to celebrate milestones and special occasions – birthdays
and anniversaries, and executive retirements or promotions at Anglo – in
fine style, surrounded by their loved ones. The arrival of HFO's first two
great-grandchildren, Samuel Benjamin and Isabel Ward – the offspring
of Jonathan Oppenheimer and his American-born wife, Jennifer Janvier
Ward – meant that the last four years of his life were not simply a season
of sorrowful farewells.

The grandchildren, too, were a source of pleasure and pride, and,
occasionally, perplexity. Harry and Bridget supported actress Rebecca's
career on the stage. On one occasion they trundled off to Yeoville, among
Johannesburg's seedier suburbs, to watch her perform in a one-woman
play. In the closing scene, as Rebecca removed her top in front of the
hushed audience to reveal herself in a bra, her grandmother almost
choked – rather audibly – on one of the butterscotch sweets that she used

to munch on compulsively. On the way back home, the driver overheard Bridget asking HFO if he had noticed the pungent smell of cannabis in the theatre. Had Harry ever partaken of the weed? she wanted to know. 'Marrah-jwana', BDO drawled disapprovingly, rolling her 'r' and pronouncing the 'j'.[31]

HFO retained a tremendous appetite for international travel. Sometimes these trips were tinged with the air of final partings. On one of their visits to New York, Harry and Bridget travelled to see Jane Engelhard at her new home in Nantucket. She was now wheelchair-bound, puffy and unwell, and there would be few future encounters. HFO's own health seemed robust enough. On arrival at John F Kennedy International Airport, he was rather chuffed when the immigration officer peered at his passport and asked him, in disbelief, 'Were you really born in 1908?' Bridget recounted the story to Albert Robinson: '"Yes" said Harry. "Well your wife must feed you very well", & then he [the officer] stood up & said "May I shake you by the hand?"'[32] The couple kept to a relentless social schedule, even at their ripened age. At a dinner with Jane Engelhard's daughter Annette (now married to the fashion designer Oscar de la Renta), Bridget sat next to Abe Rosenthal, former executive editor of the *New York Times*. He informed her that the newspaper's publisher, Arthur Sulzberger, had organised a grand lunch for Thabo Mbeki in New York, but that Mbeki had cancelled at the last minute. 'So that is the last good copy SA will get from the *NY Times*', Bridget sighed to Robinson. 'Can you believe it? You feel embarrassed.'[33]

A few months beforehand, HFO and Ogilvie Thompson, together with JOT's wife, Tessa, had embarked on a tour of India. They hosted an elaborate dinner for over three hundred diamond dealers. Bridget chose to stay at Brenthurst, but when HFO recounted the details of the extravaganza, the grande dame felt a pang of regret at having missed out. She painted a picture of the scene for Robinson: 'The Indian women wore superb saris & every diamond they possessed & Tessa wore a cotton dress that she would have gone shopping [for] in Rosebank!! (Harry's words). I should have been there with my diamonds!'[34]

The dinner parties continued to be laid on at Brenthurst, and Harry and Bridget still played host to a variety of illustrious house guests. 'The Keswicks leave Tuesday and Wednesday Bill Gates [arrives] at Blue Skies – never a dull moment,' Bridget chitter-chattered to Robinson.[35] She deemed the Microsoft co-founder and his wife, Melinda, to be 'perfectly pleasant'.[36] Even though the tempo of their social engagements remained distinctly *allegretto*, HFO began increasingly to withdraw from public life. Mandela bestowed a national order on him in 1999, but, having received notification of the accolade only 24 hours in advance, Oppenheimer was unable to receive it in person. HFO gave fewer interviews, though the press still profiled him, and he was always delighted to show off the treasures in his study at the Brenthurst Library, especially the original manuscript of Byron's 'She walks in beauty' and his first editions of John Keats (one of which had belonged to William Wordsworth and another to Charles Dickens). On his 90th birthday numerous newspapers devoted several column inches to the new-found nonagenarian. The *Business Day* ran a full-page spread with contributions from Relly, Robinson, Helen Suzman, Mangosuthu Buthelezi, Raymond Louw (on Anglo's 'hands-off' approach to its media empire) and Margie Keeton, the chief executive officer of the Anglo American and De Beers Chairman's Fund.[37] Mary paid tribute to her father on the same pages: he was, she wrote, a 'loving, concerned and extraordinarily generous' parent, albeit remarkably 'fastidious'. He disliked travelling with the kind of people who 'ate *naartjies* in cars', she noted, 'an especially painful experience for him'. Two years before he turned 90, after almost three decades of sedulous service to UCT, Oppenheimer relinquished his chancellorship. His move to step down, a decision he made hesitantly, coincided with the retirement of Stuart Saunders as the university's vice-chancellor. It was an emotional occasion; the farewell ceremony was 'rather traumatic' and Saunders was 'upset & tearful', Bridget remarked to Robinson.[38] HFO made a powerful speech. He warned against the dangers lurking in the vague imperative of 'transformation': 'In all the calls for an Afro-centric culture, we surely should be very careful not to forget the universal quality of any great university,' Oppenheimer affirmed as he presided over his last graduation ceremony at UCT.[39] His 'interest, love and pride' in the institution remained undimmed, HFO declared. Afterwards, he was tremendously pleased with the sculpture by Bruce Arnott which the university presented to him as a gift.

In the first few months of 1997, HFO took ill with a chronic throat infection. Generally, he approached bouts of ill health stoically. Once, at a hospital near Milkwood, he sat reading a Trollope novel for a couple of hours before being attended to; it turned out his appendix had perforated. But now the problems were persistent: he found it difficult to eat, and he was dogged by abdominal pain. X-rays revealed complex oesophageal strictures, a potentially perilous condition. 'Knowing Harry as I do,'

Bridget confided in Robinson, 'I am sure he wants time to tie everything up & be prepared.' 'It all sounds v. dramatic,' she continued, 'but we are sitting on a "time bomb".'[40] In April, HFO flew to London on the Gulfstream to seek specialist advice. He was accompanied by Bridget, the Robinsons and his physician of long standing, Ron Tucker. The medical experts were in agreement: surgery was urgently required. Harry and Bridget cut short their stay and returned to South Africa. The operation, performed at the Kenridge Hospital, was successful and HFO recovered fairly quickly. 'He is amazing & the talk of the Kenridge,' Bridget boasted to Robinson.[41] But the saga had given them a scare.

As Oppenheimer approached his 90th year, death's inevitable arrival weighed on him. In April 1995 he set down elaborate instructions for Bridget in a sealed letter that was to be handed to her after he died. HFO effectively scripted his own funeral, providing a carefully crafted catalogue of arrangements from the choice of hymns – William Blake's 'Jerusalem', Henry Vaughan's 'My soul, there is a country', and Henry Francis Lyte's 'Abide with me' – to which verses of the Bible should be read and by whom. 'I would like Job chapter 28, verses 9 to the end to be read. You might ask Julian Ogilvie Thompson to read it, if he is available. From the New Testament I would like the parable of the Prodigal Son (Luke 15, verses 11–24) to be read, if possible by Nicky. I would like Psalm 24 to be included.'[42] It constituted a sort of manual, a series of directives, that completely typified HFO's personality and style. The politely hedged suggestions belied his singularity of purpose. He knew exactly what he wanted and how it should be executed. To some it might appear presumptuous that HFO should attempt to author his own afterlife, but for a man so self-possessed, so mindful of his destiny, it was natural that he should seek to control his fate, even from beyond the grave. (In fact, he made it clear that he was to be cremated.) Oppenheimer followed these funereal fiats with another series of stipulations in December 1997, this lot addressed to Bridget, Nicky and Mary (and his executors, Guy Nicholson, Michael Henrey and Clifford Elphick), on the administration of the family fortune after he had died. Bridget must 'always be able to live in the manner to which she is accustomed', he instructed them.[43] His estate would be made out to Bridget alone – though arrangements were put in place for Mary and Nicky to take ownership of various assets – and she would inherit Milkwood and several other properties, as well as the horse racing and breeding interests. For all that, HFO did not wish to 'fetter' his executors' responsibility, he assured them, and he granted them discretion to make specific bequests for charitable purposes. There was just one point he sought to underscore, and he did so with consummate clarity: 'Lastly, if you will forgive a rather pompous exhortation, always work together with a proper regard for one another's interests and susceptibilities. Few spectacles are more repulsive than members of a rich family quarrelling about money.'

Decline of the Empire: Anglo's London Listing and the Privatisation of De Beers

HFO started to pull back from the business after his retirement from the board of De Beers. But he went into 44 Main Street almost every day, and he continued to make his presence felt. In London, on his biannual visits, Oppenheimer made regular appearances at 17 Charterhouse Street. There, his solicitous assistant, Olive Milling, kept a beady eye on him. Occasionally HFO would slip out of the office undetected – much to Milling's trepidation – and saunter off into the hurly-burly of Holborn Circus. He would browse around WH Smith or glance into the parade shops. 'He liked to wander off and just be free,' Milling recollected.[44] But HFO had become frail and hard of hearing, and as soon as she noticed his absence, Milling would dispatch a small troop of undercover security officers – all ex-military men – to tail him. Oppenheimer's unimposing demeanour made him inconspicuous. If there was an important dinner party taking place, and Bridget wanted to wear some of her special jewellery (kept in the basement vaults at Charterhouse Street), HFO would have it retrieved from the strongbox. The box was not so strong that it could not be prised open with a spoon. Having selected the jewels, Oppenheimer would wrap them in a pouch, and then discreetly tuck the pouch between the pages of *The Times*. The newspaper wedged inside his arm, he was chauffeured off to 80 Eaton Square as happy as a sandboy. But had De Beers' security team known about the valuables in transit, there would have been four cars on his trail.

Oppenheimer might no longer be in his prime, or at the height of his powers, but his interventions could still prove decisive. After the fiasco with Consolidated Gold Fields, Minorco's managing directors in London, Roger Phillimore and Tony Lea, began to bridle at Anglo's air of absolute authority. They wanted a greater degree of autonomy. Increasingly Phillimore and Lea began to flex their muscles outside Anglo's orbit. 'They wanted to declare UDI,' is how Elphick remembered the chain of

Anglo's executive committee, 1992. Anti-clockwise from Julian
Ogilvie Thompson (second from right) are Nicky Oppenheimer,
Graham Boustred, Peter Gush, Leslie Boyd, Mike King, Dave Rankin,
Clem Sunter, Theo Pretorius and Gavin Relly. HFO continued to
wield power like a constitutional monarch, even though he no
longer occupied the chairman's throne. *(Anglo American)*

events beginning in the early 1990s.[45] HFO viewed the impulse to self-
determination as a betrayal of the greater group. He grew more and
more annoyed. Eventually, one day towards the end of 1992, he called in
Ogilvie Thompson and said to him, 'Julian, they've got to go.' Lea would
be spared the executioner's sword – he soon remembered that his loyalties
lay with Anglo – but Phillimore, unconstrained and far less unassuming,
was summarily axed. Hank Slack became Minorco's chief executive
officer. Apropos the chapter that led to JOT giving him his marching
orders, Phillimore later revisited it with a faint whiff of rancour: 'I was
regarded as insubordinate, heretical and perhaps even treacherous.' As
to his godfather's role in the execution, Phillimore paused, then declared
matter-of-factly: 'His hand was never anywhere near a weapon.'[46]

As Anglo's regent emeritus, HFO was often called upon to perform
ceremonial duties. In September 1996 Godsell invited him and Bridget
to Western Deep Levels, for example, where HFO set off the blast
for the new deep mining project. In a sense he was Anglo's mascot,
though one possessed of more majesty and might than that term may

adequately convey. However, Oppenheimer's influence over group policy and strategy was no longer unassailable. 'Our organisation would be much weaker if we unbundled, and we're not going to do it,' HFO confidently asserted at the end of 1994.[47] But he was wide of the mark. Internationally, the investment environment was changing. The old order of mining finance houses had fallen on hard times. Investors now sought to unlock shareholder value by encouraging a move away from bulky conglomerates towards slimmed-down companies, enterprises focused on fewer commodities and shorn of their industrial baggage. In South Africa, Anglo's rival, Gencor, led the way. After having purchased Billiton International from Royal Dutch Shell, Gencor proceeded to sell its non-core, non-mining assets. It hived off its base metals and non-gold interests as Billiton, listed the company on the London Stock Exchange, and then merged separately with Gold Fields South Africa to create the world's largest gold producer. Anglo looked at Billiton's London listing and was minded to follow suit. Mike King, Anglo's finance director, undertook a detailed study of the implications, which promised to be both financially and administratively complex. Anglo would have to change the way it was run and dispel the notion that it was essentially a family business, with the Oppenheimers calling the shots. It would be subject to the close scrutiny of London shareholders, who worked according to a

HFO and Bobby Godsell at Western Deep Levels, 1996. *(Anglo American)*

different set of rules and expectations. Nevertheless, the attractions were indisputable. Anglo's competitors, the big Australian miners – Broken Hill Proprietary Company Limited (BHP) and Rio Tinto – were already there. Furthermore, it would be much easier, so the argument ran, for Anglo to raise capital in London. Anglo's new domicile would make the company a truly global entity.

As befitted HFO's status, the conclusive discussions on Anglo's London listing – the gathering of executives where the decision was agreed to – took place in the Brenthurst Library. Lore later had it that although HFO was not in favour of the move, his opposition was more than a little resigned. In fact, most of the debate surrounding the London listing (and the merger of Anglo and Minorco, which preceded it) had to do with timing. Anglo's lawyers suggested a cautious approach. Anglo and De Beers would have to be disentangled operationally (though not in terms of shareholding) if the envisaged Anglo American plc was going to be able to conduct business in the United States. That process might take up to 18 months to complete. Ogilvie Thompson saw little merit in waiting: restricted from travelling freely to the US because of De Beers' persistent antitrust challenges, he had never been comfortable transacting business there. JOT remained deeply affronted by Judge Mukasey's ruling in the Consgold matter, and he was irked by the constant threat of legal action which seemed to plague the group in the Land of Liberty. Unlike Slack, he was happy to forgo access to American opportunities if it meant the merger and the London listing could be expedited. At Brenthurst, Ogilvie Thompson proposed a version of the London move to Anglo's assembled executives, only to find – much to his astonishment – that none of them was inclined to endorse his approach. Leslie Boyd was particularly vocal in his opposition. In Tony Trahar's recollection, 'When we broke for lunch ... Julian was wandering around like a wounded buffalo.'[48] JOT was furious with Slack: he suspected him of lobbying Anglo's exco members behind his back. Nevertheless, once the final decision on the London listing had been taken by the collective, Trahar conceded, JOT drove the process to conclusion with 'great efficiency and determination'. Oliver Baring, one of several advisors on the endeavour, predicted that Anglo's share price would at the very least quadruple. 'It did,' Trahar triumphantly recalled; 'the listing was a great success.' Confidants of Ogilvie Thompson suggest that he came to regard the London listing as his crowning achievement. But for a slew of latter-day comment-ators, looking through the rear-view mirror rather than the windshield, 'disastrous' is an adjective not infrequently attached to the move. 'Anglo's London listing has been a disaster,' claimed Tim Cohen, one of South Africa's top financial journalists, in 2016.[49] Kalim Rajab, the chronicler of Oppenheimer's political thought, delivered a similarly damning verdict: 'The company is now a shell of what it once was following a disastrous London listing ... the unintended consequences of which were never fully thought through.'[50]

When Anglo listed in London, a dynastic thread began to fray. Ernest Oppenheimer had conceived of Anglo as a mining house rooted in South Africa, a vehicle to develop his adopted country's economy. The dynasty he created had at all times been overwhelmingly invested, financially and emotionally, in Anglo and De Beers. 'As a family we have always been happy to have all our eggs in one basket,' Nicky wrote several years later to Cynthia Carroll, Anglo's then chief executive, 'as long as we managed or had real influence over the basket!'[51] By the end of HFO's life, the family's grip on the basket – or at least that part of it which Anglo occupied – had started to slacken. There was little prospect of Nicky running the company, and Jonathan's path to the top seemed unclear. It was a slackening process – a 'weakened' hold, Nicky called it – which the family fully 'supported and understood', he assured Carroll. A trader at heart, Nicky had long been preoccupied with the diamond side of the business. In the latter half of the 1980s, as chairman of the Diamond Trading Company, the London office of De Beers, Nicky had found his niche. He was well liked and well respected throughout the company. Back in southern Africa, on the far-flung mines of Kleinzee and Oranjemund, the 'NFO XI' – a cricket team cobbled together by Nicky – provided entertainment for the isolated mine dwellers. These were festive occasions with larger-than-life characters from South Africa's sporting past – former first-class cricketers like Vince van der Bijl, David Dyer, Alan Kourie, and Rupert 'Spook' Hanley – and although Nicky, innately quiet and retiring, was not especially to the fore, everyone knew that he had gone to a great deal of trouble to organise the tours. He, not De Beers, absorbed all the costs. In his farewell address at the Kimberley Mine Museum, HFO had referred to JOT as a 'great chairman' of De Beers; he added that it gave him 'special pleasure' for Nicky to serve as JOT's deputy.[52] In 1998, with Nicky now firmly entrenched in De Beers and eager to tighten the family's clasp, JOT made way for him as chairman of the diamond empire.

Nicky and his son, Jonathan, were very close. They shared the same recreational interests and a bond, as Bridget once remarked, similar in intensity to but different in nature from HFO's relationship with Sir Ernest. As their leverage over Anglo declined, it was natural that Nicky's and Jonathan's attention should focus increasingly on De Beers. In any case, the diamond fields of Kimberley were where the Oppenheimer dynasty originated. The circle would be closed. If success has many fathers, but failure is an orphan, then the Oppenheimers' takeover and privatisation of De Beers in 2001 – a deal concluded almost a year after HFO's death – ought to be subjected to a paternity test. On one version, the inspiration for the idea came to Nicky while he was lying in the bath. Although the impetus for the deal undoubtedly sprang from HFO's heir, Clifford Elphick recounts that he and a small band of private equity investors from E Oppenheimer and Son hatched the takeover plan during a strategy session at the Hotel Splendido in Portofino. De Beers had healthy cash reserves – the company practically threw off cash – and a 35 per cent stake in Anglo American. That is what the market tended to ascribe as its sum value. The stockpile was discounted. Elphick and his team devised a deceptively simple stratagem whereby the oft-criticised crossholdings between Anglo and De Beers would be unwound, Anglo and the Oppenheimers would each acquire a 45 per cent holding in De Beers, and the government of Botswana would claim the remaining ten per cent. In order to increase their stake in De Beers from 2.64 per cent (this direct interest was relatively recent; the equity had originally resided in the Diamond Trading Company and was swapped out earlier in the 1990s), the Oppenheimers would need to reduce their 7.2 per cent stake in Anglo by half.

Nicky liked the proposal, and so did JOT. Ken Costa, a kingpin at Anglo's banker, UBS Warburg, was asked to dissect its every detail. He gave it the seal of approval. The plan suited the Botswana government: the administration had long suspected, not without justification, that the key decisions affecting Botswana's mining operations were taken not at Debswana board meetings in Gaborone, but in Kimberley or Johannesburg instead. Trahar warmed to the idea, but he found himself in an awkward position. He had to put aside his loyalty to the Oppenheimers in order to get the best deal for Anglo's other shareholders. Trahar later relived the negotiations: 'I was the ham in the sandwich … [it was] one of the most difficult things I've ever had to do.'[53] Presented with the proposal in embryonic form, HFO was alive to the advantages, but he expressed scepticism about its viability. He doubted that the majority of De Beers' public shareholders would allow it. Here was the first major

South African public company ever formed – the establishment of De Beers had marked the beginning of large-scale industrialisation in South Africa, and the history of the mining group spanned virtually the whole development of the country's economy – and now it was to be privatised and acquired for what seemed like far less than its actual value. A handful of analysts suspected a sleight of hand, and they protested vigorously. De Beers was worth at least $30 billion, insisted James Allan, an analyst at Barnard Jacobs Mellet, but the money on offer was in the region of $18 billion.[54] Between them various financial institutions held more than 15 per cent of the company, enough to block the deal. They began to push back. At Old Mutual, Mike Levett demanded a raised offer. Nicky stuck to his guns. In the end, on Anglo's initiative, the consortium upped the purchase price to $19.7 billion, and the deal was waved through with overwhelming shareholder support.[55] To achieve this, Anglo increased its share to 45 per cent, the government of Botswana raised its stake to 15 per cent, and the Oppenheimers settled for a slightly reduced holding of 40 per cent. Their grip was nevertheless unmistakeable. 'They ran De Beers as if it were their own company,' Trahar remarked of the family's subsequent involvement. 'It didn't always go down well with Anglo ... but we managed our way through that.'[56]

The Last Supper and God's Plan

At 44 Main Street, there would later be idle speculation that the germ of the De Beers deal had been concocted in great secrecy, that it had taken HFO by surprise shortly before his death and unsettled him. In all likelihood he would have chalked it up to predestination. The transaction certainly signalled a shift, a possible change of family fortunes. After the privatisation of De Beers, the Oppenheimers remained the largest non-institutional shareholder in Anglo American with a stake of 3.5 per cent. But the umbilical cord had effectively been cut. Nicky resigned as Anglo's deputy chairman and took up a non-executive directorship instead. De Beers was now his focus. Succeeding generations of Oppenheimers seemed destined never to steer the great ship Anglo American, the Olympian vessel built and launched by Ernest Oppenheimer in 1917, then modernised and expanded by his son. The sails had been trimmed, possibly even torn, but ultimately HFO did not bear witness to the severance. On the night of Wednesday, 16 August 2000, he and Bridget hosted a dinner party at Brenthurst for Trahar. It was a celebration of Trahar's appointment as the chief executive of Anglo American plc. During the course of the evening HFO's health took a turn for the worse. He made a warm but uncharacteristically rambling speech. Afterwards, he turned to Trahar's wife, Trish, seated at his right, and excused himself from the table. Bridget was perturbed. 'Delicious dinner but ruined by Harry having to leave after his speech,' she wrote in her guest book afterwards. 'He looked terrible. I was so upset …'[57] HFO appeared to rally a little the following day, but on the Friday he was admitted to the Kenridge Hospital complaining of abdominal pains and a severe headache. His condition deteriorated; he slipped in and out of consciousness. Family members gathered round him, preparing to bid the patriarch farewell. His minutes hastened to their end. And then, shortly after 9 pm on Saturday, 19 August, Oppenheimer drew his last breath. The debt, in Shelley's words, was due. Dust had come to claim dust.

Oppenheimer was cremated on 24 August. His memorial service at St George's, Parktown, the following day, led by Archbishop Njongonkulu Ndungane and the parish rector, Gerard Sharp, unfolded in perfect harmony with his written wishes. It was an occasion fit for a head of state – indeed, a goodly number of dignitaries and cabinet ministers attended – and the service was broadcast live on national television. Although the church was too small to accommodate all the mourners (it could only seat 200 people), a marquee in the grounds catered to the overflow of those coming to pay their respects. Oppenheimer was one of South Africa's 'cherished sons', Ndungane proclaimed in his eulogy. He had used every opportunity to castigate the National Party and its unjust policies, and 'worked tirelessly' to create a better country for all its inhabitants. 'Many of his values are the cornerstones on which our new democracy stands,' the Archbishop affirmed.[58]

It was a message repeated again and again over the ensuing weeks as tributes to Oppenheimer poured in. Heir, apprentice, magnate, monarch: Oppenheimer had inhabited all of these personae over the course of his life, but the golden thread – or so his panegyrists proposed – was his commitment to democracy and development in South Africa. Mandela observed that the preamble to the Constitution spoke of honouring those who had suffered for justice and freedom, and of respecting those who had worked 'to build and develop our country'. 'Chief among the latter', he continued, 'must stand Harry Oppenheimer and his family.'[59] It was an acknowledgement not just of the departed, but of the dynasty too. Mbeki, now the country's President, praised HFO as a pioneer of racial reconciliation, the bedrock of the Rainbow Nation's constitutional democracy. In the world's foremost newspapers, Oppenheimer's history of opposition to apartheid was praised and précised. JDF Jones, the journalist who at one stage had been in discussions with HFO about authoring his biography, wrote in the *Financial Times* that Oppenheimer was a 'rare and fascinating figure', a 'mighty tycoon whose life was dominated by his battle with the right-wing government of his own country'.[60] He was a 'Randlord who opposed the system'. In the *New York Times* Oppenheimer's obituarist Marilyn Berger described him as someone who had used his great wealth and considerable influence in 'the fight against apartheid'.[61]

There were, of course, dissenting voices. In *The Guardian*, David Pallister, surveyor of the Oppenheimer empire, maintained that although HFO had long been feted in the West as a singular beacon of reform, his vast business interests nevertheless 'stoked the economic engine' of white minority rule.[62] And in the South African press the opinion pages swelled with contesting views on Oppenheimer's legacy. One contributor, Mzimkulu Malunga, likened HFO's 'quiet diplomacy' on apartheid to Mbeki's latter-day mollification of Mugabe. 'It is amazing that Oppenheimer is praised for his muted advice to a regime so brutal that it cannot be adequately explained in words,' Malunga protested.[63] Meanwhile, HFO's critics on the left aired all the old grievances, though their objections were now tempered by a more carefully considered appraisal of the industrialist's actions. Duncan Innes, Anglo's adversarial assessor, 'unhesitatingly' paid tribute to HFO for his 'towering role' as a business leader, his philanthropic bequests, and his contribution to liberal politics. But he cautioned against whitewashing the King of Diamonds' legacy. What was far less clear-cut about HFO's historical balance sheet, Innes implied, was the extent to which Anglo and De Beers had benefited from the system, and whether Oppenheimer had done enough to utilise his power and resources to 'bring down apartheid'.[64] Eddie Webster had crossed swords with Oppenheimer at the time of the Western Deep Levels disaster in 1973. Now he conceded that he and many of his 'fellow left intellectuals' had harboured an 'over-simplified understanding' of the relationship between apartheid and business. The economic costs of the old racial order had been great, the sociologist granted, and the left had overestimated the power of business to dismantle apartheid's institutional apparatus. Even so, Webster warned, in the past there had been a tendency to demonise Oppenheimer; now the pendulum risked swinging towards his memory being sanitised. At the core of Oppenheimer's legacy, Webster recapitulated, was a paradox, an incongruity that lay at the heart of South African liberalism. 'While articulate opponents of the apartheid system, liberals were beneficiaries of that very same system.'[65]

It was an argument that had been expounded by Steve Biko and the Black Consciousness Movement in the 1970s, and by many others both before and after them. Oppenheimer would have readily yielded the point. He was a white liberal of a particular disposition. Although in the South African context he might appear to be liberal, HFO had more than once sallied, he was really 'just an old-fashioned conservative'.[66] From his overlong attachment to the qualified franchise to his companies' role in the migrant labour system, and all its attendant social injustices, Oppenheimer's advocacy of liberalism was characterised by ambiguity and contradiction, fallibility and imperfection. He was only human, after all, a man of his times, even if other contemporary liberals might have seen further ahead than he did. However, if in the thorny matter of appraising another man's legacy a biographer must weigh up his subject's pros and cons, then it seems justified to claim that Oppenheimer moved his country forward, from the murk of apartheid to the dawn of non-racial democracy. His individual and corporate philanthropy, his championship of black trade union rights, his role in the Urban Foundation and the reformist initiatives of the 1980s, and his efforts during the transition to democratic rule – all of these factors reinforce the case. Without him, or the dynasty his father created in Kimberley, South Africa's development as a modern, industrial economy might have taken a very different, less successful course. The nation might never have had the option of a viable opposition in Parliament, and the organs of public life (such as the press and the universities), along with the multiple beneficiaries of the Chairman's Fund, would have been deprived of Oppenheimer's liberalism and largesse.

In the final reckoning, Harry Oppenheimer was a man who transcended his country's parochial political arena and the confines of its corporate sphere to become a significant figure on the world stage. Much more of an internationalist than his father, he expanded Anglo's reach and De Beers' dominion. During HFO's reign, the Oppenheimer empire came to straddle the globe. In South Africa the Anglo powerhouse completely dominated the economy. For all the limitations of his liberalism – and there were many – Oppenheimer made a vital contribution to political and economic progress in a country hamstrung by rival racial nationalisms.

He was an enlightened advocate of democracy and development in a nation always turned inwards on itself, forever looking backwards towards the past. In that sense the epithet 'business statesman' was amply well deserved. What of the Oppenheimer dynasty? On the eve of HFO's memorial service, Bridget held up Nicky's arm in the drawing room at Brenthurst and presented him to the gathered guests as the new *chef de famille*. However, to all intents and purposes, Anglo American was now forever beyond his and Jonathan's grasp, and it felt as if the family's fortunes stood on the cusp between the familiar and the unknown. Perhaps HFO would have taken solace in Shelley: 'All things that we love and cherish, / Like ourselves must fade and perish'. He was a man steeped in the notion of manifest destiny. Yet his beliefs were not rigid or static. In the outline of his memoir, written some fifteen years before his death, Oppenheimer acknowledged that his concept of destiny and family had evolved. 'I used to think, generalising from the special case of my father & myself, of a family as being God's plan to ensure certainty.' 'I now realise', he penned prophetically, 'that it is God's plan to ensure change.'[67]

NOTES

INTRODUCTION

1   On the exploitation of *die geldmag*
    for political purposes by the radical
    right and the National Party going
    back to the 1930s, see PJ Furlong,
    *Between Crown and Swastika: The
    Impact of the Radical Right on the
    Afrikaner Nationalist Movement in
    the Fascist Era*, Witwatersrand
    University Press, 1991; and M Shain,
    *A Perfect Storm: Antisemitism in
    South Africa, 1930–1948*, Jonathan
    Ball Publishers, 2015.

2   Although the term 'Hoggenheimer'
    was first coined in South Africa in
    1903 – well before Ernest Oppen-
    heimer rose to prominence – the
    appellation and intonation bore a
    striking resemblance to the name
    'Oppenheimer'. On the origins of
    'Hoggenheimer', see M Shain,
    'Hoggenheimer: The making of a
    myth', *Jewish Affairs* (September
    1981), pp 112–16.

3   HF Oppenheimer, *The Fading Com-
    monwealth*, Cambridge University
    Press, 1968.

4   A Sampson, *Black and Gold: Tycoons,
    Revolutionaries and Apartheid*,
    Hodder and Stoughton, 1987, p 58.

5   N Mandela, 'Eulogy: Harry Oppen-
    heimer', *Time*, 4 September 2000.

6   I have tried to tell something of the
    story of Anglo American and De Beers
    through a narrower, biographical lens
    in Chapter 10 and Chapter 11, based
    on the archival holdings at the Brent-
    hurst Library, as well as the material
    made available to me from E Oppen-
    heimer and Son (EOSON). But these
    chapters do not pretend to offer
    anything approaching comprehensive
    corporate histories. Despite the weight
    of its (somewhat dated) ideological
    baggage, the study by Duncan Innes
    on Anglo American remains valuable:
    D Innes, *Anglo: Anglo American and
    the Rise of Modern South Africa*, Ravan
    Press, 1984. On the diamond side, I
    have relied on various secondary stud-
    ies which are referenced throughout.
    Two of the most useful are EJ Epstein,
    The Diamond Invention, Hutchinson,
    1982; and S Kanfer, *The Last Empire:
    De Beers, Diamonds and the World*,
    Hodder and Stoughton, 1994.

7   A Hocking, *Oppenheimer and Son*,
    McGraw-Hill, 1973.

8   Brenthurst Library [BL], Harry
    Oppenheimer Papers [MS/OPP/
    HFO], HFO, Outline of memoir,
    Chapter 1: 'Introduction', n.d.

9   K Rajab (ed.), *A Man of Africa: The Political Thought of Harry Oppenheimer*, Zebra Press, 2017.

10 K Rajab, 'A historical assessment', in Rajab, *A Man of Africa*, pp 53–4.

11 *Daily Mirror*, 20 May 1963.

12 Rajab, 'A historical assessment', p 43.

13 T Bloom, 'An exquisite approach: But should the gloves have come off?', in Rajab, *A Man of Africa*, p 94.

14 *Mail & Guardian*, 4 November 2011.

15 N Ferguson, *The House of Rothschild*, vol. 1: *Money's Prophets, 1798–1848*, Penguin Books, 1999, p 20 [electronic version]; R Cornwell, 'Remembering David Rockefeller', *Independent*, 20 March 2017.

16 T Mann, *Buddenbrooks: The Decline of a Family*, translated by J Woods, Vintage International, 1994 [1901].

17 Interview with Jonathan Oppenheimer, Johannesburg, 24 February 2020. For the classical expression of Ernest Oppenheimer's vision, see Anglo American Corporation of South Africa, Annual Chairman's Statement, 1954.

18 D Landes, *Dynasties: Fortune and Misfortune in the World's Great Family Businesses*, Viking Penguin, 2006, p x.

19 T Gregory, *Ernest Oppenheimer and the Economic Development of Southern Africa*, Oxford University Press, 1962.

20 This is the subtitle of an unsympathetic investigation into the corporate dynasty. See D Pallister, S Stewart and I Lepper, *South Africa Inc.: The Oppenheimer Empire*, Yale University Press, 1988.

21 BL, MS/OPP/HFO, HFO, Outline of memoir, Chapter 3: 'My father & my relationship with him'.

CHAPTER ONE

1   Brenthurst Library [BL], Harry Oppenheimer Papers [MS/OPP/HFO]/D10.6.24 'Family story', no author, n.d.

2   N Ferguson, *The House of Rothschild*, vol. 1: *Money's Prophets, 1798–1848*, Penguin Books, 1999, p 42 [electronic version].

3   A Elon, *Founder: Meyer Amschel Rothschild and His Time*, Harper-Collins, 1998, p 39.

4   F Stern, *Gold and Iron: Bismarck, Bleichröder, and the Building of the German Empire*, Random House, 1979, p 498.

5   TG Otte, '"Alien diplomatist": Antisemitism and anti-Germanism in the diplomatic career of Sir Francis Oppenheimer', *History*, 89, no. 2 (April 2004), pp 233–55.

6   M Perry and F Schweitzer, *Antisemitism: Myth and Hate from Antiquity to the Present*, Palgrave Macmillan, 2005, p 89.

7   BL, MS/OPP/HFO, HFO, 'Help thou mine unbelief: Some recollections and reflections by Harry Oppenheimer' (unpublished manuscript, c.1985), Chapter 2: Family roots.

8   Otte, '"Alien diplomatist"', pp 233–55.

9   This account draws on C Newbury, *The Diamond Ring: Business, Politics, and Precious Stones in South Africa, 1867–1947*, Clarendon Press, 1989; R Turrell, *Capital and Labour on the Kimberley Diamond Fields, 1871–1890*, Cambridge University Press, 1987; and W Worger, *South Africa's City of Diamonds: Mine Workers and Monopoly Capitalism in Kimberley, 1867–1895*, Yale University Press, 1987.

10 R Rotberg, *The Founder: Cecil Rhodes and the Pursuit of Power*, Oxford University Press, 1988, p 3.

11 E Jessup, *Ernest Oppenheimer: A Study in Power*, Rex Collings, 1979, p 14.

12 Ibid., p 7.

13 Jessup incorrectly states that Bernard joined Dunkelsbuhler when he was 20; see Jessup, *Ernest Oppenheimer*, p 5. See BL, Index to Bernard Oppenheimer Papers; and A Hocking, *Oppenheimer and Son*, McGraw-Hill, 1973, p 21 for the correct timing.

14 C Newbury, 'The origins and function of the London Diamond Syndicate,

1889–1914', *Business History*, 29, no. 1 (1987), pp 5–26.

15 G Wheatcroft, *The Randlords: The Men Who Made South Africa*, Weidenfeld and Nicolson, 1985.

16 T Gregory, *Ernest Oppenheimer and the Economic Development of Southern Africa*, Oxford University Press, 1962, p 49; and BL, MS/OPP/HFO, HFO, 'Help thou mine unbelief: Some recollections and reflections by Harry Oppenheimer', Chapter 2: Family roots.

17 Hocking, *Oppenheimer and Son*, p 18.

18 Cited in Gregory, *Ernest Oppenheimer and the Economic Development of Southern Africa*, p 50.

19 BL, MS/OPP/HFO/D12.2 Ernest Oppenheimer's school certificate issued by the Grossherzogliche Direktion der Realschule und des Progymnasiums, Friedberg, 9 May 1896.

20 BL, Ernest Oppenheimer Papers [MS/OPP/EO]/A9 Naturalisation and national registration papers, November 1901. The naturalisation certificate is dated 21 November 1901.

21 Jessup, *Ernest Oppenheimer*, p 18.

22 BL, MS/OPP/HFO, HFO, Help thou mine unbelief: Some recollections and reflections by Harry Oppenheimer', Chapter 2: Family roots.

23 B Roberts, *Kimberley: Turbulent City*, David Philip, 1976.

24 S Marks and S Trapido, 'Lord Milner and the South African state' *History Workshop*, no. 8 (1979), pp 50–80.

25 C van Onselen, *The Cowboy Capitalist: John Hays Hammond, the American West and the Jameson Raid*, Jonathan Ball Publishers, 2017, p 140.

26 Cited in Jessup, *Ernest Oppenheimer*, p 42.

27 A Yamey, 'Men of gold: The Goldmanns of Burghersdorp', *Stammbaum*, no. 31 (Summer 2007).

28 BL, MS/OPP/EO/A2 Marriage certificate, 4 July 1906.

29 BL, MS/OPP/HFO/D10.1.5 Lina Goldmann to May Oppenheimer, 26 March 1908.

30 BL, MS/OPP/HFO/D10.1.2 Lina Goldmann to May Oppenheimer, 26 June 1907.

31 BL, MS/OPP/HFO/D10.1.3 Lina Goldmann to May Oppenheimer, 9 July 1907.

CHAPTER TWO

1 Brenthurst Library [BL], Harry Oppenheimer Papers [MS/OPP/HFO], Harry Oppenheimer's baby souvenir book, 1908.

2 BL, MS/OPP/HFO/A2 Birth registration and circumcision certificate, 15 November 1908. The circumcision took place on 5 November.

3 MJ Cardo, 'Culture, citizenship and white South Africanism, c.1924–1948' (PhD thesis, University of Cambridge, 2003). For the pre-Union period, see D Schreuder, '"Colonial nationalism" and "tribal nationalism": Making the white South African state, 1899–1910', in J Eddy and D Schreuder (eds.), *The Rise of Colonial Nationalism*, Allen and Unwin, 1988.

4 DW Kruger, *The Making of a Nation: A History of the Union of South Africa, 1910–1961*, Macmillan, 1969, p 36.

5 R Chernow, *The House of Morgan: An American Banking Dynasty and the Rise of Modern Finance*, Grove Atlantic, Kindle edn, 2010, p 170.

6 T Gregory, *Ernest Oppenheimer and the Economic Development of Southern Africa*, Oxford University Press, 1962, pp 71–2.

7 Ibid., p 72.

8 E Jessup, *Ernest Oppenheimer: A Study in Power*, Rex Collings, 1979, p 60.

9 HF Oppenheimer, 'Sir Ernest Oppenheimer: A portrait by his son', *Optima*, 17, no. 3 (September 1967), p 95.

10 A Hocking, *Oppenheimer and Son*, McGraw-Hill, 1973, p 40.

11 BL, MS/OPP/HFO, HFO, 'Help thou mine unbelief: Some recollections and reflections by Harry

Oppenheimer' (unpublished manuscript, c.1985), Chapter 1: The beginnings in Kimberley.

12 Ibid.

13 BL, MS/OPP/HFO, HFO, 'Help thou mine unbelief: Some recollections and reflections by Harry Oppenheimer', Chapter 2: Family roots.

14 AM Grundlingh, 'Die rebellie van 1914: 'n Historiografiese verkenning', *Kleio*, 11, no. 1–2 (1979), pp 18–30.

15 *New Yorker*, 29 September 1956.

16 R Steyn, *Jan Smuts: Unafraid of Greatness*, Jonathan Ball Publishers, 2015, p 76.

17 HF Oppenheimer, 'Sir Ernest Oppenheimer: A portrait by his son', p 95.

18 *New Yorker*, 29 September 1956.

19 Ibid.

20 BL, Index to Sir Bernard Oppenheimer Papers.

21 HF Oppenheimer, 'Sir Ernest Oppenheimer: A portrait by his son', p 97; Hocking, *Oppenheimer and Son*, p 76.

22 Hocking, *Oppenheimer and Son*, p 81.

23 BL, MS/OPP/HFO, HFO, 'Help thou mine unbelief: Some recollections and reflections by Harry Oppenheimer', Chapter 5: The Anglo American Group.

24 *New Yorker*, 29 September 1956.

25 BL, Ernest Oppenheimer Papers [MS/OPP/EO]/C3.1 May Oppenheimer to Ernest Oppenheimer, 3 February [1919].

26 BL, MS/OPP/EO/C3.1 May Oppenheimer to Ernest Oppenheimer, 17 February [1919].

27 BL, MS/OPP/EO/C3.1 May Oppenheimer to Ernest Oppenheimer, 8 April [1919].

28 BL, MS/OPP/EO/C3.1 May Oppenheimer to Ernest Oppenheimer, 14 April [1919].

29 Ibid.

30 BL, MS/OPP/EO/C3.1 May Oppenheimer to Ernest Oppenheimer, 23 April [1919].

31 Ibid.

32 BL, MS/OPP/EO/C3.1 May Oppenheimer to Ernest Oppenheimer, 12 June [1919].

33 BL, MS/OPP/EO/C3.1 May Oppenheimer to Ernest Oppenheimer, 25 March [1919].

34 BL, MS/OPP/EO/C3.1 May Oppenheimer to Ernest Oppenheimer, 10 February [1919].

35 BL, MS/OPP/EO/C3.1 May Oppenheimer to Ernest Oppenheimer, 23 April [1919].

36 Ibid.

37 BL, MS/OPP/EO/C3.1 May Oppenheimer to Ernest Oppenheimer, 10 February [1919].

38 BL, MS/OPP/EO/C3.1 May Oppenheimer to Ernest Oppenheimer, 24 February [1919].

39 BL, MS/OPP/HFO, HFO, 'Help thou mine unbelief: Some recollections and reflections by Harry Oppenheimer', Chapter 2: Family roots.

40 Ibid.

41 Ibid.

42 BL, MS/OPP/EO/C3.2 Harry Oppenheimer to his father, 18 October [1918].

43 BL, MS/OPP/EO/C3.2 Harry Oppenheimer to his father, 6 January [1919].

44 BL, MS/OPP/EO/C3.2 Harry Oppenheimer to his father, 24 February [1919].

45 BL, MS/OPP/EO/C3.2 Harry Oppenheimer to his father, 9 February [1919].

46 BL, MS/OPP/HFO, HFO, Outline of memoir, Chapter 3: 'My father & my relationship with him'.

47 BL, MS/OPP/EO/C3.2 Harry Oppenheimer to his father, 27 January [1919].

48 BL, MS/OPP/EO/C3.2 Harry Oppenheimer to his father, 3 February [1919].

49 BL, MS/OPP/EO/C3.2 Harry Oppenheimer to his father, 11 March [1919].

50 BL, MS/OPP/EO/C3.2 Harry Oppenheimer to his father, 7 April [1919].

51 BL, MS/OPP/EO/C3.2 Harry Oppenheimer to his father, 24 March [1919].

52 BL, MS/OPP/EO/C3.2 Harry Oppenheimer to his father, 7 April [1919].

53 Ibid.

54 HF Oppenheimer, 'Sir Ernest Oppenheimer: A portrait by his son', p 101.

55 Cited in PR Randall, 'The English private school system in South Africa' (MEd thesis, University of the Witwatersrand, 1980), p 199. See also P Randall, *Little England on the Veld*, Ravan Press, 1982, p 105.

56 BL, MS/OPP/EO C3b(6.1) Bishop Clayton to Ernest Oppenheimer, 27 June 1938.

57 M Kaplan, *Jewish Roots in the South African Economy*, Struik, 1986, p 131.

58 Interview with Nicky Oppenheimer, Johannesburg, 1 February 2018; interview with Mary Slack, Johannesburg, 19 August 2019.

59 M Silberhaft, *The Travelling Rabbi: My African Tribe*, Jacana, 2012, p 129.

60 BL, MS/OPP/HFO/D10.5.1 Baptismal card for FL Oppenheimer, 28 July 1919.

61 BL, MS/OPP/HFO, HFO, 'Help thou mine unbelief: Some recollections and reflections by Harry Oppenheimer', Chapter 2: Family roots.

62 BL, MS/OPP/HFO/D10.9.1 JC Smuts to Ernest Oppenheimer, 18 December 1919.

63 Cited in Hocking, *Oppenheimer and Son*, p 91.

64 BL, MS/OPP/HFO/D10.2.76 May Oppenheimer, diary entry, 4 March 1921.

65 BL, MS/OPP/HFO, HFO, Outline of memoir, Chapter 2: 'My family roots'.

66 *The Carthusian*, 13, no. 428 (November 1922), p 361.

67 W Gilfillan, 'A diamond forever', *The Executive*, 6, no. 1 (February 1993).

68 BL, MS/OPP/HFO, HFO, Outline of memoir, Chapter 15: 'Recreation'.

69 BL, MS/OPP/HFO/D10.4.2 Charterhouse, Daviesites housemaster's report, December 1924.

70 BL, MS/OPP/HFO/D10.4.1 Charterhouse, mid-quarter report, October 1924.

71 *The Carthusian*, 34, no. 7 (March 1995), p 31.

72 BL, MS/OPP/HFO, HFO, Outline of memoir, Chapter 2: 'My family roots'.

73 BL, MS/OPP/HFO, HFO, 'Help thou mine unbelief: Some recollections and reflections by Harry Oppenheimer', Chapter 2: Family roots.

74 Ibid.

75 Ibid.

76 Ibid.

77 See, for example, BL, MS/OPP/HFO/D10.4.4 Frank Oppenheimer to his father, 21 January 1925.

78 BL, MS/OPP/HFO/D10.2.73 Harry Oppenheimer to his mother, 11 April [no year, sent from 21 Portman Square, W1].

79 BL, MS/OPP/HFO/D10.2.74 Harry Oppenheimer to his mother, 2 May [no year, sent from 21 Portman Square, W1].

80 Ibid.

81 Ibid.

82 Ibid.

83 BL, MS/OPP/HFO, HFO, 'Help thou mine unbelief: Some recollections and reflections by Harry Oppenheimer', Chapter 2: Family roots.

84 BL, MS/OPP/HFO/D10.2.74 Harry Oppenheimer to his mother, 2 May [no year, sent from 21 Portman Square, W1].

85 BL, MS/OPP/HFO/D10.4.3 Harry Oppenheimer to his father, 21 January 1925.

86 Oxford University, Christ Church College Archive [CHOX], Harry Oppenheimer file, Application for admission form, n.d.

87 The official history of the Brenthurst Gardens states that Ernest 'brought his family to the estate in 1922'. AH Smith, *The Brenthurst Gardens*, Brenthurst Press, 1988, p 9.

88 BL, MS/OPP/HFO/D10.2.73 Harry Oppenheimer to his mother, 11 April [no year, sent from 21 Portman Square, W1].

89 BL, MS/OPP/HFO, HFO, 'Help thou mine unbelief: Some recollections

and reflections by Harry Oppenheimer', Chapter 2: Family roots.

90 A Sisman, *An Honourable Englishman: The Life of Hugh Trevor-Roper*, Random House, 2010, p 20.

91 CHOX, Harry Oppenheimer file, Rev. Lancelot Allen to the Dean of Christ Church, Oxford, 28 February 1925.

92 *The Carthusian*, 14, no. 459 (June 1927), p 229.

93 *The Carthusian*, 14, no. 457 (February 1927), p 188.

CHAPTER THREE

1 Brenthurst Library [BL], Harry Oppenheimer Papers [MS/OPP/HFO] HFO, 'Help thou mine unbelief: Some recollections and reflections by Harry Oppenheimer', Chapter 2: Family roots.

2 *Oxford University Handbook* (1932), pp 152–62, cited in L Arena, 'From economics of the firm to business studies at Oxford: An intellectual history (1890s–1990s)' (DPhil thesis, University of Oxford, 2011), p 106.

3 W Gilfillan, 'A diamond forever', *The Executive*, 6, no. 1 (February 1993).

4 BL, MS/OPP/HFO, HFO, 'Help thou mine unbelief: Some recollections and reflections by Harry Oppenheimer', Chapter 2: Family roots.

5 Ibid.

6 J Curthoys, *The Cardinal's College: Christ Church, Chapter and Verse*, Profile Books, 2012.

7 Cited in C Butler (ed.), *Christ Church, Oxford: A Portrait of the House*, Third Millennium Publishing, 2006, p 25.

8 Curthoys, *The Cardinal's College*, p 303.

9 RF Harrod, *The Life of John Maynard Keynes*, Macmillan, 1951.

10 Oxford University, Christ Church College Archive [CHOX], Harry Oppenheimer file, Sir Ernest Oppenheimer to the Dean, Christ Church, Oxford, 10 March [no year].

11 Curthoys, *The Cardinal's College*, p 303.

12 Gilfillan, 'A diamond forever'.

13 BL, MS/OPP/HFO/D10.13 University lecture notes, 1930–1.

14 On Harrod, see HP Brown, 'Sir Roy Harrod: A biographical memoir', *Economic Journal*, 90, no. 357 (March 1980), pp 1–33.

15 Gilfillan, 'A diamond forever'.

16 JC Masterman, *The Double-Cross System: The Classic Account of World War Two Spy-Masters*, Vintage, 2013. See also E Harrison, 'Christ Church and the Secret Service: Sir John Masterman and MI5', *Christ Church Matters*, no. 35 (Trinity term 2015), pp 35–7.

17 JC Masterman, *On the Chariot Wheel: An Autobiography*, London, 1975, p 127, cited in B Harrison (ed.), *The History of the University of Oxford*, vol. VIII: *The Twentieth Century*, Clarendon Press, 1994, p 386.

18 Curthoys, *The Cardinal's College*, p 307.

19 A Hocking, *Oppenheimer and Son*, McGraw-Hill, 1973, p 148.

20 Interview with Nicky Oppenheimer, Johannesburg, 1 February 2018; NF Oppenheimer, 'A tribute to my father', *Optima*, 47, no. 1 (February 2001), p 19.

21 D Kynaston, *The City of London*, vol. II: *Golden Years, 1890–1914*, Vintage Digital, 2015.

22 This is the title of David Kynaston's third volume on the history of the City of London: *The City of London*, vol. III: *Illusions of Gold*, Vintage Digital, 2015.

23 Hocking, *Oppenheimer and Son*, p 148.

24 *Rand Daily Mail*, 17 April 1952.

25 Interview with Peter Oppenheimer, Oxford, 7 October 2019. See also CHOX, Harry Oppenheimer file, Harry Oppenheimer to Peter Oppenheimer, 30 December 1981; Harry Oppenheimer to Peter Oppenheimer, 29 January 1982; Harry Oppenheimer to Peter Oppenheimer, 31 January 1983.

26 BL, MS/OPP/HFO, HFO, 'Help thou mine unbelief: Some recollections and reflections by Harry Oppenheimer', Chapter 2: Family roots.

CHAPTER FOUR

1 B Eichengreen, *Golden Fetters: The Gold Standard and the Great Depression, 1919–1939*, Oxford University Press, 1992.

2 K Breckenridge, '"Money with dignity": Migrants, minelords and the cultural politics of the South African gold standard crisis, 1920–33', *Journal of African History*, 36, no. 2 (1995), pp 271–304.

3 E Dommisse, *Sir David Pieter de Villiers Graaff: First Baronet of De Grendel*, Tafelberg Publishers, 2011.

4 T Gregory, *Ernest Oppenheimer and the Economic Development of Southern Africa*, Oxford University Press, 1962, pp 113–19.

5 Ibid., p 155.

6 K Acutt, 'The boss as his colleagues see him', in B Mortimer (ed.), *HFO: Some Personal Perspectives on Harry Frederick Oppenheimer by His Colleagues and Friends*, Brenthurst Press, 1985, p 13.

7 Brenthurst Library [BL], Index to Sir Curt Michael Oppenheimer Papers.

8 I Michael, *Apple Sauce*, Brentano's, 1928.

9 BL, Harry Oppenheimer Papers [MS/OPP/HFO]/D10.9.3 Ernest Oppenheimer to Tielman Roos, 8 January 1931.

10 BL, MS/OPP/HFO/D10.9.4 Tielman Roos to Ernest Oppenheimer, 12 January 1931.

11 Ibid.

12 BL, MS/OPP/HFO/D10.9.7 Tielman Roos to Ernest Oppenheimer, 23 March 1931.

13 BL, MS/OPP/HFO/B.3.1 Diary entry, 6 January 1933.

14 C Swanepoel and PT Fliers, 'The fuel of unparalleled recovery: Monetary policy in South Africa between 1925 and 1936', *Economic History of Developing Regions*, 36, no. 2 (2021), pp 213–44; B Eichengreen, 'Gold and South Africa's Great Depression', *Economic History of Developing Regions*, 36, no. 2 (2021), pp 175–93.

15 BL, MS/OPP/HFO/B.3.1 Diary entry, 1 January 1933.

16 BL, MS/OPP/HFO/B.3.1 Diary entry, 14 February 1933.

17 BL, MS/OPP/HFO/B.3.1 Diary entry, 3 January 1933.

18 BL, MS/OPP/HFO/B.3.1 Diary entry, 1 January 1933.

19 BL, MS/OPP/HFO/B.3.1 Diary entry, 2 February 1933.

20 BL, MS/OPP/HFO/B.3.1 Diary entry, 10 February 1933.

21 BL, MS/OPP/HFO/B.3.1 Diary entry, 11 February 1933.

22 BL, MS/OPP/HFO/B.3.1 Diary entry, 13 February 1933.

23 BL, MS/OPP/HFO/B.3.1 Diary entry, 14 February 1933.

24 BL, MS/OPP/HFO/B.3.1 Diary entry, 2 January 1933.

25 BL, MS/OPP/HFO/B.3.1 Diary entry, 3 January 1933.

26 BL, MS/OPP/HFO/B.3.1 Diary entry, 15 January 1933.

27 BL, MS/OPP/HFO/B.3.1 Diary entry, 4 March 1933.

28 BL, MS/OPP/HFO/B.3.1 Diary entry, 10 January 1933.

29 BL, MS/OPP/HFO/B.3.1 Diary entry, 4 January 1933; BL, MS/OPP/HFO B.3.1 Diary entry, 9 February 1933.

30 BL, MS/OPP/HFO/B.3.1 Diary entry, 27 January 1933.

31 BL, MS/OPP/HFO/B.3.1 Diary entry, 24 February 1933.

32 BL, MS/OPP/HFO/B.3.1 Diary entry, 6 January 1933.

33 BL, MS/OPP/HFO/B.3.1 Diary entry, 2 February 1933.

34 BL, MS/OPP/HFO/B.3.1 Diary entry, 3 February 1933.

35 BL, MS/OPP/HFO/B.3.1 Diary entry, 6 February 1933.

36 BL, MS/OPP/HFO/B.3.1 Diary entry, 15 February 1933.

37 BL, MS/OPP/HFO/B.3.1 Diary entry, 26 January 1933.

38 HF Oppenheimer, 'Sir Ernest Oppenheimer: A portrait by his son', *Optima*, 17, no. 3 (September 1967), p 101.

39 BL, MS/OPP/HFO/B.3.1 Diary entry, 6 January 1933.

40 BL, MS/OPP/HFO/B.3.1 Diary entry, 8 January 1933.

41 BL, MS/OPP/HFO/B.3.1 Diary entry, 10 January 1933.

42 BL, MS/OPP/HFO, HFO, 'Help thou mine unbelief: Some recollections and reflections by Harry Oppenheimer', Chapter 5: The Anglo American Corporation.

43 BL, MS/OPP/HFO/B.3.1 Diary entry, 5 January 1933.

44 A Desai and G Vahed, *The South African Gandhi: Stretcher-Bearer of Empire*, Stanford University Press, 2016.

45 BL, MS/OPP/HFO/B.3.1 Diary entry, 5 January 1933.

46 R Turrell, 'Kimberley, labour and compounds, 1871–1888', in S Marks and R Rathbone (eds.), *Industrialisation and Social Change in South Africa: African Class Formation, Culture and Consciousness, 1870–1930*, Longman, 1982, p 45.

47 JW Cell, *The Highest Stage of White Supremacy: The Origins of Segregation in South Africa and the American South*, Cambridge University Press, 1982.

48 S Dubow, *Racial Segregation and the Origins of Apartheid in South Africa, 1919–36*, Macmillan, 1989, p 39.

49 BL, MS/OPP/HFO/D10.10.9 Ernest Oppenheimer to CAF Calvert, 17 February 1936.

50 FA Mouton, *Prophet without Honour: FS Malan; Afrikaner, South African and Cape Liberal*, Protea Book House, 2011; A Paton, *Hofmeyr*, Oxford University Press, 1964.

51 PB Rich, *White Power and the Liberal Conscience: Racial Segregation and South African Liberalism*, Ravan Press, 1984.

52 BL, MS/OPP/HFO/B.3.1 Diary entry, 20 January 1933.

53 AG Barlow, *Almost in Confidence*, Juta, 1952, p 238; AD Turrell, 'The South African Party 1932–1934: The movement towards Fusion' (MA thesis, University of Natal, 1977), p 48.

54 BL, MS/OPP/HFO/D10.9.10 JC Smuts to Ernest Oppenheimer, 28 December 1932.

55 BL, MS/OPP/HFO/B.3.1 Diary entry, 7 January 1933.

56 BL, MS/OPP/HFO/B.3.1 Diary entry, 26 January 1933.

57 BL, MS/OPP/HFO/B.3.1 Diary entry, 28 January 1933.

58 BL, MS/OPP/HFO/B.3.1 Diary entry, 31 January 1933.

59 BL, MS/OPP/HFO/B.3.1 Diary entry, 1 February 1933.

60 Ibid.

61 Ibid.

62 BL, MS/OPP/HFO/B.3.1 Diary entry, 2 March 1933.

63 BL, MS/OPP/HFO/B.3.1 Diary entry, 24 January 1933.

64 BL, MS/OPP/HFO/B.3.1 Diary entry, 28 January 1933.

65 BL, MS/OPP/HFO/B.3.1 Diary entry, 9 February 1933.

66 BL, MS/OPP/HFO/B.3.1 Diary entry, 2 March 1933.

67 EJ Epstein, *The Diamond Invention*, Hutchinson, 1982, p 77.

68 BL, MS/OPP/HFO/B.3.1 Diary entry, 13 January 1933.

69 BL, MS/OPP/HFO/B.3.1 Diary entry, 10 March 1933.

70 BL, MS/OPP/HFO/B.3.1 Diary entry, 10 February 1933.

71 BL, MS/OPP/HFO/B.3.1 Diary entry, 22 February 1933.

72 Cited in Gregory, *Ernest Oppenheimer and the Economic Development of Southern Africa*, p 514.

73 BL, MS/OPP/HFO/B.3.1 Diary entry, 29 January 1933.

74 Ibid.

75 Gregory, *Ernest Oppenheimer and the*

Economic Development of Southern Africa, pp 415–16.

76 BWE Alford and CE Harvey, 'Copper-belt merger: The formation of the Rhokana Corporation, 1930–1932', *Business History Review*, 54, no. 3 (Autumn 1980), pp 330–58.

77 BL, MS/OPP/HFO/D10.14 Journal entry, Visit to Northern Rhodesia and Congo Copper Fields and the Congo and Angola Diamond Fields, 20 June 1933.

78 BL, MS/OPP/HFO/D10.14 Journal entry, 21 June 1933.

79 Ibid.

80 BL, MS/OPP/HFO/D10.14 Journal entry, 22 June 1933.

81 BL, MS/OPP/HFO/D10.14 Journal entry, 24 June 1933.

82 Ibid.

83 BL, MS/OPP/HFO/D10.14 Journal entry, 25 June 1933.

84 BL, MS/OPP/HFO/D10.14 Journal entry, 26 June 1933.

85 BL, MS/OPP/HFO/D10.14 Journal entry, 27 June 1933.

86 Ibid.

87 RB Hagart, 'The formative years: A recollection', *Optima*, 17, no. 3 (September 1967), pp 105–11.

88 Cited in Gregory, *Ernest Oppenheimer and the Economic Development of Southern Africa*, p 310.

89 Acutt, 'The boss as his colleagues see him', p 13.

90 For Hallett's confidential account of the death, see his letter to 'Christopher' [no surname indicated]: BL, MS/OPP/HFO/D.10.5.19 John Hallett to Christopher, 18 April 1935: 'This is the whole story for yourself and *very* few as on the island only the doctor knows that the two girls had not gone home before the tragedy.'

91 BL, MS/OPP/HFO/D10.5.14 Telegram, 17 April 1935.

92 BL, MS/OPP/HFO/D10.5.15 JC Smuts to Ernest Oppenheimer, 18 April 1935.

93 BL, MS/OPP/HFO/D.10.5.20 JC Smuts to Ernest Oppenheimer, 26 April 1935.

94 BL, MS/OPP/HFO, HFO, 'Help thou mine unbelief: Some recollections and reflections by Harry Oppenheimer', Chapter 5: The Anglo American Corporation.

95 HF Oppenheimer, 'Sir Ernest Oppenheimer: A portrait by his son', p 101.

96 The best account of the 'diamond invention' remains Epstein, *The Diamond Invention*, pp 108–24. See also T Green, *The World of Diamonds*, Littlehampton, 1981; and S Kanfer, *The Last Empire: De Beers, Diamonds and the World*, Hodder and Stoughton, 1994.

97 Interview with Gary Ralfe, Johannesburg, 23 March 2021; interview with Julian Ogilvie Thompson, Johannesburg, 11 January 2018. See also J Ogilvie Thompson, 'An appreciation of Harry Oppenheimer', *Optima*, 33, no. 1 (March 1985), pp 2–7.

98 Cited in Epstein, *The Diamond Invention*, p 109.

99 Cited in Epstein, *The Diamond Invention*, p 110.

100 Epstein, *The Diamond Invention*, pp 78–9.

CHAPTER FIVE

1 NF Oppenheimer, 'A tribute to my father', *Optima*, 47, no. 1 (February 2001), p 14.

2 Brenthurst Library [BL], Harry Oppenheimer Papers [MS/OPP/HFO], HFO, Outline of memoir, Chapter 8: 'The war years'.

3 O Pirow, *James Barry Munnik Hertzog*, Howard Timmins, 1957, p 227.

4 A Paton, *Hofmeyr*, Oxford University Press, 1964, p 321.

5 Cited in ibid., p 321.

6 R Steyn, *Seven Votes: How WWII Changed South Africa Forever*, Jonathan Ball Publishers, 2020.

7 BL, MS/OPP/HFO, HFO, 'Help thou mine unbelief: Some recollections and reflections by Harry Oppenheimer', Chapter 2: Family roots.

8 Ibid., Chapter 4: Smuts.

9 Ibid.

10 Steyn, *Seven Votes*, p 66.

11 PJ Furlong, *Between Crown and Swastika: The Impact of the Radical Right on the Afrikaner Nationalist Movement in the Fascist Era*, Witwatersrand University Press, 1991.

12 M Shain, *A Perfect Storm: Antisemitism in South Africa, 1930–1948*, Jonathan Ball Publishers, 2015.

13 BL, MS/OPP/HFO/D1.2 Military training courses, 1940.

14 BL, MS/OPP/HFO/D1.2 South African Military College [notes on] Bush Warfare, 16 February 1940.

15 BL, MS/OPP/HFO/D1.2 South African Military College, Report on Course 607G for Intelligence Officers, 24 October 1940 and certificate of attendance, 9 November 1940.

16 BL, E Oppenheimer and Son Papers [EOSON], HFO to Ina Oppenheimer, 15 April 1941.

17 BL, EOSON, HFO to Ernest Oppenheimer, 25 April 1941.

18 G Young, 'Action in the Western Desert' in B Mortimer (ed.), *HFO: Some Personal Perspectives on Harry Frederick Oppenheimer by His Colleagues and Friends*, Brenthurst Press, 1985, p 53.

19 BL, EOSON, HFO to Ernest Oppenheimer, 25 April 1941.

20 BL, EOSON, HFO to Ernest Oppenheimer, 12 May 1941.

21 BL, EOSON, HFO to Ernest Oppenheimer, 13 May 1941.

22 BL, EOSON, HFO to Ernest Oppenheimer, 20 May 1941.

23 BL, EOSON, HFO to Ina Oppenheimer, 4 June 1941.

24 BL, EOSON, HFO to Ernest Oppenheimer, 20 May 1941.

25 BL, EOSON, HFO to Ernest Oppenheimer, 24 August 1941.

26 G Fletcher, 'Action in the Western Desert', in B Mortimer (ed.), *HFO: Some Personal Perspectives on Harry Frederick Oppenheimer by His Colleagues and Friends*, Brenthurst Press, 1985, pp 56–7.

27 H Skelly, 'Action in the Western Desert', in Mortimer, *HFO: Some Personal Perspectives*, pp 51–7.

28 BL, EOSON, HFO to Ernest Oppenheimer, 23 June 1941.

29 BL, Sir Ernest Oppenheimer Papers, [MS/OPP/EO]/C1.1.1 Ernest Oppenheimer to HFO, 10 August 1941.

30 BL, MS/OPP/EO/ C1.1 Ernest Oppenheimer to HFO, 4 May 1941.

31 Ibid.

32 BL, MS/OPP/EO/C1.1 Ernest Oppenheimer to HFO, 27 May 1941.

33 BL, EOSON, HFO to Ernest Oppenheimer, 23 June 1941.

34 BL, EOSON, HFO to Ernest Oppenheimer, 19 December 1941.

35 BL, MS/OPP/HFO/N4.1 JD McCarthy, Historical notes on Debshan, 1992.

36 BL, EOSON, HFO to Ernest Oppenheimer, 31 August 1941.

37 BL, EOSON, HFO to Ernest Oppenheimer, 21 July 1941.

38 BL, MS/OPP/EO/C1.1 Ernest Oppenheimer to HFO, 30 May 1941.

39 BL, EOSON, HFO to Ernest Oppenheimer, 21 July 1941.

40 BL, EOSON, HFO to Ernest Oppenheimer, 7 August 1941.

41 BL, MS/OPP/EO/ C1.1 Ernest Oppenheimer to HFO, 11 May 1941.

42 BL, EOSON, HFO to Ernest Oppenheimer, 24 August 1941.

43 BL, EOSON, HFO to Ernest Oppenheimer, 15 October 1941.

44 BL, EOSON, HFO to Ernest Oppenheimer, 15 August 1941.

45 BL, EOSON, HFO to Ernest Oppenheimer, 17 September 1941.

46 G Young, 'Action in the Western Desert', in Mortimer, *HFO: Some Personal Perspectives*, pp 53.

47 BL, EOSON, HFO to Ernest Oppenheimer, 20 September 1941.

48 BL, EOSON, HFO to Ernest Oppenheimer, 5 December 1941.

49 BL, EOSON, HFO to Ernest Oppenheimer, 3 December 1941.

50 BL, MS/OPP/HFO/ D12.13.2 C Neill to HFO, 30 October 1978.

51 BL, EOSON, HFO to Ina Oppenheimer, 4 December 1941.

52 BL, EOSON, HFO to Ernest Oppenheimer, 5 December 1941.

53 BL, EOSON, HFO to Ernest Oppenheimer, 28 January 1942.

54 BL, EOSON, HFO to Ernest Oppenheimer, 3 February 1942.

55 BL, EOSON, HFO to Ernest Oppenheimer, 19 February 1942.

56 Ibid.

57 BL, EOSON, HFO to Ernest Oppenheimer, 20 April 1942.

58 BL, EOSON, JC Smuts to Ernest Oppenheimer, 7 September 1939: 'We can talk over Harry a little later, as I am now in charge of Defence. He is the only one you have left, and that consideration should be before us …'

59 BL, MS/OPP/EO/C1.4 Ernest Oppenheimer to HFO, 22 May 1942.

60 BL, EOSON, HFO to Ernest Oppenheimer, 14 June 1942.

61 BL, EOSON, HFO to Ernest Oppenheimer, 12 June 1942.

62 Steyn, *Seven Votes*, p 113.

63 BL, EOSON, HFO to Ernest Oppenheimer, 22 June 1942.

64 BL, EOSON, HFO to Ernest Oppenheimer, 24 June 1942.

65 BL, EOSON, HFO to Ernest Oppenheimer, 10 July 1942.

66 BL, EOSON, HFO to Ernest Oppenheimer, 19 May 1942.

67 Cited in A Hocking, *Oppenheimer and Son*, McGraw-Hill, 1973, p 199.

68 Fletcher, 'Action in the Western Desert', p 57.

69 BL, EOSON, HFO to Ernest Oppenheimer, 25 April 1942.

70 BL, EOSON, HFO to Ina Oppenheimer, 30 March 1942.

CHAPTER SIX

1 C D'Este, *Warlord: A Life of Winston Churchill at War, 1874–1945*, Harper Perennial, 2009, p 602.

2 EJ Epstein, *The Diamond Invention*, Hutchinson, 1982, pp 80–6.

3 T Gregory, *Ernest Oppenheimer and the Economic Development of Southern Africa*, Oxford University Press, 1962, pp 358–9.

4 DW Kruger, *The Making of a Nation: A History of the Union of South Africa, 1910–1961*, Macmillan, 1969, p 214.

5 B Wilson, 'The Orange Free State goldfield,' in B Mortimer (ed.), *HFO: Some Personal Perspectives on Harry Frederick Oppenheimer by His Colleagues and Friends*, Brenthurst Press, 1985, pp 61–3.

6 EP Kleynhans, 'The Axis and Allied maritime operations around southern Africa, 1939–1945' (DPhil thesis, University of Stellenbosch, 2018), p 61.

7 Brenthurst Library [BL], Ernest Oppenheimer Papers [MS/OPP/EO]/C1.6 Harry Oppenheimer [HFO] to Ernest Oppenheimer, 10 August 1942.

8 Interview with Tony Leon, Cape Town, 6 October 2017.

9 BL, MS/OPP/EO/C1.6 HFO to Ernest Oppenheimer, 10 August 1942.

10 Ibid.

11 Ibid.

12 A Wessels, 'South Africa and the war against Japan: 1941–1945', *Military History Journal*, 10, no. 3 (June 1996).

13 This anecdote is reported as fact in A Hocking, *Oppenheimer and Son*, McGraw-Hill, 1973, pp 209–10. The military historian Evert Kleynhans could not corroborate the claim. He indicated that if it were true, then the incident would have been mentioned in an official naval intelligence file. Kleynhans had not come across any such file in the course of extensive research. Email communication with EP Kleynhans, 30 October 2020.

14 BL, Harry Oppenheimer Papers [MS/OPP/HFO]/D1.6.7.1 Major General Poole to HFO, 3 March 1943.

15 HMF McCall, *The Children of Ulsterman KC and Alice*, privately published, n.d., p 75.

16 Bridget started writing this memoir in April 1993, principally for her granddaughter Victoria, who she

thought 'was the only grandchild to have expressed … an interest' in family history. The memoir is written on WH Smith notepaper and runs to 48 chapter headings. BL, Bridget Denison Oppenheimer Papers [MS/OPP/BDO], Unpublished memoir, c.1993.

17 BL, MS/OPP/BDO, Unpublished memoir, c.1993.

18 Ibid.

19 Mary Slack Private Papers [MSPP], HFO to Bridget McCall, 4 January 1943.

20 Ibid.

21 MSPP, HFO diary entry, 6 March 1943.

22 BL, E Oppenheimer and Son Papers [EOSON], Comar Wilson to HFO, 21 March 1943.

23 MSPP, HFO to Bridget McCall, 4 January 1943.

24 BL, MS/OPP/BDO, Unpublished memoir, c.1993.

25 Ibid.

26 Ernest Oppenheimer to HFO, 12 September 1942, cited in Gregory, *Ernest Oppenheimer and the Economic Development of Southern Africa*, p 355.

27 Ernest Oppenheimer to HFO, 22 August 1942, cited in Gregory, *Ernest Oppenheimer and the Economic Development of Southern Africa*, p 358.

28 HF Oppenheimer, 'The Anglo American Corporation's role in South Africa's gold mining industry', *Optima*, 34, no. 2 (1986), pp 58–67.

29 Wilson, 'The Orange Free State goldfield', p 61.

30 Ibid.

31 K Acutt, 'The Orange Free State goldfield,' in Mortimer, *HFO: Some Personal Perspectives*, p 65.

32 Gregory, *Ernest Oppenheimer and the Economic Development of Southern Africa*, p 578.

33 Acutt, 'The Orange Free State goldfield', p 65.

34 Cited in K Rajab (ed.), *A Man of Africa: The Political Thought of Harry Oppenheimer*, Zebra Press, 2017, p 48.

35 BL, MS/OPP/BDO, Unpublished memoir, c.1993.

36 Ibid.

37 BL, EOSON, Ernest Oppenheimer to HFO, 28 November 1948.

38 MSPP, HFO to Bridget Oppenheimer, 26 May 1944.

39 MSPP, HFO to Bridget Oppenheimer, 25 October 1944.

40 MSPP, HFO to Bridget Oppenheimer, 10 December 1944.

41 MSPP, Robin Grant Lawson to HFO, 7 January 1944.

42 MSPP, HFO to Bridget Oppenheimer, 31 October 1944.

43 MSPP, HFO to Bridget Oppenheimer, 10 December 1944.

44 MSPP, HFO to Bridget Oppenheimer, 12 October 1944.

45 MSPP, HFO to Bridget Oppenheimer, 29 November 1944.

46 MSPP, HFO to Bridget Oppenheimer, 5 November 1944.

47 BL, MS/OPP/HFO/Diary entry, 12 November 1949 and 13 November 1949.

48 MSPP, HFO to Bridget Oppenheimer, 31 October 1944.

49 BL, MS/OPP/HFO/Diary entry, 3 December 1949.

50 MSPP, HFO to Bridget Oppenheimer, 31 October 1944.

51 MSPP, HFO to Bridget Oppenheimer, 15 November 1944.

52 MSPP, HFO to Bridget Oppenheimer, 18 November 1944.

53 BL, MS/OPP/HFO/Diary entry, 5 December 1949.

54 MSPP, HFO to Bridget Oppenheimer, 5 November 1944.

55 For more on this theme see Rajab, *A Man of Africa*, pp 3–56.

56 MSPP, HFO to Bridget Oppenheimer, 16 November 1945.

57 K Rose, *Elusive Rothschild: The Life of Victor, Third Baron*, Weidenfeld and Nicolson, 2003.

58 MSPP, HFO to Bridget Oppenheimer, 16 November 1945.

59 Interview with Nicky Oppenheimer, Johannesburg, 1 February 2018.

60 MSPP, Cynthia Barlow to Bridget Oppenheimer, n.d.

61 BL, MS/OPP/BDO, Unpublished memoir, c.1993.

62 BL, MS/OPP/HFO/Diary entry, 20 October 1949.

63 Cited in EJ Epstein, 'Have you ever tried to sell a diamond?', *Atlantic*, February 1982.

64 Ibid.

65 BL, MS/OPP/HFO/Diary entry, 19 October 1949.

66 Ibid.

67 BL, MS/OPP/HFO/Diary entry, 21 October 1949.

68 Ibid.

69 Ibid.

70 BL, MS/OPP/HFO/Diary entry, 17 October 1949.

71 BL, MS/OPP/HFO/Diary entry, 21 October 1949.

72 BL, MS/OPP/HFO/Diary entry, 30 October 1949.

73 Ibid.

74 BL, MS/OPP/HFO/Diary entry, 18 October 1949.

75 R Chernow, *The House of Morgan: An American Banking Dynasty and the Rise of Modern Finance*, Grove Atlantic, Kindle edn, 2010, p 634.

76 BL, MS/OPP/HFO/Diary entry, 28 October 1949.

77 Ibid.

78 Ibid.

79 BL, MS/OPP/HFO/Diary entry, 3 November 1949.

80 Ibid.

81 BL, MS/OPP/HFO/Diary entry, 4 November 1949.

82 Ibid.

83 Gregory, *Ernest Oppenheimer and the Economic Development of Southern Africa*, pp 570–1.

84 BL, MS/OPP/HFO/Diary entry, 3 November 1949.

85 Ibid.

86 B Bozzoli, *The Political Nature of a Ruling Class: Capital and Ideology in South Africa, 1890–1933*, Routledge and Kegan Paul, 1981.

87 G Viney, *The Last Hurrah: South Africa and the Royal Tour of 1947*, Jonathan Ball Publishers, 2018.

88 BL, MS/OPP/EO/C2 JC Smuts to Ernest Oppenheimer, 16 July 1948.

89 BL, MS/OPP/HFO/P13 Typescript, 'The glittering world of Harry Oppenheimer' (no author, c.1960).

CHAPTER SEVEN

1 Brenthurst Library [BL], MS/OPP/ HFO, Harry Oppenheimer [HFO], Outline of memoir, Chapter 9: 'Entry into Parliament'.

2 *Financial Times*, 24 June 1946.

3 BL, MS/OPP/HFO, HFO, 'Help thou mine unbelief: Some recollections and reflections by Harry Oppenheimer', Chapter 4: Smuts.

4 Ibid.

5 J Hyslop, '"Segregation has fallen on evil days": Smuts' South Africa, global war, and transnational politics, 1939–46', *Journal of Global History*, 7, no. 3 (2012), pp 438–60.

6 D O'Meara, *Volkskapitalisme: Class, Capital and Ideology in the Development of Afrikaner Nationalism, 1934–1948*, Ravan Press, 1983, pp 226–33.

7 Cited in D Welsh, *The Rise and Fall of Apartheid*, Jonathan Ball Publishers, 2009, p 19.

8 P Walshe, *The Rise of African Nationalism in South Africa*, Ad Donker, 1987, p 286.

9 Cited in O'Meara, *Volkskapitalisme*, p 237.

10 Welsh, *The Rise and Fall of Apartheid*, pp 20–3.

11 BL, MS/OPP/HFO, HFO, Outline of memoir, Chapter 9: 'Entry into Parliament'.

12 A Robinson, 'The political perspective', in B Mortimer (ed.) *HFO: Some Personal Perspectives on Harry Frederick Oppenheimer by His Colleagues and Friends*, Brenthurst Press, 1985, p 71.

13 *Rand Daily Mail*, 26 November 1946.

14 GW Plint, 'The influence of Second World War military service on prominent white South African veterans in opposition politics, 1939–1961' (MMil thesis, University of Stellenbosch, 2021), p 111.

15 Interview with Mary Slack, Johannesburg, 29 August 2022.

16 D Sher, 'The career of Graham S Eden: "Coloured representative"', *Kleio*, 23, no. 1 (1991), pp 69–84.

17 *Diamond Fields Advertiser*, 17 March 1948.

18 BL, MS/OPP/HFO/I4.13 Handwritten notes [c. April 1948].

19 *Diamond Fields Advertiser*, 27 April 1948.

20 Cited in A Paton, *Hofmeyr*, Oxford University Press, 1964, p 493.

21 Cited in WB White, 'The South African parliamentary opposition, 1948–1953' (PhD thesis, University of Natal, 1989), p 31.

22 Cited in Paton, *Hofmeyr*, p 484.

23 G Relly, 'The political perspective', in Mortimer, *HFO: Some Personal Perspectives*, p 75.

24 B Nasson, 'A flying Springbok of wartime British skies: A.G. "Sailor" Malan', *Kronos*, no. 35 (November 2009), pp 71–97.

25 Cited in A Hocking, *Oppenheimer and Son*, McGraw-Hill, 1973, p 235.

26 Paton, *Hofmeyr*, p 488.

27 WK Hancock, *Smuts*, vol. 2: *The Fields of Force, 1919–1950*, Cambridge University Press, 1968, p 498.

28 Ibid.

29 BL, MS/OPP/HFO, HFO, Outline of memoir, Chapter 9: 'Entry into Parliament'.

30 Ibid.

31 Cited in Paton, *Hofmeyr*, p 497.

32 BL, MS/OPP/HFO, HFO, Outline of memoir, Chapter 9: 'Entry into Parliament'.

33 Cited in Paton, *Hofmeyr*, p 493.

34 *The Star*, 10 February 1949.

35 BL, Bridget Oppenheimer Papers [MS/OPP/BDO], Unpublished memoir, c.1993.

36 Ibid.

37 Interview with Nicky Oppenheimer, Johannesburg, 1 February 2018.

38 See BL, MS/OPP/BDO/B2.1-B2.18 Menus and guests, Brenthurst, 1949–1992; OPP/BDO/B4.1-B4.15 Menus and guests, Milkwood House, 1970–2005.

39 BL, E Oppenheimer and Son Papers [EOSON], Ernest Oppenheimer to HFO, 28 November 1948.

40 *Cape Times*, 15 June 1949.

41 Union of South Africa, Debates of the House of Assembly [Hansard], 18 August 1948, cols. 413–14.

42 Ibid., col. 417.

43 Hocking, *Oppenheimer and Son*, p 238.

44 *Sunday Times*, 18 February 1951.

45 *The Forum*, 28 August 1948.

46 BL, MS/OPP/BDO/B1.2 Scrapbook, JC Smuts to HFO, 19 August 1948.

47 BL, MS/OPP/BDO/B1.2 Scrapbook, Margaret Ballinger to HFO, n.d.

48 BL, MS/OPP/BDO/B1.2 Scrapbook, Jan Hofmeyr to HFO, n.d.

49 *Cape Times*, 10 February 1949.

50 *Cape Argus*, 9 February 1949.

51 See E McKenzie, 'The English-language press and the Anglo American Corporation: An assessment', *Kleio*, no. 26 (1994), pp 98–107.

52 BL, MS/OPP/BDO/B1.2 Scrapbook, JC Smuts to HFO, 10 February 1949.

53 BL, MS/OPP/BDO/B1.2 Scrapbook, Cutting from *Cape Argus*, September 1948.

54 Cited in Robinson, 'The political perspective', p 71.

55 BL, MS/OPP/HFO/I6.3 United South Africa Trust Fund, Minutes of trustees' meeting, 27 January 1950. The inaugural trustees comprised PM Anderson, Eric Gallo, RB Hagart, Charles James, Claude Leon, Calvin Stowe McLean, Gerald Orpen and Buller Pagden. Two United Party men, Henry Tucker and Jack

Higgerty, were appointed at Smuts's bidding.

56 BL, MS/OPP/HFO/I6.3 United South Africa Trust Fund, Constitution, adopted on 27 January 1950.

57 BL, MS/OPP/HFO/I6.3 United South Africa Trust Fund, Minutes of trustees' meeting, 13 April 1950.

58 BL, MS/OPP/HFO/I6.3 United South Africa Trust Fund (Central Account) Income and Expenditure Account for 1 Dec. 1949 – 31 Dec. 1950.

59 Hansard, 19 February 1951, col. 1476.

60 Hansard, 19 February 1951, col. 1477.

61 *Sunday Times*, 25 February 1951.

62 *The Economist*, 19 May 1951.

63 *Die Transvaler*, 31 March 1951.

64 *The Star*, 4 April 1951.

65 *The Star*, 28 August 1951.

66 Hansard, 19 February 1952, col. 1395.

67 *Rand Daily Mail*, 21 February 1952.

68 Hansard, 19 February 1952, col. 1418.

69 Hansard, 22 January 1952, cols. 77–8.

70 FA Mouton, '"A decent man, but not very popular": JGN Strauss, the United Party and the founding of the apartheid state, 1950–1956', *Journal for Contemporary History*, 38, no. 2 (2013), pp 1–20.

71 De Villiers Graaff, *Div Looks Back: The Memoirs of Sir De Villiers Graaff*, Human and Rousseau, 1993, pp 137–8.

72 Dawie, 'Uit my politieke pen', *Die Burger*, 3 August 1957.

73 Plint, 'The influence of Second World War military service on prominent white South African veterans in opposition politics, 1939–1961', p 27.

74 Cited in O Walker, *Sailor Malan: A Biography*, Cassell, 1953, pp 163–4.

75 See, especially, M Fridjhon, 'The Torch Commando and the politics of white opposition, South Africa 1951–1953', University of the Witwatersrand, African Studies Seminar Paper, 1976; and N Roos, *Ordinary Springboks: White Servicemen and Social Justice in South Africa, 1939–1961*, Ashgate, 2005, pp 129–57.

76 *The Challenge*, 29 March 1952; *Rand Daily Mail*, 25 March 1952.

77 *Rand Daily Mail*, 15 May 1952.

78 *Rand Daily Mail*, 10 November 1951.

79 *Rand Daily Mail*, 15 March 1952.

80 *The Star*, 3 May 1952.

81 Cited in J Kane-Berman, 'The rise and fall of the Torch Commando', Politicsweb, 30 July 2018. Accessed at https://www.politicsweb.co.za/opinion/the-rise-and-fall-of-the-torch-commando.

82 Cited in White, 'The South African parliamentary opposition, 1948–1953', p 307.

83 *Sunday Express*, 18 October 1953.

84 BL, MS/OPP/HFO/B3.3 Diary entry, 13 January 1954.

85 BL, MS/OPP/HFO/B3.3 Diary entry, 16 February 1954.

86 BL, MS/OPP/HFO/B3.3 Diary entry, 17 January 1954.

87 BL, MS/OPP/HFO/B3.3 Diary entry, 10 September 1954.

88 BL, MS/OPP/HFO/B3.3 Diary entry, 8 September 1954.

89 BL, MS/OPP/HFO/B3.3 Diary entry, 10 September 1954.

90 Mouton, '"A decent man, but not very popular"', p 15.

91 BL, MS/OPP/HFO/B3.3 Diary entry, 31 January 1955.

92 BL, MS/OPP/HFO/B3.3 Diary entry, 19 May 1954.

93 BL, MS/OPP/HFO/B3.4 Diary entry, 23 March 1955.

94 BL, MS/OPP/HFO/B3.4 Diary entry, 25 March 1955.

95 Interview with Bobby Godsell, Johannesburg, 10 October 2017; B Godsell, 'Reflections: Harry Oppenheimer talks to Bobby Godsell', *Optima*, 38, no. 3 (November 1992), p 110.

96 J Morris, *South African Winter*, Faber and Faber, 2008 [1958], p 174.

97 H Suzman, *In No Uncertain Terms*, Jonathan Ball Publishers, 1993, pp 22–3.

98 Z de Beer, 'The political perspective', in Mortimer, *HFO: Some Personal Perspectives*, p 79.

99 Ibid., p 79.

100 Ibid., p 79.

101 Ibid., p 75.

102 BL, MS/OPP/HFO/B3.4 Diary entry, 22 November 1955.

103 BL, MS/OPP/HFO/B3.3 Diary entry, 19 June 1954.

104 BL, MS/OPP/HFO/B3.3 Diary entry, 4 January 1954.

105 BL, MS/OPP/HFO/B3.3 Diary entry, 10 April 1954.

106 BL, MS/OPP/BDO, Unpublished memoir, c.1993.

107 Ibid.

108 R Rudd, 'The boss', in Mortimer, *HFO: Some Personal Perspectives*, p 39.

109 BL, MS/OPP/HFO/B3.3 Diary entry, 4 January 1954.

110 BL, MS/OPP/HFO/B3.4 Diary entry, 9 November 1955.

111 BL, MS/OPP/HFO/B3.3 Diary entry, 4 January 1954.

112 BL, MS/OPP/HFO/B3.3 Diary entry, 12 February 1954.

113 BL, MS/OPP/HFO/B3.4 Diary entry, 16 November 1955.

114 BL, MS/OPP/HFO/B3.4 Diary entry, 15 September 1955.

115 BL, MS/OPP/HFO/B3.3 Diary entry, 2 November 1954.

116 JDF Jones, *Through Fortress and Rock: The Story of Gencor, 1895–1995*, Jonathan Ball Publishers, 1995, pp 118–19.

117 EJ Epstein, *The Diamond Invention*, Hutchinson, 1982, pp 128–33. The organisation was the forerunner of substantial intelligence capability in Anglo American. See J Sanders, *Apartheid's Friends: The Rise and Fall of South Africa's Secret Service*, John Murray, 2006, p 365; and J Crush, 'Power and surveillance on the South African gold mines', *Journal of Southern African Studies*, 18, no. 4 (1992), pp 825–44.

118 BL, MS/OPP/HFO/B3.3 Diary entry, 3 August 1954.

119 S Jones, 'Union Acceptances: The first merchant bank, 1955–73', in S Jones (ed.), *Financial Enterprise in South Africa since 1950*, Macmillan, 1992, pp 154–91.

120 BL, MS/OPP/HFO/J4.1.1 HFO to JNV Duncan, 3 December 1956; BL, MS/OPP/HFO/J4.1.1 HFO to Fred Searls, 3 December 1956.

121 BL, MS/OPP/HFO/J4.1.1 HFO to AC Wilson, 7 August 1956.

122 BL, MS/OPP/HFO/B3.4 Diary entry, 6 November 1955.

123 BL, MS/OPP/HFO/B3.4 Diary entry, 9 November 1955.

124 BL, MS/OPP/HFO/ J4.1.1 HFO to Nicky Oppenheimer [NFO], 19 November 1956.

125 BL, MS/OPP/HFO/B3.3 Diary entry, 9 June 1954.

126 BL, MS/OPP/HFO/B3.3 Diary entry, 12 June 1954.

127 BL, MS/OPP/HFO/B3.3 Diary entry, 10 June 1954.

128 BL, MS/OPP/HFO/B3.4 Diary entry, 6 November 1955.

129 Ibid.

130 Ibid.

131 This episode is covered very comprehensively in Hocking, *Oppenheimer and Son*, pp 289–303.

132 BL, MS/OPP/HFO/B3.4 Diary entry, 7 December 1955.

133 BL, MS/OPP/HFO/B3.5 Diary entry, date marked 17 January – 2 February 1956.

134 BL, MS/OPP/HFO/B3.4 Diary entry, 20 April 1955.

135 BL, MS/OPP/HFO/B3.5 Diary entry, date marked 17 January – 2 February 1956.

136 Ibid.

137 BL, MS/OPP/BDO, Unpublished memoir, c.1993.

138 Ibid.

139 BL, MS/OPP/HFO/B3.3 Diary entry, 21 February 1954.

140 Interview with Mary Slack, Johannesburg, 11 February 2020.

141 Mary Slack Private Papers [MSPP], Mary Oppenheimer to her parents, n.d.

142 BL, MS/OPP/HFO/B3.4 Diary entry, 9 April 1955.

143 MSPP, HFO to BDO, 29 April 1955.

144 BL, MS/OPP/HFO/B3.4 Diary entry, 9 April 1955.

145 BL, MS/OPP/HFO/B3.3 Diary entry, 18 May 1954.

146 BL, MS/OPP/HFO/B3.4 Diary entry, 20 April 1955.

147 BL, MS/OPP/HFO/B3.4 Diary entry, 23 May 1955.

148 Hansard, 26–27 May 1955, col. 6426.

149 *The Star*, 16 June 1955.

150 *The Star*, 19 January 1954.

151 BL, MS/OPP/HFO/B3.4 Diary entry, 13 June 1955.

152 Ibid.

153 BL, MS/OPP/HFO/B3.4 Diary entry, 14 June 1955. See also Ray Swart's account in his memoir, *Progressive Odyssey: Towards a Democratic South Africa*, Human and Rousseau, 1991, p 38.

154 BL, MS/OPP/HFO/B3.4 Diary entry, 15 June 1955.

155 Ibid.

156 BL, MS/OPP/HFO/B3.4 Diary entry, 21 April 1955.

157 BL, MS/OPP/HFO/B3.4 Diary entry, 13 May 1955.

158 BL, MS/OPP/HFO/B3.4 Diary entry, 20 June 1955.

159 *Rand Daily Mail*, 13 July 1955.

160 *Business Day*, 28 October 1998.

161 BL, MS/OPP/HFO/B3.4 Diary entry, 16 June 1955.

162 BL, MS/OPP/HFO/B3.4 Diary entry, 4 April 1955.

163 Cited in D Pallister, S Stewart and I Lepper, *South Africa Inc.: The Oppenheimer Empire*, Yale University Press, 1988, p 82.

164 G Relly, 'Harry Oppenheimer: An appreciation', *Optima*, 31, no. 2 (April 1983), pp 47–8.

165 BL, MS/OPP/HFO/B3.3 Diary entry, 7 February 1954.

166 BL, MS/OPP/HFO/B3.3 Diary entry, 4 February 1954.

167 A Luthuli, *Let My People Go*, Tafelberg, 2006 [1962], p 132.

168 D Everatt, *The Origins of Non-Racialism: White Opposition to Apartheid in the 1950s*, Wits University Press, 2009, pp 42–3.

169 Ibid., p 178.

170 The Freedom Charter, as adopted at the Congress of the People, Kliptown, 26 June 1955. Accessed at https://www.anc1912.org.za/the-freedom-charter-2/.

171 *Natal Witness*, 8 August 1957.

172 BL, MS/OPP/HFO/B3.3 Diary entry, 21 June 1954.

173 A Sampson, *Mandela: The Authorised Biography*, Harper-Collins, 2000, p 109.

174 Ibid., p 90.

175 Ibid., p 59.

176 BL, MS/OPP/HFO/B3.3 Diary entry, 29 June 1954.

177 BL, MS/OPP/HFO/B3.3 Diary entry, 28 June 1954.

178 BL, MS/OPP/HFO/J4.1.2 HFO to Quintin Whyte, 2 August 1957.

179 *Eastern Province Herald*, 7 August 1957.

180 BL, MS/OPP/HFO/O6.1 'The future of industry in South Africa', Address to the South African Institute of Race Relations Council Meeting, Johannesburg, January 1950.

181 Welsh, *The Rise and Fall of Apartheid*, p 22.

182 BL, MS/OPP/HFO/O6.1 'The future of industry in South Africa'.

183 Ibid.; *The Star*, 20 January 1950.

184 BL, MS/OPP/HFO/O6.3 'Industrial relations in a multi-racial society', Address to the Duke of Edinburgh's Study Conference on Industrial Relations, Oxford, July 1956. See MS/OPP/HFO/O4 for printed booklet of the speech, *Towards Racial Harmony*, 25 July 1956.

185 BL, MS/OPP/HFO/O6.3 'The role of South Africa in a changing Africa', Address to joint meeting of the Royal African Society and the Royal Commonwealth Society, London, 12 November 1950.

186 Ibid.

187 *The Star*, 8 January 1952.

188 *Rand Daily Mail*, 21 June 1954.

189 Hansard, 13 June 1952, col. 8030.

190 T Gregory, *Ernest Oppenheimer and the Economic Development of Southern Africa*, Oxford University Press, 1962, pp 578–80.

191 *Rand Daily Mail*, 17 February 1955.

192 Ibid.

193 Cited in Hocking, *Oppenheimer and Son*, pp 308–9.

194 Ibid.

195 *Rand Daily Mail*, 18 February 1955.

196 *Evening Post*, 1 October 1957.

197 BL, MS/OPP/HFO/J4.1.2 HFO to FR Tomlinson, 11 September 1957.

198 Hansard, 15 May 1956, col. 5420.

199 BL, MS/OPP/HFO/ I8 Handwritten notes for speech at the Transvaal Congress of the UP, 1956.

200 BL, MS/OPP/HFO/I9.3 HFO, handwritten notes on policies needed for a multi-racial community [c.1956]. In his notes, Oppenheimer cautioned that the word 'veto' should not be associated with the scheme, since it had 'acquired a sinister meaning in recent years'.

201 BL, MS/OPP/HFO/I9.4 HFO to JC Masterman, 3 June 1956.

202 BL, MS/OPP/HFO I9.8.2 KC Wheare to HFO, 6 November 1956.

203 BL, MS/OPP/HFO I9.9.2 Scheme for Amendment of the South African Constitution, Opinion, Sir Ivor Jennings, 15 November 1956. See also BL, MS/OPP/HFO/ I9.10 HFO to Sir Ivor Jennings, 27 November 1956, and BL, MS/OPP/HFO/I9.11 Sir Ivor Jennings to HFO, 4 December 1956.

204 BL, E Oppenheimer and Son Papers [EOSON], HFO to Zach de Beer, 13 August 1956.

205 BL, MS/OPP/HFO/ I9.6 De Villiers Graaff to HFO, 11 October 1956.

206 BL, MS/OPP/HFO/I9.7 HFO to De Villiers Graaff, 23 October 1956.

207 J Strangwayes-Booth, *A Cricket in the Thorn Tree: Helen Suzman and the Progressive Party*, Hutchinson, 1976, p 123.

208 SL Barnard and AH Marais, *Die Verenigde Party: Die groot eksperiment*, Butterworth, 1982, p 102.

209 BL, EOSON, Colin Eglin to Pieter de Kock, 25 August [1957].

210 *Rand Daily Mail*, 22 August 1957.

211 *Die Transvaler*, 21 August 1957.

212 *Cape Argus*, 28 August 1957.

213 *Die Transvaler*, 10 August 1957.

214 BL, MS/OPP/HFO/J4.1.2 HFO to Philip Brownrigg, 23 August 1957.

215 BL, MS/OPP/HFO/J4.1.2 HFO to AC Wilson, 26 November 1957.

CHAPTER EIGHT

1 Anglo American Corporation of South Africa, Annual Chairman's Statement, 1958.

2 G Gaskill, 'South Africa's King of Diamonds', *Reader's Digest*, June 1964.

3 Brenthurst Library [BL], Harry Oppenheimer Papers [MS/OPP/HFO]/J4.1.3 HFO to WA Chapple, 1 February 1958.

4 *The Star*, 9 December 1957.

5 BL, Unaccessioned, Nicky Oppenheimer to Cynthia Carroll [c.2007, soon after the Oppenheimer family sold a third of its shareholding in Anglo American to the Chinese billionaire Larry Yung]. 'Set out below is the shareholding structure that existed in 1998, just prior to Anglo's move to London.'

6 Oppenheimer Memorial Trust, 'The history of the OMT'. Accessed at https://www.omt.org.za/history/the-history-of-the-omt/. Also *Rand Daily Mail*, 5 December 1957.

7 A Hocking, *Oppenheimer and Son*, McGraw-Hill, 1973, p 334.

8 BL, Bridget Oppenheimer Papers [MS/OPP/BDO]/B1.9 Scrapbook, Michael Stern to Harry Oppenheimer, 20 June 1964.

9 K Anderson, 'My heart is in Africa, *Personality*, 7 March 1963.

10 BL, E Oppenheimer and Son Papers

[EOSON], Ernest Oppenheimer to HFO, 20 November 1948.

11 BL, MS/OPP/HFO, HFO, 'Help thou mine unbelief: Some recollections and reflections by Harry Oppeheimer', Chapter 5: The Anglo American Corporation.

12 Interview with Julian Ogilvie Thompson, Johannesburg, 11 January 2018.

13 BL, MS/OPP/HFO/J4.1.2 HFO to RB Hagart, 13 November 1957.

14 Interview with Hank Slack, Cape Town, 11 September 2019.

15 D Beckingham, 'The Group in industry: A view of diversification', Optima, 22, no. 3 (September 1972), pp 130–9.

16 BL, MS/OPP/HFO, HFO, Outline of memoir, Chapter 13: 'Diversification of the Group into industry'.

17 G Fletcher, 'The boss', in B Mortimer (ed.), HFO: Some Personal Perspectives on Harry Frederick Oppenheimer by His Colleagues and Friends, Brenthurst Press, 1985, p 24.

18 T Brown, 'Organization and group structure', in Mortimer, HFO: Some Personal Perspectives, p 189.

19 G Young, 'The boss', in Mortimer, HFO: Some Personal Perspectives, p 35.

20 Ibid.

21 Ibid.

22 Anglo American Corporation of South Africa, Annual Chairman's Statement, 1964.

23 BL, EOSON, Zach de Beer to Pieter de Kock, 10 October 1957.

24 BL, EOSON, Pieter de Kock to Zach de Beer, 22 July 1958.

25 R Rudd, 'The boss', in Mortimer, HFO: Some Personal Perspectives, p 38.

26 NF Oppenheimer, 'A tribute to my father', Optima, 47, no. 1 (February 2001).

27 Interview with Julian Ogilvie Thompson, Johannesburg, 11 January 2018.

28 BL, MS/OPP/HFO/J4.1.3 Julian Ogilvie Thompson to HFO, 20 May 1958.

29 Interview with Nicky Oppenheimer, Johannesburg, 1 February 2019.

30 BL, MS/OPP/HFO/D10.16.2 Julian Ogilvie Thompson to HFO, n.d.

31 Sunday Times, 15 January 1967.

32 Ibid.

33 D Innes, Anglo: Anglo American and the Rise of Modern South Africa, Ravan Press, 1984, p 231.

34 BL, MS/OPP/HFO, HFO, 'Help thou mine unbelief: Some recollections and reflections by Harry Oppeheimer', Chapter 5: The Anglo American Corporation.

35 G Relly, 'Organization and group structure', in Mortimer, HFO: Some Personal Perspectives, p 190.

36 BL, MS/OPP/HFO, HFO, 'Help thou mine unbelief: Some recollections and reflections by Harry Oppeheimer', Chapter 5: The Anglo American Corporation.

37 A Sampson, Black and Gold: Tycoons, Revolutionaries and Apartheid, Hodder and Stoughton, 1987, p 95.

38 BL, MS/OPP/HFO/O6.11 'Is South Africa a good risk?', Address by HFO to the Institute of Directors, Royal Festival Hall, London, 5 November 1959.

39 Anglo American Corporation of South Africa, Annual Chairman's Statement, 1959.

40 Ibid.

41 Anglo American Corporation of South Africa, Annual Chairman's Statement, 1962.

42 B Pain, 'Aftermath of Sharpeville' and M Rush, 'Aftermath of Sharpeville', in Mortimer, HFO: Some Personal Perspectives, pp 135–6.

43 Rush, 'Aftermath of Sharpeville', p 136.

44 Anglo American Corporation of South Africa, Annual Chairman's Statement, 1962.

45 R First, J Steele and C Gurney, The South African Connection: Western Investment in Apartheid, Maurice Temple Smith, 1972, p 203.

46 Anglo American Corporation of South Africa, Annual Chairman's Statement, 1963.

47 Anglo American Corporation of

South Africa, Annual Chairman's Statement, 1965.

48 *Financial Mail*, 22 July 1966.

49 Ibid.

50 Anglo American Corporation of South Africa, Annual Chairman's Statement, 1961.

51 Anglo American Corporation of South Africa, Annual Chairman's Statement, 1960.

52 G Relly, 'International diversification', in Mortimer, *HFO: Some Personal Perspectives*, p 140.

53 D Gevisser, *The Unlikely Forester: A Memoir*, Jacana, 2006.

54 *Time*, 27 January 1961.

55 BL, EOSON, HFO to Charles Engelhard, 10 September 1970.

56 Gevisser, *The Unlikely Forester*, p 83.

57 J Engelhard, 'Association with Engelhard', in Mortimer, *HFO: Some Personal Perspectives*, p 163.

58 BL, EOSON, RB Hagart to HFO, 25 July 1959.

59 BL, EOSON, HFO to Charles Engelhard, 22 February 1960.

60 K Acutt, 'International diversification', in Mortimer, *HFO: Some Personal Perspectives*, p 139.

61 Anglo American Corporation of South Africa, Annual Chairman's Statement, 1962.

62 M Rush, 'International diversification', in Mortimer, *HFO: Some Personal Perspectives*, p 140.

63 Anglo American Corporation of South Africa, Annual Chairman's Statement, 1963.

64 BL, MS/OPP/HFO/J4.1.3 HFO to Harry Winston, 24 February 1958.

65 BL, EOSON, Charles Engelhard to HFO, 25 July 1960.

66 Ibid.

67 Interview with Tony Leon, Cape Town, 6 October 2017.

68 BL, MS/OPP/BDO/B1.8 Scrapbook, Invitation card: 'The President and Mrs Kennedy request the pleasure of the company of Mr and Mrs Oppenheimer at dinner on Wednesday, May 2, 1962 at 8.15 o'clock.' The other guests were the British Ambassador to the United States, David Ormsby-Gore, and his wife, Sylvia; the Engelhards; Prince Stanisław Albrecht Radziwill (married to Jackie Kennedy's sister); and William Walton. See John F Kennedy Presidential Library and Museum [Digital] Archives [JFK], Presidential Papers, White House Staff Files of Sanford L Fox, Social Events, Dinner, 2 May 1962, JFKWHSFSLF-013-008-p0005.

69 BL, EOSON, Charles Engelhard to HFO, 11 June 1962.

70 BL, MS/OPP/BDO/B1.8 Scrapbook, Jacqueline Kennedy to HFO and BDO, 28 June 1962.

71 J Roberts, *Glitter and Greed: The Secret World of the Diamond Cartel*, Disinformation Company, 2007, pp 170–1.

72 BL, MS/OPP/HFO, Charles Engelhard to HFO, 4 March 1960.

73 Roberts, *Glitter and Greed*, p 170.

74 Ibid., p 173.

75 BL, MS/OPP/HFO, Maurice Tempelsman to HFO, 11 June 1965.

76 Anglo American Corporation of South Africa, Annual Chairman's Statement, 1965.

77 BL, MS/OPP/HFO/J4.2.3 HFO to Ellis Robins, 27 December 1959; BL, MS/OPP/HFO/J4.2.5 WD Wilson, Notes on the amalgamation of certain assets of the BSA Company, De Beers Investment Trust and Rand Selection Corporation, 4 January 1960.

78 T Gregory, *Ernest Oppenheimer and the Economic Development of Southern Africa*, Oxford University Press, 1962, pp 107–8.

79 Anglo American Corporation of South Africa, Annual Chairman's Statement, 1965.

80 Innes, *Anglo*, p 235.

81 S Jones, 'Union Acceptances: The first merchant bank, 1955–73', in S Jones (ed.), *Financial Enterprise in South Africa since 1950*, Macmillan, 1992, pp 157.

82 Ibid., pp 154–91.

83 BL, EOSON, HFO to Comar Wilson, 5 March 1955.

84 S Kell, 'The Discount House of South Africa, 1957–88: Profile of a market force', in Jones, *Financial Enterprise in South Africa since 1950*.

85 Innes, *Anglo*, p 235.

86 Gregory, *Ernest Oppenheimer and the Economic Development of Southern Africa*, pp 103–4.

87 Ibid., p 321; T Brown, 'Diversifying from mining', in Mortimer, *HFO: Some Personal Perspectives*, p 127.

88 B Freund, 'South Africa: The Union years, 1910–1948; Political and economic foundations', in R Ross, A Mager and B Nasson (eds.), *The Cambridge History of South Africa*, vol. 2: *1885–1994*, Cambridge University Press, 2012, p 248.

89 Anglo American Corporation of South Africa, Annual Chairman's Statement, 1965.

90 *Financial Mail*, 3 July 1971.

91 F Howard, 'The boss', in Mortimer, *HFO: Some Personal Perspectives*; interview with Francis Howard, London, 8 October 2019.

92 T Cross, 'Afrikaner nationalism, Anglo American and Iscor: The formation of the Highveld Steel and Vanadium Corporation, 1960–70', *Business History*, 36, no. 3 (1994), p 89.

93 G Boustred, 'The boss', in Mortimer, *HFO: Some Personal Perspectives*, p 37.

94 BL, MS/OPP/HFO, HFO, 'Help thou mine unbelief: Some recollections and reflections by Harry Oppenheimer', Chapter 5: The Anglo American Corporation.

95 BL, EOSON, Colin Eglin to Pieter de Kock, 1 December 1957.

96 *Die Burger*, 30 November 1957.

97 *The Star*, 2 December 1957.

98 BL, MS/OPP/HFO/J4.1.3 HFO to AJ Brink, 31 January 1958.

99 BL, MS/OPP/HFO/J4.1.3 HFO to JW Higgerty, 30 January 1958.

100 BL, MS/OPP/HFO/J4.1.3 HFO to Sam Cohen, 29 March 1958.

101 *Natal Mercury*, 3 December 1957.

102 Address by Harold Macmillan to Members of Both Houses of the Parliament of the Union of South Africa, Cape Town, 3 February 1960. Accessed at https://web-archives. univ-pau.fr/english/TD2doc1.pdf.

103 K Acutt, 'The Federation and UDI', in B Mortimer, *HFO: Some Personal Perspectives*, p 115.

104 Anglo American Corporation of South Africa, Annual Chairman's Statement, 1959.

105 A Cohen, *The Politics and Economics of Decolonization in Africa: The Failed Experiment of the Central African Federation*, IB Tauris, 2017.

106 LJ Butler, 'Business and British decolonisation: Sir Ronald Prain, the mining industry and the Central African Federation', *Journal of Imperial and Commonwealth History*, 35, no. 3 (2007), pp 459–84.

107 LJ Butler, 'Mining, nationalism and decolonization in Zambia: Interpreting business responses to political change, 1945–1964', *Archiv für Sozialgeschichte*, 48 (2008), p 327.

108 Robinson had left South Africa and moved in 1954 to Salisbury where, with Oppenheimer's help, he took up a clutch of directorships and enjoyed a profitable business career.

109 BL, MS/OPP/HFO/C5.2 HFO to Sir Roy Welensky, 19 July 1963.

110 Butler, 'Mining, nationalism and decolonization in Zambia', p 329.

111 Cited in Cohen, *The Politics and Economics of Decolonization*, p 182.

112 BL, EOSON, Sir Roy Welensky to HFO, 2 January 1963.

113 BL, EOSON, HFO to Rab Butler, 29 January 1963.

114 BL, MS/OPP/BDO, B1.38 Typescript of HFO's speech to senior staff after Anglo American Corporation AGM, 13 August 1982.

115 J Knight and H Stevenson, 'The Williamson diamond mine, De Beers, and the Colonial Office: A case-study of the quest for control', *Journal of Modern African Studies*, 24, no. 3 (September 1986), pp 423–45.

116 B Wilson, 'The diamond industry',

in Mortimer, *HFO: Some Personal Perspectives*, p 101.

117 BL, MS/OPP/HFO/J4.1.1 HFO to WA Chapple, 21 August 1956.

118 BL, MS/OPP/BDO/B1.38 Scrapbook, Typescript of a speech by HFO to senior staff after the Anglo AGM, 13 August 1982.

119 BL, MS/OPP/HFO/J4.1.3 HFO to IC Chopra, 13 January 1958.

120 BL, MS/OPP/HFO/J4.1.3 HFO to AC Beatty, 18 January 1958.

121 Cited in T Wilson, 'The diamond industry', in Mortimer, *HFO: Some Personal Perspectives*, p 103.

122 J Ogilvie Thompson, 'The boss', in Mortimer, *HFO: Some Personal Perspectives*, p 26.

123 T Muller, 'The Federale Mynbou–General Mining deal', in Mortimer, *HFO: Some Personal Perspectives*, p 173.

124 G Verhoef, 'Nationalism and free enterprise in mining: The case of Federale Mynbou 1952–1965', *South African Journal of Economic History*, 10, no. 1 (1995), pp 89–107; G Verhoef, 'The development of diversified conglomerates: Federale Volksbeleggings; A case study', *Journal of Contemporary History*, 24, no. 2 (1999), pp 55–78.

125 Muller, 'The Federale Mynbou–General Mining deal', p 173.

126 Verhoef, 'Nationalism and free enterprise', p 100.

127 Innes, *Anglo*, p 158.

128 Muller, 'The Federale Mynbou–General Mining deal', p 173.

129 Verhoef, 'Nationalism and free enterprise in mining', p 103.

130 *The Star*, 22 January 1964.

131 *Sunday Times*, 26 January 1964.

132 Cited in Muller, 'The Federale Mynbou–General Mining deal', p 174.

133 Muller, 'The Federale Mynbou–General Mining deal', p 174.

134 *Rand Daily Mail*, 28 August 1964.

135 *Sunday Times*, 30 August 1964.

136 *Rand Daily Mail*, 29 August 1964.

137 *Die Volksblad*, 28 August 1964.

138 Cited in D O'Meara, *Forty Lost Years: The Apartheid State and the Politics of the National Party, 1948–1994*, Ravan Press, 1996, p 123.

139 *Die Vaderland*, 1 September 1964.

140 O'Meara, *Forty Lost Years*, p 120.

141 Verhoef, 'Nationalism and free enterprise in mining'; H Giliomee, 'Ethnic business and economic empowerment: The Afrikaner case, 1915–1970', *South African Journal of Economics*, 76, no. 4 (2008), pp 765–88; H Giliomee, *The Afrikaners: Biography of a People*, Tafelberg, 2010, p 543.

142 A Robinson, 'The Federale Mynbou–General Mining deal', in Mortimer, *HFO: Some Personal Perspectives*, p 171.

143 H Adam, 'Privileging legality over legitimacy', in K Rajab (ed.), *A Man of Africa: The Political Thought of Harry Oppenheimer*, Zebra Press, 2017, p 65.

144 *Die Huisgenoot*, 15 May 1964

145 *Die Huisgenoot*, 31 July 1964.

146 *Die Huisgenoot*, 7 August 1964.

147 *Die Brandwag*, 8 May 1964.

CHAPTER NINE

1 ELW [Eric Williams], 'Harry Oppenheimer: Profile', *Optima*, 25, no. 3 (1975), pp 164–70.

2 K Rajab, 'A historical assessment', in K Rajab (ed.), *A Man of Africa: The Political Thought of Harry Oppenheimer*, Zebra Press, 2017, p 13.

3 Brenthurst Library [BL], Harry Oppenheimer Papers [MS/OPP/HFO] Unaccessioned, Memorandum entitled 'Confidential: Visit to Washington on 10 June 1965', 22 June 1965. The haircut having been completed, the meeting moved to LBJ's bedroom. HFO's PA at the time, Fran Howard, recalled HFO's subsequent report-back. LBJ lay on the bed while a machine blew oxygen into his face to revive him ahead of the evening's engagements. HFO sat on a chair beside the bed. Interview with Fran Howard, London, 8 October 2019.

4 H Macmillan, *Pointing the Way, 1959–1961*, Macmillan, 1972, p 153.

5 National Archives, United Kingdom [NAUK], Records of the Prime Minister's Office [PREM]13/1752, Correspondence on meetings with HFO, April 1965 – February 1967.

6 E Heath, *The Course of My Life: The Autobiography of Edward Heath*, Hodder and Stoughton, 1998, p 620.

7 BL, MS/OPP/HFO/P1, Interview with HFO by Joe Thompson for *Modern Jeweller*, November 1983.

8 BL, MS/OPP/HFO, Unaccessioned, Memorandum entitled 'Confidential: Visit to Washington on 10 June 1965', 22 June 1965.

9 BL, MS/OPP/HFO/P1, Interview with HFO by Joe Thompson for *Modern Jeweller*, November 1983.

10 A Special Correspondent, 'Portrait of a millionaire: "I, Harry Oppenheimer"', *Africa South*, 4, no. 3 (April–June 1960), pp 7–16.

11 M Lipton, *Capitalism and Apartheid: South Africa, 1910–1986*, David Philip, 1989, p 229. See also Rajab, 'A historical assessment', pp 23–4.

12 MC O'Dowd, 'The stages of economic growth and the future of South Africa', in MC O'Dowd, *The O'Dowd Thesis and the Triumph of Democratic Capitalism*, Free Market Foundation, 1996.

13 B Rogers, *White Wealth and Black Poverty: American Investments in Southern Africa*, Greenwood Press, 1976, p 70.

14 S Dubow, *Apartheid: 1948–1994*, Oxford University Press, 2014, p 131.

15 *The Star*, 18 January 1963.

16 *Sunday Times*, 2 June 1968.

17 BL, MS/OPP/HFO/C2 HFO to Mary Oppenheimer [Waddell] and Gordon Waddell, 21 June 1969.

18 *Sunday Express*, 28 February 1971.

19 BL, MS/OPP/HFO, Unaccessioned, HFO to GWH Nicholson, 15 November 1954; and BL, MS/OPP/HFO/J4.1.2 HFO to Raymond Oppenheimer, 26 November 1957.

20 BL, Bridget Oppenheimer Papers [MS/OPP/BDO], Unpublished memoir, c.1993.

21 University of Cape Town, Special Collections, Jagger Library [UCT], Colin Eglin Papers [BC 1103], G8.6 HFO to Colin Eglin, 16 July 1965.

22 BL, MS/OPP/BDO B1.9 Scrapbook, Mrs R Chaitowitz to BDO, 15 October 1965.

23 S Kanfer, *The Last Empire: De Beers, Diamonds and the World*, Hodder and Stoughton, 1993, p 336.

24 *Sunday Express*, 10 September 1967.

25 *Scope*, 6 October 1967.

26 Interview with Nicky Oppenheimer, Johannesburg, 1 February 2018.

27 BL, MS/OPP/BDO, Unpublished memoir, c.1993.

28 BL, MS/OPP/BDO/B1.17 Scrapbook, June 1972–1973, undated clipping 'Someone of value', no publication details.

29 BL, MS/OPP/HFO/C2 HFO to Mary and Gordon Waddell, 21 June 1969.

30 *Sunday Express*, 11 April 1971.

31 J Strangwayes-Booth, *A Cricket in the Thorn Tree: Helen Suzman and the Progressive Party*, Hutchinson, 1976, p 125.

32 BL, E Oppenheimer and Son Papers [EOSON], HFO to Pieter de Kock, 22 May 1958.

33 C Eglin, *Crossing the Borders of Power: The Memoirs of Colin Eglin*, Jonathan Ball Publishers, 2007, p 67.

34 Ibid., p 68.

35 University of Cape Town, Special Collections, Jagger Library [UCT], Harry Lawrence Papers [BC 640], H1.28 HFO to Harry Lawrence, 12 June 1959.

36 Cited in Strangwayes-Booth, *A Cricket in the Thorn Tree*, p 158.

37 BL, EOSON, Statement by HFO, n.d.; carried in *Cape Argus*, 2 September 1959.

38 University of Witwatersrand Historical Papers Research Archive [Wits], Helen Suzman Papers [A2084], Ka6.1.1 HFO to Harry Lawrence, 1 September 1959.

39 *The Times*, 3 September 1959.

40 *Cape Times*, 17 December 1959.

41 R Renwick, *Helen Suzman: Bright Star in a Dark Chamber*, Jonathan Ball Publishers, 2013.

42 BL, EOSON, Colin Eglin to HFO, 18 August 1966.

43 Ibid.

44 Eglin, *Crossing the Borders of Power*, p 119.

45 FA Mouton, "'One of the architects of our democracy": Colin Eglin, the Progressive Federal Party and the leadership of the official parliamentary opposition, 1977–1979 and 1986–1987', *Journal for Contemporary History*, 40, no. 1 (June 2015), pp 1–22.

46 Interview with Tony Leon, Cape Town, 6 October 2017.

47 *Rand Daily Mail*, 19 February 1973.

48 Frances Jowell Private Papers [FJPP], Helen Suzman to Frances Suzman, 21 June 1960.

49 FJPP, Helen Suzman to Frances Suzman, 20 November 1963.

50 UCT, BC 640, B24.2 HFO to Harry Lawrence, 6 November 1961.

51 BL, EOSON, HFO to Jean Lawrence, 22 January 1974.

52 BL, MS/OPP/HFO, D12.28 Zach de Beer to HFO, 27 September [no year]. Zach de Beer motivated for E Oppenheimer and Son to guarantee an overdraft for Steytler. In the past, De Beer noted, HFO had loaned Steytler R20 000: 'There is, of course, no earthly reason why you should feel in any way inclined to help Jannie on present grounds ... On the other hand, he did lead the party, however badly, for eleven years plus; and he did, in the end, get out reasonably gracefully.' Slabbert, for his part, received a housing loan from Oppenheimer. See A Grundlingh, *Slabbert: Man on a Mission; A Biography*, Jonathan Ball Publishers, 2021, p 147.

53 R Vigne, *Liberals against Apartheid: A History of the Liberal Party of South Africa, 1953–68*, Macmillan, 1997, pp 111–12.

54 UCT, BC 640, H1.136 Notes for

Mr HG Lawrence [from HFO], 12 November 1959.

55 Ibid.

56 D Scher, *Donald Molteno: Dilizintaba – He-Who-Removes-Mountains*, South African Institute of Race Relations, 1979, pp 71–9.

57 Cited in ibid., p 81.

58 Ibid.

59 BL, MS/OPP/HFO/I19 Interim Report of the Expert Commission Set Up by the Progressive Party to Make Recommendations on a Revised Constitution for South Africa Extending Franchise Rights to All Civilised Subjects of the Union [Molteno Report, vol. 1], November 1960.

60 T Ngcukaitobi, *The Land Is Ours: South Africa's First Black Lawyers and the Birth of Constitutionalism*, Penguin Random House, 2018.

61 BL, MS/OPP/HFO/I19, Molteno Report, vol. 1, November 1960.

62 Ibid.

63 M Cardo, *Opening Men's Eyes: Peter Brown and the Liberal Struggle for South Africa*, Jonathan Ball Publishers, 2010, p 160.

64 Ibid.

65 Cited in Scher, *Donald Molteno*, p 98.

66 Ibid.

67 *Cape Argus*, 6 September 1962.

68 BL, MS/OPP/HFO O6.15 'The conditions for progress in Africa', TB Davie Memorial Lecture by HFO, 6 September 1962.

69 Grundlingh, *Slabbert: Man on a Mission*, p 77.

70 *Financial Times*, 4 November 1960.

71 Ibid.; *The Times* [London], 4 November 1960.

72 Anglo American Corporation of South Africa, Annual Chairman's Statement, 1962.

73 *Cape Times*, 23 July 1960.

74 Ibid.

75 B Hackland, 'The economic and political context of the growth of the Progressive Federal Party in South Africa, 1959–1978', *Journal of*

Southern African Studies, 7, no. 1 (1980), p 11.

76 A Sampson, *Black and Gold: Tycoons, Revolutionaries and Apartheid*, Hodder and Stoughton, 1987, p 94.

77 H Adam, 'Privileging legality over legitimacy', in K Rajab (ed.), *A Man of Africa: The Political Thought of Harry Oppenheimer*, Zebra Press, 2017, p 65.

78 W de Villiers, 'The boss', in B Mortimer (ed.), *HFO: Some Personal Perspectives on Harry Frederick Oppenheimer by His Colleagues and Friends*, Brenthurst Press, 1985, p 20.

79 A Rupert, 'The Urban Foundation', in Mortimer, *HFO: Some Personal Perspectives*, pp 211–12.

80 E Dommisse, *Anton Rupert: 'n Lewensverhaal*, Tafelberg, 2005, p 197.

81 *Sunday Times*, 5 December 1971.

82 BL, MS/OPP/HFO, HFO, Outline of memoir, Chapter 9: 'Entry into Parliament'.

83 *Sunday Express*, 9 July 1966.

84 T Cross, 'Afrikaner nationalism, Anglo American and Iscor: The formation of the Highveld Steel and Vanadium Corporation, 1960–70', *Business History*, 36, no. 3 (1994), pp 81–99.

85 I Wilkins and H Strydom, *The Super Afrikaners: Inside the Afrikaner Broederbond*, Jonathan Ball Publishers, 2012.

86 *Financial Mail*, 25 April 1969.

87 JHP Serfontein, *Brotherhood of Power: An Exposé of the Secret Afrikaner Broederbond*, Rex Collings, 1979, p 177; Cross, 'Afrikaner nationalism, Anglo American and Iscor', p 91. O'Meara claims that Verwoerd 'secretly appointed' the 'Hoek Commission' into Anglo's holdings and role in the economy: D O'Meara, *Forty Lost Years: The Apartheid State and the Politics of the National Party, 1948–1994*, Ravan Press, 1996, p 120.

88 Cited in A Hocking, *Oppenheimer and Son*, McGraw-Hill, 1973, p 431.

89 *Rand Daily Mail*, 3 August 1968.

90 *Die Afrikaner*, 20 February 1970.

91 BL, EOSON, HFO to Mrs ZK Matthews, 23 June 1960.

92 A Sampson, *Mandela: The Authorised Biography*, HarperCollins, 2000, p 141.

93 Cited in A Hepple, *Censorship and Press Control in South Africa*, self-published, 1960, p 64.

94 R Nixon, *Selling Apartheid: South Africa's Global Propaganda War*, Pluto Books, 2016.

95 R Ainslie and D Robinson, *The Collaborators*, Anti-Apartheid Movement, 1963, p 17.

96 Ibid., pp 7–8.

97 Cited in Sampson, *Black and Gold*, p 90.

98 Interview with Julian Ogilvie Thompson, Johannesburg, 11 January 2018.

99 J Sanders, 'A struggle for representation: The international media treatment of South Africa, 1972–1979' (PhD thesis, University of London, 1997), p 88.

100 BL, MS/OPP/HFO/F1975.2 Membership certificate for the South Africa Foundation, 18 June 1975.

101 BL, MS/OPP/HFO/R7 Transcript of an interview with John Robbie, Radio 702, 11 February 1998.

102 'Foundation cream', *Africa South*, 4, no. 3 (April–June 1960), p 3.

103 S Uys, Interview with Zach de Beer, *Africa South*, 4, no. 3 (April–June 1960), p 22.

104 D Pallister, S Stewart and I Lepper, *South Africa Inc.: The Oppenheimer Empire*, Yale University Press, 1988, p 94.

105 BL, EOSON, JD Opperman [secretary, United Party] to HFO, 16 September 1960.

106 HF Oppenheimer, 'The press and society', Text of a speech delivered at the UCT Summer School, *Optima*, 23, no. 1 (March 1973), p 3.

107 BL, MS/OPP/HFO J4.1.3 HFO to Jim Bailey, 27 June 1958.

108 *The Star*, 3 February 1973.

109 E McKenzie, 'The English-language press and the Anglo American

Corporation: An assessment', *Kleio*, 26, no. 1 (1994), p 99.

110 J Mervis, *The Fourth Estate: A Newspaper Story*, Jonathan Ball Publishers, 1989, p 437.

111 *Investors Chronicle*, 26 November 1971.

112 P Pereira, 'Chairman's Fund, 1967–2020: A broad-brush history' (unpublished report for Oppenheimer Generations, 2021). Pereira dates the amalgamation to 1967; Michael O'Dowd dates it to 'about' 1973. See M O'Dowd, 'Practical social responsibility: The work of AAC and De Beers Chairman's Fund', *Optima*, no. 2 (1978), p 118.

113 Pereira, 'Chairman's Fund', citing M Keeton, 'De Beers in South Africa: A socio-political history, 1888–2006' (unpublished manuscript, 2007).

114 Anglo American Corporation of South Africa, Annual Chairman's Statement, 1968.

115 M O'Dowd, 'The Chairman's Fund', in Mortimer, *HFO: Some Personal Perspectives*, pp 195–7; P Pereira, 'Corporate charity as political intervention', *Business Day*, 22 August 2017.

116 Email communication with Gary Ralfe, 22 October 2020.

117 Pallister et al., *South Africa Inc.*, p 44.

118 History of the Oppenheimer Memorial Trust, 1960s. Accessed at https://www.omt.org.za/history/the-history-of-the-omt/1960s/.

119 BL, EOSON, HFO to the Vice-President of the John Simon Guggenheim Memorial Foundation, GT Tanselle, 15 November 1984.

120 University of the Witwatersrand [Wits], Historical Papers Research Archive [HPRA], AD1432, Bureau of Literacy and Literature Records, Index.

121 TD Mweli Skota, *The African Who's Who: An Illustrated Classified Register and National Biographical Dictionary of the Africans in the Transvaal*, 3rd edn, Central News Agency, 1964.

122 History of the Oppenheimer Memorial Trust, 1960s. Accessed at https://

www.omt.org.za/history/the-history-of-the-omt/1960s/.

123 J Jansen, 'The other Harry', in Rajab, *A Man of Africa*, pp 143–5.

124 *Varsity*, 7 June 1967.

125 *Rhodesia Herald*, 14 May 1965.

126 *Rand Daily Mail*, 21 May 1965.

127 *The Star*, 15 July 1965.

128 H Phillips, *UCT under Apartheid, 1948–1968: From Onset to Sit-In*, Jacana, 2019, p 4.

129 BL, MS/OPP/HFO D10.17.4 Professor HM Robertson to HFO, 13 October 1966.

130 BL, EOSON, Clive Corder to HFO, 14 December 1966.

131 BL, EOSON, HFO to Sir De Villiers Graaff, 19 December 1966.

132 BL, EOSON, HFO to Zach de Beer, 20 December 1966.

133 BL, MS/OPP/HFO D10.17.5 Zach de Beer to HFO, 15 October 1966.

134 *Cape Times*, 30 January 1967.

135 *Rand Daily Mail*, 11 March 1967.

136 Hocking, *Oppenheimer and Son*, p 469.

137 *Forbes*, 15 June 1973.

138 Phillips, *UCT under Apartheid*, p 4.

139 HF Oppenheimer, Address to the Congregation, University of Natal Graduation Ceremony, 25 March 1961; reprinted in *Theoria: A Journal of Social and Political Theory*, no. 16 (1961), pp 58–62.

140 *The Star*, 19 December 1966.

141 BL, MS/OPP/HFO O6.15 'The conditions for progress in Africa', TB Davie Memorial Lecture by HFO, 6 September 1962.

142 Ibid.

143 BL, MS/OPP/HFO, HF Oppenheimer, 'The fading Commonwealth', Smuts Memorial Lecture, University of Cambridge, 2 November 1967. See also HF Oppenheimer, *The Fading Commonwealth*, Cambridge University Press, 1968.

144 HF Oppenheimer, 'A reassessment of Rhodes and his relevance to the problems of Africa today', Text of lecture delivered at Rhodes

University to commemorate the 100th anniversary of the arrival of Cecil Rhodes in South Africa, *Optima*, 20, no. 3 (September 1970), pp 103–7.

145 *Sunday Times*, 17 June 1962.

146 *Varsity*, 7 June 1967.

147 K Kaunda, 'From African statesmen and leaders', in Mortimer, *HFO: Some Personal Perspectives*, p 84.

148 BL, MS/OPP/HFO, Unaccessioned, Memorandum marked 'HFO/JP' and entitled 'Confidential: Visit to Washington on Thursday 10 June', 22 June 1965.

149 *The Guardian*, 13 October 1970.

150 Anglo American Corporation of South Africa, Annual Chairman's Statement, 1968.

151 BL, EOSON, HFO to Kenneth Kaunda, 25 December 1974.

152 BL, EOSON, Kenneth Kaunda to HFO, 20 January 1975.

153 F Wilson, *Labour in the South African Gold Mines, 1911–1969*, Cambridge University Press, 1972, p 141.

154 J Nattrass, *The South African Economy: Its Growth and Change*, Oxford University Press, 1988, p 139.

155 De Villiers, 'The boss', in Mortimer, *HFO: Some Personal Perspectives*, p 20.

156 WG James, *Our Precious Metal: African Labour in South Africa's Gold Industry, 1970–1990*, David Philip, 1992, p 25.

157 *Sunday Times*, 7 April 1963.

158 *Rand Daily Mail*, 27 June 1963.

159 Anglo American Corporation of South Africa, Annual Chairman's Statement, 1973.

160 A Boraine, *A Life in Transition*, Zebra Press, 2008, pp 70–8.

161 Anglo American Corporation of South Africa, Annual Chairman's Statement, 1970.

162 *Sunday Times*, 31 May 1970.

163 Anglo American Corporation of South Africa, Annual Chairman's Statement, 1973.

164 *The Guardian*, 18 April 1972.

165 HF Oppenheimer, 'Catalysts for change in South Africa', Address to a joint meeting of the Royal Institute of International Affairs and the Royal African Society at Chatham House, *Optima*, 24, no. 1 (1974), pp 2–9.

166 HF Oppenheimer, 'South Africa's growth in the 70s: Its problems, and the opportunities that lie ahead', Address to 17th annual conference of the Trade Union Council of South Africa in Durban, 16 September 1971, *Optima*, 21, no. 4 (December 1971), p 157.

167 Anglo American Corporation of South Africa, Annual Chairman's Statement, 1973.

168 Oppenheimer, 'Catalysts for change in South Africa', p 6.

169 Anglo American Corporation of South Africa, Annual Chairman's Statement, 1971.

170 Anglo American Corporation of South Africa, Annual Chairman's Statement, 1974.

171 Ibid.

172 *Rand Daily Mail*, 6 June 1973.

173 *Financial Times*, 6 June 1973.

174 J Shilling, 'The boss', in Mortimer, *HFO: Some Personal Perspectives*, p 33.

175 E Webster to HFO, n.d., reproduced in *Bolt*, no. 10 (May 1974), pp 7–10.

176 HFO to L Platzky, n.d., reproduced in *Bolt*, no. 10 (May 1974), p 5.

177 D Horner and A Kooy, 'Conflict on South African mines, 1972–1976', University of Cape Town, South African Labour and Development Research Unit (Saldru), Working Paper no. 5 (August 1976), p 1.

178 J Kane-Berman, *South Africa's Silent Revolution*, South African Institute of Race Relations, 1990.

CHAPTER TEN

1 Cited in J Lelyveld, 'Oppenheimer of South Africa', *New York Times Magazine*, 8 May 1983.

2 *The Economist*, 1 May 1982.

3   G Relly, 'Harry Oppenheimer:
    An appreciation', *Optima*, 31, no. 2
    (1983), pp 46–9.

4   *Weekly Mail*, 7 March 1997.

5   Anglo American Corporation of
    South Africa, Annual Chairman's
    Statement, 1980.

6   J Ogilvie Thompson, Speech at a
    special company dinner in Kimberley
    on 26 November 1984 to celebrate
    HFO's 50 years as a director of De
    Beers, reprinted as 'An appreciation
    of Harry Oppenheimer', *Optima*, 33,
    no. 1 (March 1985), pp 2–7.

7   *The Star*, 22 May 1968.

8   *Fortune*, 10 September 1990.

9   'Inside the Anglo power house',
    Special survey for the *Financial Mail*,
    4 July 1969, p 17.

10 For example, *The Economist*, 1 May
    1982; and *BusinessWeek*,
    2 May 1983.

11 'Inside the Anglo power house',
    Financial Mail, 4 July 1969, p 7.

12 Cited in D Innes, *Anglo: Anglo
    American and the Rise of Modern
    South Africa*, Ravan Press, 1984,
    p 157. A politically conscious indus-
    trialist, with strong contacts across
    the colour line, Clive Menell and
    his wife, Irene, had recently worked
    with Todd Matshikiza to create the
    hit musical *King Kong*. A multiracial
    collaboration and challenge to apart-
    heid, it premiered in 1959.

13 T Moll, 'Did the apartheid economy
    "fail"?', *Journal of Southern Afri-
    can Studies*, 17, no. 2 (June 1991),
    pp 271–91.

14 N Nattrass and J Seekings, 'The
    economy and poverty in the twen-
    tieth century', in R Ross, A Mager
    and B Nasson (eds.), *The Cambridge
    History of South Africa*, vol. 2:
    1885–1994, Cambridge University
    Press, 2012, pp 541–2.

15 For a detailed discussion, see D Beck-
    ingham, 'The Group in industry:
    A view of diversification', *Optima*, 22,
    no. 3 (1972).

16 'Inside the Anglo power house', *Finan-
    cial Mail*, 4 July 1969, p 31.

17 Innes, *Anglo*, p 205.

18 J Iliffe, 'The South African economy,
    1652–1997', *Economic History Review*,
    52, no. 1 (1999), p 97.

19 D O'Meara, *Forty Lost Years: The
    Apartheid State and the Politics of the
    National Party, 1948–1994*, Ravan
    Press, 1996, p 358.

20 Brenthurst Library [BL], MS/OPP/
    HFO, Harry Oppenheimer [HFO],
    Outline of memoir, Chapter 13:
    'Diversification of the Group into
    industry'.

21 P Schmeisser, 'Harry Oppenheimer's
    empire: Going for the gold', *New York
    Times*, 19 March 1989.

22 Anglo American Corporation of
    South Africa, Annual Chairman's
    Statement, 1964.

23 Ibid.

24 Ibid.

25 Innes, *Anglo*, p 197.

26 Anglo American Corporation of
    South Africa, Annual Chairman's
    Statement, 1971.

27 Innes, *Anglo*, p 195.

28 T Cross, 'Afrikaner nationalism, Anglo
    American and Iscor: The formation
    of the Highveld Steel and Vanadium
    Corporation, 1960–70', *Business
    History*, 36, no. 3 (1994), p 89.

29 Ibid., p 88.

30 Ibid., p 90.

31 BL, MS/OPP/HFO/C2 HFO to Mary
    Oppenheimer [Waddell] and Gordon
    Waddell, 21 June 1969.

32 Ibid.

33 BL, E Oppenheimer and Son Papers
    [EOSON], HFO to Hans Coetzee,
    23 July 1969.

34 Cross, 'Afrikaner nationalism, Anglo
    American and Iscor', p 92.

35 BL, EOSON, HFO to Hans Coetzee,
    23 July 1969.

36 Cited in A Sampson, *Black and
    Gold: Tycoons, Revolutionaries and
    Apartheid*, Hodder and Stoughton,
    1987, p 99.

37 Nattrass and Seekings, 'The economy
    and poverty in the twentieth century',
    p 547.

38 Anglo American Corporation of South Africa, Annual Chairman's Statement, 1969.

39 *Rand Daily Mail*, 20 June 1968.

40 Cross, 'Afrikaner nationalism, Anglo American and Iscor', pp 93–4.

41 Ibid., p 94.

42 Anglo American Corporation of South Africa, Annual Chairman's Statement, 1971.

43 Anglo American Corporation of South Africa, Annual Chairman's Statement, 1973.

44 Anglo American Corporation of South Africa, Annual Chairman's Statement, 1972.

45 Ibid.

46 Innes, *Anglo*, p 201.

47 Ibid.

48 'Inside the Anglo power house', *Financial Mail*, 4 July 1969.

49 BL, EOSON, HFO to Charles Engelhard, 11 May 1960.

50 Innes, *Anglo*, p 214.

51 Anglo American Corporation of South Africa, Annual Chairman's Statement, 1974.

52 Anglo American Corporation of South Africa, Annual Chairman's Statement, 1973.

53 Anglo American Corporation of South Africa, Annual Chairman's Statement, 1977.

54 Anglo American Corporation of South Africa, Annual Chairman's Statement, 1975.

55 Anglo American Corporation of South Africa, Annual Chairman's Statement, 1977.

56 Anglo American Corporation of South Africa, Annual Chairman's Statement, 1965.

57 W de Villiers, 'The boss', in B Mortimer (ed.), *HFO: Some Personal Perspectives on Harry Frederick Oppenheimer by His Colleagues and Friends*, Brenthurst Press, 1985, p 20.

58 M Ferreira, 'Diversifying from mining', in Mortimer, *HFO: Some Personal Perspectives*, p 132.

59 K Middlemas, *Cabora Bassa: Engineering and Politics in Southern Africa*, Weidenfeld and Nicolson, 1975.

60 BL, EOSON, HFO to Ted Brown, 15 April 1972.

61 Ibid.

62 Anglo American Corporation of South Africa, Annual Chairman's Statement, 1970.

63 BL, EOSON, HFO to RJ Goss, 15 July 1969.

64 Anglo American Corporation of South Africa, Annual Chairman's Statement, 1969.

65 D Hoffe, 'Carlton Centre', in Mortimer, *HFO: Some Personal Perspectives*, pp 177–8.

66 Anglo American Corporation of South Africa, Annual Chairman's Statement, 1971.

67 A Sampson, *The Money Lenders: The People and Politics of the World Banking Crisis*, Penguin Books, 1983, p 200.

68 On Wesbank, see S Jones and G Scott, 'Wesbank: South Africa's leading hire purchase bank, 1968–90', in S Jones (ed.), *Financial Enterprise in South Africa since 1950*, Macmillan, 1992, pp 213–35.

69 Innes, *Anglo*, p 218.

70 Ibid., p 206.

71 S Jones, 'Union Acceptances: The first merchant bank, 1955–73', in Jones, *Financial Enterprise in South Africa*, pp 154–5.

72 BL, EOSON, HFO to Sidney Spiro, 5 March 1970.

73 BL, EOSON, Mark Norman to HFO, 3 April 1970.

74 BL, EOSON, HFO to Mark Norman, 13 April 1970.

75 Jones, 'Union Acceptances: The first merchant bank, 1955–73', p 155.

76 G Verhoef, 'Nedbank, 1945–1989: The Continental approach to banking in South Africa', in Jones, *Financial Enterprise in South Africa*, p 94.

77 *Financial Mail*, 29 March 1974.

78 BL, EOSON, HFO to Anthony Tuke, 6 June 1974.

79 Ibid.

80 On Volkskas, see G Verhoef, 'Afrikaner nationalism in South African banking: The cases of Volkskas and Trust Bank', in Jones, *Financial Enterprise in South Africa*, pp 115–53.

81 BL, EOSON, HFO to Anthony Tuke, 6 June 1974.

82 G Verhoef, *The Power of Your Life: The Sanlam Century of Insurance Empowerment, 1918–2018*, Oxford University Press, 2018, pp 163–7; personal communication with Grietjie Verhoef, 7 February 2022; JDF Jones, *Through Fortress and Rock: The Story of Gencor, 1895–1995*, Jonathan Ball Publishers, 1995, pp 149–63.

83 Cited in G Verhoef, 'Nationalism and free enterprise in mining: The case of Federale Mynbou 1952–1965', *South African Journal of Economic History*, 10, no. 1 (1995), p 104.

84 Jones, *Through Fortress and Rock*, p 162.

85 *Financial Mail*, 29 March 1974.

86 *Rand Daily Mail*, 22 March 1974.

87 *Financial Times*, 21 March 1974.

88 *Financial Mail*, 29 March 1974.

89 *Eastern Province Herald*, 25 March 1974.

90 *Rand Daily Mail*, 26 March 1974.

91 *Financial Mail*, 29 March 1974.

92 BL, EOSON, John Schlesinger to HFO, 22 November 1974.

93 BL, EOSON, John Schlesinger to HFO, 30 November 1974.

94 K Romain, *Larger Than Life: Donald Gordon and the Liberty Life Story*, Jonathan Ball Publishers, 1989, pp 87–9.

95 BL, EOSON, HFO to John Schlesinger, 6 December 1974.

96 BL, EOSON, HFO to Mandy Moross, 23 October 1975.

97 BL, EOSON, Mandy Moross to HFO, 16 October 1975.

98 BL, EOSON, HFO to Mandy Moross, 23 October 1975.

99 *The Economist*, 21 February 1976.

100 Anglo American Corporation of South Africa, Annual Chairman's Statement, 1975.

101 Innes, *Anglo*, p 217.

102 Ibid., p 221.

103 G Relly, 'Organization and group structure', in Mortimer, *HFO: Some Personal Perspectives*, p 189.

104 Ibid.

105 Anglo American Corporation of South Africa, Annual Chairman's Statement, 1974.

106 *Financial Mail*, 29 March 1974.

107 BL, MS/OPP/HFO/D10.15.2 Certificate, District Grand Lodge of South Africa, Central Division, showing HFO's initiation on 21 October 1943 and continued membership as of 5 August 1958. Name and number of Lodge: Richard Giddy No. 1574 EC.

108 A Doull, 'The boss: As his PAs see him', in Mortimer, *HFO: Some Personal Perspectives*, p 42; Skype interview with Adrian Doull, 30 August 2019.

109 N Diemont, 'The boss: As his PAs see him', in Mortimer, *HFO: Some Personal Perspectives*, p 43; Telephone interview, 11 February 2020.

110 Interview with Tony Trahar, London, 3 October 2019.

111 Interview with Gary Ralfe, Johannesburg, 23 March 2021.

112 Interview with Bobby Godsell, Johannesburg, 10 October 2017.

113 Interview with Mike Spicer, Cape Town, 19 November 2020. See also Spicer, 'Remembering the business contribution to our successful transition to democracy', in K Rajab (ed.), *A Man of Africa: The Political Thought of Harry Oppenheimer*, Zebra Press, 2017, p 99.

114 Interview with Hank Slack, Cape Town, 11 September 2019.

115 Interview with Roger Phillimore, London, 9 October 2019.

116 BL, MS/OPP/HFO, HFO, Outline of memoir, Chapter 1: 'Introduction'.

117 *Sunday Express*, 14 March 1971.

118 Ibid.

119 BL, EOSON, Adrian Doull to Bill Johnson, 26 March 1971.

120 *Sunday Times*, 19 September 1971.

121 BL, EOSON, Gavin Relly to HFO, 12 July 1979.

122 Ibid.

123 BL, MS/OPP/HFO, 'Help thou mine unbelief: Some recollections and reflections by Harry Oppenheimer', Chapter 5: The Anglo American Corporation.

124 *BusinessWeek*, 2 May 1983.

125 BL, EOSON, HFO to Philip Oppenheimer, 12 April 1980.

126 BL, EOSON, HFO to Anthony Oppenheimer, 10 June 1980.

127 BL, EOSON, HFO to Pierre Crokaert, 12 August 1980.

128 Anglo American Corporation of South Africa, Annual Chairman's Statement, 1980.

129 *Wall Street Journal*, 2 June 1982.

130 Anglo American Corporation of South Africa, Annual Chairman's Statement, 1982.

131 *Financial Mail*, 11 July 1985.

132 D Beckett, *Radical Middle: Chasing Peace While Apartheid Ruled*, ColdType.net, 2010, p 115.

CHAPTER ELEVEN

1 HF Oppenheimer, 'Sir Ernest Oppenheimer: A portrait by his son', *Optima*, 17, no. 3 (September 1967), p 103.

2 BL, Bridget Oppenheimer Papers [MS/OPP/BDO]/B1.16 Scrapbook, Handwritten note on Carlyle notepaper, March 1970 [should be 1971].

3 D Innes, *Anglo: Anglo American and the Rise of Modern South Africa*, Ravan Press, 1984, p 234.

4 BL, E Oppenheimer and Son Papers [EOSON], Memorandum in HFO's handwriting entitled 'Iran', marked 'confidential', n.d. but evidence suggests February 1976.

5 Anglo American Corporation of South Africa, Annual Chairman's Statement, 1970.

6 H Dyer, 'Diversifying from mining', in B Mortimer (ed.), *HFO: Some Personal Perspectives on Harry Frederick Oppenheimer by His Colleagues and Friends*, Brenthurst Press, 1985, p 129.

7 *The Star*, 16 May 1963.

8 EJ Epstein, *The Diamond Invention*, Hutchinson, 1982, p 150.

9 De Beers Consolidated Mines, *Annual Report*, 1971.

10 B Kantor, 'The many facets of De Beers – or why it isn't what it appears to be', Paper prepared for the School of Economics, University of Cape Town, January 1982.

11 BL, Harry Oppenheimer Papers [MS/OPP/HFO], HFO, Outline of memoir, Chapter 6: 'The diamond "monopoly"'.

12 Epstein, *The Diamond Invention*, p 91.

13 I Fleming, *The Diamond Smugglers*, Jonathan Cape, 1957.

14 Epstein, *The Diamond Invention*, p 137.

15 P Hain, *Sing the Beloved Country: The Struggle for the New South Africa*, Pluto, 1996, pp 104–7.

16 G Winter, *Inside BOSS: South Africa's Secret Police*, Penguin, 1981, pp 323–4, 462–5.

17 *Sunday Express*, 15 May 1976.

18 F Kamil, *The Diamond Underworld*, Allen Lane, 1979.

19 See https://www.pbs.org/wgbh/frontline/film/the-diamond-empire/. Accessed on 4 April 2022.

20 See http://www.shoppbs.pbs.org/wgbh/pages/frontline/programs/transcripts/1209.html. Accessed on 4 April 2022.

21 BL, MS/OPP/BDO, B1.38 Scrapbook, WJ Lear to C Elphick, 31 January 1994.

22 T Cleveland, *Stones of Contention: A History of Africa's Diamonds*, Ohio University Press, 2014.

23 Epstein, *The Diamond Invention*, p 34.

24 P Crokaert, 'The diamond industry', in Mortimer, *HFO: Some Personal Perspectives*, p 100.

25 *Financial Times*, 9 March 1983.

26 S Kanfer, *The Last Empire: De Beers, Diamonds and the World*, Hodder and Stoughton, 1994, pp 298–9.

27 C Andrew and V Mitrokhin, *The Mitrokhin Archive: The KGB in Europe and the West*, Allen Lane/The Penguin Press, 1999, p 604.

28 BL, EOSON, Serge Combard to HFO, 30 July 1965.

29 BL, EOSON, 'Proposed visit to Moscow', Memorandum marked 'Private and Confidential', no author, n.d. [but included with Combard's correspondence dated 1965].

30 Ibid.

31 BL, EOSON, Francis Howard to HFO, 14 September 1965.

32 D Pallister, S Stewart and I Lepper, *South Africa Inc.: The Oppenheimer Empire*, Yale University Press, 1988, p 146.

33 *Washington Post*, 4 August 1981.

34 *Wall Street Journal*, 7 July 1984.

35 *The Star*, 1 April 1968.

36 Cited in Kanfer, *The Last Empire*, p 371.

37 Anglo American Corporation of South Africa, Annual Chairman's Statement, 1981.

38 Anglo American Corporation of South Africa, Annual Chairman's Statement, 1982.

39 *Christian Science Monitor*, 28 December 1982.

40 J Ogilvie Thompson, 'The diamond industry', in Mortimer, *HFO: Some Personal Perspectives*, p 101.

41 P Schmeisser, 'Harry Oppenheimer's empire: Going for the gold', *New York Times*, 19 March 1989.

42 Anglo American Corporation of South Africa, Annual Chairman's Statement, 1968.

43 Anglo American Corporation of South Africa, Annual Chairman's Statement, 1974.

44 Ibid.

45 Anglo American Corporation of South Africa, Annual Chairman's Statement, 1969.

46 A Gower, 'International diversification: Expansion in South America', in Mortimer, *HFO: Some Personal Perspectives*, p 164; and Julian Ogilvie Thompson, 'International diversification: Expansion in South America', pp 166–7.

47 'I remember our visit in Brasília with President Geisel', Tempelsman wrote to HFO in 1994. BL, MS/OPP/BDO, B1.39 Maurice Tempelsman to HFO and BDO, 25 June 1994.

48 D Fig, 'The political economy of South–South relations: The case of South Africa and Latin America' (PhD thesis, London School of Economics and Political Science, 1992), p 224.

49 Anglo American Corporation of South Africa, Annual Chairman's Statement, 1975.

50 Anglo American Corporation of South Africa, Annual Chairman's Statement, 1971.

51 Ibid.

52 *Investors Chronicle*, 26 November 1971.

53 BL, EOSON, HFO to Murray Hofmeyr, 30 July 1973.

54 G Relly, 'International diversification: The Minorco–Charter restructuring', in Mortimer, *HFO: Some Personal Perspectives*, p 149.

55 M Hofmeyr, 'International diversification: The Minorco–Charter restructuring', in Mortimer, *HFO: Some Personal Perspectives*, pp 150–1.

56 Pallister et al., *South Africa Inc.*, p 123.

57 BL, EOSON, HFO to Murray Hofmeyr, 30 July 1973.

58 Ibid.

59 Anglo American Corporation of South Africa, Annual Chairman's Statement, 1975.

60 BL, EOSON, Gavin Relly to HFO, 12 July 1979.

61 N Clarke, 'International diversification: The Minorco–Charter restructuring', in Mortimer, *HFO: Some Personal Perspectives*, p 149.

62 Anglo American Corporation of South Africa, Annual Chairman's Statement, 1966.

63 E Beimfohr, 'International diversification: Association with Engelhard', in Mortimer, *HFO: Some Personal Perspectives*, pp 154–5.

64 BL, EOSON, HFO to Charles Engelhard, 19 January 1960.

65 *New York Times*, 13 September 1963.

66 Anglo American Corporation of
South Africa, Annual Chairman's
Statement, 1968.

67 BL, EOSON, Charles Engelhard to
HFO, 10 March 1969.

68 BL, EOSON, HFO to Charles Engelhard, 8 January, 1970.

69 BL, EOSON, HFO to Basil Hone,
8 January 1970.

70 BL, EOSON, HFO to Gavin Relly,
15 June 1970.

71 Anglo American Corporation of
South Africa, Annual Chairman's
Statement, 1975.

72 L Jesselson, 'International diversification: Association with Engelhard',
in Mortimer, *HFO: Some Personal
Perspectives*, p 158.

73 BL, MS/OPP/BDO]/B1.16 Scrapbook, Handwritten note on Carlyle
notepaper, March 1970 [should be
1971].

74 JH Shenefield and IM Stelzer, *The
Antitrust Laws: A Primer*, American
Enterprise Institute Press, 1993, p 1.

75 R Fraser, 'International diversification:
The New World', in Mortimer, *HFO:
Some Personal Perspectives*, p 141.

76 Anglo American Corporation of
South Africa, Annual Chairman's
Statement, 1979.

77 P Gush, 'International diversification:
The New World', in Mortimer, *HFO:
Some Personal Perspectives*, p 144.

78 Anglo American Corporation of
South Africa, Annual Chairman's
Statement, 1981.

79 Anglo American Corporation of
South Africa, Annual Chairman's
Statement, 1978.

80 *New York Times*, 4 August 1981.

81 Kanfer, *The Last Empire*, p 379.

82 *Fortune*, 10 August 1981.

83 *Washington Post*, 11 April 1982.

84 Anglo American Corporation of
South Africa, Annual Chairman's
Statement, 1981.

85 M Lewis, *Liar's Poker: Rising through
the Wreckage on Wall Street*,
WW Norton, 1989.

86 *Washington Post*, 11 April 1982.

87 Schmeisser, 'Harry Oppenheimer's
empire: Going for the gold'.

88 Interview with Oliver Baring,
London, 4 October 2019.

89 B Jamieson, *Goldstrike! The Oppenheimer Empire in Crisis*, Hutchinson
Business Books, 1990, pp 63 and 65.

90 J Ogilvie Thompson, 'Consgold and
the dawn raid', in Mortimer, *HFO:
Some Personal Perspectives*, p 201.

91 Ibid., p 202.

92 O Baring, 'Consgold and the
dawn raid', in Mortimer, *HFO:
Some Personal Perspectives*, p 204.

93 J Taylor, 'Hard to be rich: The rise and
wobble of the Gutfreunds', *New York
Magazine*, 11 January 1988, p 28.

94 *Washington Post*, 28 September 1987.

95 Kanfer, *The Last Empire*, p 402.

96 Interview with Hank Slack, Cape
Town, 11 September 2019.

97 Interview with Roger Phillimore,
London, 9 October 2019.

98 Kanfer, *The Last Empire*, p 403.

99 Cited in P Newman, 'Apartheid and
the Canada connection', *Business
Watch*, 13 February 1989.

100 Kanfer, *The Last Empire*, p 405.

101 Ibid., p 408.

102 BL, MS/OPP/BDO, B1.38 Typescript
of HFO's speech to senior staff after
Anglo American Corporation AGM,
13 August 1982.

103 *Financial Times*, 28 June 1993.

104 Cited in Schmeisser, 'Harry Oppenheimer's empire: Going for the gold'.

CHAPTER TWELVE

1 *Forbes*, 15 December 1972.

2 *The Economist*, 1 May 1982.

3 S Biko, *I Write What I Like*,
Bowerdean, 1978, pp 20–2.

4 R Fatton Jr, *Black Consciousness in
South Africa: The Dialectics of
Ideological Resistance to White
Supremacy*, SUNY Press, 1986,
pp 82–3.

5   Brenthurst Library [BL], Harry
    Oppenheimer Papers [MS/OPP/
    HFO]/O5, 'The Fifth Stock Exchange
    Chairman's Lecture', 18 May 1976.

6   Anglo American Corporation of
    South Africa, Annual Chairman's
    Statement, 1975.

7   Ibid.

8   BL, E Oppenheimer and Son Papers
    [EOSON], HFO to Hilgard Muller,
    5 November 1974.

9   BL, EOSON, Edmond de Rothschild
    to HFO, 28 July 1978.

10 BL, EOSON, HFO to Edmond de
    Rothschild, 28 August 1978.

11 As South African ambassador to the
    United Kingdom in the early 1960s,
    Muller had once hosted a dinner in
    Oppenheimer's honour and toasted
    him warmly. BL, Bridget Oppen-
    heimer Papers [MS/OPP/BDO]/B1.8
    Scrapbook, Note on South Africa
    Club dinner in honour of Mr and
    Mrs Harry Oppenheimer,
    Lancaster Room, Savoy Hotel,
    30 October 1962.

12 BL, MS/OPP/BDO/B1.21 Typescript
    of a speech delivered by HFO at the
    US-SALEP symposium on southern
    Africa, 8 March 1976.

13 BL, MS/OPP/HFO/O5, 'The Fifth
    Stock Exchange Chairman's Lecture',
    18 May 1976.

14 HF Oppenheimer, 'For South
    African national unity', *New York
    Times*, 2 June 1976.

15 *Rand Daily Mail*, 9 March 1976.

16 *Sunday Tribune*, 14 March 1976.

17 Ibid.

18 BL, MS/OPP/HFO/O5, 'The Fifth
    Stock Exchange Chairman's Lecture',
    18 May 1976.

19 BL, MS/OPP/HFO/ J4.1.1 HFO to
    Desmond Tutu, 14 September 1956.
    See also J Allen, *Rabble-Rouser for
    Peace: The Authorised Biography of
    Desmond Tutu*, Rider, 2007, pp 62–3.

20 Allen, *Rabble-Rouser for Peace*,
    pp 219–22; and K Rajab, 'A historical
    assessment', in Rajab (ed.), *A Man of
    Africa: The Political Thought of Harry
    Oppenheimer*, Zebra Press, 2017, p 27.

21 BL, MS/OPP/HFO/O5, 'The Fifth
    Stock Exchange Chairman's Lecture'.

22 H Kissinger, 'The political perspec-
    tive: From the USA', in B Mortimer
    (ed.), *HFO: Some Personal Perspec-
    tives on Harry Frederick Oppenheimer
    by His Colleagues and Friends*, Brent-
    hurst Press, 1985, p 82.

23 Ibid., p 82.

24 'Text of Kissinger's address in Zambia
    on US policy toward southern Africa',
    New York Times, 28 April 1976.

25 Ibid.

26 The phrase was coined by the Con-
    servative Prime Minister Edward
    Heath in 1973, and stuck to Lonrho.

27 US Department of State, Cable to
    Secretary of State marked 'secret',
    23 April 1976. Accessed at https://
    wikileaks.org/plusd/cables/1976LU-
    SAKA01051_b.html.

28 H Kissinger, *Years of Renewal*, Simon
    and Schuster, 1999, p 998.

29 US Department of State, Cable to
    Secretary of State marked 'confi-
    dential', 28 March 1977. Accessed
    at https://wikileaks.org/plusd/
    cables/1977LUSAKA00822_c.html.

30 A Young, 'He never gave up on peace',
    in Rajab, *A Man of Africa*, pp 169–72.

31 US Mission, United Nations, Cable
    from A Young to Z Brzeziński,
    'Appointment request for Harry
    Oppenheimer', 27 September 1977.
    Accessed at https://wikileaks.org/
    plusd/cables/1977USUNN03339_c.
    html.

32 M Friedman, Record of a trip to
    southern Africa, March 20 – April
    9, 1976, Unpublished typescript
    transcribed from a tape, dictated
    7–9 April 1976. Accessed at https://
    miltonfriedman.hoover.org/internal/
    media/dispatcher/271010/full.

33 *Newsweek*, 24 May 1976.

34 *Newsweek*, 31 March 1975.

35 A Butler, *Cyril Ramaphosa*, Jacana,
    2007, p 99.

36 A Rupert, 'The Urban Foundation',
    in Mortimer, *HFO: Some Personal
    Perspectives*, p 211.

37 D de Villiers, 'The Urban Foundation',

in Mortimer, *HFO: Some Personal Perspectives*, p 213.

38 On HFO's sponsorship of Kuzwayo, see BL, EOSON, HFO to Dr DJ du Plessis (vice-chancellor of Wits University), 16 April 1981; and BL, EOSON, Note prepared for HFO by PM Formby, 25 June 1981.

39 Cited in Butler, *Cyril Ramaphosa*, p 101.

40 Ibid.

41 N Diemont, 'The Urban Foundation', in Mortimer, *HFO: Some Personal Perspectives*, p 210.

42 BL, EOSON, Wim de Villiers to HFO, 2 December 1976.

43 BL, EOSON, HFO to Wim de Villiers, 7 December 1976.

44 *Sunday Times*, 5 December 1976.

45 S Hoogenraad-Vermaak, 'The contribution of the Urban Foundation to political reform', *Historia*, 56, no. 2 (November 2011), p 136; South African Institute of Race Relations [SAIRR], *A Survey of Race Relations in South Africa: 1977*, South African Institute of Race Relations, 1978, p 45.

46 J Steyn, 'The Urban Foundation', in Mortimer, *HFO: Some Personal Perspectives*, p 214.

47 Hoogenraad-Vermaak, 'The contribution of the Urban Foundation to political reform', p 138.

48 Butler, *Cyril Ramaphosa*, p 104.

49 This summation of the Free Market Foundation's objectives is cited in D O'Meara, *Forty Lost Years: The Apartheid State and the Politics of the National Party, 1948–1994*, Ravan Press, 1996, p 184.

50 BL, EOSON, HFO to Jan Steyn, 11 January 1979.

51 BL, EOSON, Jan Steyn to HFO, 25 November 1980: 'May I say how much I appreciate your offer of a seat on the main board of Anglos [*sic*]. As soon as I receive approval from Government to resign I will formally accept the offer.'

52 BL, EOSON, Mike Rosholt to HFO, 23 January 1981.

53 BL, EOSON, HFO to Jan Steyn, 4 November 1980.

54 BL, EOSON, Jan Steyn to HFO, 10 February 1981.

55 Ibid.

56 Steyn believed the UF should continue to put Koornhof 'under as much benign pressure as possible in order to ensure an equitable dispensation'. BL, EOSON, Jan Steyn to HFO, 8 June 1982.

57 *New York Times*, 21 February 1981.

58 Cited in D Welsh, *The Rise and Fall of Apartheid*, Jonathan Ball Publishers, 2009, p 260.

59 BL, EOSON, PGJ Koornhof to HFO, 20 November 1978.

60 BL, EOSON, DJ Louis Nel to HFO, 6 August 1984.

61 SAIRR, *A Survey of Race Relations in South Africa: 1977*, p 32.

62 Butler, *Cyril Ramaphosa*, p 103.

63 Hoogenraad-Vermaak, 'The contribution of the Urban Foundation to political reform', p 153.

64 Alan Paton wrote a history of the organisation's first ten years: *Beyond the Present: The Story of Women for Peace, 1976–1986*, Brenthurst Press, 1986. It was described as 'an ample tribute to Mrs Oppenheimer': *The Star*, 11 January 1987.

65 SAIRR, *A Survey of Race Relations in South Africa: 1976*, South African Institute of Race Relations, 1977, p 30. On the Ulster Women's Peace Movement reference, see Erica Rudden, 'Bridget wants her army to march for peace', *Sunday Express*, 14 November 1976.

66 K Rajab, 'Bridget Denison Oppenheimer, 1921–2013'. Accessed at https://www.omt.org.za/in-the-media/bridget-denison-oppenheimer-nee-mccall-1921-2013/.

67 *The Citizen*, 14 November 1976.

68 Ibid.

69 HF Oppenheimer, 'Prospects for change in Southern Africa', Address to the Foreign Policy Association, New York City, 14 October 1977. Reproduced as a supplement to *Optima*, 27, no. 3 (1977), pp 1 and 6.

70 University of the Witwatersrand

[Wits], Historical Papers Research Archive [HPRA], Helen Suzman Papers [A2084], Mb2.13.5 HFO to Helen Suzman, postmarked 26 April 1974.

71 A Boraine, *A Life in Transition*, Zebra Press, 2008, p 82.

72 BL, EOSON, Colin Eglin to HFO, 6 October 1977.

73 BL, EOSON, Colin Eglin to HFO, 11 January 1978; BL, EOSON, Colin Eglin to Hank Slack, 9 February 1978.

74 HFO, 'Prospects for change in Southern Africa', p 7.

75 HF Oppenheimer, 'Why the world should continue to invest in South Africa', Address to the International Monetary Conference, Mexico City, 22 May 1978. Reproduced as a supplement to *Optima*, no. 1 (1978), p 2.

76 A Grundlingh, *Slabbert: Man on a Mission; A Biography*, Jonathan Ball Publishers, 2021, p 77.

77 C Eglin, *Crossing the Borders of Power: The Memoirs of Colin Eglin*, Jonathan Ball Publishers, 2007, p 177.

78 Interview with Tony Leon, Cape Town, 6 October 2017; Grundlingh, *Slabbert: Man on a Mission*, p 101.

79 I Wilkins and H Strydom, *The Super Afrikaners: Inside the Afrikaner Broederbond*, Jonathan Ball Publishers, 2012 [1978].

80 Interview with Patrick Esnouf, Cape Town, 20 January 2017.

81 Anglo American Corporation of South Africa, Annual Chairman's Statement, 1975.

82 Anglo American Corporation of South Africa, Annual Chairman's Statement, 1980.

83 Anglo American Corporation of South Africa, Annual Chairman's Statement, 1976.

84 Anglo American Corporation of South Africa, Annual Chairman's Statement, 1977.

85 Cited in Rajab, 'A historical assessment', p 46.

86 Anglo American Corporation of South Africa, Annual Chairman's Statement, 1977.

87 L Flynn, *Studded with Diamonds and Paved with Gold: Miners, Mining Companies and Human Rights in Southern Africa*, Bloomsbury, 1992, p 222.

88 Wits, HPRA, A2084, Mb2.7.2.1 KM Salema to Helen Suzman, 2 March 1968.

89 Anglo American Corporation of South Africa, Annual Chairman's Statement, 1979.

90 Anglo American Corporation of South Africa, Annual Chairman's Statement, 1975.

91 On the conflict among different mining houses within the Chamber of Mines, see J Crush, A Jeeves and D Yudelman, *South Africa's Labour Empire: A History of Black Migrancy to the Gold Mines*, Westview Press, 1991, pp 186–94.

92 Interview with Bobby Godsell, Johannesburg, 10 October 2018; B Godsell, 'The classical liberal who bore the responsibilities of power', in Rajab, *A Man of Africa*, p 126.

93 AD Wassenaar, *Assault on Private Enterprise: The Freeway to Communism*, Tafelberg, 1977.

94 Godsell, 'The classical liberal who bore the responsibilities of power', p 129.

95 Ibid.

96 HF Oppenheimer, 'Towards a more just racial order in South Africa', Opening address to the 50th anniversary conference of the South African Institute of Race Relations, Johannesburg, 2 July 1979. Reproduced as a supplement to *Optima*, 28, no. 3 (August 1979), p 5.

97 T Dunbar Moodie, 'Managing the 1987 mine workers' strike', *Journal of Southern African Studies*, 35, no. 1 (March 2009), p 64.

98 O'Meara, *Forty Lost Years*, p 294.

99 *Daily Telegraph*, 3 June 1982.

100 *Time*, 3 December 1979.

101 *Financial Mail*, 14 August 1981.

102 BL, EOSON, Zach de Beer to HFO, 28 August 1981.

103 BL, Bobby Godsell Papers, MS717/5, Speech delivered by HFO at the

Prime Minister's conference, 12 November 1981.

104 BL, EOSON, HFO to Henry Kissinger, 3 February 1978.

105 BL, EOSON, Breakfast meeting with Dr Henry Kissinger, notes compiled by JOT, 22 May 1978.

106 BL, EOSON, Henry Kissinger to HFO, 23 December 1981.

107 H Kissinger, 'American global concerns and Africa', *International Affairs Bulletin*, 6, no. 3 (1982), pp 5–22.

108 Kissinger, 'The political perspective: From the USA', p 82.

109 *Rand Daily Mail*, 15 June 1983.

110 Grundlingh, *Slabbert*, p 97.

111 M Spicer, 'Remembering the business contribution to our successful transition to democracy', in Rajab, *A Man of Africa*, p 98; interview with Michael Spicer, Cape Town, 9 November 2020.

112 *Daily News*, 18 October 1983.

113 D Beckett, 'Millions of payslips', in Rajab, *A Man of Africa*, p 73.

114 BL, MS/OPP/HFO, 'Apartheid under pressure', Address to the Foreign Policy Association, New York, 11 October 1984.

115 S Saunders, *Vice-Chancellor on a Tightrope: A Personal Account of Climactic Years in South Africa*, David Philip, 2000.

116 J Matisonn, *God, Spies and Lies: Finding South Africa's Future through Its Past*, Quivertree Publications, 2015, p 141.

117 J Mervis, *The Fourth Estate: A Newspaper Story*, Jonathan Ball Publishers, 1989, p 527.

118 Ibid., pp 527–30; R Gibson, *Final Deadline: The Last Days of the Rand Daily Mail*, David Philip, 2007; A Sparks, *The Sword and the Pen: Six Decades on the Political Frontier*, Jonathan Ball Publishers, 2016, pp 422–9.

119 BL, EOSON, HFO to Peter Galliner, 22 March 1985.

120 Sparks, *The Sword and the Pen*, p 431.

121 See R Louw, 'The *Rand Daily Mail*: Convenient scapegoat', *Focus*, no. 39 (2005). Accessed at https://hsf.org.za/publications/focus/issue-39-third-quarter-2005/the-rand-daily-mail-convenient-scapegoat.

122 Rajab, 'A historical assessment', p 13.

123 W Gilfillan, 'A diamond forever', *The Executive*, 6, no. 1 (February 1993).

124 BL, MS/OPP/HFO, HFO, Outline of memoir, Chapter 15 'Recreation'.

125 Interview with Jonathan Oppenheimer, Johannesburg, 24 February 2020.

126 BL, MS/OPP/BDO/B4.5 Dinner menu and guest list, 31 December 1980.

127 Churchill Archives Centre, University of Cambridge [CHAC], Julian Amery Papers, AME/2/1/108, Julian Amery to HFO, 21 September 1981, for example.

128 Margaret Thatcher Foundation [MTF], Prime Ministerial Private Office files, PREM19/1970 f273, Julian Amery to Margaret Thatcher, 1 August 1986, enclosing HFO to Julian Amery, 24 July 1986.

129 C Moore, *Margaret Thatcher: The Authorized Biography*, vol. 2, Penguin Books, 2016, p 562.

130 MTF, Prime Ministerial Private Office files, PREM19/1965 f126, Julian Amery to Margaret Thatcher, 28 January 1986.

131 MTF, Prime Ministerial Private Office files, PREM19/1965 f245, Geoffrey Howe to Margaret Thatcher, 20 December 1985.

132 HFO warmed to Ted Koppel. See, for example, BL, EOSON, HFO to Ted Koppel, 12 April 1985: 'Bridget and I are going to be in New York … beginning 13 May and would so much like to meet you again.'

133 BL, EOSON, HFO to PW Botha, 12 February 1985.

134 BL, EOSON, Mangosuthu Buthelezi to PW Botha, 19 November 1984.

135 BL, MS/OPP/BDO/B1.31 Scrapbook, Certificate and citation, 'The Decoration for Meritorious Service', 21 March 1985.

136 BL, EOSON, HFO to Roger Smith, n.d.

137 *New York Times*, 8 May 1983.

138 BL, EOSON, Roger Smith to HFO, 12 February 1986; and BL, EOSON, Roger Smith to HFO, 27 March 1986.

139 Cited in A Sampson, *Black and Gold: Tycoons, Revolutionaries and Apartheid*, Hodder and Stoughton, 1987, p 253.

140 *New York Times*, 21 October 1986.

141 *Washington Post*, 27 April 1989.

142 Email correspondence with Bobby Godsell, 7 September 2022. See also PL Berger, *Adventures of an Accidental Sociologist: How to Explain the World Without Becoming a Bore*, Prometheus Books, 2011.

143 PL Berger and B Godsell (eds.), *A Future South Africa: Visions, Strategies, and Realities*, Westview Press, 1988.

144 BL, MS/OPP/BDO/B1.38 Typescript of HFO's speech to senior staff after Anglo AGM, 13 August 1982.

145 BL, EOSON, Draft handwritten speech by HFO entitled 'The relevance of a qualified franchise in an alternative constitution for South Africa', marked 'first draft' [internal evidence suggests 1977, just before the formation of the PFP].

146 D Welsh, 'Review of the Buthelezi Commission', H&H Publications, 1982. Accessed at https://www.sahistory.org.za/sites/default/files/archive-files2/rejul82.5.pdf.

147 'Why I back Buthelezi Report – Oppenheimer', *Daily News*, 8 July 1982.

148 BL, EOSON, Mangosuthu Buthelezi to HFO, 3 June 1985.

149 BL, EOSON, Giles Hefer [HFO's PA] to Winnie Mandela, 22 February 1985: the enclosed cheque was made out in Winnie Mandela's name. The request for funds was initiated by Humphrey Harrison.

150 Butler, *Cyril Ramaphosa*, p 276.

151 *New York Times*, 18 November 1985.

152 Cited in M Gevisser, *Thabo Mbeki: The Dream Deferred*, Jonathan Ball Publishers, 2007, p 503.

153 *Washington Post*, 14 September 1985.

154 Gevisser, *Thabo Mbeki*, p 504.

155 UCT, BC 1070, G1.91 Transcript of an interview with HFO by Patti Waldmeir, 27 October 1994.

156 T Bloom, 'An exquisite approach – but should the gloves have come off?', in Rajab, *A Man of Africa*, p 94.

157 For example, *Sunday Tribune*, 29 September 1985.

158 Bloom, 'An exquisite approach', p 95.

159 MTF, Prime Ministerial Private Office files, PREM19/1643 f37, Charles Powell [Thatcher's private secretary] to Colin Budd [Foreign and Commonwealth Office], 24 September 1985.

160 Cited in A Sampson, *Mandela: The Authorised Biography*, HarperCollins, 2000, p 342.

161 *New York Times*, 18 November 1985.

162 'Anton Harber on how Ramaphosa made history confronting Oppenheimer', *Business Day*, 30 August 2017. Accessed at https://www.businesslive.co.za/bd/opinion/2017-08-30-anton-harber-ramaphosa-made-history-confronting-oppenheimer/.

163 Butler, *Cyril Ramaphosa*, p 184.

164 Ibid.

165 Interview with Patrick Esnouf, Cape Town, 20 January 2017.

166 Grundlingh, *Slabbert*, p 109.

167 Boraine, *A Life in Transition*, pp 127–8.

168 *Sunday Times*, 9 February 1986.

169 *Sunday Times*, 19 February 1986.

170 Cited in Eglin, *Crossing the Borders of Power*, p 119.

171 FA Mouton, '"One of the architects of our democracy": Colin Eglin, the Progressive Federal Party and the leadership of the official parliamentary opposition, 1977–1979 and 1986–1987', *Journal for Contemporary History*, 40, no. 1 (June 2015), p 14.

172 Interview with Tony Leon, Cape Town, 6 October 2017.

173 *Time*, 18 May 1987.

174 BL, MS/717-5, HFO to Colin Eglin, 11 February 1988.

175 Wits, HPRA, A2084, Ma8.4.2.4 Speech delivered by HFO at a dinner to honour Helen Suzman's 35th year in Parliament, 27 March 1988.

176 T Leon, *On the Contrary: Leading the Opposition in a Democratic South Africa*, Jonathan Ball Publishers, 2008, p 154.

177 Wits, HPRA, A2084, Ma8.2.1.3 HFO to Clifford Elphick, 26 June 1989, Message for Irene Menell 'for use at Helen Suzman's meeting this evening'.

178 R Lee (ed.), *Values Alive: A Tribute to Helen Suzman*, Jonathan Ball Publishers, 1990.

179 Interview with HFO in M Albeldas and A Fischer (eds.), *A Question of Survival: Conversations with Key South Africans*, Jonathan Ball Publishers, 1987, p 338.

180 R Harvey, *The Fall of Apartheid: The Inside Story from Smuts to Mbeki*, Palgrave, 2001.

181 HF Oppenheimer, 'Four steps to democracy', Speech at the World Economic Forum conference in Davos, 31 January 1989. Reproduced as a supplement to *Optima*, 37, no. 1 (March 1989), pp 1–7.

182 Ibid., p 5.

183 Ibid., p 3.

184 RW Johnson and D Welsh (eds.), *Ironic Victory: Liberalism in Post-Liberation South Africa*, Oxford University Press, 1998.

CHAPTER THIRTEEN

1 A Sampson, *Mandela: The Authorised Biography*, HarperCollins, 2000, p 403.

2 University of Cape Town, Special Collections, Jagger Library [UCT], Herman Giliomee Papers [BC 1070], G1.91 Transcript of an interview with HFO by Patti Waldmeir, 27 October 1994.

3 *Financial Times*, 28 June 1993.

4 *Mail & Guardian*, 7 March 1997.

5 Ibid.

6 P Waldmeir, *Anatomy of a Miracle: The End of Apartheid and the Birth of the New South Africa*, Rutgers University Press, 2001. Unless stated otherwise, all quotes are taken from UCT, BC 1070, G1.91 Transcript of an interview with HFO by Patti Waldmeir, 27 October 1994.

7 CH Feinstein, *An Economic History of South Africa: Conquest, Discrimination and Development*, Cambridge University Press, 2005, p 244.

8 Cited in Sampson, *Mandela*, p 402.

9 Interview with Clifford Elphick, Johannesburg, 12 February 2020.

10 Brenthurst Library, Bridget Oppenheimer Papers [MS/OPP/BDO]/ B2.18 Menu and guests, 20 May 1991.

11 D Geldenhuys, 'The foreign factor in South Africa's 1992 referendum', *Politikon*, 19, no. 3 (1992), pp 45–63.

12 *Washington Post*, 19 March 1992.

13 Email correspondence with Bobby Godsell, 7 September 2022. Godsell recalled the Chamber's contribution being in the region of R450 000.

14 D Welsh, *The Rise and Fall of Apartheid*, Jonathan Ball Publishers, 2009, p 467.

15 C Eglin, *Crossing the Borders of Power: The Memoirs of Colin Eglin*, Jonathan Ball Publishers, 2007, p 285.

16 Welsh, *The Rise and Fall of Apartheid*, p 491.

17 Ibid., p 508.

18 Waldmeir, *Anatomy of a Miracle*, p 226.

19 HF Oppenheimer, 'Four steps to democracy', Speech at the World Economic Forum conference in Davos, 31 January 1989. Reproduced in a supplement to *Optima*, 37, no. 1 (March 1989), p 6.

20 Sampson, *Mandela*, p 435.

21 *Washington Post*, 1 April 1990.

22 Sampson, *Mandela*, p 400.

23 Mandela's rally address on his release from prison, Cape Town, 11 February 1990. Accessed at https:// archive.nelsonmandela.org/index. php/za-com-mr-s-16.

24 UCT, BC 1070, G1.91 Transcript of an interview with HFO by Patti Wald-meir, 27 October 1994; Waldmeir, *Anatomy of a Miracle*, p 241.

25 Sampson, *Mandela*, p 409.

26 Ibid., p 434.

27 UCT, BC 1070, G1.91 Transcript of an interview with HFO by Patti Wald-meir, 27 October 1994.

28 Interview with Clifford Elphick, Johannesburg, 12 February 2020.

29 UCT, BC 1070, G1.91 Transcript of an interview with HFO by Patti Wald-meir, 27 October 1994.

30 N Segal, *Breaking the Mould: The Role of Scenarios in Shaping South Africa's Future*, SUN Press, 2007. See also A Sparks, *Beyond the Miracle: Inside the New South Africa*, Jonathan Ball Publishers, 2003, pp 170–201.

31 UCT, BC 1070, G1.91 Transcript of an interview with HFO by Patti Wald-meir, 27 October 1994.

32 *Financial Times*, 28 June 1993.

33 Interview with Julian Ogilvie Thomp-son, Johannesburg, 11 January 2018.

34 RW Johnson, *South Africa's Brave New World: The Beloved Country since the End of Apartheid*, Overlook Press, 2010, p 15.

35 Sampson, *Mandela*, p 502.

36 N Mandela, 'Speech on the occasion of the donation of the Rhodes Build-ing to the Mandela Rhodes Founda-tion', August 2003. Accessed at http:// db.nelsonmandela.org/speeches/ pub_view.asp?pg=item&Item ID=NMS1074.

37 Johnson, *South Africa's Brave New World*, p 15.

38 M Padayachee, 'South Africa's inter-national financial relations, 1970–1987: History, crisis and transforma-tion' (PhD thesis, University of Natal, 1989), p 211.

39 BL, MS/OPP/BDO/B1.38 Scrapbook, Full transcript of an inter-view with HFO by *Financial Times* editorial team, 17 May 1993.

40 *Financial Times*, 28 June 1993.

41 Interview with Clifford Elphick, Johannesburg, 12 February 2020.

42 BL, MS/OPP/BDO/B1.38 Scrapbook, Full transcript of an inter-view with HFO by *Financial Times* editorial team, 17 May 1993.

43 Cited in Welsh, *The Rise and Fall of Apartheid*, p 515.

44 *USA Today*, 20 June 1994.

45 Welsh, *The Rise and Fall of Apartheid*, p 516.

46 R Mattes, H Giliomee and W James, 'The election in the Western Cape', in RW Johnson and L Schlemmer (eds.), *Launching Democracy in South Africa: The First Open Election, April 1994*, Yale University Press, 1996, p 136.

47 RW Johnson, 'The 1994 election: Out-come and analysis', in Johnson and Schlemmer, *Launching Democracy*, p 308.

48 *USA Today*, 20 June 1994.

49 T Leon, *On the Contrary: Leading the Opposition in a Democratic South Africa*, Jonathan Ball Publishers, 2008, p 191.

50 BL, MS/OPP/HFO/D12.27 Zach de Beer to HFO, 3 May [1994].

51 Leon, *On the Contrary*, p 147.

52 Interview with Tony Leon, Cape Town, 6 October 2017.

53 Ibid.

54 P Williams and I Taylor, 'Neoliber-alism and the political economy of the "new" South Africa', *New Political Economy*, 5, no. 1 (2000), pp 21–40. The literature is vast, but for varia-tions upon a theme see G Schneider, 'The post-apartheid development debacle in South Africa: How mainstream economics and the vested interests preserved apartheid economic structures', *Journal of Economic Issues*, 52, no. 2 (2018), pp 306–22.

55 BL, Bobby Godsell Papers [MS717/5], Julian Ogilvie Thompson to Donald Gordon, 16 February 1994.

56 BL, MS717/5, Report on meeting between ANC and business, Brent-hurst Library, 22 February 1994, signed by Michael Spicer. Manuel was the ANC's head of economic planning, and subsequently served for a long

period as finance minister, after a stint as the minister of trade and industry. Mboweni, another of the party's economics heavyweights, went on to become the inaugural minister of labour. Cosatu was well represented by Shilowa (general secretary) and Gomomo (president). Naidoo, a prominent trade unionist, went on to serve as the minister responsible for the ANC's Reconstruction and Development Programme. Carolus was a former UDF activist elected to the ANC's national executive committee in 1991.

57 I Uys, 'Harry O and the Brenthurst Group: The empire strikes back', *Millennium*, April 1996.

58 BL, MS717/5, Report on meeting between ANC and business, Brenthurst Library, 22 February 1994, signed by Michael Spicer.

59 Sparks, *Beyond the Miracle*, p 191.

60 BL, MS717/5, Report on meeting between ANC and business, Brenthurst Library, 22 February 1994, signed by Michael Spicer.

61 Interview with Bobby Godsell, 11 October 2017.

62 BL, MS717/7, Note from Bobby Godsell to Brenthurst Group business delegation, 4 May 1994.

63 BL, MS/OPP/BDO/B1.39 Scrapbook, Michael Spicer to Julian Ogilvie Thompson, 6 May 1994: 'Peter Sullivan … phoned me to say a reliable ANC source had given him the following as the list of Cabinet appointees …' The list was partially correct, though incomplete.

64 K Rajab, 'A historical assessment', in Rajab (ed.), *A Man of Africa: The Political Thought of Harry Oppenheimer*, Zebra Press, 2017, p 42.

65 Interview with Michael Spicer, Cape Town, 19 November 2020.

66 BL, MS717/7, Note from Julian Ogilvie Thompson for the Brenthurst Group, 14 December 1994.

67 BL, MS717/7, Note for the record, Meeting between President Mandela and business leaders, 20 July 1995, signed by Bobby Godsell.

68 SJ Terreblanche, 'The ideological journey of South Africa from the RDP to the GEAR macro-economic plan', Paper presented to workshop on 'Globalisation, Poverty, Women and the Church in South Africa', 16 February 1999. Accessed at https://www.ekon.sun.ac.za/sampieterreblanche/wp-content/uploads/2018/04/SJT-1999-From-RDP-to-GEAR.pdf.

69 Uys, 'Harry O and the Brenthurst Group: The empire strikes back'.

70 M Gevisser, *Thabo Mbeki: The Dream Deferred*, Jonathan Ball Publishers, 2007, p 686.

71 Ibid., p 687.

72 N Nattrass, 'Gambling on investment: Competing economic strategies in South Africa', *Transformation*, no. 31 (1996), p 26.

73 BL, MS/OPP/BDO/C3 Bridget Oppenheimer to Albert Robinson, 2 December 1997.

74 Ibid.

75 BL, MS/OPP/BDO/C3 Bridget Oppenheimer to Albert Robinson, 23 October 1996.

76 BL, MS/OPP/BDO/Unnumbered, Menu and guests, Dinner at Brenthurst, 22 October 1996.

77 BL, MS/OPP/BDO/Unnumbered, Menu and guests, Dinner at Brenthurst, 20 November 1996.

78 BL, MS/OPP/BDO/C3 Bridget Oppenheimer to Albert Robinson, 27 October 1996.

79 BL, MS/OPP/BDO/B1.38 Scrapbook, Full transcript of an interview with HFO by *Financial Times* editorial team, 17 May 1993.

80 Interview with Julian Ogilvie Thompson, Johannesburg, 11 January 2018.

81 *Forbes*, 6 March 2008.

82 *USA Today*, 20 June 1994.

CHAPTER FOURTEEN

1 Cited in K Rajab, 'A historical assessment', in Rajab (ed.), *A Man of Africa: The Political Thought of Harry Oppenheimer*, Zebra Press, 2017, p 42.

2 *Financial Times*, 28 June 1993; and

BL, Bridget Oppenheimer Papers [MS/OPP/BDO]/B1.38 Scrapbook, Full transcript of an interview with HFO by *Financial Times* editorial team, 17 May 1993.

3 PB Shelley, 'Death', in M Shelley (ed.), *The Poetical Works of Percy Bysshe Shelley*, Edward Moxon, 1840, p 276.

4 YouTube video embedded at https://mauritzfontein.com/our-history/.

5 NF Oppenheimer, 'A tribute to my father', *Optima*, 47, no. 1 (February 2001).

6 BL, MS/OPP/HFO, HFO, Outline of memoir, Chapter 16: 'Conclusion'.

7 'Musings of a billionaire', *Mail & Guardian*, 7 March 1997.

8 *New York Times*, 29 September 1993.

9 A Jeffery, *The Truth about the Truth Commission*, South African Institute of Race Relations, 1999.

10 K Asmal, L Asmal and RS Roberts, *Reconciliation through Truth: A Reckoning of Apartheid's Criminal Governance*, David Philip, 1996.

11 Ibid., p 155.

12 A Hocking, *Oppenheimer and Son*, McGraw-Hill, 1973, p 424.

13 BL, MS/OPP/BDO/C3 Albert Robinson to Bridget Oppenheimer, 27 October 1996.

14 BL, MS/OPP/BDO/C3 Bridget Oppenheimer to Albert Robinson, 27 October 1996.

15 BL, MS/OPP/BDO/B1.38 Scrapbook, Full transcript of an interview with HFO by *Financial Times* editorial team, 17 May 1993.

16 N Nattrass, 'The Truth and Reconciliation Commission on business and apartheid: A critical evaluation', *African Affairs*, 98, no. 392 (July 1999), pp 373–91.

17 Truth and Reconciliation Commission of South Africa, *Truth and Reconciliation Commission of South Africa Report*, vol. 4, Juta, 1998, p 1. Accessed at https://www.justice.gov.za/trc/report/finalreport/Volume%204.pdf.

18 Anglo American Corporation of South Africa, 'Submission to the Truth and Reconciliation Commission', 20 October 1997. Copy supplied by Bobby Godsell.

19 BL, MS/OPP/BDO/B1.38 Scrapbook, Full transcript of an interview with HFO by *Financial Times* editorial team, 17 May 1993.

20 Truth and Reconciliation Commission, 'Transcript of business sector hearing, Day 3', 13 November 1997. Accessed at https://www.justice.gov.za/TRC/special/business/busin3.htm.

21 Ibid.

22 Ibid.

23 Truth and Reconciliation Commission of South Africa, *Truth and Reconciliation Commission of South Africa Report*, vol. 4, p 35. Accessed at https://www.justice.gov.za/trc/report/finalreport/Volume%204.pdf.

24 Nattrass, 'The Truth and Reconciliation Commission on business and apartheid', p 389.

25 A Bernstein, 'Submission to the Truth and Reconciliation Commission', November 1997, p iii. Copy supplied by Ann Bernstein.

26 A Bernstein, *The Case for Business in Developing Economies*, Penguin Books, 2010, pp 5–6.

27 BL, MS/OPP/BDO/B1.39 HFO's speaking notes: 60th anniversary of his De Beers directorship, 21 November 1994.

28 Interview with Gary Ralfe, Johannesburg, 23 March 2021.

29 *Sunday Times*, 27 November 1994.

30 The eulogy was published in *Optima*. See HF Oppenheimer, 'A tribute to Sir Philip Oppenheimer', *Optima*, 42, no. 1 (February 1996), pp 47–8.

31 Interview with Rebecca Oppenheimer, Cape Town, 15 August 2022.

32 BL, MS/OPP/BDO/C3 Bridget Oppenheimer to Albert Robinson, 24 September 1996.

33 Ibid.

34 BL, MS/OPP/BDO/C3 Bridget Oppenheimer to Albert Robinson, 20 February 1996.

35 BL, MS/OPP/BDO/C3 Bridget

Oppenheimer to Albert Robinson,
1 March 1997.

36 BL, MS/OPP/BDO/C3 Bridget
Oppenheimer to Albert Robinson,
9 March 1997.

37 *Business Day*, 28 October 1998.

38 BL, MS/OPP/BDO/C3 Bridget
Oppenheimer to Albert Robinson,
29 June 1996.

39 BL, MS/OPP/BDO/B1.42 Scrapbook,
'Speech by HFO at UCT upon the
announcement of his retirement as
chancellor', 27 June 1996.

40 BL, MS/OPP/BDO/C3 Bridget
Oppenheimer to Albert Robinson,
28 February 1997.

41 BL, MS/OPP/BDO/C3 Bridget
Oppenheimer to Albert Robinson,
1 May 1997.

42 BL, MS/OPP/HFO, HFO to Bridget
Oppenheimer, 13 April 1995.

43 BL, MS/OPP/HFO, HFO, 'Note
for Bridget, Nicky, Mary, Guy,
Michael and Clifford in connection
with my will and related matters',
3 December 1997.

44 Interview with Olive Milling, London,
3 October 2019.

45 Interview with Clifford Elphick, Cape
Town, 7 February 2020.

46 Interview with Roger Phillimore,
London, 9 October 2019.

47 *Sunday Times*, 27 November 1994.

48 Interview with Tony Trahar, London,
3 October 2019.

49 T Cohen, 'Anglo's London disaster',
Financial Mail, 17 February 2016.

50 Rajab, 'A historical assessment', p 43.

51 BL, Unaccessioned, Nicky Oppenheimer to Cynthia Carroll, c.2007
[soon after the Oppenheimer family
sold one-third of its shareholding
in Anglo American to the Chinese
billionaire Larry Yung].

52 BL, MS/OPP/BDO/B1.39, HFO's
speaking notes: 60th anniversary of
his De Beers directorship, 21 November 1994.

53 Interview with Tony Trahar, London,
3 October 2019.

54 *JCK Magazine*, 28 March 2001; *New
York Times*, 16 February 2001.

55 *Wall Street Journal*, 21 May 2001.

56 Interview with Tony Trahar, London,
3 October 2019.

57 BL, MS/OPP/BDO, Unnumbered,
Menus and guests, Brenthurst dinner,
16 August 2000.

58 BL, MS/OPP/HFO/D9.2 Video of
HFO's memorial service, 25 August
2000.

59 Cited in Rajab, *A Man of Africa*, front
matter.

60 *Financial Times*, 21 August 2000.

61 *New York Times*, 21 August 2000.

62 *The Guardian*, 21 August 2000.

63 *Business Day*, 7 September 2000.

64 *Business Day*, 24 August 2000.

65 *Sunday Times*, 27 August 2000.

66 Cited in D Pallister, S Stewart and
I Lepper, *South Africa Inc.:
The Oppenheimer Empire*,
Yale University Press, 1988, p 82.

67 BL, MS/OPP/HFO, HFO, Outline of
memoir, Chapter 16: 'Conclusion'.

SOURCES AND BIBLIOGRAPHY

1. Archival Collections

SOUTH AFRICA

Brenthurst Library, Johannesburg
Sir Bernard Oppenheimer Papers
Sir Curt Michael Oppenheimer Papers
Sir Ernest Oppenheimer Papers
Sir Philip Oppenheimer Papers
Lady Caroline 'Ina' Magdalen Oppenheimer Papers
Lady Mary 'May' Lina Oppenheimer Papers
Bridget Denison Oppenheimer Papers
Frank Leslie Oppenheimer Papers
Harry Frederick Oppenheimer Papers
Louis Oppenheimer Papers
Mary Oppenheimer Papers
Nicholas Frank Oppenheimer Papers
Raymond Harry Oppenheimer Papers

Henry Richmond 'Hank' Slack Papers
Gordon Waddell Papers

Bobby Godsell Papers: Business leaders re change in South Africa,
    1970s–1990s
Anglo American Corporation, Annual Chairman's Statements,
    1957–1984
E Oppenheimer and Son Papers, in the process of being accessioned
    into the collections of individual family members

**Special Collections, Manuscripts and Archives,
University of Cape Town**
Colin Eglin Papers
Hermann Giliomee Papers
Harry Lawrence Papers

**Historical Papers Research Archive,
University of the Witwatersrand**
Helen Suzman Papers

Archival and Special Collections, University of South Africa
United Party Archives

Alan Paton Centre, University of KwaZulu-Natal
Alan Paton Papers

UNITED KINGDOM

Charterhouse Archive
The Carthusian

Christ Church Archive, University of Oxford
File on Harry Frederick Oppenheimer, compiled by Peter Oppenheimer

Churchill Archives Centre, University of Cambridge
Julian Amery Papers

Margaret Thatcher Foundation
Prime Minister's Private Office Files

The National Archives, Kew
Prime Minister's Office Records
Foreign Office and Foreign and Commonwealth Office Records

UNITED STATES

**John F Kennedy Presidential Library and Museum
[Digital] Archives**
John F Kennedy Presidential Papers, White House Staff Files of
Sanford L Fox, Social Events, 1961–1964

2. Private Collections

Ann Bernstein Private Papers
Bobby Godsell Private Papers
Frances Jowell Private Papers
Mary Slack Private Papers

3. Government Publications

Union of South Africa, Debates of the House of Assembly [Hansard], 1948–1957

4. Newspapers and Periodicals

Africa South
Die Afrikaner
The Atlantic
Bolt
Die Brandwag
Die Burger
Business Day
Business Watch
BusinessWeek
Cape Argus
Cape Times
The Challenge
Christian Science Monitor
The Citizen
Commentary
Daily Mirror
Daily News
Daily Telegraph
Diamond Fields Advertiser

Eastern Province Herald
The Economist
Evening Post
The Executive
Financial Mail
Financial Times
Forbes
Fortune
The Forum
The Guardian
Die Huisgenoot
Independent
Investors Chronicle
JCK Magazine
Life International
Mail & Guardian
Millennium
Natal Mercury
Natal Witness
Newsweek

New York Magazine
New York Times
New Yorker
Optima
Personality
Rand Daily Mail
Reader's Digest
Rhodesia Herald
Scope
The Star
Sunday Express
Sunday Times
Time
The Times
Die Transvaler
USA Today
Die Volksblad
Wall Street Journal
Washington Post
Weekly Mail

5. Interviews and Correspondence

Oliver Baring
Rob Darné
Nick Diemont
Adrian Doull
Clifford Elphick
Patrick Esnouf
Victoria Freudenheim
Bobby Godsell
Marcelle Graham

Francis Howard
Jessica Jell
Margie Keeton
Tony Leon
Olive May [Milling]
Alan McKerron
Julian Ogilvie Thompson
Anthony Oppenheimer
Catherine Oppenheimer

Jonathan Oppenheimer

Nicky Oppenheimer

Peter Oppenheimer

Rebecca Oppenheimer

Rupert Pardoe

Paul Pereira

Roger Phillimore

Gary Ralfe

Dick Scott

Hank Slack

Mary Slack

Rachel Slack

Michael Spicer

Clem Sunter

Tony Trahar

6. Books and Book Chapters

Albeldas, Michel and Fischer, Alan (eds.), *A Question of Survival: Conversations with Key South Africans*, Jonathan Ball Publishers, 1987.

Ainslie, Rosalynde and Robinson, Dorothy, *The Collaborators*, Anti-Apartheid Movement, 1963.

Allen, John, *Rabble-Rouser for Peace: The Authorised Biography of Desmond Tutu*, Rider, 2007.

Andrew, Christopher and Mitrokhin, Vasili, *The Mitrokhin Archive: The KGB in Europe and the West*, Allen Lane/The Penguin Press, 1999.

Asmal, Kader, Asmal, Louise and Roberts, Ronald Suresh, *Reconciliation through Truth: A Reckoning of Apartheid's Criminal Governance*, David Philip, 1996.

Barlow, Arthur G, *Almost in Confidence*, Juta, 1952.

Barnard, SL and Marais, AH, *Die Verenigde Party: Die groot eksperiment*, Butterworth, 1982.

Berger, Peter L and Godsell, Bobby (eds.), *A Future South Africa: Visions, Strategies, and Realities*, Westview Press, 1988.

Berger, Peter L, *Adventures of an Accidental Sociologist: How to Explain the World Without Becoming a Bore*, Prometheus Books, 2011.

Bernstein, Ann, *The Case for Business in Developing Economies*, Penguin Books, 2010.

Boraine, Alex, *A Life in Transition*, Zebra Press, 2008.

Beckett, Denis, *Radical Middle: Chasing Peace While Apartheid Ruled*, ColdType.net, 2010.

Biko, Steve, *I Write What I Like*, Bowerdean, 1978.

Bozzoli, Belinda, *The Political Nature of a Ruling Class: Capital and Ideology in South Africa*, Routledge and Kegan Paul, 1981.

Butler, Anthony, *Cyril Ramaphosa*, Jacana, 2007.

Butler, Christopher (ed.), *Christ Church, Oxford: A Portrait of the House*, Third Millennium Publishing, 2006.

Cardo, Michael, *Opening Men's Eyes: Peter Brown and the Liberal Struggle for South Africa*, Jonathan Ball Publishers, 2010.

Cell, John W, *The Highest Stage of White Supremacy: The Origins of Segregation in South Africa and the American South*, Cambridge University Press, 1982.

Chernow, Ron, *The House of Morgan: An American Banking Dynasty and the Rise of Modern Finance*, Grove Atlantic, Kindle edn, 2010.

Cleveland, Todd, *Stones of Contention: A History of Africa's Diamonds*, Ohio University Press, 2014.

Cohen, Andrew, *The Politics and Economics of Decolonization in Africa: The Failed Experiment of the Central African Federation*, IB Tauris, 2017.

Crush, Jonathan, Jeeves, Alan and Yudelman, David, *South Africa's Labour Empire: A History of Black Migrancy to the Gold Mines*, Westview Press, 1991.

Curthoys, Judith, *The Cardinal's College: Christ Church, Chapter and Verse*, Profile Books, 2012.

Desai, Ashwin and Vahed, Goolam, *The South African Gandhi: Stretcher-Bearer of Empire*, Stanford University Press, 2016.

D'Este, Carlo, *Warlord: A Life of Winston Churchill at War, 1874–1945*, Harper Perennial, 2009.

Dommisse, Ebbe, *Anton Rupert: 'n Lewensverhaal*, Tafelberg, 2005.

Dommisse, Ebbe, *Sir David Pieter de Villiers Graaff, First Baronet of De Grendel*, Tafelberg, 2011.

Dubow, Saul, *Racial Segregation and the Origins of Apartheid in South Africa, 1919–36*, Macmillan, 1989.

Dubow, Saul, *Apartheid, 1948–1994*, Oxford University Press, 2014.

Eglin, Colin, *Crossing the Borders of Power: The Memoirs of Colin Eglin*, Jonathan Ball Publishers, 2007.

Eichengreen, Barry, *Golden Fetters: The Gold Standard and the Great Depression, 1919–1939*, Oxford University Press, 1992.

Elon, Amos, *Founder: Meyer Amschel Rothschild and His Time*, HarperCollins, 1998.

Epstein, Edward J, *The Diamond Invention*, Hutchinson, 1982.

Everatt, David, *The Origins of Non-Racialism: White Opposition to Apartheid in the 1950s*, Wits University Press, 2009.

Fatton, Robert, Jr, *Black Consciousness in South Africa: The Dialectics of Ideological Resistance to White Supremacy*, SUNY Press, 1986.

Feinstein, Charles H, *An Economic History of South Africa: Conquest, Discrimination and Development*, Cambridge University Press, 2005.

Ferguson, Niall, *The House of Rothschild*, vol. 1: *Money's Prophets, 1798–1848*, Penguin Books, 1999 [electronic version].

First, Ruth, Steele, Jonathan, and Gurney, Christabel, *The South African Connection: Western Investment in Apartheid*, Maurice Temple Smith, 1972.

Fleming, Ian, *The Diamond Smugglers*, Jonathan Cape, 1957.

Flynn, Laurie, *Studded with Diamonds and Paved with Gold: Miners, Mining Companies and Human Rights in Southern Africa*, Bloomsbury, 1992.

Freund, Bill, 'South Africa: The Union years, 1910–1948; Political and economic foundations', in Ross, Robert, Mager, Anne K and Nasson, Bill (eds.), *The Cambridge History of South Africa*, vol. 2: *1885–1994*, Cambridge University Press, 2012.

Furlong, Patrick J, *Between Crown and Swastika: The Impact of the Radical Right on the Afrikaner Nationalist Movement in the Fascist Era*, Witwatersrand University Press, 1991.

Gevisser, David, *The Unlikely Forester: A Memoir*, Jacana, 2006.

Gevisser, Mark, *Thabo Mbeki: The Dream Deferred*, Jonathan Ball Publishers, 2007.

Gibson, Rex, *Final Deadline: The Last Days of the Rand Daily Mail*, David Philip, 2007.

Giliomee, Hermann, *The Afrikaners: Biography of a People*, Tafelberg, 2010.

Graaff, De Villiers, *Div Looks Back: The Memoirs of Sir De Villiers Graaff*, Human and Rousseau, 1993.

Green, Timothy, *The World of Diamonds*, Littlehampton Book Services, 1981.

Gregory, Theodore, *Ernest Oppenheimer and the Economic Development of Southern Africa*, Oxford University Press, 1962.

Grundlingh, Albert, *Slabbert: Man on a Mission; A Biography*, Jonathan Ball Publishers, 2021.

Hain, Peter, *Sing the Beloved Country: The Struggle for the New South Africa*, Pluto, 1996.

Hancock, William Keith, *Smuts*, vol. 2: *The Fields of Force, 1919–1950*, Cambridge University Press, 1968.

Harrison, Brian (ed.), *The History of the University of Oxford*, vol. VIII: *The Twentieth Century*, Clarendon Press, 1994.

Harrod, Roy, *The Life of John Maynard Keynes*, Macmillan, 1951.

Harvey, Robert, *The Fall of Apartheid: The Inside Story from Smuts to Mbeki*, Palgrave, 2001.

Heath, Edward, *The Course of My Life: The Autobiography of Edward Heath*, Hodder and Stoughton, 1998.

Hepple, Alex, *Censorship and Press Control in South Africa*, self-published, 1960.

Hocking, Anthony, *Oppenheimer and Son*, McGraw-Hill, 1973.

Innes, Duncan, *Anglo: Anglo American and the Rise of Modern South Africa*, Ravan Press, 1984.

James, Wilmot G, *Our Precious Metal: African Labour in South Africa's Gold Industry, 1970–1990*, David Phillip, 1992.

Jamieson, Bill, *Goldstrike! The Oppenheimer Empire in Crisis*, Hutchinson Business Books, 1990.

Jeffery, Anthea, *The Truth about the Truth Commission*, South African Institute of Race Relations, 1999.

Jessup, Edward, *Ernest Oppenheimer: A Study in Power*, Rex Collings, 1979.

Johnson, RW and Schlemmer, Lawrence (eds.), *Launching Democracy in South Africa: The First Open Election, April 1994*, Yale University Press, 1996.

Johnson, RW and Welsh, David (eds.), *Ironic Victory: Liberalism in Post-liberation South Africa*, Oxford University Press, 1998.

Johnson, RW, *South Africa's Brave New World: The Beloved Country since the End of Apartheid*, Overlook Press, 2010.

Jones, JDF, *Through Fortress and Rock: The Story of Gencor, 1895–1995*, Jonathan Ball Publishers, 1995.

Jones, Stuart (ed.), *Financial Enterprise in South Africa since 1950*, Macmillan, 1992.

Jones, Stuart, 'Union Acceptances: The first merchant bank, 1955–73', in Jones, Stuart (ed.), *Financial Enterprise in South Africa since 1950*, Macmillan, 1992.

Jones, Stuart and Scott, GW, 'Wesbank: South Africa's leading hire purchase bank, 1968–90', in Jones, Stuart (ed.), *Financial Enterprise in South Africa since 1950*, Macmillan, 1992.

Kamil, Fred, *The Diamond Underworld*, Allen Lane, 1979.

Kane-Berman, John, *South Africa's Silent Revolution*, South African Institute of Race Relations, 1990.

Kanfer, Stefan, *The Last Empire: De Beers, Diamonds and the World*, Hodder and Stoughton, 1994.

Kaplan, Mendel, *Jewish Roots in the South African Economy*, Struik, 1986.

Kell, Sue, 'The Discount House of South Africa, 1957–1988: Profile of a market force', in Jones, Stuart (ed.), *Financial Enterprise in South Africa since 1950*, Macmillan, 1992.

Kissinger, Henry, *Years of Renewal*, Simon and Schuster, 1999.

Krüger, Daniël W, *The Making of a Nation: A History of the Union of South Africa, 1910–1961*, Macmillan, 1969.

Kynaston, David, *The City of London*, vol. II: *Golden Years, 1890–1914*, Vintage Digital, 2015.

Kynaston, David, *The City of London*, vol. III: *Illusions of Gold*, Vintage Digital, 2015.

Landes, David S, *Dynasties: Fortune and Misfortune in the World's Great Family Businesses*, Viking Penguin, 2006.

Lee, Robin (ed.), *Values Alive: A Tribute to Helen Suzman*, Jonathan Ball Publishers, 1990.

Leon, Tony, *On the Contrary: Leading the Opposition in a Democratic South Africa*, Jonathan Ball Publishers, 2008.

Lewis, Michael, *Liar's Poker: Rising through the Wreckage on Wall Street*, WW Norton, 1989.

Lipton, Merle, *Capitalism and Apartheid: South Africa, 1910–1986*, David Philip, 1989.

Luthuli, Albert, *Let My People Go*, Tafelberg, 2006 [1962].

Macmillan, Harold, *Pointing the Way, 1959–1961*, Macmillan, 1972.

Mann, Thomas, *Buddenbrooks: The Decline of a Family*, translated by John E Woods, Vintage International, 1994 [1901].

Masterman, John Cecil, *On the Chariot Wheel: An Autobiography*, Oxford University Press, 1975.

Masterman, John Cecil, *The Double-Cross System: The Classic Account of World War Two Spy-Masters*, Vintage, 2013.

Matisonn, John, *God, Spies and Lies: Finding South Africa's Future through Its Past*, Quivertree Publications, 2015.

McCall, Hilary MF, *The Children of Ulsterman KC and Alice*, privately published, n.d.

Mervis, Joel, *The Fourth Estate: A Newspaper Story*, Jonathan Ball Publishers, 1989.

Michael, Ina, *Apple Sauce*, Brentano's, 1928.

Middlemas, Keith, *Cabora Bassa: Engineering and Politics in Southern Africa*, Weidenfeld and Nicolson, 1975.

Moore, Charles, *Margaret Thatcher: The Authorized Biography*, vol. 2, Penguin Books, 2016.

Morris, Jan, *South African Winter*, Faber and Faber, 2008 [1958].

Mortimer, Barry (ed.), *HFO: Some Personal Perspectives on Harry Frederick Oppenheimer by His Colleagues and Friends*, Brenthurst Press, 1985.

Mouton, F Alex, *Prophet without Honour: FS Malan; Afrikaner, South African and Cape Liberal*, Protea Book House, 2011.

Nattrass, Jill, *The South African Economy: Its Growth and Change*, Oxford University Press, 1988.

Nattrass, Nicoli and Seekings, Jeremy 'The economy and poverty in the twentieth century', in Ross, Robert, Mager, Anne K and Nasson, Bill (eds.), *The Cambridge History of South Africa*, vol. 2: *1885–1994*, Cambridge University Press, 2012.

Newbury, Colin, *The Diamond Ring: Business, Politics, and Precious Stones in South Africa, 1867–1947*, Clarendon Press, 1989.

Ngcukaitobi, Tembeka, *The Land Is Ours: South Africa's First Black Lawyers and the Birth of Constitutionalism*, Penguin Random House, 2018.

Nixon, Ron, *Selling Apartheid: South Africa's Global Propaganda War*, Pluto Books, 2016.

O'Dowd, Michael C, *The O'Dowd Thesis and the Triumph of Democratic Capitalism*, Free Market Foundation, 1996.

O'Meara, Dan, *Volkskapitalisme: Class, Capital and Ideology in the Development of Afrikaner Nationalism, 1934–1948*, Ravan Press, 1983.

O'Meara, Dan, *Forty Lost Years: The Apartheid State and the Politics of the National Party, 1948–1994*, Ravan Press, 1996.

Oppenheimer, Harry F, *The Fading Commonwealth*, Cambridge University Press, 1968.

Pallister, David, Stewart, Sarah and Lepper, Ian, *South Africa Inc.: The Oppenheimer Empire*, Yale University Press, 1988.

Paton, Alan, *Hofmeyr*, Oxford University Press, 1964.

Paton, Alan, *Beyond the Present: The Story of Women for Peace, 1976–1986*, Brenthurst Press, 1986.

Perry, Marvin and Schweitzer, Frederick M, *Antisemitism: Myth and Hate from Antiquity to the Present*, Palgrave Macmillan, 2005.

Phillips, Howard, *UCT under Apartheid, 1948–1698: From Onset to Sit-In*, Jacana, 2019.

Pirow, Oswald, *James Barry Munnik Hertzog*, Howard Timmins, 1957.

Rajab, Kalim (ed.), *A Man of Africa: The Political Thought of Harry Oppenheimer*, Zebra Press, 2017.

Randall, Peter R, *Little England on the Veld*, Ravan Press, 1982.

Renwick, Robin, *Helen Suzman: Bright Star in a Dark Chamber*, Jonathan Ball Publishers, 2013.

Rich, Paul B, *White Power and the Liberal Conscience: Racial Segregation and South African Liberalism*, Ravan Press, 1984.

Roberts, Brian, *Kimberley: Turbulent City*, David Philip, 1976.

Roberts, Janine, *Glitter and Greed: The Secret World of the Diamond Cartel*, The Disinformation Company, 2007.

Rogers, Barbara, *White Wealth and Black Poverty: American Investments in Southern Africa*, Greenwood Press, 1976.

Romain, Ken, *Larger Than Life: Donald Gordon and the Liberty Life Story*, Jonathan Ball Publishers, 1989.

Roos, Neil, *Ordinary Springboks: White Servicemen and Social Justice in South Africa, 1939–1961*, Ashgate, 2005.

Rose, Kenneth, *Elusive Rothschild: The Life of Victor, Third Baron*, Weidenfeld and Nicholson, 2003.

Rotberg, Robert I, *The Founder: Cecil Rhodes and the Pursuit of Power*, Oxford University Press, 1988.

Sampson, Anthony, *The Money Lenders: The People and Politics of the World Banking Crisis*, Penguin Books, 1983.

Sampson, Anthony, *Black and Gold: Tycoons, Revolutionaries and Apartheid*, Hodder and Stoughton, 1987.

Sampson, Anthony, *Mandela: The Authorised Biography*, HarperCollins, 2000.

Sanders, James, *Apartheid's Friends: The Rise and Fall of South Africa's Secret Service*, John Murray, 2006.

Saunders, Stuart, *Vice-Chancellor on a Tightrope: A Personal Account of Climactic Years in South Africa*, David Philip, 2000.

Scher, David, *Donald Molteno: Dilizintaba – He-Who-Removes-Mountains*, South African Institute of Race Relations, 1979.

Schreuder, Deryck, '"Colonial nationalism" and "tribal nationalism": Making the white South African state, 1899–1910', in Eddy, John and Schreuder, Deryck (eds.), *The Rise of Colonial Nationalism: Australia, New Zealand, Canada and South Africa First Assert their Nationalities, 1880–1914*, Allen and Unwin, 1988.

Segal, Nick, *Breaking the Mould: The Role of Scenarios in Shaping South Africa's Future*, SUN Press, 2007.

Serfontein, JHP, *Brotherhood of Power: An Exposé of the Secret Afrikaner Broederbond*, Rex Collings, 1979.

Shain, Milton, *A Perfect Storm: Antisemitism in South Africa, 1930–1948*, Jonathan Ball Publishers, 2015.

Shelley, Mary (ed.), *The Poetical Works of Percy Bysshe Shelley*, Edward Moxon, 1840.

Shenefield, John H and Stelzer, Irwin M, *The Antitrust Laws: A Primer*, American Enterprise Institute Press, 1993.

Silberhaft, Moshe, *The Travelling Rabbi: My African Tribe*, Jacana, 2012.

Sisman, Adam, *An Honourable Englishman: The Life of Hugh Trevor-Roper*, Random House, 2010.

Smith, Alan H, *The Brenthurst Gardens*, Brenthurst Press, 1988.

South African Institute of Race Relations, *A Survey of Race Relations in South Africa: 1976*, South African Institute of Race Relations, 1977.

South African Institute of Race Relations, *A Survey of Race Relations in South Africa: 1977*, South African Institute of Race Relations, 1978.

Sparks, Allister, *The Sword and the Pen: Six Decades on the Political Frontier*, Jonathan Ball Publishers, 2016.

Stern, Fritz, *Gold and Iron: Bismarck, Bleichröder, and the Building of the German Empire*, Alfred A Knopf, 1977.

Steyn, Richard, *Jan Smuts: Unafraid of Greatness*, Jonathan Ball Publishers, 2015.

Steyn, Richard, *Seven Votes: How WWII Changed South Africa Forever*, Jonathan Ball Publishers, 2020.

Strangwayes-Booth, Joanna, *A Cricket in the Thorn Tree: Helen Suzman and the Progressive Party*, Hutchinson, 1976.

Suzman, Helen, *In No Uncertain Terms*, Jonathan Ball Publishers, 1993.

Swart, Ray, *Progressive Odyssey: Towards a Democratic South Africa*, Human and Rousseau, 1991.

Turrell, Robert V, 'Kimberley, labour and compounds, 1871–1888', in Marks, Shula and Rathbone, Richard (eds.), *Industrialisation and Social Change in South Africa: African Class Formation, Culture and Consciousness, 1870–1930*, Longman, 1982.

Turrell, Robert V, *Capital and Labour on the Kimberley Diamond Fields, 1871–1890*, Cambridge University Press, 1987.

Van Onselen, Charles, *The Cowboy Capitalist: John Hays Hammond, the American West and the Jameson Raid*, Jonathan Ball Publishers, 2017.

Verhoef, Grietjie, 'Afrikaner nationalism in South African banking: The cases of Volkskas and Trust Bank', in Jones, Stuart (ed.), *Financial Enterprise in South Africa since 1950*, Macmillan, 1992.

Verhoef, Grietjie, 'Nedbank, 1945–1989: The Continental approach to banking in South Africa', in Jones, Stuart (ed.), *Financial Enterprise in South Africa since 1950*, Macmillan, 1992.

Verhoef, Grietjie, *The Power of Your Life: The Sanlam Century of Insurance Empowerment, 1918–2018*, Oxford University Press, 2018.

Vigne, Randolph, *Liberals against Apartheid: A History of the Liberal Party of South Africa, 1953–1968*, Macmillan, 1997.

Viney, Graham, *The Last Hurrah: South Africa and the Royal Tour of 1947*, Jonathan Ball Publishers, 2018.

Waldmeir, Patti, *Anatomy of a Miracle: The End of Apartheid and the Birth of the New South Africa*, Rutgers University Press, 2001.

Walker, Oliver, *Sailor Malan: A Biography*, Cassell, 1953.

Walshe, Peter, *The Rise of African Nationalism in South Africa*, Ad Donker, 1987.

Wassenaar, Andries D, *Assault on Private Enterprise: The Freeway to Communism*, Tafelberg, 1977.

Welsh, David, *The Rise and Fall of Apartheid*, Jonathan Ball Publishers, 2009.

Wheatcroft, Geoffrey, *The Randlords: The Men Who Made South Africa*, Weidenfeld and Nicolson, 1985.

Wilkins, Ivor and Strydom, Hans, *The Super Afrikaners: Inside the Afrikaner Broederbond*, Jonathan Ball Publishers, 2012 [1978].

Wilson, Francis, *Labour in the South African Gold Mines, 1911–1969*, Cambridge University Press, 1972.

Winter, Gordon, *Inside BOSS: South Africa's Secret Police*, Penguin, 1981.

Worger, William H, *South Africa's City of Diamonds: Mine Workers and Monopoly Capitalism in Kimberley, 1867–1895*, Yale University Press, 1987.

7. Journal Articles

Alford, Bernard William Ernest and Harvey, Charles Edward, 'Copperbelt merger: The formation of the Rhokana Corporation, 1930–1932', *Business History Review*, 54, no. 3 (Autumn 1980), pp 330–58.

Breckenridge, Keith, '"Money with dignity": Migrants, minelords and the cultural politics of the South African gold standard crisis, 1920–33', *Journal of African History*, 36, no. 2 (1995), pp 271–304.

Brown, Henry Phelps, 'Sir Roy Harrod: A biographical memoir', *Economic Journal*, 90, no. 357 (March 1980), pp 1–33.

Butler, Larry J, 'Business and British decolonisation: Sir Ronald Prain, the mining industry and the Central African Federation', *Journal of Imperial and Commonwealth History*, 35, no. 3 (2007), pp 459–84.

Butler, Larry J, 'Mining, nationalism and decolonization in Zambia: Interpreting business responses to political change, 1945–1964', *Archiv für Sozialgeschichte*, 48 (2008), pp 317–32.

Cross, Tim, 'Afrikaner nationalism, Anglo American and Iscor: The formation of the Highveld Steel & Vanadium Corporation, 1960–70', *Business History*, 36, no. 3 (1994), pp 81–99.

Crush, Jonathan, 'Power and surveillance on the South African gold mines', *Journal of Southern African Studies*, 18, no. 4 (1992), pp 825–44.

Eichengreen, Barry, 'Gold and South Africa's Great Depression', *Economic History of Developing Regions*, 36, no. 2 (2021), pp 175–93.

Geldenhuys, Deon, 'The foreign factor in South Africa's 1992 referendum', *Politikon*, 19, no. 3 (1992), pp 45–63.

Giliomee, Hermann, 'Ethnic business and economic empowerment: The Afrikaner case, 1915–1970', *South African Journal of Economics*, 76, no. 4 (2008), pp 765–88.

Grundlingh, Albert M, 'Die rebellie van 1914: ń Historiografiese verkenning', *Kleio*, 11, nos. 1–2 (1979), pp 18–30.

Hackland, Brian, 'The economic and political context of the growth of the Progressive Federal Party in South Africa, 1959–1978', *Journal of Southern African Studies*, 7, no. 1 (1980), pp 1–16.

Harrison, Edward, 'Christ Church and the Secret Service: Sir John Masterman and MI5', *Christ Church Matters*, no. 35 (Trinity term 2015), pp 35–7.

Hoogenraad-Vermaak, Salomon, 'The contribution of the Urban Foundation to political reform', *Historia*, 56, no. 2 (November 2011), pp 133–53.

Hyslop, Jonathan, '"Segregation has fallen on evil days": Smuts' South Africa, global war, and transnational politics, 1939–46', *Journal of Global History*, 7, no. 3 (2012), pp 438–60.

Iliffe, John, 'The South African economy, 1652–1997', *Economic History Review*, 52, no. 1 (1999), pp 87–103.

Kissinger, Henry, 'American global concerns and Africa', *International Affairs Bulletin*, 6, no. 3 (1982), pp 5–22.

Knight, John and Stevenson, Heather, 'The Williamson diamond mine, De Beers, and the Colonial Office: A case-study of the quest for control', *Journal of Modern African Studies*, 24, no. 3 (September 1986), pp 423–45.

Marks, Shula and Trapido, Stanley, 'Lord Milner and the South African state', *History Workshop*, no. 8 (1979), pp 50–80.

McKenzie, Elspeth, 'The English-language press and the Anglo American Corporation: An assessment', *Kleio*, 26 (1994), pp 98–107.

Moll, Terence, 'Did the apartheid economy "fail"?', *Journal of Southern African Studies*, 17, no. 2 (June 1991), pp 271–91.

Moodie, T Dunbar, 'Managing the 1987 mine workers' strike', *Journal of Southern African Studies*, 35, no. 1 (March 2009), pp 45–64.

Mouton, F Alex, '"A decent man, but not very popular": JGN Strauss, the United Party and the founding of the apartheid state, 1950–1956', *Journal for Contemporary History*, 38, no. 2 (2013), pp 1–20.

Mouton, F Alex, '"One of the architects of our democracy": Colin Eglin, the Progressive Federal Party and the leadership of the official parliamentary opposition, 1977–1979 and 1986–1987', *Journal for Contemporary History*, 40, no. 1 (June 2015), pp 1–22.

Nasson, Bill, 'A flying Springbok of wartime British skies: AG "Sailor" Malan', *Kronos*, no. 35 (November 2009), pp 71–97.

Nattrass, Nicoli, 'Gambling on investment: Competing economic strategies in South Africa', *Transformation*, no. 31 (1996), pp 25–42.

Nattrass, Nicoli, 'The Truth and Reconciliation Commission on business and apartheid: A critical evaluation', *African Affairs*, 98, no. 392 (July 1999), pp 373–91.

Newbury, Colin, 'The origins and function of the London Diamond Syndicate, 1889–1914', *Business History*, 29, no. 1 (1987), pp 5–26.

Otte, Thomas G, '"Alien diplomatist": Antisemitism and anti-Germanism in the diplomatic career of Sir Francis Oppenheimer', *History*, 89, no. 2 (April 2004), pp 233–55.

Schneider, Geoff, 'The post-apartheid development debacle in South Africa: How mainstream economics and the vested interests preserved apartheid economic structures', *Journal of Economic Issues*, 52, no. 2 (2018), pp 306–22.

Shain, Milton, 'Hoggenheimer: The making of a myth', *Jewish Affairs* (September 1981), pp 112–16.

Sher, David, 'The career of Graham S Eden: "Coloured representative"', *Kleio*, 23, no. 1 (1991), pp 69–84.

Swanepoel, Christie and Fliers, Philip T, 'The fuel of unparalleled recovery: Monetary policy in South Africa between 1925 and 1936', *Economic History of Developing Regions*, 36, no. 2 (2021), pp 213–44.

Verhoef, Grietjie, 'Nationalism and free enterprise in mining: The case of Federale Mynbou 1952–1965', *South African Journal of Economic History*, 10, no. 1 (1995), pp 89–107.

Verhoef, Grietjie, 'The development of diversified conglomerates: Federale Volksbeleggings; A case study', *Journal of Contemporary History*, 24, no. 2 (1999), pp 55–78.

Wessels, André, 'South Africa and the war against Japan: 1941–1945', *Military History Journal*, 10, no. 3 (June 1996).

Williams, Paul and Taylor, Ian, 'Neoliberalism and the political economy of the "new" South Africa', *New Political Economy*, 5, no. 1 (2000), pp 21–40.

Yamey, Adam, 'Men of gold: The Goldmanns of Burghersdorp', *Stammbaum*, no. 31 (Summer 2007).

8. Articles in *Optima*, a quarterly review published by the Anglo American Corporation and De Beers group of companies

Beckingham, Doug, 'The Group in industry: A view of diversification', *Optima*, 22, no. 3 (September 1972), pp 130–9.

Godsell, B, 'Reflections: Harry Oppenheimer talks to Bobby Godsell', *Optima*, 38, no. 3 (November 1992), pp 108–10.

Hagart, Richard B, 'The formative years: A recollection', *Optima*, 17, no. 3 (September 1967), pp 105–11.

O'Dowd, Michael, 'Practical social responsibility: The work of AAC and De Beers Chairman's Fund', *Optima*, no. 2 (1978), pp 117–28.

Ogilvie Thompson, Julian, 'An appreciation of Harry Oppenheimer', *Optima*, 33, no. 1 (March 1985), pp 2–7.

Oppenheimer, Harry F, 'Sir Ernest Oppenheimer: A portrait by his son', *Optima*, 17, no. 3 (September 1967), pp 95–104.

Oppenheimer, Harry F, 'A reassessment of Rhodes and his relevance to the problems of Africa today', Text of lecture delivered at Rhodes University to commemorate the 100th anniversary of the arrival of Cecil Rhodes in South Africa, *Optima*, 20, no. 3 (September 1970), pp 103–7.

Oppenheimer, Harry F, 'South Africa's growth in the 70s: Its problems, and the opportunities that lie ahead', Address to 17th annual conference of the Trade Union Council of South Africa in Durban, 16 September 1971, *Optima*, 21, no. 4 (December 1971), pp 154–9.

Oppenheimer, Harry F, 'The press and society', Text of a speech delivered at the UCT Summer School, *Optima*, 23, no. 1 (March 1973), pp 2–6.

Oppenheimer, Harry F, 'Catalysts for change in South Africa', Address to a joint meeting of the Royal Institute of International Affairs and the Royal African Society at Chatham House, *Optima*, 24, no. 1 (1974), pp 2–9.

Oppenheimer, Harry F, 'Prospects for change in southern Africa', Address to the Foreign Policy Association, New York City, 14 October 1977. Reproduced as a supplement to *Optima*, 27, no. 3 (1977), pp 1–8.

Oppenheimer, Harry F, 'Why the world should continue to invest in South Africa', Address to the International Monetary Conference, Mexico City, 22 May 1978. Reproduced as a supplement to *Optima*, no. 1 (1978), pp 1–8.

Oppenheimer, Harry F, 'Towards a more just racial order in South Africa', Opening address to the 50th anniversary conference of the South African Institute of Race Relations, Johannesburg, 2 July 1979. Reproduced as a supplement to *Optima*, 28, no. 3 (August 1979), pp 1–8.

Oppenheimer, Harry F, 'The Anglo American Corporation's role in South Africa's gold mining industry', *Optima*, 34, no. 2 (June 1986), pp 58–67.

Oppenheimer, Harry F, 'Four steps to democracy', Speech at the World Economic Forum conference in Davos, 31 January 1989. Reproduced as a supplement to *Optima*, 37, no. 1 (March 1989), pp 1–7.

Oppenheimer, Harry F, 'A tribute to Sir Philip Oppenheimer', *Optima*, 42, no. 1 (February 1996), pp 47–8.

Oppenheimer, Nicholas Frank, 'A tribute to my father', *Optima*, 47, no. 1 (February 2001), pp 13–19.

Relly, Gavin, 'Harry Oppenheimer: An appreciation', *Optima*, 31, no. 2 (April 1983), pp 46–9.

ELW [Eric Williams], 'Harry Oppenheimer: Profile', *Optima*, 25, no. 3 (1975), pp 164–70.

9. Theses and Working Papers

Arena, Lise, 'From economics of the firm to business studies at Oxford: An intellectual history (1890s–1990s)', DPhil thesis, University of Oxford, 2011.

Cardo, Michael, 'Culture, citizenship and white South Africanism, c.1924–1948', PhD thesis, University of Cambridge, 2003.

Fig, David, 'The political economy of South–South relations: The case of South Africa and Latin America', PhD thesis, London School of Economics and Political Science, 1992.

Fridjhon, Michael, 'The Torch Commando and the politics of white opposition, South Africa 1951–1953', University of the Witwatersrand, African Studies Seminar Paper, 1976.

Horner, Dudley and Kooy, Alide, 'Conflict on South African mines, 1972–1976', University of Cape Town, South African Labour and Development Research Unit (Saldru), Working Paper no. 5, August 1976.

Kantor, Brian, 'The many facets of De Beers – or why it isn't what it appears to be', Paper prepared for the School of Economics, University of Cape Town, January 1982.

Kleynhans, Evert P, 'The Axis and Allied maritime operations around southern Africa, 1939–1945', DPhil thesis, University of Stellenbosch, 2018.

Padayachee, Mahavishnu, 'South Africa's international financial relations, 1970–1987: History, crisis and transformation', PhD thesis, University of Natal, 1989.

Pereira, Paul, 'Chairman's Fund, 1967–2020: A broad-brush history', Report for Oppenheimer Generations, 2021.

Randall, Peter R, 'The English private school system in South Africa', MEd thesis, University of the Witwatersrand, 1980.

Plint, Graeme Wesley, 'The influence of Second World War military service on prominent white South African veterans in opposition politics, 1939–1961', MMil thesis, University of Stellenbosch, 2021.

Sanders, James, 'A struggle for representation: The international media treatment of South Africa, 1972–1979', PhD thesis, University of London, 1997.

Turrell, Athol Denis, 'The South African Party 1932–1934: The movement towards Fusion', MA thesis, University of Natal, 1977.

White, William Barry, 'The South African parliamentary opposition, 1948–1953', PhD thesis, University of Natal, 1989.

10. Online Sources

Friedman, Milton, Record of a trip to southern Africa, March 20 – April 9, 1976, Unpublished typescript transcribed from a tape, dictated 7–9 April 1976. Accessed at https://miltonfriedman.hoover.org/internal/media/dispatcher/271010/full.

The Freedom Charter, as adopted at the Congress of the People, Kliptown, 26 June 1955. Accessed at https://www.anc1912.org.za/the-freedom-charter-2/.

Kane-Berman, John, 'The rise and fall of the Torch Commando', Politicsweb, 30 July 2018. Accessed at https://www.politicsweb.co.za/opinion/the-rise-and-fall-of-the-torch-commando.

Louw, Raymond, 'The *Rand Daily Mail*: Convenient scapegoat', *Focus*, no. 39 (2005). Accessed at https://hsf.org.za/publications/focus/issue-39-third-quarter-2005/the-rand-daily-mail-convenient-scapegoat.

Mandela, Nelson, 'Rally address on release from prison', Cape Town, 11 February 1990. Accessed at https://archive.nelsonmandela.org/index.php/za-com-mr-s-16.

Mandela, Nelson, 'Speech on the occasion of the donation of the Rhodes Building to the Mandela Rhodes Foundation', August 2003. Accessed at http://db.nelsonmandela.org/speeches/pub_view.asp?pg=item&ItemID=NMS1074.

Oppenheimer Memorial Trust, 'The history of the OMT'. Accessed at https://www.omt.org.za/history/the-history-of-the-omt/.

PBS Frontline, 'The diamond empire', 1 February 1994 [Description]. Accessed at https://www.pbs.org/wgbh/frontline/film/the-diamond-empire.

PBS Frontline, 'The diamond empire', 1 February 1994 [Transcript]. Accessed at http://www.shoppbs.pbs.org/wgbh/pages/frontline/programs/transcripts/1209.html.

Rajab, Kalim, 'Bridget Denison Oppenheimer, 1921–2013. Accessed at https://www.omt.org.za/in-the-media/bridget-denison-oppenheimer-nee-mccall-1921-2013/.

Ryan, Brendan, 'Why the Oppenheimers sold out of De Beers', Miningmx, 30 December 2011 [first published 7 November 2011]. Accessed at https://www.miningmx.com/opinion/columnists/25581-why-the-oppenheimers-sold-out-of-de-beers/.

Terreblanche, Sampie, 'The ideological journey of South Africa: From the RDP to the GEAR macro-economic plan', Paper presented to a workshop on 'Globalisation, Poverty, Women and the Church in South Africa', 16 February 1999. Accessed at https://www.ekon.sun.ac.za/sampieterreblanche/wp-content/uploads/2018/04/SJT-1999-From-RDP-to-GEAR.pdf.

Truth and Reconciliation Commission, 'Transcript of business sector hearing, Day 3', 13 November 1997. Accessed at https://www.justice.gov.za/TRC/special/business/busin3.htm.

Truth and Reconciliation Commission of South Africa, *Truth and Reconciliation Commission of South Africa Report*, vol. 4 (Juta, 1998). Accessed at https://www.justice.gov.za/trc/report/finalreport/Volume%204.pdf.

United Nations, US Mission, Cable from A Young to Z Brzeziński, 'Appointment request for Harry Oppenheimer', 27 September 1977. Accessed at https://wikileaks.org/plusd/cables/1977USUNN03339_c.html.

United States Department of State, Cable to Secretary of State marked 'secret', 23 April 1976. Accessed at https://wikileaks.org/plusd/cables/1976LUSAKA01051_b.html.

Welsh, David, 'Review of the Buthelezi Commission' (H&H Publications, 1982). Accessed at https://www.sahistory.org.za/sites/default/files/archive-files2/rejul82.5.pdf.

ACKNOWLEDGEMENTS

Over the long course of researching and writing HFO's biography, my debt pile grew considerably. I would like to pay thanks to the following individuals and institutions. Nicky Oppenheimer and Mary Slack granted me unfettered access to all the family papers held at the Brenthurst Library. Both gave generously of their time to be interviewed. Nicky Oppenheimer arranged for additional photographic material to be made available for the book. Mary Slack furnished me with supplementary documentation from her private holdings, including several of her father's personal letters. Along the way she entertained a myriad of questions.

HFO's grandchildren were similarly accommodating. Rachel Slack smoothed the path for my enquiries, helped me to secure interviews, and was a vital point of contact. I badgered her with copious requests for information – ranging from the top to the bottom of the family pile – all of which she or her sister, Jessica Jell, responded to uncomplainingly. Victoria Freudenheim allowed me to consult her grandmother Bridget's marvellous collection of scrapbooks. Jonathan Oppenheimer, Rebecca Oppenheimer and Victoria Freudenheim engaged with me in lengthy interviews; I appreciated their openness and approachability.

For a biographer, the seal of authorisation can be a double-edged sword, at once empowering and potentially constraining. Yet, when I embarked upon this project, there was never any suggestion on the part of HFO's progeny that I should burnish the paterfamilias's image – nor, at the end of it, the slightest attempt to have me alter my portrait of him. Given free rein among the archived records of Oppenheimer's life, I mined the quarry and appropriated from it liberally. Mary Slack and Nicky Oppenheimer saw the draft manuscript ahead of publication, but they made no move to censor me or to impose any changes. The palette, the perspective and the profile here are entirely my own. In short, without the co-operation of HFO's children and grandchildren, I would not have been able to construct as solid a canvas on which to render my subject.

This project relied to a great extent on the toil of archivists and librarians. I consulted most of my primary material at the Brenthurst Library: its holdings are a treasure trove. My gratitude to the team under the expert direction of Sally MacRoberts is unbounded. Over a period of almost six years, Sally, Inarie de Vaal, Jennifer Kimble, Fylyppa Meyer and Desré Stead went above and beyond the call of duty to assist me. They dealt with a battery of queries, fetched and ferried hundreds of boxes of papers, scanned scores of documents, tracked down records, assisted with logistics, advised on the selection of photographs, and – all in all – eased my labours immeasurably. Together with Michael Makhado, Richard Mphephu, Yvonne Mabuza and the rest of the staff at the library, they added to the pleasure of my many intermittent visits.

As my research got under way, a long-locked vault of documents was opened at E Oppenheimer and Son, the private family firm established by Sir Ernest Oppenheimer in 1935. This unearthed further gems, including HFO's outbound correspondence from the Second World War and a substantial deposit of letters, files and memoranda that shed light on his political career and business life. I was fortunate to be able to tap into this rich seam before its transfer into the Brenthurst collections.

Through the auspices of the Brenthurst Press, I undertook a research trip to England. At Charterhouse, Catherine Smith provided me with access to the school's digital archive, and steered me towards relevant information. At the University of Oxford, the keeper of the Christ Church Archive, Judith Curthoys, and the college librarian, Steven Archer, gave me permission to consult records on HFO. They also directed me to a bevy of fruitful secondary sources. At the University of Cambridge I profited from a short spell in the Churchill Archives Centre at Churchill College. In London, at the National Archives in Kew, I drew on records from the Prime Minister's Office and the Foreign and Commonwealth Office.

In South Africa, the principal librarian at the Africana Library in Kimberley, Bernice Nagel, sent me useful newspaper cuttings. At the Library of Parliament in Cape Town I referred to the set of Hansards covering HFO's spell as the member of Parliament for Kimberley. Thea Louw, from the parliamentary library's reference unit, managed to source electronic versions of books that had long eluded my grasp.

At the University of Cape Town (UCT), I turned to UCT Libraries Special Collections, housed in the Jagger Library. This was mere months before a wildfire engulfed the eastern slopes of Table Mountain and proceeded to gut the Jagger Reading Room. Anybody who has ever undertaken research at this wonderful facility will appreciate the nature of the loss. I am indebted to Clive Kirkwood, the archivist at Special Collections, for his guidance and assistance.

At the Archival and Special Collections at the University of South Africa in Pretoria, the Alan Paton Centre at the University of KwaZulu-Natal in Pietermaritzburg, and the Historical Papers Research Archive at the University of the Witwatersrand (Wits) in Johannesburg, I collected a mountain of material for my doctoral thesis and a previous biography. Much of it pertains to the United Party, the Liberal Party, the Progressive Party and the South African Institute of Race Relations, and it has turned out to be of continuing benefit. During the course of my research for this book, Helen Suzman's daughter Frances Jowell granted me access to her mother's papers, which are archived at Wits. Gabriele Mohale, the head archivist, responded swiftly to my requests for items from the digitised collection. Frances Jowell also kindly trawled through her mother's privately held letters for references to HFO, and shared them with me.

Diane Vaubell did a superb job of combing Anglo American's archives for images. Michelle Bossenger, the senior companies secretary at De Beers Group Services, acted as an intermediary during my preliminary investigations into the company's archival holdings.

Apart from Harry Oppenheimer's offspring, I spoke to or interviewed a range of people for this book – both in England and in South Africa, or, thanks to the technological adaptability spawned by Covid-19, via Skype and Zoom. Many of them were HFO's colleagues at Anglo American, De Beers, or E Oppenheimer and Son. *Primus inter pares* is Julian Ogilvie Thompson. Appointed as HFO's personal assistant in 1958, he appeared to have perfect recall of everything that had ever taken place in the Anglosphere of 44 Main Street, the group's Johannesburg headquarters, and its international empire over the ensuing four decades. I am grateful to JOT and his late wife, Tessa, for hosting me at their home in Johannesburg; and to JOT for sharing his encyclopedic knowledge of the greater group. Similarly, I would like to thank Anthony Oppenheimer and his wife, Antoinette, at Adbury House in Newbury; Gary Ralfe in Johannesburg; and Tony Trahar in London.

In addition to those already mentioned, Oliver Baring, Rob Darné,

Adrian Doull, Clifford Elphick, Bobby Godsell, the late Alan McKerron, Rupert Pardoe, Roger Phillimore, Hank Slack, the late Michael Spicer and Clem Sunter helped me to navigate Anglo's corporate labyrinth. They yielded diverse insights into my subject. From Olive May, Harry Oppenheimer's secretary at the group's Charterhouse Street complex in London, I gained a feel for HFO's English sojourns in his later years. Both Bobby Godsell and Hank Slack read the completed manuscript: they saved me from some slip-ups and provided beneficial feedback.

I interviewed several men who served at one or other point as HFO's personal assistant. Besides Ogilvie Thompson, Doull, Slack and Elphick, the former PAs I spoke to were Francis Howard, Nick Diemont and Patrick Esnouf. They were uniformly obliging. Clifford Elphick was an indispensable guide to the last decade of HFO's life; interviewed on multiple occasions, he was the epitome of generosity.

After HFO retired as the chairman of Anglo American at the end of 1982 and of De Beers in 1984, one of the group's press attachés, Barry Mortimer, edited a compilation of tributes to the plutocrat. Published by the Brenthurst Press and billed as *HFO: Some Personal Perspectives on Harry Frederick Oppenheimer by His Colleagues and Friends*, the book – stripped of its deferential excesses – serves as a handy resource. Predominantly transcripts of recorded interviews, the contributions are conversational and anecdotal. They afforded me the opportunity to hear, as it were, from a number of HFO's key associates who are no longer alive.

In Oxford, Peter and Catherine Oppenheimer (no relation to HFO) invited me into their home and shared reminiscences of their friend and namesake. Peter Oppenheimer was a mine of information about HFO's long association with the University of Oxford. In South Africa, Tony Leon drew on a well-stocked fund of knowledge about HFO's politics, his support for the Progressive Party, and the party's various reincarnations. I have a raft of other interlocutors to thank, but I would particularly like to mention Dick Scott, Marcelle Graham, Ann Bernstein, Paul Pereira and Margie Keeton. Paul Pereira gave me sight of his unpublished research on the Anglo American and De Beers Chairman's Fund. Both he and Margie Keeton were immensely informative on Anglo's culture of corporate citizenship and philanthropy. Many other individuals responded to esoteric queries, volunteered useful information, sparked thoughts, or facilitated connections. To this end I would like to thank Hugh Amoore, Francis Antonie, Doug Band, Hugh Corder, Mark Gevisser, Dominique Herman, Hugh Herman, Peter Hodes, Adrian Horwitz, Jeremy Norman,

Laurine Platzky, Kathy Satchwell, Christopher Saunders, Rabbi Moshe Silberhaft, Rose Smuts, Paul Trewhela, James van den Heever and Adam Yamey. Jan-Jan Joubert assisted me with arbitrary translations when I feared my Afrikaans might not be up to scratch, and encouraged me in my endeavours. Ebbe Dommisse enlightened me on aspects of the Afrikaner press. For help with administrative arrangements I would like to thank Antoinette Becker, Julie Burgon, Debbie Copeland, Thelma O'Donnell, Susan Fewster and Hayley Napier from E Oppenheimer and Son (or, latterly, Oppenheimer Generations and Mary Oppenheimer and Daughters) and Colleen Cawood from the Brenthurst Press.

Several scholars enriched my appreciation of Oppenheimer's life and times. At the beginning of this project, I went to pick the brains of my former history lecturer Professor Keith Breckenridge, now at Wits. At the University of Johannesburg I drew on the expertise of Professor Grietjie Verhoef, an authority on business history. Professor Hermann Giliomee illuminated the background to the General Mining–Federale Mynbou deal for me. Professor Charles van Onselen engaged me in a stimulating back-and-forth on Oppenheimer's potential post-war networks, even if our speculations proved inconclusive. Dr Evert Kleynhans, a military historian at the University of Stellenbosch, settled a query on the Second World War. Bill Nasson, an emeritus professor in history at the same institution, read the manuscript for the publisher and commented on it with acuity and flair. I took on board many of his excellent suggestions; where I failed to, no doubt the book is the worse for it, and I readily assume responsibility for any deficiencies, superfluities and inaccuracies that remain.

I benefited from the wisdom of a cohort of UCT's professors emeriti. Professor David Welsh has long exercised an influence over my approach to the study of South African political history, and I profited from our informal conversations. Professor Brian Kantor shared his unpublished research on De Beers; I also learnt a great deal from his writing on economics. I owe a special debt of thanks to Professor Milton Shain. His friendship, encouragement and counsel played a valued role in nudging this project to a conclusion. Milton urged me to continue writing at a time when my research materials felt hopelessly onerous. Over countless coffees, he helped me to clarify my thoughts. He lent me a stack of books, acted as my 'first reader', delivered incisive comments on each chapter soon after it was finished, and had to endure endless talk of HFO. I am very grateful to him.

Owing to my responsibilities as a member of Parliament, my work on this book took place in concentrated bursts. I did not want to outsource any of the research, which in any event is the most enjoyable part; and, at the risk of sounding somewhat old-fashioned, as a biographer I drew inspiration from the great Australian historian of the British Commonwealth, Sir Keith Hancock. In the preface to his biography of Jan Smuts, the statesman who figured prominently in Oppenheimer's life, Hancock wrote that his scholarly practice was to 'hew my own wood and draw my own water'. Democratic Alliance (DA) party bosses might feel, with some justification, that my own hewing and drawing carried on rather too long. But they were remarkably tolerant. I would like to thank the Leader of the Opposition, John Steenhuisen, and former chief whip of the DA Natasha Mazzone for their indulgence. My party colleagues on the Employment and Labour portfolio, Michael Bagraim and Nceba Hinana, more than shouldered their share of our joint responsibilities. Michael also helped me to pursue a line of investigation with regard to HFO's Jewish roots in Kimberley.

Without the love of my family and the support of my friends, this book would have been a much harder task. Heartfelt thanks to Helen Cardo, Richard and Renee Cardo, and Julia and Larry Oellermann. For indulging my obsessions, I would like to thank the following friends. Mark and Kelly Vorwerg often hosted me on my trips to Johannesburg and, together with their daughters, Sophie and Lily, provided welcome distractions from my research. Gavin Davis, a long-suffering sounding board, listened perceptively while I agonised over the challenges of writing a 'big life'. Stacey Hopkins, a good Samaritan, sustained me in so many ways over this project's protracted gestation.

The team at Jonathan Ball Publishers, led by Eugene Ashton, was unwavering in its support. When I overshot my original deadline by some measure, Jeremy Boraine, the former publishing director, was a model of forbearance. His successor, Annie Olivier, piloted the book through production with warmth and aplomb, meticulously assisted by Caren van Houwelingen. Russell Martin edited the manuscript with skill and sensitivity; it was rewarding working with him. I value the role played by all those who had a hand in midwifing the book: Sean Robertson for designing the cover; Martine Barker for overall design and typesetting; Paul Wise for reading the proofs; and Rita Sephton for compiling the index.

Finally, I would not have written this biography had it not been for the man who built the publishing house: the late, great Jonathan Ball.

Over one of our regular breakfasts, for reasons that were certainly clearer to him than to me, Jonathan suggested that I should be the author of this book. He got the ball rolling on the project, oiled the wheels of the Oppenheimers' authorisation, and followed my progress keenly throughout. Sadly, Jonathan's diagnosis with cancer in December 2020 (and death five months later) meant that he did not read the completed manuscript. But it is impossible for me to divorce him from my subject. During my research, I supplied him with a steady stream of eagerly devoured gobbets from the archives, including the letter that he sent, as a young and relatively newfound publisher, to Harry Oppenheimer in 1979, soliciting the magnate's memoirs. At the time, HFO agreed to reflect upon the suggestion, but nothing concrete came of it. Over forty years later, I hope this biography serves as a modest form of recompense: a posthumous bookend, if you will, which, however imperfectly, brings closure to the publisher's original request. Over time, Jonathan became a close friend to me. He was a unique character: utterly larger than life; by turns caring and crochety; warm-hearted yet clear-eyed; and, more often than not, gloriously, uproariously funny with it. I miss him a great deal. When all is said and done, I hope to have produced a biography worthy of JB's colophon. With deepest affection and gratitude, then, this book is dedicated to the memory of Jonathan Ball.

Michael Cardo
Cape Town
March 2023

INDEX